Fire Debris Analysis

Visit the companion website for

Fire Debris Analysis:

http://books.elsevier.com/companions/9780126639711

The companion website for *Fire Debris Analysis* hosts reference chromatograms used to make comparison by superimposition with the chromatograms of Chapters 9 and 12. The reader is strongly advised to download these files, which should then be printed on transparencies. As such, the reader will be able to match the patterns exhibited by the reference chromatograms on transparencies to the patterns exhibited by the ignitable liquid and sample chromatograms presented in this book.

Fire Debris Analysis

Eric Stauffer

Julia A. Dolan

Reta Newman

With a foreword by Dr. John D. DeHaan
With a contribution by Dr. P. Mark L. Sandercock

ELSEVIER

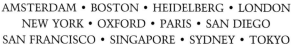
AMSTERDAM • BOSTON • HEIDELBERG • LONDON
NEW YORK • OXFORD • PARIS • SAN DIEGO
SAN FRANCISCO • SINGAPORE • SYDNEY • TOKYO
Academic Press is an imprint of Elsevier

Acquisitions Editor: Jennifer Soucy
Assoc. Developmental Editor: Kelly Weaver
Project Manager: Christie Jozwiak
Publishing Services Manager: Sarah Hajduk
Marketing Manager: Linda May
Cover Designer: Eric DeCicco

Academic Press is an imprint of Elsevier
30 Corporate Drive, Suite 400, Burlington, MA 01803, USA
525 B Street, Suite 1900, San Diego, California 92101-4495, USA
84 Theobald's Road, London WC1X 8RR, UK

This book is printed on acid-free paper. ∞

Library of Congress Cataloging-in-Publication Data
Application Submitted

British Library Cataloguing-in-Publication Data
A catalogue record for this book is available from the British Library.

ISBN: 978-0-12-663971-1

For information on all Academic Press publications
visit our Web site at www.books.elsevier.com

Printed in the United States of America
08 09 10   9 8 7 6 5 4 3 2 1

Table of Contents

Biographies

Eric Stauffer, MS, F-ABC

Eric Stauffer is a criminalist presently living in Switzerland. In 1998 he obtained his license (Master-equivalent degree) in forensic sciences from the *Institut de Police Scientifique et de Criminologie* at the University of Lausanne in Switzerland. In 1999 he moved to the United States and, two years later, obtained another Master's degree in forensic sciences from Florida International University in Miami, Florida. Mr. Stauffer is certified as a Diplomate and a Fellow of the American Board of Criminalistics, with a specialty in the area of fire debris analysis. He is also a Certified Fire and Explosion Investigator (CFEI) and a Certified Fire Investigation Instructor (CFII) both from the National Association of Fire Investigators (NAFI).

During his early career as a criminalist, Mr. Stauffer worked as a crime scene officer and a firearms and toolmarks examiner. In 2001, he moved to Atlanta and joined the private sector as a fire investigator and fire debris analyst. As such, his duties involved the investigation of numerous residential, commercial, and vehicle fire scenes to determine their origin and cause and, at the laboratory, the examination of fire debris samples for ignitable liquid residues. In 2006, he moved back to Switzerland to conduct research in forensic sciences, notably in fingermark enhancement techniques and fire investigation. He is currently pursuing doctoral studies at the School of Criminal Sciences at the University of Lausanne.

From 2003 to 2006, Mr. Stauffer was Chair of the Fire Laboratory Standards and Protocols committee of the Scientific Working Group on Fire and Explosives (SWGFEX). He also served as a subject matter expert for the development of the fire debris validation kit produced by the National Forensic Science Technology Center (NFSTC).

Mr. Stauffer is a recognized speaker and instructor in the field of forensic sciences and, more particularly, in fire investigation and fire debris analysis. He has presented his work at several conferences in both national and international forums and has authored several scientific articles and book chapters. More recently, he co-edited *Forensic Investigation of Stolen-Recovered and Other Crime-Related Vehicles* (Elsevier Academic Press), the first comprehensive book on the technical aspects of auto theft investigation. Mr. Stauffer has taught at different universities and has also served as an instructor to the official basic and advanced fire debris analysis courses offered by the Bureau of Alcohol, Tobacco, Firearms and Explosives (ATF) and the National Center for Forensic Sciences (NCFS).

Finally, Mr. Stauffer is also a volunteer fire fighter, functioning as an engineer and smoke diver. He was incorporated in the Pully City Fire Department (Switzerland) from 1993 to 1999 as well as in the Swiss Federal Institute of Technology Fire Department from 1997 to 1999. Recently, he reintegrated into the fire service and is currently incorporated in the city of Yverdon-les-Bains Fire Department (Switzerland).

Julia A. Dolan, MS, F-ABC

Julia Dolan has worked in the field of forensic sciences for eighteen years, primarily in the area of fire debris analysis. Her professional career began at the Commonwealth of Virginia, where she worked in the areas of seized drug analysis and trace evidence. Following her work at the Northern Laboratory of the Division of Forensic Science, she moved to the Federal Bureau of Alcohol, Tobacco, Firearms and Explosives (ATF), where she has focused on fire debris analysis and various aspects of fire investigation. Currently, she serves as Chief of the Arson and Explosives II section of the ATF Forensic Science Laboratory-Washington, where she oversees a variety of forensic disciplines.

In her career at ATF, Ms. Dolan has conducted research and has responded to numerous fire and explosion scenes of national significance. She has served as a member of ATF's National and International Response Teams. She has developed numerous training programs, and has served as a principal instructor for the ATF/NCFS series of fire debris courses. In this capacity, she has benefited from the opportunity to meet and work with hundreds of forensic professionals throughout the United States. Ms. Dolan has been involved in a number of professional associations, including serving in various leadership capacities in the American Board of Criminalistics (ABC) and the Mid-Atlantic Association of Forensic Scientists (MAAFS). She is a Fellow of the American Academy of Forensic Sciences (AAFS) and is a member of ASTM Committee E30 on Forensic Science, the American Chemical Society (ACS), the Chemical Society of Washington (CSW), and the International Association for Arson Investigators (IAAI), where she serves on the Forensic Science Committee. She has served in various roles in the Scientific Working Group on Fire and Explosives (SWGFEX). Ms. Dolan is certified as a Fellow of the American Board of Criminalistics, with a specialty in the area of fire debris analysis.

Ms. Dolan holds a Bachelor of Science degree in Chemistry from the University of Maryland at College Park and is a fervent Terps fan. She also holds a Master of Science degree in Chemistry from George Mason University and a second Bachelor of Science degree in Fire Science from the University of Maryland University College.

Julia is the proud mother of Michael Dolan, who she often describes as "darn-near perfect."

Reta Newman, MA, F-ABC

Reta Newman is the Director of the Pinellas County Forensic Laboratory in Largo, Florida. She has a Bachelor of Science Degree from Missouri State University. She has been a forensic chemist since 1989 and has specialized in fire debris analysis since 1991. She is a principal instructor for the NCFS-ATF Basic and Advanced Fire Debris Analysis courses that are provided annually to train forensic scientists in the complex analysis of fire debris. She is an author of the widely distributed *GC-MS Guide to Ignitable Liquids* and has authored several other book chapters and analytical papers in the area of fire debris analysis.

Ms. Newman is also very active in the quality assurance aspects of forensic sciences. She has taught workshops on QA/QC as it pertains to fire debris analysis and laboratory management. She is a legacy inspector for the American Society of Crime Laboratory Directors/Laboratory Accreditation Board (ASCLD/LAB) and an assessor for the ASCLD/LAB International ISO 17025 program. She has served on committees to develop a comprehensive validation program for forensic fire debris analysis and is a previous Chair of the Fire Laboratory Standards and Protocols Committee of the Scientific Working Group on Fire and Explosives (SWGFEX). She has also served on ASTM working groups for the revisions of the ASTM fire debris standards.

Ms. Newman is very active in the forensic science community. She is a certified Fellow in both fire debris analysis and drug analysis by the American Board of Criminalistics (ABC). She is a Fellow of the American Academy of Forensic Sciences (AAFS) and holds memberships with the American Society of Crime Laboratory Directors (ASCLD), Midwestern Association of Forensic Scientists (MAFS), the Southern Association of Forensic Scientists (SAFS), the Association of Forensic Quality Assurance Managers (AFQAM), and ASTM International. She is currently the Exam Committee Chair of the American Board of Criminalistics.

Preface

Fire debris analysis is a specialty of fire investigation and forensic sciences that is based on objective science and subjective evaluation. Objective science is used in the analytical scheme until chromatographic or mass-chromatographic data are generated. Then comes the most difficult part of the analysis: the interpretation of the results. Even though many efforts have been made to render the interpretation of the data as objective as possible (standards are available, for example), the final call whether an ignitable liquid is present or not, rests on the evaluation of the criminalist and remains subjective. Furthermore, it will probably continue to remain so forever. As such, the importance of the fire debris analyst's skills does not lie so much in his/her ability to operate a gas chromatograph-mass spectrometer, but rather in his/her capacity to determine if a set of peaks and valleys exhibited by a sample resembles closely enough those of a reference ignitable liquid. Although training in interpretation must heavily rely on practical exercises, the theoretical base must be obtained through the reading of scientific articles and books.

There is an abundance of literature in fire debris analysis; many articles are published every year in the most prestigious forensic journals worldwide. From 2001 to 2004, the detection and collection of fire debris from fire scenes represented less than 10% of the publications dedicated to fire debris analysis; the extraction techniques approximately 25%; the analytical techniques around 20%; and 50% of the publications dealt with the interpretation of the results. This underscores how important this step is and how there remains much more to do in this regard. Although periodical literature in fire debris analysis is relatively abundant, this is not so for comprehensive textbooks on the topic. For forensic scientists new to this field, it is difficult to start training by reading advanced literature that pertains to well-defined but isolated topics. I (ES) remember very well when I began my thesis: I had to gather and read about 400 articles on the topic before starting to get a clear picture of what fire debris analysis was. This is a tremendous amount of time and energy that cannot be easily devoted by the working forensic practitioner. So what about a textbook? Bertsch, Holzer, and Sellers wrote the last textbook on fire debris analysis, *Chemical analysis for the arson investigator and attorney*, in 1993. Because of the evolution of the field, this great book is no longer up-to-date. Other books mention the topic or devote a couple of chapters to it; however, today, there are no comprehensive books on fire debris analysis dedicated to the forensic practitioner. This book fills this void in the literature.

The idea that started this book arose from a social event at the 55th Annual Meeting of the American Academy of Forensic Sciences, which took place in Chicago, Illinois in February 2003. The chance encounter between an acquisitions editor from Elsevier Academic Press and one of the authors (ES) would become fruitful. Of course, the ambience created by the fantastic buffet and a couple of ethylic beverages helped to convince both parties that it was necessary to start a collaboration and write a book on the analysis of fire debris samples. The next morning, all freshened up, the future author (ES) hastened to meet with his two future co-authors (JD and RN). These two co-authors, who had much more life experience than the first one, warned him about the hard work ahead and placed some reserves on starting this journey. However, the enthusiasm was clearly there, and all three authors quickly agreed to write this book. It took almost five years to complete this work. Today, more than 170,000 words, more than 330 figures, and more than 70 tables have been mixed together to create this volume. This book was a long time in coming for many reasons, but mostly the authors wanted this book to be as comprehensive as possible and fully accurate. Therefore, it was decided not to compromise the quality of this writing for a quick release.

After an introductory chapter (Chapter 1), the reader is exposed to an informative history of fire debris analysis (Chapter 2). Then, a brief review of organic chemistry is included (Chapter 3) to provide the minimum knowledge needed to understand this field. Chapter 4 presents the concepts of the chemistry and the physics of fire. It finishes with an introduction to the development of a typical room fire. These concepts may appear superfluous at first, but the fire debris analyst will quickly realize that they actually are necessary to fully understand the work conducted in the laboratory. The techniques used to detect ignitable liquid residues at a fire scene are presented in Chapter 5 and the collection of samples in Chapter 6. These two chapters provide the laboratory analyst with some ideas of the work carried out by the fire investigator at the scene. They also provide the basics of good packaging practices for fire debris samples. Basic concepts of the refining of petroleum products are presented in the following chapter (Chapter 7), along with a brief classification of the petroleum products. Again, it is crucial for the fire debris analyst to have a basic idea of the origins and manufacturing schemes of finished petroleum-based ignitable liquids. Then, a review of the theory of the analytical instruments used in fire debris analysis is provided (Chapter 8). Gas chromatography and mass spectrometry are explained to some extent. This chapter, as for Chapter 3, provides a minimum of knowledge needed by all fire debris analysts.

After the first part of the book, which provides basic theoretical concepts and background information, the second part directly addresses the analysis of ignitable liquids and their residues. Chapter 9 introduces the reader to the different ignitable liquids, along with their characteristics. It teaches how to interpret chromatograms and correctly identify a neat ignitable liquid. Then, the too often forsaken but very important, preliminary examination of the debris is presented (Chapter 10), followed by the extraction techniques used to isolate ignitable liquid residues from their debris (Chapter 11). The reader may wonder whether or not the ordering of Chapters 9, 10, and 11 is correct. This ordering was a deliberate decision: Because the influence of the debris and the extraction technique can only be observed in the final output, the chromatogram, it was decided to present Chapter 9 first to guarantee a good flow and understanding of the concepts presented in the subsequent chapters. Finally, the interpretation of chromatograms from extracts from fire debris samples is presented in Chapter 12, along with the imperative concept of interfering products.

In the third part of the book, one can learn about the other techniques used in fire debris analysis and the future of this field (Chapter 13). Then, other particular examinations that are less frequently conducted are also presented (Chapter 14). These include the analysis of vegetable oil residues, automotive fluids, homemade chemical bombs, and flare residues. The last three chapters present the concepts of certification, accreditation, and standardization (Chapters 15 to 17).

It is hoped that this volume is both comprehensive and as succinct as possible regarding the topic of fire debris analysis. Of course, the entirety of the field could not be covered due to space constraints. Neural networks used in the interpretation of the results have not been presented. Appendices with chemical characteristics and molecule properties have not been included. All brands and models of analytical instruments used in fire debris analysis have not been covered. Questions regarding safety in the laboratory have been skipped. Finally, a chapter on how to write a report has not been incorporated. These were deliberate choices, which do not decrease the quality of the information presented. Indeed, the most accurate and recent information was included throughout the whole book.

This book has been designed to provide the theoretical basis required for the criminalist starting in fire debris analysis as well as the practical basis for the experienced fire debris analyst, who wishes to have a resource at hand for the vast majority of the issues that he/she may encounter. While it has been designed to teach the forensic scientist almost everything one wants to know about fire debris analysis, it was also written in clear and easy language so that students or non-scientists will also benefit from it. As a result, this book is a great asset for forensic scientists, fire investigators, prosecutors, attorneys, and instructors who wish to gain knowledge of the field.

Eric Stauffer, Julia A. Dolan, and Reta Newman

Acknowledgments

Eric Stauffer

When engaging in a big adventure, such as the writing of this book, many people become involved by providing their technical, administrative, logistical, and personal help. Thus, if the list of people to thank is quite long, it is only the reflection of the many great scientists who contributed to this publication through their experience, knowledge, and kindness. No words are sufficient enough to thank them.

First, we would like to thank the team at Elsevier Academic Press who believed in this book and who exhibited an incredible, almost unimaginable, patience. Jennifer Soucy led this project from almost its inception to its publication. Thank you so much for your fantastic work and your determination. Without you, this book would not be in print today. Kelly Weaver has also contributed a lot to this publication. She was always available and did excellent work. Christie Jozwiak handled the final phase of the publication process, particularly the production, which led to a beautiful final outcome. Thanks again to everyone at Elsevier Academic Press. It has been an immense pleasure to work with you and it is great always to be able to count on you.

Second, I would like to personally thank Dr. P. Mark L. Sandercock, Manager of Operations Support for the Royal Canadian Mounted Police, one of the greatest forensic scientists and fire debris analysts I know. Dr. Sandercock has dedicated an incredible amount of time and energy reviewing this book and providing critical and pertinent feedback and ideas. I have the utmost respect for his science and knowledge, which render his contribution to the forensic community priceless.

Third, I would like to thank all the other forensic scientists who reviewed the book, or portions of the book. Their work has been invaluable and their comments very much appreciated. Thanks to (in alphabetical order): Doug Byron, President of Forensic & Scientific Testing; Gretchen Lajoie with the Maine State Police Crime Laboratory; Dr. Olivier Delémont with the School of Criminal Sciences (ESC) at the University of Lausanne; and Sue Hetzel with SEA Limited. We also would like to deeply thank Dr. John D. DeHaan, President of Fire-Ex Forensics, for his review and then writing the foreword to this book.

Fourth, I would like to thank the people who provided material for the book. Particularly, I think of Dr. Glenn Frysinger, Professor at the US

Coast Guard Academy, who has conducted groundbreaking research in the application of GCxGC-MS in fire debris analysis. Dr. Frysinger has exceptional knowledge of the analysis of petroleum products and never ceases to amaze me with his ideas and discoveries. He is a front-runner whose contribution to the field of fire debris analysis will likely spark a new vision of the interpretation of fire debris analysis data. I also would like to thank (in alphabetical order): Steven J. Avato with the Bureau of Alcohol, Tobacco, Firearms and Explosives; Dr. Andy Becue with the ESC; Keith Bell with Holland Investigations; Colleen Carbine with the Crime Laboratory Bureau of the Miami-Dade Police Department; Laura Conner; Dr. Ronald Coulombe formerly with the Laboratoire de sciences judiciaires et de médecine légale (Québec, Canada); Blair Darst with Cunningham Investigative Services; Céline De La Porte; Emre Ertan with the Neuchâtel State Police (Switzerland); Florence Jolliet with the ESC; Dr. Stéphanie Lociciro with the ESC; Kristin A. McDonald with the Forensic Investigations Division of the New York Police Department Crime Laboratory; François Perbet, fire investigator in France; François Rey with the ESC; H. Kelly Wilson with Rimkus Consulting Group; and John H. Woodland, chemist in Iowa (USA).

Then, I would like to thank my partners in crime, Julia Dolan and Reta Newman for blindly accepting to join in this adventure. Reta and Julia were there for me many years ago when I was struggling with my master's degree research and they gave me direction, motivation, and encouragement to finish my research. Without them, I would have never been attracted to the field of fire debris analysis. There is nothing I can say to thank you for that. Your presence in my life is priceless and I will be forever grateful to you for that. The next time a project like this arises, we will all think twice before accepting it . . . I would like to also thank all my colleagues and friends involved in forensic sciences and fire debris analysis with whom I had many opportunities to discuss problems and solutions over the years. This interaction is invaluable and greatly helps me to conduct research and improve fire debris analysis. Thank you, thank you, and thank you, again. I hope we will have many more discussions in the future!

Finally, I would like to thank Dr. Sarah Brown, who has always been here for me, who has always been supportive of what I do, and whom I love very much. Sarah has also spent countless hours, day and night, to read and reread the text of this book to provide grammatical suggestions. Sarah, thank you so much for your incredible work and support.

Julia A. Dolan

I would like to thank my mentors, who have helped and encouraged me, and planted in me the love of the challenge of forensic sciences, especially Eileen Davis and Mary Lou Fultz. For my parents who always believed that I could do anything—my mom, Ella Agnes McCarthy Harris, who passed away while this book was in progress; my dad, James Edgar Harris, and stepmother Anna Clyde Fraker. I appreciate your faith and encouragement. My dear friend and technical expert in everything, Special Agent (ATF) Steven Avato who has taught me so much about fire investigation, philosophy, logic and has provided so much more than friendship. I especially want to thank Mick, who was so patient when I was writing and who is my absolute favorite person on the planet, Mom loves you. Finally, my co-authors Eric and Reta who have been so many things to me: teachers, inspirations, and of course friends. I love you guys. Still.

Reta Newman
I must thank the following people, for without them, my participation in this book would not have happened. First, to Mary Lou Fultz, my friend and my mentor for she is the reason I became so active in the fire debris analysis world. Second, to Julia Dolan, my dear friend, co-author, and my Mom's Club confidant for she travels the same roads and is an inspiration. Third, to Eric Stauffer, first student, then friend, now mentor, the most brilliant person in the fire debris community, for getting us into this project, for keeping it going, and for pushing it (kicking and screaming) to the end. Be very proud of this accomplishment, my friend—you have earned it! To Luke, my husband, my love, for putting up with all the projects for all these years—I will learn to say "no" sometime, I promise. To Christine, my step-daughter, my friend, how lucky I am to have you in my life. And, finally to Katie, my baby, my joy, for the wonderful child that you are and the great young lady you are becoming. I am so lucky–"cuz God gave me you!"

Foreword

It is a shock to one's sense of place to review some 40 years of progress in a discipline you pursued and contributed to for most of that time, all in one massive volume. One of my first assignments as a criminalist in 1970 was to analyze fire debris. There's the oven, there's the GC, and here's a syringe. There are the cans and jars of debris. Punch a hole in each lid, warm them in the oven, draw out a sample and inject it. That was the training. The column was a packed glass tube about 2 m long, the oven was isothermal, and the data "system" was a strip chart recorder connected to an FID detector. A pattern of 12 peaks or so, all on scale, was considered a successful chromatogram. (A steam distillation device was available if you thought you needed it.) You generated your own reference library for identifications. Gas chromatography had only been introduced to crime labs fewer than ten years previously. There were no courses (except for Perkin-Elmer's mini-courses), no reference books, and very few experts (defined as anyone who had done this kind of analysis for more than a year). You applied the best scientific approach and asked as many questions as you could. There were few, if any, standard procedures. You learned by doing. Luckily, the GC systems were simple (at first) and you learned by fixing and trying (and sometimes failing). When I first discovered "patterns" of peaks that didn't match any of my reference charts, there was no resource to turn to. Back to the GC with a variety of burned substrates, and *sometimes* the puzzles were solved by empirical testing.

As more criminalists did more samples, results were shared through Academy and regional meetings and publications, and as data systems and gas chromatography got better (thank you, Walt Jennings!), we developed more reliable and reproducible techniques, improved sensitivity, and got faster turn-around as well. By the 1980s capillary columns and computer-based data systems were becoming the norm. The sensitivity (detection limit) was always an issue. "I could smell it in my sample and you're telling me it's negative!" was a common refrain. The introduction of canines and their superior detection limits (but very limited specificity) brought new but similar challenges. Mass spectrometry has helped enormously to sort out both selectivity (accuracy) and sensitivity issues. We now can claim part per billion sensitivity in fire debris analysis with accuracy to match. And what have we discovered? The modern world is filled with volatile compounds, some of which mimic known petroleum products, some of which are the *same* products, left as traces from the production processes. So, even if we can identify minute residues of "gasoline" in a suspect's footwear, what is the significance? Does it mean the wearer splashed it on his shoes while setting the fire or just had the bad luck to buy shoes made in some foreign land where gasoline was used as an industrial solvent for the glue used to put them together?

We have also discovered what a complex and irascible event a fire can be. Despite the fact that we have been using fire as a (more-or-less) controllable part of our human existence for 30,000 years or so, there is still so much we don't know. The pyrolysis and combustion products produced in a fire can vary enormously depending on the fuel involved, its temperature, the presence or absence of oxygen at the burning surface, the intensity and duration of its exposure to radiant heat and flames, even its orientation and location in the fire environment. Post-flashover conditions produce radiant heat intensities and temperatures far in excess of conditions in a simple flame, and they change continually during a fire with turbulent mixing and changing ventilation conditions. Extinguishment methods play varied and complex roles in determining what volatile products remain after a fire.

The amazing thing is that we, as a multi-disciplinary forensic science community, have come to understand so much about fire-related evidence (and to appreciate the limits of what we do not yet know). It is not until you see such accumulated knowledge in one place that you appreciate the progress made in the last 40 years or so. The fire debris analyst of today has to know so much about so many different topics to do the job properly!

I cannot think of three authors better qualified to bring this knowledge together. Among them they have dealt with fire evidence (and fire investigations!) on the local, national and international level. They have researched many of the critical topics themselves and published their results widely and in many different forms. They have taught these topics to a wide variety of audiences so they can appreciate the needs of students and tailor their material appropriately. The breadth and depth of their knowledge and experience is reflected in this volume. From the chemistry of ignitable liquids and their production, to scene examination and collection, and to separation, analysis and characterization, it is all here. So much of the knowledge involved in high quality fire debris analysis comes from disparate disciplines, and it is good to see it condensed into a useful compendium. But this book accomplishes more—as it puts "fire debris analysis" into the wider context of a criminalistics inquiry. Far too often such analysts develop a single-focus mindset, blinded to the real challenge of finding the answer to the big question: how can the cause of this fire (be it intentional or accidental) be determined fairly and accurately? To their great credit, Eric, Reta and Julia have devoted two chapters to looking beyond the elusive volatiles in the can. To open the can, assess the contents, describe it and evaluate it—that is the right way. There has been great progress made in latent fingerprint and DNA techniques that make it possible to wring information out of fire "debris" that can identify a *person* responsible. Toolmarks, physical matches, chemical incendiary residues, even questioned documents can also play a role in finding the answers—but only if we look for them.

There is a look to the future as well. There are always new techniques being offered, some of which have potential. Others do not appear to help answer the important questions—what is it, does it belong there, how did it get there, and is it of evidentiary significance? Thanks to these authors, we can appreciate those important questions and the techniques and knowledge necessary to find the answers.

John DeHaan, PhD

CHAPTER 1

Introduction

"The journey of a thousand miles begins with a single step."
Lao Tzu, Chinese philosopher (604 BC–531 BC)

1.1 THE OTHER USE OF GASOLINE AND DIESEL FUEL

For a small single story building, the prescription is two incendiary devices each using 5 gallons of accelerant. [. . .] It is usually unnecessary and a waste of precious time to gather up flammable materials at the scene (e.g. fenceposts, branches, wooden furniture). It is much more valuable to bring more fuel if you are concerned about the success of your fire. Gasoline and diesel are perfectly suited to delivering large quantities of heat, not too fast and not too slow.

These lines, found in the 2001 publication of the Earth Liberation Front entitled, "Setting fires with electrical timers," summarize relatively well why ignitable liquids often are used as accelerants in committing arson [1]. Fortunately, the average layperson does not comprehend the chemistry and physics of fire and, more particularly, the use of ignitable liquids as accelerants. Thus, it is frequent that a criminal willing to set a structure (building) or a vehicle on fire douses it with an incredibly large amount of gasoline. Although this practice is highly inefficient from a combustion perspective, the resulting fire scene may contain a great amount of gasoline residues—an advantageous situation from a forensic perspective—which can be detected by the fire investigator with the help of the crime laboratory. The identification of ignitable liquid residues (ILR) from fire debris samples collected at a fire scene constitutes the practice of fire debris analysis.

Gasoline was not developed for intentional use by arsonists. As a matter of fact, it was developed in the early 1800s to fight against lice and their eggs pharmaceutically. However, this use was discontinued when it was discovered that gasoline was carcinogenic and led to a greater risk of dermatitis. Additionally, its use against lice usually was not carried out in a very safe manner from a fire safety perspective, which led to serious injuries and deaths [2]. In 1855, Benjamin Silliman Jr. (New Haven, Connecticut, USA) patented the distillation of crude oil into a number of products, including gasoline [3]. As the car industry expanded, gasoline underwent a significant evolution to become the fuel of choice for automotive vehicles. In 1919, gasoline became the most commonly produced petroleum-based product in the United States. In 2006, more than three billion barrels were produced in the United States [4].[1]

Gasoline is one of the accelerants of choice for arsonists. Actually, it is the most commonly encountered accelerant in probably every country around the world. The reasons lie in the fact that it is readily available, inexpensive, easy to transport, and more importantly, it is easy to ignite and it provides the necessary energy to accelerate a fire. Arsonists do not travel great distances to find the perfect accelerant; they use whatever works. Although gasoline is the most used accelerant, it is clear that many other ignitable liquids also are used to start fires, such as charcoal lighter fluids, paint thinners, lamp oils, diesel fuels, alcohols, and many other solvents.

Arson v. Incendiary, Intentional, or Deliberate Fire

The term "arson"—from the medieval Latin term *arsio*, which comes from the Latin verb *ardere* (to burn)—is a legal term in many countries. Thus, its exact definition varies from one jurisdiction to another. However, a general definition commonly accepted for arson is a criminal act of deliberately setting fire to a property. Arson implies that there is criminal intent and deliberate burning of some object, usually a structure or a vehicle. In some instances, the terms "intentional fire," "incendiary fire," or "deliberate fire" are used interchangeably with arson. These terms are used in order to avoid citing the term arson, which would imply a legal meaning. Setting some dead leaves on fire in the backyard (respecting the jurisdiction's regulations) or lighting a grill to cook some meat are two examples of fires intentionally started. However, typically these are not labeled arson as they do not include a criminal element. Indeed, when the term intentional fire is used, the criminal intent of the fire often is implied, even if not directly stated. Thus, when statistics present "intentional" or "deliberate" fires rather than simply arson, one should consider that they include only fires that have a criminal connotation.

Nevertheless, some jurisdictions prosecute fires that have been accidentally set by a human being. Thus, although these fires are part of a criminal prosecution, they typically do not involve a criminal intent and are not classified as part of the intentional fires nor as part of arson. Throughout this book, the terms arson, deliberate, intentional, and incendiary fires are used interchangeably unless otherwise stated.

---

[1]A barrel is a unit used in the petroleum industry. It is equivalent to 42 gallons or 159 liters and it is abbreviated bbl.

Unfortunately, arson is a problem that goes much beyond property crime. It also takes the lives of many people and animals every year, it produces feelings of insecurity to citizens, and it costs enormous amounts of money in damages, victim's compensation, government services (firefighting, law enforcement, government insurance, etc.), and private insurance services. Nevertheless, it is a crime difficult to prosecute because, by its very nature, it destroys evidence. In the United States, though relatively accessible, statistics in fire and arson investigation are not very accurate and one must be very prudent when interpreting the figures provided. One of the main reasons for such precaution is that the reporting system is based on fire department reports rather than fire investigation reports [5]. Thus, the fire chief responding to the scene may declare a fire electrical without having been trained to investigate fire. The scene might later reveal that the fire was incendiary when subsequently investigated by the fire marshal or a private fire investigator. Furthermore, there is a significant number of fires for which the exact cause remains unknown. The field of fire investigation is very prone to differences of opinion. Thus it is never truly known what caused some fires even after thorough investigation. Finally, though general statistics about fires are readily available (numbers, locations, types, etc.), specific data regarding the use of ignitable liquids or the types of ignitable liquid used in criminal fires is not readily available.

Accelerant v. Ignitable Liquid

The term "accelerant" is often wrongfully used synonymously with "ignitable liquid." It is important to remember that a material is defined as an ignitable liquid based upon its physical and chemical properties, but a material is defined as an accelerant based upon how it is used. An accelerant is [10]: "a fuel (usually a flammable liquid) that is used to initiate or increase the intensity or speed of spread of fire." Therefore, not all flammable liquids found at a fire scene are accelerants and conversely, not all accelerants used to commit arson are liquids. A paper trail used by an arsonist to set a house on fire is an accelerant. However, the presence of gasoline on a piece of carpet placed in a garage under vehicles to collect oil stains is not an accelerant; rather, it is defined as an incidental liquid present on the substrate.

As an example, a criminalist in the laboratory receives two liquid samples from an investigator: A and B. Following analysis, both samples are identified as gasoline. At that point, the scientist can state with no further information that both samples A and B are ignitable liquids. The inves-

tigator, knowing the sources of the liquids, can infer whether or not they are accelerants. Sharing the information that sample A was retrieved from the gasoline tank of the suspect's lawnmower, and that sample B was recovered from glass bottle fragments with a wick protruding from the neck portion found at a fire scene, the investigator can infer whether they were used as accelerants or not. Sample B was used for the purpose of initiating a fire; therefore, it is an accelerant. Conversely, sample A simply was used as a fuel for an internal combustion engine, and is therefore not an accelerant. Both samples are ignitable liquids and have the same chemical composition, yet one is an accelerant, and the other is not. It is crucial that the criminalist not refer to ignitable liquids as accelerants based solely on their chemical and physical properties. The term accelerant necessarily refers to the context of the fire and the investigation. This is why, throughout this text, the terms "ignitable liquids" and "ignitable liquid residues" usually are used; only under the rare and appropriate circumstances, do the authors refer to "accelerants."

Table 1-1	The different types of ignitable liquids found at fire scenes in a study carried out in the United States between 1994 and 1998 [7]. Values are provided as annual average number of fires. The last column is the proportion of fires that are either intentional or suspicious in nature for each category of liquid. This means that 52.6% of the fires where gasoline is found are intentional or suspicious in nature. Note that the categories used in this table do not correspond to the ignitable categories commonly used in fire investigation and forensic sciences.

Class	Description	Examples	Annual average number	Intentional or suspicious [%]
Gasoline	—	—	5,800	52.6
IA flammable liquid	Flash point below 73°F (22.8°C) and boiling point below 100°F (37.8°C)	Ethyl ether, pentane, ethylene oxide	900	39.0
IB flammable liquid	Flash point below 73°F (22.8°C) and boiling point at or above 100°F (37.8°C)	Acetone, ethyl alcohol, JP-jet fuel (gasoline excluded)	500	20.5
IC flammable liquid	Flash point at or above 73°F (22.8°C) and below 100°F (37.8°C)	Butyl alcohol, propyl alcohol, styrene, turpentine	500	25.3
II combustible liquid	Flash point at or above 100°F (37.8°C) but less than 140°F (60°C)	Kerosene, most paint thinners	4,000	8.5
IIIA combustible liquid	Flash point at or above 140°F (60°C) but less than 200°F (93.4°C)	Fuel oil 4, 5, and 6, cottonseed oil, creosote oil	500	0
IIIB combustible liquid	Flash point at or above 200°F (93.4°C)	Cooking oil, motor oil, lubricating oil	4,400	0

In spite of this, it is always interesting to look at some of these numbers and to have a rough, even if knowingly inaccurate, idea of the proportion of different factors surrounding fire and arson investigation and, more particularly, the use of ignitable liquids at fire scenes. In 2005, Hall reported that less than 10% of the intentionally set structure fires involved the use of incendiary devices [6]. Table 1-1 presents some data extracted from an older report including US home fires that occurred between 1994 and 1998 (average annual values are reported) [7]. It shows the breakdown of different classes of ignitable liquids and their use in intentional or suspicious fires. As previously stated, gasoline is the most frequently encountered accelerant used in arson cases, followed by light flammable liquids, which are usually the most readily available and efficient products.

Again, these figures must be cautiously interpreted, as there was an annual average of 80,000 structure fires that were caused by arson during this period and fewer than 4,000 arson cases were reported to involve the use of ignitable liquids [8]. In practice, it seems that the proportion of arson fires involving the use of ignitable liquids as accelerants is much higher than the 5% value reported. As a matter of fact, statistics provided by the Office of the Ontario Fire Marshal show that approximately 10% of the 4,985 fires investigated by that agency between 1995 and 2005 involved an ignitable liquid as the first material ignited [9]. Also note the fact that this agency is likely to handle a greater proportion of intentional/suspicious fires than a regular fire department, thus there is a higher proportion of fires involving an ignitable liquid.

1.2 FIRE INVESTIGATION

1.2.1 Principle

Whenever a fire occurs, an investigation almost always ensues. Depending on the laws in place within the jurisdiction, parties responsible for the fire are prosecuted under penal law if the fire was set intentionally or even, in some instances, if the fire was set accidentally. All the forensic sciences have goals of determining if a crime has been committed, identifying its victim(s) and perpetrator(s), and identifying the modus operandi of the perpetrator(s) [11]. Fire scene investigation, also referred to origin and cause investigation, is a specialized discipline of forensic sciences, it is carried out mainly to answer the question of whether or not a crime has been committed and what the modus operandi of the perpetrator is.[2] The identification of victim(s) and perpetrator(s) is usually performed using a traditional criminalistic approach and does not concern the origin and cause investigation itself.[3] Therefore, the goals of fire scene investigation are to answer the following two specific questions: "Where did the fire start?" and "Why did the fire start?"

---

[2] It is important to specify that while public agencies are mostly concerned with investigating a fire to determine whether a crime has been committed or not, there are many private fire investigators who are concerned with the accidental aspect of the fire and who work in the context of a civil litigation rather than a criminal one. As such, when considering its broad definition, fire (scene) investigation is no longer just applied in the context of a criminal activity, but also to fully comprehend and identify the factors and circumstances that led to the fire in order to provide sufficient information for the judge or jury to assess the responsibility of each party at trial.

[3] However, it is part of the overall investigation. This is the reason why a fire should always be investigated with a general criminalistic approach in order to properly exploit the scene and its evidence. This can be carried out in a team setting with a fire investigator accompanied by crime scene investigators and/or criminalists, or by one person whose competency includes all aspects.

A/ Origin of the Fire

The first question refers to the determination of the origin of the fire. The fire investigator must identify the first material ignited and its location, which is called the point of origin (or the seat of fire). It is critical to identify the point or area of origin because without it, it is impossible, except under some particular circumstances, to answer the second question. When it is not possible to identify an area of origin or a very precise point, the subsequent process is thus greatly complicated.

B/ Cause of the Fire

The second question refers to the determination of the cause of the fire. The fire investigator must identify the ignition source that ignited the combustible which first caught fire, and the circumstances that brought the two together. The ignition source is found at the point of origin unless it has been subsequently removed. In order to determine which possible sources of ignition are present and which ones are suitable to ignite the surrounding combustible, it is essential for the investigator to be aware of the different sources of thermal energy, their transfer, and the properties of the materials available in the area of origin.

1.2.2 Investigative Agencies and Investigators

In most countries, it is the responsibility of the police department to determine if a crime (arson) has been committed or if a fire was accidental or resulted from negligence. The fire department is usually the first entity to arrive at the scene to carry out rescue and extinguishment activities. Once these operations terminated the responsibility of the scene is transferred to the investigative authority. In the United States as well as in some other countries, such as England and Australia, fire departments are given the legal authority to conduct fire (and explosion) scene examinations and to proceed with a complete criminal investigation. Such departments usually have sworn law enforcement officers carrying weapons who are responsible for conducting the investigation. Even though they are not part of the police department *per se*, they can fulfill all the functions of a police detective. In other countries, the investigation of fires and explosions is mostly the responsibility of the police department, which may have specialized units dedicated to that duty.

Although origin and cause investigation is a specialized discipline of forensic sciences, many fire investigators are not forensic scientists and did not undergo specific forensic training. This is particularly true in jurisdictions where fires and explosions are investigated by fire departments such as in the United States. Thus, their approach to the examination of the fire scene is purely from a fire perspective, which consists in determining the origin and the cause of the fire. In this fashion, they may not always investigate a fire scene with a comprehensive criminalistic approach and may not answer the other main goals of forensic sciences, namely, identifying the victim(s) and perpetrator(s). This might also be one of the reasons why arson crimes do not present a significant rate of clearance.

1.2.3 Investigation Steps

Figure 1-1 shows the typical steps of a fire investigation. The investigation of a fire starts with the occurrence of a fire or an attempted fire. In general, the fire department is called first to proceed to the extinguishment and other rescue operations. It is important for the investigator to be aware of the fire department intervention so he or she can evaluate the modifications brought to the scene through the action of the firefighters. At some point, the investigator is summoned to the scene. He or she may arrive during the extinguishment operation or at a later time.

Before the investigator actually starts the examination of the scene, it is crucial to gather as much background information as possible regarding the fire. Background information includes interviews of victim(s) and witness(es), owner(s) of the premises, and collection of information from the fire department, police department, and other official entities. Fire departments usually prepare a run report of the intervention, which contains a limited amount of information. It is also crucial for the investigator to interview firefighters as well as the chief in charge. The ultimate goal of the collection of background information is to establish the most detailed account of the circumstances surrounding the fire, most importantly the chronology of the different events preceding the fire.

Then, the observation of the scene begins. The scene is examined from general to particular and from the least burned area to the most burned area. First, the investigator goes around the scene to comprehend the extent of the fire. Then, the investigator observes fire and smoke patterns in order to identify the origin of the fire. Once an area of origin is determined, the investigator proceeds to the identification of all ignition sources within that area and determines the potential causes of the fire.

At any time during the observation of the scene, the investigator may call other specialists to assist in the investigation. These specialists can be forensic scientists or other individuals with particular skills and knowledge relevant to the investigation. These include engineers, chemists, electricians, mechanics, and the like.

Also, during the investigation, different items of evidence usually are collected. One of the very commonly collected items of evidence is a fire debris sample in order to determine the presence of ignitable liquid residues. Other types of evidence may also be collected such as electrical wiring, remnants of a timing device, mechanical parts, and such.

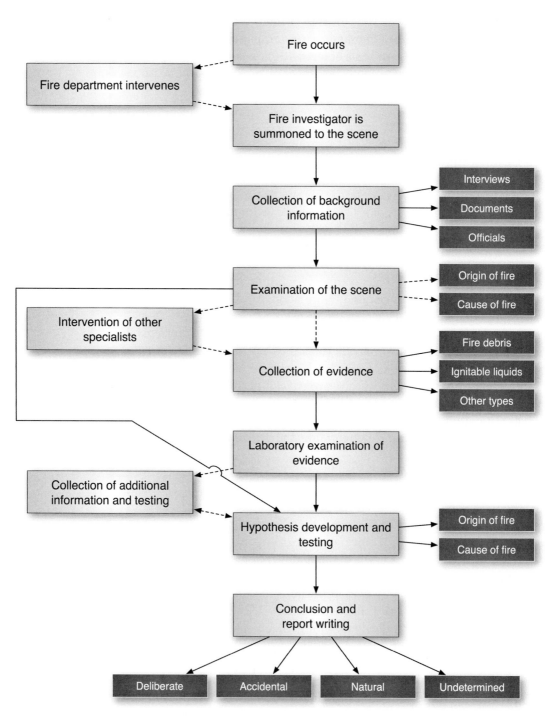

FIGURE 1-1 *The different steps of a typical fire investigation.*

Next, the evidence is forwarded to the laboratory for examination. The investigator should personally contact the criminalist(s) performing the examination of the evidence to communicate information regarding the circumstances of the fire and the evidence and to ensure that the most pertinent examinations are conducted. Also, in some instances, the forensic scientist may request additional items of evidence.

During the scene investigation, the investigator usually develops a hypothesis or a series of hypotheses regarding the origin and cause of the fire. Information provided by specialists at the scene and results from the crime laboratory are integrated into this process. These hypotheses are then tested using the scientific method and are refined as necessary. The goal is to validate the hypothesis in order to reach a conclusion. At that point, the investigator may want to gather more information pertinent to the case. Additionally, testing might be necessary to determine if a hypothesis is valid or not.

Finally, once the investigation is complete and the most suitable hypothesis validated, it is possible to reach a conclusion and write a fire investigation report. The four possible conclusions—from a legal perspective—with respect to the cause of a fire are deliberate, accidental, natural, or undetermined. The proportion of undetermined fires is actually quite significant, due to the destructive nature of fire.

1.3 WHAT IS FIRE DEBRIS ANALYSIS?

1.3.1 Definition

Fire debris analysis (FDA) is the science related to the examination of fire debris samples performed to detect and identify ignitable liquid residues (ILR). When fire debris samples suspected to contain traces of ignitable liquid are collected from the fire scene, they are forwarded to the crime laboratory along with the request to identify the presence of any possible ILR.

For most criminalists, the analysis of fire debris samples starts at the laboratory when the sample is brought in by the scene investigator. However, the story of the sample begins much earlier. Its history actually starts at the moment when the materials constituting the sample are produced and assembled together. Then, it undergoes fire (possibly preceded by a generous dousing of ignitable liquid) and often fire extinguishment procedures. Finally, it is sampled by the fire investigator and brought to the laboratory. Chapters 4 through 6 and Chapter 12 describe some of these steps, leading to a better understanding of what constitutes a fire debris sample.

1.3.2 Examination Steps

The examination of fire debris is carried out in five steps as shown in Figure 1-2.

FIGURE 1-2

FIGURE 1-2

The different steps of the examination of fire debris samples in order to determine the presence of ignitable liquid residues.

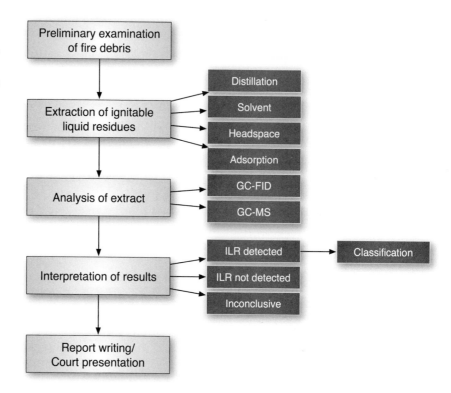

A/ Preliminary Examination

Before performing any types of destructive or nondestructive analysis of the sample, the criminalist proceeds to a preliminary examination of the debris (see Chapter 10). This usually consists of simply observing the content of the debris and possibly conducting an olfactory examination. The goal of this examination is threefold: First, it is to obtain any information regarding the possible presence of an ignitable liquid. This information is vital to the choice of the proper extraction technique. Second, it is to determine the nature of the debris. This is useful in the choice of the proper extraction technique and it is needed to properly interpret the final results. Finally, it is to determine whether other physical evidence of forensic interest are present and if so, to proceed with their preservation and to identify the proper sequence of examination in integration with ILR extraction.

B/ Extraction

This step, also referred to as isolation, consists of removing any (volatile or semivolatile) ignitable liquid residues that may be present in the debris so that it is in a form suitable for their subsequent analysis (see Chapter 11). Traces of ignitable liquid present in a sample are adsorbed onto the substrate, which is not in a suitable form for the instrumental analysis. Thus, it is necessary to isolate the ILR into a proper form, either in a liquid state (pure or in solution) or in a gaseous state. The different techniques available for the extraction step are based either on distillation (mostly obsolete), solvent extraction, headspace, or adsorption.

C/ Analysis

Once ILR are in a suitable form, analysis proceeds. This step is carried out using gas chromatographic (GC) techniques (see Chapter 8). Ignitable liquids usually are composed of tens or hundreds of different compounds (see Chapter 7), thus it is not possible to analyze the extract without first separating its components and then detecting them. Modern instrumental analysis allows for such a separation and GC is the most and only suitable technique to carry out this mission. The detection of the analytes normally is performed either by flame ionization detection (FID) or preferably, by mass spectrometry (MS).

D/ Interpretation of Results

Once the analytical data have been generated, it is possible to proceed with the most important, difficult, and delicate step of fire debris analysis: the interpretation of results (see Chapters 9 and 12). The interpretation of results consists of reviewing and analyzing the data to determine whether or not an ignitable liquid is present in the sample. The data usually consists of chromatograms obtained by the GC analysis, mass spectra obtained by the MS, and any other observations made during the examination of the debris. Whenever available, the circumstances around which the evidence was discovered and collected must be integrated into the interpretation. The criminalist does not stop at determining whether an ignitable liquid is present or not. He or she must characterize the liquid present in the debris, which typically is done by categorizing it, for example following the classification of ASTM International [12, 13].

E/ Report Writing and Court Presentation

Once the data have been interpreted and the conclusion reached, the criminalist prepares a report outlining the items of evidence examined, the examinations carried out, the results obtained, and the conclusions reached. This report must be succinct but comprehensive and understandable to the layperson.

Additionally, in some countries, and more particularly in the United Kingdom and the United States, the criminalist often is called to testify in court. In such instances, the expert witness must appear at trial. After qualifying as an expert, he or she must explain the examinations performed on the different items of evidence and present the results obtained as well as the conclusions reached. It is usually at this stage that any irregularities in the work performed or any misinterpretations of the results are brought to light, which may invalidate the criminalist's work. This reminds any forensic scientist how important it is to perform any forensic examinations with the greatest care, to use solely validated scientific techniques, to follow the scientific method, and to maintain the highest standard of ethical practice.

1.3.3 Other Examinations

The main goal of fire debris analysis is to determine whether or not an ignitable liquid is present in a fire debris sample; however, there are other laboratory examination requests that are closely related to fire debris analysis. These include:

- The determination of the function of an ignitable liquid.
- The physical and chemical characterization (such as flash point or boiling point) of an ignitable liquid.
- The determination of the source of an ignitable liquid.
- The identification of an unknown liquid.
- The examination of fire debris to determine the presence of chemicals susceptible of undergoing spontaneous ignition.
- The determination of the propensity of a liquid to undergo self-heating and spontaneous ignition.
- The examination of fire debris for the presence of other sources of ignition such as flare residues and timing device remnants.

The main reasons these examination requests are forwarded to the criminalist handling fire debris samples are either because they require the same type of instrumentation used to perform fire debris analysis or because this person is the laboratory point of contact for the fire investigator.

A/ Determination of the Function of an Ignitable Liquid

The determination of the function of an ignitable liquid (charcoal starter fluid, paint thinner, fuel, etc.) is not usually possible; however, characterization of the liquid through examination may provide some indications. Unfortunately, chemically and physically similar or even identical liquids can be used for two or more different purposes. For example, a certain liquid may be used as either a lamp oil or as a charcoal starter fluid. Additionally, a liquid intended for one particular purpose can present two different chemistries. Chapter 9 deals with this topic and presents the limitations of such a determination.

B/ Physical and Chemical Characterization of an Ignitable Liquid

In some instances, the investigation requires more information regarding a liquid than just its nature. For example, the determination of the flash point of a kerosene sample might be crucial in the evaluation of the proper functioning of a water heater (see Chapter 14). In another case, the determination of the melting point of a given fuel needs to be known to corroborate or refute a certain hypothesis. Also, the autoignition temperature of a liquid may be required information in order to evaluate a scenario involving its ignition on a hot surface. There are many examinations that can be performed on ignitable liquids and many of these fall outside the capabilities of a typical public service crime laboratory. Some crime laboratories are equipped to measure flash points, but that is about all the services available in this regard. Using private or government assay laboratories with specialized capabilities may be necessary if such examinations are requested.

C/ Determination of the Source of an Ignitable Liquid

Often, fire investigators would like to know where a given ignitable liquid comes from. It is not uncommon that a jug containing remnants of gasoline is found at a fire scene or within the vehicle of a suspect. Many times, the investigator also collects gasoline from a gas station and submits all these samples to the crime laboratory, asking whether or not the samples of gasoline have a common source. Determination of the identity of a source in fire debris analysis is a very delicate field and is usually not possible. It is often possible to exclude a common source between two samples, but the ability to infer common source between two samples is extremely limited. Detailed information regarding such examination and the subsequent interpretation of results is provided in Chapter 9.

D/ Identification of Unknown Liquids

It is not uncommon for the criminalist at the laboratory to receive an unknown liquid with the request to identify it. The liquid in question might not even be ignitable, but the submitter may not even know this. The reason these unknown liquids end up on the desk of a fire debris analyst is because the use of GC-MS along with Fourier transform infrared spectroscopy (FTIR) is one of the most suitable instruments to proceed with such a determination. In such instances, the fire debris analyst might work in collaboration with another criminalist from the trace evidence section for example.

E/ Residues of Liquids Undergoing Spontaneous Ignition

A few crime laboratories also examine samples for residues of liquids capable of undergoing spontaneous ignition, commonly referred to as vegetable oil residues (VOR) [14, 15]. This type of analysis might bring important answers to an investigation, where the presence of vegetable or animal oils is suspected as the cause of the fire. Chapter 14 introduces this concept and presents the examination scheme.

F/ Propensity to Self-Heat

In some other instances, investigators have a liquid that they would like to evaluate to determine its propensity to self-heat and possibly to spontaneously ignite [16]. This type of examination is typically outside of the capabilities of most crime laboratories and requires some specific apparatus. If this is the case, the investigator must resort to fire-testing laboratories with specialized capabilities in this type of examination.

G/ Other Sources of Ignition

Fire debris samples may contain remnants of the source of ignition such as road flare residues, matches, or timing devices [17]. They may also contain other evidence of forensic interest. The criminalist must be trained to recognize and preserve such evidence. Often, the examination of such evidence requires the intervention of another forensic specialist.

1.4 WHO PERFORMS FIRE DEBRIS ANALYSIS?

1.4.1 Providers (Laboratories)

Fire debris analysis services are found in most crime laboratories in the United States and in almost all major crime laboratories in other countries. The only expensive analytical equipment required to perform fire debris analysis is a gas chromatograph or gas chromatograph-mass spectrometer (see Chapter 8). Other pieces of equipment include a hood, an oven big enough to accommodate fire debris containers, and small laboratory items that mostly depend on the extraction technique used (see Chapter 11). If the laboratory offers a larger range of services related to fire debris analysis such as flash point determination, additional pieces of equipment may be required (see Chapter 14).

In the United States, crime laboratories with fire debris analysis capability are found at national, state, and local levels. The laboratories operated by the Bureau of Alcohol, Tobacco, Firearms and Explosives (ATF) are probably among the most advanced and experienced laboratories conducting such examination at a national level in the United States. Most state crime laboratories offer fire debris analysis as part of their basic services. In some states, such as Florida or Ohio, however, is possible to find laboratories operated by the fire marshal's office rather than the state police or state law enforcement agency. These laboratories are specialized in assisting fire investigators and can typically provide high quality fire debris analysis as well as explosive analysis. Moreover, they might be able to provide additional assistance when compared to a regular crime laboratory by carrying extra instruments such as a flash point determination apparatus.

Using Public Resources

Public investigators representing smaller jurisdictions may not have access to a full service forensic science laboratory capable of providing fire debris analysis. The option will always exist to utilize pay-for-service private laboratories; however, public investigators may have other options available. When addressing investigations that have a direct public interest, these investigators may be able to take advantage of laboratory services offered by their state or by the federal government. Many state laboratory systems will accept evidence from smaller agencies within their state when the purpose benefits the public. In the United States, the federal government's interests in fire investigation fall under the primary jurisdiction of either the Bureau of Alcohol, Tobacco, Firearms and Explosives (ATF) or the Federal Bureau of Investigation (FBI). Both the ATF and the FBI have forensic science laboratories providing fire debris analysis services. Although their primary function is to support federal investigations, public investigators requesting their services may sometimes use these laboratories. To inquire about accessing the services of a federal laboratory, the public investigator should contact the corresponding local field office.

In other countries, where fewer crime laboratories are usually present, fire debris analysis is offered in most major laboratories. In Canada, the Royal Canadian Mounted Police (RCMP) laboratories, the Centre of Forensic Sciences' laboratories in Toronto and Sault Ste Marie (Ontario), the *laboratoire de sciences judiciaires et de médecine légale* in Montréal (Québec), all have excellent fire debris analysis practices. In France, the laboratories of the *Préfecture de Police de Paris*, *Police Nationale*, and *Gendarmerie Nationale* (IRCGN) provide this service. In Switzerland, only three laboratories (University of Lausanne, University of Bern, and the *Wissenschaftlicher Dienst* of the Zurich Police) have such capabilities.

Government laboratories are not the only forensic laboratories to offer fire debris analysis services. In the United States and in the United Kingdom particularly, it is possible to find many private (or semiprivate) laboratories providing fire debris analysis either as part of their practice or as their sole service. More than a dozen private laboratories offer fire debris analysis in the United States.

Most government laboratories carry out forensic examinations free of charge to public agencies, but private laboratories charge a fee per sample—typically between 100 and 200 USD—or, less commonly, per hour. Public agencies should contact their local crime laboratories or national ones such as the ATF to obtain information regarding the level and conditions under which services are offered. Public agencies can also use private laboratories, but they will most likely have to pay a fee. It is worthy to note, though, that some private laboratories perform analyses on samples at a discounted price for public agencies. In some instances, it is desirable for public agencies to use private laboratories because the turnaround time is normally much shorter. Some public laboratories have an extreme turnaround time of several months, but most of them can provide verbal response or a written report within a couple of weeks. When working with private laboratories, a verbal response is commonly provided within 24 to 48 hours following receipt of the sample. This could present a great advantage in a given investigation and this is the reason why many private laboratories contract samples for some public agencies on a regular basis.

It is important for the investigator desiring to submit samples to a public or private laboratory to ensure that the work performed is of great quality. Some laboratories provide the best work possible and are extremely reliable entities for such examination. However, some laboratories have been known to provide substandard work, which could have disastrous consequences to the investigation and subsequent trial. The investigator must therefore be very careful of the laboratory chosen. This is why it is crucial for the fire investigator to clearly communicate with the criminalist and to obtain clear explanation of the work performed at the laboratory, the certifications held by the personnel, the accreditations carried by the laboratory, the (standard) methods used to examine fire debris samples, and the participation to Round Robin or other proficiency testing (see Chapters 15–17). Additionally, it is excellent practice for fire debris analysts to communicate among themselves to ensure that the laboratory is using up-to-date techniques and is aware of the latest advances in fire debris analysis.

1.4.2 Examiners (Fire Debris Analysts)

Personnel performing the analysis of fire debris samples are forensic scientists or criminalists. Often, the examiner is referred to as a fire debris analyst or more simply, an analyst. Some practitioners consider the term criminalist as applying only to the generalist, working in several fields of forensic sciences. It is however important to keep in mind that many practitioners use the term fire debris analyst to designate an examiner who solely performs fire debris analysis. Even though these concepts are understood and respected, be aware that this book uses the terms forensic scientist, criminalist, fire debris analyst, and analyst almost interchangeably. Chapter 15 presents the education and training requirements for a scientist to become a fire debris analyst.

REFERENCES

1. Fireant Collective (2001) *Setting fires with electrical timers: An earth liberation front guide.*
2. Pray SW (1999) Head lice: Perfectly adapted human predators, *American Journal of Pharmaceutical Education*, **63**(2), pp 204–9.
3. Schiff JA (2005) How Yale launched the oil economy, *Yale Alumni Magazine*, **69**(2).
4. Energy Information Administration (2006) *Petroleum Supply Monthly–November 2006*, US Department of Energy, Washington, DC.

5. TriData Corporation (1997) *Uses of NFIRS: The many uses of the National Fire Incident Reporting System*, US Fire Administration–National Fire Data Center, Emmitsburg, MD.

6. Hall JR (2005) *Intentional fires and arson*, National Fire Protection Association, Quincy, MA.

7. Rohr KD (2001) *Selections from the U.S. home product report (forms and types of materials first ignited in fires) flammable or combustible liquids*, National Fire Protection Association, Quincy, MA.

8. United States Fire Administration/National Fire Data Center (2004) *Fire in the United States 1992–2001*, 13th edition, Department of Homeland Security–Federal Emergency Management Agency, Emmitsburg, MD.

9. Merkley D (2006) *Personal communication of April 10, 2006 to Eric Stauffer*, Office of the Ontario Fire Marshal (retired).

10. DeHaan JD (2002) *Kirk's fire investigation*, 5th edition, Prentice Hall, Upper Saddler River, NJ.

11. Stauffer E (2006) *Traces and their evidentiary value. In: Forensic investigation of stolen-recovered and other crime-related vehicles*, editors Stauffer E and Bonfanti M, Elsevier Academic Press, Burlington, MA.

12. ASTM International (2006) ASTM E 1387-01 *Standard test method for ignitable liquid residues in extracts from fire debris samples by gas chromatography*, Annual Book of ASTM Standards 14.02, West Conshohocken, PA.

13. ASTM International (2006) ASTM E 1618-06 *Standard test method for ignitable liquid residues in extracts from fire debris samples by gas chromatography-mass spectrometry*, Annual Book of ASTM Standards 14.02, West Conshohocken, PA.

14. Stauffer E (2005) A review of the analysis of vegetable oil residues from fire debris samples: Spontaneous ignition, vegetable oils, and the forensic approach, *Journal of Forensic Sciences*, **50**(5), pp 1091–100.

15. Stauffer E (2006) A review of the analysis of vegetable oil residues from fire debris samples: Analytical scheme, interpretation of the results, and future needs, *Journal of Forensic Sciences*, **51**(5), pp 1016–32.

16. Jones JC (1999) Recent developments and improvements in test methods for propensity towards spontaneous heating, *Fire and Materials*, **23**, pp 239–43.

17. Dean WL (1984) Examination of fire debris for flare (fusee) residues by energy dispersive x-ray spectrometry, *Arson Analysis Newsletter*, **8**(2), pp 23–46.

CHAPTER 2

History

"The moments of the past do not remain still; they retain in our memory the motion which drew them towards the future, towards a future which has itself become the past, and draw us on in their train."

Marcel Proust, French writer, essayist, and critic (1871–1922)

2.1 PREAMBLE

2.1.1 Why Learn Some History?

It is important to understand where fire debris analysis comes from and how it evolved into today's technology and practice. Looking back at the history of a scientific branch can be quite interesting, not to mention quite shocking. How predecessors did things makes one realize how much progress has been made. It also helps the modern criminalist to orient future research and developments in forensic sciences.

These are some of the reasons why the authors strongly believe it is important for every fire debris analyst to have a basic knowledge of the history of current practice. This chapter is intended to provide this information. When desired, the reader is encouraged to read further into the articles cited throughout the text to obtain more information about the past. Researching literature in the past is not always an easy task. Fortunately, the bulk of forensic sciences are quite young (about 120 years old) and fire debris analysis even younger (about 70 years old). Thus, the task is much easier than researching ancestral Roman Empire customs. The chapter limits the extent of the information presented to major milestones in fire debris analysis as well as to some noteworthy text extracts, which are often amusing. The research conducted to gather this material has been relatively thorough, however, it is not, and probably can never be, fully comprehensive.[1] Also, as a general rule, the older the information, the less reliable it is. Whenever available, controversies in history of fire debris analysis have been presented. The reader is also invited to return to this chapter once proficient in fire debris analysis, as it will make the reading much more entertaining.

2.1.2 Starting with Bread Crumbs

In 1945, H. Rethoret wrote in his fire investigation book [1]:

> *The sense of taste can also be used to good advantage. Prior to relying on the sense of taste, it has been recommended that fresh bread-crumbs be chewed for a while and then expectorated in order to get a clean taste in one's mouth. The suspected place is then lightly touched with a piece of bread which, in turn, is chewed for a while. The taste of combustible material is then noted, even if only a slight trace of it adheres to the bread. While this is an unappetizing method, it is useful. Practically everyone can recall from time to time tasting kerosene if their food accidentally touched that liquid.*

Although the sniffing of ashes by fire investigators was very common at the beginning of the century, and is still somewhat common today, the tasting of possible ignitable liquid was not so common. Rethoret's text is as good as it gets in this regard. A more "scientific" approach than the one offered by Rethoret is presented by Battle and Weston in 1954 [2]: "Investigators can quickly learn to recognize the odors of various flammable liquids by placing small amounts in wide-mouthed glass jars. By shutting their eyes, opening a jar, and guessing as to its contents they'll soon build up an experience which will permit them to make prompt identification."

The same year, Myren publishes his book in which he presents a case [3]: "In the burning of a dry goods store in North Carolina, one of the firemen noted that some of the stock of clothing appeared to be saturated with kerosene. He sealed several of the garments in a can, marked the can so that he could identify it, and turned it over to the solicitor. [. . .] Imagine the effect on the jury when the odor of kerosene from that can reached their nostrils."

Apparently, the olfactory examination was not only good for the fire investigator, but it was also excellent for convincing a jury during court proceedings.

---

[1] Most English literature has been thoroughly researched, as well as some German and French literature. However, the authors did not have enough resources to properly search important collections such as *Archiv für Kriminologie* and the *Archives d'anthropologie criminelle* of Professor Lacassagne. It is almost certain that if the German and French literature were to be extensively searched, pertinent information and contemporaneous discoveries would be developed.

The reliance on one's own sense of smell was a recommended practice from the beginning of fire investigation and is found in many early books treating the topic. However, one might think that with the progresses that started in the early 1940s and the advent of gas chromatography in 1960, the reliance on olfactory examination would be confined to the field investigator and to a very preliminary examination at the laboratory (see Chapter 10). Unfortunately, in 1978, although fire debris analysis was quite well-developed, it was still possible to find marginal procedures presented in forensic books such as [4]:

> *Infrared spectrophotometers are also used in the crime laboratory for identifying unknown liquids used as accelerants in cases of arson. Sometimes, however, quick tests can be easily done by investigators with only a limited knowledge of laboratory techniques.*
>
> *TEST 1 Any object suspected of containing a flammable substance may be heated in water to a temperature of 70°C. When the container is opened, it is often possible to determine the type of flammable material by its odor.*
>
> *TEST 2 A suspected substance may be broken into pieces and put into a distillation flask with a little water. The flask is then heated so that the material inside is distilled. The fractions passing off may be roughly identified by odor—gasoline being the more volatile will come first, then kerosene a few fractions further on.*

In 1978, infrared spectrometers were not commonly used at the crime laboratory to identify ignitable liquid residues (ILR), and, though a quick olfactory examination may prove useful with all samples, the procedures presented in the cited text should not be applied to fire debris samples.

2.1.3 The Very Beginning

One of the difficulties encountered in reconstructing an accurate timeline for the development of fire debris analysis is that there are many chronological inconsistencies in the information presented in the different publications related to fire investigation. As presented in the previous paragraph, setbacks (old and obsolete techniques published in newer books) are often found. Prior to the 1940s, it is extremely difficult to find any books or articles that describe any possible examination for the identification of the presence of ILR or even suggest the collection of debris.

In his *Manuel de police scientifique* from 1911, Reiss, founder of the now School of Criminal Sciences of the University of Lausanne in Switzerland, described the technique used to search for petroleum products in fire debris [5]. This is the oldest account of distillation techniques applied to fire debris analysis found by the authors, and the methods were well ahead of Reiss' time.

In 1923, Locard, in his manual on scientific police, referred the reader to the text of Reiss [6]: "We found traces of the fuel oil that was used to set the fire (Reiss)."[2] No other mention of the possible collection and analysis of fire debris was given.

In 1938, Bischoff gave a great explanation regarding the presence of ILR at the scene, their detection, and collection [7]:

> *A considerable portion of the liquid cannot be absorbed by the substrate onto which it is poured so the excess flows onto the floor and forms puddles. The liquid also follows declivities and seeps in cracks in the wood flooring, between floor tiles, and even penetrates the ground. These are the reasons why we can almost always retrieve sufficient quantities of this liquid in order to characterize it and to demonstrate its use. It is not rare that, after completely removing the debris, when lifting a wooden floor or digging up the ground we can perceive an odor characteristic and revealing of the ignitable liquid used by the arsonist. One must remember this smell when collecting debris that will be forwarded to a chemist for analysis performed in order to isolate and characterize the liquid.*[3]

In 1949, Turner advised the criminalist to secure liquids or samples that are believed to be impregnated with an inflammable material and to send them to the forensic laboratory for analysis [8]. He also recommended collecting undamaged or unimpregnated samples as controls. Interestingly, no description of any analytical techniques applied to fire debris analysis is found in his book.

It is important to remember that fire investigation is as contemporary as forensic sciences. As a matter of fact, in the United States, one of the oldest published articles relating to the possible investigation of fires is a letter written by Thomas Edison to the New York Board of Underwriters and dated 1881 [9]. Edison warns them about the possible danger of electricity in starting a fire. The science of fire investigation probably started prior

---

[2] Text translated by the authors. The original French text reads [6]: *"On a retrouvé la trace du pétrole avec lequel on avait mis le feu (Reiss)."*

[3] Text translated by the authors. The original French text reads [7]: *"Ces quantités considérables de liquide ne peuvent pas être absorbées par les matières sur lesquelles on les verse de sorte que l'excédent coule sur le sol, forme de véritables flaques, suit les déclivités et surtout pénètre dans les fentes des planchers, entre des carreaux, voire même imprègne le terrain. C'est grâce à cela du reste que l'on arrive presque toujours à retrouver des quantités suffisantes de ces corps pour pouvoir les caractériser et affirmer leur emploi. Il n'est pas rare que, après avoir complètement déblayé les décombres si l'on soulève un plancher ou si l'on creuse le sol, on perçoive une odeur caractéristique et révélatrice du combustible liquide employé par l'incendiaire. Il faut se souvenir de cet élément pour la saisie des matériaux que l'on confiera à un chimiste pour les analyses destinées à isoler et à caractériser le liquide en question."*

to this date and likely outside the United States, however no formal publications were retrieved from that time.

2.1.4 Evolution of Fire Debris Analysis

With the development of more formal forensic sciences and the progress made in chemistry and subsequently in instrumental analysis, the science of fire debris analysis gradually improved starting in the middle of the twentieth century.

The analysis of fire debris started with the mere detection of odors at fire scenes. When "evidentiary" odors were detected, debris was collected as evidence, but no further analysis was performed. Typical sentences found in the literature stated that:[4] "We immediately noticed that the apron and the shoes strongly smelled of petroleum." It is important at this stage to understand that in the early 1900s, there were very little artificial (petroleum-based) polymers used in household goods. Most of the building materials consisted of natural materials, such as stone, concrete, mortar, wood, cotton, straw, and paper. Therefore, it is understandable that the issues encountered today in fire debris analysis generated by the production of volatile organic compounds (VOC) from modern polymers were not encountered at that time. So, after all, the sense of smell was less likely to be subjected to false positive interpretation than it is today.

The more "laboratory-advanced" side of fire debris analysis started with the isolation of ignitable liquid residues from fire debris samples. During the early years of such attempts, once isolated, these extracts would simply be smelled, as was done at the scene with raw debris. Figure 2-1 shows some of the milestones in the development of the extraction of ILR from fire debris. The evolution of the techniques went from distillation and solvent extraction to headspace, and finally to adsorption techniques.

Once ILR were isolated from fire debris, it was time to develop the proper manner of analyzing them. Figure 2-2 shows some of the milestones in the development of the analysis of ILR. As can be seen, residual liquids were analyzed first by boiling point, specific gravity, and refractive index. At the very beginning, the use of infrared spectrometry and mass spectrometry was also cited, but no further details are available and it was not possible to find any formal publications validating these two techniques. Several scientists attempted to detect the presence of lead (from the lead tetraethyl) in order to ascertain the presence of gasoline; this was performed by emission spectroscopy and paper chromatography. Gas chromatography was the solution of choice and started to be used in 1960. Since then, mostly technical advancements of gas chromatography have been developed, such as the use

---

[4] Text translated by the authors. The original French text reads [5]: "... et a pu constater immédiatement que tablier et pantoufles sentaient fortement le pétrole."

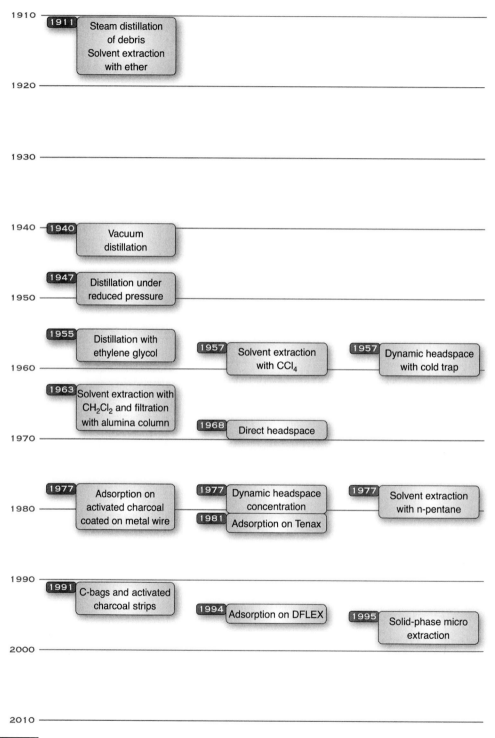

FIGURE 2-1   *Major milestones in the evolution of extraction of fire debris samples.*

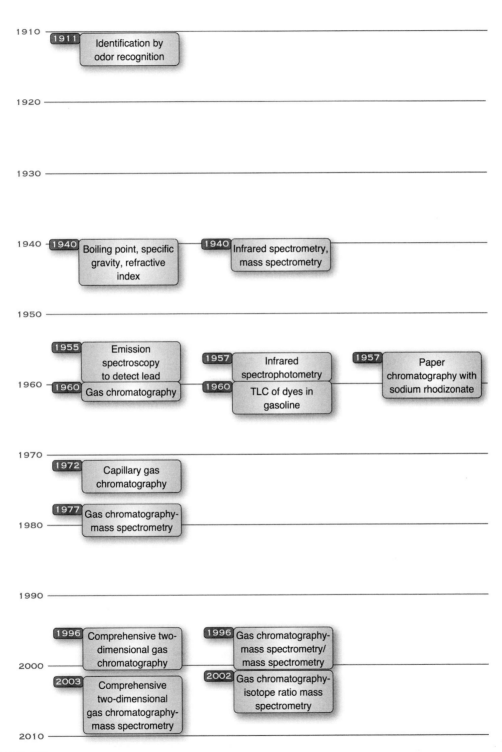

FIGURE 2-2 *Major milestones in the evolution of the analysis of extracts (ignitable liquid residues).*

of capillary columns, mass spectrometry as a detection technique, and finally, the use of comprehensive two-dimensional gas chromatography.

Other important developments occurred in fire debris analysis, such as the detection of debris at the scene and, more importantly, the study of interferences from fire debris samples, which is a significant factor in the interpretation of results. Some of these milestones are presented in Figure 2-3.

The technical evolution of the analysis of fire debris has been very intense. In general, it parallels the technical evolution of analytical chemistry, albeit a few years behind. However, the main issues in fire debris analysis do not pertain to the techniques themselves, but rather to the interpretation of the results and the significance of what is found. These issues followed a certain evolution as shown in Figure 2-3, though they also have been behind the technology. Scientists have always admired their new tools. This often leads to some sort of blind trust in these tools rather than questioning them and, more importantly, making sure that the results obtained from them are fully integrated within the circumstances of the case. This lack of interest in the interpretation of the results also comes from the fact that it is much easier to carry out analytical technique development than to carry out the difficult study of evidence interpretation, not to mention that with analytical development, the reward is almost instantaneous. Eventually, some scientists did question their results and the significance of fire debris analysis made a huge step forward. Unfortunately, such advancement always comes with a certain delay.

In 1954, Lieutenant Glenn D. Bennett, Commanding Officer of the Arson Squad of the Detroit Police and Fire Department in Michigan, USA, related three arson cases in an interesting article [10]. This article is the summary of a verbal presentation made by the same author in the previous year. In one of the cases, he explained that they collected a rug from which they extracted gasoline by vacuum distillation. The laboratory also identified a liquid contained in a jug as gasoline. Because the investigation identified a suspect who bought gas at a gas station, they collected gasoline from the station tanks and compared it to the gasoline from the rug and the jug. Bennett stated that [10]: "A sample of gasoline was taken from the station tanks, analyzed and found to be identical to the gasoline contained in the jug found near the scene of the fire as well as the sample extracted from the rug." One can only hope that they performed more than boiling point, specific gravity, and refractive index determination on these samples. One can also safely assume that the fact that the suspect was mentally incompetent greatly helped to prevent any opposition to this opinion. Also note that Bennett did not clearly infer an identity of source, but simply declared the two samples "identical."

The same year, Battle and Weston cited a lecture given in 1949 by Lloyd M. Shupe, police chemist with the Columbus Police Department in Ohio, USA [2]:

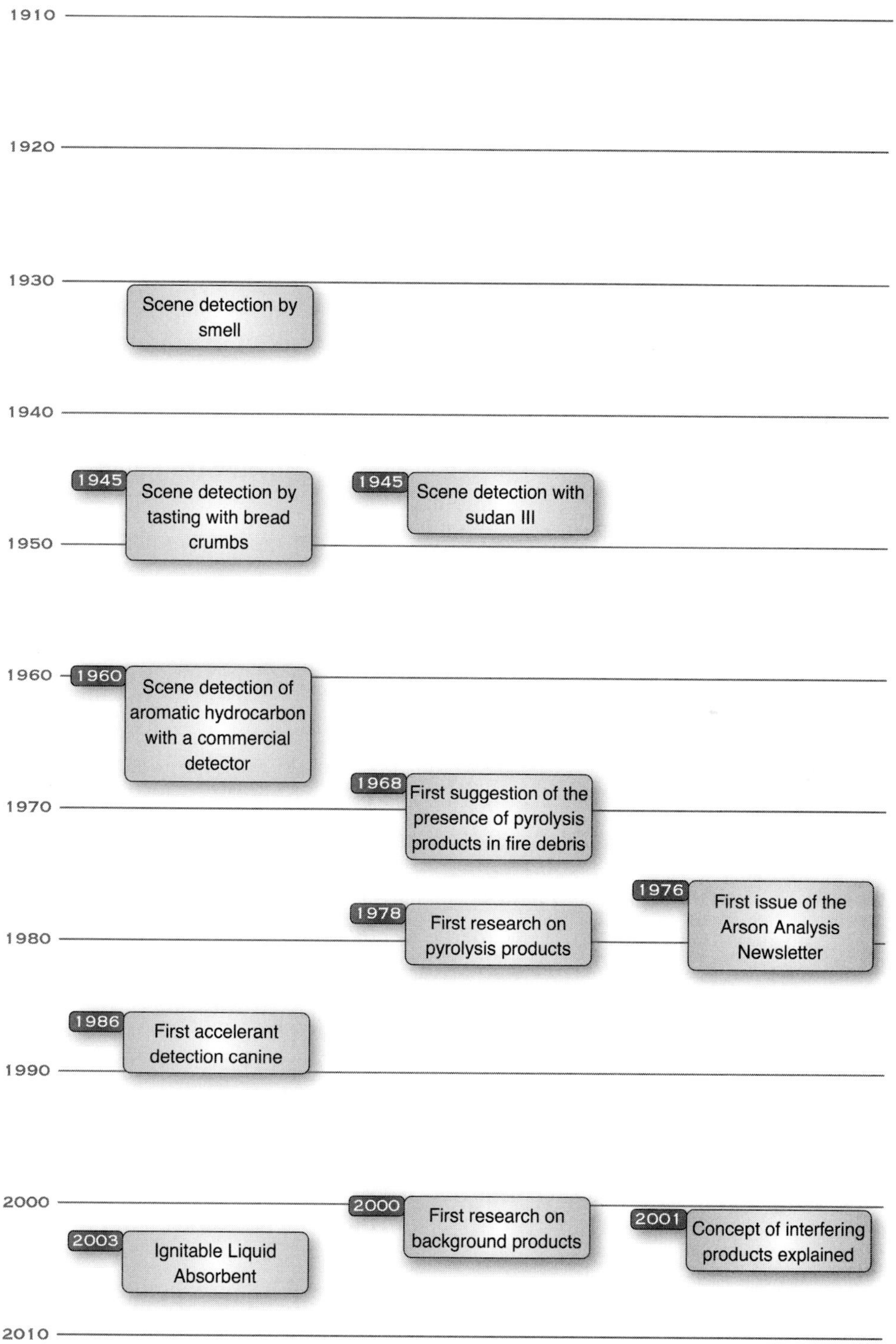

FIGURE 2-3 *Other major milestones in the evolution of fire debris analysis.*

[5] Text translated by the authors. The original French text reads [5]: "*Ajoutons qu'une analyse chimique des pantoufles et du tablier a pleinement confirmé les premières constatations. Cette analyse doit être faite par distillation du pétrole. Pour cela on fera arriver sur l'objet suspect de contenir du pétrole, des vapeurs d'eau chauffée à 100'. On les recueille ensuite dans un tube réfrigérant à direction descendante. Les vapeurs d'eau entraînent les composants à bas point d'ébullition du pétrole, qu'on recueille, avec l'eau, dans un récipient, après condensation dans le réfrigérant. L'odeur très caractéristique de ces produits indique nettement la présence de pétrole sur l'objet examiné. Il vaut mieux faire arriver les vapeurs d'eau sur l'objet suspect que d'introduire cet objet dans le récipient même qui contient l'eau.*

Les composants à haut point d'ébullition du pétrole peuvent être recueillis par extraction avec de l'éther. A ce propos, il est à re-marquer que ces composants restent très longtemps sur les objets, même si ceux-ci ont été très près du feu. Il est donc possible de les déceler par analyse chimique, même si les composants à bas point d'ébullition se sont évaporés."

I was able to extract some oil from the wood and examination of the specific gravity and refractive index showed it to be the same as the sample of kerosene submitted from a Shell Service Station in the neighborhood. One of the attendants at the station remembered selling the suspect a five-gallon can of kerosene a few days before and when confronted to this evidence the suspect confessed his guilt.

Shupe stated that the two samples are the same, but he did not clearly infer a common source. However, at least the suspect probably made that inference of identity of source since he confessed based on the knowledge of the analytical results. As was demonstrated many years later, the comparison of ignitable liquids to determine identity of source is a very complicated and, unfortunately, extremely limited process. This is one more example in science of how the interpretation of the results was (and is still today) behind the technology.

2.2 SAMPLE ANALYSIS

2.2.1 1911

Rodolphe-Archibald Reiss of the University of Lausanne described the use of steam distillation and solvent extraction applied to fire debris samples in a paragraph of his *Manuel de police scientifique* [5]. He stated [5]:

Let's add that a chemical analysis of the shoes and of the apron fully confirmed the first observations. This analysis must be carried out by distillation of petroleum. This is performed by exposing the items suspected of containing petroleum to water vapors heated to 100°C. These vapors are then collected in a refrigerated tube. Steam carries petroleum compounds with a low boiling point, which are collected with the water, in a container after condensation in the refrigerant. The odor of these products is very characteristic of the presence of petroleum on the examined item. It is better to expose the object to steam than to introduce the object in the same container that has the water.

Petroleum components with high boiling points can be collected by extraction with ether. In this regard, these components persist a long time on fire debris, even when these have been closely exposed to fire. It is thus possible to detect them by chemical analysis, even though low boiling point components have already evaporated.[5]

This statement would thus represent one of the first times steam distillation and solvent extraction were described in the forensic literature.

There appears to be some controversy regarding the first scientist who ever analyzed fire debris for residual ignitable liquid. According to Internet sources and some American literature, Dr. Vincent Hnizda, a chemist with the Ethyl Corporation in Detroit, Michigan, USA, is credited with this discovery in 1947 [11, 12]. However, these sources do not aptly recognize Reiss' book published approximately 30 years prior to Dr. Hnizda's work.

Further research in more recent literature revealed Karl Popp, a chemist from Frankfurt, Germany, who specialized in the analysis of tobacco products, to be the first person to perform fire debris analysis. Harry Söderman wrote [13]: "Whether he ever identified the ash of a Trichinopoli cigar I do not know, but Popp was the first to analyze ashes and other residues in cases of suspected arson in order to ascertain the presence of inflammable oils." Söderman also described Popp as the German authority in forensic chemistry. This same discovery was presented in Eckert's *Introduction to Forensic Sciences* [14]: "Carl Popp, a commercial chemist in Germany, developed an interest in the forensic application of chemistry as well as serologic and toxicologic examinations. He further identified fingerprints and applied photography to forensic fields. He was one of the first to analyze debris for evidence in cases involving explosives and arson." Unfortunately, there are no references to this statement and it is not clear exactly which year Karl Popp would have tried such examination.

2.2.2 1940s

The different sources that mentioned Hnizda's work clearly attribute the year 1940 to his discovery. Bennett wrote [12]:

> Let me describe briefly some simple tests conducted by Dr. Vincent Hnizda, one of the head research chemists at the Ethyl Corp. in Detroit, who, with the consent of his employer, has also assisted us in numerous murder and arson cases with his scientific knowledge. [. . .] Back in 1940 we were confronted with the problem of what to do with some petroleum-soaked articles recovered as evidence in an arson murder. Dr. Hnizda solved the problem by placing the evidence in a large glass dessicator which he connected by tubing to a series of three vapor traps with volumetric graduations which were submerged in coolants contained in wide-mouth De War flasks. The traps in turn were connected with a mercury manomoter and a small vacuum pump. This method of extraction is not new in the laboratory field, but to our knowledge it was the first time ever applied in this field of arson detection.

Interestingly enough, Ethyl Corporation was not named so until 1942 [15]. According to Bennett's article, dated 1958, it appears that Hnizda's extraction of fire debris was followed by the testing of the residues through the determination of the boiling point, specific gravity, and refractive index [12]. Bennett also mentions the use of infrared spectrometry and mass spectrometry, however it is not clear if this is contemporaneous to the article's date or to Hnizda's quoted work.

2.2.3 1955

Katte and Specht, scientists with the Bayerisches Landeskriminalamt (LKA) in München, Germany, proposed that the presence of tetraethyl lead or monomethylaniline be detected in extracts from fire debris to demonstrate the presence of gasoline [16]. They used steam distillation to extract the debris and emission spectroscopy to detect the presence of lead.

2.2.4 1957

Donald Adams, a scientist with the Indiana State Police Laboratory, published the first article describing the use of infrared spectrometry to analyze ILR [17].

Werner Katte used paper chromatography to separate the components of extracts from steam distillation and to detect the presence of tetraethyl lead by reaction with sodium rhodizonate [18]. The paper chromatography was conducted with a solution of 2:1 butanol:hydrochloric acid (3.5M) and lasts for 16 to 24 hours.

2.2.5 1960

Douglas M. Lucas of the Attorney's General Laboratory (now Centre of Forensic Sciences) in Toronto, Canada, published the article entitled: "The identification of petroleum products in forensic science by gas chromatography" in *Journal of Forensic Sciences* [19]. This was the first article that presented the application of gas chromatography to the analysis of fire debris samples. Lucas concluded that [19]: "Gas chromatography appears to have great potential in the identification of a type of petroleum product and in the differentiating of different brands of a type. Only part of this potential has been revealed by this work."

In 1960, only packed columns were available. Lucas used a gas chromatograph (GC) Beckman model GC-2 with a Beckman C-22 firebrick packed column and a thermal conductivity detector [19]. Figures 2-4 and 2-5 show some of the chromatograms presented in the article. One can appreciate the difference in resolution with modern chromatographic techniques when compared with the chromatograms shown in Chapters 9 and 12.

In the following issue of *Journal of Forensic Sciences*, an article by Cadman and Johns reported the application of gas chromatography in criminalistics [20]. Among the different applications cited, fire debris analysis

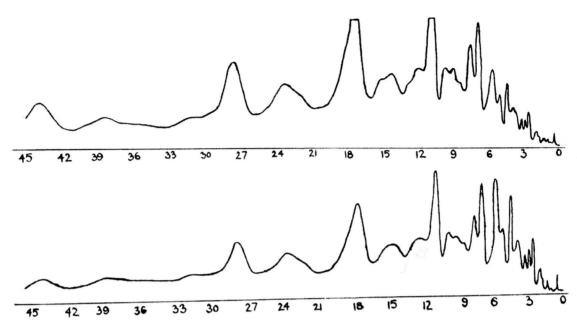

FIGURE 2-4 *Stove oil chromatogram (top) and kerosene chromatogram (bottom). (Source: Lucas DM (1960) The identification of petroleum products in forensic science by gas chromatography,* Journal of Forensic Sciences, *5(2), pp 236–47. Reprinted with permission of ASTM International, West Conshohocken, Pennsylvania, USA.)*

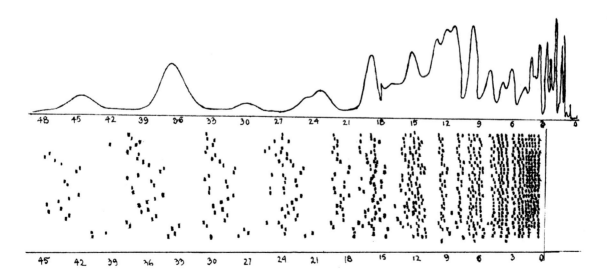

FIGURE 2-5 *Chromatogram of gasoline (top) and the differences in peak position of 28 gasoline samples and 3 grades of aviation gasolines (bottom). (Source: Lucas DM (1960) The identification of petroleum products in forensic science by gas chromatography,* Journal of Forensic Sciences, *5(2), pp 236–47. Reprinted with permission of ASTM International, West Conshohocken, Pennsylvania, USA.)*

was one of them. Nevertheless, Cadman and Johns revealed that [20]: ". . . it may be possible to determine brands of gasoline at a particular season through comparison with known standards. It also appears possible to determine batch differences within the same brand of gasoline." They were just at the beginning of what has been the subject of scientific research for the last 40 years. They presented a case where a suspect was apprehended with a five-gallon jerry can running away from a parked truck. The suspect denied being involved in any theft of gasoline, so the gasoline from the jerry can was sent to the laboratory along with samples of gasoline from the left and right tanks of the truck. They concluded that [20]:

> Gas chromatographic determinations indicated that while the standards from the right and left tanks were similar, they were not identical, indicating the same brand of gasoline was contained in both. The questioned sample was found to be very similar to the standard from the right tank. The slight differences which were noted in the C4's to C6's region could be attributed to the large air space left above the right tank standard in the vial in which it was submitted. The suspect pleaded guilty upon being confronted with the evidence.

As presented in Chapter 9, comparison of gasoline brands is unfortunately much more complex than that and such conclusions cannot be made in modern days.

Finally, they mentioned taking a headspace sample from debris and injecting it in the GC. This is extremely interesting as no literature mentioned the use of headspace until Ettling and Adams' article in 1968 (see Section 2.3). However, although the headspace provided them with preliminary results, they still followed up with the distillation in ethylene glycol (see Section 2.3.4), collection of some fractions from the GC, and analysis by infrared spectrometry. They identified α- and β-pinenes.

2.2.6 1972

The main purpose of Chisum and Elzerman's article was to present the advantages of a digital log electrometer as compared to a linear electrometer, but it also appeared to be the first mention of the use of a GC capillary column in fire debris analysis [21]. Note that the use of the capillary column increased the total run time to 102 minutes.

After this date, many papers dealing with the use of capillary columns in gas chromatography for the analysis of ILR were published. In 1975, Cain presented a very convincing article on the improved resolution offered by capillary columns versus the ones resulting from packed columns in the analysis of different samples of kerosene [22].

2.2.7 1977

M.H. Mach, a scientist with Aerospace Corporation in El Segundo, California, USA, was the first person to publish a paper presenting the use of gas chromatography-mass spectrometry (GC-MS) for the analysis of ILR [23]. Amusingly, Mach did not use a capillary column with his GC-MS. So, although the power of the mass spectrometric detection was demonstrated, the low resolution of the packed column was still present. Also, Mach published his article with the scope of studying polyaromatic hydrocarbons (PAH). The article represented some preliminary work in a attempt to demonstrate the hypothesis that a specific pattern of PAH was created by burned gasoline. If observed, this pattern, not found in burned debris free of gasoline, would demonstrate the presence of gasoline. Mach's article, though the first one to introduce the concept of applying GC-MS to fire debris analysis, did not fully realize the whole power of this technique. For this, the field waited five more years for Smith's article [24].

2.2.8 1996

The year 1996 was an exciting year for the field of fire debris analysis. Phillips et al. presented the application of comprehensive two-dimensional gas chromatography (GCxGC) at the Pittsburgh Conference in Chicago, Illinois, USA [25]. Unfortunately, this preliminary work went on standby for a few years until Dr. Frysinger and Dr. Gaines from the US Coast Guard Academy built some interest in its application to fire debris.

The same year, Bertsch published the first article mentioning the possible application of GC-MS/MS to fire debris analysis [26]. One year later, it was followed by the first article entirely devoted to the application of GC-MS/MS in fire debris analysis [27].

2.2.9 2002 and 2003

In 2002, the first paper addressing the application of GCxGC to the analysis of ILR was published by Frysinger and Gaines, professors at the US Coast Guard Academy in Connecticut, USA [28]. The paper presented the incredible potential of GCxGC when applied to the analysis of ILR.

Then, in 2003, Frysinger presented the application of comprehensive two-dimensional gas chromatography-mass spectrometry to the analysis of fire debris (GCxGC-MS) at the 55th Annual Meeting of the American Academy of Forensic Sciences in Chicago, Illinois, USA [29].

2.3 SAMPLE EXTRACTION

2.3.1 1940

Dr. Vincent Hnizda is believed to be the first to extract liquid accelerants from fire debris using a vacuum distillation apparatus [12, 30, 31].

2.3.2 1947

Loren G. Farrell, Assistant Fire Marshal for the City of Detroit Fire Department in Michigan, USA, describes the use of a reduced-pressure distillation apparatus to recover flammable liquids from fire debris [32]. He explained that the process of steam distillation is not convenient as it is hard to place items in flasks and that it results in severe mutilation of the evidence. The apparatus consisted of a 30-gallon cast iron container (to hold the fire debris) connected to copper tubing immersed first in saline ice and, second, in a carbon dioxide bath to trap the vapors, and that is finally connected to a vacuum pump. He further suggested the use of an infrared lamp if it was necessary to heat the sample. Interestingly, the article stated that this apparatus was in use for eight years, which would set the first extraction of fire debris in about 1939.

2.3.3 1952

Macoun, a scientist with the Customs Excise Laboratory in Ottawa, Canada, described a technique to extract small amounts of flammable hydrocarbons from fire debris that was allegedly better than steam distillation [33]. The procedure consisted of soaking the debris in 95% alcohol overnight, adding three times as much water, mixing, and distilling slowly. To the first few fractions collected by distillation, potassium dichlorate and hydrochloric acid were added. The contents were mixed thoroughly and left to rest overnight. The next morning, the hydrocarbons would be in a layer separate from the aqueous one. The flammability of the extracts was then tested, along with their refractive index, specific gravity, and boiling range.

2.3.4 1955

J.W. Brackett, Jr., a criminalist at the Laboratory of Criminalistics of the Office of the District Attorney in San Jose, California, USA, described the extraction of fire debris by distillation with ethylene glycol [34]. He concluded that it presented significant advantages when compared to regular steam distillation and vacuum distillation. It saved time, required simpler apparatus, and yielded more complete recoveries. The extracts were still characterized by refractive index. Table 2-1 shows the refractive indices measured by Brackett [34]. To date, the authors have not been able to find a publication that provides some guidelines as to how to interpret refractive index and what would constitute an identification. As a comparison, glycerin has a refractive index of 1.47 and an approximately 50% sugar solution has an index of 1.43.

2.3.5 1957

Adams' article presented in the previous section also described two extraction techniques [17]. The first one, recommended for light ignitable liquids

Table 2-1	Refractive Indices (RI) found by Brackett [34]		
Liquid	RI at 25°C	RI after steam distillation	RI after ethylene glycol distillation
White gasoline	1.399	1.405	—
Regular gasoline	1.419	1.434	—
Premium gasoline	1.416	1.434	1.429
Stoddard solvent	1.428	1.429	—
Kerosene	1.442	1.442	1.442
Stove oil	1.464	1.464	1.463
Diesel fuel	1.481	1.480	1.471
SAE 10 motor oil	1.480	—	1.476

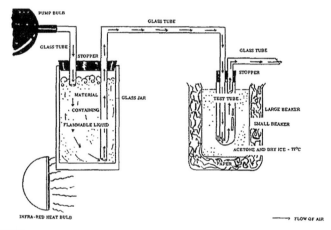

FIGURE 2-6 *Setup used for the dynamic headspace technique.* (Source: Adams DL (1957) The extraction and identification of small amounts of accelerants from arson evidence, The Journal of Criminal Law, Criminology and Police Science, **47**(5), pp 593–6. Reprinted by special permission of Northwestern University School of Law, The Journal of Criminal Law and Criminology.)

such as gasoline, consisted of an early version of a dynamic headspace with a cold trap. The apparatus used is shown in Figure 2-6.

The debris was brought to the laboratory in the container, which was set up as shown in the diagram. A manual pump provided the airflow flushing the sample's headspace to the cold trap located on the right part of the diagram. The residues were then recuperated in a solid or liquid state. A second procedure was proposed for samples with heavier components such as fuel oils. It was simply a solvent extraction with carbon tetrachloride

(CCl$_4$) as the solvent. Adams also stated that if the first procedure did not yield any residues, the second one should be applied.

Specht (working for the LKA in Germany) published an article that described the extraction by distillation with water or diethyl ether [35].

2.3.6 1963

Bruce Ettling described a solvent extraction of fire debris using methylene chloride (CH$_2$Cl$_2$) [36]. He proposed the following: soak the debris for about 20 minutes in methylene chloride, collect the solvent after filtration, add some hexane, decant the solution in a column containing dry activated alumina, flush the column, and finally evaporate the solvent. The remaining residue is air-dried and weighed. The use of the alumina column allowed for the elimination of all polar compounds and the resulting eluant was constituted, according to the author, of pure hydrocarbons. Ettling also added that it is possible to analyze the residues by infrared spectrophotometry or gas chromatography. Finally, he illustrated the article with a case for which he extracted some charred debris from a residence and obtained 1,760 ppm of hydrocarbons. He obtained comparison samples of mahogany wood, finished and unfinished, and obtained 63 and 73 ppm of hydrocarbons, respectively. Although Ettling did recognize that it was not possible to determine what exact amount of hydrocarbons would be considered as suspicious in a given sample, he definitely used the fact that an abnormally excessive amount of hydrocarbons found in a sample as an indication of added hydrocarbons. Fortunately, he also warned the reader that under some circumstances, it might be expected to have incidental ignitable liquids in samples.

2.3.7 1968

Ettling and Adams published an article in *Journal of Forensic Sciences* regarding the study of ILR in fire debris [37]. They used a direct headspace sampling of the debris by pulling two ml of headspace from the jar into which debris were kept. They injected this volume directly in the GC. The samples were not heated in this experiment.

In 1969, one year after Ettling and Adams' article was published, Paul Kirk published the first edition of what would become (with the subsequent outstanding involvement of Dr. John D. DeHaan[6]) the world reference in fire investigation [39]. His book, simply entitled *Fire investigation*, com-

---

[6] Dr. Paul Kirk passed away in 1970 with his book in its first edition. In 1983, Dr. John DeHaan published a second edition of the book. He renamed the book, *Kirk's Fire Investigation*, in order to preserve the memory of the original author. *Kirk's Fire Investigation* is now in its sixth edition and has undergone a tremendous improvement since its very first edition [38].

prises 255 pages covering many aspects of the scene and laboratory investigation of a fire. Chapter 12 includes a section on laboratory examination
that reads [39]:

> *Extraction with a very volatile solvent could be used, but the*
> *method is neither easy nor commercial. One possible shortcut that*
> *probably could be used, although to this writer's knowledge has not*
> *been, is to enclose the debris in a closed container, heat it somewhat*
> *to volatilize the liquid and saturate the internal gaseous phase, sample*
> *the vapor, and analyze it by gas chromatography. This procedure*
> *would require special equipment also and would not be expected to*
> *detect some of the less volatile fractions of mixed fuels. It would,*
> *however, in all probability be successful in many, possibly most,*
> *instances.*

Kirk cited Ettling and Adams' article as presenting a procedure similar
to the one suggested and explained that the method used appeared to
produce very useful results. Kirk described simple headspace extraction in
his book; however, it is quite interesting to note that although he read Ettling
and Adams' work, he still stipulates that nobody carried out the procedure
he described. The only difference was that Ettling and Adams had not heated
their samples.

2.3.8 1977

John D. Twibell and Janet M. Home of the Home Office Central Research
Establishment in Berkshire, United Kingdom, published the first article
describing the use of passive headspace concentration extraction for fire
debris samples in *Nature* [40]. They proposed the use of a ferromagnetic
wire coated with a thin layer of activated charcoal. The wire was exposed
for a couple of hours to the headspace above the fire debris, where it adsorbed
the VOCs. Once the extraction terminated, the wire was placed in a Curie
point apparatus, which inductively heated the wire, thermally releasing the
adsorbed compounds directly into the GC. Five years later, the two scientists, along with a third one, followed up with another article published in
Journal of the Forensic Science Society, which demonstrated the much
increased sensitivity of the adsorption wire technique versus steam distillation and regular headspace [41].

Another important first use of a technique is described by Joseph E.
Chrostowski and Ronald N. Holmes, both scientists with the then Bureau
of Alcohol, Tobacco, and Firearms Philadelphia laboratory in Pennsylvania,
USA [42]: the first use of dynamic headspace concentration extraction of
fire debris samples. For this purpose, they use activated coconut charcoal
placed in a disposable pipette between two glass wool plugs. Heated nitrogen
is injected in the container with the debris and the charcoal tube is placed

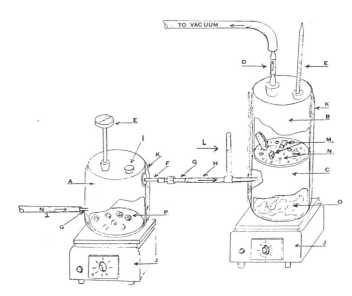

FIG. 2 - Accelerant vapor collection system: A- gallon paint can; B- unused metal container (paint can in pint, quart, or gallon size); C- unused metal container (paint can in pint, quart, or gallon size); D- collection column; E- thermometer; F- 1/8" copper tubing; G- ¼" copper tubing; H- silicone rubber tubing; I- rubber stopper; J- hot plate; K- insulation; L- flowmeter; M- debris; N- 8 penny nail holes; O- aluminum foil; P-glass marbles.

at the top of the can, connected to a vacuum pump. The illustrations presented in the article are shown in Figures 2-7 and 2-8.

The system described by Chrostowski and Holmes was a hybrid system between a positive-pressure and a negative-pressure system (see Chapter 11). The collection time was set between 30 and 60 minutes and the nitrogen rate was set at approximately 3 liters per minute. Note that after the extraction was complete, the charcoal was desorbed with carbon disulfide

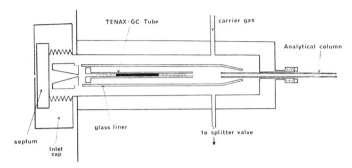

FIGURE 2-9 *Tenax insert inside a GC injection port. (Source: Russell LW (1981) The concentration and analysis of volatile hydrocarbons in fire debris using tenax-GC,* Journal of the Forensic Science Society, *21(4), pp 317–26. Reprinted with permission of The Forensic Science Society, Harrogate, North Yorkshire, United Kingdom.)*

(CS_2) and the extract was analyzed by gas chromatography and infrared spectroscopy.

2.3.9 1981

L.W. Russell published the first article dealing specifically with the use of Tenax (see Chapter 11) as an adsorption medium for fire debris samples [43]. Tenax began being used in 1973, however no scientist published any article mentioning its use in fire debris analysis until 1981 [44]. Russell utilized the same sampling system as used by Bertsch et al. to monitor VOCs found in the cabin atmosphere of Skylab 4, a NASA mission that lasted 84 days [45]. It is interesting to note here that Bertsch would become a renowned fire debris analyst a few years later. Tenax was placed in an insert tube and the headspace of the sample was drawn through the tube using a large plastic syringe (dynamic headspace of reduced volume) [43]. The insert was then directly placed in the injection port of the GC (preheated at 250°C) as shown in Figure 2-9.

Russell demonstrated the highly improved sensitivity of Tenax compared to Brackett's distillation and vacuum distillation for hydrocarbon-based ignitable liquids. Conversely, he expressed concerns for nonhydrocarbon products such as alcohols for which preliminary studies did not show any promising results. Also, he showed that the laboratory workload is highly reduced with Tenax.

2.3.10 1982

John A. Juhala of the Michigan State Police Crime Laboratory in Bridgeport, Michigan, USA, published an article presenting an improved carrier for the activated charcoal used in passive headspace concentration [46]. Instead of the usual metal wire utilized to this point, he used plexiglas beads coated with fine particles of activated charcoal. The beads were coated using a dental amalgamator. After extraction, the beads were desorbed using carbon disulfide.

2.3.11 1991

William R. Dietz of the then Bureau of Alcohol, Tobacco, and Firearms in San Francisco, California, USA, published the first article presenting both the C-bag and the activated charcoal strip used for passive headspace concentration extraction [47]. The C-bag consists of a small piece of filter-type paper into which is placed activated charcoal. Then, the paper is folded and suspended in the container with the fire debris. This is illustrated in Figure 2-10.

FIGURE 2-10

Manufacturing of C-bags. (Source: Dietz WR (1991) Improved charcoal packaging for accelerant recovery by passive diffusion, Journal of Forensic Sciences, ***36**(1), pp 111–21. Reprinted with permission of ASTM International, West Conshohocken, Pennsylvania, USA.)*

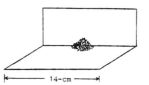

|← 14-cm →|

1. Cut paper into a 11-cm by 14-cm rectangle.
2. Fold paper in half lengthwise (14-cm edges together).
3. Place activated charcoal on the center fold.

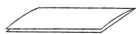

4. Bring the 14-cm edges together. This is the "open edge".

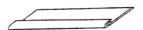

5. Fold the open edge back 1/3 of the distance toward the center fold.

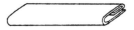

6. Fold the bottom edge once more to meet the center fold. The paper will measure approximately 2-cm by 14-cm.

7. Fold the 2-cm edges together. The bulk of the paper will be on the interior of this fold. The charcoal will be visible from the outside.

8. Fold the 2-cm edge back 1-cm.
9. Lay the end of string across this fold.
10. Staple string in place on this fold.

The original charcoal strip comes from charcoal membranes found in organic vapor badges. They measure 4 by 32 millimeters and weigh approximately 0.08 grams. Dietz eluted both adsorption media with carbon disulfide. Although passive headspace concentration was used (mostly with coated wires) in fire debris analysis from 1977 on, this is the first article describing what would become the modern activated charcoal strips used by most laboratories. Dietz understood one of the greatest advantages of this method, as he stated [47]:

> Since C-bags and charcoal strips are so easy to work with, two or more may be placed into an evidence container at the same time. One advantage of this is that it would allow periodic sampling of the adsorbed vapors over time. A second advantage would be that additional C-bags or charcoal strips not used for immediate instrumental analysis could be sealed and preserved for future examinations by other analysts (such as review chemists or defense experts).

Three years later, Demers-Kohls et al. were the first ones to publish an article evaluating the Diffusive Flammable Liquid Extraction (DFLEX) device manufactured by Albrayco (Cromwell, Connecticut, USA) that is commonly used by most laboratories today (see Chapter 11 for recent developments) [48].

2.3.12 1995

In 1995, Furton et al. published the first article demonstrating the use of solid-phase micro extraction (SPME) to extract fire debris samples [49].

2.4 STUDY OF INTERFERENCES

2.4.1 1968

Ettling and Adams studied the amounts and kinds of hydrocarbons that can be extracted from charred materials in an article from *Journal of Forensic Sciences* [37]. They state that [37]: "For example, it is known that some hydrocarbons may be produced by pyrolysis of wood." The idea behind the research was to determine the presence of accelerant based on the weight of hydrocarbons extracted from the debris. Each material gave different amount of hydrocarbons and they classify them from the least amount to the greatest amount as follows: wood (except for pitch pine), polyester and wrapping paper, cotton and wool, and finally, newspaper. However, they observed that [37]: "In most cases, the amount of hydrocarbons extracted from the original material was greater than that extracted from the charred material with or without accelerant." The determination of the presence of hydrocarbons on a weight basis was an extremely dubious procedure and fortunately, they concluded [37]: "The most important finding was that the amount of hydrocarbons in the char does not necessarily indicate added accelerant."

2.4.2 1976

Clodfelter and Hueske published a paper that aimed to compare pyrolysis products released by burning substrates with different "accelerants" such as gasoline, diesel fuel, kerosene, or jet fuel [50]. Analysis performed by GC-FID show complex chromatograms for each extract of 30 to 60 peaks. No attempt has been made to identify the different peaks of pyrolysis products. Eventually, a free burning test was made with nylon carpet and compared to the sample charred through the charring apparatus. In conclusion, the authors stated that the chromatograms obtained from different substrates were easily distinguishable from the chromatograms of "accelerants."

2.4.3 1978

Thomas warned fire and arson investigators about the necessity of collecting control samples when submitting fire debris samples to the laboratory for analysis [51]. His foundations stated that [51]: ". . . not all hydrocarbon vapors come from flammable liquids. Examples included in this group are hydrocarbons given off from burning carpet or smoldering mattress. These hydrocarbons may also be detected by the GC but should not be confused by the analyst with any of the more common flammable liquids."

2.4.4 1982 and 1983

Smith published two of the most important articles at the time in fire debris analysis [24, 52]. He provided some of the basic criteria needed to identify ILR by GC-MS. He also presented some studies made on authentic arson samples in which he detected different chemicals similar to those usually found in ILR. He observed that the presence of styrene and other low-boiling alkylbenzenes arise from pyrolysis of styrene-containing polymer (carpet or carpet backing for example).

2.4.5 1984

Stone and Lomonte discussed the false positive in fire debris analysis [53]. They reported the necessity of taking control samples at the fire scene in order to improve the interpretation of the laboratory analyses. They cited a case reported by Nowicki and Strock [54], in which a vinyl floor was submitted to the laboratory for analysis. The sample revealed an "accelerant" that in fact was naturally produced by the floor when burning. The authors also affirmed that they very often detected turpentine in wood samples, especially for pine wood, that was not attributed to any added liquid, but rather to the pyrolysis products of the wood itself. Finally, the authors recommended the use of GC-MS in order to identify the peaks and to decrease the number of false positives in FDA.

2.4.6 1988

DeHaan and Bonarius published the first and quite complete article about the study of pyrolysis products by trying to answer two basic questions [55]:

Whether, in the absence of any petroleum distillate accelerant, volatile products occur in the debris of combustibles most common in structure fires-carpets, pads (underlay) and floor-coverings, and whether in the presence of petroleum distillates, these pyrolysis products cause any interference or difficulty in identifying the accelerant.

The experiments carried out by the authors consisted of real-size fires of house trailers. Different substrates were placed on the floor prior to ignition. They were mainly constituted of nylon carpet (with jute, polypropylene [PP] or polyethylene/polypropylene [PE/PP] backing), rubber, or polyurethane pads and nylon turf with styrene-butadiene backing. In one trailer, the fire was ignited simply with a match; in the second the ignition was helped by pouring gasoline, paint thinner, and camp fuel. Extractions were done by both direct headspace and dynamic headspace concentration and the analysis performed with a GC-FID. Some samples were confirmed by GC-MS.

The authors made the following remarks [55]:

- Nylon carpet produced traces of volatiles and isolated peaks in the middle petroleum distillate range. Benzene, toluene, and xylenes are easily identifiable on the resulting chromatogram.
- The presence of a pad did not affect the chromatogram. However, these pads were made of natural fibers such as hair, jute, and cotton.
- The urethane pad showed only traces of isolated compounds on direct headspace, while it revealed a complex mixture in the medium-range petroleum distillate when extracted by dynamic headspace concentration. Oxygenated compounds seemed to be present, also.
- Synthetic turf (PE/PP) presented a complex mixture in the middle petroleum distillate range.
- In the fire initiated with accelerant, polyester and nylon carpet samples showed very complex chromatograms of moderate concentration. Chromatograms of gasoline, paint thinner, and camp fuel, however, were readily identified.

According to the authors, the mixtures of substrates did not pose a problem in identifying accelerant. However, they produced peaks in the chromatograms that occupy mid-range distillates. They added that nylon and unbacked PE/PP floor coverings produce little volatiles. Conversely, urethane, rubber-backed PE/PP, and polyester and nylon shag carpets produced a high amount of volatiles.

In conclusion, they offer some solutions to discriminate chromatograms of PyP from accelerant:

- Major peaks don't have a Gaussian distribution
- Peak distribution is irregular
- Large unresolved groups of peaks (and some present tailing due to oxygenated compounds)
- Absence of particular peaks associated with common blend
- Presence of prominent single peaks such as styrene

2.4.7 1995

Raymond Keto, forensic chemist for the then Bureau of Alcohol, Tobacco, and Firearms, advocated the use of extracted ion chromatograms in order to help the identification of ILR in the presence of contaminated arson debris [56]. He stated [56]: "Another hazard is that petroleum like isomer profiles may not originate from petroleum distillate at all." He added [56]: "Petroleum distillate pattern matches of this type occur frequently in polymer pyrolyzates, and make it evident that these isomer patterns are not characteristic of petroleum distillate alone." The author presented a very interesting concept of peak ratio between two peaks eluting very close to one another. He showed that these ratios are constant for ILR and proper for each class. This is not the case with the pyrolyzates, where these ratios are not the same. A lot of examples are shown and are very demonstrative. The author presented a list of 43 target compounds proper to all the classes of ILR according to ASTM. Finally, he recommended the use of both extracted ion profiling as well as target compound analysis for the identification of ILR in presence of high background.

2.4.8 1997

Tranthim-Fryer and DeHaan published a paper reporting the identification of carpet and underlay pyrolysis products to which canines had responded falsely positive [57]. Carpet and carpet underlay were burned and examined for pyrolysis products. These same substances were analyzed by pyrolysis gas chromatography. They also created pyrolysis products by heating the substrate inside a U-shaped tube. They provided a list of some pyrolysis products for different materials such as nylon 6/6, styrene-butadiene, ethylene-vinylacetate-indene, polypropylene, styrene-butadiene-isoprene, poly(1-butene)-polyethylene, sourced from carpet pile fibers, adhesives, plastic mesh backing material, rubber underlays, and rubber backing materials. They concluded that the dogs can respond positively to these samples.

2.4.9 2000

Lentini, Dolan, and Cherry published a new concept in fire debris analysis [58]. They defined two sources for interfering products [58]: "actual liquid petroleum products that are present in the substrate material, and substrate materials that pyrolyze to form interfering volatile compounds in the range of common ignitable liquids." The authors tested a great number of household products. They extracted these products unburned and analyzed the extracts by GC-MS. They found that a great number of petroleum products can be found in unburned samples and thus, affect the identification of an ILR. They explained it by the presence of organic solvent within the objects, even if not specified on the manufacturer's label. According to the authors, the only commonly encountered ignitable liquid that was not found in these objects was gasoline. However, they again recommend the use of a control sample when samples are submitted to the laboratory, and stated that caution be used when interpreting the chromatograms.

2.4.10 2001

Detailed research on interfering products in fire debris analysis was conducted and published [59]. Interfering products were defined as constituted of substrate background, pyrolysis, and combustion products. For the first time, fire debris analysts have a comprehensive scheme regarding interfering products with appropriate explanations [60, 61]. The theory behind the interfering products is constantly being updated and the latest developments are presented in Chapter 12 [62].

REFERENCES

1. Rethoret H (1945) *Fire investigations*, Recording & Statistical Corporation, Limited, Toronto, Canada.
2. Battle BP and Weston PB (1954) *Arson: A handbook of detection and investigation*, Greenberg, New York, NY.
3. Myren RA (1954) *Investigation of arson and other unlawful burnings*, Institute of Government, The University of North Carolina, Chapel Hill, NC.
4. Califana AL and Levkov JS (1978) *Criminalistics for the law enforcement officer*, McGraw-Hill Book Company, New York, NY.
5. Reiss R-A (1911) *Manuel de police scientifique (technique)—I Vols et homicides*, Librairie Payot & Cie, Lausanne, Switzerland.
6. Locard E (1923) *Manuel de technique policière*, Payot, Paris, France.
7. Bischoff M (1938) *La police scientifique*, Payot, Paris, France.
8. Turner RF (1949) *Forensic science and laboratory technics*, Charles C. Thomas, Springfield, IL.
9. Edison TA (1881) *Letter to the New York Board of Underwriters*, May 6, 1881.
10. Bennett GD (1954) Physical evidence in arson cases, *Journal of Criminal Law, Criminology and Police Science*, **44**, pp 652–60.
11. Rudin N and Inman K (2002) *Forensic science timeline*, available from http://www.forensicdna.com/Timeline020702.pdf, last access performed on December 17, 2006.

12. Bennett GD (1958) The arson investigator and technical aids, *Journal of Criminal Law, Criminology and Police Science*, **49**, pp 172–7.
13. Söderman H (1957) *Policeman's lot: A criminologist's gallery of friends and felons*, Longmans, Green and Co, London, England.
14. Eckert WG (1997) *Historical development of forensic sciences*. In: *Introduction to forensic sciences*, editor Eckert WG, CRC Press, Boca Raton, FL.
15. Ethyl Corporation (2004) *Our history*, available from http://www.ethyl.com/About+Ethyl/Our+History.htm, last access performed on December 17, 2006.
16. Katte W and Specht W (1955) Die chemische Identifizierung von Benzinrückständen in Brandresten, *Archiv für Kriminologie*, **115**, pp 116–17.
17. Adams DL (1957) The extraction and identification of small amounts of accelerants from arson evidence, *Journal of Criminal Law, Criminology and Police Science*, **47**(5), pp 593–6.
18. Katte W (1957) Zur Aufklärung von Brandstiftungen: Vorschlag eines papierchromatographischen Nachweises von Bleibenzin-Spuren in Brandresten und Brandruss, *Archiv für Kriminologie*, **120**, pp 106–8.
19. Lucas DM (1960) The identification of petroleum products in forensic science by gas chromatography, *Journal of Forensic Sciences*, **5**(2), pp 236–47.
20. Cadman WJ and Johns T (1960) Application of the gas chromatograph in the laboratory of criminalistics, *Journal of Forensic Sciences*, **5**(3), pp 369–85.
21. Chisum WJ and Elzerman TR (1972) Identification of arson accelerants by gas chromatographic patterns produced by a digital log electrometer, *Journal of Forensic Sciences*, **17**(2), pp 280–91.
22. Cain PM (1975) Comparison of kerosenes using capillary column gas liquid chromatography, *Journal of the Forensic Science Society*, **15**(4), pp 301–8.
23. Mach MH (1977) Gas chromatography-mass spectrometry of simulated arson residues using gasoline as an accelerant, *Journal of Forensic Sciences*, **22**(2), pp 348–57.
24. Smith MR (1982) Arson analysis by mass chromatography, *Analytical Chemistry*, **54**(13), pp 1399A–409A.
25. Phillips JB, Tang Y, and Cerven JF (1996) *Prospective new method for fire debris analysis using comprehensive two-dimensional gas chromatography*, Pittsburgh Conference, Chicago, IL.
26. Bertsch W (1996) Chemical analysis of fire debris: Was it arson?, *Analytical Chemistry News & Features*, September, pp 541A–5A.
27. Sutherland DA (1997) The analysis of fire debris samples by GC/MS/MS, *Canadian Society for Forensic Science Journal*, **30**(4), pp 185–9.
28. Frysinger GS and Gaines RB (2002) Forensic analysis of ignitable liquids in fire debris by comprehensive two-dimensional gas chromatography, *Journal of Forensic Sciences*, **47**(3), pp 471–82.
29. Frysinger GS and Gaines RB (2003) *Analysis of ignitable liquids in fire debris with comprehensive two-dimensional gas chromatography-mass spectrometry (GCxGC/MS)*, 55th Annual Meeting of the American Academy of Forensic Sciences, Chicago, IL.
30. Inman K and Rudin N (2001) *Principles and practice of criminalistics: The profession of forensic science*, CRC Press, Boca Raton, FL.
31. Midkiff CR (1997) *Laboratory examination of arson evidence*. In: *More chemistry and crime: From marsh arsenic test to DNA profile*, editors Gerber SM and Saferstein R, American Chemical Society, Washington, DC.
32. Farrell LG (1947) Reduced pressure distillation apparatus in police science, *Journal of Criminal Law and Criminology*, **38**(4), pp 438.
33. Macoun JM (1952) The detection and determination of small amounts of inflammable hydrocarbons in combustible materials, *The Analyst*, **77**, pp 381.

34. Brackett JW (1955) Separation of flammable material of petroleum origin from evidence submitted in cases involving fires and suspected arson, *Journal of Criminal Law, Criminology and Police Science*, **46**(4), pp 554–61.

35. Specht W (1957) Der Nachweis von Zünd- und Brandmitteln, *Archiv für Kriminologie*, **119**, pp 88–95.

36. Ettling BV (1963) Determination of hydrocarbons in fire remains, *Journal of Forensic Sciences*, **8**(2), pp 261–7.

37. Ettling BV and Adams MF (1968) The study of accelerant residues in fire remains, *Journal of Forensic Sciences*, **13**(1), pp 76–89.

38. DeHaan JD (2006) *Kirk's fire investigation, 6th edition*, Prentice Hall, Upper Saddler River, NJ.

39. Kirk PL (1969) *Fire investigation*, John & Wiley Sons, Los Angeles, CA.

40. Twibell JD and Home JM (1977) Novel method for direct analysis of hydrocarbons in crime investigation and air pollution studies, *Nature*, **268**(5622), pp 711–3.

41. Twibell JD, Home JM, and Smalldon KW (1982) A comparison of the relative sensitivities of the adsorption wire and other methods for the detection of accelerant residues in fire debris, *Journal of the Forensic Science Society*, **22**, pp 155–9.

42. Chrostowski JE and Holmes RN (1979) Collection and determination of accelerant vapors from arson debris, *Arson Analysis Newsletter*, **3**(5), pp 1–16.

43. Russell LW (1981) The concentration and analysis of volatile hydrocarbons in fire debris using Tenax-GC, *Journal of the Forensic Science Society*, **21**(4), pp 317–26.

44. Caddy B, Smith FP, and Macy J (1991) Methods of fire debris preparation for detection of accelerants, *Forensic Science Review*, **3**(1), pp 57–68.

45. Bertsch W et al. (1974) Concentration and analysis of organic volatiles in Skylab 4, *Journal of Chromatography*, **99**, pp 673–87.

46. Juhala JA (1982) A method for adsorption of flammable vapors by direct insertion of activated charcoal into the debris samples, *Arson Analysis Newsletter*, **6**(2), pp 32–6.

47. Dietz WR (1991) Improved charcoal packaging for accelerant recovery by passive diffusion, *Journal of Forensic Sciences*, **36**(1), pp 111–21.

48. Demers-Kohls JF et al. (1994) Evaluation of the DFLEX® device for fire debris analysis, *Canadian Society for Forensic Science Journal*, **27**(3), pp 99–123.

49. Furton KG et al. (1995) A simple, inexpensive, rapid, sensitive and solventless technique for the analysis of accelerants in fire debris based on SPME, *Journal of High Resolution Chromatography*, **18**, pp 625–9.

50. Clodfelter RW and Hueske EE (1976) A comparison of decomposition products from selected burned materials with common arson accelerants, *Journal of Forensic Sciences*, **22**(1), pp 116–18.

51. Thomas CL (1978) Arson debris control samples, *Fire and Arson Investigator*, **28**(3), pp 23–5.

52. Smith MR (1983) Mass chromatographic analysis of arson accelerants, *Journal of Forensic Sciences*, **28**(2), pp 318–29.

53. Stone IC and Lomonte JN (1984) False positive in analysis of fire debris, *Fire and Arson Investigator*, **34**(3), pp 36–40.

54. Nowicki J and Strock C (1983) Comparison of fire debris analysis techniques, *Arson Analysis Newsletter*, **7**, pp 98–108.

55. DeHaan JD and Bonarius K (1988) Pyrolysis products of structure fires, *Journal of the Forensic Science Society*, **28**(5–6), pp 299–309.

56. Keto RO (1995) GC/MS data interpretation for petroleum distillate identification in contaminated arson debris, *Journal of Forensic Sciences*, **40**(3), pp 412–23.

57. Tranthim-Fryer DJ and DeHaan JD (1997) Canine accelerant detectors and problems with carpet pyrolysis products, *Science & Justice*, **37**(1), pp 39–46.
58. Lentini JJ, Dolan JA, and Cherry C (2000) The petroleum-laced background, *Journal of Forensic Sciences*, **45**(5), pp 968–89.
59. Stauffer E (2001) *Identification and characterization of interfering products in fire debris analysis*, Master's thesis, International Forensic Research Institute, Florida International University, Miami, FL.
60. DeHaan JD (2005) Review of: Fire investigation, *Journal of Forensic Sciences*, **50**(1).
61. Stauffer E (2004) *Sources of interference in fire debris analysis*. In: *Fire investigation*, editor Nic Daeid N, Taylor and Francis, Boca Raton, FL.
62. Stauffer E (2006) *Interferences in fire debris samples*, 58th Annual Meeting of the American Academy of Forensic Sciences, Seattle, WA.

CHAPTER 3

Review of Basic Organic Chemistry

"Let us learn to dream, gentlemen, and then perhaps we shall learn the truth."

Friedrich August Kekulé von Stradonitz, German chemist (1829–1896)

3.1 INTRODUCTION

The term organic chemistry historically has been used to describe the chemistry of compounds derived from life forms. Until German Professor Friedrich Wöhler synthesized urea in 1828, it was thought that all organic compounds had to have originated from a living organism, thus the term "organic" [1]. Although numerous organic compounds have since been synthesized from nonliving materials, the term organic has remained in use. The only common feature of the compounds derived from living sources was the presence of the element carbon. Thus, the science of organic chemistry is now simply understood to be the chemistry of carbon and its compounds [1].

It is crucial for the fire debris analyst to have a strong foundation in organic chemistry. Virtually all ignitable liquids are composed of organic compounds or blends of organic compounds. Similarly, common solid fuels or ordinary combustibles are typically organic compounds. The reactions occurring during a fire involve organic molecules and, to understand them, one must understand their underlying chemistry. This chapter by no means covers all of the necessary organic chemistry background; however, it emphasizes some of the most relevant terms and concepts required to understand the chemical reactions involved during a fire and to perform the identification of ignitable liquid residues.

Terminology used by the petroleum industry and in some older textbooks is different from that of the International Union of Pure and Applied Chemistry (IUPAC) system. In fire debris analysis, the terminology used is somehow a mix of older terminology still in use in the petroleum industry and IUPAC nomenclature. Because of the potential for confusion, this chapter includes a section on proper nomenclature of organic compounds and whenever possible, both common terminology and IUPAC terminology are presented.

3.2 CHEMICAL BONDS

3.2.1 Principle

A chemical bond is the force that holds atoms together in a molecule [2]. Chemical bonds are formed in order to provide a stable electronic configuration through the formation of an outer shell that is filled with electrons. A full outer shell is the most stable configuration of electrons, and therefore chemical bonds that will satisfy this condition are formed. There are two fundamental ways by which this stable electronic state can be achieved: by the transfer of electrons or through sharing electrons [1]. When one or more electrons are transferred from one atom to another to form a molecule, the bond is called an ionic bond. When electrons are shared between the atoms of a molecule, the bond is called a covalent bond. It is also important to understand that ionic and covalent bonds are not completely discrete; some ionic bonds can display a covalent character and vice versa.

For most atoms, the electronic configuration of chemically bonded atoms is more stable (lower energy) than that of the unbonded atoms in their ground state. This means that when bonds are formed, a lower state of energy is achieved and energy is released. The formation of bonds is therefore an exothermic process. Conversely, energy is required to break chemical bonds. Thus, reactions such as pyrolysis (discussed in Chapter 4) are endothermic. These important concepts are useful in understanding the chemistry of fire and its related reactions.

Endothermic v. Exothermic Reactions

A chemical reaction will either absorb energy from its surroundings or release energy into its surroundings. A reaction that absorbs energy is said to be endothermic. In an endothermic reaction, the starting materials (reactants) are more stable than the products; they are in a lower energy state. In order for the higher energy products to be formed, energy must be acquired from the environment. A reaction that results in products of greater stability (lower energy) than the reactants gives off energy and is said to be exothermic. The combustion reaction is the exothermic reaction that occurs during fire, releasing energy in the form of heat and light. Endothermic reactions such as pyrolysis also play an important role in the chemistry of fire and must be clearly understood. Each of these reactions and how they relate to one another is discussed in greater detail in Chapter 4.

Table 3-1	Electronic shells and their characteristics.			
Shell number	Orbital type	Orbital electron capacity	Shell electron capacity	Total electron capacity
1	s	2	2	2
2	s p	2 6	8	10
3	s p d	2 6 10	18	28
4	s p d f	2 6 10 14	32	60
5	s p d f	2 6 10 14	32	92
6	s p d	2 6 10	18	110
7	s p	2 6	8	118

Atoms are constituted of a nucleus—containing protons and neutrons—and electrons that are constantly revolving around the nucleus [3]. These electrons occupy different energy levels referred to as shells. Table 3-1 presents the various electronic shells and their electron capacities.

Each ground state atom[1] has a different electron configuration, which can be obtained from the periodic table of the elements, a simplified version of which is shown in Figure 3-1.

The row of the periodic table of the elements indicates the number of shells possessed by the atom. For example, hydrogen (H) and helium (He) have one shell, carbon (C) has two shells, and sodium (Na) has three shells. The outermost shell of an atom is called the valence shell and is responsible for the bonding characteristic of the atom. The column number indicates the number of electrons present on the outermost orbital of the valence shell of the atom. Here are some examples of ground state atoms electronic configurations (Figure 3-2 shows the corresponding schematic):

---

[1] An atom is said to be in its ground state when all of its electrons are in their lowest energy state. Conversely, an atom is said to be in its excited state when one or more electrons are in a higher energy shell.

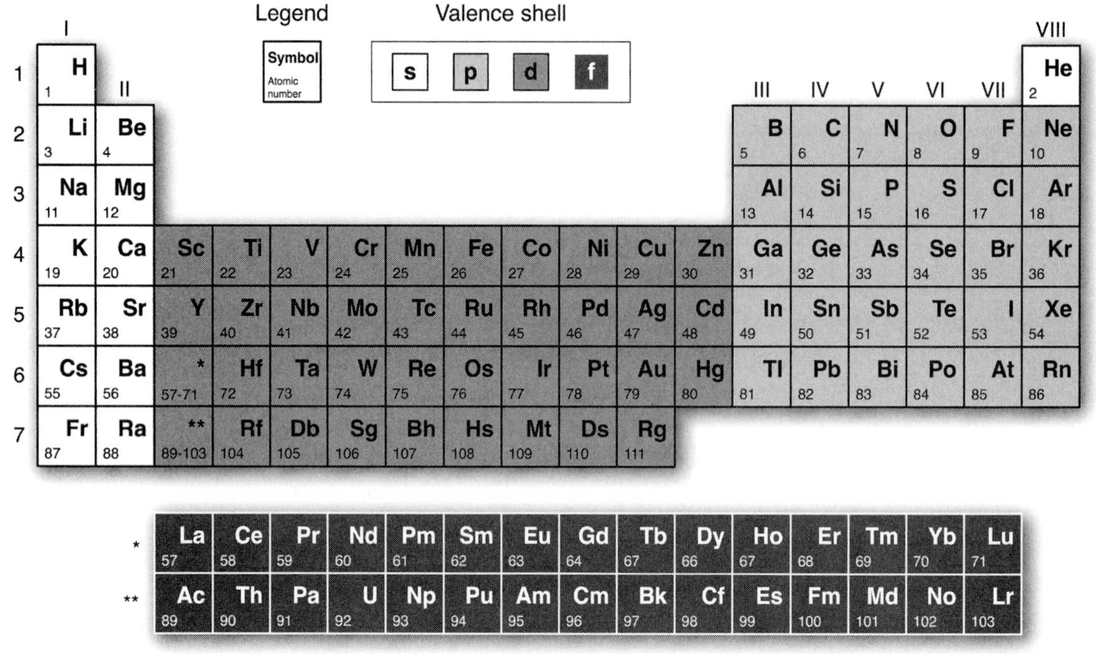

FIGURE 3-1 *Simplified periodic table of the elements.*

- Hydrogen: $1s^1$
- Carbon: $1s^2\ 2s^2\ 2p^2$
- Oxygen: $1s^2\ 2s^2\ 2p^4$
- Neon: $1s^2\ 2s^2\ 2p^6$
- Chlorine: $1s^2\ 2s^2\ 2p^6\ 3s^2\ 3p^5$

A stable electronic state is attained for a molecule when the valence shells of its atoms are full. The only atoms that are electronically stable in their ground state are the noble gases (last column). These atoms meet the requirement of having a full outer shell as shown with the example of neon in Figure 3-2. The theory behind the combination of atoms to form molecules is based upon the octet rule: atoms tend to combine in such a way that their valence shell has eight electrons (except for the first shell, which is limited to two electrons).

The valence electrons of an atom are the electrons available for creating bonds with the valence electrons from another atom. The number of valence electrons for each element can be determined from the periodic table of the elements. Without taking into account the columns of the transition metals, the column number of the table indicates the number of valence electrons. Thus, beryllium (Be) has two valence electrons, aluminum (Al) has three,

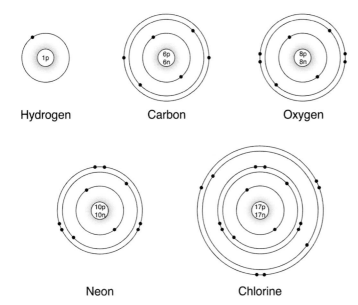

FIGURE 3-2

Schematic of the electronic configuration of ground state atoms of hydrogen, carbon, oxygen, neon, and chlorine.

and carbon (C) has four. Noble gases have eight; their valence shells are already full.

The periodic table of the elements also provides information regarding the total number of electrons contained within each atom. The atomic number (abbreviated Z) reflects the number of protons present in the nucleus and, because every element has a neutral charge when in ground state, the number of electrons equals the number of protons.

3.2.2 Ionic Bonds

An ionic bond is formed by the complete transfer of some electrons from one atom to another. The atom losing one or more electrons becomes a cation—a positively charged ion. The atom gaining one or more electron becomes an anion—a negatively charged ion. When the transfer of electrons occurs, an electrostatic attraction between the two ions of opposite charge takes place and an ionic bond is formed.

A salt such as sodium chloride (NaCl) is a good example of a molecule with ionic bonding (see Figure 3-3). The atomic number of the element sodium (Na) is 11, meaning that a sodium atom possesses eleven protons and eleven electrons. Its electronic configuration is $1s^2\ 2s^2\ 2p^6\ 3s^1$. In this state, there is only one electron in the valence shell. The tendency is for sodium to lose an electron so that the new resulting valence shell (2) is in its most stable state (full octet). This loss of an electron results in the ionization of sodium, to form the positively charged ion Na^+.

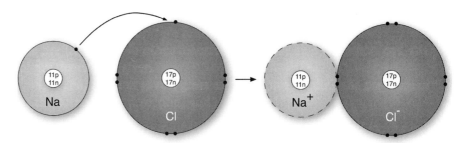

FIGURE 3-3 *Schematic representation of the principle of ionic bonds with the example of sodium chloride. Note that only valence orbitals are shown and that the valence orbital of Na in NaCl is shown in dash line to reflect the fact that it no longer exists due to an absence of electrons.*

The other atom of the salt is chlorine (Cl), which has the atomic number 17, and the electronic configuration $1s^2 \, 2s^2 \, 2p^6 \, 3s^2 \, 3p^5$. This configuration shows that the chlorine atom has seven electrons in its valence shell. Its tendency is to pick up an electron to form an octet, thus completing its third shell. In doing so, chlorine becomes the negatively charged ion Cl⁻. Because of the propensity of sodium to lose an electron and of chlorine to gain an electron, the elements are well suited to bond with one another. This transfer of electrons results in the formation of the ionic bond holding Na⁺ and Cl⁻ together. Ionic bonding is very common in inorganic chemistry but is encountered much less frequently in organic chemistry.

3.2.3 Covalent Bonds

Covalent bonds are the most important means of bonding in organic chemistry. The formation of a covalent bond is the result of atoms sharing some electrons. The bond is created by the overlapping of two atomic orbitals [1]. This process is illustrated in Figure 3-4. In this type of bond, each shared electron will be counted toward both atoms' valence shells for the purpose of satisfying the octet rule. In a single bond one pair of electrons is shared, with one electron being contributed from each of the atoms. Double bonds share two pairs of electrons and triple bonds share three pairs of electrons. Bonds sharing more than one pair of electrons are called multiple covalent bonds.

In a single covalent bond, when the electrons are shared between two *s* orbitals, the resulting bond is a sigma (σ) bond as shown in Figure 3-4. Sigma bonds are the strongest covalent chemical bonds. Sigma bonds also occur when an *s* and a *p* orbital share a pair of electrons or when two *p* orbitals that are parallel to the internuclear axis share a pair of electrons (see Figure 3-4). A pi (π) bond is the result of the sharing of a pair of electrons between two *p* orbitals that are perpendicular to the internuclear axis

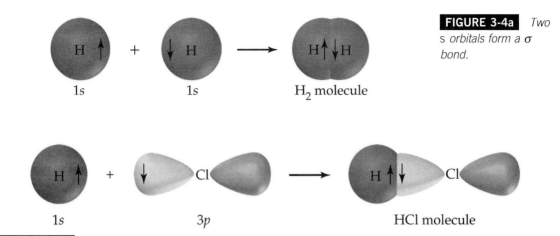

FIGURE 3-4a *Two s orbitals form a σ bond.*

1s   1s H_2 molecule

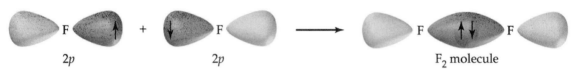

1s   3p   HCl molecule

FIGURE 3-4b *An s orbital and a p orbital also form a σ bond.*

2p   2p F_2 molecule

FIGURE 3-4c *Two p orbitals parallel to their internuclear axis also form a σ bond. (Source: McMurry J and Fay RC (2003) Chemistry, 4th edition Prentice Hall, Upper Saddle River, NJ. Reprinted with the permission of Prentice Hall, Upper Saddle River, New Jersey, USA.)*

(see Figure 3-5). In double and triple bonds, the first bond is a σ bond and the second and third ones are π bonds. Pi bonds are weaker than sigma bonds, however a double bond has the combined strength of the σ and π bonds. Analogously, a triple bond has the combined strength of a σ and two π bonds. As an example, each of the hydrogen atoms in water (H_2O) is bonded to the oxygen via a single bond (σ bond) whereas the oxygen atoms in carbon dioxide (CO_2) are bound to the carbon atom via double bonds, each consisting of a σ bond and a π bond.

3.2.4 Bond-Dissociation Energy

IUPAC defines bond-dissociation energy *(D)* as [4]: "the enthalpy (per mole) required to break a given bond of some specific molecular entity by homolysis." Homolysis is the cleavage of a bond in such a fashion that each resulting fragment retains one of the formerly bonded electrons [5]. As seen previously, when a bond is created, energy is released because the bonded atoms are of lower energy level than the individual atoms. Thus, in order to break the bond, energy must be provided to the molecule (bond-dissociation energy). As a matter of fact, the amount of energy required to break the bond is the same as that released upon formation of the bond.

FIGURE 3-5a
Two p orbitals perpendicular to the internuclear axis form a π bond.

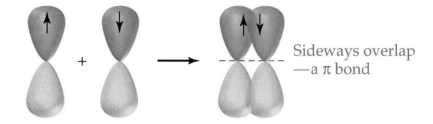

Sideways overlap
—a π bond

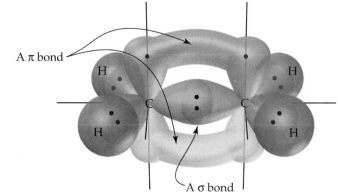

A π bond

A σ bond

FIGURE 3-5b *In double bonds, the first bond is a σ bond and the second bond is a π bond. The diagram clearly explains why a double bond can no longer rotate on itself.*

[2] kJ stands for kilojoule. A joule is the système international (SI) unit of energy or work. One joule is equivalent to one newton-meter (Nm), which is the work done when applying a one-newton force for a distance of one meter. kcal stands for kilocalorie. A calorie (cal) is a unit of energy or work defined as the energy required to raise one gram of water by one degree C at 15°C. One calorie is equal to 4.1868 joules. The unit kilocalorie (abbreviated Cal or kcal) is more often used than the unit calorie. The abbreviation mol refers to a mole: The SI unit defined by the amount of substance equal to the quantity containing as many elementary units as there are atoms in 0.012 kg of ^{12}C. This number, referred to as Avogadro's number, is 6.0221415· 10^{23}.

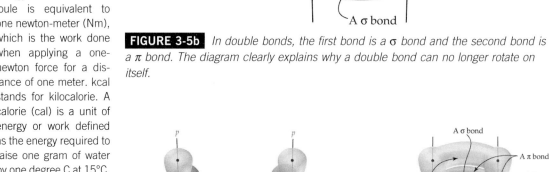

A σ bond

A π bond

A π bond

FIGURE 3-5c *In triple bonds, the first bond is a σ bond and the last two bonds are π bonds. (Source: McMurry J and Fay RC (2003) Chemistry, 4th edition Prentice Hall, Upper Saddle River, NJ. Reprinted with the permission of Prentice Hall, Upper Saddle River, New Jersey, USA.)*

D is expressed in either kJ/mol or kcal/mol[2]. D is also dependent on the temperature and it is normally given for a temperature of 25°C.

The concept of bond-dissociation energy is important to understand because it is one of the fundamental principles of pyrolysis. Knowledge of pyrolysis is required in order to understand the complex nature and formation of interfering products found in fire debris samples. The cleavage that most concerns fire debris analysts is homolysis. When homolysis occurs, two radicals are formed.

The more stable a bond, the greater the amount of energy that is required to break it. As expected, different bonds exhibit different bond-dissociation energies. Table 3-2 presents some bond-dissociation energies for some commonly encountered bonds in organic chemistry [6–8]. It is important to understand that the value of D for a given bond varies depending on other bonds present on both atoms. For example, the bond C–H requires $410\,kJ/mol$ to be broken in C_2H_6, but requires $528\,kJ/mol$ when

Table 3-2	Bond-dissociation energies (D) for commonly encountered bonds in organic chemistry [6–8].		
Bond	**D [kJ/mol]**	**Bond**	**D [kJ/mol]**
$H_3C–CH_3$	377	H–F	570
$H_3C–C_2H_5$	371	H–Cl	432
$H_3C–C_3H_7$ (iso)	367	H–Br	366
$H_3C–C_4H_9$ (tert)	366	H–I	298
$H_3C–C_6H_5$	434	$H–CF_3$	450
$H_3C–CH_2C_6H_5$	332	$H–CCl_3$	393
$H_3C–COCH_3$	354	H–OH	497
$H_2C=CH_2$	728	$H–NH_2$	453
HC≡CH	965	$H–OCH_3$	436
NC–CN	536	$H–COCH_3$	374
$CH_3–NO$	167	$H–CH_3$	439
$CH_2=N_2$	<175	$H–C_2H_5$	410
HC≡N	880	$H–C_3H_7$	410
$H_3C–OH$	389	$H–CH_2CH(CH_3)_2$	410
$H_5C_2–OH$	385	$H–CH(CH_3)_2$	396
$H_7C_3–OH$	381	$H–C(CH_3)_3$	389
O=CO	532	HO–OH	213
$CH_3–SH$	313		
C–F	450		
C–Cl	330		
C–Br	270		
C–I	240		

broken from HCN. Similarly, a C–C bond in C_2H_6 requires 377 kJ/mol to be cleaved, however the middle C–C bond in C_8H_{18} requires only 301 kJ/mol.

Some trends can be drawn from this table. For example, with the series of halogens, D decreases in the order F > Cl > Br > I. Finally, it is crucial to understand that these values relate to a homolysis of the bond and not a heterolysis. In a homolytic cleavage, two radicals are formed as the electrons stay with each atom. In contrast, in a heterolytic cleavage, the electrons stay paired and remain with one of the two fragments, thereby forming one positive and one negative ion. Some molecules containing a bond with a significant bond-dissociation energy for homolytic cleavage actually might readily be broken by heterolysis. For example, the bond H–F requires significant energy to dissociate by homolysis, but it is readily dissociated via heterolysis, into H^+ and F^- when placed in water. This phenomenon is highly dependent on the nature of the bond.

3.3 CLASSIFICATION OF ORGANIC COMPOUNDS

3.3.1 Principle

Millions of organic compounds are known to exist. As such, organic chemistry could appear quite intimidating. However, by organizing these compounds into logical classes based upon their formulae and structures, the study of organic chemistry is much more manageable. Organic compounds can be separated into two main categories: hydrocarbons and nonhydrocarbons. Hydrocarbons are molecules containing only carbon and hydrogen atoms with the general formula C_xH_y [9]. These are the molecules most commonly encountered in fire debris analysis as constituents of ignitable liquids. Nonhydrocarbon organic compounds contain other atoms, in addition to carbon and hydrogen, such as oxygen, nitrogen, chlorine, or sulfur. These atoms may be arranged in particular combinations, called functional groups, that will dictate the reactivity or the behavior of the molecule. Nonhydrocarbons, particularly those that contain oxygen, also are encountered in the field of fire debris analysis. Figure 3-6 is an illustration of the main classes of organic compounds.

In both categories, it is possible to further classify the compounds into aliphatic and aromatic compounds. Aliphatic compounds include all acyclic[3] or cyclic, saturated or unsaturated, carbon compounds, excluding aromatics [10]. By contrast, all aromatic compounds contain a ring structure and are unsaturated. They include benzene and all compounds that due to their similar electronic configurations behave like benzene. IUPAC

---

[3] Acyclic compounds are compounds that do not incorporate a ring as part of their structure.

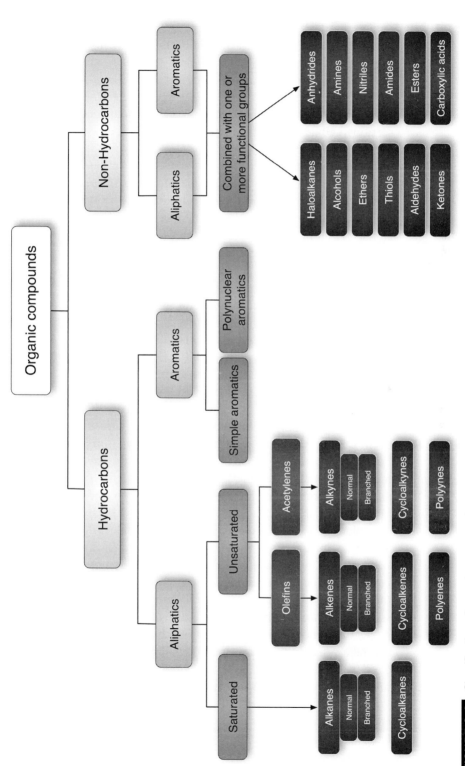

FIGURE 3-6   *Classification of organic compounds.*

defines aromatic compounds as having a chemistry typified by benzene [11]. Because of their unique electronic configuration, aromatic compounds exhibit a special stability and do not undergo the reactions typical of unsaturated aliphatic compounds. Although the fire debris analyst does not need to be proficient in every aspect of organic chemistry, there are some classes of organic compounds that must be clearly understood. The following subsections will address each important compound class.

3.3.2 Alkanes

Alkanes naturally occur in crude oil and are a major component of many fuels and solvents derived from petroleum. Alkanes are acyclic aliphatic hydrocarbons having the general molecular formula C_nH_{2n+2} [12]. They are characterized by C–C and C–H single bonds. Because they use only single bonds, alkanes contain the maximum number of hydrogen atoms relative to the number of carbon atoms, and are therefore said to be saturated. The term paraffin, although deemed obsolete by IUPAC, is still a commonly used synonym for alkane in the petroleum industry [13]. It is generally recommended that those in the fire debris analysis community use the IUPAC terminology alkanes rather than paraffins.

The simplest alkane is methane (CH_4), which consists of a single carbon atom covalently bonded to four hydrogen atoms. A homologous series of alkanes may be formed by adding additional methylene groups ($–CH_2–$). The series continues in this manner to include ethane (C_2H_6), propane (C_3H_8), butane (C_4H_{10}), among others. Although a more in-depth discussion of chemical nomenclature is presented in Section 3.4, it is practical to mention how alkanes are named. Alkane names—with the exception of the four first members of the series (methane, ethane, propane, and butane)—are composed of a numerical prefix followed by the termination -ane. The numerical prefixes used are from the Greek or Latin roots corresponding to the number of carbons in the molecule as presented in Table 3-3 [14].

Thus, the homologous series of alkanes continues with pentane, hexane, heptane, octane, nonane, decane, and so on. Remembering that there must be one bond per hydrogen and four bonds per carbon, one can see that for the three simplest alkanes, there is only one configuration, or molecular structure that can exist, as shown in Figure 3-7.

As the carbon chain gets longer and the molecules increase in size, atoms can be arranged in different ways, while still satisfying the basic tenets of covalent bonding. For example, both butane (C_4H_{10}) and pentane (C_5H_{12}) have more than one chemical structure that can exist, as shown in Figure 3-8.

Chemical compounds that have the same molecular formula, but different molecular structures are said to be isomers. Butane, with four carbons, has two possible molecular structures, whereas pentane has three different structures. The number of potential isomers increases dramatically as the number of carbons increases (see Table 3-4).

Table 3-3	Numerical prefixes used to name the number of carbon atoms in the main aliphatic chain [14].		
Number	**Prefix**	**Number**	**Prefix**
1	mono-	21*	henicosa-
2	di-	22	docosa-
3	tri-	23	tricosa-
4	tetra-	24	tetracosa-
5	penta-	25	pentacosa-
6	hexa-	26	hexacosa-
7	hepta-	27	heptacosa-
8	octa-	28	octacosa-
9	nona-	29	nonacosa-
10	deca-	30	triaconta-
11	undeca-	31	hentriaconta-
12	dodeca-	32	dotriaconta-
13	trideca-	33	tritriaconta-
14	tetradeca-	40	tetraconta-
15	pentadeca-	50	pentaconta-
16	hexadeca-	60	hexaconta-
17	heptadeca-	70	heptaconta-
18	octadeca-	80	octaconta-
19	nonadeca-	90	nonaconta-
20*	Icosa-	100	hecta-

*Note that the nomenclature eicosa- and heneicosa- is also very widely used throughout the scientific community and will be used in this text.

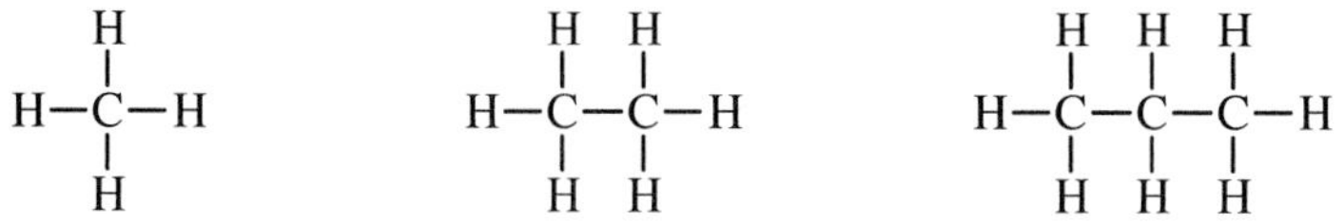

FIGURE 3-7 Chemical structures of methane, ethane, and propane.

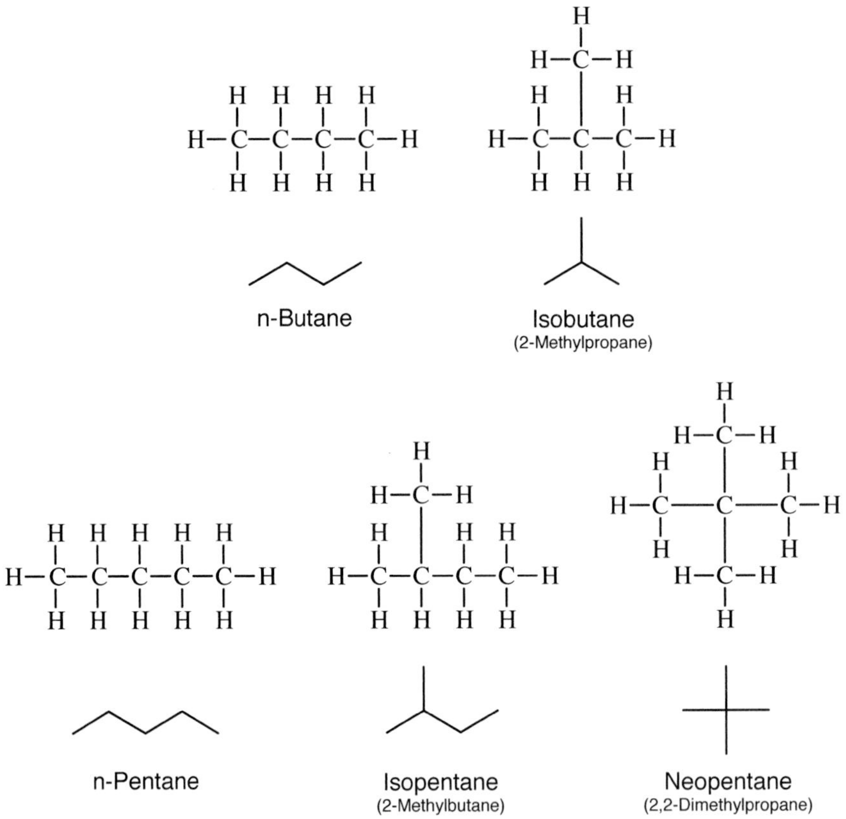

FIGURE 3-8 *Chemical structures of n-butane, isobutane, n-pentane, isopentane, and neopentane. Note that the full structure (shown above for each molecule) comprises all atoms; however due to space constraint, it is not often used. In fact, a simplified structure is often used as shown below the full structure for each molecule. This structure basically represents the carbon-to-carbon bonds without mentioning the letters C and H for carbon and hydrogen atoms. Carbon-to-hydrogen bonds do not appear. If a functional group is present, it will be "spelled out"; however, one must infer the presence of the carbon and hydrogen atoms by knowing the basic bonding rules.*

Isomers

Isomers are molecules of the same formula but having a different arrangement of their atoms [15]. There are several types of isomers:

Constitutional or structural isomers differ in the configuration (bonding) of their atoms. For example, n-pentane, isopentane, and neopentane are structural isomers.

When isomers differ only by their spatial configuration rather than by a change in their (bonding) structure, they are referred to as stereoisomers or spatial isomers. Enantiomers are molecules that are mirror images of each other (like the two hands on a person). Diastereoisomers are molecules that present the same configuration of atoms (same bonds throughout the molecules) but that are not mirror images of each other.

Table 3-4	Number of possible isomers for selected alkanes.	
Compound name	Molecular formula	Number of isomers
Methane	CH_4	1
Ethane	C_2H_6	1
Propane	C_3H_8	1
Butane	C_4H_{10}	2
Pentane	C_5H_{12}	3
Hexane	C_6H_{14}	5
Heptane	C_7H_{16}	9
Octane	C_8H_{18}	18
Nonane	C_9H_{20}	35
Decane	$C_{10}H_{22}$	75
Dodecane	$C_{12}H_{26}$	355
Pentadecane	$C_{15}H_{32}$	4,347
Eicosane	$C_{20}H_{42}$	366,319
Triacontane	$C_{30}H_{62}$	4,110,000,000

Physical properties of alkanes are consistent with their chemical structure. Since alkanes consist exclusively of carbon and hydrogen held together by single covalent bonds, they tend to be nonpolar and relatively unreactive. Hence, alkanes are fairly stable compounds. At room temperature and at atmospheric pressure, the C_1 (methane) through C_4 (n-butane) alkanes are gaseous; the C_5 (n-pentane) through C_{17} (n-heptadecane) alkanes are liquid; and the alkanes from C_{18} (n-octadecane) are solid (see Table 4-2 for more information). Branching affects physical properties; an increase in branching generally results in a decrease in boiling point among isomers. For example, the boiling point of n-pentane, isopentane, and neopentane decrease from 36°C to 28°C to 10°C, respectively, which is due to the increasing branching of the molecule.

3.3.3 Alkenes

Alkenes are acyclic (branched or unbranched) hydrocarbons having one carbon-to-carbon double bond (C=C) and the general molecular formula C_nH_{2n} [16]. Because alkenes contain less than the maximum possible number of hydrogen atoms per carbon atom, they are said to be unsaturated. An older term that is still used in the petroleum industry to designate alkenes is olefins (see text box). To be consistent in language, it is recommended that fire debris analysts use the IUPAC nomenclature whenever possible.

Alkenes and Olefins

The terms alkenes and olefins often are used interchangeably; however, this is not quite accurate. According to IUPAC, alkenes include all aliphatic hydrocarbons exhibiting one and only one double bond [16]. Olefins encompass a larger set of compounds as shown in Figure 3-6, including alkenes [17]. As a matter of fact, olefins include all aliphatic (both acyclic and cyclic) hydrocarbons having one or more carbon-to-carbon double bonds: alkenes, cycloalkenes, and polyenes (compounds exhibiting more than one double bond). When an alkene has more than one double bond, the nomenclature changes to alkadiene, alkatriene, and so on [16]. Alkadienes often are encountered in fire debris analysis as pyrolysis products of some polymers (see Subsections 4.4 and 12.3 for more detail).

As with alkanes, alkenes form a homologous series consisting of molecules of increasing molecular weight by the addition of methylene ($-CH_2-$) units. The simplest molecule in the alkene series is ethene, more commonly known as ethylene (C_2H_4); it is followed by propene, also commonly referred to as propylene (C_3H_6), butene, also known as butylene (C_4H_8), pentene (C_5H_{10}), and so on. The naming system for alkenes is similar to that for alkanes, with the termination -ene indicating that the compound is an alkene.

In addition to the different isomers that can be formed based on chain branching, alkenes will also have isomers based on other factors. One such factor is the location of the double bond. For example, whereas n-butane exhibits only one possible structure, the corresponding n-alkene butene can have two different structures, both of which incorporate the straight chain backbone: one with the double bond between the first and second carbons (1-butene) and one with the double bond between the second and third carbons (2-butene). This is shown in Figure 3-9. When the double bond is located at the end of a molecule, it is referred to as a terminal alkene. By contrast, alkenes that do not have their double bond located at the end of the molecule are called internal alkenes.

The other factor contributing to an increased number of isomers for alkenes is the nature of the carbon-to-carbon double bond itself. Whereas a single bond allows for free rotation—it almost acts like an axle—the same is not true for a double bond. Because of the nature of how the π bond forms the second bond, free rotation cannot occur. Therefore, there exists another pair of isomers for the 2-butene structure, as shown in Figure 3-10.

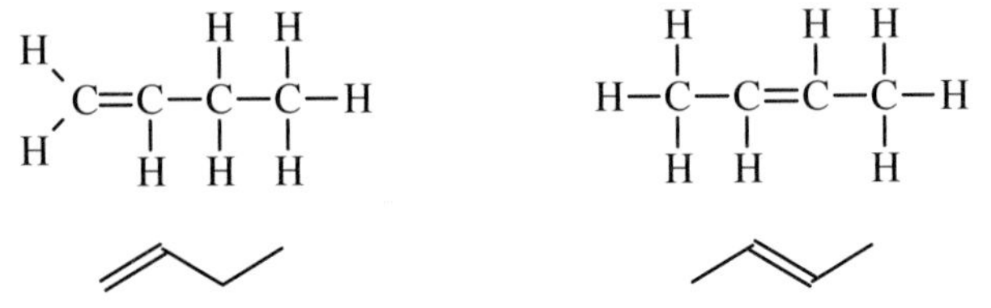

FIGURE 3-9

Chemical structures of 1-butene and 2-butene.

1-Butene

2-Butene

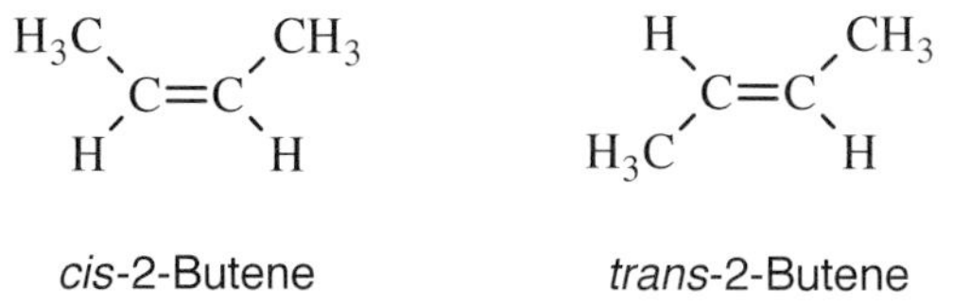

$$H_3C \diagdown \diagup CH_3$$
$$C=C$$
$$H \diagup \diagdown H$$

cis-2-Butene

$$H \diagdown \diagup CH_3$$
$$C=C$$
$$H_3C \diagup \diagdown H$$

trans-2-Butene

FIGURE 3-10

Example of stereoisomerism with cis- *and* trans-2-butene.

The difference between these isomers depends on whether the methyl groups are on the same side (*cis*) of the double bond, or on opposite sides (*trans*). The presence of a double bond therefore will result in a significantly greater number of isomers as compared with the analogous alkane. Using butene as an example, there are four isomers for the alkene (1-butene, *cis*-2-butene, *trans*-2-butene, and isobutene), whereas there are only two for the corresponding alkane (n-butane and isobutane).

Alkenes are defined by the carbon-to-carbon double bond, and it is this bond that is responsible for many of the specific properties of the alkenes. The double bond is a shorter, and therefore stronger, bond than the analogous single bond; a greater amount of energy is required to break a double bond than to break a single bond. Another important property of double bonds is their reactivity. Double bonds are more reactive than their single bond counterparts, and are particularly susceptible to addition reactions, including polymerization. Because of this tendency to react, alkenes are not commonly found in crude oils. For the same reason, it is not usually desirable to have alkenes in finished products, as they could react, affecting the viscosity and other properties of the fuel. Alternatively, products such as some varnishes or wood floor finishes purposely incorporate molecules with double bonds, so that a polymerization reaction will occur and form the desired hard film on the surface.

3.3.4 Alkynes

Alkynes are acyclic (branched or unbranched) aliphatic hydrocarbons having one carbon-to-carbon triple bond and, thus, the general molecular formula C_nH_{2n-2} [18]. Following the trend, triple bonds are shorter and stronger than double bonds. The extra π linkage (alkynes have two π bonds) makes the triple bond even more reactive. Thus, alkynes are very reactive, and with the exception of ethyne, commonly referred to as acetylene (C_2H_2), they are not commonly encountered. The naming system for alkynes follows the conventions for the alkanes and alkenes, however the presence of the triple bond is indicated by the -yne termination.

Similarly to polyenes, acyclic hydrocarbons with two or more triple bonds would be called polyynes, however due to the extreme reactivity of the triple bond, such compounds are not expected to be encountered. In any case, alkadiyne, alkatriyne, and so on constitute the proper nomenclature to use [18].

Alkynes and Acetylenes

The terms alkynes and acetylenes correspond to the terms alkenes and olefins for triple bond-bearing compounds. Acetylenes encompass all acyclic and cyclic hydrocarbons with one or more carbon-to-carbon triple bond [19]. As such, they include alkynes (branched and unbranched), cyclic alkynes, and polyynes.

Acetylenes must not be confused with the molecule acetylene (C_2H_2), the simplest of all acetylenes, whose name was given in the middle of the nineteenth century and has long been accepted as such. The systematic name of acetylene is ethyne.

3.3.5 Alicyclic Hydrocarbons

Alicyclic compounds refer to aliphatic compounds (saturated or unsaturated) in which some of the carbon atoms are in a ring formation (cycle), but may not be a benzenoid or other aromatic system [20]. Saturated alicyclic hydrocarbons go by several names, including cycloalkanes, cycloparaffins, and naphthenes. Cycloalkanes, although they are saturated (all bonds are single bonds), have the general formula C_nH_{2n}. Their reactivity is similar to that of their open-chain alkane counterparts. Unsaturated alicyclic hydrocarbons include cycloalkenes and cycloalkynes.

Naphthene v. Naphthalene

It is important not to confuse the terms naphthene and naphthalene. Naphthalene is a specific organic compound: a polynuclear aromatic hydrocarbon of formula $C_{10}H_8$ with a chemical structure that can be envisioned as two benzene rings fused together. Naphthene, on the other hand, is the older common terminology used to

describe a class of chemical compounds: the cycloalkanes and more particularly cyclopentane and cyclohexane [21]. Although the term naphthene is still widely used in the petroleum industry, it is strongly recommended that fire debris analysts use IUPAC terminology in order to prevent any confusion.

Cycloalkanes naturally occur in crude oil and are present in a variety of fuels and solvents derived from crude oil. Compounds based on cyclopentane and cyclohexane are encountered most commonly. This is due to the fact that five- and six-membered rings are fairly stable because their ring shapes allow for bond angles with minimal bond strain. Naming conventions for alicyclic compounds follow the same patterns as for their acyclic counterparts, however the prefix cyclo- is added to front of the name, before the carbon numerical prefix.

3.3.6 Aromatic Hydrocarbons

Aromatic hydrocarbons constitute a special category of organic compounds. Aromatic compounds contain a planar unsaturated ring of atoms that is stabilized due to a delocalization of π electrons. The most fundamental aromatic compound is composed of six carbon atoms in the form of a ring, with each carbon atom being bonded to two other carbon atoms and a hydrogen atom. It is called benzene and is illustrated in Figure 3-11. Aromatic compounds are compounds with a chemistry typified by benzene [11]. A synonym for aromatic compounds often used is arenes [22].

Discovery of Benzene

Benzene was discovered by British Professor Michael Faraday in 1825, while he was pyrolyzing whale oil [23]. He obtained a colorless liquid and gave it the name "bicarburet of hydrogen." Out of mere curiosity, he tried to ignite the liquid and it burned. The name benzin (the English translation would later become benzene) was given by German Chemist Eilhard Mitscherlich in 1833 [24]. The cyclic structure of benzene remained a mystery until 1865 when German Professor Friedrich August Kekulé elucidated it when he dreamt of a snake biting its own tail [23]. However, Kekulé did not discover the presence of interactions between the double bonds [25]. One had to wait until 1931 for American Professor Linus Pauling to propose that benzene exhibited a hybrid structure composed of delocalized electrons [26, 27]. This was a refinement of Kekulé's discovery. Benzene has a somewhat pleasant, sweet smell, however it is carcinogenic.

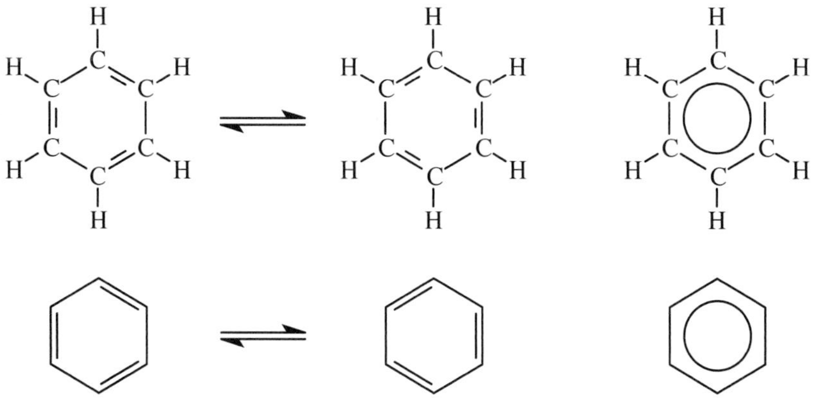

FIGURE 3-11 *Structure of benzene. Contrary to what Kekulé first thought, there are not three single bonds and three double bonds in a resonance state as shown in the two structures on the left and in the middle. As a matter of fact, benzene consists of 6 equivalent bonds that are delocalized. For this reason, it is more proper to use the structure shown on the right.*

If benzene were the cyclohexatriene structure originally proposed, the single and double bonds would be clearly demarcated, resulting in alternating bond lengths. However, as the electrons of the six p orbitals (perpendicular to the ring plane) are delocalized, a general orbital cloud is formed all around the ring. Consequently, there is no distinction between single and double bonds and the bond lengths in benzene are thus identical. One manner of representing this situation is shown on the right in Figure 3-11. This delocalization is the reason for the particular inherent stability of benzene and of aromatic compounds in general, which is not encountered with unsaturated aliphatic compounds. Aromatic compounds undergo electrophilic substitution reactions, but do not easily undergo addition reactions. Although they are unsaturated, aromatic compounds do not undergo the reactions that are typical of unsaturated aliphatics, such as the alkenes.

In more common language, aromatic compounds also are referred to as "benzene and its derivates." However, this is not completely accurate as there are other compounds considered to be aromatics, such as azulene ($C_{10}H_8$), whose chemical behavior mimics that of benzene, but that are not derived from it. Aromatic compounds must obey the Hückel[4] rule, which states that [1]: "a molecule will be aromatic only if it has a planar, monocyclic system of conjugation with a p orbital on each atom, and only if the p orbital system contains $4n + 2$ π electrons, where n is an integer (n = 0, 1, 2, 3) . . .)." Thus, cyclic compounds with 2, 6, 10, 14, . . . pi electrons have the potential to be aromatic.

When more than one benzene ring is fused together, the molecule formed is part of the class of polycyclic aromatic hydrocarbons (PAH). A synonym for PAH is polynuclear aromatic (hydrocarbon) or PNA. One of the most commonly encountered PAH in fire debris analysis is naphthalene. It is important to keep in mind that if a molecule with multiple benzene rings is not a hydrocarbon, then it is not correctly classified under neither the PAH nor the PNA denomination.

3.3.7 Nonhydrocarbons

When an organic compound contains a functional group with atoms other than carbon and hydrogen, it is no longer considered a hydrocarbon. There are several different functional groups in organic chemistry, each of which imparts different properties to the molecule. Functional groups often are referred to as the controllers of the reactivity of organic compounds.

When performing fire debris analysis, the criminalist most commonly encounters hydrocarbons, such as alkanes, cycloalkanes, alkenes, aromatics,

---

[4] Erich Hückel (1896–1980) was a German professor of physics and physical chemistry and is known for his contribution to the calculations of molecular orbitals on π electron systems.

Name	Suffix	Structure
Alkane	-ane	R—H
Alkene	-ene	$\diagup$C=C$\diagdown$
Alkyne	-yne	—C≡C—
Arene	-	R—⬡
Alcohol	-ol	R—OH
Alkyl halide	-halide	R—X
Ether	ether	R—O—R'
Amine	-amine	R—NH_2
Aldehyde	-al	$\overset{O}{\overset{\|}{R-C-H}}$
Ketone	-one	$\overset{O}{\overset{\|}{R-C-R'}}$
Carboxylic acid	-oic acid	$\overset{O}{\overset{\|}{R-C-OH}}$
Ester	-oate	$\overset{O}{\overset{\|}{R-C-OR'}}$
Amide	-amide	$\overset{O}{\overset{\|}{R-C-NH_2}}$

Table 3-5 *Some functional groups in organic chemistry.*

and polynuclear aromatic hydrocarbons. Thus, the study of functional groups might not be of the greatest interest. In spite of this, the analyst will encounter some molecules with nonhydrocarbon groups, particularly halogenated and oxygenated compounds. Thus, it is important to be aware of the different functional groups as presented in Table 3-5.

When starting with a hydrocarbon compound, if a hydrogen atom of an organic compound is replaced by a functional group, this process is called *substitution*. Substitution is an important concept to understand as it is present in many applications such as the derivatization of fatty acids when

analyzing fire debris for vegetable (and animal) oil residues (see Section 14.2).

3.4 IUPAC NOMENCLATURE

3.4.1 General Principle

It is crucial to properly name organic molecules. With the enormous number of different molecules, a systematic manner of naming them needed to be developed. This was carried out by IUPAC and it is now widely accepted as a standard around the world [28]. IUPAC refers to its publication regarding the nomenclature of organic compounds as "The Blue Book" [29]. A version of the IUPAC blue book is available online free of charge [30].

Because the systematic naming of organic molecules is quite new when compared with the development of science and the discovery of chemical compounds, the IUPAC nomenclature is not always followed; so, there are many synonyms available for some molecules, not to mention that there are trivial names still deeply anchored in the common language. For example, benzene has more than 30 synonyms available. Even the simplest organic molecule, methane, has several synonyms as shown in Table 3-6 [31, 32].

Table 3-6	*Some synonyms of benzene and methane [31, 32].*
Benzene	**Methane**
[6]annulene; AI3-00808; Benzeen; Benzen; Benzin; Benzine; Benzol; Benzol 90; Benzole; Benzolene; Benzolo; Bicarburet of hydrogen; CCRIS 70; Carbon oil; Caswell No. 077; Coal naphtha; Cyclohexatriene; Fenzen; HSDB 35; Mineral naphtha; Motor benzol; NCI-C55276; NSC 67315; Nitration benzene; Phene; Phenyl hydride; Polystream; Pyrobenzol; Pyrobenzole; RCRA waste number U019; UN 1114.	Biogas; Fire damp; Marsh gas; Methyl hydride; R 50; UN 1971; UN 1972.

It is not the goal of this section to offer a comprehensive guide to the nomenclature of organic compounds, since it has already been done and actually takes hundreds of pages. The aim is just to remind the reader of the main principles behind the nomenclature of organic compounds, with an emphasis on examples of compounds commonly encountered in fire debris analysis. The fire debris analyst is encouraged to consult the aforementioned IUPAC publications for more information or other available reference books [33, 34].

The name of an organic compound is composed of the stem (the main name, typically the longest chain in the molecule) onto which prefixes,

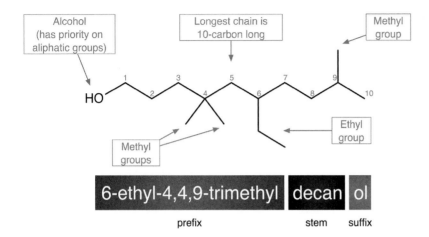

FIGURE 3-12

Structure of the name of an organic compound.

suffix, and numerical indices are attached as shown in Figure 3-12. The name is built in two general steps:

1. The stem is named based on the longest carbon chain in the molecule (the parent chain).
2. Prefixes, suffix, and their respective numerical indices are added in order to indicate the nature and the position of extraneous atoms and/or functional groups on the chain.

3.4.2 Prefixes and Suffixes of Functional Groups

Only one suffix is allowed,[5] whereas several prefixes may be used, depending on the number of functional groups. Thus, when a molecule exhibits several functional groups, it is necessary to prioritize which one will be placed in the suffix and which ones will be placed in the prefix and in which order. This assignation is performed based on the priority list (sometimes referred to as seniority of the functional groups) shown in Table 3-7 [14]. The group closest to the top of the list gets to be named in the suffix and all other groups are cited in the prefix. Once the suffix is chosen, the smallest carbon number of the main carbon chain is assigned to it.

It should be noted that some functional groups are always cited in the prefix (these groups are called subordinate groups) and never in the suffix [14]. Table 3-8 presents the list of these groups.

---

[5] When one of the functional groups is an alkene or alkyne, it is possible to combine the terminations "-ene" and "-yne" with one more suffix chosen from the list in Table 3-7.

Table 3-7	Prefixes and suffixes and priority order (seniority) of some principal functional groups. Note that the suffix of alkenes and alkynes can be combined to one of the suffix in the table. This is the reason why these two functional groups are not in the table.

Priority order	Functional group	Suffix (priority)	Prefix (nonpriority)
1	Carboxylic acids	-oic acid -carboxylic acid	carboxy-
2	Esters	-oate	R-oxycarbonyl-
3	Amides	-amide	carbamoyl-
4	Nitriles	-nitrile	cyano-
5	Aldehydes	-al	formyl-
6	Ketones	-one	oxo-
7	Alcohols and Phenols	-ol	hydroxy-
8	Thiols	-thiol	sulfanyl-
9	Amines	-amine	amino-

Table 3-8	Subordinate functional groups are always expressed in the prefix.

Functional group	Formula	Prefix (nonpriority)
Halogens	F Cl Br I	fluoro- chloro- bromo- iodo-
Nitro compounds	NO_2	nitro-
Nitroso compounds	NO	nitroso-
Ethers	O-R	R-oxy-

3.4.3 Naming Alkanes and Nonhydrocarbon Saturated Aliphatics

How simple alkanes are named was previously demonstrated (see Subsection 3.3.2). When the alkane is substituted (and may not be an alkane anymore), the following rules must be followed:

1. Identify the longest continuous carbon chain in the molecule and name it (stem of the name).
2. Identify all the substituent groups attached to the chain and name them.

3. Starting at the end nearest one of the substituent groups, consecutively number the carbon of the longest chain.
4. Determine the location of each substituent group by the appropriate carbon (location) number.
5. Identify which substituent will be in the suffix. Add the suffix to the stem separated by the location number in between two dashes.
6. Build the prefix by first listing the substituent groups in alphabetical order. Then, each substituent group is named with its location number preceding it, separated by a dash. The substituent groups are separated from each other by a dash. The prefix qualifiers used to designate several groups of the same kind are not considered when alphabetizing.

Prefix and Suffix Qualifiers

When there is a repetition of identical functional groups, such as two methyl substituents on an alkane chain, it is possible to use the qualifiers di-, tri-, tetra-, and so on, to designate them. In such instances, these prefix and suffix qualifiers are not taken into account when alphabetizing.

Also, the carbon numbers assigned to the different groups are separated by commas, keeping the dash only between the last number and the prefix or suffix (see examples hereafter).

Also, some subrules may be applicable:

I. If there are two or more longest chains of equal length, the one with the largest number of substituent groups is designated as the main chain.
II. If both ends of the root chain have equidistant substituents: (a) The chain numbering begins at the end nearest a third substituent, if one is present. (b) The chain numbering begins at the end nearest the first cited group (alphabetical order).

Figure 3-13 presents a few molecular structures with their respective names.

3.4.4 Naming Cycloalkanes

Cycloalkanes are named in two parts: the prefix cyclo- is followed by the alkane name (cyclobutane, cyclopentane, cyclohexane).

1. If the cycloalkane is monosubstituted, the ring constitutes the stem name and the substituent group is named as previously described. For obvious reasons, it is not useful to indicate a location number.

FIGURE 3-13

Examples of chemical structures and nomenclature of alkanes and nonhydrocarbons saturated aliphatics.

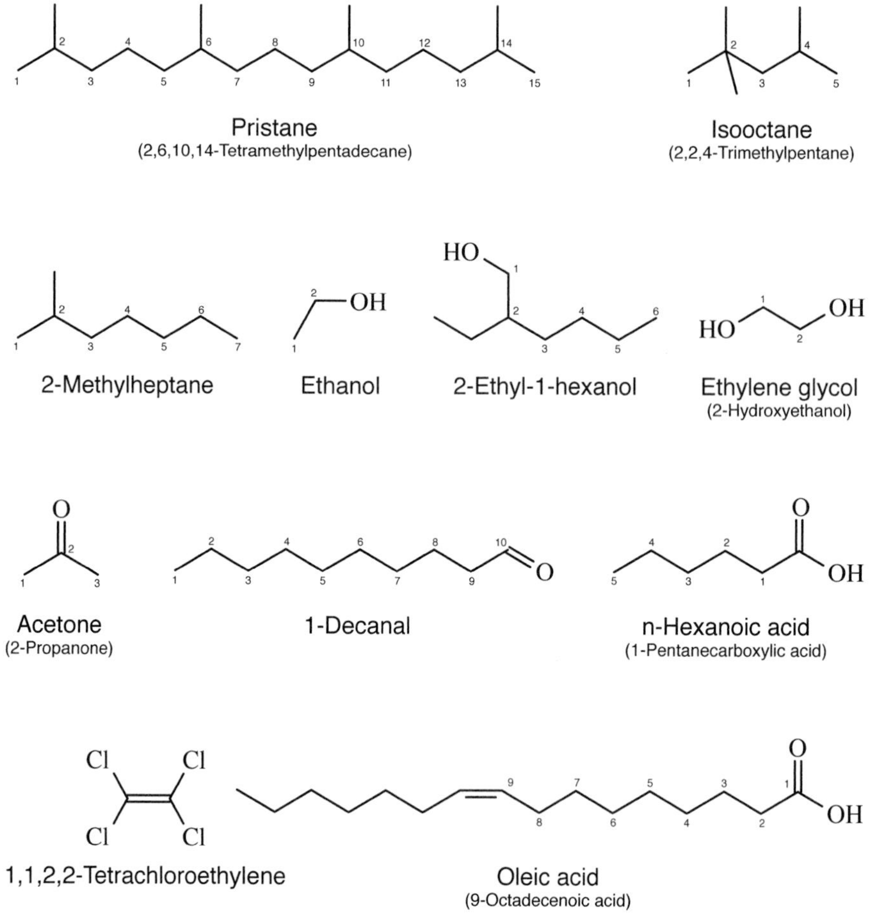

2. If the alkyl substituent is very complex, it is possible to invert the situation and name the ring as a substituent group on an alkane.

3. If the ring possesses two different substituents, they are listed in alphabetical order, and the first cited substituent is arbitrarily assigned to carbon number 1. The numbering of ring carbons is then continued in the (clockwise or counterclockwise) direction that assigns the lowest possible location number to the second substituent.

4. If the ring possesses several substituents, they are listed in alphabetical order. Location numbers are assigned to the substituents so that one of them is at carbon number 1 and the other have the lowest possible location numbers, counting in either a clockwise or counterclockwise direction.

5. Build the name by first listing the substituent groups in alphabetical order followed by the name of the cycloalkane. Each substituent group is named with its location number preceding it, separated by a dash.

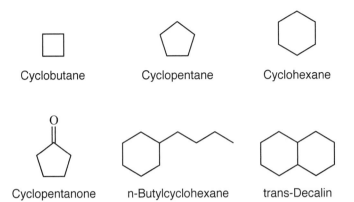

FIGURE 3-14

Examples of chemical structures and nomenclature of cycloalkanes.

The substituent groups are separated from each other by a dash. The prefix qualifier used to designate several groups of the same kind are not considered when alphabetizing.

Figure 3-14 presents a few molecular structures with their respective names.

3.4.5 Naming Unsaturated Aliphatics
Alkenes, alkynes, cycloalkenes, and cycloalkynes follow the rules for the alkanes and cycloalkanes very closely.

1. The -ene (-yne) suffix indicates an alkene (alkyne) or cycloalkene (cycloalkyne).
2. When choosing the main chain for the stem, it must include both carbon atoms of the double (triple) bond.
3. The main chain must be numbered starting from the end nearest a double (triple) bond carbon. If the double (triple) bond is in the center of the chain, the nearest substituent rule is used to determine the end where the numbering will start.
4. The smaller of the two numbers designating the carbon atoms of the double (triple) bond is used as the double (triple) bond location number.
5. When multiple double (triple) bonds are present, a location number is assigned to each of them. The suffix is also adapted (addition of a qualifier) to reflect the number of double (triple) bonds: -diene (-diyne), -triene (-triyne), and so on.
6. With cycloalkenes (cycloalkynes), the double (triple) bond carbons are arbitrarily assigned ring locations number 1 and 2. The position 1 is assigned based on the nearest substituent rule.
7. Substituent groups containing double bonds are: (i) Vinyl group: $H_2C=CH-$; (ii) Allyl group: $H_2C=CH-CH_2-$. Substituent groups con-

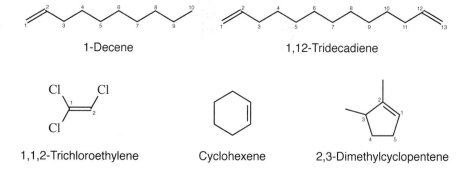

Examples of chemical structures and nomenclature of alkenes and cycloalkenes.

1-Decene

1,12-Tridecadiene

1,1,2-Trichloroethylene

Cyclohexene

2,3-Dimethylcyclopentene

Examples of chemical structures and nomenclature of alkynes and cycloalkynes.

2-Butyne

1-Heptyne

Cyclooctyne

taining triple bonds are: (i) Ethynyl group: HC≡C–; (ii) Propargyl group: HC≡C–CH$_2$–.

Also, some subrules may be applicable:

I. The main chain is the one containing the maximum number of multiple bonds.

II. If more than one such chain is found, the longest chain is chosen as the main chain.

III. If the chains have equal length, the one with the most substituents is chosen.

Figures 3-15 and 3-16 present a few unsaturated aliphatic structures with their respective names.

3.4.6 Naming Aromatics

The nomenclature of substituted benzene ring compounds is less systematic than that of the alkanes, alkenes, and alkynes. When dealing with simple aromatic molecules, the stem of the name is based on benzene. The benzene ring has six hydrogen atoms that can be substituted. When one of them is substituted, the benzene is said to be monosubstituted, when two are substituted, it is said to be disubstituted, and so on. When the benzene group itself is used as a substituent, it is named phenyl, and when toluene (methylbenzene) is used as substituent, it is named benzyl.

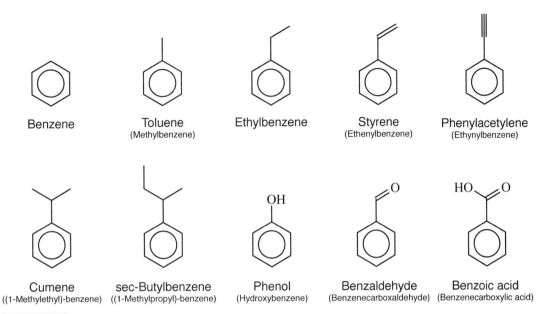

| Benzene | Toluene (Methylbenzene) | Ethylbenzene | Styrene (Ethenylbenzene) | Phenylacetylene (Ethynylbenzene) |

| Cumene ((1-Methylethyl)-benzene) | sec-Butylbenzene ((1-Methylpropyl)-benzene) | Phenol (Hydroxybenzene) | Benzaldehyde (Benzenecarboxaldehyde) | Benzoic acid (Benzenecarboxylic acid) |

FIGURE 3-17 *Examples of chemical structures and nomenclature of monosubstituted benzenes.*

A/ Monosubstituted Benzenes

With monosubstituted benzene, the position of the substituent cannot be determined and is not specified in the name. Many names are built with the substituent prefix followed by the word benzene, such as in chloroben-zene or methylbenzene. Some names use the substituents in the suffix position, such as in benzenol or benzenamine. Although one should aim to use IUPAC names most often, there are many names that are widely used and generally accepted in lieu of the official systematic nomenclature. For example, phenol is used instead of benzenol, benzaldehyde instead of ben-zenecarbaldehyde, and benzoic acid instead of benzenecarboxylic acid. Toluene is another example of an accepted name for methylbenzene. One must remember names that are commonly attributed to monosubstituted benzenes because they usually are accepted by IUPAC names even if they do not follow the exact nomenclature rules. Figure 3-17 presents a few examples with their respective names.

B/ Disubstituted Benzenes

With disubstitued benzenes, there are three possible arrangements of the sub-stituents. They can be in positions 1 and 2, 1 and 3, or 1 and 4. For example, dimethylbenzene can be 1,2-dimethylbenzene, 1,3-dimethylbenzene, or 1,4-dimethylbenzene. Another very common manner of characterizing the position of the two substituents is the use of the Greek prefixes ortho-, meta-, and para-, abbreviated o-, m-, and p-. They correspond to (1,2-), (1,3-), and

FIGURE 3-18
Examples of chemical structures and nomenclature of disubstituted benzenes.

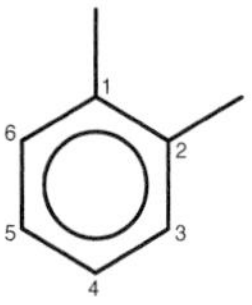

o-Xylene
(1,2-Dimethylbenzene)

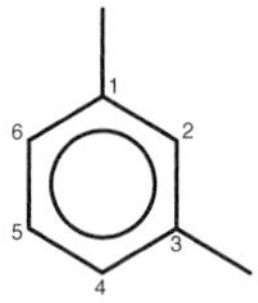

m-Xylene
(1,3-Dimethylbenzene)

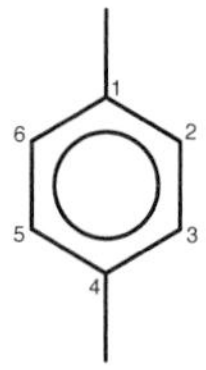

p-Xylene
(1,4-Dimethylbenzene)

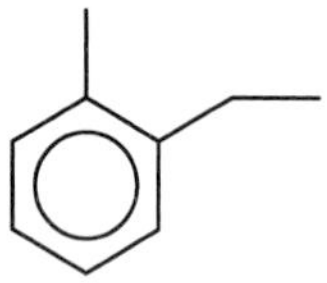

2-Ethyltoluene
(1-ethyl-2-methylbenzene)

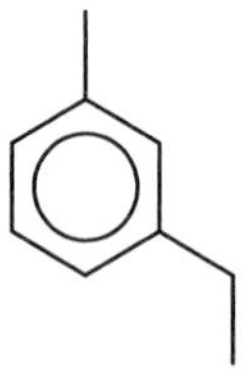

3-Ethyltoluene
(1-ethyl-3-methylbenzene)

4-Ethyltoluene
(1-ethyl-4-methylbenzene)

p-Cymene
(1-methyl-4-(1-methylethylbenzene))

(1,4-) respectively. Thus, the common names of 1,2-dimethylbenzene, 1,3-dimethylbenzene, or 1,4-dimethylbenzene are o-xylene, m-xylene, and p-xylene, three important molecules in fire debris analysis.

The attribution of the position 1 is given by priority of the functional groups, as presented in Tables 3-7 and 3-8, and when similar functional groups are present, to the longest one. If both functional groups are identical it does not matter, as the molecule is symmetrical. The substituents then are organized alphabetically in the name using the aforementioned rules. Figure 3-18 presents several examples of disubstituted benzenes.

C/ Highly Substituted Benzenes

When the benzene is tri- or more substituted, the carbon atoms are numbered in such a way as to assign the substituents the lowest possible numbers. Substituents are listed alphabetically in the final name. If the substitution is symmetrical the numbering then must correspond to the alphabetical order. Examples of chemical structures with their respective names are shown in Figure 3-19.

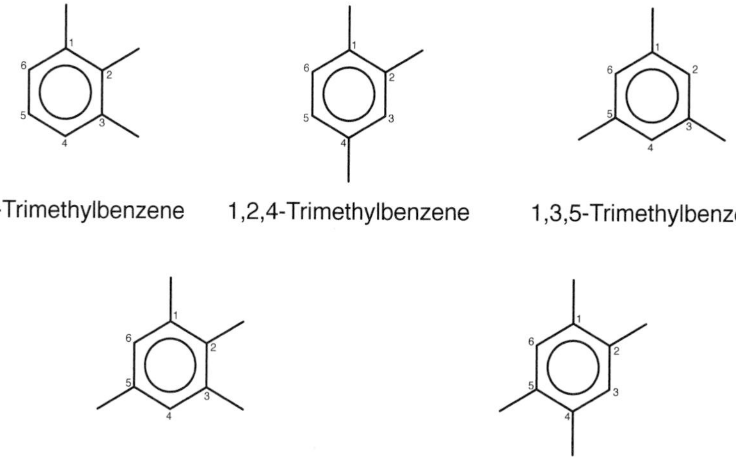

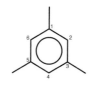

FIGURE 3-19

Examples of chemical structures and nomenclature of tri- and more substituted benzenes.

1,2,3-Trimethylbenzene   1,2,4-Trimethylbenzene   1,3,5-Trimethylbenzene

1,2,3,5-Tetramethylbenzene   1,2,4,5-Tetramethylbenzene

D/ Indanes and Indenes

A particular set of compounds important to know in fire debris analysis are indanes and indenes. The compounds referred to as indanes and indenes are those that are based on the compounds indane (C_9H_{10}) and indene (C_9H_8). These compounds are comprised of a six-membered ring and five-membered ring fused to one another. In both compounds, the six-membered ring is a benzene-type ring (aromatic); indene however, also has additional unsaturation in its five-membered ring (a double-bond). Figure 3-20 shows the structures of indane, indene, and substituted indane compounds with the numbering system. Note where the carbon location number starts. Also, the two carbons located in the fusion between the two rings do not count in the chain numbering as they cannot be bonded to any other atoms. Indanes are naturally occurring in crude oil, and the methylindanes and dimethylindanes are found in a variety of petroleum products.

E/ Polynuclear Aromatic Hydrocarbons

When dealing with polynuclear aromatic hydrocarbons, the situation can quickly become complicated. The simplest of the PAH is naphthalene. Many of the PAH names are based on naphthalene using the same principle as benzene. Note that the two carbons located in the fusion between the two rings do not count in the chain numbering as they cannot be bonded to any other atoms. Figure 3-21 presents some chemical structures of PAH commonly encountered in fire debris analysis along with their names.

F/ Other Compounds

Many other compounds that are commonly encountered in fire debris analysis are presented along with their names in Figure 3-22. It is recommended that the criminalist become familiar with these names.

80 **CHAPTER 3:** Review of Basic Organic Chemistry

FIGURE 3-20

Examples of chemical structures and nomenclatures of indanes and compounds based on indane.

Indane   4-Methylindane   5-Methylindane

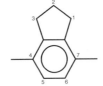

4,7-dimethylindane    Indene

FIGURE 3-21

Examples of chemical structures and nomenclature of PAH.

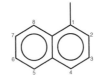

Naphthalene   1-Methylnaphthalene   2-Methylnaphthalene

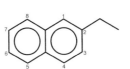
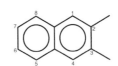
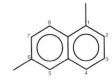

2-Ethylnaphthalene   2,3-Dimethylnaphthalene   1,6-Dimethylnaphthalene

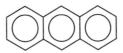
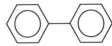

Anthracene   Biphenyl   Biphenylene

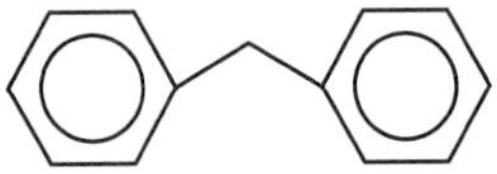

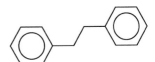

Diphenylmethane   Bibenzyl

FIGURE 3-22

Some important molecules in fire debris analysis and their nomenclature.

Pentanal

Tetraethyl lead

Propylene glycol
(1,2-Propanediol)

α-pinene

β-pinene

Camphor

Furfural
(2-Furancarboxaldehyde)

5-Methyl-
2-furancarboxaldehyde

d-Limonene
(4-Isopropenyl-1-methyl-cyclohexene)

3-Methoxyphenol
(1-Hydroxy-3-methoxybenzene)

Diethylphthalate

Caprolactam

For the less commonly encountered and more complex polynuclear aromatic hydrocarbons, refer to the IUPAC references provided.

REFERENCES

1. McMurry J (1988) *Organic chemistry*, 2nd edition, Brooks/Cole Publishing Company, Pacific Grove, CA.
2. International Union of Pure and Applied Chemistry (1997) Bond, *IUPAC Compendium of Chemical Terminology*, Research Triangle Park, NC.
3. International Union of Pure and Applied Chemistry (1997) Atom, *IUPAC Compendium of Chemical Terminology*, Research Triangle Park, NC.

4. International Union of Pure and Applied Chemistry (1997) Bond-dissociation energy, *IUPAC Compendium of Chemical Terminology*, Research Triangle Park, NC.

5. International Union of Pure and Applied Chemistry (1997) Homolysis (homolytic), *IUPAC Compendium of Chemical Terminology*, Research Triangle Park, NC.

6. McMurry J and Fay RC (1998) *Chemistry*, 2nd edition, Prentice Hall, Upper Saddle River, NJ.

7. Cottrell TL (1958) *The strengths of chemical bonds*, Butterworths Scientific Publications, London, England.

8. McMillen DF and Golden DM (1982) Hydrocarbon bond dissociation energies, *Annual Reviews of Physical Chemistry*, **33**, pp 493–532.

9. International Union of Pure and Applied Chemistry (1997) Hydrocarbons, *IUPAC Compendium of Chemical Terminology*, Research Triangle Park, NC.

10. International Union of Pure and Applied Chemistry (1997) Aliphatic compounds, *IUPAC Compendium of Chemical Terminology*, Research Triangle Park, NC.

11. International Union of Pure and Applied Chemistry (1997) Aromatic, *IUPAC Compendium of Chemical Terminology*, Research Triangle Park, NC.

12. International Union of Pure and Applied Chemistry (1997) Alkanes, *IUPAC Compendium of Chemical Terminology*, Research Triangle Park, NC.

13. International Union of Pure and Applied Chemistry (1997) Paraffin, *IUPAC Compendium of Chemical Terminology*, Research Triangle Park, NC.

14. Leigh GJ, Favre HA, and Metanomski WV (1998) *Principles of chemical nomenclature: A guide to IUPAC recommendations*, Blackwell Science, Oxford, United Kingdom.

15. International Union of Pure and Applied Chemistry (1997) Isomer, *IUPAC Compendium of Chemical Terminology*, Research Triangle Park, NC.

16. International Union of Pure and Applied Chemistry (1997) Alkenes, *IUPAC Compendium of Chemical Terminology*, Research Triangle Park, NC.

17. International Union of Pure and Applied Chemistry (1997) Olefins, *IUPAC Compendium of Chemical Terminology*, Research Triangle Park, NC.

18. International Union of Pure and Applied Chemistry (1997) Alkynes, *IUPAC Compendium of Chemical Terminology*, Research Triangle Park, NC.

19. International Union of Pure and Applied Chemistry (1997) Acetylenes, *IUPAC Compendium of Chemical Terminology*, Research Triangle Park, NC.

20. International Union of Pure and Applied Chemistry (1997) Alicyclic compounds, *IUPAC Compendium of Chemical Terminology*, Research Triangle Park, NC.

21. International Union of Pure and Applied Chemistry (1997) Naphthenes, *IUPAC Compendium of Chemical Terminology*, Research Triangle Park, NC.

22. International Union of Pure and Applied Chemistry (1997) Arenes, *IUPAC Compendium of Chemical Terminology*, Research Triangle Park, NC.

23. Roberts RM (1989) *Serendipity: Accidental discoveries in science*, John Wiley & Sons, New York, NY.

24. Encyclopedia Britannica (2006) C_6H_6 *Benzene*, available from http://encyclopedia.jrank.org/BEC_BER/BENZENE_C6H6.html, last access performed on December 29, 2006.

25. International Union of Pure and Applied Chemistry (1997) Kekulé structure (for aromatic compounds), *IUPAC Compendium of Chemical Terminology*, Research Triangle Park, NC.

26. Brush SG (1999) Dynamics of theory change in chemistry: Part 1. The benzene problem 1865–1945, *Studies in History and Philosophy of Science Part A*, **30**(1), pp 21–79.

27. Brush SG (1999) Dynamics of theory change in chemistry: Part 2. Benzene and molecular orbitals, 1945–1980, *Studies in History and Philosophy of Science Part A*, **30**(2), pp 263–302.

28. International Union of Pure and Applied Chemistry (1979) *Nomenclature of organic chemistry*, 4th edition, Pergamon Press, Headington Hill Hall, Oxford, United Kingdom.

29. Panico R, Powell WH, and Richer J-C (1994) *A guide to IUPAC nomenclature of organic compounds, recommendations 1993*, 2nd edition, Blackwell Scientific Publications, Oxford, United Kingdom.

30. Advanced Chemistry Development (1997) *IUPAC nomenclature of organic chemistry*, available from http://www.acdlabs.com/iupac/nomenclature/, last access performed on December 19, 2006.

31. National Institute of Standards and Technology (2005) *Benzene*, available from http://webbook.nist.gov/cgi/cbook.cgi?Name=benzene&Units=SI, last access performed on June 3, 2007.

32. National Institute of Standards and Technology (2005) *Methane*, available from http://webbook.nist.gov/cgi/cbook.cgi?Name=methane&Units=SI, last access performed on June 3, 2007.

33. Fox RB and Powell WH (2001) *Nomenclature of organic compounds: Principles and practice*, American Chemical Society, Washington, DC.

34. Pal SC (2006) *Nomenclature of organic compounds*, Alpha Science International, Oxford, United Kingdom.

CHAPTER 4

Chemistry and Physics of Fire and Liquid Fuels

"Nothing is too wonderful to be true if it be consistent with the laws of nature."

Michael Faraday, English chemist and physicist (1791–1867)

4.1 DEFINITION OF FIRE

4.1.1 Basic Conditions

Fire is an exothermic reaction involving a combustible substance (fuel) and an oxidizer that occurs at a rate rapid enough to produce both heat and light. In order for a fire to occur, several conditions must be fulfilled. There are two main models used to describe fire: the fire triangle and the fire tetrahedron [1]. Other models such as the fire pentagon and the life cycle of fire also exist, but they are not widely accepted [2, 3].

A/ Fire Triangle

The fire triangle is the oldest and most well known theory. Basically, it states that in order for a fire to occur, three conditions must be present and interact together:

- Combustible (fuel)
- Oxidizer (for example oxygen)
- Activation energy (heat source)

Each condition is represented by one side of the triangle as shown in Figure 4-1. When the three conditions are brought together (assembly of the three sides to form a triangle), fire occurs.

This model is simple and works well. The fact that each side is connected to the others symbolizes the continuous interaction between all three conditions. A fire is stopped by breaking one side from the triangle, which therefore inhibits the interaction of this condition with the other two. This is the principle of fire extinguishment [4]. If the fuel (combustible) is removed

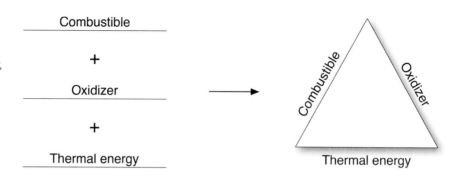

Fire Triangle. When the three sides (combustible, oxidizer, and thermal energy) interact all together (assembly of the triangle), fire occurs.

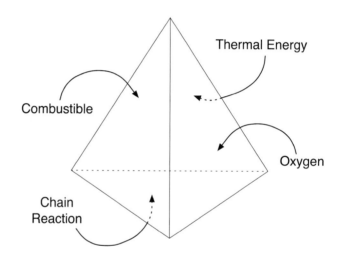

Fire Tetrahedron. Each side of the tetrahedron represents one of the four conditions required for a fire to occur: combustible, oxidizer, thermal energy, and an uninhibited chain reaction.

the triangle is not complete, and, without fuel, no fire is possible. If the oxidizer is removed, again, the triangle is not complete, and therefore no fire occurs. If a combustible and oxidizer are present together without suffi-cient thermal energy, the triangle is not complete, and no fire results. In the everyday world, combustibles are almost always in contact with oxidiz-ers—such as oxygen in the ambient atmosphere—however fire does not spontaneously occur. Only with the addition of a sufficient thermal energy (ignition source) does combustion and thus, the exothermic reaction, begin.

B/ Fire Tetrahedron

In the fire tetrahedron, as shown in Figure 4-2, the extra side corresponds to the concept of uninhibited chemical chain reactions. All four sides are connected together, forming a tetrahedron or pyramid.

The same principle as the fire triangle is applied here. The only differ-ence is that the uninterrupted chemical chain reaction between the combustible, oxidizer, and thermal energy is represented as a distinct component, whereas it simply is implied in the overall construction of the fire triangle.[1] If any one of the sides is missing, then the tetrahedron is not complete and fire either does not occur, or is extinguished.

4.1.2 Combustibles

Combustibles are comprised of any materials existing in a chemical state in which they can be oxidized in the presence of a suitable ignition source [1]. Combustibles, or fuels, are present almost everywhere. Some common fuels such as gasoline or wood are well known. However, there are many combustible materials that are not commonly thought of as combustible, such as some metals and other inorganic compounds [3].

Fuels can be found in the solid, liquid, or gaseous phase.[2] Fuels can be organic or inorganic materials. They can be simple elements or complex molecules. Since the goal of this book is to address fire debris analysis, and since ignitable liquids are the most commonly encountered accelerants, emphasis will be placed on liquid fuels. It will be explained in Chapter 7 that most ignitable liquids are composed of organic compounds, such as petroleum products and their derivatives.

4.1.3 Oxidizers

The most common oxidizer is the oxygen gas (O_2) present in the air. Earth's atmosphere contains approximately 21% oxygen [5]. Oxygen is present virtually everywhere and, therefore, it is the oxidizer present in most fires. However, it is important to note that other oxidizers, such as molecules containing oxygen or some halogens, exist [3]. For example, methane is known to burn with chlorine, resulting in the formation of hydrochloric acid.

As a general rule, if the level of oxygen drops below 10%, flaming combustion will cease [6]. Only glowing fire can survive in an atmosphere containing less than approximately 10% oxygen [7]. Further details about these two types of fire are provided later in this chapter.

4.1.4 Thermal Energy or Ignition Source

If the thermal energy present is sufficient and adequate, it becomes an ignition source. As part of the fire triangle or tetrahedron, it initiates the com-

---

[1] Another perspective in the difference between the fire triangle and the fire tetrahedron is that the first one solely concerns the start of the combustion process, and the second one concerns the sustained process of combustion.

[2] It will be explained later in this chapter that most liquid and solid fuels must undergo a phase or chemical change to the gaseous phase before they can burn in a flaming fire.

Table 4-1	The different sources of ignition with some examples
Source	**Example**
Mechanical	Heat produced by the friction of an axle onto its seat, when improperly lubricated
Electrical	Arc created between two contacts when a switch is opened or closed
Biological	Bacterial activity within hay
Chemical	Exothermic reaction between sodium hypochlorite and glycol
Nuclear	Fission reaction occurring with uranium

bustion process. Identifying the source of ignition is often the key element in the determination of the cause of a fire [8]. Sources of ignition can be classified into different categories as shown in Table 4-1.

It is important to understand that the mere presence of a source of ignition within an ignitable atmosphere does not guarantee the ignition of that atmosphere. In order for ignition to occur, the source of ignition needs to be suitable: It must have the capability of transferring enough energy to the combustible to bring it to its autoignition temperature, and therefore, ignite it. Many sources of ignition are not suitable for some given materials. For example, a hot surface does not commonly ignite gasoline [9]. A glowing cigarette is a great source of ignition for latex foam, and it will ignite a few gases, however neither gasoline nor methane are ignitable by a lit cigarette [10]. Similarly, an electrical arc or spark may be of sufficient temperature, but, because of its brief duration, is often not sufficient to ignite ordinary combustibles.

4.2 COMBUSTION

4.2.1 Oxidation Reaction

The term "oxidation reaction" was once commonly defined as the interaction of a reactant with oxygen [11]. However, a more accurate definition is provided by IUPAC as [12]: "An increase in the oxidation number of any atom within any substrate." Also, IUPAC provides another definition for oxidation, which applies particularly well in this context [12]: "Gain of oxygen and/or loss of hydrogen of an organic substrate." The following reaction is an example of oxidation, with the oxidation number of each atom written below it:

$$\underset{-IV+I}{CH_4} + \underset{0}{2\,O_2} \rightarrow \underset{+IV-II}{CO_2} + \underset{+I\ -II}{2\,H_2O}$$

In this chemical equation, the carbon in methane has an oxidation number of –IV. The carbon atom present in the carbon dioxide has an oxidation number of +IV, meaning that it has been oxidized. In every oxidation reaction, another atom must be reduced. For this reason, these reactions also are referred to as oxidation-reduction reactions, or redox reactions. Oxygen, which has an oxidation number of 0 in O_2, has an oxidation number of –II in carbon dioxide (CO_2) as well as in water (H_2O). Therefore, the oxygen was reduced. The oxidation number of the hydrogen atoms did not vary. In this example, the reaction generally is described as an oxidation reaction since the compound of interest, methane, is oxidized (from a carbon perspective).

4.2.2 Types of Fire

Combustion is applicable to two types of fire: Flaming combustion and smoldering combustion [13]. It is important to have a good understanding of the chemical mechanisms of each of these types of fire.

A/ Flaming Combustion

Flaming combustion is the most common type of combustion. It is the open-flame fire, such as the one seen in a gas burner. Chemically, it is a gas-to-gas reaction, meaning that the fuel has to be in the gaseous state in order to react with the oxidizer, which is already in the gaseous state. This is a very important concept because liquids and solids do not burn in an open flame, only their vapors do.[3] If the fuel is a solid or a liquid to begin with, it has to undergo either a phase change or a chemical change to become a gas prior to participating in the exothermic combustion reaction. In order for a flaming fire to occur, at least 10% oxygen must be present in the air, assuming oxygen is the oxidizer. Figure 4-3 is a diagram of a typical flaming combustion. It shows the different zones and their respective relationships.

B/ Smoldering Combustion

The smoldering, or glowing, combustion occurs without the generation of flames. It is the typical glow on the charcoal briquettes in a backyard grill after the flames die down. Chemically, it is a solid-to-gas reaction, where the surface of the solid combustible reacts directly with the gaseous oxidizer. Smoldering combustion often occurs due to a deficiency of oxidizer. Glowing combustion can be sustained at a much lower concentration of oxygen than the 10% required for flaming combustion.

4.2.3 Partial or Incomplete Combustion

Combustion is a very complex phenomenon involving the creation of many chemical species through different mechanisms [14]. In theory, complete

---

[3] Some finely divided metals and inorganic fuels are capable of burning in their solid state, but for most ordinary combustibles, they must be in the gaseous state.

Representation of a fire plume (flaming combustion). (Source: DeHaan JD (2002) Kirk's fire investigation, 5th edition, Prentice Hall, Upper Saddle River, NJ, Figure 3.1, p 23. Reprinted with permission of Prentice Hall, Upper Saddle River, New Jersey, USA.)

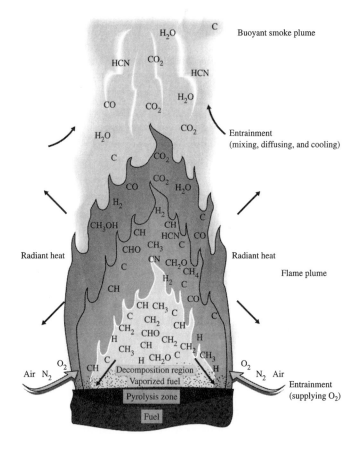

combustion of some organic materials, such as petroleum products, yields only carbon dioxide and water [13]. However, this rarely occurs outside of laboratory conditions. Combustibles and oxidizers are hardly ever perfectly mixed or present in stoichiometric[4] ratios and, thus, the oxidation reaction cannot go to completion. This results in the production of many combustion products—in addition to carbon dioxide and water, such as carbon monoxide (CO)—referred to as products of incomplete combustion [15].

When the oxidizer is deficient, the reaction is called partial or incomplete combustion. The following examples illustrate the difference between complete and incomplete combustions.

$$C_4H_{10} + \frac{13}{2}O_2 \rightarrow 4CO_2 + 5H_2O$$

---

[4] A stoichiometric ratio implies that molar ratio for each reactant taking part of a chemical reaction is respected as in a balanced chemical equation. In such instances, because no reactant is present in excess, there is complete conversion of the reactants into products.

Butane (C_4H_{10}) reacts completely with oxygen to produce only carbon dioxide and water. A stoichiometric mixture of butane:oxygen of $1:6.5$ exists. No further oxidation of the butane can occur. It should be noted however that complete oxidation is not guaranteed, even in the presence of sufficient oxygen. There also must be adequate interaction between the fuel and the oxidizer.

$$C_4H_{10} + \frac{9}{2}O_2 \rightarrow 4CO + 5H_2O$$

In this reaction, the available oxygen is not sufficient to satisfy the stoichiometric ratio of a complete reaction. Therefore, the reaction yields carbon monoxide rather than carbon dioxide. This is an incomplete combustion reaction because the carbon monoxide can undergo further combustion into carbon dioxide as follows:

$$2CO + O_2 \rightarrow 2CO_2$$

Carbon monoxide is not only a poisonous gas, but also very flammable. The release of carbon monoxide from incomplete combustion is a phenomenon very well known to fire investigators, which causes many deaths every year [16, 17]. Additionally, the release of carbon monoxide from smoldering fires and incomplete combustion also has been reported to create an explosive atmosphere [18].

$$C_4H_{10} + \frac{5}{2}O_2 \rightarrow 4C + 5H_2O$$

In this last reaction, even less oxygen is available. The products of combustion are thus carbon and water. Further combustion of the carbon, therefore, is possible as shown here:

$$C + O_2 \rightarrow CO_2$$

Carbon has long been observed as a product of incomplete combustion [19]. The bright orange color of the flame of a candle is due to the burning of carbon particles resulting from an incomplete combustion of the candle wax. When the amount of oxygen provided to an oil lamp or to an acetylene torch is reduced, the amount of soot (carbon) is highly increased.

Figure 4-4 shows the flame from an acetylene torch with different degrees of oxygen available. Figure 4-4a shows a flame with a great deficiency of oxygen, resulting in a bright orange flame and an enormous production of soot as evidenced by the black smoke rising from the flame. Figure 4-4b shows a bright orange flame as the amount of oxygen is slightly reduced. However, the production of soot is almost nonexistent. Figure 4-4c shows a blue flame with no soot produced. This flame produces almost exclusively carbon dioxide and water. This is due to the fact that oxygen is available in

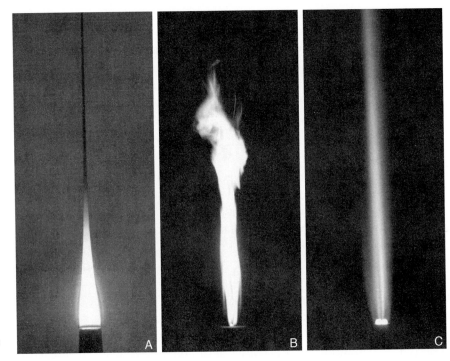

FIGURE 4-4

Example of complete, partial, and incomplete combustion with an acetylene torch where the availability of oxygen is increased from the left to the right. A/ The generation of heavy soot is typical of an incomplete combustion. B/ The bright yellow flame is due to the incandescence of some carbon particles. C/ The blue flame shows a complete combustion, where no particles of carbon are generated. (For a full color version of this figure, please see the insert.)

a stoichiometric ratio or even slightly in excess and is intimately mixed with the acetylene.

The combustion of butane is a very simple example that yields many different combustion products. The chemical equations previously described are very theoretical in the sense that the combustion process does not produce only one sort of molecule such as carbon dioxide or carbon monoxide. It is generally a mixture of different molecules with one being more prevalent than the others, depending primarily upon the amount of available oxygen [14]. With bigger molecules, the diversity and raw number of possible combustion products can be enormous. Soot and smoke condensates constitute the visible evidence of incomplete combustion products.

Smoke Condensates v. Soot

When the smoke resulting from combustion is deposited onto a cooler surface, it is referred to as smoke condensates. Often, smoke condensates are confused with soot. Soot is composed exclusively of carbon particles. Smoke condensates commonly are composed of very complex molecules, such as polynuclear aromatics. Pinorini et al. demonstrated the value of studying the contents of soot and smoke condensates in fire debris analysis [20, 21]. The black "smoke" seen escaping a fire is composed of both soot and smoke.

It should be noted that there are several chemicals that do burn to completion and leave almost no combustion products other than carbon dioxide and water. A good example of such a chemical is methanol. Methanol burns with a blue flame and produces neither smoke nor soot. Ethanol products also have been reported to burn without any smoke [22]. This is due in large part to the fact that these compounds contain oxygen as a significant part of their molecular structure.

4.2.4 Spontaneous Ignition

Spontaneous combustion differs from the aforementioned combustion processes only in the manner of ignition. Although the term spontaneous combustion often is used interchangeably with the term spontaneous ignition, the latter is actually a more accurate term. Spontaneous ignition is defined as [23]: "the chemical or biological process that generates sufficient heat to ignite the reacting material." In such instances, the ignition occurs without the presence of an external ignition source: It is solely attributable to the self-heating process of the material. It is not to be confused with the term autoignition (see next Subsection).

The spontaneous ignition process is due to either biological or chemical activities. It is very common with vegetable oils [24]. The exothermic biological or chemical reaction will ignite the surrounding material if it produces heat at a rate faster than the rate at which the heat is dissipated [25]. This situation leads to thermal runaway, which increases the temperature of the material until eventually the material reaches its autoignition temperature [15]. A typical scenario of fire resulting from such a phenomenon involves carelessly discarded rags impregnated with a vegetable oil-based floor staining product. Overnight, the vegetable oil present on the cotton rag self-heats to the point where the ignition temperature of the cotton rag is reached and fire breaks out. This usually is preceded by the release of acrid fumes for many minutes or hours.

The phenomenon of spontaneous ignition is important to the fire investigator and fire debris analyst, as it is the cause of many fires every year [26–29]. In some instances, the crime laboratory might be asked to assist in the investigation of such a fire by identifying the chemicals involved [30, 31]. More information is provided in Section 14.2 on this particular type of fire debris analysis.

4.2.5 Autoignition

Autoignition is the ignition of a material in the absence of a piloted source of ignition, such as a flame or a spark. It occurs simply by surrounding heat. Autoignition also often is referred to as nonpiloted ignition. It is important to understand that every single combustible must reach its autoignition temperature in order to burn. Even in the case of a piloted ignition when, for example, a lighter is applied to a piece of paper, a small portion of the paper is brought to its autoignition temperature for the flaming fire to begin. However, it would be possible to ignite the same paper by placing it into an oven and raising the temperature of the oven to the autoignition temperature of the paper, at which point it would ignite. Whereas spontaneous ignition does not require a transfer of energy from an external source (because this energy is generated within the combustible through chemical or biological heating process), autoignition requires such a heat transfer. The two terms should not be confused.

This type of ignition, due to an external (nonpiloted) heat source bringing a material to its autoignition temperature, is a significant factor in fire spread. Radiant heat from a burning object often provides sufficient energy to raise the temperature of nearby combustibles to their autoignition temperature. This results in fire spread without direct flame impingement (often referred to as ignition of remote fuels).

4.3 PHASE CHANGES

4.3.1 Definition

The three common phases of matter are solid, liquid, and gas[5] [32]. A solid is rigid and its shape and size is independent of the container in which it is located; that is, it has both fixed volume and shape. A liquid is a fluid and takes the shape of the container in which it is present. Liquids have fixed volumes, and therefore are considered to be incompressible fluids. A gas is also a fluid, but it fills the totality of the container into which it is present and it can be readily compressed. Therefore, both the volume and shape of a gas can change.

A change of phase is the physical transformation of a substance from one phase to one of the others. There are six possible phase changes: fusion (melting), solidification (freezing), vaporization (boiling), condensation, sublimation, and deposition. Figure 4-5 illustrates the different phase changes and their relationships. Although phase changes do not alter the chemical composition, it is still necessary for the fire debris analyst to understand them, as they may play an important role in the investigation.

4.3.2 Vapor and Gas

Unfortunately, the terms vapor and gas often are used interchangeably; however, there is an important difference. A vapor is the gaseous phase of a substance in a state of equilibrium with its liquid and/or solid state at a

---

[5]Other phases exist, such as plasma and supercritical fluid, but they are not applicable to this discussion.

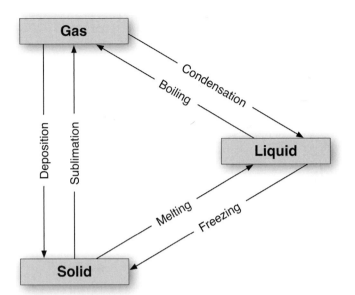

FIGURE 4-5

The different possible phase changes.

temperature below its boiling point [11]. Therefore, in order to have vapors, the liquid or solid phase of the same substance must be present. For example, the fog above the water on a lake is water vapor, since the body of liquid water is present below. When there is no liquid phase present or when the system is not in a state of equilibrium, then the proper terminology is gas.

Above absolute zero (−273.15°C or 0°K), every liquid has vapors above it in a state of equilibrium. The amount of vapor is dependent on the vapor pressure of the particular material, as well as the temperature. The concept of vapor pressure is introduced later in this chapter.

4.3.3 Chemical and Physical Transformations to the Gaseous Phase

As previously seen, solids and liquids must be transformed into gases prior to being able to burn in flaming combustion (with a few limited exceptions) [14]. This transformation can occur through the different processes shown in Figure 4-6.

It is important to realize that this figure combines both physical and chemical transformations. Physical transformations include the phase changes as shown in Figure 4-5, and the chemical transformations are represented by pyrolysis. This phenomenon is purely a chemical decomposition and its understanding is fundamental to the science of fire debris analysis [33]. For this reason, the next section is dedicated to a detailed discussion of the concept of pyrolysis.

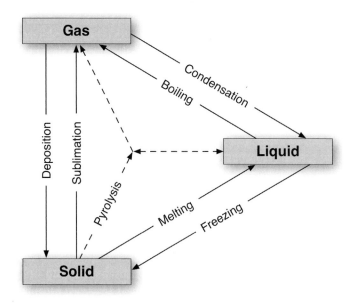

FIGURE 4-6

Passage of a solid or liquid to the gaseous phase by chemical and physical changes. The chemical changes are represented by the dotted lines and the physical changes by the solid lines.

4.4 PYROLYSIS

4.4.1 Definition

Pyrolysis is a process by which a solid (or a liquid) undergoes thermal degradation into smaller volatile molecules, without interacting with oxygen or any other oxidants [34]. Pyrolysis is a necessary process for the combustion of most solid fuels. Pyrolysis of a given material can produce many different thermal degradation products, called pyrolysis products. It significantly contributes to the chemicals recovered from fire debris samples during the laboratory analysis.

It is important to understand that pyrolysis is not a phase change; it is a chemical process. More correctly, it is a thermal degradation process, as it occurs under heat and degrades larger molecules into smaller ones. Pyrolysis is influenced by many variables including substrate type, presence of oxygen or other chemicals, rate of temperature rise, and temperatures reached [35]. Pyrolysis commonly follows three main degradation mechanisms: random scission, side-group scission, and monomer reversion.

4.4.2 Random Scission

In the random scission mechanism, the carbon-to-carbon bonds constituting the long carbon chain are randomly broken down. The scission is random in nature because all the carbon-to-carbon bonds are of the same strength. Figure 4-7 illustrates this phenomenon with the example of polyethylene (PE).

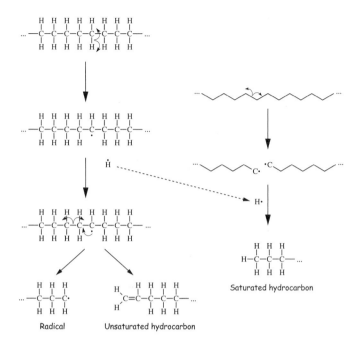

FIGURE 4-7

Random scission mechanism illustrated with the example of polyethylene. (Source: Stauffer E (2003) Basic concepts of pyrolysis for fire debris analysts, Science & Justice, 43(1), pp 29–40. Reprinted with permission of The Forensic Science Society, Harrogate, North Yorkshire, United Kingdom.)

Saturated hydrocarbon

Radical

Unsaturated hydrocarbon

Polyethylene is a chain of carbon atoms, each of which is bonded to two hydrogen atoms (except for the two terminal groups). Because each element of the chain is identical ($-CH_2$), each carbon-to-carbon bond is of the same strength, and the scission occurs randomly along the chain. The resulting molecules are shorter in length and some of them are unsaturated. The reason is that a hydrogen atom is necessary to complete the terminal group of a saturated chain, leaving one of the fragments with a deficiency of two electrons. This chain then rearranges in a double-bond configuration, as shown in the figure. In such instances, an alkene is created. When such a phenomenon occurs at both ends of the same chain, an alkadiene is created. Thus, the resulting products of random scission on polyethylene are a series of alkanes, alkenes, and alkadienes. More information is provided in Chapter 12.

4.4.3 Side-Group Scission

In the side-group scission mechanism, it is the carbon-to-side element bond rather than the carbon-to-carbon bond that is first broken apart. Figure 4-8 shows this phenomenon with polyvinyl chloride (PVC).

PVC is a polymer consisting of a carbon-to-carbon chain where every other carbon is bonded to one atom of chlorine and one atom of hydrogen. The remaining carbons are bonded to two atoms of hydrogen. In accordance with the bond dissociation energies (D values) presented in Table 3-2, the first bond to break is a carbon-to-chlorine bond—it has a bond dissociation

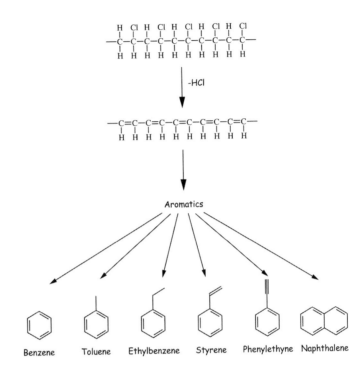

FIGURE 4-8

Side-group scission mechanism illustrated with the example of polyvinyl chloride. (Source: Stauffer E (2003) Basic concepts of pyrolysis for fire debris analysts, Science & Justice, 43(1), pp 29–40. Reprinted with permission of The Forensic Science Society, Harrogate, North Yorkshire, United Kingdom.)

energy of approximately 330 kJ/mol compared to more than 350 for a C–C bond and more than 400 for a C–H bond. During this process, the adjacent carbon-to-hydrogen bond also breaks, thus freeing a hydrogen radical, which will combine with the chlorine radical to form hydrogen chloride. Chlorine gas (green fumes) is produced when PVC is heated above 250°C [36]. When this bond cleavage is repeated along the carbon chain, the resulting backbone is a carbon chain with a series of conjugated double bonds. This unsaturated chain then rearranges in aromatic molecules as shown in Figure 4-8. Thus, the resulting products are aromatic compounds ranging from benzene to PAH.

4.4.4 Monomer Reversion

Monomer reversion, also called depolymerization, consists of reversing the polymerization process and breaking the chain into its monomeric elements. Figure 4-9 illustrates this phenomenon with polymethyl methacrylate (PMMA).

In this instance, the carbon-to-carbon bonds break at every other carbon, leaving the monomeric element (methylmethacrylate) alone. This pyrolysis mode is not necessarily the most interesting to the fire debris analyst because it typically creates only one compound (the monomer) rather than a series of different molecules.

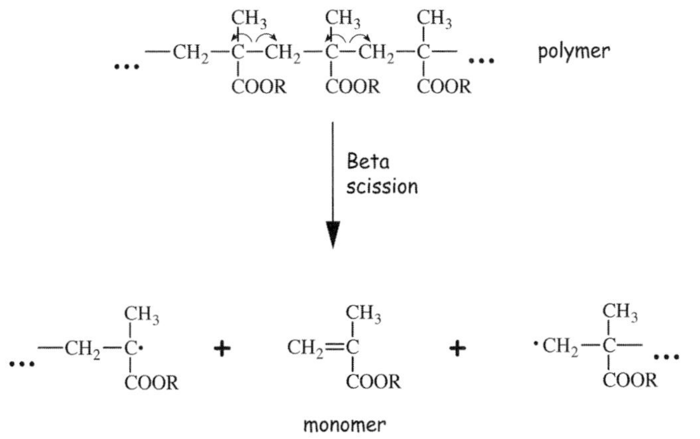

FIGURE 4-9 *Monomeric reversion mechanism illustrated with the example of polymethyl methacrylate. (Source: Stauffer E (2003) Basic concepts of pyrolysis for fire debris analysts,* Science & Justice, *43(1), pp 29–40. Reprinted with permission of The Forensic Science Society, Harrogate, North Yorkshire, United Kingdom.)*

4.4.5 Understanding Pyrolysis

There are some other mechanisms of pyrolysis that have been described in the literature. One of these mechanisms—called cross-linking or char formation—produces very few volatile organic compounds [37]. Other mechanisms have been described for which the presence of contaminants, such as water or nitrogen, lead to a particular breakdown of the molecules [35]. These other mechanisms do not influence the resulting pyrolysis products in a significant manner. Therefore, this book will not further describe these mechanisms, as they are not pertinent to the analysis of fire debris samples. In any case, the three main mechanisms previously described are the most important and influential in fire debris analysis. They result in the formation of the majority of pyrolysis products found in fire debris samples.

Some polymers are more prone to one mechanism of degradation than others, due to their molecular structure. However, it should be noted that most polymers undergo more than one type of pyrolysis. This chapter only intends to present pyrolysis and to explain the main degradation mechanisms leading to the different molecules. It is important for the fire debris analyst not only to know these mechanisms, but also to understand why and when they occur [33]. This will be discussed in much greater detail in Chapter 12, and it will be directly applied to the context of fire debris analysis.

4.5 FIRE DEVELOPMENT

4.5.1 Principle

Fire development is another important concept of fire science. Because no two fires are identical, it is impossible to provide an exact model that would accurately describe all fires. Nonetheless, the following paragraphs provide a general representation of how a typical compartment fire evolves. Also, this provides the basic knowledge needed to understand the effects that fire has on items of potential evidence.

The sequence of events in a common room fire can be divided into five distinct steps [38]:

1. Incipient stage
2. Ceiling layer development
3. Preflashover
4. Flashover
5. Postflashover

Ignition of the fire is the seminal event of all fires. However, it is important to note that not all fires can or will go to flashover and other fully developed stages of fire. In fact, some may not develop beyond the incipient stage.

4.5.2 Incipient Stage

Figure 4-10 is a view of a room that contains a typical fuel package consisting of a couch, two tables, a chair, and some small items. The room is open toward the front. Ignition of a trashcan behind the couch on the left has just occurred and the flame is relatively small.

FIGURE 4-10

Incipient stage of a room fire. (Photograph courtesy of Steven J. Avato, Bureau of Alcohol, Tobacco, Firearms and Explosives, Falls Church, Virginia, USA.) (For a full color version of this figure, please see the insert.)

Small flames progress upward and produce hot gases that are rising due to buoyancy. The smoke starts to accumulate in the ceiling, and it is possible to see this through the blurriness of the top of the black lamp. No other items in the room are on fire, and the average temperature of the room is just above ambient.

4.5.3 Ceiling Layer Development

The flame on the couch grows and starts to spread horizontally. The smoke produced by the flame increases and accumulates at the ceiling level. The smoke spreads horizontally on the ceiling, making a uniform layer. It eventually reaches the front of the room (opening) and, as the layer grows (downward) in depth, some of it escapes through the opening, as shown in Figure 4-11. It is important to understand that this layer of smoke is very hot, and is transferring energy to its surroundings, including items in the room. This transfer of heat via radiation is an important part of how fire spreads.

The lampshade is not yet burning, but the poster on the left already suffers from the heat of the hot layer of smoke. The hot smoke coming out of the opening as well as the consumption of air create a negative pressure in the room, which is compensated by the intake of fresh air through the lower part of the front opening. At this point, if the rate at which smoke is produced is equal to the rate at which the smoke escapes, the smoke layer will not grow any further. However, if the rate of smoke production is greater, then the smoke layer will continue to grow downward until it reaches the bottom part of the upper threshold. The room's temperature can be roughly divided into two zones: the hot smoke layer and the much cooler lower layer. The temperature of the lower portion of the room gradually increases, but is still much lower than that of the upper layer of smoke. It is also possible

FIGURE 4-11

Ceiling layer development. (Photograph courtesy of Steven J. Avato, Bureau of Alcohol, Tobacco, Firearms and Explosives, Falls Church, Virginia, USA.) (For a full color version of this figure, please see the insert.)

to see some flames inside the hot layer, particularly close to the opening, where more oxygen is available. These flames are part of a phenomenon called rollover.

4.5.4 Preflashover

As the fire keeps growing and spreading horizontally, more smoke and hot gases are produced and accumulate at the ceiling level. The hot gas layer at the ceiling has reached a much higher temperature (about 400 to 500°C) and the rate of heat transfer (to all exposed items in the room, including those at floor level) by radiation increases. Figure 4-12 illustrates this situation.

At this point, there is enough air coming into the room through the opening to sustain combustion. In such instances, the burning is fuel-controlled. That is, the burning rate is limited by the amount of ready-to-burn fuel. If the opening was closed, the amount of oxygen available would not be sufficient to sustain the burning and the fire would be ventilation-controlled. In that situation, the fire usually dies after a few moments, even though fuel is still available. However, if more oxygen in introduced into this underventilated environment, such as through the opening of a door, for example, then the combustion process is revived, and a backdraft, or "smoke explosion" may occur.

In the case illustrated in the photograph, the smoke layer continues to develop and the radiation is greater and greater. Some furniture and objects are already burning, for example by the couch and the lampshade. Other objects, such as the tables and chair, and items located at floor level, such as the carpet, pyrolyze as a result of the radiant heat flux from the smoke layer. This pyrolysis can be observed by the smoke coming out of the carpet (notice the blurriness in front of the table leg in the middle) and the

FIGURE 4-12

Preflashover condition. (Photograph courtesy of Steven J. Avato, Bureau of Alcohol, Tobacco, Firearms and Explosives, Falls Church, Virginia, USA.) (For a full color version of this figure, please see the insert.)

table on the left (notice the smoke on the right side of the table). While the fire is very intense, flashover has not yet occurred at this point.

4.5.5 Flashover

With the fire growing, the hot gas layer eventually reaches the critical temperature of approximately 600°C (1,100°F). At this point, the hot gas layer ignites, thus significantly increasing the radiant heat transferred to the floor level. In turns, the pyrolysis products released by the objects at floor level ignite. The whole room is suddenly and completely engulfed in fire, as shown in Figure 4-13. This is called flashover.

This transition usually lasts only a couple of seconds, thus is usually a very fast and impressive phenomenon. At that point, all the objects in the room are burning, except the protected areas that were not exposed to radiant heat. This is shown in the photograph by the area under the table on the left and under the chair on the right. However, the carpet in the middle that was exposed to the radiant heat of the hot gas layer is on fire as well as all the other objects in the room.

4.5.6 Postflashover or Full-Room Involvement

With the dynamic of the gas flow around the room and the intense heat produced by all the burning items, every piece of combustible material in the room burns. This situation is called full-room involvement and is illustrated in Figure 4-14. Only objects that were shielded (protected) from the direct impact of the radiant heat are spared.

In this room, for example, the areas under the couch and under the legs of the tables and chair are protected from the fire. These areas may be

FIGURE 4-13

Flashover. (Photograph courtesy of Steven J. Avato, Bureau of Alcohol, Tobacco, Firearms and Explosives, Falls Church, Virginia, USA.) (For a full color version of this figure, please see the insert.)

"clean" or undamaged, allowing for postfire reconstruction of the scene or replacement of objects to their prefire positions. It should be noted that some areas may be somewhat protected by the influx of cool air, such as the carpet near an open doorway or other vent. It also should be noted that not all fuels are necessarily consumed, only those that are ignited.

4.5.7 Accelerated v. Nonaccelerated Fires

For many years it has been believed that if a fire was accelerated with an ignitable liquid, such as gasoline, it would burn much hotter. This misconception can be found in early texts on fire investigation, but, unfortunately, also in some modern texts. It is crucial for the fire debris analyst not to get misled by these old unscientific statements.

Gasoline burns at approximately the same temperature as wood or most other household combustibles. As a matter of fact, most modern household furniture is made of petroleum-based polymers, thus exhibiting a chemistry somewhat similar—in terms of temperatures reached during their combustion—to that of gasoline. A typical house fire will result in temperatures up to about 1,000°C (1,900°F), although in some instances, higher temperatures may be reached.

As an illustration, Figure 4-15 is a graphic representation of temperature measurements taken in two fires: one accelerated with gasoline and one nonaccelerated. Both rooms were identical with identical fuel load, except for the added accelerant. The temperature was measured at the ceiling using a thermocouple.

The nonaccelerated fire shows a typical slow fire development curve; in this case the temperature gradually increases until flashover is reached in

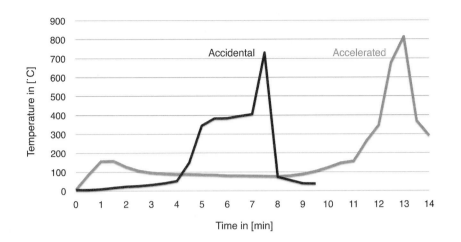

FIGURE 4-15
Graph showing the variation of temperature during the development of an accelerated and a nonaccelerated fire.

about 7.5 minutes. In both fires, the extinguishment procedure started immediately after flashover, thus the sharp decrease in temperature. With the accelerated fire, one can fully appreciate the influence of the added accelerant in the fire development: The addition of an accelerant results in a much more rapid increase in temperature, compared with the nonaccelerated fire. In this particular case, the temperature began to show a rapid increase, but then the fire became oxygen deprived, and there was no significant additional increase in temperature until around 10 minutes, at which time a window was opened, to introduce additional oxygen to the fire. Although both fires reach a similar temperature, the primary difference is the rate of temperature increase. An accelerant, such as gasoline, has a much higher heat release rate (HRR) than ordinary combustibles. So although it may release the same amount of heat, and it may achieve the same temperatures, the temperature will increase much more quickly in a typical accelerated fire. This scenario shows the beginning of this rapid increase in temperature, but because of the limited amount of accelerant and mostly oxygen, the temperature did not peak as quickly as it typically occurs in an accelerated fire. In the end, the temperature reached by the accelerated fire was very slightly higher than for the nonaccelerated fire. However, this temperature difference is not significant and surely not in the 1,500°C (2,800°F) or higher range necessary to melt iron, as was claimed by some investigators in the past.

4.6 LIQUID FUEL PROPERTIES

4.6.1 Melting and Boiling Points
The melting point of a substance is defined as the temperature at which a substance changes from solid phase to liquid phase; that is, undergoes fusion. It is also called the freezing point.

The boiling point of a substance is defined as the temperature at which a liquid boils and, thus, changes from liquid phase to gas phase. Another definition involves the concept of vapor pressure and states that the boiling point is the temperature at which the vapor pressure of the liquid is equal to the surrounding pressure. More details are provided in Subsection 4.6.5.

Melting and boiling points are dependent on the surrounding pressure. Usually values found in the literature unless otherwise specified refer to conditions at standard temperature and pressure (STP).[6]

There is a great range of melting and boiling points among combustibles. With hydrocarbon compounds and their derivatives, there are some correlations between their melting/boiling points and their molecular formulae. Here are a few general rules that can be used to better understand the variation of the boiling and melting points:

- Within the same class of compounds, the melting and boiling points increase with the number of carbons (molecular weight [MW]).
- Branching commonly decreases melting and boiling points. This is due to the fact that branched molecules do not fit together as well as linear molecules. Thus, there are many gaps between the molecules and they are easier to separate.
- Double-bonds and triple-bonds usually decrease both the melting and the boiling points. As with the branching, the presence of double- and triple-bonds in the molecules interrupt the regular structure, and the molecules do not nestle together as well.
- Aromaticity usually increases the melting and boiling points. The greater polarity of aromatic compounds increases the forces between the molecules, making them harder to separate.
- The addition of an alcohol group can greatly increase the melting and boiling point. The presence of the alcohol group increases the polarity of the molecule, thus allowing for significant hydrogen bonding.
- The presence of a cyclic group decreases boiling and melting points. The presence of a ring does not allow the molecules to fit together as neatly as within a linear chain, and, therefore, creates gaps that weaken their intermolecular attractions.

To illustrate, Figure 4-16 shows examples of the variation of boiling and melting of different molecules starting from n-decane $(C_{10}H_{22})$.

The trend in melting and boiling points from n-decane $(C_{10}H_{22})$ (in the center of the figure) to n-undecane $(C_{11}H_{24})$ and n-tetradecane $(C_{14}H_{30})$ is to increase due to the longer carbon chains. In examining some C_{10} isomers, note that the change from n-decane to 2,7-dimethyloctane $(C_{10}H_{22})$ results

---

[6] Standard temperature and pressure conditions are provided by the IUPAC and are 0°C and $1 \cdot 10^5$ Pa for temperature and pressure, respectively. However, values often found in the literature refer to a standard temperature of 25°C.

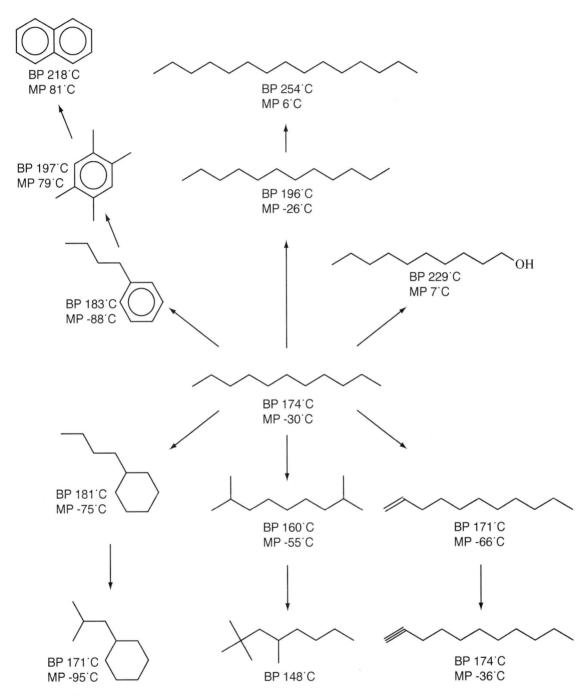

FIGURE 4-16 *Illustration of the effects of chemical structure variations on melting and boiling points.*

in a decrease in melting and boiling points. Further branching, such as with the isomer 2,2,4-trimethylheptane ($C_{10}H_{22}$), leads to an even greater decrease in the melting and boiling points. This is consistent with branching generally causing a decrease in the melting and boiling points. A change such as the addition of an alcohol group, such as to 1-decanol ($C_{10}H_{21}OH$) results in a substantial increase in the melting and boiling points. The presence of double and triple bonds such as in 1-decene and 1-decyne show only slight variations in boiling point, and a decrease in the melting point. When a ring structure is present (naphthene), there is a significant decrease in the melting point, however in this case there is little change to the boiling point. Finally, it is possible to see that, in general, aromaticity increases boiling and melting points. n-Butylbenzene is an exception to this general rule, however, as its melting point is substantially decreased when compared with n-decane.

Table 4-2 presents the boiling and melting points of some hydrocarbons. It is interesting to observe the different trends and to compare the values within a series of similar compounds and from one class of compounds to another.

4.6.2 Specific Gravity

The specific gravity of a liquid is the relative weight of that liquid compared to an equal volume of water. The specific gravity of water is de facto 1. Liquids that are lighter than water have a specific gravity less than 1 and those heavier than water have a specific gravity greater than 1. Specific gravity is dependent on the temperature, and most of the values found in the literature refer to STP conditions.

Density v. Specific Gravity

Although the two terms often are used interchangeably, there is a technical difference between specific gravity and density. Density is defined as the mass per unit volume of a substance. Water has a density of 1 kg/l at 4°C. When the specific gravity is defined based on water at 4°C, then the specific gravity is equal to the density of the liquid. However, if the specific gravity is expressed at different temperatures, it will no longer be equal to the density. Although there is a difference between specific gravity and density, for the most part the values are similar enough to be used interchangeably in most situations.

Specific gravity is an important concept to know when mixtures of immiscible liquids, such as gasoline and water, are present. It is possible that the particular location of a liquid within a mixture is of interest in a case. Petroleum products, in general, have a low specific gravity, and will float on water. With an increasing number of carbons, the specific gravity of petroleum products increases. However, the specific gravity does not exceed one until products such as asphalt are considered.

Table 4-2	*Melting and boiling points of some alkane, aromatic, alcohol, cyclo-alkane, and isoalkane compounds*	
Alkanes	**Melting point [°C]**	**Boiling point [°C]**
Methane	-182	-164
Ethane	-183	-89
Propane	-190	-42
n-Butane	-138	-1
n-Pentane	-130	36
n-Hexane	-95	69
n-Heptane	-91	98
n-Octane	-57	126
n-Nonane	-51	151
n-Decane	-30	174
n-Undecane	-26	196
n-Dodecane	-10	216
n-Tridecane	-6	235
n-Tetradecane	6	254
n-Pentadecane	10	271
n-Hexadecane	18	287
n-Heptadecane	22	302
n-Octadecane	28	316
n-Nonadecane	32	330
n-Eicosane	37	343
n-Docosane	44	369
n-Tricosane	47.6	380
n-Tetracosane	54	391
n-Dotriacontane	70	467
Aromatics		
Benzene	6	80
Toluene	-95	111
Ethylbenzene	-95	136
Styrene	-31	145
Phenylethyne	-45	142
o-Xylene	-25	144

Table 4-2 continued	Melting and boiling points of some alkane, aromatic, alcohol, cycloalkane, and isoalkane compounds	
Aromatics	**Melting point [°C]**	**Boiling point [°C]**
1,2,3-Trimethylbenzene	-25	175
n-Propylbenzene	-100	159
Indane	-51	178
Indene	-2	183
Naphthalene	81	218
1-Methylnaphthalene	-22	245
2-Methylnaphthalene	34	241
Anthracene	217	340
Alcohols		
Methanol	-94	65
Ethanol	-117	79
n-Propanol	-127	97
Isopropanol	-90	82
n-Butanol	-90	117
Cycloalkanes		
Methylcyclohexane	-127	101
Propylcyclohexane	-95	157
n-Butylcyclohexane	-95	171
n-Pentylcyclohexane	-58	203
Branched alkanes		
2,2,4-Trimethylpentane	-107	99
2,2,4-Trimethylheptane	—	148
2,7-Dimethyloctane	-55	160

Table 4-3 shows a list of compounds with their particular specific gravities. Note that the rule of the increasing carbon number works well with the n-alkanes; however it is much more difficult to find a clear trend with other classes, such as the aromatics. Also, note that aromatics exhibit a much greater specific gravity than their corresponding (in number of carbon atoms) aliphatics. Finally, compounds with chlorine or sulfur typically exhibit a very high specific gravity, despite a small number of atoms.

Table 4-3	*Specific gravities of different chemical compounds*
Aliphatics	**Specific gravity [kg/l]**
Pentane	0.626
Hexane	0.660
Octane	0.703
2,2,4-Trimethylpentane	0.716
Decane	0.730
Dodecane	0.749
Tetradecane	0.763
Methylcyclohexane	0.769
Octadecane	0.777
Pristane	0.783
Eicosane	0.789
Docosane	0.794
Tetracosane	0.799
Hexacosane	0.803
Octacosane	0.807
Nonacosane	0.808
Dotriacontane	0.812
d-Limonene	0.841
Adamantane	1.070
Aromatics	
4-Ethyltoluene	0.861
1,3,5-Trimethylbenzene	0.864
Toluene	0.867
Ethylbenzene	0.867
1,2,4-Trimethylbenzene	0.867
Benzene	0.877
o-Xylene	0.880
1,2,3,5-Tetramethylbenzene	0.890
1,2,3-Trimethylbenzene	0.894
Styrene	0.906
4,7-Dimethylindane	0.949
4-Methylindane	0.958

Table 4-3	Specific gravities of different chemical compounds continued
Aromatics	**Specific gravity [kg/l]**
Indane	0.964
1,2,3,4-Tetrahydronaphthalene	0.970
Indene	0.996
2,3-Dimethylnaphthalene	1.003
1-Methylnaphthalene	1.020
Naphthalene	1.162
Anthracene	1.283
Oxygenates	
Diethyl ether	0.714
Isopropanol	0.786
Ethanol	0.789
Acetone	0.790
Methanol	0.791
Methyl isobutyl ketone	0.798
n-Propanol	0.804
Methyl ethyl ketone	0.805
n-Butanol	0.810
Cyclopentanone	0.949
Propylene glycol	1.036
Benzaldehyde	1.042
Dibutyl phthalate	1.047
Furfural	1.159
Dimethyl phthalate	1.191
Others	
Carbon disulfide	1.263
Dichloromethane	1.327
Chloroform	1.483
Tetrachloromethane	1.594
Tetrachloroethylene	1.623

4.6.3 Vapor Density

Vapor density is the weight of a volume of pure vapor or gas compared to an equal volume of dry air at the same temperature and pressure. It is obtained by dividing the molecular weight of the vapor by the average molecular weight of air thus, it is unitless. The average molecular weight of air is considered to be about 29 g/mol. Table 4-4 shows the typical composition of air, which explains the average molecular weight although it can be more easily approximated by using only the two major components [39].

Table 4-4	Chemical composition of air			
Gas	Formula	Concentration [%]	Molecular weight [g/mol]	Molecular mass in air [g/mol]
Nitrogen	N_2	78.08	28	21.86
Oxygen	O_2	20.95	32	6.70
Argon	Ar	0.93	40	0.37
Carbon dioxide	CO_2	0.031	44	0.014
Neon	Ne	0.0018	20	0.00036
Methane	CH_4	0.00020	16	0.000032
Helium	He	0.00052	4	0.000021
Krypton	Kr	0.00011	84	0.000092
Hydrogen	H_2	0.00005	2	0.000001
Xenon	Xe	0.0000087	131	0.000011
Air	—	100	28.94	—

The vapor density gives a good idea of the behavior of a gas once released in the air. If the vapor density is below 1, the gas will rise; if the vapor density if above 1, the gas will settle at floor level. When the vapor density is close to 1, the gas will mix with the air and no neat demarcation will occur. It is also important to remember that conditions do not always involve still air, and therefore, motions in the air created by wind and other pressure differences can make a heavier gas rise or a lighter gas settle. Figure 4-17 shows different situations of gas accumulation.

There are only 14 gases and vapors with a vapor density less than one, meaning that they are lighter than air. These are acetylene, ammonia, carbon monoxide, diborane, ethylene, helium, hydrogen, hydrogen cyanide, hydrogen fluoride, methane, methyl lithium, neon, nitrogen, and water. Among these gases, nine are flammable. Table 4-5 displays the characteristics of these gases. Also, seven of these gases have a density of 0.75 and

FIGURE 4-17

Behavior of gases with different vapor densities. (a) Natural gas (methane) in a room (density < 1). (b) Gasoline in a room (density > 1). (c) Gasoline in a room with various elevations (density > 1). (Source: DeHaan JD (2002) Kirk's fire investigation, 5th edition, Prentice Hall, Upper Saddle River, J, Figure 4.4, p 65. Reprinted with permission of Prentice Hall, Upper Saddle River, New Jersey, USA.)

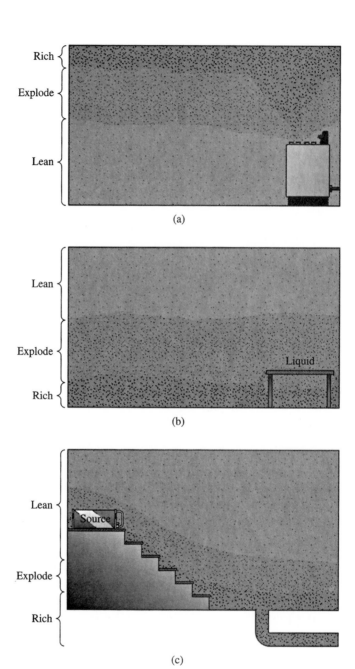

greater. When the density is so close to 1, these gases will not readily rise in the air, they will rather mix.

Table 4-6 presents some gases or vapors that are heavier than air. Although gasoline is a mixture, octane may be used to approximate its average molecular weight as 114. Thus, gasoline would have a vapor density of

Table 4-5	Gases or vapors lighter than air; gases in gray are not ignitable		
Gas	**Formula**	**Molecular weight [g/mol]**	**Vapor density**
Hydrogen	H_2	2.016	0.07
Helium	He	4.003	0.14
Methane	CH_4	16.043	0.55
Ammonia	NH_3	17.031	0.59
Water	H_2O	18.016	0.62
Hydrogen Fluoride	HF	20.006	0.69
Neon	Ne	20.180	0.70
Methyl lithium	$LiCH_3$	21.980	0.76
Acetylene	C_2H_2	26.038	0.90
Hydrogen cyanide	HCN	27.026	0.93
Diborane	B_2H_6	27.670	0.96
Carbon monoxide	CO	28.005	0.97
Nitrogen	N_2	28.013	0.97
Ethylene	C_2H_4	28.054	0.97

Table 4-6	Some flammable gases or vapors that are heavier than air		
Gas	**Formula**	**Molecular weight [g/mol]**	**Density**
Methanol	CH_3OH	32.04	1.11
Propane	C_3H_8	44.10	1.52
Ethanol	C_2H_5OH	46.07	1.59
Butane	C_4H_{10}	58.12	2.01
Acetone	CH_3COCH_3	58.08	2.01
Propanol	C_3H_7OH	60.10	2.08
Pentane	C_5H_{12}	72.15	2.49
Diethyl ether	$C_2H_5COC_2H_5$	74.12	2.56
Benzene	C_6H_6	78.11	2.70
Hexane	C_6H_{14}	86.18	2.98
Toluene	$C_6H_5CH_3$	92.14	3.18
o-Xylene	$C_6H_4(CH_3)_2$	106.17	3.67
Octane	C_8H_{18}	114.23	3.93
1,2,3-Trimethylbenzene	$C_6H_3(CH_3)_3$	120.19	4.15

approximately 3.9 (if it evaporates completely). Note that the vapor density quickly escalates to 2 and greater. Besides methanol, which has a density close to 1, all other compounds will not rise in air. Therefore, almost all vapors of flammable (and combustible) liquids will settle at floor level when escaping from a container.

4.6.4 Flammability Limits

As previously stated, three conditions are required in order to have a fire: the presence of combustible (fuel), an oxidizer, and sufficient thermal energy (ignition source). However, there are some important qualifiers to the fire triangle that must be satisfied for a flaming fire to occur. When the oxidizer is oxygen gas, it must be present at a minimum concentration of 10% in the atmosphere. With regard to the combustible gas or vapor, not only is there a minimum amount required below which no fire will occur, but there is also a maximum amount above which no fire will occur. These limits are called the lower flammability limit (LFL) and the upper flammability limit (UFL). The portion between these two limits is called the flammability range. Below the LFL, the mixture is too lean, and above the UFL, the mixture is too rich, so no fire occurs, even with a proper source of ignition. Figure 4-18 illustrates this principle. As illustrated, the LFL of gasoline is 1.5% and the UFL is 7.6%. In a scenario where gasoline vapors are present outside the range of 1.5 to 7.6%, fire cannot occur.[7]

Table 4-7 shows a series of ignitable substances with their respective LFLs and UFLs [40].

As a general rule, within a given class of hydrocarbons, increasing the number of carbon atoms decreases the LFL and the UFL. Aromaticity, unsaturation, branching, and cycling have different effects on the LFL and the UFL. Note that most hydrocarbon compounds have a UFL less than 10%. One notable exception is acetylene, which has a substantially higher UFL than most compounds (81%), rendering this gas extremely dangerous.

4.6.5 Vapor Pressure (VP)

Every liquid vaporizes to some extent until the pressure developed by its vapor (standing above the liquid) reaches equilibrium. Once this equilibrium

---

[7]Other sources may indicate different values of LFL and UFL for gasoline, for example, 0.7% and 8.7%, respectively. This illustrates very well the fact that these values must be taken with precaution as they may vary depending on the exact laboratory conditions under which they have been obtained. Furthermore, even though values for pure compounds may not vary as much, values for mixtures of compounds such as gasoline or diesel fuel may exhibit an important variation because, in addition to laboratory testing parameters, these mixtures may present significant differences in composition depending on their source.

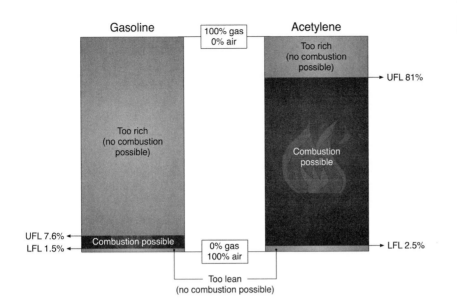

FIGURE 4-18

Illustration of the concepts of lower flammability limit (LFL) and upper flammability limit (UFL) with the examples of gasoline and acetylene.

Table 4-7 *Some LFL and UFL of gases and liquids [40]*

Aliphatics	LFL [%]	UFL [%]
Methane	5.3	14.0
Ethane	3	12.5
Ethylene	3.1	32
Acetylene	2.5	81.0
Propane	2.2	9.5
Cyclopropane	2.4	10.4
Propylene	2.4	10.3
Allylene (1-propyne)	1.74	n/a
Butane	1.9	8.5
Isobutane	1.8	8.4
Butylene	1.98	9.65
Butadiene	2.0	11.5
Pentane	1.5	7.8
Isopentane	1.4	7.6
Amylene (1-pentene)	1.65	7.70
Hexane	1.2	7.5
Cyclohexane	1.30	8.0

Table 4-7	Some LFL and UFL of gases and liquids [40] continued	
Aromatics	**LFL [%]**	**UFL [%]**
Cyclohexene	1.22	4.81
Methylcyclohexane	1.20	n/a
Heptane	1.2	6.7
Octane	1.00	3.2
Nonane	0.83	2.9
Decane	0.67	2.6
Dodecane	0.6	n/a
Tetradecane	0.5	n/a
Benzene	1.4	7.1
Toluene	1.27	6.75
Styrene	1.10	6.10
o-Xylene	1.00	6.00
Naphthalene	0.90	n/a
Anthracene	0.63	n/a
Mixtures		
Gasoline	1.5	7.6
Naphtha	1.10	6.0
Kerosene	1.0	5.0
Diesel fuel	0.52	4.09
Others		
Hydrogen	4	75
Carbon Monoxide	12.5	74
Ammonia	15.5	26.6
Hydrogen Sulfide	4.3	45.5
Carbon disulfide	1.25	44

is reached, the pressure of the vapor is called the vapor pressure (VP) of the liquid. It is necessary to see the surface of a liquid as a dynamic situation. At equilibrium, for each molecule that vaporizes into the headspace, another one condenses from the headspace into the liquid. The faster the process of vaporization/condensation, the greater the vapor pressure.

Vapor Pressure of a Mixture of Liquids

When the vapor pressure of a mixture of liquids is known, it is possible to calculate the individual contribution of each component to the total vapor pressure (and vice versa). In order to do this calculation, the nature and relative amounts of each component must be known. It is also assumed that no interaction between the liquids take place. The calculation is based on Raoult's Law, the name given after the French scientist François-Marie Raoult, who discovered the relationship of partial pressures [11]. The law states that the vapor pressure of a mixture is the sum of the vapor pressures of the individual components multiplied by their molar fraction:

$$P_{total} = \sum P_N \cdot \chi_N$$

P_N = Vapor pressure of a liquid within the mixture in [mmHg]
χ_N = Molar fraction of a liquid within the mixture
P_{total} = Vapor pressure of the mixture in [mmHg]

This concept is important because the composition of the vapor phase (headspace) of a mixture of liquids will not be the same as the one from the liquid phase. This can greatly influence the flash point. For example, a mixture of decane and benzene has a vapor pressure of 34 mmHg at 25°C (see Figure 4-19). Vapor pressures of decane and benzene are found in the literature to be:

$$P_{Decane} = 1.4 \, mmHg \text{ at } 25°C$$
$$P_{Benzene} = 110 \, mmHg \text{ at } 25°C$$

Given that the mixture exhibits a vapor pressure of 34 mmHg at 25°C, it is possible to calculate their molar fraction in the mixture using the aforementioned formula:

$$\chi_{Decane} = 0.7$$
$$\chi_{Benzene} = 0.3$$

Therefore, the partial pressures are: 1 mmHg for decane and 33 mmHg for benzene. This means that the headspace is composed of 0.13% decane, 4.34% benzene, and 95.5% air. These calculations might become important when a question, such as whether the LFL was reached, is raised.

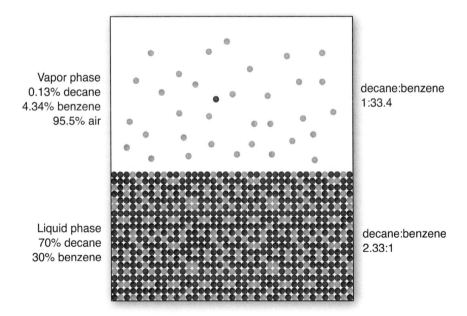

Vapor phase
0.13% decane
4.34% benzene
95.5% air

decane:benzene
1:33.4

Liquid phase
70% decane
30% benzene

decane:benzene
2.33:1

FIGURE 4-19 *Illustration of the concept of the vapor pressure of a mixture of two liquids.*

The vapor pressure is highly dependent not only on the nature of the liquid, but also on its temperature: It increases with increasing temperature. In such instances, it increases until it matches the ambient pressure above the liquid (usually 1 atm or 760 mmHg). At that point, the vapor pressure is strong enough to repel the atmosphere and to create its own space, meaning that for each molecule that vaporizes, there is no need for another molecule to condense. The temperature at which the vapor pressure equals the ambient pressure is called the boiling point. Because vapor pressures vary with temperature, they usually are reported for a temperature of 25°C.

There is a formula used to calculate vapor pressure. A very useful resource for vapor pressure information is the web site of Dr. Shuzo Ohe at http://s-ohe.com, where it is possible to obtain the vapor pressure of many liquids at different temperatures.

4.6.6 Flash Point

The flash point of a liquid is defined as the lowest temperature at which a substance generates a sufficient amount of vapor to form a (vapor/air) mixture that can be ignited (piloted ignition). At that temperature, the vapor pressure of the liquid provides a vapor concentration that equal to the lower flammability limit. If ignition is attempted when the liquid reaches its flash point, a flash flame will occur but the flame will not sustain. The cloud will burn and the fire will self-extinguish because the energy released by the combustion and transferred to the remaining fuel is not sufficient to produce enough vapors to sustain the flame.

The flash point is an important concept in fire investigation and fire protection because it is the lowest temperature at which a risk of fire exists with a given liquid. It is crucial in many circumstances to establish the presence of some liquids and to know their flash point during the investigation process.

Flash points usually are found in the literature. MSDS[8] are particularly good resources for flash point values of commercial chemicals and products. As a general rule for hydrocarbons, the simpler the molecule, the lower the flash point. Although some equations have been developed to calculate flash point, their utility is limited due to significant variations in their accuracy.

---

[8] An MSDS is a material safety data sheet. This is a document that includes information on the chemical identity of a given product as well as some of its chemical and physical properties, particularly with regard to its hazard, handling, and safety requirements. It also contains the name and contact information of the manufacturer of the product.

Calculating Flash Points

The following formula allows for the calculation of flash points [41]:

$$\frac{1000}{T_F + 273} = B_0 + B_1 \cdot \log_{10} P_{25}$$

T_F = Flash point

B_0 and B_1 = constant (see table below)

P_{25} = Vapor pressure of liquid at 25°C

This particular calculation is, unfortunately, not very accurate (variation with measured values can be as high as 100°C!) and requires the knowledge of the constants in Table 4-8 as well as the knowledge of the vapor pressure of the compound. Another more simplistic mathematical calculation starts with the autoignition temperature (AIT) in degrees Celsius of the compound [41]. It is shown in Table 4-9.

K = a variant (9 for each first branch CH_3 and 21 for each second branch CH_3, 16 for each first branch CH and 12 for each second branch CH_2)

nHr = number of hydrogen in radicals

Table 4-8	Constants for flash point calculations [41]. (*These values produce more accurate results and were obtaned by excluding 2,2-dimethylbutane, naphthalene, dodecane, diphenylmethane, tetradecane, nonylbenzene, and decylbenzene.)	
Class	**B_0**	**B_1**
Acetates	2.976	0.380
Acids	2.777	0.491
Alcohols	2.953	0.323
Phenols	2.953	0.323
Aldehydes	2.924	0.443
Alkanes	3.142	0.319
Alkanes*	2.948	0.470
Aromatics	3.142	0.319
Aromatics*	2.948	0.470
Alkenes	3.097	0.424
Amines	3.077	0.322
Esters	2.948	0.385
Ethers	3.056	0.357
Ketones	3.033	0.381

Table 4-9	Calculations of flash point [41].
Class	**Flash point [°C]**
Paraffinic hydrocarbons and olefins in gaseous state at NTP	350 – AIT
Paraffinic hydrocarbons and olefins in liquid state at NTP	250 – AIT
Benzene series	550 – (AIT + K)
Alcohols (MW ≤ 60)	8 + nHr
Alcohols (60 < MW ≤ 88)	11 + 2nHr
Alcohols (MW > 88)	29 + 3nHr

Flash point values found in the literature are the result of measurements made in the laboratory at equilibrium, via a standard test method. Chapter 14 provide more detailed descriptions for determining flash points by laboratory tests. Flash point values for a given chemical or product may vary depending on the measurement technique used. It is important to understand that these conditions might not be reproduced in a particular practical situation, and the flash point values cannot always be applied *per se*.

When a liquid is composed of a mixture of different chemicals, such as gasoline, the flash point of the mixture will be strongly influenced by the flash point of the components having the lowest flash point [42, 43]. This is due to the distribution of the components of the mixture in the vapor, which is dependent on their vapor pressure, as previously described.

Flash point is an important concept in fire investigation and fire debris analysis, not only for the classification of the ignitable liquids, but also for the evaluation of hazardous situations. The National Fire Protection Association (NFPA) defines a liquid with a flash point below 100°F (37.8°C) as flammable, and a liquid with a flash point equal to or above 100°F (37.8°C) as combustible [44]. Combustibles are further separated into Category I Combustible (flash point below 200°F or 93.3°C) and Category II Combustible (flash point above 200°F or 93.3°C). Other countries have different definitions of flammable and combustible liquids. For example, the *Commission Universitaire pour la Santé et la Sécurité au Travail Romande* in Switzerland defines flammable liquids as having a flash point lower than or equal to 55°C (131°F) and combustibles as having a flash point above 55°C (131°F) [45]. They also have further subclassifications such as "easily flammable," where the flash point is below 30°C (86°F).

4.6.7 Fire Point (Flame Point)

The fire point is the lowest temperature at which a substance will generate a sufficient amount of vapors to form an ignitable mixture that will sustain combustion once ignited (piloted ignition). Therefore, when a liquid reaches its fire point and is ignited, combustion will sustain until the combustible is totally consumed or other extinguishing action is taken. The fire point is always greater than the flash point. As a general rule, it is a few degrees above the flash point. It is possible to calculate the fire point based on the principle that it corresponds to the temperature at which the concentration of the vapors equals 1.5 times the stoichiometric value [46].

4.6.8 Ignition and Autoignition Temperatures

The ignition temperature of a fuel is defined as the minimum temperature at which it ignites. This ignition can be reached by the use of external ignition sources, such as a spark or a flame (piloted ignition). Both the ignition and autoignition temperatures are the same value for a given fuel at given conditions. However, the term autoignition temperature (AIT) most often is used when there is no direct external ignition source (nonpiloted ignition).

When a liquid is heated to its flash point or fire point and no external source of ignition is brought within the vapor cloud, no ignition occurs. For example, gasoline often is stored at temperatures significantly above its flash and fire points, yet it does not just ignite. If an ignition source is brought within the vapors and can raise the vapor cloud or even an infinitesimally small area of the cloud to its ignition temperature, ignition occurs. There is no need to heat the whole combustible area. At this point, if the liquid has reached its flash point, vapors will burn as a momentary flash, but the combustion will not sustain. On the contrary, if the liquid has reached its fire point, combustion will sustain. Actually, in many fires, only an extremely small portion of the flammable mixture is ignited at first. However, this combustion reaction is exothermic, so the heat it releases causes an increase in vapor pressure. If no external ignition source is brought in the cloud and if the temperature of the vapors is increased passed the fire point to the AIT (by means of increased surrounding temperature), they will ignite without an external (piloted) source of ignition.

Table 4-10 presents flash point, AIT, and vapor pressure values for several compounds. As a general rule, the AIT of a hydrocarbon decreases with the increasing size of the hydrocarbon. The smaller the molecule, the higher the AIT. Note the variations in the different values within the same class of compounds and between classes. Also, note the trend of one value compared to another. For example, within the aliphatic class, as the molecular weight increases, the vapor pressure diminishes, which is expected. By contrast, the flash point increases, which is also expected, however the AIT diminishes.

Table 4-10	Some organic compounds and their flash points, autoignition temperatures, and vapor pressures			
Combustible	**Molecular Weight**	**Flash point [°C]**	**Autoignition temperature [°C]**	**Vapor pressure at 25°C [mmHg]**
Aliphatics				
Methane	16.04	−188	537	gas
Ethane	30.07	−135	510	gas
Ethylene	28.05	−136	543	gas
Acetylene	26.04		335	gas
Propane	44.10	−104	468	gas
Butane	58.12	−60	430	gas
Isobutane	58.12	−81	543	gas
Pentane	72.15	−49	260	512.54
Isopentane	72.15	−56	420	688.03
Cyclopentane	72.15	−37	385	317.41
Hexane	86.18	−23	247	151.28
Cyclohexane	86.18	−18	259	97.60
Heptane	100.20	−4	223	45.67
Octane	114.23	14	220	13.95
Aromatics				
Benzene	78.11	−11	580	100.84
Toluene	92.14	4.4	552	28.47
Ethylbenzene	106.17	15	477	9.51
o-Xylene	106.17	32	475	6.62
m-Xylene	106.17	25	465	8.29
p-Xylene	106.17	27	496	8.75
Oxygenates				
Methanol	32.04	11	470	127.05
Ethanol	46.07	13	426	59.02
Propanol	60.10	15	439	20.46
Isopropanol	60.10		456	42.74
Acetone	58.08	−18	538	229.52

Oxygenates	Molecular Weight	Flash point [°C]	Autoignition temperature [°C]	Vapor pressure at 25°C [mmHg]
Diethyl ether	74.12	−45	186	501.87
Methyl ethyl ketone	72.11	−6	516	90.00
Butanol	74.12	29	367	6.15
Ethylene glycol	62.07	114	413	0.07
Ethyl acetate	88.11	−4	486	94.63
Others				
Hydrogen	2.02		580	gas
Hydrogen sulfide	34.08		260	gas
Ammonia (anhydrous)	17.03		379	
Carbon disulfide	76.14	−30	100	
Carbon monoxide	28.01		651	gas
Dichloroethylene	96.94		458	

Table 4-10 continued *Some organic compounds and their flash points, autoignition temperatures, and vapor pressures*

Gasoline v. Diesel Engines

The diesel engine is based on the concept of the autoignition of diesel fuel. In contrast to the gasoline engine, which has spark plugs that provide an electric spark to ignite the gasoline-air mixture, the diesel engine does not have spark plugs. When the diesel-air mixture is compressed, its temperature increases (due to Charles' Law) to its point of autoignition.

By looking at Table 4-10, it is possible to understand why the diesel engine can rely on the autoignition of the fuel by compression and why the gasoline engine cannot. Gasoline is made mostly of aromatic compounds ranging from benzene to dimethyl- and ethylnaphathalenes. Diesel fuel is composed mostly of aliphatic compounds ranging from octane to docosane. Thus, gasoline has an autoignition temperature much higher than diesel fuel. This temperature would not be reached by simply compressing the vaporized gasoline in the cylinder, and, therefore, the spark is necessary to ignite the mixture.

Ignition temperatures provided in Table 4-10 are not exact temperatures. This is because they are dependent upon several parameters, such as the method of measurement, oxygen concentration, rate and duration of heating, or time delay. One study resulted in variations in the AIT of hexane from 225 to 510°C depending on which measurement technique was used [41]. In the same study, the AIT of pentane varied from 548°C when it was at 1.5% in air to 476°C when it was present at 7.65% in air. Therefore, as with flash point, it is important to understand that these values are condition-dependent.

Calculating Autoignition Temperatures

It is possible to calculate, or reasonably estimate, the AIT of chemicals, as shown in Table 4-11 [47].

nC = number of carbon atoms
C' = number of carbon atoms branched from the original structure

C'' = number of compounds branched from a C_3 carbon compound
AIT = autoignition temperature in [°C]

Table 4-11	*Calculations of AIT*
Class	**AIT [°C]**
Paraffinic hydrocarbons in gaseous state at standard pressure	$\dfrac{660}{\sqrt[3]{(nC)}}$
Paraffinic hydrocarbons in liquid state at STP	$\dfrac{660}{\sqrt[3]{(nC)}} - 100$
Olefins in gaseous state at standard pressure	$\dfrac{660}{\sqrt[3]{(nC+1)}}$
Olefins hydrocarbons in liquid state at standard pressure	$\dfrac{660}{\sqrt[3]{(nC+1)}} - 100$
Iso-hydrocarbons	$\dfrac{660}{\sqrt[3]{(nC-1)}}$
Benzene series	$\dfrac{660}{\sqrt[3]{(nC)}} + 200 - 10 \cdot C' - 30 \cdot C''$
Alcohols	$\dfrac{660}{\sqrt[3]{(nC+1)}} - 40$
Acetylene series	$\dfrac{660}{\sqrt[3]{(nC)}} - 200$

4.6.9 Minimum Ignition Energy

In order to ignite a liquid, it needs to be at least at its flash point and a suitable source of ignition must bring some portion of the vapors to the fuel's autoignition temperature. The energy that this ignition source must provide to bring the smallest portion of an ignitable mixture to its autoignition temperature is called the minimum ignition energy (MIE). This energy varies enormously depending on the vapor-air concentration, as well as some other parameters, including the size of the fuel particles and the spark configuration [41]. Table 4-12 shows a list of minimum ignition energies

Table 4-12	MIE of some compounds [41]	
Compounds	MIE at 25°C [mJ]	MIE at 150°C [mJ]
Acetone	0.406	0.188
Benzene	0.23	0.145
Cyclohexane	0.24	0.145
Cyclohexanol	—	0.282
Ethane	0.292	0.208
Ethanol	0.40	0.13
Heptane	0.26	0.082
Hydrogen	0.0011	0.0051
Methane	0.3	0.167
Toluene	0.26	0.106
o-Xylene	—	0.26

for some common chemicals. Logically, these values decrease with increasing temperature, since less energy is required to make up for the difference of temperature.

The minimum ignition energy will vary according to the following rules [41]:

- It decreases with unsaturation (alkanes > alkenes > alkynes)
- It increases with chain length and branching
- It decreases with conjugation
- It increases when radicals are substituted (amine > chloride > alcohol > mercaptan)
- It decreases with the presence of nitrite and nitro groups
- Aromaticity has little effect when compared to the same number of carbon atoms in a linear structure
- It decreases with 3-membered rings
- It increases with 6-membered rings
- It increases with the presence of esters and ketones
- It increases with ethers and thioethers

REFERENCES

1. Thatcher PJ (2000) *Fire investigation: Chemistry of fire*. In: *Encyclopedia of forensic sciences*, editors Siegel JA, Saukko PJ, and Knupfer GC, Academic Press, London, United Kingdom, pp 900–5.
2. Bertsch W, Holzer G, and Sellers CS (1993) *Chemical analysis for the arson investigator and attorney*, Hüthig Buch Verlag, Heidelberg, Germany.

3. Davletshina TA and Cheremisinoff NP (1998) *Fire and explosion hazards handbook of industrial chemicals*, Noyes Publications, Westwood, NJ.

4. Haessler WM (1974) *The extinguishment of fire*, National Fire Protection Association, Quincy, MA.

5. Troost L (1904) *Précis de chimie*, Masson et Cie, Paris, France.

6. Martin J-C (1996) *Incendie et explosion d'atmosphère*, Institut de police scientifique et de criminologie, Université de Lausanne, Lausanne, Switzerland.

7. Mahoney E (1992) *Fire suppression practices and procedures*, Brady, Englewood Cliffs, NJ.

8. Martin J-C and Pepler RS (2000) *Fire investigation: Physics/thermodynamics.* In: *Encyclopedia of forensic sciences*, editors Siegel JA, Saukko PJ, and Knupfer GC, Academic Press, London, United Kingdom, pp 928–33.

9. American Petroleum Institute (2003) *Ignition risk of hydrocarbon liquids and vapors by hot surfaces in the open air*, American Petroleum Institute, Washington, DC.

10. Holleyhead R (1996) Ignition of flammable gases and liquids by cigarettes: A review, *Science & Justice*, **36**(4), pp 257–66.

11. Atkins P (1992) *Chimie générale*, InterEditions, Paris, France.

12. International Union of Pure and Applied Chemistry (2004) *IUPAC compendium of chemical terminology*, available from: http://www.iupac.org, last access performed on October 9, 2004.

13. Simmons RF (1995) *Fire chemistry.* In: *Combustion fundamentals of fire*, editor Cox G, Academic Press, San Diego, CA, pp 403–73.

14. Drysdale D (1985) *An introduction to fire dynamics*, John Wiley and Sons, Chichester, England.

15. Quintiere JG (1997) *Principles of fire behavior*, Delmar Publishers, Albany, NY.

16. The ESCO Institute (2004) *Carbon monoxide: A clear and present danger*, ESCO Press, Mount Prospect, IL.

17. Homer CD et al. (2005) Carbon monoxide-related deaths in a metropolitan county in the USA: An 11-year study, *Forensic Science International*, **149**(2–3), pp 159–65.

18. DeHaan JD (2002) *Kirk's fire investigation*, 5th edition, Prentice Hall, Upper Saddle River, NJ.

19. Faraday M (1993) *The chemical history of a candle*, Cherokee Publishing Co, Atlanta, GA.

20. Pinorini MT (1992) *La suie comme indicateur dans l'investigation des incendies*, PhD thesis, Institut de police scientifique et de criminologie, Université de Lausanne, Lausanne, Switzerland.

21. Pinorini MT et al. (1994) Soot as an indicator in fire investigations: Physical and chemical analyses, *Journal of Forensic Sciences*, **39**(4), pp 933–73.

22. Fire Findings (1998) Alcoholic beverages burn efficiently, but don't prove to be very effective accelerants, *Fire Findings*, **6**(3), pp 1–3.

23. DeHaan JD (1997) *Kirk's fire investigation*, 4th edition, Brady Prentice Hall, Upper Saddle River, NJ.

24. Fire Findings (1994) Spontaneous combustion not instantaneous, *Fire Findings*, **2**(2), pp 1–3.

25. Ettling BV and Adams MF (1971) Spontaneous combustion of linseed oil in sawdust, *Fire Technology*, **7**(3), pp 225–36.

26. American Insurance Association Engineering and Safety Service (1985) Spontaneous ignition, *Fire and Arson Investigator*, **36**(2), pp 6–8.

27. Bapst S (2001) *Étude de cas de combustion spontanée*, travail de séminaire, Institut de police scientifique et de criminologie, Université de Lausanne, Lausanne, Switzerland.

28. Bowes PC (1984) *Self-heating: Evaluating and controlling the hazards*, Elsevier Science Publishers, Amsterdam, The Netherlands.
29. Dixon B (1992) Spontaneous combustion, *Le Journal de l'Association Canadienne des Enquêteurs Incendie*, March, pp 18–21.
30. Stauffer E (2005) A review of the analysis of vegetable oil residues from fire debris samples: Spontaneous ignition, vegetable oils, and the forensic approach, *Journal of Forensic Sciences*, **50**(5), pp 1091–100.
31. Stauffer E (2006) A review of the analysis of vegetable oil residues from fire debris samples: Analytical scheme, interpretation of the results, and future needs, *Journal of Forensic Sciences*, **51**(5), pp 1016–32.
32. McMurry J and Fay RC (1998) *Chemistry*, 2nd edition, Prentice Hall, Upper Saddle River, NJ.
33. Stauffer E (2003) Basic concept of pyrolysis for fire debris analysts, *Science & Justice*, **43**(1), pp 29–40.
34. Stauffer E (2001) *Identification and characterization of interfering products in fire debris analysis*, Master's thesis, International Forensic Research Institute, Florida International University, Miami, FL.
35. Moldoveanu SC (1998) *Analytical pyrolysis of natural organic polymers*, Techniques and instrumentation in analytical chemistry, vol 20, Elsevier, Amsterdam, The Netherlands.
36. Madorsky SL (1964) *Thermal degradation of organic polymers*. In: *Polymer reviews*, editors Mark HF and Immergut EH, vol 7, John Wiley & Sons, New York, NY.
37. Wall LA (1972) *Pyrolysis of polymers*. In: *The mechanisms of pyrolysis, oxidation, and burning of organic materials*, editor Wall LA, National Bureau of Standards, Washington, DC, pp 47–72.
38. National Fire Protection Association (2004) *NFPA 921 guide for fire and explosion investigations*, Quincy, MA.
39. Department of Environmental Resources Management (2005) *Chemical composition of air*, available from: http://www.co.miami-dade.fl.us/derm/air, last access performed on January 31, 2005.
40. Babrauskas V (2003) *Ignition handbook*, Fire Science Publishers, Issaquah, WA.
41. Bond J (1991) *Sources of ignition: Flammability characteristics of chemicals and products*, Butterworth-Heinemann, Jordan Hill, Oxford, United Kingdom.
42. Lentini JJ and Waters LV (1991) The behavior of flammable and combustible liquids, *Fire and Arson Investigator*, **42**(1), pp 39–45.
43. Carson PA and Mumford CJ (1994) *Hazardous chemicals handbook*, Butterworth-Heinemann, Oxford, England.
44. Cote AE (2003) *Fire protection handbook*, 19th edition, National Fire Protection Association, Quincy, MA.
45. Commission Universitaire pour la Santé et la Sécurité au Travail Romande (2001) *Inflammables*, available from: http://www.cusstr.ch, last access performed on August 21, 2004.
46. Jones JC (2001) A means of calculating the fire points of organic compounds, *Journal of Fire Sciences*, **19**(1), pp 62–8.
47. Shimy AA (1970) Calculating flammability characteristics of hydrocarbons and alcohols, *Fire Technology*, **6**, pp 135–9.

CHAPTER 5

Detection of Ignitable Liquid Residues at Fire Scenes

"We probably would have missed it without the Sniffer."
David Burd of the California State Crime Laboratory cited by
William W. Turner, Invisible witness: The use and abuse of the new
technology of crime investigation (1968)

5.1 INTRODUCTION

The detection of ignitable liquid residues (ILR) at fire scenes can be a useful step in the investigation of a fire and more particularly in the selection of fire debris samples. Often, in the United States as well as in Canada, the fire scene examination is performed by the scene investigator and not by the laboratory personnel analyzing fire debris. In other countries, and more particularly in some European countries, sometimes the fire scene investigator and laboratory personnel are the same person or are members of a common team. When laboratory personnel are not at the scene, it is important that they have a good understanding of the principles underlying the detection of ILR at fire scenes. This helps to establish a better communication between the scene and laboratory personnel. It also helps the criminalist to understand and possibly to explain any discrepancies between the scene detection results and the laboratory results to the fire scene investigator.

Unless a suitable portable gas chromatograph(-mass spectrometer) is brought to the scene, there is no scene detector that can provide a definitive identification of ILR. All detectors used at fire scenes must be considered to be presumptive tests for ILR and therefore will have their share of false negatives and false positives. A positive response from such a detector can be interpreted only as a possibility that an ILR is present.[1] The reason

---

[1] Indeed, a negative response does not necessarily imply that no ILR are present.

for this is that these detectors, though offering great sensitivity, are not specific to ignitable liquids. Most of them respond to combustible gases or volatile compounds, which do not necessarily originate from an ignitable liquid. This is a very important concept to grasp. For example, when a substrate burns, pyrolysis products are released as explained in Section 4.4. These products present very similar, if not identical, chemical structures to the chemicals found in ignitable liquids, and therefore, engender a positive response from most of the detection techniques used at the fire scene.

Presumptive v. Confirmatory Tests

A presumptive test is not 100% specific to the analyte of interest. A presumptive test suffers from false positives; that is, other analytes that are not the one(s) of interest trigger a positive response. A confirmatory test is specific to the analyte of interest to the exclusion of all others. The concept of presumptive and confirmatory tests is well known to forensic serologists or drug analysts. For example, luminol and phenolphthalein are presumptive tests used to detect blood. These techniques will yield a positive response when in the presence of blood, however other contaminants such as some metals and fruit or vegetable juices might also produce a positive response [1]. Thus, a positive response from luminol indicates only that blood might be present. Conversely, the Takayama and Teichman tests are confirmatory tests for blood, performed on stains, and will identify the presence of blood to the exclusion of all other possible sources [1]. The negative response from a presumptive test indicates that the analyte of interest either is not present or is not detectable (for example, because it is below the limit of detection).

Sometimes, presumptive tests are more sensitive than confirmatory tests. Thus, it is possible that a presumptive test exhibits a positive response due to the actual presence of the analyte, however the confirmatory test exhibits a negative response because the analyte of interest is present at a concentration below the test's limit of detection.

From a fire investigation perspective, all detection techniques presently used at the scene should be considered as presumptive tests for ignitable liquids. These techniques are useful in helping an investigator select quality samples, however with regard to the identification of ILR, only an analysis by gas chromatography or gas chromatography-mass spectrometry can provide a definitive identification.

It is often the role of the fire debris analyst to teach this concept to the fire scene investigator. Many fire scene investigators do not entirely grasp the chemical and physical properties of ignitable liquids, and have even less understanding of the concept of interferences among fire debris. Additionally, they are often not trained in the technology behind these detectors and may not fully understand the concepts of specificity and sensitivity. However, many investigators will use ignitable liquid detectors on a daily basis and blindly trust their reliability. When the laboratory issues a negative result on a sample that provided a positive signal with the scene detector, the investigator might question the laboratory's capabilities. This type of situation arose when the first accelerant detection canines (ADC) were used

[2, 3]. At that point, it is necessary for the scientist to have the cognizance of the technology behind these detectors, so that he or she can shed some light on the investigator's doubts. It is also crucial to understand that scene detectors and laboratory instruments do not fulfill the same goals and are more complementary rather than competitive techniques. For this reason, it would not be pertinent to compare every aspect of each.

The three main principles behind the detection of ignitable liquids at fire scenes are as follows:

I. Detection can be done based on the visual recognition of the residual burn pattern left by the pouring of a liquid.

II. Detectors can react to the presence of volatile organic compounds (VOCs) that are present in the headspace above the sample due to vapor pressure.

III. Detectors can react to the fluorescence produced by the aromatic content of some ignitable liquids when subjected to UV light.

As of today, there are no detectors integrating all three principles. Table 5-1 summarizes the different types of detectors. Each detection technique is explained briefly and its particular limitations are presented.

Table 5-1	Different types of detectors and their respective principle of detection
Principle of detection	**Detector Type**
Pattern	Burn pattern observation
Headspace	Electronic sniffers Colorimetric tubes Accelerant detection canines Ignitable liquid absorbent
Fluorescence	UV light

5.2 BURN PATTERNS

Burn patterns are used by fire investigators in the determination of the origin of a fire. Fire patterns are a larger category than burn patterns because they include other patterns, such as smoke patterns. Fire patterns are defined as [4]: "the visible or measurable physical effects that remain after a fire." As one can imagine, fire can create an enormous number of different patterns. The National Fire Protection Association (NFPA) *Guide for Fire and Explosion Investigations* defines numerous different patterns [4]. There are patterns that indicate the direction of travel of the fire and some that indicate the intensity of heat.

There are also patterns indicating that an ignitable liquid has been poured at a scene. However, other patterns often are misinterpreted as pour patterns. It was once believed that all irregularly shaped patterns were an indication of the pour of an ignitable liquid. Examples of such patterns are shown in Figure 5-1.

This is unfortunately not true as the patterns shown in Figure 5-1 are not due to the pour of an ignitable liquid. Such irregular patterns are often the results of post-flashover conditions. As stated in Chapter 4, once flashover occurs, practically all surfaces in the room begin burning. Melting and smoldering debris, as well as other heat exposures, can create such irregular patterns without any ignitable liquids. Two interesting reports produced by the National Institute of Justice (USA) illustrate the different patterns that can be obtained with and without ignitable liquids and in full-room involvement [5, 6]. Figure 5-2 shows examples of actual pour patterns. Note that there is not very much difference between Figures 5-1 (particularly b) and 5-2. It is easy to understand how that confusion may arise between such patterns.

The only rare circumstances under which an irregular pattern can be called a pour pattern are:

- When the presence of a nonincidental ignitable liquid in the pattern is subsequently demonstrated at the laboratory.
- When fire damage is extremely limited (flashover did not occur), and no other possibility than the pour of a liquid can explain such a

FIGURE 5-1a

These irregularly shaped patterns are the results of particular ventilation conditions. Because of the important crawl space below the flooring, fresh air was brought from the bottom, thus accelerating the burning of holes in the wooden planks. (For a full color version of this figure, please see the insert.)

In this case, burning material falling from the ceiling created these irregularly shaped burn patterns. (For a full color version of this figure, please see the insert.)

This room underwent flashover, thus creating these irregularly shaped burn patterns. None of these three burn patterns were the results of the pour of an ignitable liquid. (For a full color version of this figure, please see the insert.)

FIGURE 5-2a

This irregularly shaped pattern is part of a trailer of ignitable liquid that was poured on the floor of an apartment. (For a full color version of this figure, please see the insert.)

FIGURE 5-2b

The irregularly shaped patterns present in this room are actual pour patterns, confirmed by laboratory analyses positive for gasoline. Note that the general shapes very closely resemble the ones presented in Figure 5-1.
(Photographs courtesy of Blair Darst, Cunningham Investigative Services, Grayson, Georgia, USA.) (For a full color version of this figure, please see the insert.)

FIGURE 5-3
This pool-shaped pattern is the result of the pour of an ignitable liquid. Note the close resemblance to Figure 5-1b. (For a full color version of this figure, please see the insert.)

FIGURE 5-4 *This pool-shaped pattern presents spots where the carpet was protected and did not sustain burns. These areas were protected because of the presence of difference objects. If the floor is uneven, a raised area usually burns prior to a lower area, because the liquid accumulates in the latter and protects it from burning. The resulting pattern would be called a doughnut-shaped pattern. (Photograph courtesy of Keith Bell, Holland Investigations, Atlanta, Georgia, USA.) (For a full color version of this figure, please see the insert.)*

pattern. Even in these instances, it is always delicate to call such a pattern a pour pattern. Figures 5-3 and 5-4 show pool-shaped patterns that are both genuine pour patterns. Also, when a liquid forms a nice puddle (this applies as well on uneven surfaces), a doughnut-shaped pattern can appear. This pattern is created by the more rapid burning of the liquid in the circumference of the circle, while the center is cooled by the liquid and, thus, protected.

As a result, the presence of an ignitable liquid must not be drawn solely from the shape of a fire pattern, unless exceptional circumstances allow for this. Also, many times an investigator might think there is a liquid involved as he or she observes irregularly shaped patterns. In such instances, the laboratory analyst should not necessarily expect a positive identification of an ignitable liquid because these patterns might be created by factors other than the pouring of a liquid. Besides flashover, these factors may include melting from a polymer present on the ceiling of a room or from a particular venting configuration.

5.3 ELECTRONIC SNIFFERS

5.3.1 Definition
Electronic sniffers, also called electronic noses, combustible gas detectors, portable gas detectors, or, wrongly, mechanical sniffers, have been in use for about 50 years. They were first developed for atmospheric analysis in potentially hazardous situations, and eventually found their way into the field of fire investigation as well. The fire scene is scanned with such a detector: The headspace above the surface is drawn into the detector, which reacts to the presence of combustible gas or volatile organic compounds.

There have been very few formal validation studies published regarding the use of electronic sniffers for fire investigation purpose [7–9]. A recent review of different electronic noses used to detect explosives shows an impressive number of different technologies that eventually could be applied to ignitable liquid detection [10]. There are many different types of detectors used in the field. The most common types—catalytic combustion, flame ionization detection, and photoionization detection—are reviewed hereafter. Other types of detectors exist, such as one with a sensor based on a metal oxide semiconductor, but these are not commonly used in fire investigation [11].

The overall functioning principle of an electronic sniffer is shown in Figure 5-5. A probe is used to selectively pump the atmosphere above the surface to be sampled through the action of a vacuum pump. The sampled atmosphere is brought to a detector, which provides output through a small display and/or connection to a computer system.

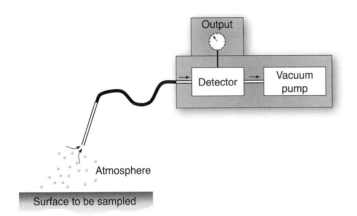

FIGURE 5-5
Overall functioning principle of an electronic sniffer.

5.3.2 Operating Principle

A/ Catalytic Combustion Detector

An oxidizable (combustible) gas is pumped to a catalyst-coated resistance element, which oxidizes the gas as shown in Figure 5-6 [12]. The heat resulting from this oxidation reaction (combustion) engenders a change in the resistance of the element, which is proportional to the amount of combustible gas passing through it. An identical reference element, not subjected to the combustible gas, is incorporated in a Wheatstone bridge with the measuring element, and leads to a difference of potential, which is measurable and proportional to the amount of combustible gas. This is illustrated in Figure 5-7. Results are expressed in volumetric concentration, usually ppm. These detectors typically offer a long life, but they are also very sensitive to changes in humidity.

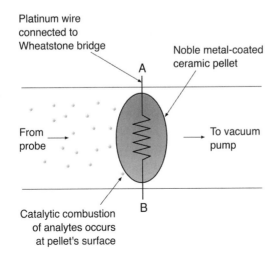

FIGURE 5-6
Schematic representation of the functioning of a catalytic combustion detector. The ceramic pellet is coated with a noble metal, which acts as a catalyst when heated. When analytes contact the catalyst, they will combust, inducing a temperature increase of the pellet and the platinum wire contained within.

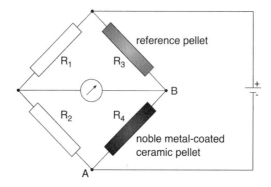

FIGURE 5-7 *The resistance of the platinum wire is a function of its temperature. As a result, a temperature change generates a resistance change, which is detected by the Wheatstone bridge: If the ratio R_2/R_1 is equal to the ratio R_4/R_3, then the difference of potential between the midpoints is null. As soon as R_4 varies, a difference of potential is generated and detected by the voltmeter at the center of the bridge. In regular catalytic combustion detectors, the reference pellet R_3 is identical to R_4, with the exception of the catalyst coating. As such, it is not subject to temperature changes induced by catalytic combustion and it keeps the same electrical properties.*

FIGURE 5-8

*The TLV electronic sniffer. Note the (stick) probe in front of the apparatus.
(Photograph courtesy of Laura Conner.)*

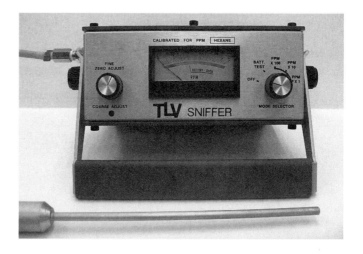

The TLV sniffer (Scott Instruments, Monroe, North Carolina, USA) is based on catalytic combustion (see Figure 5-8) [13]. It is capable of detecting flammable vapors at concentrations as low as 2 ppm. This instrument is usually calibrated with hexane, but can also be calibrated with methane or hydrogen. It is operated with a pump that can create a flow up to 1,750 ml/minute.

FIGURE 5-9 *A Pragmatics 626 Trooper 2 instrument. The main body of the instrument also includes a flashlight. Notice the two cups and the search (sampling) and reference sensors. In this instrument, R_3 (from Figure 5-7) is represented by the reference sensor, thus R_3 is a ceramic pellet with a catalyst coating identical to R_4. (Photograph courtesy of Oliver Seth, KWJ Engineering Inc, Newark, California, USA.)*

A very interesting concept has been developed by Pragmatics (KWJ Engineering, Newark, California, USA) using the catalytic combustion detector [14]. Rather than having the usual surrounding atmosphere running through the reference element (baseline or background), it is possible to select a specific background to use in lieu of the typical reference background. By doing this, the system can effectively cancel out the effect of the interferences from the substrate to be sampled. These instruments use two independent systems, one directed to the sampling element and one to the reference element (see Figure 5-9). Also, the typical stick-style probe has been replaced by a cup system, improving the headspace sampling of the surface. The catalytic combustion detectors have been integrated in the probe, which eliminates the long dead times generated by the traveling of the analytes through a tube to reach the main unit. As a result, when one suspects a certain pattern to contain an ignitable liquid and the substrate of this pattern is constituted of carpet for example, it is possible to place the sampling (search) sensor on top of the alleged pour pattern and the reference sensor on top of the same carpet in a spot not suspected to contain any ignitable liquid (comparison location). Thus, the background provided by the carpet on the reference element will be considered as the baseline. This background will be used to define a baseline for the signal produced by the sampling (search) element and the analytes additional to the baseline will be clearly seen. Such an instrument definitely decreases the false positive rate.

B/ Flame Ionization Detector

The flame ionization detector is a very common detector used in gas chromatography. The functioning principle of this detector is shown in Figure 8-21. The sample is brought to the detector via a pumping action, and it is burned in a flame. The flame commonly is generated with hydrogen and air. When a chemical compound is burned, it produces ions and electrons. These electrons are located between two electrodes to which a difference of potential of a few hundred volts is applied. As a result, the newly produced ions generate a current that can be recorded. The intensity of the current is directly proportional to the amount of analytes (ions) present in the detector. The operating principle of the overall unit closely resembles what was presented in Figure 5-5.

This type of detector is sensitive to almost all compounds, mostly combustible ones [15]. There are, however, a few compounds to which the detector has very little, if any, sensitivity. These include O_2, N_2, CS_2, H_2S, SO_2, NO, N_2O, NO_2, NH_3, CO, CO_2, and H_2O. The insensitivity to these compounds is an advantage in the fire debris analysis application.

C/ Photoionization Detector

The photoionization detector uses ultraviolet light to irradiate the sample, thus ionizing it [16]. The analysis chamber is composed of two plates between which a difference of potential is applied. Upon production of ionized molecules, a current is created and recorded as illustrated in Figure 5-10. The intensity of the current is a direct measure of the amount of ionized molecules. Except for the mode of ion production, the principle of this detector is very similar to that of the FID.

Although the exact response of the detector depends on the lamp ionization energy and the molecules ionization potential, this detector responds

FIGURE 5-10

Schematic representation of the functioning of a photoionization detector. Analytes are ionized by the UV light source and a current is created and recorded.

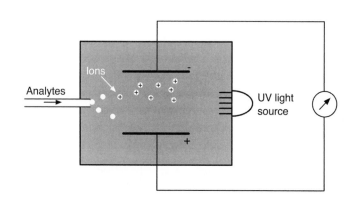

to almost all VOCs, many of which are not components found in ignitable liquids. Consequently, false positives are relatively common.

5.3.3 Use

All these detectors operate in approximately the same manner. They are usually very portable and consist of four main parts: the probe, the pump, the detector, and the recording or reporting device.

The probe can vary in size, but some are pretty long and allow for easy screening of the scene by just walking around holding the probe on one hand and the detector on the other, as shown in Figure 5-11.

The pump is usually battery-powered and can pump volumes up to a few liters per minute. The detector itself differs, depending on the type. Some might require a warm-up period whereas others might require extra accessories. For example, the flame ionization detector requires a hydrogen tank and an air or oxygen tank in order to produce the flame. The photoionization detector needs more battery power to operate the UV lamp. Some devices have an integrated recording device that prints results

FIGURE 5-11 *A fire investigator holding an FID electronic sniffer with a stick probe at a fire scene. (For a full color version of this figure, please see the insert.)*

on paper, but most have just a live, contemporaneous output device, such as an LCD screen, that shows the concentration of the analytes detected. Many systems also are equipped with a speaker that will emit a sound when a certain level of concentration is reached.

The use of these detectors is very simple. Once turned on, the investigator just places the probe close to the area to be screened and waits for a reading. It is also possible to walk around with the detector and screen a larger area. Some detectors offer a very short reaction time, almost instantaneous, and some offer a more delayed reaction time, in the order of a few seconds. The user needs to be aware of this parameter, so he or she can take this into account when using the detector.

5.3.4 Advantages and Drawbacks

Byron tested three types of detectors: a simple filament type (Electronic Nose), a catalytic combustion type (TLV Sniffer), and a photoionization type (LIS Combustible Gas Detector) [7]. In addition, he described the catalytic combustion type as [7] "time-consuming and ineffective." He concluded that the photoionization detector is the only advantageous one at the scene. He found that the simple filament type is [7] "nearly useless for fire scene work since it lacks selectivity and seems to respond to practically everything."

Hilliard and Thomas reported a lack of sensitivity from a J.W. Combustible Gas Detector for some heavy petroleum distillates [8]. Also, they reported that the detector gave a positive answer for ignitable liquids where none existed. This is, of course, not unexpected with presumptive tests. Finally, they concluded that [8]: "no conclusion concerning the presence or absence of flammable liquids should be drawn until specimens of debris submitted to the laboratory have been analyzed and a report received."

Indeed, some manufacturers recognize the limitations of their instruments, as Scott and Bacharach state in their application note [17]: "Upon locating possible physical evidence (a piece of cloth or portion of a floor board, for example) the 'sample' can be sent out for laboratory clarification." This is, however, an understatement: Every sample must be sent to the laboratory if positive identification of ignitable liquid is sought.

More recently, Casamento et al. tested a photoionization detector and showed that it failed to detect 100% of samples that were positive when subsequently analyzed by GC-MS [9]. Conner et al. also tested the TLV Sniffer (Bacharach Inc., Pittsburgh, Pennsylvania, USA) and the tpi Pocket Combustible Gas Leak Detector (Professional Equipment Inc., Hauppauge, New York, USA) [11, 18]. They concluded that [18]: "The TLV Sniffer® is a relatively inexpensive, commercially available electronic nose, which has been demonstrated to have some utility in the detection of accelerants in fire debris." They do not believe the tpi instrument would be useful at a fire scene. Finally, they compared the TLV sniffer to the standards used for an accelerant detection canine (Canine Accelerant Detection Association

[CADA] proficiency test) and although it performed adequately, it did not function as effectively as an ADC [18].

The main drawback of these detectors is their lack of specificity and, in some instances, sensitivity. Though the solution offered by Pragmatics might decrease the number of false positives, it certainly does not make it a confirmatory test for ignitable liquids. Also, each of these detectors will have their particular problems or limitations such as sensitivity to humidity or contamination, which must be known prior to their use.

The advantages of these detectors are that they are relatively easy to use and there is minimal required maintenance. The scanning process may be time-consuming and it may be difficult to identify the exact location where ILR are present. In spite of this, these detectors can improve in the selection of fire debris samples by sorting them according to the response of the detector. This is useful when priority in laboratory analysis is required. The price of these instruments ranges from a few hundred to several thousand dollars.

5.4 COLORIMETRIC TUBES

5.4.1 Definition
Devices, such as Dräger tubes, can be useful at fire scenes in order to detect or determine the possible presence of ignitable liquids. These colorimetric tubes can be very convenient and offer greater specificity to some chemicals than the electronic noses. These devices consist of glass tubes filled with a powder designed to react by changing color upon the presence of a specific chemical or class of chemicals.

5.4.2 Operating Principle
Figure 5-12 illustrates colorimetric tubes in various stages of use. The headspace or atmosphere suspected to contain the chemical is drawn via a pumping action through the tube, which is filled with a chemical mixture. If the analyte of interest is present in the headspace, it reacts with the chemical mixture present in the tube, which will change color. In some instances, the tube is calibrated with a scale along its side. When a given amount of headspace is drawn through the tube, it is possible to estimate the concentration of the analyte of interest. Some systems have electronic readers that provide a digital output to the user.

Dräger makes a great number of different tubes that are designed for different chemicals [19]. Figure 5-13 shows two such tubes (one unreacted and one reacted).

5.4.3 Use
The tube is placed just above the sample that needs to be tested. A given amount of the sample's headspace is forced through the tube using a manual or electrical pump as shown in Figure 5-14.

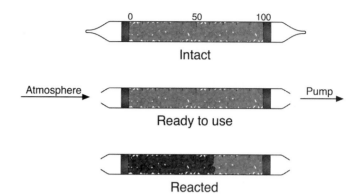

FIGURE 5-12 *Schematic representation of the functioning of a colorimetric tube. Top: An intact tube. Middle: The two ends of the tube are broken off and the tube is connected to the pump. A specified volume of atmosphere is drawn through the tube. Bottom: The analytes reacted with the powder inside the tube and a colorimetric reaction occurred. It is possible to read the concentration of the analytes with the graduation and the limit of coloration.*

FIGURE 5-13 *Examples of unreacted and reacted Dräger tubes. Note the dark coloration of the reactant inside the bottom tube, indicating the positive reaction. Also, note the scale along the side of the top tube. (For a full color version of this figure, please see the insert.)*

FIGURE 5-14

A pump used with Dräger tubes.

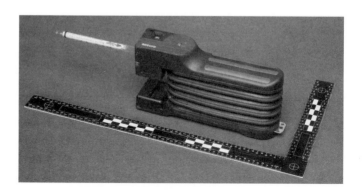

In some instances, these tubes can be used at the laboratory to perform preliminary assessment of the debris. This is particularly convenient when the debris exhibits a strong but unrecognized odor. If needed, the sample can be preheated prior to analysis; this allows the headspace of the sample to be more concentrated.

5.4.4 Advantages and Drawbacks

These tubes are usually inexpensive and a manual pump is also reasonably priced (a couple of hundred USD). If an electrical pump with an electronic reader is chosen, the cost can be significant. Usually, each tube is designed for one particular chemical class, which could be convenient when the user would like to check for a given chemical rather than ignitable liquids in general. However, be aware that false positives may occur. Most of these tubes are not exclusively specific to the chemical for which they are designed. The manufacturer's notice explains that there are possibilities of detecting false positives. Colorimetric tubes must be considered as presumptive tests. This specificity can also be a drawback to the investigator who is looking for ignitable liquids in general. In such instances, a combination of several tubes needs to be used, which might become cumbersome and expensive.

The sensitivity of the technique might also be a problem. Casamento et al. recently revealed that the colorimetric tube technique failed to reveal any samples identified as containing ignitable liquid by the GC-MS [9]. The sensitivity problem potentially could be due to the sampling technique rather than the tubes themselves.

These tubes are also particularly convenient when operating in an explosive atmosphere or in spaces close to the lower limit of flammability because they do not require any electrical sources. Finally, it is definitely not feasible to screen a whole fire scene with such tubes, because this means of screening relies upon taking discrete samples. One needs to think of using colorimetric tests more for one precise area or a given fire debris sample rather than for the scene as a whole, where a continuous sampling method would be more appropriate.

5.5 ACCELERANT DETECTION CANINES

5.5.1 Definition

Accelerant detection canines (ADC) are one of the most successful tools used at fire scenes to detect ILR. There are presently more than 300 ADCs used in the United States [20]. Unfortunately, they are sparingly used overseas [21]. ADC capabilities have been developed since 1986 in a joint program between the Connecticut State Police and the then Bureau of Alcohol, Tobacco and Firearms [22, 23]. This means of detection is very versatile and offers a great efficiency at the fire scene, although training, maintenance, and upkeep can be both costly and time-consuming.

5.5.2 Operating Principle

The principle of detection lies in the fact that the canine's olfactory organ is much more developed than that of humans. They possess a relatively low threshold for the detection of odors of ignitable liquids [24]. In order for an odor to be detected, it needs to reach the sensory apparatus of the canine. This process is achieved by the act of sniffing.

5.5.3 Use

The canine team consists of a dog handler and an ADC. The team screens the fire scene for any smell of ILR as shown in Figure 5-15. Once an odor is detected, the dog will manifest a positive alert using different signals, depending on the training received. Usually the dog will sit or stand still in front of the area designated, however there are other means by which the dog can signal its findings.

Once the detection is complete, the dog is rewarded either by being fed or by playing with its handler. This is shown in Figures 5-16 and 5-17.

Once the samples have been collected, they may be aligned at a reasonable distance from each other and away from the scene, in order to be checked again by the canine, as shown in Figure 5-18. At this stage, if the canine does not confirm a sample for which it indicated a positive hit earlier, the sample may be discarded. The team may elect to rework the area of the scene from which the nonconfirmed sample was collected. If the canine continues to alert in that area, it may indicate that the collected samples did not contain the material of interest. In this case, additional samples may be collected.

FIGURE 5-15

Dusty, a 5-year old Springer Spaniel ADC screening a fire scene for the presence of ILR. (Photograph courtesy of Inspector Emre Ertan, Forensic Unit, Neuchâtel State Police, Switzerland.)

FIGURE 5-16

Dusty is trained to stand still when he detects something. In this case, the handler rewards the dog by petting him. (Photograph courtesy of Inspector Emre Ertan, Forensic Unit, Neuchâtel State Police, Switzerland.)

FIGURE 5-17

The handler rewards the dog by playing with him. (Photograph courtesy of Inspector Emre Ertan, Forensic Unit, Neuchâtel State Police, Switzerland.)

FIGURE 5-18

Once samples have been collected, they are placed at a certain distance from each other and the ADC confirms the presence of ILR again. (Photograph courtesy of Inspector Emre Ertan, Forensic Unit, Neuchâtel State Police, Switzerland.)

5.5.4 Advantages and Drawbacks

The use of canines has shown an improvement in the proportion of positive confirmations from samples submitted to the laboratory [25]. Casamento et al. published a confirmatory rate of 84% for ADC [9]. Due to the canine's great sensitivity, every forensic laboratory receiving samples from a canine team should analyze them by GC-MS. This recommendation was made by Schultz, Ercoli, and Cerven in 1996 [26]. According to these authors, if the laboratory uses a GC-FID, the rate of confirmation will be much lower than by GC-MS, thus increasing the frustration of the canine team.[2] Another advantage of accelerant detection canines is that they offer good selectivity. A properly trained canine team will also train on common debris samples that produce interfering compounds to encourage a negative response from the canine.

The dogs offer an excellent sensitivity, but their selectivity does not approach that of modern instrumentation [2, 27]. There have been multiple scientific experiments conducted in order to estimate the canine's selectivity [27–29] and their reliability has been questioned [30]. Although ADCs offer better selectivity than most tools used for the indication of ILR on scene, they are not infallible, and false positives will occur. Some of the issues relating to both the sensitivity and selectivity of canines was addressed in 1995 when the International Association of Arson Investigators Forensic Science Committee published a position letter in *Journal of Forensic Sciences* [3]. The committee stated that [3]: "Some early testing indicates that the limits of detection for a well trained and maintained canine may be below those of some forensic laboratory methods utilized for recovery and detection of ignitable liquids." With regard to selectivity, the committee

---

[2] Although GC-FID and GC-MS have comparable lower limit of detection (although GC-FID has an even lower limit with some compounds when compared to GC-MS in full scan mode; see Chapter 8), because of the mass spectral information provided by the mass spectrometer, it is possible to improve the identification of ignitable liquid residues from fire debris samples with GC-MS over GC-FID.

related that [3], "The discrimination ability of the canine to distinguish between pyrolysis products and accelerants is remarkable but not infallible." The committee finally concluded that every positive hit from the canine must be confirmed by the laboratory. If the laboratory's finding is negative, then the canine positive hit is not relevant and should be ignored.

The canine is a great tool for the fire investigator, however it is only a tool that can assist in the investigation, more precisely in the selection of samples. It should never be used as the sole basis for the determination of the presence of ignitable liquid residues at a fire scene.

5.6 IGNITABLE LIQUID ABSORBENT

5.6.1 Definition

A new tool for the fire investigation community made its appearance with the Ignitable Liquid Absorbent (ILA), developed by John H. Woodland and patented on March 25, 2003 under the title *Method and Composition for Detecting Ignitable Liquids* [31]. ILA consists of a powder that is designed to be spread onto a substrate and that has the capability of both absorbing ILR and indicating their presence.[3]

5.6.2 Operating Principle

ILA is composed of two powders that must be mixed together prior to use. The first one is white powder that acts as the absorbent and as a contrasting background for the color indicator. The second is a dark powder used to indicate the presence of ignitable liquids. Table 5-2 shows the original composition of the absorbent powder [31, 32]. It should be noted that the

Table 5-2 Different components of the original formula of the absorbing powder of ILA

Compounds	Examples	Ideal proportion (by weight)	Function
Hydrophobic polymers	Polypropylene Polyethylene Polystyrene Polyethylene terephthalate	70–80%	Absorbing substrate
Long-chain carboxylic acid	Stearic acid	10–25%	Attracts polar, semipolar and nonpolar solvents
Hydrophobic white metallic oxide	Aluminum oxide Titanium dioxide	9–14%	Contrast agent for the solvent indicator dye

[3] Even though it is not clear if ILA actually absorbs, adsorbs, or absorbs and adsorbs, the term absorbent will be used to simplify the reading.

composition of that powder recently has been changed. It is now composed of nonhydrocarbon-based mineral material [33].

The indicator powder is composed of a hydrophobic solvent indicator dye, usually a metal complex, such as solvent blue. It is present at ideal proportions between 0.03 to 1% by weight [31]. The purpose of the dye is to indicate the presence of absorbed solvents.

When a solvent is absorbed onto the ILA, the indicator turns blue, revealing the presence of absorbed solvents. Once the ILA absorbs the solvent, it can be collected and brought to the laboratory for ignitable liquid residues analysis.

5.6.3 Use

An ILA kit comes in two containers as shown in Figure 5-19. Prior to use, it is necessary to create a homogeneous mixture of both powders [34]. The ILA then is spread onto the surface of the substrate of interest. If ignitable liquid residues are present above the sample, they are absorbed by the ILA.

5.6.4 Advantages and Drawbacks

ILA is convenient to use. The can is easily transportable and the mixture is readily prepared at the scene and spread onto the surface of interest. A one-quart can covers about 100 square feet (about 9 square meters) and costs between USD 20 and 25. The material can be stored for quite a long period of time prior to combining the two powders. The indication of the presence

FIGURE 5-19

ILA comes in two containers: The white powder is located in the quart metal can and the blue powder in the small glass vial, which is attached to the quart can. Both powders must be mixed together prior to use.

of ignitable liquid can be pretty obvious, however it is not always the case. It is also subject to false positives.

To a certain extent and with the proper training, the user can differentiate some false positives and understand the patterns exhibited by ILA. For example, in the presence of a uniform surface releasing pyrolysis products, ILA turns uniformly blue. By contrast, if a clear pattern of ignitable liquid is present, neat blue delineations appear on the ILA. This is illustrated in Figures 5-20 and 5-21. Unfortunately, it is always possible to obtain false positives, and thus ILA can be used only as an indicator or presumptive test, and laboratory analyses need to be performed in order to demonstrate the presence of ILR. Also, ILA cannot be used on a hot surface. If the surface is too hot, first of all, ILA will turn blue and second, it can melt. This last problem should have been resolved with the new powder formulation [33].

As ILA is a relatively recent innovation, there has been little published pertaining to it. Byron demonstrated that ILA does not produce significant interference in the chromatogram [35]. Only a few extra peaks were present and easily distinguishable from any patterns from ignitable liquids that were present. Thomas et al. presented contradictory data with regard to the interference of ILA [36]. They demonstrated that ILA produced several branched alkanes and n-heptadecane. Again, note that the presence of interfering products should be strongly diminished if not suppressed with the

FIGURE 5-20

Example of the use of ILA with 500 μl of diesel fuel. The neat blue delineation indicates the presence of diesel fuel. (Photograph courtesy of François Rey, Institut de Police Scientifique, École des Sciences Criminelles, Université de Lausanne, Switzerland.) (For a full color version of this figure, please see the insert.)

Example of the use of ILA on wood after a short exposure to water. The neat blue delineations indicate the presence of 85% weathered gasoline. (Photograph courtesy of François Rey, Institut de Police Scientifique, École des Sciences Criminelles, Université de Lausanne, Switzerland.) (For a full color version of this figure, please see the insert.)

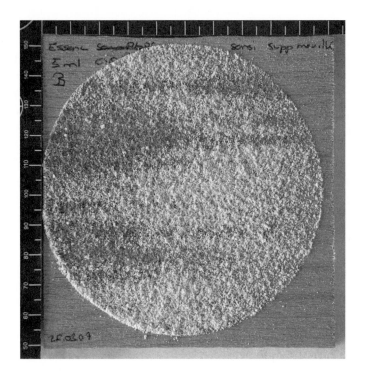

new powder formulation. Thomas et al. also showed that ILA prevents the recovery of ignitable liquid when using headspace technique [36]. This phenomenon is expected as the ILA's function is to absorb ILR; it will prevent a good release of these analytes in the headspace. When extracting the ILA using a solvent, Thomas et al. observed the presence of n-heptadecane as well as the presence of a few fatty acids [36]. Finally, they performed some field evaluation in which the color change was not always obvious. They often observed the color change in the underlayer of the ILA, once it was being removed.

Very recently, an article by Nowlan et al. studied the use of ILA at a fire scene [37]. The authors showed that the ILA indicator dye did not perform as well as they would have expected. As a matter of fact, among many substrates with different ignitable liquids on them, it indicated only a paint thinner on carpet. Moreover, their research also included a part in which the absorbing capability of ILA was tested. In this regard, they found that it absorbed paint thinner and camp fuel in five out of six and in four out of six wood panels, respectively. However, they noted that the amount of recovered ignitable liquid is quite small compared to the amount that was present on the panel before the collection. Finally, the ILA did not absorb any gasoline from wood panels, even though gasoline was still there before and after the ILA was applied.

The degree of false positives and false negatives produced by ILA has not been evaluated. Research and the ILA literature warns the user that pyrolysis products might be absorbed and might turn the indicator dye to blue [34, 35]. Thus, the user needs to interpret the pattern exhibited by the indicator dye to develop his or her opinion regarding the presence of ignitable liquids. No study has evaluated the proper recovery of ignitable liquids from ILA. One important aspect of ILA is the fact the original powder formula melts at about 69°C [32]. This might be a serious inconvenience during the extraction process as many laboratories usually proceed at temperatures above 70°C [38]. In such instances, the extraction processes would have to be performed at lower temperatures, resulting in a lower recovery of heavy compounds. More information is provided in Chapter 11 about the extraction techniques used in fire debris analysis. Another issue is the compatibility of ILA with different solvents. If, for the reason explained earlier, a headspace technique is not suitable to extract ignitable liquids from ILA, a solvent extraction would be the next best solution. Unfortunately, ILA is composed of petroleum-based polymers, and therefore, will be dissolved in most solvents used in fire debris analysis.

Before ILA can be used on a routine basis to absorb ILR and to collect them for laboratory analysis, more research needs to be performed and published. This research must address the absorption of ignitable liquid by ILA, and the extraction of these liquids from ILA for fire debris analysis. Until this occurs, the fire scene investigator should use ILA with great caution and make the laboratory analyst aware of its use.

5.7 ULTRAVIOLET DETECTION

5.7.1 Background

The use of ultraviolet (UV) light to detect pour patterns of ignitable liquids at fire scenes has been reported as early as the mid 1970s [39]. Yet, this technique never underwent a tremendous development for this application and, as a result, no formal research has ever been published demonstrating the use of this technique at fire scenes. This is probably because it is relatively inefficient. Recent developments, published by Saitoh and Takeuchi, are very interesting and offer a promising future for the UV detection of stains of ignitable liquid [40]. However, it requires the use of a time-resolved fluorescence system equipped with a pulsed Nd-YAG laser, which is quite complex and expensive equipment that is not designed to be operated in the field [40].

5.7.2 Operating Principle

Most ignitable liquids are petroleum-based and, thus, contain many compounds that fluoresce when exposed to UV light. The fluorescence of a compound is intimately linked to the presence of double bonds. In general, the more conjugated double bonds, the more intense the fluorescence. As a result, aromatics, and more particularly polynuclear aromatics, exhibit interesting and intense fluorescence spectra. This is the concept behind the detection of ignitable liquids with UV light. Figure 5-22 shows the emission and excitation spectra of gasoline and diesel fuel. Notice the similarities between the fluorescence of the liquids.

The fluorescence of a chemical compound is due to the displacement of electrons from the electron clouds present around the atoms. More information on the phenomenon of fluorescence is presented in Chapter 13. Takeuchi et al. showed that gasoline, kerosene, and diesel fuel fluoresce in the spectral range between UV and the shorter wavelengths of the visible range [41].

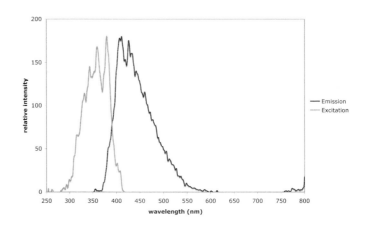

FIGURE 5-22a

Excitation and emission spectra of gasoline. Excitation spectrum was obtained with observation fixed at 408 nm and emission spectrum was obtained with excitation fixed at 355 nm.

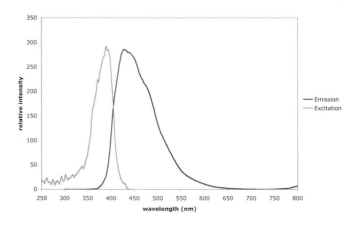

FIGURE 5-22b

Excitation and emission spectra of diesel fuel. Excitation spectrum was obtained with observation fixed at 430 nm and emission spectrum was obtained with excitation fixed at 355 nm.

5.7.3 Use

The original (and unfortunately not very fruitful) use of such a technique is pretty simple. Any portable UV light is suitable for use. It is a good idea to find a light source that is capable of producing both long and short UV [42]. Long UV ranges from approximately 300 to 400 nm and short UV from 200 to 300 nm. It is necessary to operate UV light wearing safety goggles, as UV light will damage the eyes upon exposure. Also, it is necessary to operate UV light in (almost) total darkness, and if necessary, the scene can be darkened by using black polyethylene sheets. Lane recommends the use of a 4-mil black polyethylene sheet [39].

It is possible to photograph fluorescing patterns and surfaces. As the emitted light is in the visible range, it is not necessary to obtain particular photographic equipment to record it: A regular camera is suitable. When using conventional photography, high-speed films (800 ISO or higher) or a very long exposure time (60 seconds and above) may be required as the fluorescence is often very weak, and these techniques might compensate for the low light condition. It is important to remember that a more powerful UV light source might also greatly help with photography conditions. When the fluorescence permits it, a system composed of two cameras can be used. Although both cameras record the fluorescence, one is then turned off and a quick flash is given and recorded by the second camera. This provides two photographs, one with the fluorescence only and one with the background and the fluorescence. This technique has been described for luminol by Mosher and Engels [43]. It is important to keep in mind that the fluorescence of ignitable liquid is most often extremely weak and, thus, this technique may not apply in most instances. This is the reason why it had been forgotten for many years.

Recently, Takeuchi et al. performed some extensive research on the visualization of petroleum-based ignitable liquids by fluorescence [41]. They showed that it was possible to observe the fluorescence of gasoline, kerosene, and diesel fuel under UV light with an image-intensified CCD camera. They also determined that the fluorescence lifetime of petroleum-based ignitable liquids was much longer than those exhibited by common background materials (paper, cotton glove, and carpet). The fluorescence lifetime for ignitable liquids ranges from 6.4 to 26.8 ns, and the lifetime for background materials ranges from 1.5 to 4.8 ns [40]. Thus, they developed a system based on time-resolved fluorescence imagery. Because the fluorescence of petroleum products is actually very weak, a simple UV light does not suffice to produce a recordable image. Thus, Saitoh and Takeuchi use a Nd:YAG laser as an excitation source at mostly 266 nm [40]. As a result, they were able to clearly observe the presence of gasoline, kerosene, and diesel fuel stains on unburned and on some burned materials.

5.7.4 Advantages and Drawbacks

If the mere use of a UV light at a scene was as successful as it is simple, it would be used every single day at fire scenes. Unfortunately, this is not the case and there has been no formal scientific research published validating the use of UV light to detect ILR. The reasons for that are probably three-fold:

I. Fluorescence phenomena occur only with particular molecules having the ability to produce fluorescence. Although most ignitable liquids are petroleum-based and contain some aromatics capable of fluorescing, their emitted fluorescence is extremely weak. Thus, it may not be detectable when excited with a simple UV light under the conditions encountered in fire investigation.

II. Fluorescence of ignitable liquids may be significantly hampered when the ignitable liquid is spread and absorbed onto a substrate. The substrate may act as a quencher to the fluorescence of the ignitable liquid. Thus, the liquid's fluorescence might be further diminished.

III. Molecules among ignitable liquid that are most likely to fluoresce are aromatics. When modern polymers burn, they produce a great number of aromatic products through pyrolysis. This means that the substrate contains many different aromatic compounds adsorbed onto it. Even unburned, substrates fluoresce mostly above 400 nm, but main peaks of fluorescence are observed under 400 nm for gasoline, kerosene, and diesel fuel [40]. As a result, the whole substrate might fluoresce, which requires the time-resolved imagery to distinguish it from the fluorescence of ignitable liquids.

The research undertaken by Saitoh and Takeuchi is extremely promising, however it uses much more complicated equipment (Nd:YAG laser and time-resolved imagery) than merely UV light [40, 41]. This technique appears valid, however its complex equipment will certainly not lead to routine use.

In any case, the criminalist receiving samples identified as positive by the fire investigator under UV light should not expect these samples to be either positive or negative.

5.8 PORTABLE GAS-CHROMATOGRAPH (-MASS SPECTROMETER)

Technological advances in gas chromatography and mass spectrometry led to the miniaturization of the instruments and to the increase of their portability. Today, portable gas chromatographs and gas chromatograph-mass spectrometers are available. For example, the Hapsite field portable gas chromatograph-mass spectrometer (Inficon, East Syracuse, New York,

USA) weighs approximately 20 kg and is one of the most advanced portable GC-MS systems [44, 45]. Other less expensive systems do not include a mass spectrometer, such as the Photovac Voyager (Photovac Inc., Waltham, Massachusetts, USA), which offers PID detection or the Automated Field Systems hand-held gas chromatograph, equipped with detectors based on the MEMS technology. Chapter 8 is dedicated to the analysis of fire debris by GC and GC-MS, so no further details of their operating principles are presented here.

The advantage of bringing the laboratory to the scene lies in the rapidity at which results are generated for the field investigator. The investigator can sample debris from the scene and have quasi-live results whether ignitable liquids are present or not. With the advance of fast GC technology, most of these portable systems run chromatograms in a couple of minutes or in less than one minute in some instances. Some systems have an integrated headspace sampling probe.

These systems are relatively recent and require a good knowledge of chemistry and chromatographic techniques to be used optimally. Thus, in the rare instances where these systems are used, it is usually crime laboratory personnel operating them, rather than fire investigators. It should be noted that most of these systems presently are applied in fire investigation at the experimental stage rather than the operational stage. Very little literature has been published with regard to the fire debris analysis application. Casamento et al. presented a very recent study where the Inficon Hapsite was tested and compared to a benchtop GC-MS system [46]. They concluded that the major limitations of the system were the temperature range at which it operates and the sampling program. They also showed that the chromatographic resolution of the system did not reach the same level as the one exhibited by a benchtop instrument. Finally, they recommend several improvements to this instrument prior to its use in the field, where it should be operated by someone familiar with chromatographic techniques, such as a chemist.

REFERENCES

1. Lee HC (1982) *Identification and grouping of bloodstains*. In: *Forensic science handbook*, editor Saferstein R, Prentice Hall Regents, Englewood Cliffs, NJ.
2. Kurz ME et al. (1994) Evaluation of canines for accelerant detection at fire scenes, *Journal of Forensic Sciences*, **39**(6), pp 1528–36.
3. International Association of Arson Investigators Forensic Science Committee (1995) IAAI Forensic Science Committee position on the use of accelerant detection canines, *Journal of Forensic Sciences*, **40**(4), pp 532–4.
4. National Fire Protection Association (2004) *NFPA 921 guide for fire and explosion investigations*, Quincy, MA.
5. Putorti Jr AD (1997) *Full scale room burn pattern study*, National Institute of Justice, Law Enforcement and Corrections Standards and Testing Program, Washington, DC.

6. Putorti Jr AD (2001) *Flammable and combustible liquid spill/burn patterns*, National Institute of Justice, Office of Science and Technology, Washington, DC.

7. Byron MM (1982) Three commonly used accelerant detectors, *The National Fire & Arson Report*, **1**(2), pp 6–14.

8. Hilliard R and Thomas C (1976) The combustible gas detector (sniffer): An evaluation, *Arson Analysis Newsletter*, **26**, pp 48–50.

9. Casamento S et al. (2005) The use of accelerant detection aids at the fire scene, *17th Meeting of the International Association of Forensic Sciences*, Hong Kong, China.

10. Yinon J (2003) Detection of explosives by electronic noses, *Analytical Chemistry*, **75**(5), pp 99A–105A.

11. Conner L (2005) *Evaluation of field sampling and analysis methods for fire investigation including electronic noses and adsorption sampling/gas chromatography mass spectrometry*, Master's thesis, Florida International University, Miami, FL.

12. Bacharach Inc. (1990) *Instruction manual TLV sniffer*, Instruction 23-9613, Rev. 2, Pittsburgh, PA.

13. Scott Instruments (2002) *TLV sniffer: Portable combustible gas survey & arson investigation instrument*, application note, Pittsburgh, PA.

14. Pragmatics (2004) http://www.pragmatics-arson.com/, last access performed on September 30, 2004.

15. McNair HM and Bonelli EJ (1969) *Basic gas chromatography*, Varian, Palo Alto, CA.

16. Skoog DA and Leary JJ (1992) *Principles of instrumental analysis*, 4th edition, Saunders College Publishing, Fort Worth, TX.

17. Scott/Bacharach (year unknown) *The TLV sniffer and arson investigation*, Tech notes, Pittsburgh, PA.

18. Conner L, Chin S, and Furton KG (2006) Evaluation of field sampling techniques including electronic noses and a dynamic headspace sampler for use in fire investigations, *Sensors and Actuators B*, **116**(1–2), pp 121–9.

19. Dräger Safety (2005) *Draeger-tubes® and accuro® pump*, Draeger Safety, Inc., Pittsburg, PA.

20. DeHaan JD (1997) *Kirk's fire investigation*, 4th edition, Brady Prentice Hall, Upper Saddle River, NJ.

21. Gregory C (1998) STAR le premier chien d'investigation sur incendies d'Europe, *Pol Cant Information—Bulletin de la Police cantonale vaudoise* (33), pp 23–5.

22. Berluti AF (1989) Sniffing through the ashes, *Fire & Arson Investigator*, **4**(June), pp 31–5.

23. Whitstine WH (1992) *Sniffing the ashes—K-9's in the fire service*, International Society of Fire Service Instructors, Ashland, MA.

24. Furton KG and Myers LJ (2001) The scientific foundation and efficacy of the use of canines as chemical detectors for explosives, *Talanta*, **54**(3), pp 487–500.

25. Jacobs S (1993) K-9 s prove their worth, *Fire & Arson Investigator*, **Spring**, p 50.

26. Schultz BW, Ercoli JM, and Cerven JF (1996) Letter to the editor: Commentary on "Evaluation of canines for accelerant detection at fire scenes", *Journal of Forensic Sciences*, **41**(2), p 187.

27. Tindall R and Lothridge K (1995) An evaluation of 42 accelerant detection canine teams, *Journal of Forensic Sciences*, **40**(4), pp 561–4.

28. Kurz ME et al. (1996) Effect of background interference on accelerant detection by canines, *Journal of Forensic Sciences*, **41**(5), pp 868–73.

29. Tranthim-Fryer DJ and DeHaan JD (1997) Canine accelerant detectors and problems with carpet pyrolysis products, *Science & Justice*, **37**(1), pp 39–46.
30. Katz SR and Midkiff CR (1998) Unconfirmed canine accelerant detection: A reliability issue in court, *Journal of Forensic Sciences*, **43**(2), pp 329–33.
31. Woodland JH (2003) *Method and composition for detecting ignitable liquids*, United States patent US 6,537,497 B1, March 25, 2003.
32. Ancarro (2004) *MSDS for ignitable liquid absorbent*, Ancarro, Indianola, IA.
33. Woodland JH (2006) Change in composition of ILA, *personal communication to Eric Stauffer*, November 3, 2006.
34. Woodland JH (2004) *Manual of ILA*, Ancarro, Indianola, IA.
35. Byron DE (2004) An introduction to the new Ignitable Liquid Absorbent (ILA), *Fire and Arson Investigator*, **54**(3), pp 31–2.
36. Thomas SA, Lee S, and Najam A (2004) Ignitable Liquid Absorbent (ILA): A new collection tool for fire investigators at the crime scene, *4th Annual TWGFEX Symposium on Fire and Explosion Debris Analysis and Scene Investigation*, Orlando, FL.
37. Nowlan M, Stuart AW, Basara GJ, and Sandercock PML (2007) Use of a solid absorbent and an accelerant detection canine for the detection of ignitable liquid burned in a structure fire, *Journal of Forensic Sciences*, **52**(3), pp 643–8.
38. Tindall Newman R, Dietz WR, and Lothridge K (1996) The use of activated charcoal strips for fire debris extractions by passive diffusion. Part 1: The effects of time, temperature, strip size, and sample concentration, *Journal of Forensic Sciences*, **41**(3), pp 361–70.
39. Lane CM (1975) Ultra-violet light—Gem or junk?, *Fire and Arson Investigator*, **26**, pp 40–2.
40. Saitoh N and Takeuchi S (2005) Fluorescence imaging of petroleum accelerants by time-resolved spectroscopy with a pulsed Nd-YAG laser, *Forensic Science International*, **163**(1–2), pp 38–50.
41. Takeuchi S et al. (2005) Visualization of petroleum accelerants in arson cases, *17th Meeting of the International Association of Forensic Sciences*, Hong Kong, China.
42. Ultra-Violet Products Inc. (1997) *Use of ultraviolet light in arson detection*, Application bulletin UVP-AB-107, Upland, CA.
43. Mosher SL and Engels R (1994) Luminol photography, *IABPA News*, **10**(4), pp 7–16.
44. Inficon (2004) *Hapsite chemical identification system*, Inficon, East Syracuse, NY.
45. Casamento S et al. (2005) Evaluation of a portable gas chromatograph for the detection of ignitable liquids, *Canadian Society of Forensic Science Journal*, **38**(4), pp 191–203.
46. Casamento S et al. (2005) The Hapsite: A portable GCMS for accelerant detection, *17th Meeting of the International Association of Forensic Sciences*, Hong Kong, China.

CHAPTER 6

Sample Collection

"... the investigator should be certain to send as much of the evidence as possible. It is far better to send a whole rug rather than a small piece, a half a door rather than a small panel from it, ..."

Brendan P. Battle and Paul B. Weston, Arson:
A handbook of detection and investigation (1954)

6.1 INTRODUCTION

The role of the criminalist at a fire scene may vary from agency to agency, and from scene to scene. At the vast majority of fire scenes, even those in which evidence is collected for forensic examination, laboratory personnel are seldom present. In some organizations, laboratory personnel trained in the examination of fire debris for the presence of ILR may routinely be dispatched to scenes to assist in the origin and cause determination and are responsible for all aspects surrounding evidence collection. Still other agencies may provide laboratory assistance to fire scene investigators only when circumstances dictate, such as major fire losses or fires involving chemicals.

Regardless of a fire debris analyst's involvement in actual fire scene processing, it is imperative that all laboratory personnel tasked with the forensic analysis of fire debris have a general understanding of the evidence collection process. They must understand how evidence is selected, collected, preserved, and transported, and how these processes can potentially affect their findings. In addition, many examiners are called upon to provide training to field investigators regarding various aspects of evidence collection and preservation. Investigators often look to the scientists in the laboratory as experts in evidence collection and expect them to be able to provide guidance on various issues regarding the samples ultimately submitted to the laboratory. Therefore, even for the criminalist who may never set foot on a fire scene, there is a need to understand the different steps pertaining to fire scene evidence and related issues in order to be well versed in fire debris analysis.

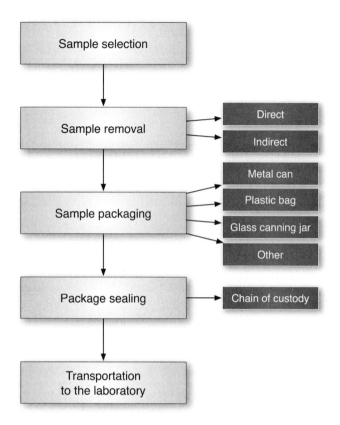

The collection of fire debris is a process that includes several steps as shown in Figure 6-1. It spans from the selection of the debris, usually based on one of the techniques presented in Chapter 5, to its transportation to the forensic laboratory. This chapter describes each step in detail.

6.2 SAMPLE SELECTION

6.2.1 Making the Right Choice

The proper collection of evidence first begins with the determination of the best sample to collect. The selection of appropriate evidence is affected by many factors, such as the ignitable liquid properties, the substrate properties, and the location and configuration of the sample. Chapter 5 covered the different tools and techniques used by the fire investigator at the fire scene to determine the possible presence of ignitable liquids. However, these tools and techniques have a great propensity for both false negative and false positive responses, therefore their utility may be limited [1].

Once the investigator determines an area of origin, it is important to carefully select the exact samples to be taken. In some instances, the area of origin can be as small as a few square decimeters. In other instances, it can be as large as a room. The selection of a sample is based mostly on the location where it is suspected that an ignitable liquid has been poured. However, within that region, it is important to take into account other factors, such as the properties of the different substrates constituting the area. These factors must be thoroughly understood as they apply to the preservation of evidence as well.

6.2.2 Consideration of Ignitable Liquid Properties

The properties of ignitable liquids govern not only the selection of appropriate samples, but also the development of guidelines to prevent the loss of the possibly present ignitable liquids and to avoid contamination. Volatility is the major factor affecting the survivability of ignitable liquids, their potential for loss between the times of collection and processing, and the possibility of their contamination.

Volatility significantly affects how a liquid fuel burns and its potential for having detectable quantities that survive a fire. It is this property that also makes ignitable liquids valuable fuels and effective accelerants. More volatile liquids, such as a light petroleum distillate-type camp stove fuel, vaporize more readily during the combustion process, and thus, burn more easily, quickly, and completely than a less volatile product, such as the heavy petroleum distillate diesel fuel. Therefore, there is proportionally less of a more volatile product that survives the combustion process.

A second factor to consider is postfire survivability. Although it is recommended that the investigation take place and samples be collected as soon as possible after the fire, this is not always feasible. Thus, it is important to consider the effect that volatility has on the postfire survival of ILR. All conditions being equal, by definition, more volatile liquids evaporate more readily than less volatile liquids. Consequently, the postfire survivability of more volatile products—those referred to as "light"—will not be as good as that of the "heavy" products, those which tend to evaporate less readily. Naturally, the fire investigator and the laboratory personnel have no control over the type of ignitable liquids used at the fire scene; however they must understand the concepts of volatility and survivability when interpreting results of ILR analysis.

6.2.3 Consideration of Substrate Properties

One other key factor in the survivability of ILR is the type of substrate on which these are found along with its configuration and location relative to the fire (see next subsection). Absorbent materials, such as carpet and wood, are good at retaining ignitable liquids. Because an ignitable liquid can soak into an absorbent, rather than merely remaining on its surface, a portion of the liquid is somewhat protected from direct exposure to the fire. A less absorbent, or nonporous, material provides less protection for the ignitable liquid, and consequently does not retain ILR as well. In addition to the degree to which a substrate can protect a residue, the nature of the substrate material may also affect the survival of an ILR and the ability to detect it. During a fire, a highly complex synthetic matrix undergoes pyrolysis and partial combustion leading to breakdown products, which may interfere with the ability to identify low levels of ILR (see Chapters 4 and 12).

Other substrates causing concerns to the fire debris analyst include soils and organic matter containing microbes capable of breaking down petroleum products. Soil is usually considered a very good substrate for the retention of ILR. Additionally, it is relatively free of contamination, which renders the interpretation of the chromatograms fairly easy. In spite of this, microbial degradation of ILR in soil has been shown to occur in as little as three days [2]. This may result in the consumption of an ignitable liquid to the extent that it cannot be identified. This degradation of petroleum products does not necessarily take place in all soil samples; it is dependent upon the types of microbes naturally present in the particular soil. Thus, one must be careful when collecting soil samples and ensure that they are transported to the laboratory in the shortest possible amount of time. Additionally, soil samples should be frozen during transportation or as soon as they arrive at the laboratory in order to retard the degradation caused to hydrocarbons within the sample.

6.2.4 Consideration of Sample Location

Finally, the physical position of a material should be considered when selecting samples. Samples that are protected from the fire can better retain ILR than those that are exposed to the fire. Similarly, samples found at lower levels often contain a greater quantity of ILR due to the natural spread of a liquid by gravity.

When considering the origin of the fire, the investigator should not take the most burned part as a sample. If the substrate is charred completely beyond recognition, there is little chance that any ignitable liquid has survived. When ignitable liquids are poured on floor coverings, they burn often leaving some sort of pool pattern (see Chapter 4). If extinguished early enough in the fire, this pattern presents neat delineation between the burned and unburned material. When collecting from such a pattern, it is important to obtain material from the edge of the pattern [3]. Usually, it is possible to cut a rectangle with one-half burned and one-half unburned. It is also crucial to take as much of the underlay as possible as the liquid usually travels downward by gravity and lower levels are typically more protected. Figures 6-2a and 6-2b present an example of the proper selection of an area from such a burn pattern.

FIGURE 6-2a

The best samples usually are found at the edge of the burn and should contain about half of the substrate burned and half unburned. This photograph shows the burn pattern before collection of samples.

FIGURE 6-2b

This photograph has been taken after collection of the samples to illustrate their exact locations. On the left, the sample was chosen to include deep layers from the baseboard, a location where ignitable liquids often seep through the cracks and where residues may be well-preserved. On the right, the sample was taken at the edge of the burn pattern to include a burned and an unburned portion. (Photographs courtesy of H. Kelly Wilson, Rimkus Consulting Group, Atlanta, Georgia, USA.)

It is always crucial to think logically when choosing the right location to collect the sample. The liquid will find any interstices to seep through the floorboard or floor coverings by gravity. This is why it is important to collect samples with a certain depth of material. Also, if dealing with items such as floorboards, baseboards, or thresholds, it is good practice to collect underlying material to ensure that all possible liquids that would have seeped through are found. Finally, when dealing with floor coverings present on top of concrete slab, it is good practice, although not as easy, also to sample the first few centimeters of concrete rather than the floor covering only.

6.3 SAMPLE REMOVAL

6.3.1 General Principle

The actual process of extracting the evidence from the fire scene varies depending on the nature of the evidence. Often evidence collected for determination of ILR is a sample removed from a larger item such as a piece of carpet, wood, or furniture. Other times, the entire item may be collected, such as glass fragments from a Molotov cocktail or ignition devices. It is also possible to collect only ILR at the scene without taking the debris. So, two different sampling processes can be defined:

- *Direct*: When the substrate itself is removed and preserved as evidence, along with its ILR content.
- *Indirect*: When only the possible ILR portion of the sample is collected via an absorbing medium, which is preserved as evidence.

The majority of debris is collected by direct sampling and forwarded to the crime laboratory as is. However, some investigators favor the collection of a sample by indirect sampling. In some instances, indirect sampling may be the only practical technique. Therefore, the criminalist must be aware of the differences between the two techniques so he or she will not be surprised when receiving particular samples at the laboratory.

6.3.2 Documentation

Regardless of the nature of the evidence, an important part of the collection process is documentation. Documentation of evidence collection is part of the scene examination documentation and should include notes, sketches, and photographs. Sketches or diagrams are often the most useful way of showing the location from which a sample was taken. The investigator's notes may supplement the diagram and should include evidence locations with measurements and the types of material taken. Photographs of the evidence should be taken before its collection, showing it in place (as shown in Figure 6-2).

Additional photographs may be useful as well; many agencies take photographs during the collection of the debris and of the packaged evidence as well. The extent of photographic documentation should be dictated by policy and commonsense; if something needs to be shown, it should be photographed. Photography should include overall shots to aid in determining relative location in addition to the close-up shots necessary to provide sufficient detail of the sample itself. Documentation of standard procedures, such as putting on new gloves, is generally not necessary, but may provide an added level of comfort for some (see Section 6.5).

6.3.3 Direct Sampling

The goal of direct sampling is to get a portion of material from the fire scene into a container. Samples of materials that are easily subdivided, such as soil and some debris, may simply be picked up and placed into an appropriate container. More commonly, a sample must be removed from a larger item. Materials such as carpeting, flooring, baseboards and furniture will require cutting, breaking, disassembling, or pulling apart to get a sample of appropriate size. In these situations, the use of tools often is required; shovels, rakes, saws, chisels, hammers, drills, and even chainsaws are some of the tools that may be used to aid in the collection of samples from a fire scene. When using tools, especially reusable tools, the investigator must be aware of contamination issues (see Subsection 6.3.7). Other materials may pose more of a challenge.

When samples are removed from larger items, such as carpeting or flooring, sample size should be taken into consideration. A bigger sample is not always better. If the sample seems to have a relatively high concentration of ignitable liquid, a large sample is not needed: A sample of approximately 100 cm^2 would be appropriate. If there is no discernible odor, it may be useful to collect a larger sample. When selecting the sample, the investigator should keep in mind the limitations of the size of the container to be used, and aim for a sample that will fill the container to no more than two-thirds to three-quarters full, in order to allow for adequate headspace, which is an important concern to the laboratory analyst.

6.3.4 Indirect Sampling

A/ Generic Powders

Porous materials such as concrete may have absorbed/adsorbed ignitable liquids, but are more difficult to sample. As always, the best evidence is the actual material itself; therefore, when possible, either a chisel or a core-style drill bit should be used to collect a sample of concrete. When this is not feasible, it has been shown that ignitable liquids can be collected in the field through the use of an absorbent/adsorbent material.[1] Tontarski recommends the use of flour, calcium carbonate, or sweeping compounds [4]. However, it is crucial not to use self-rising flour, which may release carbon dioxide and lead to the bursting of the evidence container. When using sweeping compounds, Tontarski warns the user regarding scented compounds [4]. These contain volatile compounds that may interfere with the chromatogram. ILA also is advertised as a tool used to collect ILR (see later) [5]. Cat litter (constituted of clay) has also been recommended [6]. Other materials may be more efficient at collecting sample vapors, but these materials offer the significant advantage of being readily available. All absorbent/adsorbent materials should be validated for such applications prior to their use. In any case, it is important for the fire investigator to submit a blank sample of the absorbing/adsorbing material with the fire debris sample.

To collect a sample using an absorbent/adsorbent material, the collection material is sprinkled on the area of interest for a period of time (usually minimum 30 minutes to approximately 1 hour) to allow absorption to take place. This material is then simply swept up and packaged. It is important to ensure that the surface is quite dry, otherwise the material may clump together and the presence of water may prevent a proper absorption/adsorption of ILR. It is recommended to extract these absorbent/adsorbent materials using a passive or active headspace extraction (see Chapter 11).

B/ Portable Arson Sampler

Another product designed to aid the investigator in recovering ignitable liquid residues samples is the Portable Arson Sample or P_AS (Portable Arson Samplers, Tooele, Utah, USA). This product is marketed as a means of performing a dynamic extraction of debris in the field [7]. It is based on the use of an adsorption tube, which has been described previously in the literature [8]. The apparatus consists of a reusable chamber lined with Teflon. The debris is placed in the chamber, which is heated. The chamber is connected to a vacuum system, pumping the headspace above the sample area through a tube filled with adsorbent, usually activated charcoal or Tenax, thus trapping the vapors. Figure 6-3 is an illustration of a P_AS. The temperature of the chamber and the extraction time can be directly set on the instrument. Usually, a temperature of 60°C and an extraction time of at least 10 minutes are recommended.

This sampling device aims to simplify the collection of evidence by sampling the vapors rather than the substrate material itself. When the P_AS is used, the investigator would submit only the adsorbent tubes rather than the actual debris. The main advantage of this device is the tremendous

---

[1] It is not always clear if these materials absorb or adsorb ILR. A recent study claims that clay does both; however it fails to substantiate this statement. For this reason, both terms are used in this particular instance.

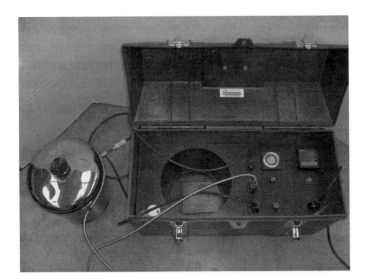

FIGURE 6-3

A Portable Arson Sampler is a device used to collect indirect samples of ILR at fire scenes. (Photograph courtesy of Laura Conner.)

difference in the size of the evidence to be brought back to the lab. Twenty adsorbent tubes fit in one pocket whereas 20 one-gallon cans take half the size of a car's trunk. Additionally, this results in the production of samples that require only desorption, rather than a comprehensive extraction at the laboratory, a situation most advantageous for routine work in a high-volume laboratory. According to the literature advertising the device, another advantage is that the chamber can be placed over a surface in an inverted position and the system turned on [9]. In this fashion, it is possible to collect headspace from a surface (such as concrete) without having to dig into the material.

Individual dynamic sampling in the field, while offering the advantage of minimizing the time delay between the fire and the extraction of a sample and avoiding the need for transportation of bulky samples of fire debris, results in new challenges to the investigator, including an increase in the investigator's time for sampling, contamination concerns (such as the chamber cleaning procedure), as well as sample preservation issues. One main issue is the fact that the debris is not collected as evidence, and therefore, cannot be evaluated by the fire debris analyst at the laboratory. This will very likely result in a much more limited interpretation of the data by the criminalist. Additionally, this indirect sampling technique may result in insufficient extraction of the debris, and therefore, poor recovery of ILR [10]. Conner et al. also determined that the P_AS is not the most suitable method to collect low levels of ILR as well as heavy ignitable liquids such as diesel, due to their low vapor pressures [11]. Nonetheless, she observed that the use of the device in an inverted fashion on concrete surface was particularly efficient, except for heavy compounds [11]. Practical application of field sampling through a product such as the P_AS would necessitate the development of guidelines to ensure that contamination due to the reusable sample chamber would not occur and that some means of evidence preservation takes place. In addition, its sensitivity limit must be well known and compared to standard laboratory extraction techniques (see Chapter 11).

C/ Ignitable Liquid Absorbent

More recently, another product designed for passive adsorption in the field has been introduced. The product called Ignitable Liquid Absorbent or ILA (Ancarro, Indianola, Iowa, USA) is an absorbent/adsorbent material designed not only to indicate the presence of an ignitable liquid residue at a fire scene, but also to absorb/adsorb the residue for later testing by a laboratory. It was extensively described in Section 5.6. ILA is essentially a method for performing a passive adsorption-style extraction in the field with the aid of a visible indicator to assist in sample selection. For that matter, it is an upgraded version of the absorbent/adsorbent powders presented earlier. A recent paper studied a few absorbing/adsorbing powders and determined that cat litter (clay) was more efficient than calcium sulfate, baking soda, and the original formulation of ILA [6].

Although ILA is intended to collect and trap the vapors of ILR, the marketing literature still recommends that the substrate be collected as well, which can only be considered as sage advice [5]. Before the investigator decides to use ILA in actual casework, it is advised that independent research be conducted to verify that it functions as intended. Finally, before utilizing any new collection medium, the investigator should check with the laboratory conducting the analysis to ensure that it will accept evidence of that type and to determine its impact on the interpretation of the results.

D/ Swabbing

Another common means of collecting ILR from a fire scene is through swabbing. The most commonly used materials for swabbing are gauze pads marketed for first aid use and cotton tipped applicators. Because these materials are not specifically marketed for this application, it is imperative that sample of an unused swab be submitted along with the collected samples to serve as a comparison sample (see Subsection 6.3.6). This is important because some cotton-tipped applicators have been shown to contain isoparaffinic products, and some gauze pads have been shown to contain heavy petroleum distillate products, specifically those marketed as nonadhering. Swabbing is most applicable when there is a relatively high concentration of ignitable liquid on a surface that may not be amenable to removal. To collect a sample via swabbing, the investigator rubs the surface of interest with the selected swabbing medium, then packages the swab in a container suitable for ILR samples. Swabs generally should not be moistened prior to use.

E/ Others and Future Developments

Mann and Putaansuu describe a technique that consists in creating an "impermeable" volume above the surface to be sampled with nylon bags into which an activated charcoal strip is placed [6]. The volume is then heated with a halogen light. However, although this method appears efficient with low-boiling point compounds, it is not sufficient to collect heavier compounds such as the ones found in heavy petroleum distillates [6]. Interestingly, this method was developed to sample ILR from concrete, however it is much more efficient and prudent to collect concrete samples using a hammer and a chisel. Since concrete constitutes one of the best supports not only for retaining ILR but also for extracting ILR (because of its low interference) at the laboratory, it would be unwise not to collect the sample directly.

Research continues with the hope of developing field sampling products that will maximize the chances of ILR recovery. Although many means of sampling exist, it is important to recognize the fact that when new techniques are introduced, new quality assurance needs arise. By its nature, indirect sampling prevents the laboratory analyst from selecting the most advantageous extraction procedure for a specific sample. Additionally, contamination becomes of even greater concern, as highly adsorptive media are present in the environment of a fire scene. For these reasons, it is important that a proactive approach be taken with the development of quality assurance and quality control procedures to use these products. Regardless of how samples are collected—whether extracted in the field or simply packaged—it is imperative that the submission of samples be done in a manner acceptable to the laboratory performing the fire debris examination.

6.3.5 Sampling on Suspects

Sometimes, a suspect in an arson case quickly is identified and arrested. In such instances, it may be desirable to examine his or her clothing, shoes, and hands for traces of an ignitable liquid that may have been used during the commission of the arson. As a matter of fact, it is not uncommon for an arsonist using ignitable liquid to come in contact with it at some point, usually during the pouring of the liquid at the scene [12].

The collection of shoes and clothing must be carried out right away—as soon as the suspect is identified and in custody. Each item must be packaged separately (one shoe per package, one clothing item per package) in the same containers as the ones used for fire debris analysis. Generally, only the outer layers of clothing should be submitted (i.e., not underwear), unless circumstances dictate otherwise. These items are then forwarded to the laboratory. The criminalist must be extremely careful when interpreting results from clothing and, most particularly, shoes. This will be discussed in Chapter 12.

Although collecting shoes and clothing is a relatively simple task, it is not quite the same when one needs to collect ILR from a person's hands. In this instance, the sampling must be indirect, however it still needs to be carried out as soon as possible since more than 90% of the gasoline present on someone's hand is lost within 30 minutes [13]. Additionally, when the hands are washed with soap and water, up to 85% of the initial amount of gasoline may be lost [13]. Several procedures to collect ILR from hands have been recently studied. The use of a gauze pad impregnated with pentane swiped on the hands has shown to be extremely inefficient and thus is not recommended [14]. When one wants to collect ILR from hands, the technique of wearing disposable gloves on the hands for a given time is most efficient.

Darrer used PVC gloves in her study and Rolph et al. prescribe nitrile gloves [13, 15, 16]. In a very recent study, Montani demonstrated that both PVC and nitrile gloves exhibited significant interferences and were not suitable for collecting ILR from hands [14]. Important amounts of mostly heavy petroleum distillates were present in the background of these gloves. She found that latex gloves (powdered and powder-free) offered the least amount of interferences.[2] She developed a very convenient kit comprised of the following items placed in a metallic quart-can [14]:

- A pair of gloves (powder-free latex gloves from VWR International) used by the person conducting the collection. These gloves constitute the control sample.
- Another pair of identical gloves used by the person whose hands are examined. This person wears the gloves for about 20 minutes.
- Two nylon bags used for fire debris into which each pair of gloves is placed after use. The bags are then sealed and forwarded to the laboratory.

Gloves are extracted using passive headspace concentration extraction with an activated charcoal strip (see Chapter 11). A metallic frame is placed in the bags prior to the extraction in order to guarantee a good exposure of the glove's surface to the headspace.

Another technique presented consists of placing the suspect's hand into a vapor-tight bag and sampling the contents via solid phase microextraction (SPME) [17]. Unfortunately, there are some practical limitations associated with this technique, and consequently, it has not gained widespread use.

Sester et al. observed that when filling a tank, contamination of hands with gasoline occurred [18, 19]. However, a more recent study showed that among eight people filling a jerrycan of gasoline, none exhibited a detectable level of gasoline on their hands [14]. The same recent study showed that

---

[2] One must be careful with people who are allergic to latex and take all necessary dispositions in this regard.

among eight people who had actually poured gasoline from a container, only one exhibited clear identifiable gasoline on his hands [14]. Regarding clothing, studies have shown that contamination of clothing may very well occur during the pouring of an ignitable liquid. This is particularly true for the lower half of the body and for the shoes, as demonstrated by Coulson and Morgan-Smith [20]. Whereas the persistence of gasoline on hands is very limited, clothing retains it longer, where it may last up to a couple of days [12, 21].

Forensic scientists in crime laboratories should make an effort to discuss with their fire investigators the various methods of collecting ILR on suspects' hands. It may prove beneficial to provide fire investigators with a kit for this purpose, and to train them regarding its proper use.

6.3.6 Comparison Samples

There are several reasons why it is a good practice to collect comparison samples for each type of evidence. A comparison sample can provide information to the laboratory analyst regarding what is normally present in a specific substrate material [22]. There are numerous examples of common household materials containing detectable levels of petroleum products [23]. Without an appropriate comparison sample, it is difficult for the analyst to form an opinion as to whether or not a recovered ignitable liquid is incidental or foreign to the tested material. By having a sample of the same substrate material, the criminalist is able to determine what, if any, ILR are inherent to that specific substrate. In addition, some materials may produce significant pyrolysis and partial combustion products that may interfere with the analyst's ability to interpret the data [24]. By having a comparison sample, the analyst can see what components of the pattern can be attributed to the substrate material, and use that information to "subtract" those contributions from the pattern. Material collected to serve as comparison samples is removed using the same techniques as for direct sampling.

Comparison samples may be used for other reasons, as well. For example, some soils may contain microbes capable of degrading petroleum products. If a soil sample was submitted for ILR analysis, and the product recovered showed significant degradation, it might be difficult to identify it. With a comparison sample of the same soil, the forensic scientist can use it to degrade a known petroleum product, thereby making more suitable reference ILR for comparison. This would allow for the identification of a significantly degraded product by comparison to an appropriate standard. Comparison samples may provide an abundance of information about the test samples, and should be collected whenever possible.

The term control sample has been used for many years to mean a comparison sample [22]. Control sample was a term widely accepted by the fire investigation community until recently. The use of that term in this context has been discontinued because it does not reflect a true control. Unless a comparison sample is definitely known as a control sample, the term control sample should not be used.

Comparison v. Control Samples

A comparison sample is a sample that contains the same substrate as the sample collected for ILR analysis (test sample), but that is believed by the investigator to be free of ignitable liquid. For example, if it is suspected that an ignitable liquid has been poured on a certain area of a carpet, a sample of that carpet at the edge of the burn is collected (test sample). A comparison sample to that sample would be a portion of the carpet away from the area suspected to contain the ignitable liquid. This comparison sample contains the same carpet, the same substrate as the test sample with the exception of having the suspected ignitable liquid present.

Control samples are used in scientific testing to show how a particular test or procedure reacts on a sample of known composition (whether a negative or positive control).

The content of a control sample is not left to random events, but is under complete control of the scientist. Because the samples collected at fire scenes for comparison purposes are not unequivocally known to be free of foreign ignitable liquids, the term "control sample" should not be used in this context. Even if two carpet samples are collected a few meters away from each other and are constituted of the exact same carpet, it is not known if one area underwent a different history at some point in time than the other area in regard to incidental ignitable liquids. The only situation where a comparison sample can be referred to as control sample is if there is a set of circumstances that demonstrate an identical history—except for the pouring of the suspected ignitable liquid—between the regular sample and the aptly named control sample.

There are many times when comparison samples are unnecessary; however it is often not known if such samples will be beneficial until after the laboratory analysis of the evidence has begun. At this point, it is not always possible to obtain comparison samples; therefore, it is recommended that comparison samples be taken at the same time as the test samples. If submitting excess samples is considered a problem, these comparison samples may be retained by the investigator, and submitted to the laboratory upon request. Judicious use of comparison samples can provide a wealth of information and they may be as important as the other items of evidence.

Finally, it is good practice to collect unburned comparison samples. This enables the criminalist to first analyze the sample unburned, to burn it, and to reanalyze it burned. In some instances, it can reveal very pertinent information regarding the interfering products found in the debris. The role of the criminalist is to talk with the investigator and request the routine collection of comparison samples.

6.3.7 Contamination

The issue of contamination has arisen with increasing frequency. Contamination of physical evidence is always a concern; however, it becomes an even greater concern when dealing with trace amounts of materials. Advances in extraction techniques and instrumental capabilities have provided fire debris analysts with the ability to detect extremely low levels of ignitable liquids. This means that if low-level contamination had occurred in the past, it might never have been detected, but it would be detected today with the latest technology. Adding to this concern is the fact that vapors from ignitable liquids may be easily transferred, even in the absence of direct physical contact. It is incumbent on the investigator to minimize the possibility of contamination.

Spoliation of Evidence

Spoliation is defined as [25]: "The destruction or material alteration of, or failure to save, evidence that could have been used by another in future litigation." It is imperative that the forensic scientist is aware of the concept of spoliation, and the need to preserve evidence so that it may be available for subsequent examination by another interested party. In fire debris analysis, spoliation generally is avoided through the use of examinations that are essentially nondestructive; that is, they do not alter the evidence in such a manner that it cannot be reexamined. Extraction methods such as passive headspace concentration have been demonstrated to cause minimal change to the evidence, and, therefore, would not prevent subsequent testing by another party [26, 27]. When examinations are used that can potentially substantially modify the evidence, it is strongly advised that the criminalist preserve a portion of the sample prior to testing. Spoliation does not only apply to laboratory analyses, but also to the entire fire scene examination. It is recognized that the thorough examination of a fire scene will result in some changes to it; however, allegations of spoliation can be minimized if the fire scene and the investigative activities affecting it are properly documented. Failure to take reasonable precautions to preserve evidence could result in its lack of admissibility or even in sanctions to the responsible party.

One important part of the standard operating procedure for any fire scene examination and laboratory examination is following specific steps to minimize the potential for contamination during evidence collection and packaging. The first step is to ensure that procedures are in place to check that all evidence collection tools and packaging materials begin contaminant-free. The issue of contamination of packaging material is discussed in Section 6.4.

For collection tools, the best course of action is to use disposable items. Although this may be practical for items such as gloves, it is not usually economically feasible for more durable items, such as shovels, trowels, and saws. By using new gloves for the collection of every sample, one can be assured that the gloves did not transfer ILR from one location at the scene to another. For items that must be reused, there must be measures in place to decontaminate them between scenes or between samples. When there is no indication of gross contamination, most tools can be cleaned effectively by scrubbing them with dish detergent and water [28]. In cases of gross contamination, the tool should be subjected to an extremely rigorous cleaning, after which it should be tested for residual contamination. If the tool fails to be decontaminated, it must be disposed of.

Placing Gloves in the Container?

In the past, some investigators recommended placing used gloves in the sample container along with the collected evidence. The idea behind this recommendation was to show that good contamination prevention practices were in place. By preserving the gloves along with the evidence, it was demonstrated that for each sample a new pair of gloves was used, thus no gloves were reused. Others also stipulated that the idea was to ensure that no contamination was generated through the use of gloves. This recommendation actually was included in the 1992 version of the NFPA 921 *Guide for Fire and Explosion Investigations*.

Naturally, the problem with this was what to do with the gloves in the laboratory. Should they be considered as part of the evidence? Should they be included in the extraction process, or removed prior to extraction? Different laboratories had different policies.

Even though the gloves do not transfer any interference to the debris through regular manipulation when extracted as part of the evidence, their presence in the sample can contribute to significant interferences. Research has shown high levels of interfering products in some gloves [14]. Nevertheless, gloves are designed to bring a clean layer of protection between the hands of the fire investigator and the debris. By placing the gloves in the sample after manipulating the debris, basically it is exposed to any possible contamination present on the hands of the fire investigator from the inside of the gloves. This may jeopardize the integrity of the sample. After much discussion among laboratory scientists and investigators, this recommendation was abandoned. It was determined that there are better ways to demonstrate that measures were taken to reduce the possibility of contamination.

Incorporating steps, such as wearing new gloves and cleaning tools between each sample, may add a few minutes to the collection of each sample; however it saves a lot of time and frustration for the investigator on the witness stand, and, more importantly, it may even save the evidence from being inadmissible.

6.4 SAMPLE PACKAGING

6.4.1 General Principles

Following collection of the evidence, it is important for the collected materials to be properly preserved pending laboratory analysis. The proper preservation of collected samples is necessary to ensure that the condition of the evidence does not undergo harmful changes prior to its examination in the laboratory. Selection of the appropriate type of packaging is vital to this process. Ideally, the sample's condition must be the same when being examined as it was when collected at the fire scene.

Harmful changes that may occur to the sample during its storage and transportation generally fall into two broad categories: diminution (loss) and contamination [29]. When considering ignitable liquids, the category of diminution includes the evaporation or dissipation of ILR from the evidence collected. The problem of contamination refers to the unintentional addition of materials for which the items of evidence are being tested. Means to reduce these types of evidence alteration are discussed in further detail later. A third category of harmful change—not as common as the first two—is degradation, which has been mentioned briefly in the previous section. Degradation occurs when the sample contains microbes, mostly from soil, which attack petroleum products.[3]

A/ Purposes of the Container

This section focuses on the preservation of the evidence selected for collection. The purpose of the container is three-fold:

I. To provide a safe means of preserving and transporting the evidence.
II. To protect against the loss of ILR from the sample.
III. To prevent contamination of the sample by foreign ignitable liquids.

These three goals are fulfilled through the use of a container, which provides a physical barrier and that is impermeable to vapors, particularly to volatile organic compounds. The most commonly used containers for fire debris include metal cans (paint cans) with friction lids, plastic (mostly nylon or polyester) bags, and glass canning jars. Polyethylene plastic bags, such as those commonly used for food storage, are not suitable because they do not adequately retain vapors. Vials with Teflon-lined screw caps are well suited for collecting liquid samples. The most critical feature of the container is to prevent permeation of vapors in either direction, but other features are beneficial as well. The ideal container should be readily available, inexpensive, easy to transport and store, easy to seal and unseal, free of contamination, and resistant to damage, breakage, puncture, or cutting. This section reviews each type of commonly used container, along with its advantages and disadvantages.

B/ Filling of the Container

Regardless of which type of container is used to collect evidence, it is crucial that the fire investigator not fill it to its maximum capacity. Most techniques used to extract ILR from fire debris samples are based on collecting vapors from the headspace (see Chapter 11). Therefore, it is necessary to have sufficient space above the sample to properly perform the

---

[3] Other forms of degradation may occur depending on the nature of the sample. For example, with vegetable oil residues, polymerization may occur, possibly compromising the identification of the liquid. In this section, only degradations applicable to typical ignitable liquids are presented.

extraction. A sufficient amount of sample should be collected; however, the size of the container will dictate the amount of sample that may be placed into it. If an amount of sample greater than what can fit into the container is required, the sample may be split and placed into several containers. Most evidence can be collected and properly preserved with little difficulty if the investigator has a well-stocked evidence collection kit. If a container is filled completely to the top, the fire debris analyst will either split the sample into two containers or transfer the sample into one larger container in order to effectively extract it. The criminalist must document this and understand that it may render the interpretation of the results more difficult. As a general rule, it is recommended not to fill the container to more than 70% of its capacity.

C/ General Container Issues

As stated in Subsection 6.3.7, the issue of contamination is of great concern. It is addressed with each type of container in the following subsections. However, general rules apply to all container types. It is good practice to order packaging materials in bulk and to test a representative sample to demonstrate that the manufacturing process did not leave any detectable residues that could interfere with the analysis. Doing this shows that the containers (cans, bags, and so on) are contamination-free at a specific point in time; however it cannot provide information about the packaging materials at the time they are used. The containers must be stored in such a manner as to prevent contamination. Generally, storage requirements may include precautions such as keeping the lids on cans, keeping the containers in a closed box, and other similar steps. Nevertheless, it is always good practice to send an empty container (blank) with the evidence to demonstrate the absence of contamination during transportation. Additional measures can be taken in an attempt to show a lack of contamination. By addressing all these measures in a standard procedure, the investigator has the benefit of knowing that he or she has taken all logical and reasonable precautions to minimize the possibility of contamination, and will also have the confidence to defend his or her actions after having followed a well thought-out procedure.

6.4.2 Metal Cans

Metal cans are one of the most commonly used containers for fire debris samples in the United States. Many different sizes of cans are available, but the most commonly used are one-quart (0.946 liters) and one-gallon cans (3.785 liters). Figure 6-4 presents some new metal cans typically available on the market.

Cans are purchased empty from retailers and are normally ready to use. The user usually chooses between lined and unlined cans, each of which having both benefits and drawbacks.

FIGURE 6-4
Metal cans are one of the most popular fire debris packages in the United States.

Lined v. Unlined Cans

Unused metal cans (paint cans) with friction lids have long been one of the preferred packaging methods for debris samples in the United States. They meet many of the desired requirements; they are rugged, puncture resistant, and reasonably airtight. There has been some dispute over whether it is preferable to use cans that bear a protective lining, or those that are made of unlined metal. When some lined cans were used, coextraction of interferences from the can's lining had contributed to sample extracts, resulting in concerns about contamination. Consequently, for many years, unlined cans were recommended so as to avoid this potential problem. Unfortunately, unlined cans presented their own set of problems. With no protection between the often wet debris and the metal can, unlined cans were prone to rapid deterioration (rust). The problems due to extracting lining contaminants are greatly lessened when the passive headspace concentration technique is used for extraction. Because lined cans will last much longer and the contamination concern has been greatly minimized due to the overwhelming use of passive headspace concentration as the preferred extraction method, lined cans are now generally preferred over unlined cans. It is still necessary that a representative sample from a batch of cans be analyzed in order to demonstrate that the lining will not contribute to the extract.

Metal cans offer many advantages: they are rigid and highly resistant to puncture; they are easily stackable, opened and closed; and they are relatively inexpensive. Some of the main drawbacks of metal cans are the fact that they may quickly rust when wet samples are contained; they are bulky due to their rigid structure; and they cannot easily accommodate large items or items with unusual shapes. The corrosion problem with cans is an issue that cannot be ignored. The use of lined cans diminishes the potential for corrosion. However, if the debris contains sharp items, it is likely that the lining inside the can will be compromised, opening the door to corrosion. Figure 6-5 shows a can that has undergone extensive corrosion. Note that corrosion easily creates holes in the can, therefore compromising the integrity of the sample by allowing vapors to pass through.

FIGURE 6-5

Corrosion can be a significant issue with metal cans. This can was stored for a long period of time under conditions that did not prevent it from rusting. When the case went to a private laboratory for reanalysis, the integrity of the container was seriously compromised and all ignitable liquid residues that were possibly present in the debris at a prior time had disappeared.

In general, metal cans offer a very good physical barrier against loss and contamination [29]. When compared with plastic bags and glass canning jars, however, Mann reported that metal cans offered the least amount of protection from loss and contamination [30]. Although he observed leakage during storage—where the seal from the friction lid may not always have been good—cross-contamination occurred only under extreme circumstances, and did not occur under sample storage conditions that were most consistent with actual evidence storage. He finally concluded that even though loss occurs, metal cans offer enough protection to retain minute amounts of ILR if the extraction procedure is carried out in a timely manner.

The contamination of new, unused metal cans varies greatly from one manufacturer to another and from one batch to another. It is best to check every batch of cans for background contamination. Manufacturers use petroleum-based oil in the machines that handle the metal sheeting and form the cans. Although metal cans are supposed to be cleaned after manufacture, in some instances, residues of oil may remain [30]. To decontaminate cans, it is a good practice to "bake" the cans overnight at a minimum of 150°C. This drives off most residues that may be present and is particularly effective for any residues that may be in the boiling point range of ignitable liquids of interest. Metal cans may also be decontaminated by rinsing them with a solvent, which is a long and tedious operation. In general, if the contamination present in the metal can is not removed by simple baking, a different manufacturer should be sought.

6.4.3 Plastic Bags

Although plastic bags are very commonly used throughout Europe, they are much less common in North America. They present the advantage of being transparent, therefore allowing the crime laboratory analyst to quickly identify what is in the sample. Also, they are flexible and allow for much larger objects or objects with unusual shapes to be packed than with a canning jar or a metal can. Bags are usually available in individual sets or as a roll stock that can be cut to the user's desired length (see Figure 6-6). Different sizes of bags exist up to about a 30 cm wide and a meter (or even a couple of meters if roll stocked) long. They take very little space when stored or transported prior to use, and they do not rust. They do not break when dropped, however they may be punctured or torn apart when sharp objects are present in the bag.

The material constituting the bags is of extreme importance, as it is the physical barrier that must fulfill the three goals of an evidence container. When choosing plastic bags as containers, those specially designed for the packaging of fire debris are the best choice. They have been designed for the specific purpose of being impermeable to ILR and VOCs. Common plastic bags, such as food storage bags made of polyethylene, do not

FIGURE 6-6

Plastic bags are found in various sizes and even in a roll stock, allowing for the packaging of large or unusually shaped items. (Photograph courtesy of École des Sciences Criminelles, Université de Lausanne, Switzerland.)

adequately block the passage of ignitable liquid vapors. As an example, Tontarski tested some polyethylene cups and showed that significant losses of ignitable liquid occurred along with the possibility of contamination [31]. Similarly, Kocisko studied the possibility of using multilayered polyethylene/polyvinylidene chloride bags for fire debris samples [32]. She observed that ILR was partially adsorbed onto the bag material itself, thus significantly reducing the amount recovered during extraction. This eventually rendered the bags not suitable for such use. Stackhouse and Gray evaluated the use of polyester bags and compared them to regular metal cans and canning jars [33]. They recognized the efficiency of the bags in fulfilling the goals of a fire debris container and noted a few advantages, but they also claimed that these are more of a convenience to the field investigator than to the fire debris analyst [33]. Demers-Kohls et al. published a comprehensive evaluation of six different bags [34]. At the time, they recommended the use of WinPak bags (WinPak, Winnipeg, Manitoba, Canada), because they offered the best results of the study. Since that time, problems have arisen with WinPak bags, which are made of a polyethylene/nylon laminate, and they are no longer recommended.

In general, nylon or polyester bags show excellent resistance to vapor loss. However, nylon bags do not retain alcohols and other similar polar compounds [29]. Until recently, the most commonly used bags in the United States were Kapak bags (now Ampac, Minneapolis, Minnesota, USA).[4] However, this has not always been the case, and Kapak earned its reputation through many different failures. These bags have been the subject of many contamination problems and some loss of volatiles. In 1980, the first Kapak bags were successfully tested for their efficiency. DeHaan found that the only loss encountered through his testing concerned methanol, which would escape the bags even at room temperature [35]. Originally, Kapak bags were made of polyethylene-lined polyester [33]. In the mid 1980s, there were questions regarding the level of background contamination in Kapak bags. Potts discovered a medium petroleum distillate in the background of the bags [36]. In 1988, Dietz and Mann also reported the presence of a medium petroleum distillate in Kapak bags [37]. They state that bags manufactured prior to 1985 were free from contamination. As a result, the company manufacturing the plastic films used in the bags, 3M (St. Paul, Minnesota, USA), began an investigation and discovered that, in production, the film underwent a change. In 1989, 3M changed its manufacturing process and Kapak produced a new generation of their bags for fire

---

[4] Kapak was purchased by Ampac Corporation in 2005, which continued to market the Kapak fire debris bag under the name Fire DebrisPAK. However, the market for this product was too small and so they discontinued it and it is no longer available.

debris samples [38]. Scientific testing of these new bags demonstrated that they were free from any significant contaminants [38]. Lastly, Ampac bags for fire debris samples were made of a two-layered film (cast nylon and acrylonitrile/methacrylate sealant) held together with an adhesive [39]. In Europe, bags made of nylon 11 (similar to Rilsan) and provided by BVDA (Haarlem, The Netherlands) are very popular and quite efficient [40]. They present some minute level of background interferences such as methyl iso-butyl ketone (MIK), toluene, and limonene [14].

It is important to understand that the quality and overall efficiency of plastic bags can frequently change. Although some manufacturers are now aware of the use of their bags for fire debris samples, some others are not. As a consequence, they may change some portion of the manufacturing process, which may either introduce contamination to the bags or cause a decrease in the volatile loss prevention. It is, therefore, important to check every new batch of bags. As an example, one of the authors tested several bags from Grand River Products (Grosse Pointe, Michigan, USA) in early 2000 and noticed a serious contamination with one peak: caprolactam. Caprolactam is the monomer used in the manufacturing of nylon 6-6, the material constituting the bag. Although this compound may not be mistaken for an ignitable liquid, since it is an oxygenated compound and was present in significant concentration, it had the tendency to present a peak with serious tailing, which obscured a good part of the chromatogram. More recently, the Edmonton laboratory of the Royal Canadian Mounted Police tested the Grand River's nylon bags and found them to be the cleanest bags ever tested. As a result, they recommend these bags to their investigators [41].

Besides the material used to manufacture the bag, the other significant parameter in the bag's ability to retain vapors is how it is closed. There are four main sealing techniques commonly used in the fire investigation community (see Figure 6-7):

- Heat seal
- Swan or goose neck seal (with cable tie)
- Regular knot
- Fold and tape seal

Stryjnik and Hong-You studied the effectiveness of the different seals with Grand River brand nylon bags on the loss of ILR from the bags [42]. They ranked the seals in the following order of decreasing effectiveness: heat seal > fold and duct tape seal > swan neck with duct tape seal > swan neck seal. They observed a loss of ignitable liquid vapors with a swan neck seal, independent of the liquid's nature [42]. Double bagging the sample did not improve the effectiveness of the seal. They also tested cross-contamination

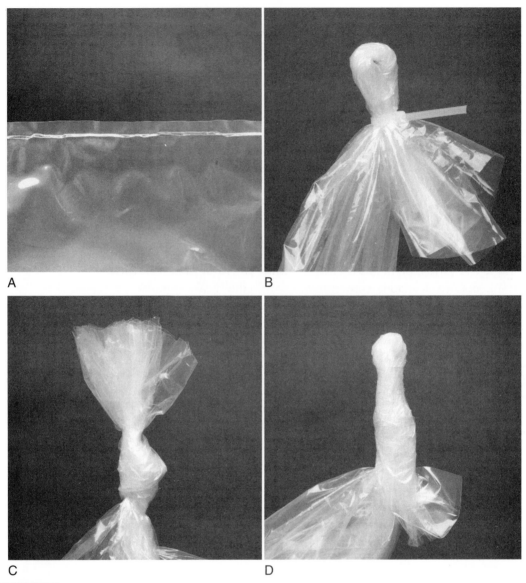

FIGURE 6-7 *Examples of the different sealing techniques used with plastic bags. A/ Heat seal. B/ Swan neck with cable tie. C/ Regular knot. D/ Fold and taped.*

between bags left adjacent to one another in a cardboard box at room temperature for five months: no cross-contamination was detected [42]. Finally, it is important to remember that if a swan neck or a fold and tape seal is used, the usable bag volume is significantly reduced.

The heat seal is the most efficient seal, but one must realize that if not properly performed, the heat seal can either leak or create volatile

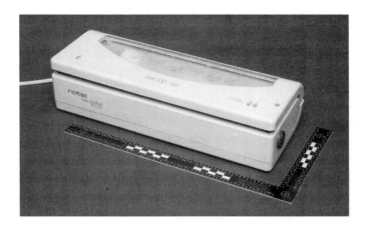

FIGURE 6-8

Heat sealers are more affordable today and some manufacturers produce portable ones. (Photograph courtesy of École des Sciences Criminelles, Université de Lausanne, Switzerland.)

compounds inside the bag's headspace, which might interfere with the subsequent analysis. Today, heat sealers are relatively inexpensive and some manufacturers provide portable ones (see Figure 6-8).

As with other containers, it is important for the user to remember that enough headspace must be present in the bag. Also, when using passive headspace adsorption techniques, it might be more difficult to place the charcoal strip in an optimal manner inside the container. The use of a Diffuse Flammable Liquid Extraction (DFLEX) device (Albrayco, Cromwell, Connecticut, USA) or some sort of metal wire frame placed inside the bag may help.[5]

Finally, when opening the bag to place and/or extract the adsorption device, it is possible to cut a small hole somewhere and to seal it back with tape. Interestingly, although there are many studies on the efficiency of the bag's material to retain vapors and on the seals themselves, no one has really studied the impact of using regular tape to seal holes cut in such a fashion. However, no extra interfering products were found from the tape when using dynamic headspace extraction [41]. If the bag is heat-sealed, a better practice consists of cutting a slot just below the seal and resealing the bag with heat.

6.4.4 Glass Canning Jars

Glass canning jars are found very commonly in the fire investigation community in Canada and to a lesser extent in the United States and Europe. As with plastic bags, they are transparent, and therefore one can view the sample without opening the container, which can be considered a benefit (see Figure 6-9). However, they are only available in limited sizes (usually

---

[5] At the time of writing of this book, DFLEX devices are no longer sold. See Chapter 11 for more information in this regard.

FIGURE 6-9 *Canning jars also often are used as fire debris containers. The model shown here does not exhibit a two-part lid, so it is not possible to reverse the inner lid.*

one liter or smaller) and are prone to breakage. In addition, special precautions must be taken to ensure that the rubber seals are not in contact with petroleum vapors, as they may seriously degrade.

Lang studied the contamination of glass canning jars and determined that no significant contamination was present in the containers [43]. She demonstrated that a small cluster of heavy peaks may be present, accompanied by some peaks in the medium to heavy range, but not sufficient to result in the identification of an ignitable liquid. These peaks, which are present at extremely low concentrations, are not likely to interfere with ILR identification. These contaminants might originate from the rubber seal present on the lid, therefore many fire investigators reverse the inner lid of the glass canning jar, therefore exposing the rubber seal to the outside of the jar. Although this practice might prevent the unlikely contamination of the debris by the rubber seal, it definitely contributes to a diminished ability to retain ILR and to prevent contamination from entering. The seal is effective only when the gasket is used as intended. When necessary, glass canning jars can be cleaned prior to use by washing them with hot water.

6.4.5 Others

Other containers are used to collect fire debris in unusual circumstances. For example, a quilt or other debris that are much larger than any of the containers previously described present a packaging challenge. Whenever possible, these items should be subdivided and packaged separately. However, this is not always feasible. When a much larger container is required, one should use metal containers such as lard cans (typically 5 to 10 gallons [19–38 liters]) or 30-gallon (113 liters) steel drums. When such containers are required, the investigator must ensure that they are free from contamination prior to use. These containers typically are not obtained in batches and normally are not free from contamination [44]. Therefore, it is necessary to proceed to their cleaning with a solvent wash, followed by a regular ILR extraction and analysis. This would allow the investigator to be certain that the container is totally free from contamination prior to use. Also, it is important that these containers are properly sealed. In many instances, it is good practice to use tape for this.

Packaging with DFLEX Devices

It is pertinent to mention at this point that some investigators place an adsorbing device in the container at the time of the collection. One such device is typically the DFLEX, which consists of an activated charcoal strip encased in a metal container between semipermeable membranes (see Chapter 11). It is designed so that the field investigator may place the device into the sample container along with the evidence. The idea is that the extraction procedure can begin immediately, thereby reducing the chances of irrecoverable vapor loss. It should be noted however, that the parameters of the extraction process are less controlled when the extraction is started in the field. Therefore, even though the extraction procedure is the same as the one used in the forensic lab, it is still advisable to check with the specific laboratory that will be analyzing the samples prior to using DFLEX in the field.

6.4.6 Liquids

In some instances, the fire investigator has to collect liquid samples. This may be done using a pipette, if practical, or using an absorbent material, such as a gauze pad.

Generally, only a small amount of a liquid sample is required, so laboratory vials are the best choice for packaging liquids. It is important however, to ensure that appropriate vial caps are used. Not all lids are designed to resist petroleum products, however, Teflon-coated lids perform well in this regard, and are highly recommended. To minimize the possibility of breakage, it is also recommended that these vials be placed in a small can with packing material such as Styrofoam peanuts or, better, vermiculite.[6] Even though very small amounts of liquid—typically in the µl or ml range—are required to perform a GC or GC-MS analysis, the investigator should not necessarily limit the sample to such an amount. Larger amounts may be required, depending on the examination requested. If evaporation studies or flash point determinations are requested, the amount needed may be greater. For a typical ignitable liquid identification, 2 to 20 milliliters are recommended.

---

[6]Vermiculite will also act as an absorbent, should a leak arise, which is a necessary requirement to comply with North American regulations of dangerous goods transportation.

Gauze Pads

When first aid-type gauze pads are used, they must not be labeled "nonstick." Pads specifically designed not to stick to wounds often have been shown to contain petroleum distillates, typically in the heavy range. The use of regular gauze pads is recommended. The investigator is advised to contact the laboratory and have the pads tested prior to use. The laboratory can also take proactive measures to test some pads that will later be recommended or forwarded to the field investigator.

It should be pointed out that when any foreign material is used to aid in the collection of evidence, whether it is a swab, gauze pad, or absorbent material, a comparison sample of the material must be submitted as well. This allows the laboratory analyst to ensure that it does not contain any contamination, and if it does, to estimate the extent of the contamination within and integrate that factor in the interpretation of the results.

6.4.7 Inappropriate Containers

In a fire debris analyst's career, he or she will encounter many fire debris samples that are submitted to the laboratory in inappropriate containers. Some samples are received in such a condition that the criminalist will first assume that the investigator is playing a joke on the laboratory. However, one must realize that some investigators are simply oblivious to proper packaging techniques. Figures 6-10 through 6-13 show some examples of evidence that have been received by the laboratory in inappropriate conditions.

In most instances, the investigator either was misled in what types of containers should be used for fire debris samples or was ignorant of the proper practices. One of the problems originates from outdated literature that recommends inappropriate containers, such as coffee cans with plastic lids [45].

FIGURE 6-10

This debris was received in this cardboard box. The debris was tightly packed into a regular low-density polyethylene (grocery) bag. Stains were observed throughout the interior of the box as liquid material leaked from the bag.

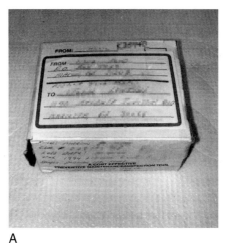

A   B

C

FIGURE 6-10
continued

A

B

FIGURE 6-11

These six samples, including one comparison sample, were individually packaged in zipper-lock bags, which are not appropriate containers because they are not impermeable to volatile organic compounds. One or more of the samples had a relatively strong presence of gasoline, and contaminated all the other samples in the cardboard box, including the comparison sample.

FIGURE 6-12 *This metal can obviously underwent heavy mechanical stress during (or prior to) its transportation to the laboratory. As a result, the lid was no longer sealed. This could have contributed to either loss of ignitable liquid residues, or worse, contamination by the surrounding environment.*

A

B

FIGURE 6-13 *Two examples of containers that have been overfilled. In these cases, it is necessary for the investigator to either repackage the debris in a larger container or to split the debris into multiple parts and extract them separately.*

Receiving Improperly Packaged Evidence

Sometimes, items of evidence that are not properly packaged are submitted to the laboratory. In fire debris analysis, this could be a metal can that rusted through and has developed big holes, a comforter brought in an open trash bag, or numerous items of debris strongly smelling of gasoline packaged together (including the comparison samples) in self-sealing bags. The question of what to do in such instances remains.

Most laboratories will have policies and procedures in place to guide the analyst in these situations. First and foremost, laboratory policies must be followed. Many laboratories have developed policies that mandate not analyzing any items of evidence that are not properly packaged. The philosophy behind such policies is that because the integrity of the evidence cannot be assured, there is little benefit to analyzing it. Though this could be absolutely true, one cannot evaluate the extent of this contamination, and, more importantly, its significance, until confronted with the results of the analysis. As such, this policy is not necessarily based on sound, scientific, and logical thinking. Hence, it may be more appropriate to have policies in place with greater flexibility that would allow the criminalist to use some discretion. For example, if two samples,

along with an additional comparison sample are packaged together, and only one shows gasoline, and the other sample and the comparison sample were negative, then it can be inferred that the gasoline present in the sample was not the result of cross-contamination. If gasoline was detected in both samples, yet the comparison sample was negative, there would be no reason to believe that cross-contamination occurred. This is yet another example demonstrating the value of comparison samples.

For this reason, it is often not wise to refuse a sample simply based on the fact that it was improperly packaged. However, it is necessary to integrate this information into the interpretation of the results, which may be significantly hampered in some instances. Nevertheless, in most cases it is only once the analysis is performed and the results are known that one can fully appreciate how the potential for contamination influences the significance and the pertinence of the results. If one thinks his or her laboratory's policy seems overly restrictive with regard to cases of improperly packaged evidence, he or she is encouraged to discuss the policy with the laboratory quality manager; however, one must comply with the policy, even when disagreeing with it.

6.5 EVIDENCE ADMINISTRATION AND TRANSPORTATION

6.5.1 Sealing and Labeling

The use of an appropriate vapor-tight container is only one part of ensuring that the sample is properly preserved. The other important part of preservation involves labeling and sealing the container. Once evidence is placed into an appropriate container, and the container is closed, loss or contamination is unlikely. However, in order to demonstrate that the package has not been opened in the interim, it is necessary to seal the container. Although it is the physical closure that actually prevents the loss and contamination, it is the seal that documents the fact that the evidence has been properly packaged and preserved. An intact seal shows that the package has not been opened or tampered with. Similarly, proper labeling documents the origin of a sample. By using unique identifiers, usually a case number and an exhibit number, the particular item of evidence is identified in such a way that it can be unequivocally linked to the fire scene and to

FIGURE 6-14

A typical evidence label that is affixed onto the container with the fire debris. (Illustration courtesy of Doug Byron, Forensic & Scientific Testing, Lawrenceville, Georgia, USA.)

EVIDENCE

FORENSIC & SCIENTIFIC TESTING INC.
275 N. PERRY STREET, LAWRENCEVILLE, GA 30045, USA
OFFICE + 1 (800) 225 1302 FAX + 1 (770) 449 4433
HTTP://WWW.FAST-LAB.COM

Evidence ID: _____   Date of collection: _____

Collected by: _____   Time of collection: _____

Project: _____   Project No. _____

Client: _____   Client No. _____

Description and origin of the evidence:

Storage conditions and/or particular disposition:

the notes, photographs, diagrams, and other evidentiary items taken at the scene.

Evidence labels should include, at a minimum, the case identifier, the unique evidence identifier, the date on which the sample was collected, and the name of the person who collected the sample. It is good practice to add the location of the sample collection and a description of the sample. An example of a good evidence label is shown in Figure 6-14.

To ensure admissibility into a court of law, it is necessary to demonstrate that appropriate measures were taken to avoid contamination of fire debris evidence. A proper label and seal, in conjunction with the accompanying chain of custody documentation, are critical in establishing that the evidence analyzed at the lab, and later shown in court, is the evidence that was recovered from the scene in question.

6.5.2 Transportation

It is important for the fire investigator to ensure which means of transportation are approved by the laboratory. Most laboratories accept walk-ins, which is often preferable because it stays in the custody of the investigator until delivered to the laboratory. If the samples are sent to the laboratory via a common courier, it should be one that provides tracking in order to maintain an intact chain of custody. Some laboratories will not even accept packages that were not sent via a trackable carrier. Shipping companies such as DHL, FedEx, and UPS offer tracking capability on every single package. Official government post offices should also offer such capability upon request.

Finally, the investigator must be made aware that there are possibly time-sensitive materials in the samples. Examples are samples containing soils and samples containing residues of vegetable oils (see Section 14.2).

In these situations, the submitter must ensure that the package will be properly preserved (usually refrigerated) during transit in order to minimize the sample's degradation.

6.5.3 Submission of Evidence

Submission of evidence to the laboratory must be in accordance with the receiving laboratory's policies. In general, paperwork accompanying the evidence should provide sufficient identifying information for the evidence and a summary of the examinations required. For ignitable liquid testing, this paperwork should include a unique item number for each item of evidence, as well as a description of the material and the location from which it was recovered. This information will allow the criminalist to better understand the circumstances surrounding the evidence, and potentially the significance (or lack thereof) of any ILR recovered. In addition, items collected as comparison samples should be listed as such. The accompanying documentation must also clearly state what examinations are requested. A well-trained criminalist is able to appropriately prioritize the examinations when several disciplines are involved. Similarly, with sufficient background information, the thorough analyst may be able to suggest additional testing to provide additional pertinent information.

REFERENCES

1. Thatcher PJ and Kelleher JD (2000) *Fire investigation: Evidence recovery at the fire-scene*. In: *Encyclopedia of forensic sciences*, editors Siegel JA, Saukko PJ, and Knupfer GC, Academic Press, London, United Kingdom, pp 905–11.
2. Mann DC and Gresham WR (1990) Microbial degradation of gasoline in soil, *Journal of Forensic Sciences*, **35**(4), pp 913–23.
3. O'Donnell JF (1985) The sampling of burned areas for accelerant residues analysis, *Fire and Arson Investigator*, **35**(4), pp 18–20.
4. Tontarski Jr RE (1985) Using absorbents to collect hydrocarbon accelerants from concrete, *Journal of Forensic Sciences*, **30**(4), pp 1230–2.
5. Woodland JH (2004) *Manual of ILA*, Ancarro, Indianola, IA.
6. Mann DC and Putaansuu ND (2006) Alternative sampling methods to collect ignitable liquid residues from non-porous areas such as concrete, *Fire and Arson Investigator*, **57**(1), pp 43–6.
7. Portable Arson Sampler (2000) http://www.trilobyte.net/pas/, last access performed on August 16, 2005.
8. Frenkel M and Tsaroom S (1986) Field sampling of arsons area by the adsorption tube method, *Arson Analysis Newsletter*, **9**(2), pp 33–41.
9. Johnston WK (year unknown) Portable Arson Samplers, Tooele, UT.
10. Conner L (2005) *Evaluation of field sampling and analysis methods for fire investigation including electronic noses and adsorption sampling/gas chromatography mass spectrometry*, Master's thesis, Florida International University, Miami, FL.
11. Conner L, Chin S, and Furton KG (2006) Evaluation of field sampling techniques including electronic noses and a dynamic headspace sampler for use in fire investigations, *Sensors and Actuators B*, **116**(1–2), pp 121–9.

12. Folkman TE et al. (1990) Evaporation rate of gasoline from shoes, clothing, wood and carpet materials and kerosene from shoes and clothing, *Canadian Society for Forensic Science Journal*, **23**(2&3), pp 49–59.

13. Darrer M (1998) *La persistance de l'essence sur les mains*, séminaire de 4ème année, Institut de police scientifique et de criminologie, University of Lausanne, Lausanne, Switzerland.

14. Montani I (2006) *La collection de liquides inflammables sur les mains de suspects*, travail de Master, Institut de police scientifique, École des sciences criminelles, University of Lausanne, Lausanne, Switzerland.

15. Rolph E (2000) *Petrol on hands: Handling method and validity of results*, research project, Department of Chemistry, University of Technology, Sydney, Australia.

16. Rolph E et al. (2001) Petrol on hands: Handling method and validity of results, *13th INTERPOL Forensic Science Symposium*, Lyon, France.

17. Wang J (1998) *Variable influencing the recovery of the ignitable liquid residues from simulated fire debris and human skin using solid phase microextraction/gas chromatography*, Master's thesis, Department of chemistry, Florida International University, Miami, FL.

18. Sester N et al. (2000) Evaluation of gasoline traces transferred on hands during car tank filling, *2nd European Academy of Forensic Science Meeting*, Cracow, Poland.

19. Sester N (2000) *Évaluation des traces d'essence transférées sur les mains lors du remplissage d'un réservoir*, séminaire de 4ème année, Institut de police scientifique et de criminologie, University of Lausanne, Lausanne, Switzerland.

20. Coulson SA and Morgan-Smith RK (2000) The transfer of petrol on to clothing and shoes while pouring petrol around a room, *Forensic Science International*, **112**(2–3), pp 135–41.

21. Terrapon F (1997) *Persistance de l'essence sur des jeans*, séminaire de 4ème année, Institut de police scientifique et de criminologie, University of Lausanne, Lausanne, Switzerland.

22. Thomas CL (1978) Arson debris control samples, *Fire and Arson Investigator*, **28**(3), pp 23–5.

23. Lentini JJ, Dolan JA, and Cherry C (2000) The petroleum-laced background, *Journal of Forensic Sciences*, **45**(5), pp 968–89.

24. Stauffer E (2003) Basic concept of pyrolysis for fire debris analysts, *Science & Justice*, **43**(1), pp 29–40.

25. DeHaan JD (2002) *Kirk's fire investigation*, 5th edition, Prentice Hall, Upper Saddler River, NJ.

26. Waters LV and Palmer LA (1993) Multiple analysis of fire debris samples using passive headspace concentration, *Journal of Forensic Sciences*, **38**(1), pp 165–83.

27. Newman RT (1995) An evaluation of multiple extractions of fire debris by passive diffusion, *Proceedings of the International symposium on the forensic aspects of arson investigations*, George Mason University, Fairfax, VA.

28. DeMent JL (1996) *Cross contamination*, Bureau of Alcohol, Tobacco and Firearms, Hyattsville, MD.

29. Carlsson G et al. (1993) *Conserving samples of fire debris suspected of containing accelerants*. In: *Advances in Forensic Sciences—Proceedings of the 13th meeting of the IAFS Düsseldorf*, editors Jacob B and Bonte W, International Association of Forensic Sciences, Berlin, Germany, pp 187–90.

30. Mann D (2000) In search of the perfect container for fire debris evidence, *Fire and Arson Investigator*, **50**(3), pp 21–5.

31. Tontarski Jr RE (1983) Evaluation of polyethylene containers used to collect evidence for accelerant detection, *Journal of Forensic Sciences*, **28**(2), pp 440–5.

32. Kocisko MJ (2001) Absorption of ignitable liquids into polyethylene/polyvinyl-dine dichloride bags, *Journal of Forensic Sciences*, **46**(2), pp 356–62.

33. Stackhouse CC and Gray CI (1988) Alternative methods for processing arson samples in polyester bags, *Journal of Forensic Sciences*, **33**(2), pp 515–26.

34. Demers-Kohls JF et al. (1994) An evaluation of different evidence bags used for sampling and storage of fire debris, *Canadian Society for Forensic Science Journal*, **27**(3), pp 143–70.

35. DeHaan JD (1981) Evaluation of Kapak plastic pouches, *Arson Analysis Newsletter*, **5**(1), pp 6–11.

36. Potts M (1988) Contaminant in Kapak bags, *Tieline*, **13**(1), pp 17–27.

37. Dietz WR and Mann DC (1988) Evidence contaminated by polyester bags, *Scientific Sleuthing Newsletter*, **12**(3), pp 5–6.

38. Kinard WD and Midkiff CR (1991) Arson evidence container evaluation: II. "New generation" Kapak bags, *Journal of Forensic Sciences*, **36**(6), pp 1714–21.

39. Kapak Corporation (2001) *Kapak adhesive lamination technical data—NG38*, Kapak Corporation, Minneapolis, MN.

40. BVDA (2006) Fire debris bags, available from http://www.bvda.com/EN/sect13/en_13_1a.html, last access performed on December 23, 2006.

41. Sandercock PML (2007) Testing of Grand River bags, *Personal communication to Eric Stauffer*, June 13, 2007.

42. Stryjnik A and Hong-You R (2004) Evaluation of the effectiveness of nylon bags as packaging for fire debris, *56th Annual Meeting of the American Academy of Forensic Sciences*, Dallas, TX.

43. Lang T (1999) A study of contamination in fire debris containers, *Canadian Society for Forensic Science Journal*, **32**(2&3), pp 75–83.

44. Juhala J (1981) Contaminated sample containers?, *Arson Analysis Newsletter*, **5**(4), p 57.

45. Hurteau WK (1973) The arson evidence package, *Fire Journal*, July, pp 47–54.

CHAPTER 7

Flammable and Combustible Liquids

"What we see depends mainly on what we look for."
John Lubbock, English biologist and politician (1834–1913)

7.1 INTRODUCTION

In order for a fire debris analyst to effectively analyze the assortment of evidence that may be submitted to the forensic laboratory, he or she must have expertise in a wide variety of areas. Although by definition an accelerant can be any material used to initiate a fire or increase the rate of growth or spread of a fire, the most commonly used accelerants are ignitable liquids and the most commonly used ignitable liquids are petroleum-based products [1, 2]. It is important then for the forensic scientist conducting ignitable liquid examinations to have a thorough understanding of petroleum products including the composition of crude oil, the refinery process, and the composition and classification of petroleum products. Less frequently, ignitable liquids from nonpetroleum sources may be encountered; therefore the criminalist should also have some familiarity with the variety of ignitable liquids from sources other than petroleum that may be encountered.

Many different types of petroleum products exist in order to fill many different needs. In addition, new products are continuously developed. Because these products come from a common source—crude oil—they will have similar compositions. What makes one product different from another are the refinery processes producing these fuels and solvents. They have a substantial effect on their ultimate composition and properties. Familiarity with the variety of procedures that are used to create usable products from crude oil is a major asset to the criminalist tasked with interpreting complex data, often representing mixtures of literally hundreds of different chemical compounds.

This chapter provides an overview of the petroleum refining process and an introduction to the types of products derived from crude oil. In addition, a consensus-based system for classifying ignitable liquids is presented in terms of chemical composition. More detailed information on classifying ignitable liquids based upon analysis of instrumental data is presented in Chapter 9.

7.2 HISTORY

The raw material for the ignitable liquids of most interest to the fire debris analyst is crude oil, also called petroleum. Crude oil is found underground and is the result of millions of years of decomposition of various life forms. Mankind's use of petroleum has a history dating back thousands of years. Use of asphalt for waterproofing and as an adhesive occurred as early as the fourth century BC. Petroleum-derived liquids had their use as incendiary weapons and lamp oils documented in the second century BC [3]. The beginning of the modern era of petroleum can be considered to be 1859, the year in which petroleum was discovered in America. However, crude oil in its natural state is not a very useful product. Thus, shortly after Americans discovered sources of crude oil, the first attempts to refine it began.

Refining technology has greatly changed since its humble beginnings. The first efforts at making usable products from petroleum focused on distillation. Distillation is a method for physically separating a mixture of liquids based on differences in boiling points. In these initial refinery operations, distillation was simple and was done in discrete batches. Kerosene was rapidly replacing whale oil and was the most economically valuable fraction obtained from petroleum. Distillation efforts focused solely on its recovery; the remainder of the crude was considered waste. Improvements to the distillation process in the 1880s brought about the introduction of the continuous distillation process and the cracking, or destructive distillation, of the heavier fractions leading to a greater kerosene production [3]. Fractional distillation was introduced in the early 1900s and is still used in modern refineries today. Changes in refinery operations have continued to occur, primarily focusing on maximizing the economic value of a barrel of crude oil. Today, modern integrated refineries use a variety of physical separation and chemical conversion methods to achieve this goal.

7.3 SOURCES OF CRUDE OIL

Petroleum was created over many millions of years as a result of the decay of organic matter, primarily aquatic plants and animals. As these prehistoric forms of life died, they produced a layer rich in organic material in the seabed, which became covered with sand and mud, eventually forming sedimentary rock.[1] As this process repeated itself, forming layer upon layer, the pressure and temperature increased for the underlying layers. Bacteria helped to decay the organic material, resulting in molecules consisting primarily of carbon and hydrogen. It is important to realize, however, that only a small portion of the organic carbon actually became part of these sediments. The conditions of elevated temperature and pressure were necessary to accomplish the conversion to crude oil. Temperature generally increases with depth, and most petroleum is found in layers where the temperature is in the range of 107 to 177°C (225 to 350°F) [5].

Consequently, the formation of crude oil was not spontaneous. In addition to proper temperature and pressure conditions, there had to be adequate source rock (a shale rich in organic matter); a means for the oil to migrate into a porous reservoir rock; and finally, an impervious layer to trap the oil. The geological history of the resulting petroleum will be reflected in its characteristics. The original source of the organic material that formed the crude oil has a major effect on the oil's ultimate composition. For this reason, there is a wide variation between crude oils from different regions. The composition of crude oil affects how it is eventually refined into useable products.

Petroleum may be found throughout the earth's crust all around the world. The majority of recoverable crude oil, however, is found primarily in the Middle East. This region of the world contains almost two-thirds of the accessible petroleum. Latin America is described as the next region with the greatest source of recoverable oil, with approximately 13% of the world's supply [6]. Canada also has a tremendous reserve of oil in the Athabasca oil sands, just north of Alberta in British Columbia, however it is found under the form of bitumen. As a result, the oil must be extracted, a long and costly process. However, the estimation of the reserve contained in this bitumen would place Canada as the second largest oil reserve in the world after Saudi Arabia [7]. Although the United States is one of the world leaders in terms of production and refining operations, their supply of recoverable oil is much smaller. In fact, the continents of North America, Europe, Asia, and Africa each account for only four to eight percent of the world's recoverable petroleum resources [6].

---

[1] A different theory about oil production can be found in the book *The deep hot biosphere*, written by Thomas Gold with contribution by Freeman Dyson [4]. This will not be covered in this chapter, however the interested reader is invited to read Gold's contribution.

7.4 COMPOSITION OF CRUDE OIL

Petroleum is composed primarily of hydrocarbons, although hydrocarbon derivatives containing oxygen, nitrogen, or sulfur are also present. Additionally, some metals are present at trace levels. Different sources of petroleum exhibit different compositions, however the major hydrocarbon classes (alkanes [paraffins], cycloalkanes [naphthenes], and aromatics)[2] are found in all sources of crude oil. Although the composition of crude oil varies from location to location, and even within a single well, the basic elemental composition of crude oil shows little variation from one source to another (see Figure 7-1) [3].

The variations in composition that have an effect on the properties of the crude oil and how it is processed do not lie in the elemental composition, but rather in the proportions of the various types of compounds present.

The abundance of alkanes, including both straight chain (n-paraffins) and branched (isoparaffins) varies within a given crude oil. However, the general trend for all crude oils is that the proportion of alkanes decreases as molecular weight increases. Thus, the relative proportion of paraffinic compounds is greater in the more volatile fractions of crude oil than in the heavy fractions as illustrated in Figure 7-2 [3].

FIGURE 7-1

Basic elemental composition of crude oil, which typically exhibits little variation from source to source.

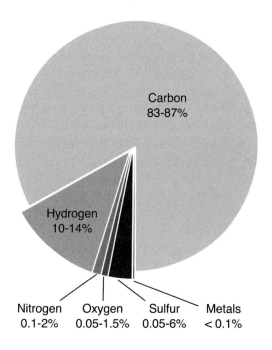

Carbon
83-87%

Hydrogen
10-14%

Nitrogen   Oxygen   Sulfur   Metals
0.1-2%   0.05-1.5%   0.05-6%   < 0.1%

---

[2] Because this chapter is about petroleum refining, common terminology to petroleum industry is sometimes used. As a result, terms such as paraffins and naphthenes will exceptionally be used. However, this chapter should not affect the information provided in Chapter 3 on nomenclature.

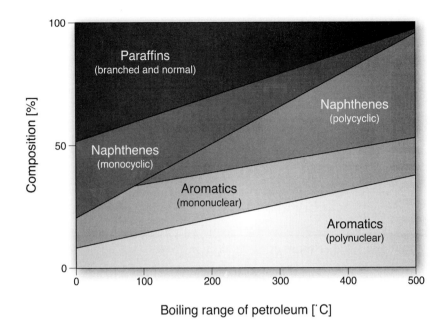

FIGURE 7-2

Graphical representation of change in composition by compound class as boiling point increases. Although there is significant variation in the relative amounts of paraffins from one crude oil source to another, the trends regarding change in composition with boiling point range are reasonably consistent [3].

In general, normal paraffins are present in most crude oils, and the less branched isoparaffins are better represented than their more highly branched isomers. Not surprisingly, the most abundant cycloalkanes are those based on the cyclopentane and cyclohexane rings, because of their minimal bond strain. Alicyclic compounds may have one or more rings, as well as alkyl chain(s) attached to the ring(s). Higher molecular weight fractions are richer in polycyclic species. Aromatic species are also an important constituent of crude oil and may have alkyl chains and/or saturated rings. They may also be condensed ring structures (polynuclear aromatic hydrocarbons or PAH). This immense combination of chemical compounds is of little use as is; however, by refining the crude oil, many different types of useful fuels and solvents can be developed.

7.5 REFINING PROCESSES

7.5.1 Principle

The purpose for refining crude oil is to produce useful and therefore, marketable products. As the market for various petroleum-based products has changed, so have the refining methods. Although not all refineries use all the same processes—some may be equipped to deal with special challenges, such as sour crude oil refining—a discussion of the general procedures used in an integrated refinery follows.

Sweet and Sour Crude Oil

Sour crude oils usually are defined as crude oils containing high levels of undesirable sulfur-based impurities such as hydrogen sulfide or mercaptans. A crude oil is deemed sour if the total amount of sulfur exceeds one percent [8]. Sour crude oil usually presents a rotten egg smell (due to the hydrogen sulfide) and may be quite corrosive. Sweet crude oil refers to an oil exhibiting very low levels of hydrogen sulfide or carbon dioxide. An oil is deemed sweet if it contains less than 0.5% of sulfur. Because sour oil must undergo extra steps in its refining process, not all refineries are equipped to process it. Sour crude can generally be purchased at a lower cost per barrel than sweet, but it requires additional capital equipment to process it; therefore it is more expensive to refine. Sweet crude oil is found mostly in Romania, Sudan, the United Kingdom, and the United States.

Each of the procedures used to refine petroleum can be thought of as accomplishing one or more of three basic purposes:

   I. Separating compounds based on boiling point.
   II. Changing the size of molecules in order to increase the amount of product within a desirable boiling point range.
   III. Modifying the type of molecules present in order to increase desirable properties.

Figure 7-3 is a simple schematic diagram showing some of the major refinery processes. Both atmospheric and vacuum distillations are used to separate the feedstock based on boiling point range. Procedures such as cracking and alkylation are used to decrease or increase the size of molecules in order to favorably affect the amount of material within a particular boiling point range. Finally, procedures such as reforming and isomerization are used to improve the quality of the products.

7.5.2 Fractional Distillation
A/ Process
Fractional distillation is one of the most important parts of the refinery process. As found in nature, petroleum may contain hydrocarbons from low molecular weight gaseous compounds, such as methane, up to much higher molecular weight solid compounds, such as those present in asphalt. With such a wide range of molecular weights and properties, petroleum has little practical use without refinement. Fractional distillation is a means of physically separating petroleum into fractions based on differences in boiling point ranges.

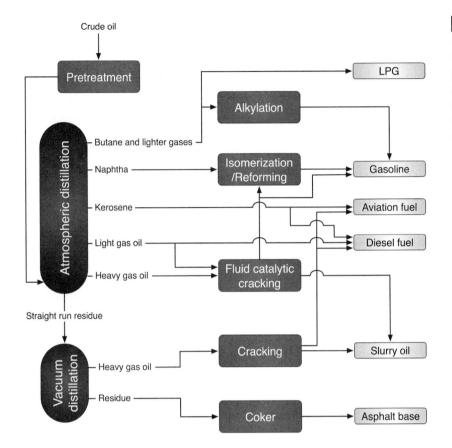

FIGURE 7-3

Overall schematic of major refinery processes. It has been extremely simplified compared to the very complex refinery operation.

Pretreatment of Crude Oil

Although distillation often is thought of as the first major step in the refining process, it is important to remember that a pretreatment of the oil is required prior to processing with distillation. Pretreatment involves the removal of salt, water, and other impurities from the crude oil and is necessary to prevent corrosion of the distillation apparatus. Various methods are used for the removal of salt, water, suspended solids, and hydrogen sulfide. Following initial pretreatment, the petroleum is ready for fractional distillation.

Fractional distillation, also referred to as fractionation, can be thought of as multiple separate distillations occurring within a single system. To better understand the more complex concept of fractional distillation, it is useful to review what occurs during the more simple distillation of a two-component mixture. Consider a mixture that is half ethanol and half water. Because ethanol has a lower boiling point than water, when this mixture is heated, the vapors above the liquid are richer in ethanol molecules than water molecules. When this vapor is cooled, it condenses and it can be collected separately from the original mixture. The recovered liquid has a greater ethanol concentration than the starting mixture. This is due to the difference in boiling point of the two liquids. Fractional distillation is based on this principle, however it is a much more complex process.

Moonshine and Distillation

Early moonshiners understood the concept of distillation. The term "moonshine" is derived from the fact that because distilling whiskey was unlawful, it had to be done at night . . . under the light of the moon. To make moonshine, a grain (typically corn), sugar, water, and yeast are combined and allowed to ferment. The fermentation process produces ethanol. The alcohol in this mash is then concentrated by a simple distillation process. The still is the distillation apparatus; in its simplest form, it contains a pot for the source material (mash), a condens-

ing tube, and a receiving container to collect the distillate (moonshine). When the fermented mixture is heated to a temperature near the boiling point of ethanol, the vapors above the liquid are richer in the more volatile component—in this case, alcohol. The vapors then are collected and cooled in a condenser. The recovered liquid has a higher alcohol content than the original mixture because of the distillation process. It may then be enjoyed as moonshine or further distilled for a higher quality product.

Fractional distillation differs from the simple distillation described in the text box in two important ways. First, the separation of petroleum is inherently more complex, as it involves a mixture of literally hundreds of different components rather than two or three. Second, the objective of fractional distillation is not to end up with a pure chemical compound, but rather to separate a highly complex mixture of very broad boiling point range into usable fractions of relatively narrow boiling point range. Although fractional distillation differs from the simple batch distillation process, it still relies upon the same basic concept: At lower temperatures, compounds with lower boiling points vaporize more readily than compounds with higher boiling points, resulting in a vapor with a composition different than that of the source material. Fractional distillation utilizes these physical properties to efficiently separate crude oil into economically viable products.

B/ Atmospheric Distillation

Fractional distillation requires a long and tall column for the separation to occur as shown in Figure 7-4. This column is heated at the bottom.

A temperature gradient exists within this column; the bottom of the column is hot, and the temperature gradually decreases along the height of the column. Distributed from the bottom to the top of the column are perforated trays. These trays allow for vapors rising from the bottom of the column to bubble through and mix with the liquid present in the tray. Along

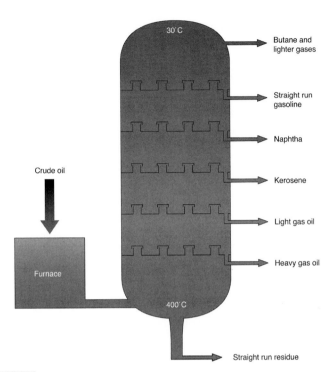

FIGURE 7-4 *Schematic of a fractional distillation tower used to carry out atmospheric distillation. The column represents a temperature gradient, from very hot at the bottom, to near ambient at the top. Fractions that boil at temperatures below 400°C are vaporized at the bottom of the tower. They rise up the tower, through the perforations in the trays and mix with the liquids in the trays. When they approach a temperature near their boiling point, they will condense and become liquid. Overflow liquids are allowed to drain through a tray down to the next lower level. During this process vaporization and condensation may occur many times. This is necessary for an effective separation. Separated fractions are drawn off from the side.*

various points in the column are side draws (areas from which fractions are removed). By referring to Figure 7-4, it is possible to imagine the path taken by a particular chemical compound, such as n-decane, which has a boiling point of 174°C (345°F): At the bottom of the tower, the temperature is much higher than the boiling point of n-decane, so it vaporizes; As n-decane vapors rise in the column, they bubble through several series of trays, and eventually come to a point (or more accurately a range) where the temperature is near n-decane's boiling point. At this area of the column, the vapors condense and revert to their liquid form. The resulting liquid may then be drawn off as part of that fraction. n-Decane will not make it all the way to the top of the column as methane would, yet it will rise higher than would a compound such as n-eicosane (n-$C_{20}H_{42}$) with a boiling point of 344°C

(651°F). Thus, the complex mixture that is petroleum can be separated into fractions based upon boiling point range.

The boiling point ranges of the separated fractions are determined by cut points, which are refinery specifications that can be changed to accommodate various economic needs or market specifications. The two temperatures of interest in fractional distillation are the initial boiling point (IBP) and the end point (EP) [9]. The initial boiling point is the temperature at which a given fraction begins to boil and the end point is the temperature at which the fraction is fully vaporized. These points serve as virtual boundaries for the various fractions. The end point of a lighter fraction is the initial boiling point of the next heavier fraction. It is important to note that these cut points are not absolute temperatures, but rather somewhat narrow ranges. Thus, chromatographic analysis of a product distilled from crude oil generally exhibits a Gaussian distribution rather than a sharp beginning and end.

Exact cut points and the resulting fractions vary from refinery to refinery and season to season. They may also depend upon the nature of the crude being processed and specific product demands. Some typical cut points and their fractions are shown in Table 7-1 [3].

Most of these fractions will undergo additional processing in other parts of the refinery or may become part of a blending stock for gasoline. Straight run residue may be separated under vacuum conditions to make it more suitable for additional refinement.

When fractional distillation takes place under atmospheric pressure, it is referred to as atmospheric distillation. This method of physically separating crude oil into fractions works very well for compounds with boiling points below approximately 350°C (660°F). At temperatures above approximately 350°C (660°F), thermal decomposition of some molecules in crude

Table 7-1	General parameters for typical initial boiling point (IBP) and end point (EP) values, and the resulting petroleum fractions. Cut points for various fractions may vary depending the season, or a particular product's specifications	

Initial Boiling Point [°C]	End [°C]	Point Fraction
<32	32	Butane and lighter gases
32	104	Straight run gasoline
104	157	Naphtha
157	232	Kerosene
232	343	Light gas oil
343	427	Heavy gas oil
427	>427	Straight run residue

oil occurs. This means that rather than simply volatilizing the high-boiling components of the mixture, carbon-to-carbon bonds start to break. This pyrolytic reaction (see Chapter 4) is referred to as cracking, and is not desirable in the fractionating column.

C/ Vacuum Distillation

Vacuum distillation is the technique used to separate higher boiling fractions of crude oil. The underlying theory and the process are analogous to those used to separate the lighter fractions in the atmospheric distillation process. The difference between the two physical separation methods is that atmospheric distillation occurs under atmospheric pressure, whereas vacuum distillation occurs at a significantly reduced pressure, thus reducing the boiling point of a substance. Hence, high boiling components can be boiled at lower temperatures, without the risk of cracking. Vacuum towers are much shorter than atmospheric towers in order to minimize the pressure differential from top to bottom. Generally, the pressure used in vacuum distillation is in the range of 50 to 100 mmHg, although some lubricating oil stocks may require even lower pressure operating conditions [3]. Fractions recovered from the vacuum distillation process usually are divided into gas oil, lubricating oil, and asphalt. The combination of the atmospheric and vacuum distillation processes is an important first step in converting crude oil into useful and economically valuable products.

Refineries and Market

Refineries are in the business to make a profit. Thus, many refining operation parameters may be shifted in order to maximize the production of specific products based on market demand. Economics also has played an important role in the development of refinery operations. The earliest refineries were simple topping refineries, in which the distillation process allowed for the recovery of the most economically desirable kerosene fraction; there was little need for the remainder of the crude. Since then, much has changed. Today, the widespread use of the automobile has made gasoline the most important product from crude oil, although heating oil, jet fuel, and diesel fuel are also of significant economic value. Many of the processes in place in today's integrated refineries exist for the purpose of maximizing the amount and quality of gasoline blending stock that can be obtained from a barrel of crude oil. Refineries have become more efficient in order to obtain as much high-value product as possible from each barrel. This generally is achieved by increasing the yield of product in the gasoline and distillate fuel ranges. To accomplish these goals, more than just physical separation is necessary: Chemical conversions are used to increase the proportion of the more valuable "transportation range" products.

7.5.3 Chemical Conversions

A/ Principle

Many different conversion reactions can be used to increase the production of valuable fuel products. Not all refineries use all available methods, and not all crude oils require the use of all conversion methods. Chemical reactions can be used to achieve two basic goals:

I. To increase the yield of materials in the appropriate boiling point range. The primary purpose of this category of reactions is to decrease the size of large molecules or to increase the size of small molecules via chemical reactions. The desired products are primarily molecules in the C_5 to C_{13} range.

II. The other category of reactions aims not so much to change the size of a molecule, but rather to change its configuration to one that has more desirable properties as a component of gasoline. In most cases, this means producing chemical compounds that have high octane ratings (see Subsection 7.6.3 for a definition of octane number).

B/ Catalytic Cracking

Catalytic cracking, also called cat cracking, is the breaking of large molecules into smaller ones at elevated temperatures via the use of a catalyst. As discussed in the previous subsection, molecules will crack when subjected to severe thermal conditions without a catalyst. However, the presence of a catalyst allows for a more controlled reaction. Thermal cracking reactions are free-radical reactions, whereas catalytic cracking reactions proceed via the carbonium ion and are therefore more predictable and better controlled. Additionally, the product from cat cracking is of a higher octane rating than the product obtained with thermal cracking. For these reasons, cat cracking is the preferred method and has almost entirely replaced thermal cracking.

Catalyst

A catalyst can be described as a substance that increases the rate of a chemical reaction, but that does not itself undergo a permanent chemical change. Sometimes, catalysts may be present at very low levels and yet still have a significant effect on a large scale reaction. Catalysts generally offer a pathway for a reaction with a lower activation energy, thereby allowing for an increased rate of reaction. Some catalysts such as the Lewis acid $AlCl_3$ are somewhat generic in nature and can be used to catalyze a variety of reactions. Other catalysts, including the biochemical protein enzymes, may be very specific, thus being useful for only one specific reaction.

Physically, there are three basic components involved in cat cracking: the reactor, the regenerator, and the fractionator. The reactor is where the feedstock comes in contact with the catalyst and where the cracking reaction occurs. The regenerator processes spent catalyst and regenerates it, so that this very expensive material will have a longer lifetime. Finally, there is a fractionator so that the cat-cracked product may be separated into fractions based upon boiling point. Each of these parts plays an important role in the efficiency of the cat cracker.

Because the cracking reaction takes place at an elevated temperature, both the feedstock and the catalyst are preheated prior to coming into contact with one another in the reaction zone. Even though this reaction takes place at an elevated temperature, it is not to be confused with thermal cracking. In thermal cracking, molecular bonds break as a result of heat alone, whereas in cat cracking, an elevated temperature makes the catalytic reaction proceed more efficiently and with a greater rate of reaction. Catalysts have changed over the years, but are primarily zeolites or a blend of the crystalline zeolites with amorphous catalyst [10]. Today, the most commonly used cat cracking process is called the fluid catalytic cracking (FCC). This is a continuous process in which the size of the catalyst particles is so small that they act like a fluid. The cracking reaction produces a variety of chemicals including coke, which results in a layer of coke forming on the catalyst. Coke is a solid residue consisting primarily of carbon, which may be used as a fuel. This layer of coke leads to a substantial reduction in catalyst activity; consequently, the catalyst needs to be regenerated. In the FCC process, this is done on a continuous basis. The regeneration process is quite simple, burning off the carbon that is adhering to the surfaces of the catalyst particles. This is, as are all combustion reactions, an exothermic process. The heat energy released from the regeneration of the catalyst often is used to provide the heat needed for the endothermic cracking process. This is another example of the remarkable efficiency of refinery operations. Chemical engineers are continually striving to use every bit of energy released, and every chemical byproduct to the maximum extent possible. Minute savings in energy when applied to large scale operations can result in significant cost savings.

Zeolites

Catalysts used in the cracking of crude oil are usually hydrated aluminum silicates. Zeolites, or molecular sieves, are hydrated aluminosilicates having a very porous crystalline structure, in which water molecules are trapped. The word "zeolite" comes from the Greek word *zein*, which means "to boil," because trapped water would be released from them upon heating. Because zeolites are highly porous, they are used for a variety of applications that take advantage of their physical structure. They are commonly used as absorbents, as molecular sieves for separating mixtures by selective absorption, as well as catalysts in petroleum processing.

The specific products of cat cracking are highly dependent upon the composition of the feedstock and the reaction conditions, including temperature and residence time. The most common reaction for alkanes is the cleavage of a carbon-to-carbon single bond (C–C), generally resulting in the formation of a smaller alkane and olefin, although the formation of aromatic compounds may occur as well [3]. Olefins are very prone to catalytic cracking, whereas aromatic compounds are fairly resistant. Cycloalkanes compounds undergo catalytic cracking as well, which may result in ring opening and/or side-chain cleavage. The catalytic cracking process results in a good quantity of high octane rating products in the gasoline range. Other products, such as the low molecular weight olefin gases, are very useful as polymer precursors or can be used to produce polymer gasoline. Slightly larger olefins in the butane range can be used in the alkylation process to produce relatively high octane rating blending stock rich in isoparaffins. Catalytic cracking is one of the most important processes in the modern integrated refinery because of its ability to produce substantial quantities of high quality blending stocks for gasoline.

Polymer Gasoline

The term "polymer gasoline" originally referred to a gasoline that included the product resulting from the innovative refinery process of polymerization. This process was developed to make use of the light gaseous hydrocarbons, which otherwise were of limited value. The polymerization process transforms monomers such as ethylene into dimers, trimers, or tetramers. The resulting hydrocarbon mirrors its monomers in structure, but is of greater molecular weight making it suitable as a gasoline blending stock.

Today's gasolines are made up of many different blending stocks resulting from many different processes, including the products of the polymerization reaction. Consequently, the term "polymer gasoline" is now more appropriately applied to the gasoline blending stock produced from the polymerization process, rather than the final product itself.

The fractionation of the materials produced during the catalytic cracking process is similar to the atmospheric distillation process. Products generally are separated into gaseous compounds, gasoline/naphtha blending stock, and heavier gas oil. The latter will be recycled through the cracking process again.

C/ Alkylation

Whereas cracking reactions seek to decrease the molecular weight of large molecules in order to get them into the gasoline range, alkylation seeks to increase the molecular weight of smaller molecules, in hopes of increasing the quantity of products in the gasoline range. However, alkanes will not easily combine with one another; they lack the necessary reactivity. For alkylation to occur, one of the reactants must be of the more reactive olefin type. The carbon-to-carbon double bond (C=C) that exists in olefins is much more reactive than the C–C single bonds of alkanes, thus much

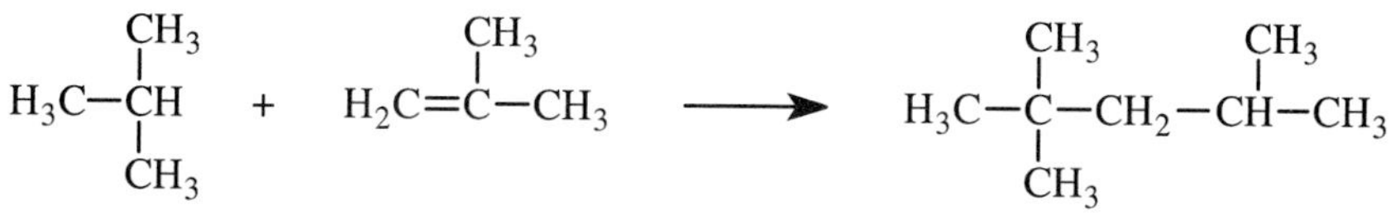

FIGURE 7-5 *The most common reaction in the alkylation process is the combination of butane and isobutylene to produce isooctane (2,2,4-trimethylpentane).*

more likely to undergo this type of reaction. Because of the highly reactive nature of the olefins, this reaction can actually occur without the aid of a catalyst. However, because the reaction would require high temperatures and pressures, it is economically more practical to use a catalyst. A typical alkylation reaction is the reaction of isobutane with isobutylene to form isooctane, as shown in Figure 7-5.

Similar reactions using propylene, pentylene, or isopentane as reactants are also possible, but usually not as advantageous as the isobutane-isobutylene reaction. One reason is that isopentane is already a useful component of gasoline, having desirable octane rating and vapor pressure qualities, so it is not economically profitable to use it as a reactant [10]. In addition, the octane ratings of the products from the propylene or pentylene reactions are not as high as those of the products from the butylene reaction [3].

One interesting phenomenon of the alkylation process is the resulting reduction of volume. The volume and density of the product are different from those of the reactants and because two smaller molecules combine to form a larger one, there is also a reduction in the number of moles. The change of volume is of great importance in the refinery industry, because volume is the primary measurement used. Reductions in volume may be in the order of 20%: When one barrel goes in as reactant, 0.8 barrel comes out as product. The converse occurs in the cracking reaction; it is said to have an expansion of volume.

Alkylation and Organic Synthesis

It should be pointed out that the term "alkylation" used in the petroleum refining industry is different than the same term used in synthetic organic chemistry. In organic chemistry, alkylation is known as the addition or substitution of an alkyl group to an aromatic ring, such as via the well-known Friedel Crafts alkylation reaction. In terms of petroleum refining, alkylation refers to the combination of a small olefin with a small isoparaffin, typically isobutane, to create a gasoline-range isoparaffin. The alkylation process yields a product rich in high octane rating isoparaffins, and is therefore a valuable gasoline blending stock.

Several catalysts can be used for the alkylation reaction such as aluminum chloride ($AlCl_3$), sulfuric acid (H_2SO_4), or anhydrous hydrofluoric acid (HF). When acid catalysts are used, there must be a tertiary carbon atom in the alkane that is to react with the olefin, such as in isobutane and isopentane. The mechanism goes through a carbonium ion, which needs to be in the tertiary form in order to "spread out" the charge. The use of these catalysts allows for the reaction to occur at relatively low temperatures. The alkylation reaction takes place with the presence of isoparaffins in significant excess relative to the olefins; the purpose is to minimize undesirable polymerization reactions. The olefins for the reaction, propylene and/or butylenes, generally come from the cat cracking process and combine with the isobutane in a chiller. Following the reaction, the acid is separated out and recycled, and the products of the reaction are treated with a caustic wash to neutralize any remaining acid. The desired end product is then separated from light gases by fractionation.

The end result from the alkylation process is a product called alkylate. Alkylate is a high octane rating blending stock with a relatively narrow boiling point range. In addition to having a high octane value, alkylate has no olefins, no sulfur, and no benzenes, however it exhibits a high vapor pressure [9]. Alkylate consists primarily of isoparaffins and is very desirable for blending into gasoline.

D/ Isomerization

The isomerization process differs from the cat cracking and alkylation processes previously discussed in one fundamental way: whereas the primary goal of the previous reactions was to change the size of molecules, the primary goal of the isomerization process is not to change the size of a molecule, but rather its structure. Because the octane number of a paraffin is related directly to the amount of branching it has, it is better to have a greater proportion of highly branched alkanes rather than normal alkanes. Thus, it is beneficial to have a process for converting straight chain alkanes to branched alkanes, which is exactly what an isomerization unit does. By converting normal paraffins to isoparaffins, the octane rating is improved, which is important to the production of high quality motor gasoline. This process generally is used on a light straight run (LSR) fraction (C_5 to C_6 range) to produce a higher quality blending stock for gasoline. A typical isomerization reaction is shown in Figure 7-6. The isomerization process can also be used with n-butane in order to produce additional isobutane as feedstock for the alkylation unit.

In order to shift the equilibrium of the conversion to favor isoparaffins, the process must occur at relatively moderate temperatures, thus requiring a catalyst [10]. Catalysts for these reactions are typically aluminum chloride or platinum, which are active enough to provide reasonable rates of reaction, even at relatively low operating temperatures. Because of the catalyst's high

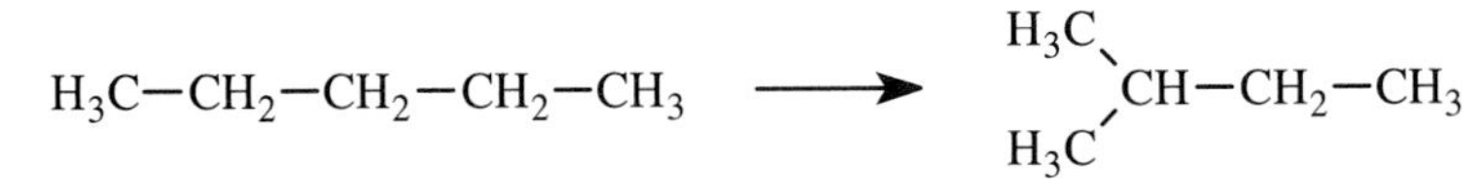

$$H_3C-CH_2-CH_2-CH_2-CH_3 \longrightarrow \begin{array}{c} H_3C \\ \diagdown \\ H_3C \diagup \end{array} CH-CH_2-CH_3$$

n-Pentane   Isopentane

RON 62   RON 92

FIGURE 7-6 *A typical isomerization reaction consisting of the conversion of n-pentane into isopentane (2-methylbutane) with a resulting increase in octane number (RON) from 62 to 92.*

activity, however, there is the problem of undesirable side reactions, such as the formation of olefins. These side reactions can be reduced by providing hydrogen or other inhibitors along with the feedstock.

The benefits of the isomerization process are primarily the increase of the octane number of an LSR fraction for blending and the production of additional isobutane for alkylation reactions. The octane number of LSR can be improved from about 70 to about 82 in the isomerate or even to the upper 80s if the normal paraffins are recycled [10]. This makes the isomerization process very useful for improving the quality of gasoline being produced.

E/ Reforming

Reforming, like isomerization, does not aim to change the molecular weights of compounds or the boiling point range of a fraction, but rather aims to improve the octane rating by changing the chemical structure of some compounds. The primary reforming reaction is the production of aromatic compounds from cycloalkanes. Whereas isomerization was performed primarily on feedstock in the C_4 or C_5 to C_6 range, by necessity, reforming requires higher molecular weights for the efficient production of aromatic compounds. Although other reactions occur in the reformer, the primary outcome is an improved octane rating due to an increase in aromatic compounds and a decrease in alicyclic compounds.

The major reactions taking place in the reformer involve dehydrogenation, isomerization, and cracking. When n-alkanes are isomerized as in the isomerization process utilized for their lower molecular weight counterparts, there is an increase in octane rating with no significant change in boiling point range or molecular size. This is a desirable reaction. The dehydrocyclization of alkanes to cycloalkanes is also a desired reaction, not because cycloalkanes are useful, but because they are then easily converted to aromatics via a relatively simple reaction. The conversion of cycloalkanes to aromatics is a reaction involving the change from a saturated ring to an aromatic ring. Because of this loss of hydrogen, this is referred to as a dehydrogenation reaction. Figure 7-7 shows a typical dehydrogenation

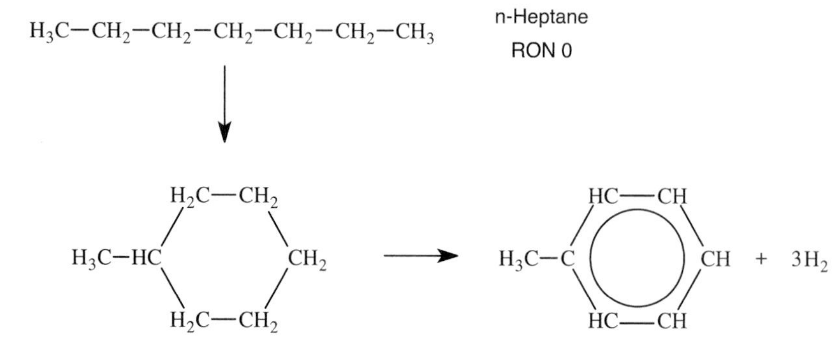

$H_3C-CH_2-CH_2-CH_2-CH_2-CH_2-CH_3$ n-Heptane
RON 0

Methylcyclohexane   Toluene
RON 70   RON 120

FIGURE 7-7 *The reforming process consists of converting alkanes to cycloalkanes and cycloalkanes to aromatics. In this typical example, the low octane paraffin n-heptane (RON 0) is converted to methylcylcohexane (RON 72), which is then converted to toluene (RON 120) with the release of hydrogen.*

reaction of a cycloalkane to an aromatic. Reaction conditions can be modified to favor the production of aromatics resulting in an almost complete conversion of alicyclic compounds to aromatic compounds.

The most common catalyst for reforming reactions is platinum, supported by alumina or silica-alumina. As with other catalysts previously discussed, catalyst poisoning can be a problem, primarily due to hydrogen sulfide; however, it is a reversible process, since the catalyst can be regenerated. The removal of sulfur from the feedstock is beneficial for a variety of reasons, not the least of which is that catalysts will last longer.

In general, the product of reforming reactions is a high-octane blending stock. How high an octane number the reformate will obtain may be affected by a variety of process variables, but is actually most dependent upon the composition of the feedstock [3]. A feed that is rich in cycloalkanes undergoes a relatively easy and efficient conversion to a product that is rich in aromatics. A feed that is more highly paraffinic has to undergo additional reactions, including the isomerization and dehydrocyclization of normal alkanes to branched alkanes and cycloalkanes, prior to their conversion to aromatic compounds. Therefore, the resulting reformate is not as rich in aromatics, and has a lower octane rating. Figure 7-8 shows the change in composition for a typical feedstock having gone through a catalytic reforming process.

F/ Blending

One of the most critical tasks that remains for the economically efficient production of automotive gasolines and other refined products is the

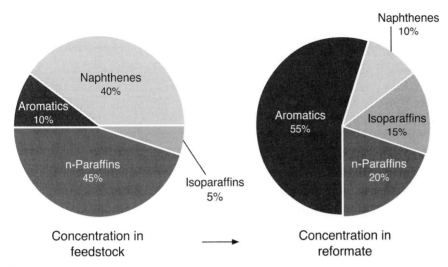

FIGURE 7-8 *Changes from feedstock to product in terms of chemical composition as a result of reforming reactions. In the reforming process, normal paraffins will be converted to isoparaffins and/or cycloalkanes (naphthenes). Naphthenes are very efficiently converted to aromatics, with a resulting production of hydrogen.*

blending process. The final specifications of a product depend heavily on the blending process. How products are blended will depend on many variables, including the location where a product is to be marketed, the season of use, the product specifications, and the environmental regulations, to name just a few. The blending process can also be used to affect how a refinery's yields are allocated to different products. Effective blending provides flexibility to allow for greater amounts of specific products when there is an increased demand [10]. Decisions regarding blending parameters can have a major economic impact on a refinery's profits, and for this reason its importance cannot be overlooked. Because many of the issues surrounding blending are dependent upon achieving particular specifications in the finished product, blending is discussed in Subsection 7.6.5, after the introduction of some of the major petroleum tests used to measure product specifications.

7.6 PETROLEUM PRODUCT PROPERTIES

7.6.1 Principle

Petroleum products must meet a variety of specifications depending on their end use. Manufacturers of products that utilize petroleum-based solvents may require a minimal level of sulfur or aromatic content or a desired flash point, depending on their specific application. Some applications require ease of vaporization, and products designed with this scope have a relatively high vapor pressure as well as a relatively low flash point. For other applications however, it is often best to have a flash point in the combustible range, rather than the flammable range. This eases shipping and transportation requirements, resulting in lower costs. Products designed as cleaning solvents or degreasers require a higher solvating power, often measured by the kauri-butanol value, in order to effectively dissolve materials. Other products, such as those used in indoor applications (for example, oils for liquid candles) have different requirements; generally they need to be low-odor and low smoke products. Gasoline and transportation fuels have their own requirements, which involve specific performance parameters, as well as specific vapor pressure, sulfur content, aromatic content, and so on. In order to test all these parameters, a wide variety of tests exist, a few of which are presented in the following subsections.

Kauri-Butanol Value

The kauri-butanol value, abbreviated Kb, is defined as the volume of solvent required to reach the cloud point of the solution when added to 20 g of a solution of 20% w/w kauri resin in n-butanol. Kauri resin is extracted from the kauri tree, found in New Zealand. ASTM International has developed the standard D 1133-04 for determining Kb value [11].

The Kb value often is used to evaluate the dissolving ability of hydrocarbons and the aromaticity of solvents. The Kb value usually increases in the following sequence: aliphatics < cycloalkanes < aromatics. The higher the Kb value, the stronger the dissolving power of the solvent. A mild cleaner will have a relatively low value, whereas a powerful degreaser will have a significantly higher Kb value. Examples of the Kb values for some common solvents are shown in Table 7-2 [12].

Table 7-2	Kauri-butanol value
Solvent	**Kb value**
n-Octane	24.5
n-Heptane	25.4
n-Hexane	26.5
n-Pentane	33.8
Cyclohexane	54.3
d-Limonene	68
Xylenes	95
Toluene	105
Trichloroethylene	129
Dichloromethane	136

7.6.2 Flash Point

Flash point testing is important for a variety of product applications and there are several specific tests designed to measure flash point. Because of slight variations within these test methods, whenever flash point is reported, the test method used should be reported along with the value. Flash point has been defined in Subsection 4.6.6 as "the lowest temperature at which a substance generates a sufficient amount of vapor to form a (vapor/air) mixture that can be ignited." It should be added that this lowest temperature is determined through specific laboratory tests.

Flammable, Combustible, and Ignitable Liquids

Flash point is an important concept for both the fire investigator and the fire debris analyst. The definitions of the terms "flammable liquid" and "combustible liquid" are both dependent upon flash point as explained in Subsection 4.6.6: In the United States, the primary criterion for determining if an ignitable liquid is flammable or combustible is whether its flash point is less than 100°F (37.8°C) or equal to or greater than 100°F (37.8°C), respectively. Because a liquid at or above its flash point is ready to burn, products with flash points below ambient temperature are more hazardous, and specific precautions must be taken during their shipment.

For years, fire investigators and criminalists struggled with the awkwardness of the phrasing "flammable or combustible liquids." In addition, the legal definitions of flammable and combustible liquids vary from one country to another. The use of the term "ignitable liquid" provides a solution and has gained acceptance as the preferred terminology especially when flash point testing has not been conducted.

Although the specifics of flash point testing vary depending on the particular test method used, most rely upon the same basic methodology. The liquid being tested is held at a temperature below its expected flash point and a spark or flame is applied at the liquid surface. If there is no "flash" or momentary flame, then the temperature is raised incrementally, and the spark or flame applied again. The process is repeated until the vapors above the liquid are sufficient to produce the momentary flash. The temperature at which this occurs is deemed the flash point.

Flash point is often an important specification of petroleum-based products and is one of the most commonly reported values used to describe a product. Flash point testing is not commonly performed on fire scene evidence, although with the advent of testing equipment requiring minimal volumes, it may become a more frequently utilized test. A discussion of flash point testing as it relates to the forensic examination of evidence appears in Section 14.6.

7.6.3 Octane Number Testing

In the previous sections discussing refinery procedures, and how gasoline is made, a lot of emphasis was placed on procedures that produced a high octane rating blending stock. Octane number, also called octane value or octane rating, is one of the critical measures of a gasoline's performance. It is a measure of a fuel's resistance to knock or to ignite prematurely.

Historically, as people wanted more powerful engines, there were several ways that could be used to get additional power from an engine, but most early attempts were aimed at making bigger engines, with more cylinders. Eventually, it was realized that increasing output in this fashion could not continue indefinitely, and so engine manufacturers aimed at increasing the compression ratio. The problem with increasing the compression ratio of the engine is that the fuel has a much greater tendency to ignite prematurely or to "knock," which negatively impacts engine performance, and could also result in serious engine damage such as crankshaft or valve breakage [3]. Consequently, anti-knock properties of fuel became increasingly important, as more powerful engines with increased compression ratio became the norm.

There are two different performance-based tests used to determine the octane number of a fuel. The motor octane number (MON) and the research octane number (RON) both represent how a gasoline product performs under specific test conditions. These performances then are compared with mixtures of varying ratios of standard reference fuels. Both the motor and the research test utilize the same standard test engine; however the operating parameters are different. The MON test was developed first and is a more rigorous test aimed at simulating highway driving conditions, whereas the RON test is less rigorous and attempts to simulate city driving conditions [10]. In general, the MON of a modern gasoline is approximately 8 to 10 points lower than its RON.

In most countries, the octane number placed at the gas pump is the RON as shown in Figure 7-9. In the United States and a few other countries, the octane number posted at the gas pump is neither the RON nor the MON; it is the arithmetic average of the MON and RON as shown in Figure 7-10. This octane number generally is called the pump octane number (PON), the road octane number (RdON), or even the anti-knock index (AKI).

FIGURE 7-9

In Switzerland, like in most countries around the world, the octane number shown at the gas pump is the RON (mentioned as ROZ on the handle).

FIGURE 7-10

Photographs of the explanatory label for the octane number of the gasoline found on a gas pump in Atlanta, Georgia, USA.

FIGURE 7-11

In the United States, the displayed octane number is the PON and thus, results in lower values than in other countries (compare with Figure 7-9).

This explains why the displayed octane number in the United States is usually much lower than in other countries (see Figure 7-11).

The standard liquids used for the octane number tests are n-heptane, which has very poor knock resistance, and is thus assigned a value of 0, and isooctane (2,2,4-trimethylpentane), which exhibits excellent knock resistance, and is thus assigned a value of 100. The anti-knock performance of the fuel being tested is then compared to mixtures of the two standards; if its performance is equivalent to a mixture that is 89% isooctane and 11% n-heptane, it would have an octane number of 89.

Octane Numbers above 100

There are several hydrocarbon compounds, and even some commercial gasolines, that have octane numbers greater than 100. For compounds and blends with octane numbers outside the range of 0 to 100, a different means of testing octane number is necessary. This is done by adding tetraethyl lead (TEL) to pure isooctane. By doing this, an extended range of octane standards was developed. For example, when one milliliter of TEL is added to a gallon of isooctane, the resulting blend has a standard octane number of 108.6; when 2 ml are added, the standard octane number is 112.8; when 6 ml are added, the resulting blend has a standard value of 120.3 [3]. By using this different set of standards octane numbers can be determined for fuels having values well over 100.

Octane characteristics of different chemical compounds can widely vary, but tend to follow a few basic trends. Figure 7-12 shows some of the basic variation tendencies of the octane number for different types of compounds.

Aromatic compounds tend to have the highest octane ratings of the hydrocarbons, whereas straight chain saturated hydrocarbons are among the

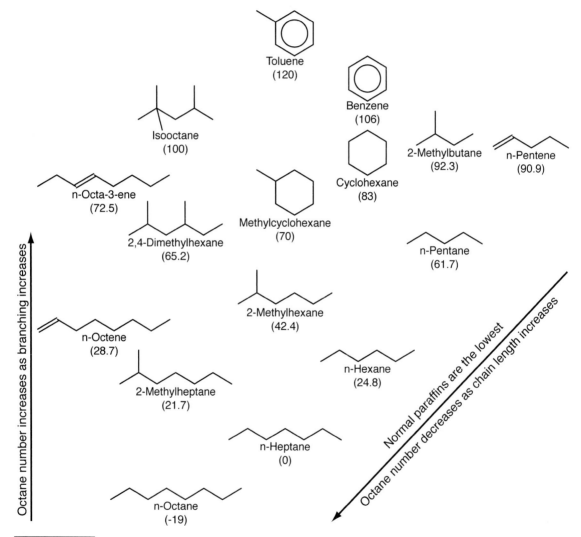

FIGURE 7-12 *Octane number (in this case RON) follows several general trends. Normal paraffins have the lowest octane ratings, and the longer the hydrocarbon chain, the lower the octane value. Branching has a tendency to increase octane number, and the more extensive the branching, the greater the improvement in octane rating. The octane number of an olefin is better than that of its corresponding paraffin, and an internal double bond results in a greater increase than a terminal double bond. Aromatics are by far superior to their aliphatic counterparts.*

worst. For normal paraffins, the bigger the homolog, the lower the octane number. Isoparaffinic compounds are vastly superior to their straight chain counterparts and the octane number generally improves with increased branching. Olefins and cycloalkanes are somewhat better than their corresponding alkanes; however olefins are undesirable for other reasons—primarily their reactivity. Perhaps it is now more clearly understood why the isomerization and reforming processes yield such high quality blending stocks for gasoline and why straight run gasoline is no longer suitable for the powerful engines of today.

Getting the Lead Out

Tetraethyl lead (TEL) was a very valuable additive to gasoline for many years. TEL is an organo-metallic compound, consisting of four ethyl groups attached to a central lead atom with the formula $Pb(CH_2CH_3)_4$. This compound was able to substantially increase the octane rating of a fuel with the addition of a very small volume. However, this was not a perfect solution. When tetraethyl lead was added to a fuel, it was also necessary to add 1,2-dibromoethane ($C_2H_4Br_2$) so that a vapor phase product, $PbBr_2$, could leave the engine without leaving behind lead residues.

As it turns out, the environmental effects of the exhaust gases of leaded gasoline engines proved to be extremely detrimental to the environment and to human health. As a result, leaded gasoline is no longer used, although some leaded gasolines are still available for use in specialty applications. Also, in some locations,

it is possible to buy TEL additives to be added to the gas tank along with regular unleaded gasoline. This particular application is used with classic and vintage vehicles, for which the well-being of the engine requires the use of leaded gasoline as lead would deposit on the valve seats in order to protect them against wear. Note that some aviation gas may still contain TEL, such as in 100LL (100 low lead, 100 being the octane number), however it is being gradually replaced with unleaded avgas [13].

The United Nations Environment Programme (UNEP) also is trying to completely phase out leaded gasoline and as of June 1, 2006, only three countries (Yemen, Afghanistan, and North Korea) are exclusively using leaded gasoline and about a dozen other countries are using both leaded and unleaded gasolines [14]. All other countries use exclusively unleaded gasoline.

7.6.4 Reid Vapor Pressure

Another important characteristic of the fuel for an internal combustion engine is its vapor pressure. Vapor pressure is the force (pressure) exerted onto the walls of a closed container due to the vapor phase of a liquid [3]. Another way of thinking of vapor pressure is to consider how much pressure is needed to keep the liquid from vaporizing [9]. Vapor pressures vary from liquid to liquid—for example, pentane is much more volatile than dodecane, and thus has a higher vapor pressure. It is also important to remember that vapor pressure is temperature dependent: vapor pressure increases with temperature. For this reason, when vapor pressures are reported, they should be done at a standard temperature. Finally, vapor pressure is perhaps most simply described as a way of measuring the volatility of a fuel.

In an internal combustion engine, fuel must provide sufficient vapors so that there is an ignitable fuel/air mixture in the cylinder. If the vapor pressure of the liquid is too low, there will be insufficient fuel in the mixture, and ignition may not occur (cold start capability). Conversely, if there is too much vapor, the mixture becomes too rich, and ignition cannot occur (vapor lock). Remembering, however, that the amount of vapor given off is highly dependent upon ambient temperature conditions, it is important to realize that a fuel suitable for summers in the hot weather of Florida may not work so well during the cold winters of Alaska. For this reason, vapor pressure ranges vary by location and season.

The specific testing for the volatility of gasolines is the Reid vapor pressure (RVP), which is a measure of vapor pressure at 37.8°C (100°F) in kilo-Pascals (kPa) [15]. The requirements for RVP are not only determined by what is required for the engine to run, but also by environmental standards. The higher the RVP, the more volatile the fuel, and therefore, the more hydrocarbons can be released into the environment when pumping gasoline. Because of this, it is desirable for environmental reasons to have lower RVPs and there are strict guidelines regulating seasonal maximum RVPs [16]. The Reid vapor pressures of many of the blending stocks for gasoline are fairly low (in the range of 1 to 11 psi) [9]. In order to boost the values, butane is the most commonly used blending agent. Butane has an RVP of 52 psi and is easily blended into gasoline to increase its vapor pressure without detrimental effects to the final product. RVP therefore is controlled with relative ease, by changing the amount of butane used in the blending process to meet the requirements for the market and season.

7.6.5 Gasoline Blending

Considerations for gasoline blending are driven primarily by the needs of the automobile engine, the requirements set forth by environmental regulations, and the refiners' economic concerns. In the United States, the 1990 Clean Air Act Amendment (CAAA) encompassed many regulations regarding gasoline, including mandates to reduce gasoline emissions of volatile organic compounds [17]. These objectives can be met by reducing RVPs and aromatic content and by adding oxygenated compounds. Reductions in RVP require lower amounts of 4-carbon and 5-carbon compounds in the finished product. Other requirements of the CAAA included strict controls on the permissible amount of benzene in gasoline (maximum 1%) and that there be a minimum amount of oxygen (2% by weight) blended into reformulated gasoline (RFG) [17]. In addition to these requirements and because of environmental and health reasons, gasoline blending must also take into account the production of various grades, or octane numbers, of fuel.

In order to effectively function in an engine, the vapor pressure of a gasoline must be high enough to provide sufficient vapors for ignition, but low enough to avoid vapor lock and to comply with environmental regulations. Different blending stocks have different RVP values, which are taken into consideration during the blending process in order to achieve the desired final RVP value. Blending stock such as a typical straight run gasoline has an RVP of approximately 11.1 psi; alkylate is in the range of 4.6 psi; reformate is around 2.8 psi; and butanes are 52.0 and 71.0 psi for the normal and branched compounds, respectively [9]. A blend of these components will result in a product with an RVP equivalent to the weighted average of the components. Therefore, when it is necessary to increase the volatility of the product, butane is the blending agent of choice. Normal butane is preferred to isobutane for increasing RVP even though its value is lower. The main reason is that the straight chain isomer is more abundant, and the branched isomer can be better used in the alkylation process [9]. If RVP were the only property to consider in the blending process, it would be a relatively straightforward process. Unfortunately, it is not so.

The process of blending gasoline also takes into account the octane number. Gasoline sold at retail stations is available in several grades, primarily distinguished by their octane number. Various blending stocks exhibit fairly significant differences in octane numbers, and these can be calculated based on the proportions used in the final product. Typical octane numbers (MON/RON) for common blending stocks are 61.6/66.4 for straight run gasoline; 84.4/94.0 for reformate; 78.1/87.4 for n-butane; and 76.8/92.3 for cat-cracked gasoline blending stock [9]. To meet both RVP and octane specifications, several algebraic expressions must be simultaneously satisfied.

In order to comply with the requirements for RFG, oxygenates must also be blended in. Typically, the most commonly used oxygenates have been methyl *tert*-butyl ether (MTBE) and ethanol, although other oxygenated compounds have been explored such as ethyl *tert*-butyl ether (ETBE). Methanol had shown some promise, but its tendency to phase-separate in the presence of water and the toxicity of some of its combustion products made it a less desirable option. Ethanol is readily available and inexpensive and has the additional advantage of exhibiting a high octane number. Also, ethanol has a fairly high RVP however, and when used, it necessitates adjusting other parameters such as eliminating C_4-compounds and severely limiting the amount of C_5-compounds that can be present in the finished product. MTBE has the advantages of a high octane number and relatively low RVP, although it is more expensive and not as easily produced as ethanol. In addition, MTBE has been found in groundwater supplies, raising environmental concerns [18]. The choice of oxygenate will affect the RVP and octane values, thereby making the blending process even more complex.

Methyl *tert*-Butyl Ether

MTBE started to be used in gasoline in the early 1980s as a substitute for tetraethyl lead as an anti-knocking agent [19]. It provided oxygen to the combustion reaction, thereby reducing exhaust emissions, although the impact of this is negligible with today's modern engines. With the advent of the Clean Air Act Amendment (CAAA) of 1990, producers had to increase the level of oxygenates in reformulated gasoline (RFG) to at least 2% (w/w) [17]. However, the CAAA did not specify how this level of oxygenate was to be achieved [20].

MTBE initially was chosen by most manufacturers—as of 1999, 85% of RFG used MTBE to meet the oxygen content requirement and only about 8% used ethanol [21]—primarily due to its low cost. Problems quickly arose with the use of MTBE, however. Because the regulations for the storage of RFG in underground tanks were not very stringent—they do not require a no leak policy, but rather tolerate a limited leak (such as 5 gallons per day)—

contamination of the groundwater occurred. Although the groundwater is affected only minimally by the hydrocarbon portion of gasoline, MTBE has a much greater persistence and mobility due to its more polar nature and increased solubility.

As a consequence, a panel of experts, called the Blue Ribbon Panel on Oxygenates in Gasoline, was formed to study this issue. They conclude that [21] "... the use of MTBE in the program has resulted in growing detections of MTBE in drinking water, with between 5% and 10% of drinking water supplies in high oxygenate use areas showing at least detectable amounts of MTBE." Based on their recommendations, the EPA recently removed the 2% oxygenates requirement in gasoline in order to [22] "provide U.S. oil refiners with greater flexibility in producing clean-burning gasoline." At this time, MTBE is not being used in gasolines in the United States.

It is important to keep in mind that the blending technique is one of the most crucial steps in the entire refining process. Blending should maximize the efficiency of all the supporting processes, so that the various products can be blended according to the current market demand. This requires flexibility and the use of computer models in order to maximize the economic value of the products, while still adhering to product specifications. Product blending is dependent upon every other process within the refinery and has a major effect on the specifications, quality, and performance of the final product.

With this fundamental understanding of crude oil, some of the major aspects of the refining process, and some of the specifications for petroleum-based products, it is now possible to begin to apply this knowledge to fire debris analysis. An in-depth discussion of data interpretation is provided in Chapters 9 and 12; however, the following section is an introduction to the classification of petroleum products in terms of the manufacturing process. It will serve as a foundation for the section on data interpretation.

7.7 THE ASTM CLASSIFICATION SCHEME

7.7.1 Principle

The forensic science community, through ASTM International, has developed consensus guidelines for the analysis of fire debris, and for the classification of ignitable liquids and their residues. These standards are an important aspect of quality in forensic sciences and are discussed in greater detail in Chapter 16. One important aspect of the fire debris standards is the ignitable liquid classification scheme, which is contained in ASTM standard test methods E 1387 and E 1618[3] [24, 25]. This system for organizing ignitable liquids recovered from fire-related evidence is an important tool in understanding the similarities and differences in petroleum-based ignitable liquids. The current system for the classification of ignitable liquids is the result of the work of many dedicated analysts striving for improved quality in their field. As part of an ASTM standard test method, this classification scheme will continue to undergo regular reviews to ensure that it reflects the variety of ignitable liquids encountered.

How Does Classification Work?

The classification of ignitable liquids is by necessity based upon chemical composition and boiling point range and not on the commercial use of the product. This is due to the fact that an ignitable liquid of a given chemical composition may be marketed as many different end-use products. Marketing practices dictate that a product must meet certain specifications and rarely that it must have a specific chemical composition. Therefore, a paint thinner, a cleaning solvent, and a charcoal starter fluid may all be made from the same exact chemical composition. The fire debris analyst, in examining this product, may be able to describe it based on its chemical content, but will not be able to unequivocally state what its original intended use was. The classification of petroleum products will be based upon the general volatility of the product, expressed as a boiling point range, and upon the families of chemical compounds that are present in the product. The criteria for classifying ignitable liquids are discussed in greater detail in Chapter 9.

There are seven general categories of ignitable liquids, each of which is defined based upon criteria related to chemical composition. These classifications include six categories that are then further characterized based on boiling point range as light, medium, or heavy [25]. The other major classification is gasoline, which is a unique product with a unique use. As such, it is the only category within this classification system that describes not only chemical composition, but also market use of a product. In addition, an extra category called "miscellaneous" exists to address ignitable liquids that cannot be placed into any of the other seven categories. The criminalist

---

[3] ASTM changed its classification system in 2006 based on the recommendation of the Fire Laboratory Standards and Protocols Committee of the Technical Working Group for Fire and Explosions [23]. At the time of this writing, however, the ASTM standards E 1618 and E 1387 have not yet been brought into agreement with one another: ASTM International did not mirror the changes made to the classification system of E 1618 to E 1387. Thus, the user is now left with two different classification systems. This book refers to the classification system presented in the new modified system (available in E 1618).

with a strong background in chemistry and with a good foundation of knowledge of the petroleum refining techniques will be well equipped to understand and apply this classification system.

There are two important concepts related to the composition of products originating from crude oil that must be well understood.

I. The refinery process begins with distillation, consequently, most products encountered, with very few exceptions, will be limited to a relatively narrow boiling point range. Thus, most products initially are described as falling within the light, medium, or heavy range. It is recognized that not all products will fall neatly within one of these ranges and this issue is addressed in the ASTM standards. For products overlapping or falling between ranges, it is explicitly stated that terms such as "light to medium" and "medium to heavy" are acceptable and in some cases may even be preferable [25]. It should be noted that some classifications generally tend to have much broader boiling point ranges than others; even in these cases, the range is narrow (typically spanning a maximum of 15 carbon numbers) relative to that of the original crude oil (several dozens of carbon numbers).

II. Regarding the ultimate composition of products originating from crude oil, all compounds present in petroleum within the limited boiling point range of the product will be present in the product, unless specific efforts have been made to remove them. The refining process is substantially responsible for changing the relative amounts of the types of compounds present within a specific product, however the removal of a class of compounds is usually the result of additional processing at a petrochemical facility.

These two basic rules of composition are helpful in understanding the criteria for the various classifications of ignitable liquids. Figure 7-13 is a very simplified schematic representation of the different ASTM classes of ignitable liquids and their relationships to one another and to crude oil. This figure should help the analyst have an overall understanding of what types of chemical compounds are present in each class.

7.7.2 Gasoline

Gasoline is one of the most highly refined products leaving the refinery. Originating from relatively light fractions (C_4–C_{12}), automotive gasoline is the result of blending the products of a variety of refinery operations, including the products of isomerization, reforming, cracking, and alkylation reactions. If gasoline were simply the product of straight run fractional distillation, it would differ significantly in composition and would be a poor fuel for the internal combustion engine. Since lead-based compounds can

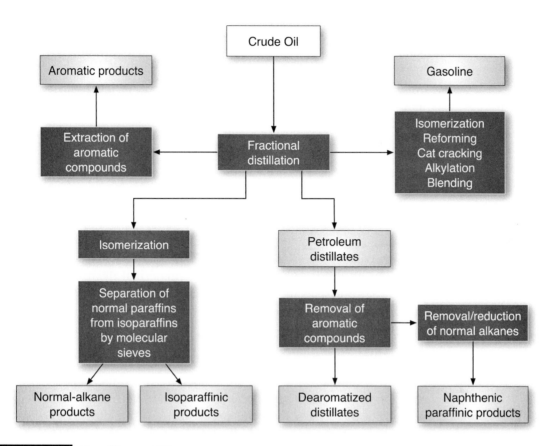

FIGURE 7-13 *The different ASTM classes used to classify ignitable liquid in relation to crude oil and the refining process. This figure is an over-simplified representation of the processes leading to these classes, as they are much more complicated than presented. However, it helps the fire debris analyst to understand better the different compounds present in each class of liquid.*

no longer be added to most gasolines, the octane number of gasoline is increased primarily by augmenting the relative proportion of aromatic compounds and isoparaffins. Gasoline contains essentially all classes of hydrocarbons in the C_4 to C_{12} range, but is dominated by aromatic compounds, with the alkylbenzenes being the most abundant and with a lesser abundance of naphthalene-based and indane-based compounds.

7.7.3 Distillates

A/ Regular Distillates

Distillates undergo relatively little refining, other than physical separation based upon boiling point. Consequently, the composition of distillates generally mirrors the composition of the crude oil from which it was distilled. Distillate products are rich in aliphatic content, yet contain aromatic compounds as well. Normal paraffins are particularly well represented, however there is a significant presence of isoparaffinic compounds and cycloalkanes as well. Because distillate products do not undergo specific processing to remove any one class of compounds naturally occurring in crude oil, all classes of compounds present within a given boiling point range of crude oil are normally present in a distillate product.

B/ Dearomatized Distillates

Similar to their distillate counterparts just discussed, dearomatized distillates are comparable in composition to the fraction of petroleum from which they were derived. The major difference, as the name implies, is the specific and intentional removal of aromatic compounds. Aromatics may be removed by solvent extraction methods or by adsorption methods using a silica gel. Consequently, dearomatized distillates are rich in normal alkanes, with a significant presence of isoalkanes and cycloalkanes. These types of products contain virtually no aromatic compounds; neither mononuclear, nor polynuclear.

7.7.4 Naphthenic Paraffinic

Naphthenic paraffinic products are derived from distillate products, but undergo additional processing to remove not only the bulk of aromatic compounds, but also a significant portion of the normal alkanes. With the removal of these classes of compounds, the resulting product is composed almost exclusively of branched alkanes and cycloalkanes. A more appropriate name for this class of products would be naphthenic isoparaffinic, to clearly distinguish this type of product from the similarly composed dearomatized distillates [23]. Although the production of naphthenic paraffinic products includes the removal of normal alkanes and aromatic compounds, there may still often be a certain amount of normal alkanes present in the finished product.

7.7.5 Isoparaffinic Products

Isoparaffinic products are one of the classes of ignitable liquids that results from significant processing. This type of product consists entirely of branched alkanes (isoparaffinic compounds). The removal of aromatic, cycloalkanes, and normal alkanes results in a low odor, clean burning product suitable for a variety of uses. Technically, it is not all the other compounds that are removed; rather, the isoparaffins are removed and recovered as a relatively pure fraction. The feedstock for the production of isoparaffinic products is the isomerate stock, as it is rich in the desired components. This is then passed through a molecular sieve, upon which the isoparaffins are retained. They can then be removed via a solvent extraction. Isoparaffinic products tend to be very narrow range products, and have very low levels of other compounds.

7.7.6 Normal Alkane Products

Normal alkane products, as the name implies, are products consisting virtually entirely of straight chain paraffins. They often are used for applications
in which a low soot burning is required, such as for liquid candle oils.
Normal paraffins are separated from their feedstock via a molecular sieve.
They tend to have somewhat narrow boiling point ranges, and generally
only a few compounds.

7.7.7 Aromatic Products

Aromatic solvents often are desired for their solvating ability. This type of
product is highly refined and completely lacks aliphatic components. Aromatic products generally are manufactured from a feedstock rich in aromatics such as the reformate. There are several means for accomplishing the
production of aromatic solvents. Extractive distillation and the Udex process
are both procedures involving fractional distillation in the presence of a
solvent as means of removing aromatic compounds [3]. Another method for
the recovery of aromatic compounds is to remove them from a refinery
stream onto an appropriate adsorbent material, such as silica gel. The pure
aromatic fraction can then be desorbed using a solvent [3].

7.7.8 Oxygenated Products

The classification of oxygenated products contains a variety of ignitable
liquids, including single solvents as well as solvent blends. Products such
as alcohols, ketones, and ethers will fall into this class, as will petroleum
products blended with at least one oxygenated compound, present at a significant concentration. Many of the liquids falling under this classification
do not originate from the refinery of crude oil.

7.7.9 Miscellaneous

While the vast majority of ignitable liquids commonly used as accelerants
can be classified into one of the previous categories, there will always exist
products that cannot be neatly classified. Two of the major types of ignitable
liquids that may be encountered in a fire investigation include vegetable oils
and turpentine. Turpentine is a product distilled from pine wood, consisting
primarily of terpene-related compounds such as α-pinene. The challenge to
the forensic scientist regarding the analysis of turpentine lies in the fact that
it is a natural product, and the commercial liquid product can generally not
be distinguished from the terpenes extracted from wood in fire debris samples
[26, 27]. Vegetable oils pose a different challenge, as they are blends of saturated and unsaturated fatty acids. Although they are ignitable liquids, this
is not the primary reason why they are of concern to the fire investigator.
The major concern with these types of oils is that they pose a risk of spontaneous ignition as discussed in Chapter 4. The analysis of vegetable oils

requires a different analytical procedure than that used for the analysis of ILR. Similarly, the approach to data interpretation for vegetable oil residues is different than that used for petroleum-based liquids. Vegetable oils are discussed in greater detail in Chapter 14.

REFERENCES

1. Bertsch W, Holzer G, and Sellers CS (1993) *Chemical analysis for the arson investigator and attorney*, Hüthig Buch Verlag, Heidelberg, Germany.
2. Coulson SA and Morgan-Smith RK (2000) The transfer of petrol on to clothing and shoes while pouring petrol around a room, *Forensic Science International*, **112**(2–3), pp 135–41.
3. Speight JG (1999) *The chemistry and technology of petroleum*, 3rd edition, Marcel Dekker, New York, NY.
4. Gold T (1999) *The deep hot biosphere*, Springer-Verlag, New York, NY.
5. Chevron USA (2006) *What is crude oil?*, available from http://www.chevron.com/products/learning_center/crude, last access performed on April 19, 2006.
6. McGrath KA and Travers B (1999) *World of scientific discovery*, Thomson Gale, Farmington Hill, MI.
7. Wikipedia (2007) *Athabasca oil sands*, available from http://en.wikipedia.org/wiki/Athabasca_Tar_Sands, last access performed on June 10, 2007.
8. Society of Petroleum Engineers (2007) *Glossary of industry terms*, available from http://www.spe.org/spe/jsp/basic/0,,1104_1710,00.html, last access performed on March 21, 2007.
9. Leffler WL (2000) *Petroleum refining in nontechnical language*, 3rd edition, PennWell Corporation, Tulsa, OK.
10. Gary JH and Handwerk GE (1994) *Petroleum refining technology and economics*, 3rd edition, Marcel Dekker, New York, NY.
11. ASTM International (2006) *ASTM D 1133-04 Standard test method for kauri-butanol value of hydrocarbon solvents*, Annual Book of ASTM Standards 06.04, West Conshohocken, PA.
12. VWR International (2006) *Technical tables—Kauri butanol values*, available from http://uk.vwr.com/app/Header?tmpl=/technical_services/table_kauri_butanol.htm, last access performed on December 23, 2006.
13. Aircraft Owners and Pilots Association (2006) *Avgas (100LL) alternatives*, available from http://www.aopa.org/whatsnew/regulatory/regunlead.html, last access performed on December 23, 2006.
14. United Nations Environment Programme (2006) *Leaded petrol phase-out: Global status*, available from http://www.unep.org/pcfv/Data/Data.htm#leaded, last access performed on December 23, 2006.
15. ASTM International (2006) *ASTM D 323-99a Standard test method for vapor pressure of petroleum products (Reid method)*, Annual Book of Standards 05.01, West Conshohocken, PA.
16. Environmental Protection Agency (2005) *Guide on federal and state summer RVP standards for conventional gasoline only*, Environmental Protection Agency, Washington, DC.
17. United States Congress (1990) *Amendments to the Clean Air Act*, Environmental Protection Agency, Washington, DC.
18. The Blue Ribbon Panel on Oxygenates in Gasoline (1999) *Achieving clean air and clean water*, Environmental Protection Agency, Washington, DC.
19. Davidson JM and Creek DN (2000) Using the gasoline additive MTBE in forensic environmental investigations, *Environmental Forensics*, **1**(1), pp 31–6.

20. Oge MT (1999) *Office of Transportation and Air Quality U.S. Environmental Protection Agency before the Subcommittee on Energy and Environment of the Committee on Science*, House of Representatives, Environmental Protection Agency, Washington, DC.

21. The Blue Ribbon Panel on Oxygenates in Gasoline (1999) *Executive summary and recommendations*, Environmental Protection Agency, Washington, DC.

22. Office of Transportation and Air Quality (2006) *Removal of reformulated gasoline oxygen content requirement and revision of commingling prohibition to address non-oxygenated reformulated gasoline*, Environmental Protection Agency, Washington, DC.

23. Fire Laboratory Standards and Protocols Committee (2004) *Letter to John J. Lentini, Chair of ASTM Committee E30*, Technical and Scientific Working Group for Fire and Explosions.

24. ASTM International (2006) *ASTM E 1387-01 Standard test method for ignitable liquid residues in extracts from fire debris samples by gas chromatography*, Annual Book of ASTM Standards 14.02, West Conshohocken, PA.

25. ASTM International (2006) *ASTM E 1618-06 Standard test method for ignitable liquid residues in extracts from fire debris samples by gas chromatography-mass spectrometry*, Annual Book of ASTM Standards 14.02, West Conshohocken, PA.

26. Trimpe MA (1991) Turpentine in arson analysis, *Journal of Forensic Sciences*, **36**(4), pp 1059–73.

27. Chanson B et al. (2000) Turpentine identification in fire debris analysis, *2nd European Academy of Forensic Science Meeting*, Cracow, Poland.

CHAPTER 8

Gas Chromatography and Gas Chromatography–Mass Spectrometry

"Like light rays in the spectrum, the different components of a pigment mixture, obeying a law, are resolved on the calcium carbonate column and then can be qualitatively and quantitatively determined. I call such a preparation a chromatogram and the corresponding method the chromatographic method."

Mikhail Semenovich Tswett, Russian botanist (1872–1919)

8.1 INTRODUCTION

Gas chromatography-mass spectrometry has become unquestionably the technique of choice for the analysis of ignitable liquids and their residues. The reasons for this are many, most notably that the nature of ignitable liquids (IL) requires that a separation be part of the analytical process, and the fact that a mass spectrometer can provide a relatively quick, straightforward, and inexpensive means of identifying the separated components.

In the previous chapter, a great deal of attention was given to the composition of petroleum products, and with good reason. One way of looking at it is that the compositions of the variety of petroleum products that have the potential for use as an accelerant in a fire are very similar to one another; they are volatile, nonpolar mixtures containing primarily hydrocarbons. But, clearly, it is possible to differentiate products into categories based on their chemical composition. Different classes of products may have many common components, although not all. Indeed, even in cases in which there is significant overlap, there will be definite differences in the relative amounts of the various components and in the nature of some of them. As an example, automotive gasoline and a medium petroleum distillate (MPD) each have the C_8, C_9, and C_{10} normal alkanes: Yet, in the MPD, they will be present as a major feature of the product, whereas in gasoline they will be minor.

Similarly, aromatic compounds such as the C_2- and C_3-alkylbenzenes will be present in the distillate, but at very low levels compared to their aliphatic counterparts. In contrast, gasoline will be very rich in these aromatic compounds. Because of this phenomenon, a chromatographic separation is essential. It is not any one single component that allows one to identify a petroleum product, but rather the presence of many components in the appropriate relative ratios. Gas chromatography is uniquely suited to this task.

It is important to understand that gas chromatography is not an analytical tool in itself: it is merely a separation technique. It is necessary to couple it to another device—called a detector—in order to obtain a signal, and thus data. Once coupled to a detector, such as a mass spectrometer, a full analytical technique is obtained. This chapter discusses the theory of the primary instruments used in the analysis of IL. Both gas chromatography (GC) and mass spectrometry (MS) will be examined in detail, as well as the unique benefits associated with the hyphenated technique gas chromatography–mass spectrometry (GC–MS). A thorough understanding of the appropriate instrumental theory will guide the fire debris analyst not only in data interpretation, but also in the development of methods and appropriate quality control measures for incorporation into standard protocols.

8.2 CHROMATOGRAPHIC THEORY

8.2.1 Principle

Chromatography has a long and rich history as a separation technique. The word "chromatography" was first used by Tswett in 1906; it is derived from the Greek words *chroma* (color) and *graphien* (to write) [1]. Early applications of chromatography included noninstrumental techniques, such as column and paper chromatography. As the name implies, these techniques often were used for the separation of colored components in a mixture. Today these techniques are still used; however there is a greater focus on instrumental techniques, such as gas chromatography, high performance liquid chromatography (HPLC), and supercritical fluid chromatography (SFC) [2].

Chromatography is defined as [7]: "A physical method of separation in which the components to be separated are distributed between two phases, one of which is stationary (stationary phase) while the other (the mobile phase) moves in a definite direction." Although there are numerous types of chromatographic methods, there are several factors that are common to all types. All chromatographic systems have a mobile and a stationary phase. Regardless of the type of chromatography, samples are dissolved in the

Tswett, Inventor of Chromatography

Mikhail Semenovich Tswett was born during a family trip in northern Italy on May 14, 1872 [1]. His mother died soon after the birth and his father (who was Russian) took him to Switzerland where he would spend the next 24 years between Lausanne and Geneva. In 1896, he received his PhD in botany from the University of Geneva and he immediately returned to Russia. While there, he pursued research in the separation of chlorophylls, carotenes, and xanthophylls for which he invented column chromatography [1]. He first presented the concept of chromatography during a lecture in Russia in 1903 [3]. However, his new technique was not published until 1906, when two articles appeared in the *Berichte der Deutschen Botanischen Gesellschaft* [4, 5]. Unfortunately, the growth of this new method was hindered by Tswett's death in 1919, World War I, and the fact that his book was available only in Russian [6]. The renaissance of chromatography began in 1931, when German postdoctoral fellow Edgar Lederer published three important articles describing chromatography after reading Tswett's publications [6].

mobile phase, which travels through the stationary phase. Separation is possible because different compounds have different affinities for the mobile and stationary phases, thereby affecting their distribution between the two phases and their resulting behavior in the system.

8.2.2 Distribution Constant

The separation occurring in the chromatographic system is a result of differences in the distribution constant (K_c) of each species to be separated. The distribution constant, also called partition coefficient, is defined for a given chemical compound in a specific chromatographic system. It is the ratio of the solute concentration in the stationary phase to its concentration in the mobile phase, as shown in Equation 8-1 [8]:

$$K_c = \frac{c_s}{c_m} \qquad \text{(Equation 8-1)}$$

where c_s is the concentration of the analyte in the stationary phase and c_m is its concentration in the mobile phase. This value can then be used to describe the relative retention of a particular component. This means that, at equilibrium in a particular chromatographic system, a compound with a distribution constant above one has a greater concentration in the stationary phase than in the mobile phase and a compound with a distribution constant below one has a greater concentration in the mobile phase than in the stationary phase. In practical terms, the higher the K_c, the slower a compound moves through the chromatographic system, and the lower the K_c, the faster the compound moves through the system.

Stationary and Mobile Phases Analogy

It may be helpful to use an analogy to illustrate the concept of how distribution constants affect a separation. Picture two groups of 100 people each that embark on a one-mile walk, which represents the chromatographic system length. Group A represents a compound with a high K_c; at any point in time, 50 people will be resting (in the stationary phase) while 50 will be walking (in the mobile phase). Group B, which represents a low K_c compound, will have 10 members of its group resting at any point in time, while the other 90 are walking. The walking speed, which represents the velocity of the mobile phase, is not variable, nor is it dependent upon the group. The average speed of each individual, however, will be determined by how much time is spent resting and how much time is spent walking.

So if the walking speed of all individuals is 4 mph (mobile phase velocity), and the Group A walkers rest 50% of the time, then their average speed will be 2 mph,

and it will take them 30 minutes to walk the one-mile distance (see Figure 8-1). Group B also walks at a rate of 4 mph, but spends only 10% of their time resting, therefore this group achieves an average speed of 3.6 mph. As a result, Group B finishes their mile walk in 16.7 minutes. Even though the members of the two groups started out mixed together, they are now separated into two distinct groups, since one of the groups finished almost 15 minutes before the other one.

This example illustrates the following:

- When in the mobile phase, the velocity of a compound is constant and is equal to the velocity of the mobile phase.
- Separation can be achieved if the proportion of time spent between the stationary phase (resting) and the mobile phase (moving) is different for different compounds.

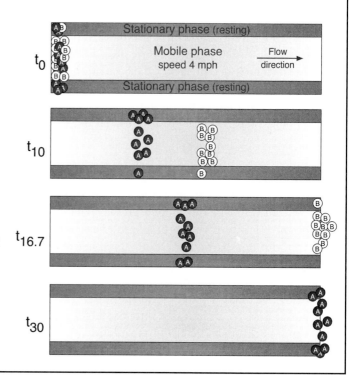

FIGURE 8-1

Illustration of the concept of distribution constant for two different groups of compounds. At time t = 0, all the molecules are grouped together. After a few minutes, group B is already separated from group A as it travels faster. After 16.7 minutes, group B elutes from the system and group A comes out after 30 minutes. Note that at all times, 50% of the members of group A are in the stationary phase, while only 10% of the members of group B are immobile in the stationary phase. This is the reason why group B travels faster through the chromatographic system than group A.

Distribution constants are the basis for all chromatographic separations, and it is important to understand the concept well. The greater the difference in distribution constant between two species, the more easily they can be separated. It is important to remember that K_c values are dependent upon a specific chromatographic system. If two species have very similar K_c values with a given system, it may be possible to use a different set of chromatographic conditions to modify these values and, thus, enhance an *a priori* difficult separation.

8.2.3 Retention Time and Abundance

Because chromatography separates compounds based on the difference in time when they elute,[1] a system has been adopted to express this difference. The simplest one is the retention time (t_R)—or the uncorrected retention time—which is a measure of the time from the injection of the sample into the system to the moment it elutes from the column and is detected. It is also possible to use the adjusted retention time (t_R'), which is calculated by subtracting the retention time of an unretained compound (symbolized t_M) from the retention time t_R. Figure 8-2 illustrates the different retention times used in a chromatographic system. In some instances, retention indices, which are simply relative retention times (one compound's retention time divided by a reference compound's retention time), are used.

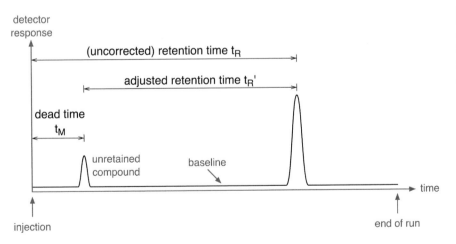

FIGURE 8-2

Illustration of the different retention times used in chromatography.

---

[1] One uses the term "to elute" to designate when a compound exits from the chromatographic system and is detected.

Unretained Compound

The concept of unretained compound is important for some chromatographic equations and to determine the linear velocity of a chromatographic system. An unretained compound is an analyte that, theoretically, does not spend any time in the stationary phase. As such it has a K_c value approaching zero. Thus, this analyte travels through the chromatographic system at nearly the speed of the mobile phase. It also represents the shortest amount of time for any analyte to go through the system. It can also be referred to as the dead time. In practice, air or methane often is considered an unretained compound in chromatographic systems used in fire debris analysis.

The adjusted retention time is required for certain chromatographic equations; however for the qualitative analysis of ignitable liquids and their residues, the (uncorrected) retention time value is used. The retention time of a compound is not entirely specific to it, because other compounds may have the same retention time. Also, the retention time will change from system to system. Nonetheless, it can provide some information about an unknown material based on the chromatographic system.

The abundance of a peak is a relative measure of the amount of the compound present. Abundance may be represented by either peak height or peak area, depending on the type of detectors (see Subsection 8.3.6). Although peak area is the only accurate measurement for mass sensitive detectors, it is still possible to use peak height as a good approximation, especially when the peak is narrow and has an appropriate shape. Depending on the type of detector used and the nature of the compound being detected, a relative amount can be estimated. If a true quantitation is desired, however, one must develop a calibration curve based on the analysis of known quantities of that compound. To ensure accuracy in a quantitative analysis, an internal standard must be included in the calibration mixtures as well as in the sample being tested. Accurate quantitative analysis is not necessary (and is generally not possible) for IL analyses, however it is important to have an understanding of how peak height/size relates to relative amount. This concept is important in pattern recognition, in which the relative amounts of the components of a mixture are a characteristic feature (Chapter 9).

8.2.4 Efficiency

The efficiency of a column is measured by the number of theoretical plates (N), or more often, the height equivalent to a theoretical plate (HETP or H). The theoretical plate number (N) usually is expressed by one of two equations [9]:

$$N = 16 \cdot \left(\frac{t_R}{w_b} \right)^2$$
(Equation 8-2)

or

$$N = 5.545 \cdot \left(\frac{t_R}{W_h}\right)^2 \qquad \text{(Equation 8-3)}$$

where t_R refers to the retention time of the peak and W_b refers to the peak width at baseline in Equation 8-2 and W_h its width at half-height in Equation 8-3. Figure 8-3 illustrates the values used with these equations. The higher the plate number N, the greater the efficiency of the column. One can understand quickly that the narrower the peak (low W), the higher N, and thus the efficiency. Efficiency is thus a measure of peak broadening; an efficient system will result in narrow peaks, whereas a less efficient column will contribute to band broadening.

The height equivalent to a theoretical plate (HETP) can be calculated when both N and the column length (L) are known [10, 11]:

$$HETP = \frac{L}{N} \qquad \text{(Equation 8-4)}$$

As a result, the lower the HETP, the better the resolution and the more efficient the separation. Efficiency is optimized when N is maximized and HETP is minimized. The van Deemter equation is another way of expressing efficiency; it takes into account three factors that, along with the mobile phase linear velocity, will affect efficiency and, therefore, the HETP value [13]. These factors are represented by the variables A, B, and C in the van Deemter equation [10]:

$$HETP = A + \frac{B}{\mu} + C \cdot \mu \qquad \text{(Equation 8-5)}$$

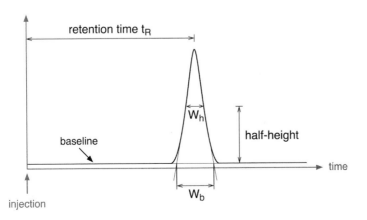

FIGURE 8-3

The different values used to calculate the plate number (N).

Theoretical Plate Concept

Historically, the concept of the number of plates as a measure of efficiency is based upon separation by distillation. The ability to separate by distillation was reflected in the number of plates, within each of which distinct equilibria occurred. The greater the number of plates, the better the potential for separation. Imagine a distillation column with two plates, then one with 100 plates (refer to Figure 7-4, which shows a simplified schematic of a distillation tower with only five plates). Clearly, more plates allow for improved separation as a more refined gradient of temperatures can be used. This concept was adapted to chromatography by Martin and Synge in 1941 [12]:

The behaviour of a column consisting of a number of "theoretical plates", within each of which perfect equilibrium between the two phases occurs, can be described with great simplicity. Peters [1922] showed that the continuous or packed type of distillation column (in which equilibrium is not established at any point) could be divided up into a number of layers each of which was equivalent to one theoretical plate, and the height of such a layer was called the H.E.T.P. or

"height equivalent to one theoretical plate". For the present purpose the H.E.T.P. is defined as the thickness of the layer such that the solution issuing from it is in equilibrium with the mean concentration of solute in the non-mobile phase throughout the layer. It can be shown from diffusion arguments that the H.E.T.P. is a constant through a given column except when the ratio of the concentrations of the solution entering and leaving the plate differs greatly from unity [cf. Sherwood, 1937]. It may be taken as constant for the chromatogram without serious error.

The theoretical plate concept is a good way to express relative efficiency, although it is important to understand that this model has limitations. When using the term "theoretical plates" one must remember that there are not actual distinct equilibria being achieved. Another concern with the theoretical plate model is that it does not adequately account for band broadening. However, the number of theoretical plates or the HETP is still used today as a means for expressing the efficiency of a chromatographic system.

in which A represents the Eddy diffusion phenomenon[2] in the column, B represents molecular (or axial) diffusion, C relates to the resistance to mass transfer, and μ is the linear velocity of the mobile phase through the chromatographic system [10]. The linear velocity is calculated based on the following equation [15]:

$$\mu = \frac{L}{t_M}$$

(Equation 8-6)

---

[2] The Eddy diffusion is the process by which substances are mixed in a fluid system due to Eddy motion, a turbulent motion in which part of the fluid moves in a way different than the main flow [14]. In gas chromatography, Eddy diffusion is also referred to as multipaths effect or flow anisotropy. In fact, this only applies to packed columns, normally no longer used in fire debris analysis. The reason for the influence of the Eddy motion to band broadening is the fact that [2]: "individual flow paths must diverge to navigate around the particles such that individual flow streams are of unequal lengths."

where L is the length of the column [cm] and t_M is the retention time[s] of an unretained analyte (dead time). The mobile phase linear velocity, μ, therefore is expressed in cm/s.

Using the van Deemter equation, one can plot the efficiency of a carrier gas in terms of HETP as the dependent variable (y-axis) against the linear velocity as the independent variable (x-axis). This plot is referred to as a van Deemter plot, and can be used to compare the efficiency of one carrier gas to another (see Figure 8-4).

All three parameters (A, B, and C) lead to band broadening: the spreading apart of a group of identical analytes throughout the system. By minimizing band broadening, identical analytes stick together and a better separation is obtained because peaks are narrow rather than broad. With Figure 8-4, one can quickly appreciate the influence of the mobile phase flow rate on each parameter. The A term in the van Deemter equation is relevant only to packed column systems and thus is constant for a given column. Nevertheless, it is independent of the linear velocity μ as indicated by Equation 8-5 and Figure 8-4. The B term represents the natural tendency of the analytes to redistribute themselves from a region of high concentration to a region of lower concentration in the mobile phase [2]. Finally, the C term, resistance to mass transfer, represents the fact that the transfer of an analyte from the mobile to the stationary phase and vice versa is not instantaneous and has a certain inertia. As a result, the analyte concentration profile of the stationary phase is slightly behind the equilibrium position and the analyte concentration profile of the mobile phase is slightly ahead of the

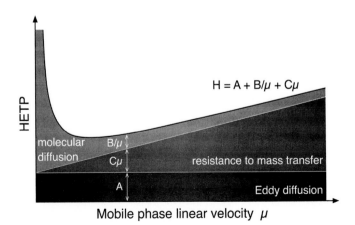

FIGURE 8-4 *A van Deemter plot showing the effect of each variable from the corresponding equation. Note that the Eddy diffusion is independent of the linear velocity, thus it is constant. Because the resistance to mass transfer (C) is multiplied by the linear velocity, it increases with μ. The invert occurs with the molecular diffusion (B).*

equilibrium position [2]. As expected, the C term increases with the flow rate as shown in Figure 8-4.

Since the Eddy diffusion does not apply to capillary columns, it may be useful to become familiar with the Golay equation, in which the A term has been removed and the C term has been expended [8]:

$$HETP = \frac{B}{\mu} + (C_s + C_m) \cdot \mu \qquad \text{(Equation 8-7)}$$

where C_s is the mass transfer from the stationary phase to the mobile one and C_m is the mass transfer from the mobile phase to the stationary one.

Another important chromatographic concept is that of resolution. The resolution, R, is a measure of the true separation of two consecutive peaks [10]. One can calculate the resolution of a chromatographic system from two consecutive peaks using the following equation:

$$R = \frac{2 \cdot d}{W_1 + W_2} \qquad \text{(Equation 8-8)}$$

where d is the separation between two peaks (measured from top to top) and W_1 and W_2 are the widths at baseline of the two peaks. This is illustrated in Figure 8-5.

The goal in chromatography is to avoid coelution. This is an issue because two coeluting peaks will mix together in the detector. For example, each compound's contribution to the overall structural information provided by the mass spectrometer will not be distinguishable, thus their identification will be hampered. This is the reason why it is important to achieve baseline resolution (R = 1.5) as the ultimate goal for all peaks. In fire debris

FIGURE 8-5

The measures used to calculate the resolution (R) of a chromatographic system.

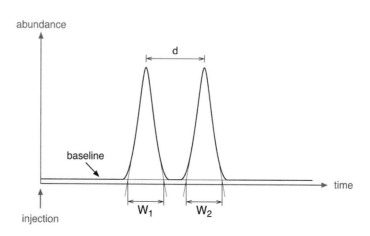

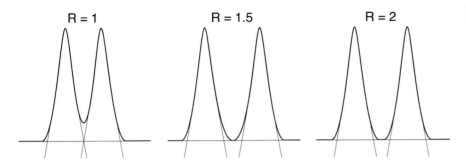

FIGURE 8-6

The effect of resolution (R) on the separation of two consecutive peaks.

analysis, this goal can never be achieved in practice, however it is important to adjust the chromatographic parameters to approximate it as closely as possible. A resolution below 1.5 will not provide complete separation and a resolution above 1.5 does not offer any extra advantages to the separation. Figure 8-6 shows the peak configurations for three different values of R.

8.3 GAS CHROMATOGRAPHY

8.3.1 Principle

Gas chromatography (GC) is a separation technique capable of separating highly complex mixtures based primarily upon differences of boiling point/ vapor pressure and of polarity. Even though chromatography was invented at the beginning of the twentieth century and Martin and Synge did not see any reason why the mobile phase should not be a gas in their 1941 publication, GC was not developed until 1952 [16]. That year, James and Martin published the first article demonstrating the use of GC to separate volatile fatty acids [17]. Gas chromatography—also referred to as gas-liquid chromatography (GLC)—is a specific type of chromatography that utilizes an inert gaseous mobile phase and a liquid stationary phase.[3] Instrumentation continues to improve, but the basics of a gas chromatograph—the instrument used to perform GC that bears the same abbreviation—have not changed and remain fairly simple. The GC is composed of several basic components as shown in Figure 8-7. A photograph of a modern GC is shown in Figure 8-8.

A GC operates by introducing a sample via an injection port into the inlet (also called injector). Carrier gas, which is the mobile phase, passes through the inlet, and sweeps the sample onto the column, where the stationary phase is. The column is enclosed in a temperature-controlled oven.

---

[3] Gas-solid chromatography (GSC) also exists, however its practical application is extremely limited and its use is insignificant when compared with GLC.

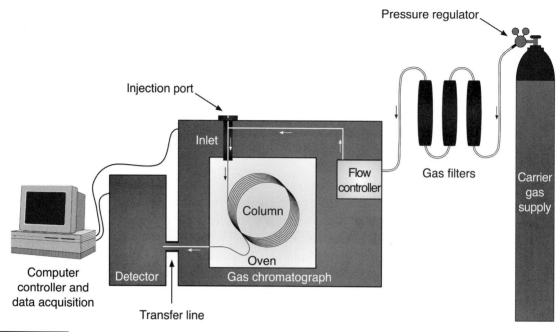

FIGURE 8-7 *A gas chromatograph and its main components.*

FIGURE 8-8

An Agilent 6890N-5975 gas chromatograph-mass spectrometer. An Agilent 7683B autosampler is present above the GC on the left.

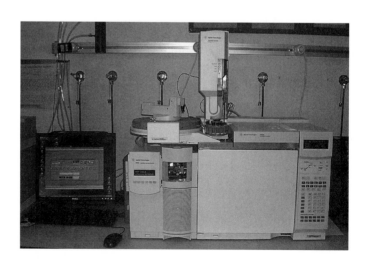

The chromatographic separation takes place as the mixture travels through the column. When the separated components of the sample exit the column, they enter a detector, which provides an electronic signal proportional to the amount of eluting analytes. Each constituent is described in more detail in the following subsections.

8.3.2 Carrier Gas

The mobile phase in a gas chromatographic system is referred to as the carrier gas. The carrier gas is inert and does not interact with the analytes. This is different from most other chromatographic systems in which the mobile phase may play an important role in the separation based upon its chemical properties. The choice of a carrier gas is limited based on the type of detector used, or when several gases may be suitable, on its efficiency and availability.

The most commonly used carrier gases for capillary gas chromatography are helium (He), hydrogen (H$_2$), and nitrogen (N$_2$). The efficiency of a chromatographic system with a given carrier gas varies with the flow rate (in ml/min), also expressed in terms of average linear velocity (in cm/sec). That is to say, one carrier gas may not always be more efficient than another, but it may be more efficient for a given range of average linear velocities. Therefore, the selection of an appropriate carrier gas depends on how it performs under specific operating conditions.

A useful way to compare the efficiencies of the different carrier gases is to use a van Deemter plot. One can generate a van Deemter plot by running the same solute through the gas chromatograph, keeping all the chromatographic conditions the same except for the flow rate, which is varied incrementally. The efficiency in terms of HETP can then be calculated for various linear velocities from the data obtained using Equations 8-2 or 8-3 along with Equation 8-4. A typical van Deemter plot comparing helium, hydrogen, and nitrogen for a given system is shown in Figure 8-9.

From the figure, one can readily appreciate the differences in efficiency for each gas. Although nitrogen typically offers the best resolution, it does

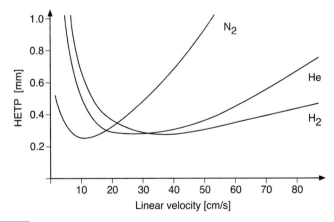

FIGURE 8-9 *Example of a van Deemter plot comparing the efficiency in terms of HETP of three carrier gases. It is important to understand that a van Deemter plot is specific for a given system (mostly based on column characteristics). Nevertheless, this plot is somewhat representative of what would be expected with a column used in fire debris analysis.*

so at a very slow linear velocity (about 12 cm/sec), thus leading to extremely long analysis times. Also, the range for which the resolution is maximum is very short and a small deviation in either direction quickly decreases the efficiency of the system. Hydrogen also offers very good efficiency, and at a much higher linear velocity (about 37 cm/sec). Its high resolution spans a much wider range from about 30 to 50 cm/sec. Finally, helium offers quite a wide range, spanning from about 20 cm/sec to 40 cm/sec, for which the resolution is very similar to that offered by hydrogen.

Most scientists performing fire debris analysis use helium as the carrier gas. Though it does not offer the best resolution, it is relatively inexpensive and allows for the system to run at a good velocity (usually in the range of 30 cm/sec), resulting in an acceptable analysis time. If one were to choose nitrogen, the run time would easily double, hence decreasing the productivity of the instrumentation, which may be detrimental to backlog. Some laboratories utilize hydrogen as a carrier gas. Not only can hydrogen be generated in-house, a great advantage over helium tanks that must be ordered and replaced on a regular basis, but it also leads to faster chromatography without loss of resolution. The two main disadvantages to using hydrogen are the hazardous situation created by the flammable gas itself and the possible need to use a more powerful vacuum pump for the mass spectrometer because of the much higher volume of gas to be pumped out of the system. However, good hydrogen generators have significant built-in safety features, thus minimizing the hazard, and some recent GC-MS instruments, such as the Agilent 6890-5973N (inert), are already set up for hydrogen as a carrier gas.

Other factors that are crucial in the selection of a carrier gas are its purity and the type of detector used. When using a flame ionization detector, helium and nitrogen are suitable whereas hydrogen is not [18]. Water and oxygen are some of the most common and most damaging contaminants. Their presence in a carrier gas can degrade expensive chromatographic columns, in addition to causing unnecessarily high background and spurious peaks. Contaminants can be removed and the purity of the gas increased fairly easily in the lab by using in-line gas purifiers or filters [19]. Usually, these purifiers consist of a moisture trap, a hydrocarbon trap, and an oxygen trap. Often, several of these may be combined into one trap, possibly with an indicator of the efficiency of the purification. An excellent resource for selecting carrier gas filters (as well as detector gas filters whenever applicable) produced by Agilent is *Maintaining your Agilent GC and GC/MS systems*, and is available free of charge on the Agilent web site at http://www.agilent.com/chem [19].

8.3.3 Injector (Inlet)

The means for introducing a sample into the column would ideally allow for an immediate and complete transfer of a variety of sample types into the column. Gases and liquids can be introduced directly into the inlet with a syringe, however solids must first be dissolved in a suitable solvent in order to be injected as a liquid solution.[4] In order to guarantee a good injection [10], "the sample should be introduced instantaneously as a 'plug' onto the column." Although there are several different types of inlets for gas chromatographic systems, each with its own purpose, the split/splitless inlet (or injector) is used almost exclusively in the analysis of fire debris samples, therefore the discussion of injection techniques will be limited to it.[5] The modern gas chromatograph utilizes quite a complex system to provide good and consistent injections. The typical split/splitless inlet is composed of several important components, as shown in Figure 8-10 [20].

A/ Septum

The top of the injector port houses a septum that is used to seal the inlet and maintain the carrier gas head pressure, which is necessary to establish the flow through the column. Septa typically are made of heat-resistant polymeric silicone capable of self-sealing following an injection by a syringe. Septa are disposable and have a limited lifetime and, therefore, need to be changed somewhat frequently depending on the amount of instrument use. Although some manufacturers advertise that some septa are good for up to 1,000 injections, it is recommended that the septa be changed about every 100 injections. When a septum is no longer efficient, many problems may occur, such as leaks, decomposition, sample loss, change in split ratio, ghost peaks, and column degradation. There are many different types of septa and the analyst must wisely choose the right one for his or her instrument [19].

Merlin Microseal

An alternative to the short-lived polymeric septum is the Merlin Microseal septum manufactured by Alltech (Deerfield, IL). Designed for use with Hewlett-Packard (now Agilent) systems, the Merlin Microseal replaces the traditional septum and septum nut. Unlike traditional polymeric septa, the Merlin Microseal typically lasts for more than 10,000 injections on most systems and may even last for up to 25,000 injections when used with a properly aligned autosampler [21]. The septum actually is designed in two parts, one of which includes an o-ring to ensure the proper seal with the syringe's needle, and the other part contains a spring-loaded slot. The Merlin Microseal offers many benefits as a replacement for traditional disposable septa, although it is compatible with only a limited number of instruments and the initial cost is much higher.

---

[4] As an alternative to dissolving the solid compound, it is also possible to pyrolyze it and inject its resulting pyrolysis products. This technique, however, does not allow for an analysis of the original solid compound, but of its degradation products. Pyrolysis-gas chromatography (Py-GC) is a widely used technique, particularly in the analysis of polymers.

[5] Because fire debris analysis is carried out on capillary columns, which have a very low capacity, it is necessary that the inlet system allow for a fast sample introduction and vaporization that it is suitable for very small sample sizes. Split/splitless inlet types meet these requirements.

FIGURE 8-10

Typical configuration of a split/splitless injector. The flow regulators/valves are used to configure the inlet as split or splitless.

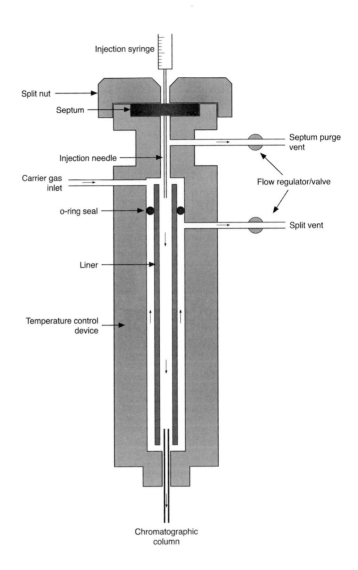

B/ Liner

The second most important part of the inlet is the liner. The liner is defined as [19]: "the centerpiece of the inlet system in which the sample is evaporated and brought into the gas phase." In fact, a liner is simply a glass tube between the septum and the column where flash vaporization takes place. Again, there are many types of liners available on the market, each of which has a particular application [22]. When choosing a liner, in addition to the instrument's characteristics, one must take into account the following three parameters:

Liner volume: A typical liner has a volume of approximately 900 µl [19]. Some liners may have a reduced volume for some particular applications. Liner volume is typically not an important issue in fire debris analysis as long as reasonable volumes (1 to 2 µl) of solvent are injected. However, if one injects direct headspace and uses larger volumes, it is crucial to know the capacity of the liner in order not to exceed it (see text box "Calculating Injection Volumes"). Introducing a volume larger than the liner's capacity may result in bad chromatography and overpressure in the system.

Liner treatment: Today, most liners are deactivated in order to reduce the reactivity of the glass with the analytes introduced in the inlet. One should use a deactivated liner, even though most analytes encountered in fire debris analysis are not too prone to reaction with the glass. Nondeactivated liners are used for particular applications.

Liner design: There are several liners compatible with both split and splitless injection modes and some others that are not cross-compatible. One must be careful when choosing the liner to make sure that it will work for the desired injection mode. Different designs (straight, tapered, baffled, with and without glass wool) are available and the user must make a wise choice [22]. Figure 8-11 shows some of these designs. When using solid phase microextraction (see Chapter 11), one must avoid the use of tapered liners as they are usually too small to allow for the introduction of the SPME fiber, unless otherwise specified.

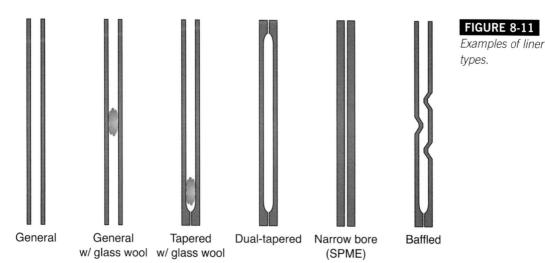

General   General   Tapered   Dual-tapered   Narrow bore   Baffled
           w/ glass wool w/ glass wool   (SPME)

FIGURE 8-11

Examples of liner types.

Calculating Injection Volumes

If the criminalist does not know the maximum amount of solvent he or she may inject without overloading the liner, it is a good exercise to calculate the volume of the solvent once it is in the gas phase. The calculation is quite easy, however it requires the knowledge of a few parameters. Of course, the criminalist can always use the Agilent software FlowCalc 2.0 available for free download at http://www.chem.agilent.com/cag/servsup/usersoft/main.html. The software is divided in two parts: the first one calculates mobile phase flow rate and the second one vapor volumes for liquid injections [23]. Figure 8-12 shows an example of vapor volume calculations from the FlowCalc 2.0 software.

Of course, it is possible to perform the quick calculations by hand using Equation 8-9:

$$V_g = V_l \cdot 22414 \cdot \frac{\rho}{MW} \cdot \frac{15}{P_{head}+15} \cdot \frac{T_{inj}+273}{273}$$

(Equation 8-9)

where:

V_g = resulting gas volume in μl
V_l = initial liquid volume in μl
ρ = density of the solvent in g/cm³
MW = molecular weight of the solvent in g/mol
P_{head} = column head pressure in psi
T_{inj} = injector temperature in °C

This equation can be derived quickly using the ideal gas law and by knowing that one mole of gas at STP takes a volume of 22.414 liters.

FIGURE 8-12

Example of a vapor volume calculation using Agilent FlowCalc 2.0 software. In this case, 2μl of methylene chloride (also called dichloromethane) would overload an 850-μl single-tapered liner.

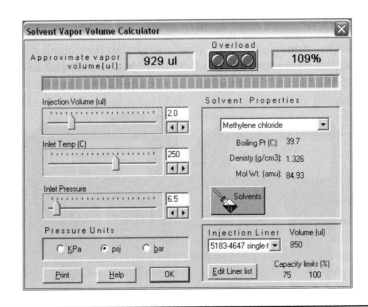

C/ Injection Modes

Split and splitless injections are carried out on the same type of inlet, however they require the set up of different parameters and present their own advantages and disadvantages. A splitless injection involves the nearly complete introduction of the sample into the column. By contrast, a split injection implies that the sample is divided in the inlet and, as a result, only part of the sample is swept into the column. This is achieved by simply separating the carrier gas flow inside the inlet into a split flow and a column flow. The split flow is evacuated into the atmosphere via the split vent while the column flow is introduced inside the chromatographic column. The split ratio[6] is defined as [24]:

$$Split\ ratio = \frac{Split\ flow}{Column\ flow} \qquad \text{(Equation 8-10)}$$

Typical split ratios are within the range of 20:1 to 80:1, although lower or higher values are also successfully used. The proportion of the sample introduced into the column can be easily changed by adjusting the split flow. The higher the split ratio, the smaller the portion of the sample going into the column. In a splitless injection, the split valve is closed, therefore the split flow is zero and the total flow is equal to the column flow. Hence, the entire sample is going into the column.

With older GCs, such as the HP 5890, the user had to adjust mechanical valves while monitoring a bubble meter in order to set the split ratio—an extremely long and tedious process. However, modern GCs usually are equipped with an electronic pressure control (EPC) inlet, rendering the setup of a split injection extremely easy: The user just has to enter the desired parameters (column flow and split ratio) in the computer and the inlet is automatically programmed. As such, split ratios can be readily changed for various chromatographic methods.

Figures 8-13 and 8-14 show the operating principles of a splitless and split injection, respectively.

Because septa produce decomposition products (some due to the plasticizers included in the silicone for better flexibility) which may generate ghost peaks in the chromatogram, a small flow of carrier gas is created under the septum to drive off these compounds [24]. This is called the septum purge and it is found in both split and splitless injection modes.

In the splitless inlet, the injection is carried out in two steps (from a gas flow perspective). First, the split vent is turned off so that only the septum purge flow and the column flow are present (as represented in Figure 8-13). The sample is then injected and is entirely introduced into the column. After a fixed period of time (decided by the user), the split vent is opened, allowing for a thorough flushing of the liner and the interior of the inlet

---

[6] A typical split flow would be 20:1, meaning that the split flow is 20 ml/min while the column flow is 1 ml/min. Thus, about 1/20th of the sample is introduced into the column. Often, the difference between the split flow and the total flow is negligible in comparison to the column flow. Thus, the split ratio is calculated as the total flow divided by the column flow. As an example, the difference between a split ratio of 50:1 or 51:1 may be considered negligible. As the split ratio decreases, this difference becomes more significant.

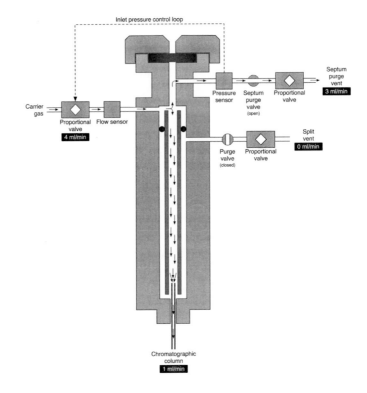

FIGURE 8-13

Operating principle of a splitless inlet. This schematic represents the first step in the splitless injection. The inlet purge valve is turned off and the split vent is 0 ml/min. Thus, all flow entering the liner goes into the column. After a given time, the inlet is purged by opening the purge valve. At that point, the situation is identical to the one shown in Figure 8-14.

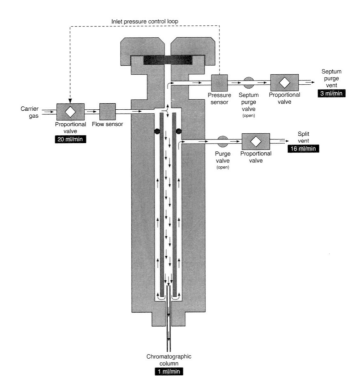

FIGURE 8-14

Operating principle of a split inlet. The inlet purge is open, thus only part of the flow entering the liner actually goes into the column. The majority of it is purged through the split vent.

(also called the inlet purge)—this purging mode grossly corresponds to the split mode as shown in Figure 8-14. The next time an injection is prepared, the split vent is turned off again.

The gas flow perspective is much simpler in the split inlet (see Figure 8-14) as it does not change throughout the injection process. The total flow is first divided between the septum purge and the "inlet flow." Then, the flow going through the inlet again is divided between the column flow and the split flow. At all times, only a fraction of the total flow or "inlet flow" actually is introduced into the column.

Both split and splitless injections are applicable to the analysis of fire debris. Selection of one technique over the other requires an examination of the advantages of both modes of sample introduction. The use of the split technique permits the injection of a strong sample without dilution and with minimal risk of column overload. This is often a significant advantage in capillary gas chromatography, which has only a very limited sample capacity. Conversely, when a sample of low concentration is being analyzed, a splitless technique would normally be preferred because the entirety of the sample is introduced into the column, thus increasing the amount reaching the detector and the overall sensitivity of the instrument. Effects can also be used with splitless techniques, such as solvent trapping, however they are usually not pertinent in fire debris analysis. One main disadvantage of splitless injection is the fact that it may strongly contribute to a tailing[7] effect of the peaks, thus significantly diminishing the resolution of the chromatogram. As such, one must consider the types of samples analyzed when determining the most appropriate type of inlet.

D/ Autosamplers

Introduction of a sample into a gas chromatograph may be done manually, via a handheld syringe, or more frequently via an automated device, called an autosampler (see Figure 8-15). The use of an autosampler offers many advantages. It allows the instrument to run continuously without user intervention, resulting in a higher sample throughput and greater efficiency. In addition, autosamplers are more precise than manual injections, thus leading to a much better reproducibility of the injection [20]. As a direct result, the retention shift between two chromatograms is almost null with an autosampler, whereas it could easily reach one-tenth of a second or more with a manual injection. Autosamplers effectively duplicate the process of a manual injection, including cleaning the syringe with solvent between samples.

---

[7] Tailing of a peak is defined as an asymmetry, relative to the baseline, in which the front of the peak is steeper than the rear [25]. Conversely, fronting is defined as an asymmetry, relative to the baseline, in which the rear of the peak is steeper than the front [26].

FIGURE 8-15

An Agilent 7683 autosampler.

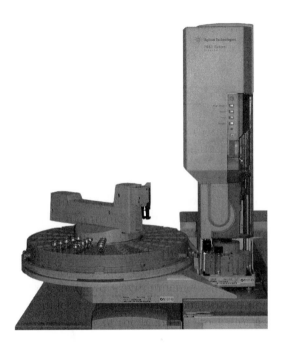

8.3.4 Column

The column is the heart and soul of the gas chromatograph. Originally, gas chromatography used exclusively packed columns—columns that were filled with an inert solid support that was coated with the liquid stationary phase [16]. In 1958, Golay invented the open-tubular (OT) column—more commonly referred to as a capillary column—which is now used in most gas chromatographs because of its incomparable resolution [27]. On a side note, compare Figure 2-5 with Figure 9-20a to have an idea of the gain in resolution between a packed column and a capillary column. It is interesting to compare packed and capillary columns in terms of their respective HETP capabilities. A packed column can exhibit a maximum of about 3,000 plates per meter, which would correspond to an HETP of 300 μm [8]. Because these columns typically do not exceed 5 meters in length, they can reach about 15,000 plates. A capillary column may have an HETP slightly below 100 μm, which is only a moderate increase over their packed counterparts. However, given the fact that they are usually much longer (usually in the range of 20 to 60 m), they can exhibit between 150,000 to 500,000 plates [8]. This clearly demonstrates the gain in efficiency obtained with a capillary column compared to a packed column. Capillary columns are required by ASTM standard methods for fire debris analysis [28]. Independent from this fact, it would be ill-advised to use a packed column in lieu of a capillary one to perform fire debris analysis in modern times. Therefore, this subsection limits its discussion to capillary columns.

The column is where the chromatographic separation takes place. The liquid stationary phase is coated on the inside wall of the OT column and the inert mobile phase flows through the hollow tube. The chemical nature of the stationary phase has a great impact on the quality of the separation. Appropriate column selection is one of the most important decisions to make in setting up a chromatographic system. The choice of a column is entirely based on the types of samples to be analyzed. There are four main variables regarding column selection: chemical nature of the stationary phase, its thickness, column length, and diameter. When taking into account all these parameters, there are literally hundreds of columns from which to choose. Because all these factors will affect the separation, it is important to clearly define what types of compounds are analyzed and what the goal of the analysis is. Fortunately, major chromatographic column manufacturers offer extensive selection guides on their web sites.[8] The most important concept to remember is that the stationary phase must have sufficient interaction with the analytes; otherwise, there will be limited retention, and therefore, limited separation. Table 8-1 shows some typical stationary phases along with their respective applications. Some columns also are sold with "MS" as part of their name, usually meaning that they are extremely low-bleed columns particularly suited for use with a mass spectrometer.

Table 8-1 *Some typical OT capillary columns along with their respective stationary phase compositions and applications*

Agilent J&W	Supelco	Restek	Phase	Application
DB-1 HP-1	SPB-1	Rtx-1	100% dimethylpolysiloxane	Non-polar compounds
DB-5 HP-5	SPB-5	Rtx-5	5% phenylpolysiloxane 95% dimethylpolysiloxane	Non-polar compounds (slightly more polar column than DB-1)
DB-35 HP-35	SPB-35	Rtx-35	35% phenylpolysiloxane 65% dimethylpolysiloxane	Midpolar compounds
DB-17 HP-50+	SPB-17	Rtx-50	50% phenylpolysiloxane 50% dimethylpolysiloxane	Midpolar compounds
DB-1701 HP-1701	SPB-1701	Rtx-1701	14% cyanopropyl-phenylpolysiloxane 86% dimethylpolysiloxane	Low/midpolar compounds
DB-wax HP-wax	Supelcowax	Rtx-wax	Polyethylene glycol (PEG)	High polar compounds, typically fatty acid methyl esters
HP-PLOT Molesieve	—	Rtx-Msieve 5A	Molecular sieve	Permanent gases, typically natural gas

[8] For examples, see http://www.agilent.com, http://www.supelco.com, or http://www.restek.com.

Also, the letters "HT" typically are used to mention a column designed to handle high temperatures, thus to separate compounds with very high boiling points.

Figure 8-16 represents a cross-section of a chromatographic column. All capillary columns are made of a fused silica open cylinder covered with an exterior polyimide coating. The stationary phase is chemically bonded to the inner wall of the cylinder.

Typical dimensions for columns range from 15 to 60 meters in length and from 0.20 to 0.53 mm in internal diameter. The stationary phase usually has a thickness ranging from 0.1 to 1 μm. When the dimensions of the column are known, the internal volume can quickly be calculated (because the thickness of the stationary phase is negligible, the internal diameter of the column is used to calculate the cross-sectional area). The volume of the column is useful data to have when one needs to check the flow rate of a system. For convenience, some volumes (in ml) for the most common column dimensions are shown in Table 8-2.

FIGURE 8-16

Cross-section of a capillary column showing its different components.

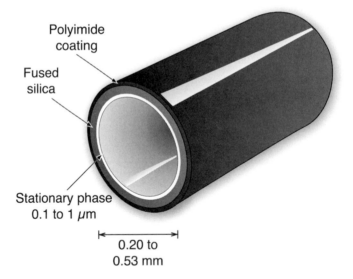

Polyimide coating

Fused silica

Stationary phase 0.1 to 1 μm

0.20 to 0.53 mm

Table 8-2 *Volumes in [ml] of some OT columns based on their internal diameter and length*

	Column length [m]			
Column diameter [mm]	15	25	30	60
0.20	0.47	0.78	0.94	1.88
0.25	0.74	1.23	1.47	2.94
0.32	1.21	2.01	2.41	4.82
0.53	3.31	5.5	6.62	13.23

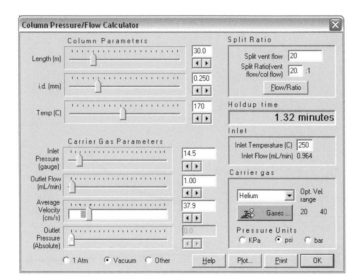

FIGURE 8-17

*Example of flow and
dead time (mentioned
as holdup time in the
figure) calculations
using the Agilent
FlowCalc 2.0 software.*

Alternatively, it is possible to use the first function of the previously described FlowCalc software. It allows for direct calculation of the dead time (identified as hold time in Figure 8-17). However, one must be careful with the figures provided by the software as some parameters may not be fully accurate, such as the length of the column, which is often shorter than its original length due to cutting during installation and maintenance.

Because of the polyimide coating, typically OT columns do not resist temperatures much higher than 350°C. Also, at high temperatures, bleeding of the column's stationary phase may occur. It is simply the degradation of the chemically bonded phase that contributes to a higher baseline toward the end of a chromatogram, as shown in Figure 8-18. New columns sold with MS in their name, such as DB-1 ms and DB-5 ms, are characterized by a very low bleeding, perfectly suited for mass spectrometric detection. Although the stationary phase is the same in terms of composition as shown in Table 8-1, the functional groups have been rearranged into a different configuration (based on Sveda's work, a chemist at DuPont) resulting in a decrease in thermal degradation [8].

The efficiency of a column will follow some general trends. It will generally increase with a decrease in diameter or in film thickness. Conversely, it increases with an increasing length.

8.3.5 Oven

The GC column is housed within an oven capable of temperature programming. The temperature of the oven may be held static throughout the analysis, referred to as isothermal analysis, or the temperature may be

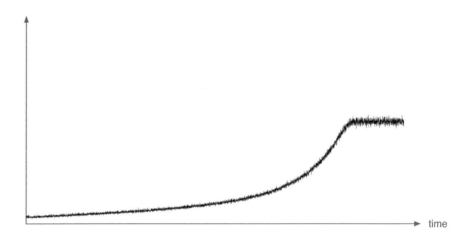

FIGURE 8-18 *A typical blank chromatogram showing the behavior of the baseline as temperature increases. Note the sharp increase toward the end of the run, due to a faster heating rate of the oven and increased bleeding at high temperature.* Chromatogram courtesy of Céline De La Porte, Institut de police scientifique, École des Sciences Criminelles, Université de Lausanne, Switzerland.

precisely increased via a temperature program. The temperature of the oven can be easily changed to suit various applications and should be high enough so that the samples have a significant vapor pressure, thereby allowing for their separation to take place within a reasonable time frame. For samples with numerous analytes over a wide boiling point range, there is not a single best temperature. A low temperature that allows for adequate retention of the more volatile components results in an excessively long retention time and band broadening for the less volatile components, if they were even able to elute at such a low temperature. Conversely, if a higher temperature more suitable for the higher-boiling compounds is used, these heavy analytes would elute with appropriate retention times and peak shapes, but the earlier components would not be adequately retained and would likely not separate from each other or possibly even from the solvent front. The solution to this problem is temperature programming: starting at a low temperature, then gradually increasing it. An appropriate program will start at a temperature suitable for the most volatile components of the mixture and end at a temperature appropriate for the least volatile ones. This principle is illustrated in Figure 8-19.

When dealing with unknown samples, a broad temperature program is often the best approach. The temperature is a very important analytical condition, but fortunately, it is one of the easiest parameters to change. It is especially important for the separation of highly complex mixtures, such as ignitable liquids, which tend to have a broad boiling point range, but have

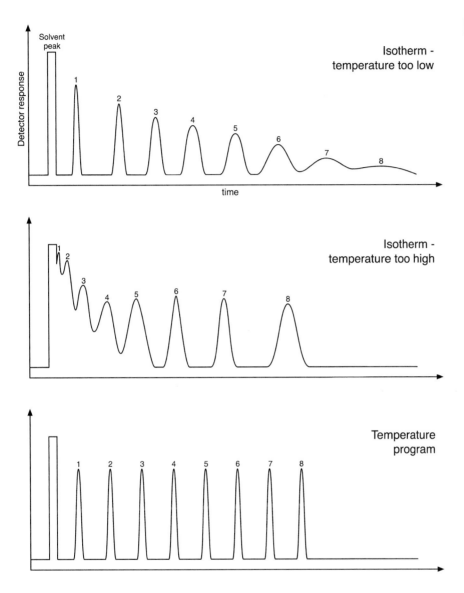

FIGURE 8-19

Illustration of the consequences of an isothermal versus a temperature program.

components that are chemically similar to one another. All GCs have ovens capable of controlling the temperature of the analysis; the challenge lies in developing a method appropriate to the desired separation.

8.3.6 Detectors

The role of a GC detector is to produce a measurable electronic signal in response to species eluting from the column. There are a variety of detectors available for GC applications. Some detectors are sensitive only to specific types of chemical compounds, whereas others are considered "universal" in

Table 8-3	The most commonly used detectors coupled with gas chromatography and some of their characteristics			
Detector	**Selectivity**	**Sensitivity**	**Linear (dynamic) range**	**Concentration or mass sensitive**
Flame ionization detector (FID)	Most organic compounds	10–100 pg	10^7	Mass
Electron-capture detector (ECD)	Halides, nitrates, nitriles, peroxides, anhydrides, organometallics	50 fg	10^5	Concentration
Thermal conductivity detector (TCD)	Universal	1 ng	10^7	Concentration
Flame photometric detector (FPD)	S, P, Sn, B, As, Ge, Se, Cr	100 pg	10^3	Mass
Nitrogen-phosphorus detector (NPD)	N, P	10 pg	10^6	Mass
Photo-ionization detector (PID)	Aromatics, ketones, esters, aldehydes, amines, heterocyclics, organosulphurs, some organometallics	2 pg	10^7	Concentration
Mass spectrometer (MS)	Universal Selective*	1 ng (scan) 1 pg (SIM)	10^3 10^3	Mass

*When a mass spectrometer is operated in SIM mode, it becomes selective based on the ions scanned. Although the MS becomes more sensitive, it loses its universal nature when in SIM mode.

that they are capable of detecting almost everything. Detectors also vary in their limits of detection. As a general rule, the more selective the detector, the greater its sensitivity. For example, electron capture detectors (ECD), which are sensitive only to electronegative species such as halogen-containing compounds, may detect down to a level of 10^{-13} grams (<pg), whereas universal detectors such as the flame ionization detector (FID) and the thermal conductivity detector (TCD) have sensitivities in the 10^{-11} g and 10^{-9} g ranges, respectively [10]. Table 8-3 is a list of the most common detectors used with a GC along with some of their characteristics.

Selective detectors, such as the ECD and the nitrogen phosphorous detector (NPD), are both very sensitive to some specific compounds. However, because most ignitable liquids are composed primarily of hydrocarbons, it is necessary to use a universal detector, such as the FID. Mass spectrometers also are used in conjunction with gas chromatographs and may be considered a sensitive and selective detector when used in the selected ion monitoring (SIM) mode, or a less sensitive universal detector, when used in the regular full scanning mode. It should be noted that in fire debris analysis,

Mass v. Concentration Sensitive Dectors

It is important to distinguish between the two categories of detectors because their functioning influences the quantitative interpretation of the chromatograms. Because mass sensitive detectors actually take into account every analyte reaching them, the measured abundance of the analytes corresponds to the area of the peak. With concentration sensitive detectors, the concentration of the analytes is measured, thus the height of the peak is the correct abundance. This is illustrated in Figure 8-20. Both FID and MS detectors are mass sensitive.

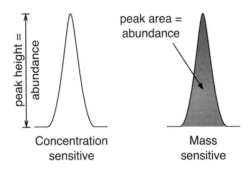

FIGURE 8-20

Illustrations of the different measures of abundance in mass and concentration sensitive detectors.

besides the mass spectrometer, which is the current state-of-the-art detector, only the FID has been used on a routine basis.[9] Because of the extreme value of the hyphenated GC-MS technique and because of the complexity of mass spectrometry, it will be discussed in much greater detail in Section 8.5. The FID, because of its important role in fire debris analysis, is discussed in the next subsection.

The flame ionization detector was developed in 1958 almost simultaneously in Australia and South Africa [30]. FID is still in use for the analysis of ILR in some laboratories, although it has lost its position as the most dominant detector to the mass spectrometer. The FID historically has been the most popular GC detector not only for fire debris analysis, but also for a wide variety of other applications. Today, its use in fire debris analysis is declining due to the increased capabilities and ready availability of relatively inexpensive and easy to operate benchtop mass spectrometers. Figure 8-21 shows an FID and its components.

An FID responds to compounds mostly containing carbon and hydrogen, although it also responds to some compounds containing carbon and no hydrogen [30]. Its operation is dependent upon the conversion of column

---

[9] A paper relating the use of a tandem PID/FID applied to fire debris analysis demonstrated that the alkanes did not give any response on the PID, thus providing two sets of data [29]: one chromatogram with aromatic compounds only (PID) and one chromatogram with all compounds (aliphatics + aromatics) (FID). However, this technique is cumbersome to carry out, complicated to interpret, and, more importantly, totally obsolete with the invention of mass spectrometry, already widely available at the time of that study.

FIGURE 8-21

Schematic of a flame ionization detector (FID). (Source: McMinn D (2000) Detectors: General: Flame ionization detectors and thermal conductivity detectors. In: Encyclopedia of separation science, Wilson I, Poole C, and Cooke M, editors. Academic Press, San Diego, CA, pp 443–7. Reproduced with the permission of Elsevier Academic Press, Burlington, MA.)

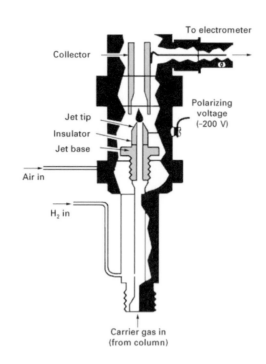

effluent (eluting compounds) to a current. When compounds elute from the column, they enter the FID where they are burned by a hydrogen-fed flame. Upon their combustion, ions are formed, which enter the collector. This collector consists of two plates to which a difference of potential is applied. As ions penetrate the space between the two plates, a current is established and detected. When nothing elutes from the column, there should be no ions formed, and therefore, no current, although slight impurities in the carrier gas may result in a very low level current [10]. Because the current produced by the FID is based upon a combustion process, there are two important factors to consider when using this type of detector. One is that the combustion reaction will produce water vapor; therefore the temperature of the FID must be set high enough that condensation does not occur. Minimally, an FID should be set at about 125°C, although they are more commonly set at 250°C or above [10]. The other important consideration is that the signal is more or less proportional to the amount of carbon detected (approximately 0.015 C/g), therefore a large molecule will produce a greater signal than a small molecule, such as methane [30]. The FID meets the two major requirements for a GC detector to be applicable for the analysis of ILR: (1) it is a universal detector and responds adequately to hydrocarbons; and (2) it is of sufficient sensitivity that it can be used in conjunction with capillary systems to detect low levels of ILR.

8.4 MASS SPECTROMETRY

8.4.1 Principle

The mass spectrometer (MS) is an important tool in ILR analysis. Whereas the detectors mentioned in the previous section merely record the presence of analytes, the MS provides additional structural information regarding the chemical composition of the detected compounds. Mass spectrometers can be applied to quantitative analyses, however they are used more often for qualitative analyses. The information provided by the mass spectrometer is, in many cases, sufficient to uniquely identify an unknown chemical compound. Although there is a vast array of mass spectrometers available to meet a variety of different needs, those commonly used in the analysis of fire debris are relatively inexpensive and easy to use.

A mass spectrometer offers structural information regarding chemical compounds through a series of processes yielding a mass spectrum. Chemical compounds entering the mass spectrometer are imparted with energy that causes their ionization and fragmentation into many ions. These ions are then sorted based on their mass-to-charge ratio (m/z) and detected. The relative amount of ions of various m/z values is organized and presented in the form of a mass spectrum: a visual representation of the mass-to-charge ratio on the x-axis against the abundance of the ions on the y-axis. Figure 8-22 shows an example of a mass spectrum.

The most intense peak in the spectrum is commonly normalized to a value of 100%. This peak is called the base peak. All other peaks are expressed as a percentage of the base peak. The mass spectrum may be considered a form of identification for most organic compounds, however in case of isomers, it may be difficult to differentiate them, especially with stereoisomers.

Although there are many types of mass spectrometers, the quadrupole is the one most commonly used in fire debris analysis and is used throughout this text to describe the functioning principle of an MS [31]. Figure 8-23 shows a schematic representation of a quadrupole MS. The sample is intro-

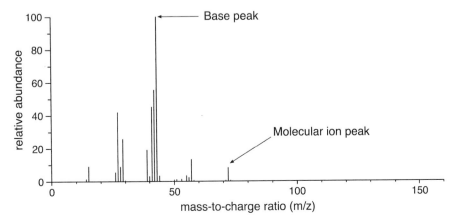

FIGURE 8-22

Example of the mass spectrum of pentane. The base peak is normalized to 100% and all other peaks are expressed as a percentage of the base peak. The molecular ion peak is the unfragmented ion.

FIGURE 8-23
The general schematic of a mass spectrometer.

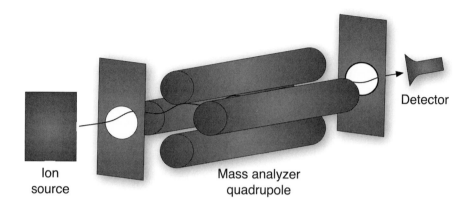

Detector

Ion
source

Mass analyzer
quadrupole

duced into the ionization chamber through the interface. It is here that ionization and fragmentation occur. Ions are then accelerated toward the mass filter (analyzer), where they are separated based upon their mass-to-charge ratio. Following separation, they reach the detector, where the abundance is measured and recorded. The entire system is kept under vacuum (usually in the range of 10^{-5} to 10^{-6} torr) [31].

Modern mass spectrometers have all of their parameters controlled by an easy-to-use computer system. In addition, the computer compiles millions of pieces of data in a reasonable amount of time, thereby allowing the system to collect data continuously throughout a lengthy GC analysis. The following subsections provide a more detailed examination of each of the steps involved in creating a mass spectrum.

8.4.2 Sample Introduction

One important component of a mass spectrometer is the means by which the sample is introduced. Mass spectrometers are capable of analyzing a wide variety of matrices, although some types of material require a special means of introducing the sample. When coupled with a GC, the introduction of samples is carried out directly from the outlet of the chromatographic column. In fact, the column is connected to the MS via a heated interface, thus the introduction of the sample into the MS is continuous.[10] A variant of the continuous-inlet system is the membrane introduction. In this case, some sample discrimination occurs because of the nature of the membrane. Compounds capable of permeating the membrane pass through it and enter the mass spectrometer; those that are not permeable will not enter the

---

[10] The other main type of MS injection is discrete (batch-inlet introduction), for which the sample is injected once. This is not used when the MS is coupled with a GC. With discrete injection, one of the most common techniques is the direct-inlet probe (DIP), for which the sample is directly introduced into the ionization chamber of the MS and the data acquisition is then started.

system, thereby allowing for a certain sample selectivity [32]. These means of sample introduction are particularly advantageous when analyzing multicomponent samples that may be easily separated via the selected means of a continuous inlet system.

8.4.3 Ionization

Once the sample has been introduced in the MS, it must be ionized. The ion source converts intact molecules into charged molecules and molecule fragments. It is this process that creates the ions that are represented in the mass spectrum. Ionization may be hard or soft. Hard ionization imparts greater energy to the molecules, resulting in greater fragmentation. Conversely, soft ionization is designed to transfer less energy to the molecules being analyzed. As a result, the charged particles are in a state of slight excitation and tend to have much less fragmentation. A hard ionization, called electron ionization or electron impact (EI), is used in fire debris analysis.[11]

In electron impact ionization, molecules entering the source are bombarded with electrons from a high-energy electron beam [33]. Figure 8-24 shows the configuration of a typical ionization chamber. Electrons are created by the filament—usually a simple tungsten coil wire—that is heated to about 200°C [31]. These electrons are then accelerated into the ionization chamber because of the difference of potential applied between the filament and the chamber. In the ionization chamber, the electrons collide with the analytes. This electron beam knocks an electron off the molecules and transfers some energy to them, resulting in excited positive ions. Because of the excess energy, some of these ions may further fragment or even rearrange. The degree of fragmentation depends upon many factors, including the stability of the molecular ion (the intact ion bearing a positive charge), the stability of the different fragments, and the energy of the electrons impacting the molecule. So, for a typical compound, there will be some molecular ions and some fragmented ions. This process is consistent for a given chemical compound under the same ionization conditions (see text box "Standard EI Conditions"). The ions are then accelerated into the mass analyzer or mass filter by the repeller's action. The trap collects residual electrons.

---

[11] All references to mass spectrometry in this text deal with electron impact (EI) mass spectrometry, because this technique is generally accepted as the most appropriate means of ionization in the field of fire debris analysis. However, ionization can also be achieved by chemical ionization (CI), using a reagent gas (such as methane), which, by virtue of it being present in excess, receives the initial ionization. Chemical ionization is a softer technique, resulting in less fragmentation and is often most useful for very fragile compounds fragmenting excessively under EI conditions. To date, there has been no research demonstrating any advantage to using CI in fire debris analysis.

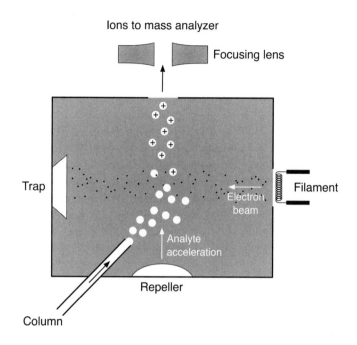

FIGURE 8-24

Schematic representation of an ionization chamber. Analytes elute from the chromatographic column and are bombarded with electrons, thus creating ions. These ions are accelerated to the mass analyzer.

Standard EI Conditions

In order to be able to compare spectra from instrument to instrument as well as to data libraries, it is necessary to standardize the fragmentation of the molecules. However, the fragmentation of a given molecule is dependent on the speed (energy) at which electrons impact it. When traveling at low speed, electrons will impact the molecule with less energy, resulting in limited fragmentation. When traveling at high speed, electrons will impact the molecule with higher energy, resulting in greater fragmentation. Thus, it is necessary to standardize the speed of the impacting electrons. This is achieved by standardizing the acceleration of the electrons. The value of 70 electron Volts (eV) is the conventional standard difference of potential used to accelerate the electrons. Since this value is almost universally used, it is possible to compare a mass spectrum from one system to another. Consequently, the most extensive mass spectra library is available with EI and an acceleration of the electrons set at 70 eV.

8.4.4 Mass Filtering

After the analytes have been ionized, the resulting ions (molecular or fragment) must be sorted in order to create a usable mass spectrum. The mass filter allows for the separation and sorting of the fragments based on their mass-to-charge ratio (m/z). There are a few types of mass filters used in mass spectrometers, most of which are suitable for fire debris applications. A mass filter for use as part of a GC-MS must be capable of producing mass spectra at a rate sufficient to collect data on the narrow, well-resolved peaks eluting from the GC. Quadrupole, ion trap, and time-of-flight systems will fit this bill. However, because the analysis of fire debris does not require ultra-high resolution or other special features, often the main criteria for selecting a system are cost, ease of use, and applicability to other types of analyses. Consequently, most GC-MS systems in use in forensic laboratories for the analysis of fire debris are quadrupole systems, followed by ion trap systems.[12] A brief description of the operating principles of these two most commonly used systems follows.

A/ Quadrupole

Quadrupole mass spectrometers are available in benchtop models that are relatively robust, inexpensive, and user-friendly. The quadrupole derives its name from the physical features of the mass filter. It requires four longitudinally parallel surfaces, with the interior of the surfaces approaching a perfect hyperbola. The desired cross-section was achieved by combining four parallel rods and, more recently, a one-piece integrated quadrupole. The quadrupole was represented in Figure 8-23.

The quadrupole creates an electromagnetic field capable of deviating ions depending on their m/z value. Ions of different m/z are separated by adjusting the electronic parameters so that only fragments of a narrow m/z range will successfully pass through the length of the quadrupole from the ion source to the detector, as illustrated in Figure 8-25. The electronics are fairly complex and are, therefore, beyond the scope of this text; however, there are several good references that can provide the interested reader with additional details.[13] In the simplest terms, the ions that are accelerated from the source toward the detector will experience an electric field in the x and y directions due to a combination of direct-current (DC) and radiofrequency (RF) fields. That is, they will be pushed and pulled toward the surfaces of the quadrupole as they traverse its length. The parameters are set such that for a given pair of DC and RF voltages, only a narrow range of m/z values will be able to pass through the entire length of the quadrupole without colliding (see Figure 8-25).

It follows, however, that this mass filter is fairly inefficient, because as parameters are set to allow one m/z range to pass through, all other ions will not make it to the detector. Consequently, for typical scan parameters, significantly less than 1% of the ions formed will reach the detector and be counted. Parameters can be adjusted to favor either sensitivity or mass

---

[12] Time-of-flight mass spectrometers are particular in the sense that they do not operate in the same manners as other detectors. As a result, they allow for an extremely rapid acquisition time, exceeding those of other mass spectrometers. Unfortunately, the resolution may not be as good as with other systems. In fire debris analysis, time-of-flight mass spectrometers are used in conjunction with two-dimensional comprehensive gas chromatography for their fast acquisition capabilities (see Chapter 13) [34].

[13] For example, *Introduction to Mass Spectrometry* by J. Throck Watson is an excellent introductory text and provides an understandable overview of the operating principles of the most common mass spectrometers available [32].

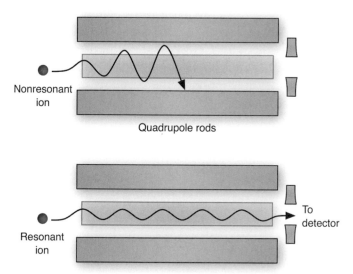

FIGURE 8-25   *Simplified schematics of the functioning principle of the quadrupole mass analyzer. The ion whose mass-to-charge ratio does not lead to a reasonance state will hit one of the four rods before reaching the detector. The reasonant ion will pass through the analyzer in an overall straight path and be recorded by the detector.*

resolution. By allowing a broader range of m/z values to traverse the quadrupole, there will be greater sensitivity; but the mass resolution will suffer. Conversely, by allowing a very narrow range of m/z values to pass through, there will be greater separation of m/z values, however the sensitivity will be reduced. Typically, unit mass resolution is achieved. As a mass spectrometer scans, these parameters are changed rapidly so that an entire mass range can be scanned usually two to three times per second. The quadrupole mass spectrometer is one of the most common mass spectrometers used in fire debris analysis. It is easy to operate, scans quickly enough for the fire debris analysis application, requires reasonable vacuum conditions, offers sufficient resolution, and is reasonably priced. Quadrupole mass spectrometers are available on Agilent and Thermo Finnigan GC-MS.

B/ Ion Trap

The second most commonly used mass spectrometer in fire debris analysis is the ion trap. The design of the ion trap is quite different from that of the quadrupole (see Figure 8-26). It is constituted of two end caps and a ring electrode to which the DC and RF voltages are applied [31]. After ionization, the ions are kept in the center of the trap, oscillating in a stable orbit. Then, by increasing the amplitude of the RF, the ions are incrementally forced out of their stable orbits into the detector. As a matter of fact, with the increas-

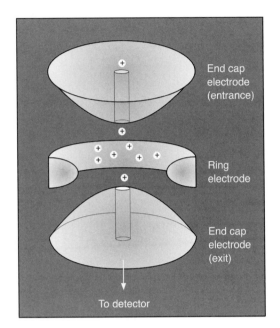

FIGURE 8-26

Simplified schematics of an ion trap.

ing RF, their trajectory increases in diameter until they are ejected into the detector.

The popularity of the ion trap is due primarily to its ability to meet the analytical requirements at a relatively low cost, not to mention that it greatly contributes to a miniaturization of the instrument. The instruments are fairly robust and will provide the necessary resolution. Although quadrupole analyzers have been the primary mass analyzers used in fire debris analysis, there is an increasing presence of ion trap instruments. However, in general, ion traps present some technical subtleties that make them not perform as well as quadrupole when applied to the analysis of ILR. Ion traps are mostly found on Varian instruments.

8.4.5 Detection

Following the separation of ions based on their mass-to-charge ratios, the ions reach their final destination as they enter the detector. The detector provides a relative measure of their abundance. It is important for a detector to have a fast response time so that it can accurately measure filtered ions from rapidly changing scan conditions. To achieve this, the detector converts the signal resulting from the ions into a measurable electric current. This current is recognized by the computer/data analysis system and represents the abundance of the detected ions of a particular m/z value at a particular point in time. Depending on the application, accuracy may be an important factor in the type of detector needed; a Faraday cup provides the

FIGURE 8-27

Principle of an electron multiplier detector.

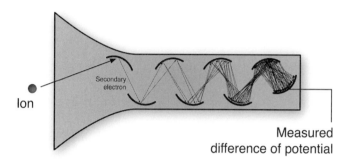

Ion

Secondary electron

Measured difference of potential

requisite accuracy for isotope work, whereas the electron multiplier is not suitable [32]. The electron multiplier (EM), however, is more sensitive than the Faraday cup and offers excellent precision, so it is a good choice for many applications, including fire debris analysis.

An EM amplifies the signal from each ion as the result of a cascading effect. The EM can be viewed as a series of plates—constituted of metal or coated with lead oxide—configured in a funnel shape (see Figure 8-27). When an ion penetrates the detector, it will hit one of the plates of the detector, thus inducing electron emission. Because a difference of potential is applied from one plate to another, these electrons are accelerated and when colliding with the next plate, induce the emission of more electrons. Thus, for each iteration, the impacting electrons cause an emission of a greater number of electrons, resulting in a significant amplification of the original signal. This yields an avalanche of electrons proportional to the number of impacting ions. These electrons generate a current that is measured by the instrument. The signal increase is usually 10^6 to 10^8 [31]. Because of this mechanism, this detector also is called an avalanching ion detector.

This sensitivity makes this detector particularly advantageous for mass spectrometers. Users may adjust gain settings, which affect the degree to which the original signal is amplified. This offers increased sensitivity; however it also results in increased noise. One disadvantage of the EM is that it does not offer a uniform response to ions of various masses. As a result, it discriminates against high mass ions; however, the user can adjust instrument parameters, while tuning the instrument, in an attempt to compensate for this effect.

8.5 PARAMETERS USED IN FIRE DEBRIS ANALYSIS

There is not a set of parameters that can be applied in a standard manner on a GC or GC-MS that will satisfy all fire debris analysts. If the ASTM methods E 1387 and E 1618 are followed, the configuration of the GC or GC-MS must meet certain criteria, such as these [28, 35]:

- The GC must be equipped with either an FID or an MS.
- The GC must be equipped with a split/splitless inlet or possibly an on-column inlet. A split inlet is highly recommended.
- A capillary column designed for the separation of nonpolar (or relatively nonpolar) compounds must be used.
- The carrier gas must be helium or hydrogen.

Of course, in order to produce good chromatograms, the GC or GC-MS must offer a good separation of the analytes of interest; this is achieved through the configuration of the instrument, mostly the temperature program. Some analysts would rather have a short program around 20 minutes, whereas others prefer a long one reaching 60 minutes and offering a slightly better separation. As long as the chromatograms are of good quality and the identification criteria are clearly observable, the exact configuration of the instrument does not matter. For further information, three different configurations currently in use in crime laboratories are provided in Table 8-4. Again, the forensic scientist can follow one of these, or better, explore the influence of each parameter when configuring the instrument in order to find the most suitable configuration.

8.6 DATA ANALYSIS AND INTERPRETATION METHODS IN GAS CHROMATOGRAPHY–MASS SPECTROMETRY

8.6.1 Preamble

The gas chromatograph–mass spectrometer, as a hyphenated instrument, is a very powerful technique; however, without a computer capable of organizing the vast quantities of data it generates, this information would be of minimal value. Because the data analysis system efficiently compiles data, the forensic scientist may examine the data in a variety of ways, depending on the type of information sought. The information available in GC-MS data is presented from three different perspectives:

- Looking at data analogous to GC-FID data
- Looking at data of mass spectra at discrete points in the chromatogram
- Taking advantage of the synergistic nature of the GC-MS hyphenated technique by combining retention times and structural data

All these techniques for analyzing data supplied by the GC-MS are of value and are used by the fire debris analyst. Each of them is introduced hereafter. Chapter 9 offers additional information on the specific applications to the analysis of ignitable liquids.

Table 8-4	Three different sets of GC-MS parameters used to analyze ILR		
Parameter	**Program 1**	**Program 2**	**Program 3**
Instrument	Agilent 5890-5970	Agilent 6890-5973	Agilent 6890-5975
Injection			
Type	Autosampler 7673	Autosampler 7673	Autosampler 7673
Inlet type	Split 50:1	Split 20:1	Split 25:1
Volume	2.0 µl	1.0 µl	1.0 µl
Injector temperature	250°C	250°C	250°C
Split flow	25.5 ml/min	24.0 ml/min	23.1 ml/min
Total flow	28.0 ml/min	28.2 ml/min	27.1 ml/min
Gas saver flow	—	20.0 ml/min	15.0 ml/min
Gas saver time	—	2.00 min	2.00 ml/min
Autosampler			
Sample washes	1	1	3
Sample pumps	2	2	5
Syringe size	10.0 µl	5.0 µl	10.0 µl
Post injection solvent A washes	2	10	3
Solvent A	Methanol	Pentane	Dichloromethane
Post injection solvent B washes	2	10	3
Solvent B	Methanol	Pentane	Dichloromethane
Plunger speed	Fast	Fast	Fast
Column			
Gas type	Helium	Helium	Helium
Type	DB-1MS	DB-1MS	HP-5MS
Length	25 m	30 m	30 m
Internal diameter (ID)	0.20 mm	0.25 mm	0.25 mm
Film thickness	0.33 µm	0.25 µm	0.25 µm
Initial flow	0.5 ml/min	1.2 ml/min	0.9 ml/min
Average velocity	30.25 cm/sec	40 cm/sec	35 cm/sec
Oven			
Initial temperature	45°C for 3 min	40°C for 2 min	50°C for 30 min
Ramp	20°C/min to 320°C	5°C/min to 120°C 12°C/min to 300°C	5°C/min to 250°C
Final temperature	320°C for 7.25 min	300°C for 5 min	250°C for 20 min

Table 8-4	*Three different sets of GC-MS parameters used to analyze ILR continued*		
Parameter	Program 1	Program 2	Program 3
Total run time	24.00 min	38.00 min	63.00 min
Post run temperature	—	60°C	150°C
Transfer line temperature	280°C	280°C	280°C
Mass spectrometer			
Type	Quadrupole	Quadrupole	Quadrupole
Quadrupole temperature	150°C	150°C	150°C
Source temperature	280°C	230°C	230°C
Scan range	33–400 m/z from 2.00 to 24.00 min	15–100 m/z from 0.00 to 1.64 min 33–300 m/z from 1.85 to 38.0 min	10–450 m/z from 0 to 63.00 min
Threshold	1500	50	20
Tune file	atune.u	atune.u	atune.u
Sample number	2	3	3
EM offset	0	0	0

8.6.2 Total Ion Chromatogram

Most commonly, GC-MS data first is examined in the form of a total ion chromatogram (TIC), also referred to as a reconstructed ion chromatogram (RIC) or total ion current. When examining data in the form of a TIC, the information obtained is most analogous to data from a GC equipped with a flame ionization detector or any other universal detector.[14] This data is of enormous value to the fire debris analyst and must never be discounted. In examining a TIC, the analyst has two types of data,[15] which are represented graphically in a two-dimensional format of abundance versus time. For example, Figure 9-3 shows the total ion chromatogram of a medium

---

[14] In the absence of a detector providing structural information, such as a mass spectrometer or a Fourier transform infrared spectrometer (FTIR), the GC-detector instrument provides two basic pieces of information for each chemical compound analyzed: retention time and abundance, which can be used as a relative measure of the amount of each substance. As such, no other information is hidden behind the chromatogram: "What you see is what you get."

[15] A third "type" of data may be obtained depending on the specificity of the chromatographic system. In fire debris analysis, for example, an oxygenated compound typically exhibits some tailing on a GC system equipped with a nonpolar or relatively low polar column (such as a DB-1 or DB-5). This information, although it should be carefully considered, is useful to quickly pinpoint peaks that may be oxygenates and, thus, are not usually present in a petroleum product.

petroleum distillate. By examining the TIC and comparing it with reference standard data, the analyst uses retention times in combination with pattern recognition techniques to identify the major n-alkanes present in this ignitable liquid. When analyzed under standard chromatographic conditions, including the use of a nonpolar column with a temperature program, more information can be gleaned from the examination of a TIC. Comparison with n-alkane reference standards provides information relating to the approximate boiling point range, often expressed in terms of a product's n-alkane range (see Section 9.3).

Examination of a TIC also provides basic information regarding the relative amounts of the components constituting the IL. Pattern recognition techniques rely on a well-trained criminalist with access to a broad range of reference liquids for comparison. In many cases, the information contained in a TIC pattern is sufficient to identify or classify complex ignitable liquids of petroleum origin.

Unfortunately, when in presence of fire debris samples, substantial amounts of interfering products sometimes can preclude the identification of an ILR based solely upon the information contained in the TIC. In such situations, the forensic scientist shall use the additional information provided by the mass spectrometer and rely upon the use of mass chromatography, as described in Subsection 8.6.4. In cases in which there is only one or a few compounds present, pattern recognition techniques cannot be applied, although retention time data can provide boiling point range information and the possible presence of specific compounds. It should be emphasized that a single peak on a chromatogram will represent at least one chemical compound. If coelution occurs, then the peak represents at least two compounds that were not adequately separated. Because not all chemicals have a unique retention time, gas chromatography cannot be used as a stand-alone technique to identify an unknown compound or simple mixture. When retention times are compared with known reference materials, or if a Kovats' retention index is determined, it can provide an indication as to the substance's identity; however, a matching retention time on a single chromatographic system is not adequate to identify an unknown chemical component. In this case, the fire debris analyst must incorporate the extra information provided by the mass spectrum of each of the individual components.

8.6.3 Mass Spectrum

The mass spectrometer portion of the GC-MS provides structural information for a particular time within a chromatogram. When the compound eluting from the column is a true unknown, the mass spectral data can provide a wealth of information. A criminalist with sufficient interpretation skills may be able to examine a mass spectrum and identify the unknown compound based on the fragmentation pattern. In other cases, identification may not be so easily achieved. However extensive information regarding the structure of the unknown may be learned, such as its empirical formula, its family, and the presence of significant functional groups. In ILR analysis, it is not necessary to identify all the components comprising a product, although individual component identification is very important in some situations. Ignitable liquids, such as normal alkane products and others containing only a few components, are not suitable for identification based solely on pattern recognition techniques due to their simple nature. In order to identify this type of product, the forensic scientist needs to supplement pattern recognition techniques with true identification of the components via mass spectrometric techniques. This is also necessary when analyzing an oxygenated product, since the identification of one or more oxygen-containing components is required for classification in accordance with the ASTM standards [28].

Most often, however, the forensic scientist is not tasked with the interpretation of a mass spectrum without help. In cases of a true unknown, he or she will likely rely upon the power of the computer system to conduct a library search. Although there are significant limitations to the value of a library search, it can provide indications of possible identifications. The best approach to the study of a mass spectrum is to have a basic understanding of mass spectral interpretation and how common classes of compounds fragment. This knowledge can be used later along with a computer-based library search.

A/ Basic Mass Spectral Interpretation

A mass spectrum provides information that can be represented visually in the form of a graph; abundance versus mass-to-charge ratio (m/z). Even though a complete primer on mass spectral interpretation is beyond the scope of this text, the fire debris analyst should be familiar with basic features of a mass spectrum and have a general understanding of how these features correlate to molecular structure.[16] Figure 8-28a shows the mass spectrum of methylcyclohexane and will be used to show the three most important features of a mass spectrum: the molecular ion peak, the base peak, and the molecular ion isotopic peak.

Methylcyclohexane has a molecular weight of 98; therefore the peak occurring at m/z = 98 represents the unfragmented, but positively charged

---

[16] The interested reader is strongly encouraged to read *"Interpretation of Mass Spectra"*, currently in its fourth edition, by Fred W. McLafferty and František Tureček [36]. It is an excellent primer on all aspects of mass spectral interpretation and provides a wealth of information on the specific characteristics of the different types of compounds routinely encountered in fire debris analysis. *Spectrometric identification of organic compounds*, written by Silverstein and Webster is another a great reference text, although not limited to mass spectrometry [37].

Mass spectrum of methylcyclohexane.

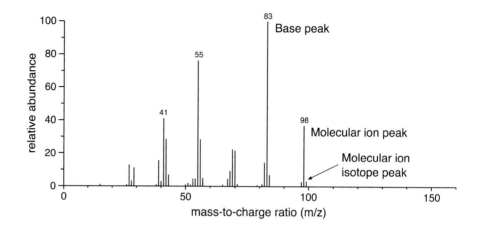

Fragmentation paths of methylcyclohexane leading to some of the ions present in the mass spectrum.

molecule (see Figure 8-28b). This peak is called the molecular ion, and is represented by the symbol $M^{+\bullet}$. Identifying the molecular ion is an important part of mass spectral interpretation: It provides the molecular weight of the unknown compound, which is critical for its identification. In EI mode, the molecular ion peak is the largest m/z (except for isotope peaks, as explained in the text box hereafter). The molecular ion can also provide important information regarding the structure of the unknown compound. Because the molecular ion is the result of a molecule that has received excess energy yet remained intact, the relative abundance of the molecular ion is

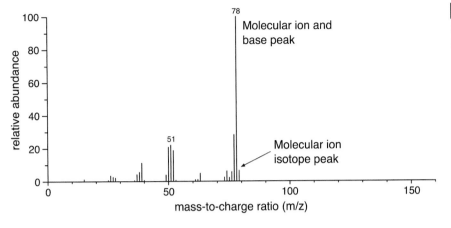

FIGURE 8-29a

Mass spectrum of benzene.

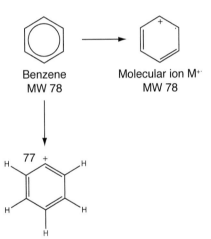

FIGURE 8-29b

Fragmentation paths of benzene leading to some of the ions present in the mass spectrum.

indicative of the compound's stability. For example, aromatic compounds such as benzene and naphthalene are very stable not only due to the presence of a ring structure, which would require multiple cleavages to achieve fragmentation, but also because this ring is fortified by π-bonds, which provide additional strength to the C-C (σ) bonds. These are the reasons for the particular stability associated with aromatic rings. Because of this inherent stability, both benzene and naphthalene exhibit abundant molecular ion peaks (see Figures 8-29a and 8-30a).

In contrast, a highly branched aliphatic compound will readily fragment, resulting in a very small or even nonexistent molecular ion peak. Figure 8-31a shows the mass spectrum of 2,2,4-trimethylpentane (isooctane), which has a molecular weight of 114. Figure 8-31b shows its corresponding fragmentation paths. Examination of Figure 8-31a shows no $M^{+\bullet}$ peak at m/z

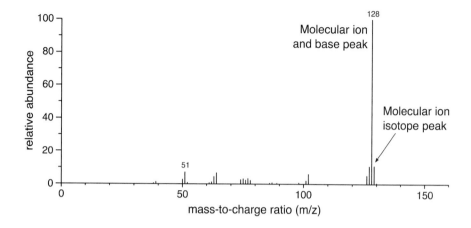

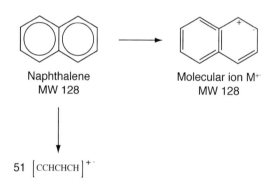

114. In general, aliphatic rings, aromatic rings, and other unsaturated compounds exhibit a more abundant molecular ion than acyclic saturated alkanes. In summary, a simple examination of the molecular ion can provide not only molecular weight information, but also a good indication of the stability of the molecule, and possibly its class.

Another important feature of the mass spectrum is the base peak, defined as the most abundant ion in the spectrum. Examination of Figure 8-28a shows that the base peak is 83. Often the base peak can provide important information regarding the presence of structural groups on the unknown compound. In this case, the base peak shows the presence of the cyclohexyl fragment, indicative of a cyclic compound. Figures 8-29a and 8-30a show the base peak being the same as the molecular ion peak: this is a sign of great stability of the compound in question. With saturated aliphatic compounds, the base peak is often m/z 43 or 57, again, a good indication of the presence of alkyl chains, and, more likely, a saturated aliphatic. With unsaturated compounds, the corresponding base peaks will be decreased by two

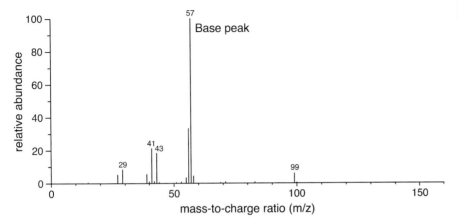

FIGURE 8-31a

Mass spectrum of 2,2,4-trimethylpentane (isooctane).

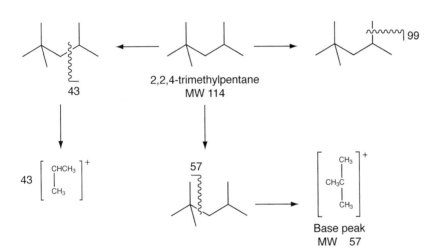

FIGURE 8-31b

Fragmentation paths of 2,2,4-trimethylpentane (isooctane) leading to some of the ions present in the mass spectrum.

m/z for each double bond. As a result, alkenes often have a base peak at m/z 41 or 55.

Finally, when examining the spectrum of an unknown compound, the analyst should look for isotopic patterns. Because of the existence of naturally occurring stable isotopes, it is accepted that some fragments will contain heavier isotopes, such as ^{13}C rather than the more common ^{12}C isotope. The number of fragments containing one or more heavy isotopes will be proportional to their naturally occurring abundance. This fact can be used in conjunction with established charts of isotope abundances to help determine the elemental composition of the unknown compound. In the case of hydrocarbons, the most important isotope ratio to know is that of

^{13}C, which has a natural abundance of approximately 1.1%. This means that for every 1,000 carbon atoms, on average, 989 will be ^{12}C and about 11 will be ^{13}C. In the methylcyclohexane example shown in Figure 8-28a, there is a peak at m/z 99 representing the positively charged intact molecule, with one of its seven carbon atoms being the heavier ^{13}C isotope. Because of the natural abundance of ^{13}C, the M+1 ion of a molecule containing seven carbon atoms is expected to have an abundance of about 7% of the M$^{+\bullet}$ ion. This type of information is most valuable when tabulated data is available, and although there is a margin of error, these isotope clusters can help to determine an empirical formula.

Isotope Peak

In the interpretation of the mass spectra of hydrocarbons, ^{13}C is the only isotope to know, because there is no significant contribution from hydrogen. It is relatively simple to use this information by remembering that an M+1 abundance of a hydrocarbon containing 10 carbon atoms will be approximately 11% of the M$^{+\bullet}$ abundance. When elemental composition is not restricted to only carbon and hydrogen, the use of isotope clusters becomes more interesting. Oxygen's most common isotope is ^{16}O, but it also has ^{18}O (an M+2 isotope) with a natural abundance of roughly 0.2%. Even more interesting are the halogens chlorine and bromine. Unlike carbon and oxygen that are constituted primarily of one largely dominant isotope, chlorine's natural abundance is about 75% ^{35}Cl and about 25% ^{37}Cl, and bromine occurs at nearly a 50:50 split of ^{79}Br and ^{81}Br. This results in very unusual cluster patterns for fragments containing either chlorine or bromine. Other elements having significant isotopes include nitrogen, silicon, and sulfur. Table 8-5 shows some of these isotopes [38].

Table 8-5	*Different isotope ratios commonly encountered in mass spectrometry and fire debris analysis*			
	Different isotopes and their ratios			
Element	**M**	**M+1**	**M+2**	**M+4**
Hydrogen	^{1}H *99.99%*	^{2}H *0.01%*		
Carbon	^{12}C *98.89%*	^{13}C *1.11%*		
Nitrogen	^{14}N *99.64%*	^{15}N *0.36%*		
Oxygen	^{16}O *99.76%*	^{17}O *0.04%*	^{18}O *0.20%*	
Fluorine	^{19}F *100%*			
Sulfur	^{32}S *95.0%*	^{33}S *0.76%*	^{34}S *4.22%*	^{36}S *0.02%*
Chlorine	^{35}Cl *75.77%*		^{37}Cl *24.23%*	
Bromine	^{78}Br *50.69%*		^{81}Br *49.31%*	
Iodine	^{127}I *100%*			

Besides these three basic features of a mass spectrum, Silverstein and Webster provide a few rules that greatly help to interpret mass spectral data [37]:

I. For aliphatic compounds of the same number of carbon atoms, straight-chain configuration offers the greatest abundance of the molecular ion peak (compare Figures 8-31a and 8-33a, even though there are two atoms of difference). As branching increases, the molecular ion peak's relative abundance decreases.

II. In a homologous series of molecules, the higher the molecular weight, the lower the abundance of the molecular ion peak (with the notable exception of fatty acid esters).

III. The bonds from alkylsubstituted carbon atoms are cleaved first. This is due to the stability of the following cations (in decreasing order): $R_3C^+ > R_2CH^+ > RCH_2^+ > CH_3^+$. Larger substituents are eliminated first due to the increased stability of a larger resulting ion.

IV. Aromatic, cyclic compounds, and double bonds increase the stability of the molecules.

V. With saturated rings, the cleavage most likely occurs at the alpha position.

VI. With alkylsubstituted aromatic compounds, the cleavage most likely occurs at the beta position. The resulting fragments rearrange in a tropylium ion of m/z 91 (see Figure 8-32), which is very stable.

VII. When dealing with a heteroatom, the adjacent C–C bond often is cleaved.

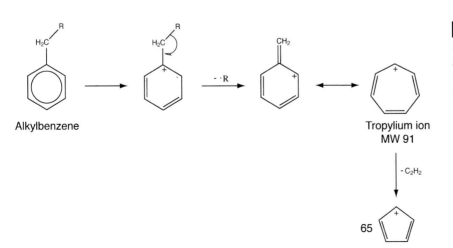

Alkylbenzene

Tropylium ion
MW 91

$- C_2H_2$

65

FIGURE 8-32

Formation of the very stable tropylium ion from a substituted benzene ring.

The base peak and other major peaks present in a mass spectrum can be used to determine the presence of specific functional groups or their lack thereof. Some m/z values can be indicative of particular fragments. For example, an alkane such as decane will break into alkyl groups having m/z values of 43, 57, 71, 85, 99, and so on, as shown in Figure 8-33a. The presence of this series of ions with a difference of 14 m/z between each represents alkyl groups, and is highly indicative of an alkane. It should be noted, however, that these ions are present in other components' spectra, because alkyl groups may fragment from other types of compounds as well.

Another m/z value that is particularly indicative of a class of compounds is ion 91: it represents the tropylium ion that is formed as an extremely stable fragment from the alkylbenzenes (see Figure 8-32). In addition to ion 91, the series of ions having m/z values in increments of +14, indicating an additional methylene group, represent alkylsubstituted tropyliums, and are also indicative of alkylbenzenes. Figures 8-34a and 8-34b show the mass spectrum of 1,2,4-trimethylbenzene and the corresponding fragmentation paths. Note the presence of the base peak at m/z 105, representative of methyltropylium, a very stable ion.

Alkylbenzenes also tend to have a fairly abundant molecular ion due to the inherent stability of the aromatic ring structure. With simple aromatics,

FIGURE 8-33a

Mass spectrum of decane.

FIGURE 8-33b

Fragmentation paths of decane leading to some of the ions present in the mass spectrum.

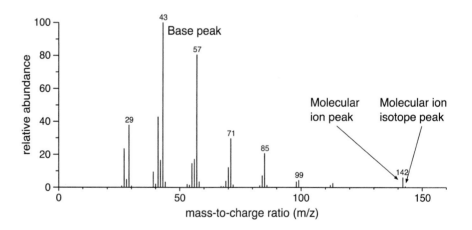

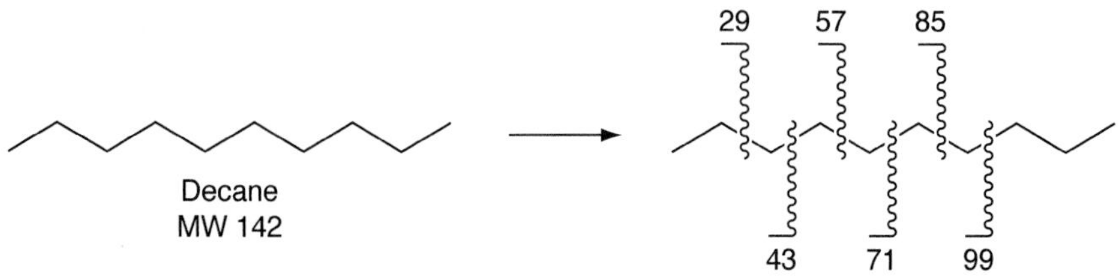

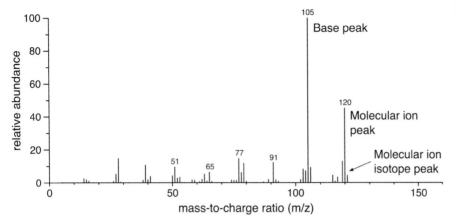

FIGURE 8-34a

Mass spectrum of 1,2,4-trimethylbenzene.

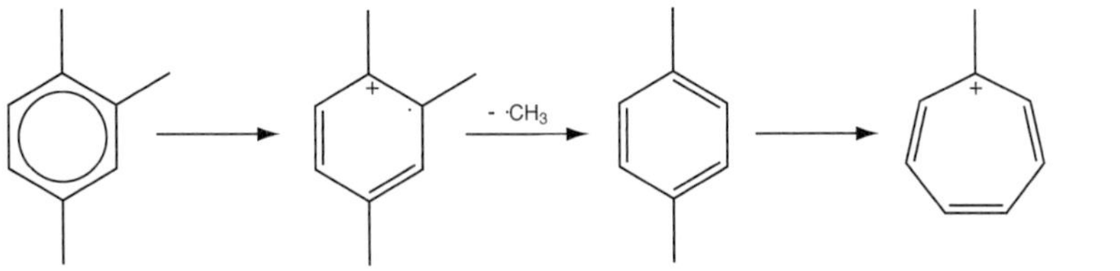

FIGURE 8-34b

Fragmentation paths of 1,2,4-trimethylbenzene leading to some of the ions present in the mass spectrum.

the M-1 ion, due to the loss of a hydrogen, is also present in a relatively significant proportion. Cycloalkanes, based upon the cyclohexane ring, are well represented by ion 83, which corresponds to the cyclohexyl fragment (refer back to Figure 8-28b). Both cycloalkanes and alkenes share an empirical formula of C_nH_{2n}, which results in their sharing some indicative ions. The ion series usually starting at m/z 41 and going by increments of 14 represents the unsaturated fragments resulting from the presence of the double bond of the original alkene. These same unsaturated fragments will also appear as a result of the presence of an aliphatic ring in a fragment.

The presence of specific various ions does not mean that the associated class of compounds is absolutely identified, but, rather, it is used as an indicator of that class. Besides the classes just described, which are often encountered in fire debris analysis, other families of compounds may have ions that are strong indicators, such as m/z 149 for phthalates or m/z 93 and 136 that appear in terpenes. Similarly, functional groups present in alcohols, aldehydes, and other classes of compounds often clearly are represented in their respective spectrum. Understanding the fragmentation patterns of the types of compounds frequently encountered in fire debris analysis is a necessary part of mass spectral interpretation, which also provides a solid foundation for the application of mass chromatography to the analysis of ignitable liquids.

B/ Mass Spectral Libraries

Although the ability to interpret a mass spectrum from scratch is a valuable skill, more often than not, the forensic scientist takes advantage of the system's data analysis ability to rapidly search electronic databases of reference spectra to suggest a possible identity for unknown compounds. The use of a good reference library can be a valuable tool in the interpretation of ignitable liquid chromatograms, which may contain hundreds of individual components. However, using the computer has its limitations.

The primary advantage offered by a reference library is the access to thousands of spectra and the ability to rapidly search the stored spectra for similarities with an unknown. Library searches often result in the proper identification of a compound; however with hydrocarbons, such as the ones frequently encountered in IL analysis, similar isomers often cannot be differentiated from one another.[17] Often, the compounds presented as high quality matches for an unknown will include the correct answer as well as other closely related compounds. When absolute identification of a particular compound is required, it is generally necessary to obtain a reference standard that can be run on the same instrument, under identical conditions, thereby allowing for the comparison of not only spectra, but also retention times. Even in cases in which a library does not have the unknown compound in its collection, a library search often can provide a very good indication as to the class of compound, thereby giving the criminalist a good starting point for spectral interpretation.

The examination of fire debris often involves the analysis of complex mixtures containing literally hundreds of individual chemical components. In cases such as this, the absolute identification of the compounds generally is not required.[18] A library search may still be useful though. One practical application of computer-based library searches is that they can easily run automated searches of all detected peaks that meet specific criteria, such as minimum peak area, within a given set of data. Because this search can be automated, minimal human intervention is required. The advantage to using a search of this type is that it may provide general indications as to

---

[17] Isomers that are often extremely difficult to differentiate based solely on their mass spectra can sometimes be identified based on their retention time. This is yet another benefit of the combined used of GC and MS techniques.

[18] A downside of the fact that some IL present so many peaks is that coeluting may happen and hamper the proper identification of a compound because the mass spectrum for the particular peak is actually constituted of two different compounds.

the types of compounds constituting an unknown sample. For example, an automated search of the data from a debris sample containing numerous peaks may indicate that the majority of the peaks are olefins and styrene-related compounds. This information can be used by the criminalist in conjunction with traditional pattern recognition techniques to conclude that the peaks present are primarily substrate-related. This would provide additional support that no IL are present. Similarly, a library search of a highly complex pattern may indicate a significant number of cycloalkanes and branched alkanes, suggesting the presence of a naphthenic/paraffinic product. Again, this information is used to supplement traditional pattern recognition techniques, not replace them.

Commercial reference libraries have improved greatly since they first became widely available and now offer much stricter levels of quality control. With so many spectra and the ability to search them so rapidly, the computer-based library search is an extremely valuable tool for the fire debris analyst.

8.6.4 Combined GC and MS Data

There are several ways in which data analysis can take advantage of the strengths of both the GC and the MS. In the simplest manner, one can use retention time in combination with spectral interpretation to help determine which particular isomer is represented in the unknown sample. In cases of IL analysis, however, combined GC and MS data becomes a very powerful tool, because one may take advantage of the strengths of GC pattern recognition and of the structural information provided by the mass spectrometer. In fire debris analysis, the two manners by which this data is observed are target compound chromatography (TCC) and mass chromatography (MC).

A/ Target Compound Chromatography

Target compound chromatography (TCC) is useful for applications in which there are a limited number of compounds of interest being sought. In this technique, computer software is provided information regarding the selected target compounds, including retention time and several significant ions with their relative abundances. Compounds selected as target compounds for fire debris analysis must be reliably present in the ignitable liquid and not commonly encountered as interfering products. When an unknown sample is analyzed with this method, the software examines the acquired data to determine if any peaks meeting the preestablished requirements are present. Usually, the retention time will specify a fairly narrow time window, and the expected relative abundances of the specified ion masses will also provide a range of acceptable values. When these criteria are met, the software identifies the peak as target compound and transfers data regarding the tentative identification, retention time, and abundance to a table or chart. In other applications, it is this tabulation of target compound data that is used primarily for data analysis; however in its application to fire debris analysis, the tabulated data is represented in a graphical form to simulate a chromatogram and to aid the analyst accustomed to visual pattern recognition. The graphical representation of the data is simply a bar graph, with retention time or peak identity along the x-axis, and the abundance represented in the y-axis. As with every technique, it offers both advantages and disadvantages.

TCC offers the advantage of finding compounds of interest in the presence of excessive interferences. By using care in the selection of the compounds to be targeted by this technique, the analyst may avoid components such as the xylenes, which are commonly contributed as interferences from the burned substrate. Consequently, the target compound chromatogram (bar graph) is a much cleaner visual representation of the components likely due to the presence of an IL. This is a major advantage when dealing with particularly complex samples that have significant contributions from the debris.

The resulting output can be represented visually in the form of a pseudo-chromatogram rather than the usual tabulated list. By using this additional step, the fire debris analyst has the data in usual graphical form, making the application of pattern recognition possible. Although this technique does offer some benefits, several disadvantages are associated with it. Although it is still taught, it is not widely applied to the analysis of fire debris. One difficulty with the use of TCC is that only a limited number of compounds are preselected, so that the forensic scientist may need to develop target compound lists for a variety of potential IL. As the variety of IL commonly encountered continues to increase, the criminalist would need to develop numerous separate target compound lists for each of the major classifications, and likely for the various boiling point ranges, as well. In addition, an unknown would need to be run through numerous sets of target compounds in order to detect an IL, or to determine that one is not present. Another drawback of this technique is that many of the compounds expected to be seen in a pattern are not included, either because they are commonly encountered as interferences, or simply because only a limited number of compounds can be targeted. As a result, the experienced examiner cannot easily transfer his or her acquired pattern recognition skills to the examination of the TCC data. Similarly, the pseudo-chromatogram created as a bar chart from the target compound data is not as analogous to a chromatogram as theorized, and therefore, requires significant additional training to develop the skills necessary to analyze data in this form.

Target compound chromatography offers a unique approach to data analysis incorporating both retention time and structural information. However, it is not as commonly applied as the technique of mass chromatography discussed in the following section. The authors do not recommend its use unless the criminalist is extremely well versed in the analysis of fire debris and clearly understands its limitations.

B/ Mass Chromatography

The concept of mass chromatography (MC) is based upon the fact that structural features specific to (or rather indicative of) a given family of chemical compounds are represented in the mass spectrum, and that this information can be used to extract chromatograms—from the total ion chromatogram—that represent those chemical classes. This technique has been termed mass chromatography because of how it efficiently and cohesively integrates mass spectral data into chromatograms. Mass chromatography is the creation of a chromatographic chart showing abundance versus time for a specific ion or set of ions. Therefore, when an ion such as $m/z\,91$, which is well represented in toluene and the other alkylbenzenes, is extracted, the result is a chromatogram emphasizing those particular components, and not showing any compounds that do not have m/z 91 in their spectra.

Acronyms and Abbreviations

There are numerous acronyms and abbreviations used to describe the different methods of analyzing GC-MS data: TIC, EIC, EIP, RIC, MC, and SIM. This can become very confusing, particularly to the beginning fire debris analyst. However, it is important to clearly understand these terms and their differences.

- TIC refers to the total ion chromatogram. This is the term used for the chromatogram that shows everything that was detected during a particular analysis. Of all the data examined by the fire debris analyst, it is arguably the most important as it represent the "big picture." The TIC is most analogous to the chromatogram obtained with a GC-FID.
- EIC is the commonly used abbreviation for the extracted ion chromatogram. It refers to data that has been drawn from the TIC. It is a chromatogram for a particular m/z value, such as for ion 55, 57, 83, or 105.
- EIP refers to an extracted ion profile. Although the terms EIC and EIP often are used interchangeably, it is more common to refer to an EIC when one specific m/z value

is displayed, and to use EIP when one is combining several different m/z values into a single display, which is indicative of a particular class of compounds. Gilbert uses the terms EIC and EIP interchangeably, however he specifies whether they are summed or individual [39].

- RIC means reconstructed ion chromatogram and is synonymous with TIC. The term RIC tends to be favored by mass spectroscopists.
- MC refers to mass chromatography, although the abbreviation is used less frequently than the full name. It refers to either extracted ion chromatography (EIC) or extracted ion profiling (EIP). The terminology recognizes the value of the combined mass spectral and chromatographic data.
- SIM refers to the technique of selected ion monitoring. Unlike the techniques just listed, which describe methods of analyzing data, SIM refers to a method of acquiring data. The technique of selected ion monitoring acquires data for preselected m/z values. SIM is a useful and sensitive technique but only when the analytes of interest are known ahead of time.

This technique is especially useful in the analysis of IL for several reasons. Most importantly, this data—presented in a format that effectively screens out many interferences—is not selectively collected; that is, this is not a selected ion monitoring (SIM) technique. Full scan data is collected, and from this full range of data (the TIC), the forensic scientist can select various ways of examining the data to emphasize components of interest. Another reason that MC is particularly applicable to ILR analysis is that many of the commonly encountered IL are derived from petroleum, and as such may contain hundreds of individual components that can be grouped into a relatively few basic groups, depending upon the characteristics of the general chemical family. Because of this, the criminalist can look at complete data and examine full mass spectra, and may also pull out relatively simple data of interest from seemingly complicated chromatograms, thus maintaining a data analysis technique that is still based on pattern recognition. The task of extracting data actually is not overwhelming, and commonly is conducted by simple computer macros. For these reasons, when IL data analysis is presented in Chapter 9, total ion chromatograms are presented along with extracted ion chromatograms or profiles.

Mass chromatography can be conducted in two basic ways. One way involves extracting data from individual ions, and examining the chromatograms for each single ion selected independently. The resulting data from an individual ion is referred to as extracted ion chromatogram (EIC). The other way is to select several ions that, together, represent a class of chemical compounds, and to present the data from these ions in a single chromatogram that is representative of that particular class. In the case of summed ions, the resulting data is referred to as extracted ion profile (EIP). Both techniques accomplish the same basic objectives, and the selection of one technique over the other is largely a matter of personal preference.

For both the individual ion (EIC) and the summed ion (EIP) techniques, the same essential ions will be used. Based upon the reproducible fragmentation patterns discussed in Subsection 8.6.3, particular ions will be consistently created for the specific classes of compounds routinely seen in petroleum products. It is these ions that are used in MC. Although the examiner has some discretion in the selection of ions used in data analysis, there are definite benefits to choosing ions that have been widely used and generally accepted within the field (see Table 8-6) [28]. Use of these recognized ions offers the benefit of not only being good representatives of the variety of compounds encountered in ignitable liquids, but also of the advantage that data comparison among various sources is possible.

Understanding the benefits of EIC and EIP is best accomplished through the use of examples. These will be presented in Chapter 9.

Table 8-6	Typical ions extracted for each class of compounds to produce mass chromatograms of interest to fire debris analysis. Ions in bold are the most indicative of that particular class. Note that for most series, the increment between two ions is m/z 14, which is due to methyl groups addition

Compound type	ions (m/z)
Alkanes	29, **43**, **57**, 71, 85, 99
Cycloalkanes	41, 55, 69, **83**
Alkenes	41, **55**, 69, 83, 97
Alkylbenzenes	**91**, 92, **105**, 106, **119**, 120
Naphthalenes	128, **142**, **156**, 170
Indanes	**117**, 118, **131**, 132
Terpenes	93, 136
Alcohols	**31**, **45**, 59
Ketones	**44**, **58**, 72, 86

REFERENCES

1. Ettre LS (2003) Milestones in chromatography—M.S. Tswett and the invention of chromatography, *LCGC North America*, **21**(5), pp 459–67.
2. Poole CF (2000) *I/Chromatography: Chromatography*. In: *Encyclopedia of separation science*, editors Wilson I, Poole C, and Cooke M, Academic Press, San Diego, CA, pp 40–64.
3. Vinet B (2003) Mikhail S. Tswett et l'invention de la chromatographie, *Annales de biologie clinique du Québec*, **40**(2), p 23.
4. Tswett M (1906) Physikalisch-chemische Studien über das Chlorophyll. Die Adsorptionen, *Berichte der Deutschen Botanischen Gesellschaft*, **24**, pp 316–23.
5. Tswett M (1906) Adsorptionsanalyse und chromatographische Methode. Anwendung auf die Chemie des Chlorophylls, *Berichte der Deutschen Botanischen Gesellschaft*, **24**, pp 384–93.
6. Meyer VR (2000) *II/Chromatography: Liquid: Historical development*. In: *Encyclopedia of separation science*, editors Wilson I, Poole C, and Cooke M, Academic Press, San Diego, CA, pp 663–70.
7. International Union of Pure and Applied Chemistry (1997) Chromatography, *IUPAC Compendium of Chemical Terminology*, Research Triangle Park, NC.
8. Jennings W (2000) *II/Chromatography: Gas: Column technology*. In: *Encyclopedia of separation science*, editors Wilson I, Poole C, and Cooke M, Academic Press, San Diego, CA, pp 427–34.
9. International Union of Pure and Applied Chemistry (1997) Plate number (in chromatography), *IUPAC Compendium of Chemical Terminology*, Research Triangle Park, NC.

10. McNair HM and Bonelli EJ (1969) *Basic gas chromatography*, Varian, Palo Alto, CA.

11. International Union of Pure and Applied Chemistry (1997) Height equivalent to a theoretical plate, *IUPAC Compendium of Chemical Terminology*, Research Triangle Park, NC.

12. Martin AJP and Synge RLM (1941) A new form of chromatogram employing two liquid phases 1. A theory of chromatography, *Biochemical Journal*, **35**(12), pp 1358–64.

13. van Deemter JJ, Zuiderweg FJ, and Klinkenberg A (1956) Longitudinal diffusion and resistance to mass transfer as causes of nonideality in chromatography, *Chemical Engineering Science*, **5**, pp 271–89.

14. International Union of Pure and Applied Chemistry (1997) Eddy dispersion (diffusion), *IUPAC Compendium of Chemical Terminology*, Research Triangle Park, NC.

15. Schomburg G (1990) *Gas chromatography: A practical course*, VCH Verlagsgesellschaft, Weinheim, Germany.

16. Adlard ER and Poole CF (2000) *II/Chromatography: Gas: Historical development*. In: *Encyclopedia of separation science*, editors Wilson I, Poole C, and Cooke M, Academic Press, San Diego, CA, pp 513–20.

17. James AT and Martin AJP (1952) Gas-liquid partition chromatography: The separation of volatile fatty acids from formic acid to dodecanoic acid, *Biochemical Journal*, **50**(5), pp 679–90.

18. Sevcik J (1976) *Detectors in gas chromatography*. In: *Journal of Chromatography Library*, **4**, Elsevier Scientific Publishing Company, Amsterdam, Netherlands.

19. Agilent Technologies (2005) *Maintaining your Agilent GC or GC/MS Systems*, Agilent Technologies, Palo Alto, CA.

20. Vérette E (2000) *II/Chromatography: Automation*. In: *Encyclopedia of separation science*, editors Wilson I, Poole C, and Cooke M, Academic Press, San Diego, CA, pp 343–52.

21. Alltech (1998) *Merlin Microseal septum*, data sheet U80060, Alltech Associates, Deerfield, IL.

22. Supelco (1997) *Capillary GC inlet liner selection guide*, Sigma-Aldrich, Bellefonte, PA.

23. Agilent Technologies (2004) *GC pressure/flow calculator software*, available from http://www.chem.agilent.com/cag/servsup/usersoft/files/GCFC.htm, last access performed on December 31, 2006.

24. Davies IW (2000) *II/Chromatography: Gas: Sampling systems*. In: *Encyclopedia of separation science*, editors Wilson I, Poole C, and Cooke M, Academic Press, San Diego, CA, pp 550–8.

25. International Union of Pure and Applied Chemistry (1997) Tailing (in chromatography), *IUPAC Compendium of Chemical Terminology*, Research Triangle Park, NC.

26. International Union of Pure and Applied Chemistry (1997) Fronting (in chromatography), *IUPAC Compendium of Chemical Terminology*, Research Triangle Park, NC.

27. Ettre LS (2005) M.J.E. Golay and the invention of open-tubular (capillary) columns, *Journal of High Resolution Chromatography*, **10**(5), pp 221–30.

28. ASTM International (2006) *ASTM E 1618–06 Standard test method for ignitable liquid residues in extracts from fire debris samples by gas chromatography-mass spectrometry*, Annual Book of ASTM Standards 14.02, West Conshohocken, PA.

29. Butler JC (1998) *A new forensic tool for arson analysis, the tandem PID/FID*, ThermoQuest CE Instruments, Austin, TX.

30. McMinn D (2000) *II/Chromatography: Gas: Detectors: General (flame ionization detectors and thermal conductivity detectors)*. In: *Encyclopedia of separation science*, editors Wilson I, Poole C, and Cooke M, Academic Press, San Diego, CA, pp 443–7.

31. Busch KL (2000) *I/Mass spectrometry*. In: *Encyclopedia of separation science*, editors Wilson I, Poole C, and Cooke M, Academic Press, San Diego, CA, pp 174–89.

32. Watson JT (1997) *Introduction to mass spectrometry*, Lippincott-Raven, Philadelphia, PA.

33. Clench MR and Tetler LW (2000) *II/Chromatography: Gas: Detectors: Mass spectrometry*. In: *Encyclopedia of separation science*, editors Wilson I, Poole C, and Cooke M, Academic Press, San Diego, CA, pp 448–55.

34. Frysinger GS and Gaines RB (2003) Analysis of ignitable liquids in fire debris with comprehensive two-dimensional gas chromatography-mass spectrometry (GCxGC/MS), *55th Annual Meeting of the American Academy of Forensic Sciences*, Chicago, IL.

35. ASTM International (2006) *ASTM E 1387–01 Standard test method for ignitable liquid residues in extracts from fire debris samples by gas chromatography*, Annual Book of ASTM Standards 14.02, West Conshohocken, PA.

36. McLafferty FW and Tureček F (1993) *Interpretation of mass spectra*, 4th edition, University Science Books, Mill Valley, CA.

37. Silverstein RM and Webster FX (1998) *Spectrometric identification of organic compounds*, 6th edition, John Wiley & Sons, New York, NY.

38. Bruice PY (2004) *Organic chemistry*, Prentice Hall, Upper Saddle River, NJ.

39. Gilbert MW (1998) The use of individual extracted ion profiles versus summed extracted ion profiles in fire debris analysis, *Journal of Forensic Sciences*, **43**(4), pp 871–6.

CHAPTER 9

Interpretation of Data Obtained from Neat Ignitable Liquids

"Things should be made as simple as possible, but not any simpler."

Albert Einstein, German-born physicist (1879–1955)

9.1 INTRODUCTION

This chapter provides the mechanisms for the identification and classification of ignitable liquids (IL) as defined in ASTM E 1618-06 standard test method for ignitable liquid residues in extracts from fire debris samples by gas chromatography–mass spectrometry [1]. Also, although the ASTM E 1387-01 standard test method for ignitable liquid residues in extracts from fire debris samples by gas chromatography is covered de facto in the following text, it will not be referenced directly (see also the footnote in Subsection 7.7.1) [2]. Even though analysis of IL and ILR by GC-FID is still valid, GC-MS is, by far, the preferred technique. Thus, this chapter will be limited to the identification of the various ASTM classes of ignitable liquids based upon GC-MS data.

Limitations in Using GC-FID and ASTM E 1387-01

It should be recognized that when using a GC-FID instead of a GC-MS, not only may it become quite difficult to distinguish some classes of liquids, but it also may be impossible to identify some ILR when in the presence of a significant amount of interfering products. For this reason, it is recommended that today all IL and ILR should be analyzed by GC-MS. Furthermore, with the availability of reasonably priced benchtop GC-MS, the cost-savings between the two instruments is negligible, when considered in the context of the structural information that is gained.

The following discussion is limited to pure ignitable liquids; isolation and recognition of ILR in the presence of background matrices is presented in Chapter 12. Recognizing and classifying pure IL based upon their chemical properties constitutes the foundation of the more complex data interpretation of ILR extracted from fire debris samples and thus its importance cannot be diminished by its relative simplicity.

The ASTM IL classification system provides for categorization based on chemical composition and boiling point range. Composition is defined by the types of compounds present (i.e., alkanes, aromatics, etc), which is determined to great extent by the manufacturing process. The IL classes as defined by ASTM E 1618 are gasoline, petroleum distillates, isoparaffinic products, naphthenic paraffinic products, aromatic products, normal-alkanes products, oxygenated solvents, and a generic "others-miscellaneous" class [1]. Table 9-1 shows the different ASTM classes with examples of IL found on the market. The ASTM E 1618 classification criteria do not address all

Table 9-1 *ASTM E 1618-06 ignitable liquid classification scheme [1]*

Class	Light (C_4-C_9)	Medium (C_8-C_{13})	Heavy (C_8-C_{20+})
Gasoline	Fresh gasoline is typically in the range of C_4-C_{12}		
Petroleum distillates (including dearomatized)	Petroleum ether Some cigarette lighter fluids Some camping fuels	Some charcoal starters Some paint thinners Some dry cleaning solvents	Kerosene Diesel fuel Some jet fuels Some charcoal starters
Isoparaffinic products	Aviation gas Some specialty solvents	Some charcoal starters Some paint thinners Some copier toners	Some commercial specialty solvents
Naphthenic paraffinic products	Cyclohexane-based solvents/products	Some charcoal starters Some insecticide vehicles Some lamp oils	Some insecticide vehicles Some lamp oils Industrial solvents
Aromatic products	Some paint and varnish removers Some automotive parts cleaners Xylenes-based products Toluene-based products	Some automotive parts cleaners Specialty cleaning solvents Some insecticide vehicles Fuel additives	Some insecticide vehicles Industrial cleaning solvents
Normal-alkanes products	Solvents: Pentane, hexane, heptane	Some candle oils Some copier toners	Some candle oils Carbonless forms Some copier toners
Oxygenated solvents	Alcohols Ketones Some lacquer thinners Fuel additives Surface preparation solvents	Some lacquer thinners Some industrial solvents Metal cleaners/gloss removers	
Others–miscellaneous	Single component products Some blended products Some enamel reducers	Turpentine products Some blended products Some specialty products	Some blended products Some specialty products

ignitable liquids: it is limited to what is most likely to be recovered and identified in a routine fire debris sample. Therefore, this chapter is also limited to IL defined in the standard; other ignitable liquids and ignitable materials, including vegetable oils, are described in Chapter 14. It also should be noted that other classification schemes exist and may be adopted by different crime laboratories around the world. The ASTM classification is not a perfect solution that fits every country and situation possible. However, it is a well-conceived classification system that has proven to be of great use for more than 10 years. It is thus appropriate to base this chapter on it as it gives a great starting point (and common ground) to all fire debris analysts.

It should be noted that the products listed in the various categories of IL in Table 9-1 are examples of known commercial applications of these products. This list does not constitute a comprehensive or exhaustive scheme. As a matter of fact, the business of solvents and ignitable liquids is extremely dynamic and new products are brought to market each year.

ASTM E 1618 is also a dynamic standard and is changing on a regular basis. The 20 version reflects the last changes in the classification scheme compared to its previous version developed in 2001 [1, 3]. The classes of dearomatized distillates and distillates have been merged together following the recommendation of the *Fire Laboratory Standards and Protocols Committee* of the Scientific Working Group for Fire and Explosives (SWGFEX) that was based on recent research [4–6]. Back in 2001, the classification was also completely revamped compared to its antecedent, the 1997 version [7]. Therefore, it is important to keep in mind that the ASTM classification scheme may adapt with time and with market changes.

9.2 PETROLEUM v. NONPETROLEUM IGNITABLE LIQUIDS

As introduced in Chapter 7, ignitable liquids can be organized into classes based upon origin and chemical composition. ASTM E 1618-06 separates ignitable liquids into eight classes based on chemical composition and boiling point range. However, a higher level distinction among IL exists and should be noted. At the uppermost level there is a division between two specific groups of IL: Petroleum- and nonpetroleum-based products. Petroleum-based products include all products obtained by the petroleum industry through the refinement of crude oil. Nonpetroleum-based IL include those extracted or derived from all other sources. The analytical technique used in fire debris analysis does not differ between these two groups, however data interpretation differs significantly.[1]

---

[1]Vegetable oils are a notable exception. Their analysis is discussed in Chapter 14.

Petroleum-based IL contain all the compounds found in refined crude oil within a given boiling point range unless specific steps have been taken to remove them (see Subsection 7.5.3 on chemical processes). As a result, data from petroleum-based products generally consist of a significant number of peaks, often extended over a wide boiling point range. These products are composed exclusively of aliphatic and aromatic hydrocarbons, with the exception of some natural contaminations such as sulfuric compounds and metals, which are present in extremely low concentrations, and therefore are not pertinent to fire debris analysis.

Conversely, nonpetroleum-based IL greatly vary in composition. They all fall into the oxygenated and others–miscellaneous classes of the ASTM system. The most common representatives of these classes include single- or few-compound mixtures of oxygenated species (ethanol, acetone, methyl ethyl ketone); compounds distilled, extracted, or derived from other natural products (turpentine, limonene, essential oils); and some petrochemicals. Ignitable liquids that are not petroleum-based tend to have much simpler patterns, and a much wider variety range of chemical compounds represented. Thus, their identification often is based on specific individual compounds rather than the pattern recognition techniques generally used for the identification of petroleum products.

Petrochemicals v. Petroleum Products

Petroleum products are those refined from distilled crude oil. They generally contain a mixture of aromatic and/or aliphatic compounds encompassing a relatively broad boiling point range. It is important not to use interchangeably the terms petroleum products and petrochemicals. A petrochemical is any single chemical derived or purified from fossil fuel [8]. Petrochemicals are used as feedstock in the manufacture of numerous products, notably polymers.

9.3 BOILING POINT RANGE

One of the single most important characteristics of an ignitable liquid is the boiling point range in which it elutes from the chromatographic system: It is defined as the region where the majority of the compounds in the liquid boils in comparison to normal alkanes. Since nonpolar columns are used for GC analysis of IL, separation of nonpolar alkanes is related directly to their boiling point. Figure 9-1 shows the separation of the homologous series of normal alkanes from n-hexane (C_6H_{14}) to n-pentacosane ($C_{25}H_{52}$).[2] For simplicity, the abbreviation "C" followed by the subscritped number of carbon atoms of the corresponding n-alkane has been established and is

---

[2] Unless specified otherwise, all chromatographic data presented in this chapter have been obtained using the GC-MS conditions presented under program 1 in Table 8-4.

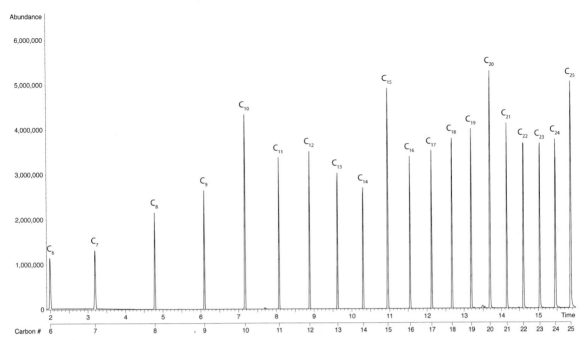

FIGURE 9-1 *Chromatogram showing the elution from C_6 (n-hexane) to C_{25} (n-pentacosane). Note the time scale at the bottom along with a carbon number scale. The latter is used to express the IL boiling point range. This figure is available for download on the publisher's web site (see note at beginning of book).*

Table 9-2	Subclasses based on boiling point range as defined by ASTM E 1618-06 [1]	
ASTM subclass	**Normal-alkane range**	**Approximate boiling point range [°C]**
Light	C_4-C_9	0 to 150
Medium	C_8-C_{13}	120 to 240
Heavy	C_8-C_{20+}	120 to 350+

accepted within the community to refer to these compounds. As an example hexane is represented as C_6, heptane as C_7, and decane as C_{10}. Since the separation is achieved via a temperature program, the elution time between each member of this homologous series is "relatively" constant. This, in turn, renders the interpretation of the chromatogram much easier. The ultimate luxury consists in designing a temperature program to have the n-alkanes eluting at the time corresponding to their number of carbons (n-dodecane eluting at 12 minutes, n-pentadecane eluting at 15 minutes, and so on). However, this may prevent a good resolution in some parts of the chromatogram with some ignitable liquids.

Three boiling point ranges—light, medium, and heavy—have been defined for the subclassification of IL as shown in Table 9-2. These ranges were not arbitrarily assigned; they are designated based upon the propensity of the petroleum industry to market products in these boiling point ranges. Light products are marketed for high flammability, high evaporation rates, lower flammability limits, and high solvency. Medium range products are produced for different solvency requirements and moderate flammability. Heavier products are marketed for higher boiling temperatures, greater heat production, and lower evaporation rates.

Detecting Light Products

Light products are defined as C_4–C_9, but for practical purposes many laboratories establish a lower limit of routine analysis at n-hexane (C_6). This is due to the fact that passive headspace concentration extraction on activated charcoal often is utilized, which necessitates the use of a solvent to desorb the activated charcoal strip (see Section 11.5). With the use of a mass spectrometer as a detector, it is necessary to let sufficient time for the solvent to elute during which the instrument does not collect data. This is called the solvent delay and typically it is set up to last from the start of the analysis until the solvent peak has passed, which often corresponds to approximately n-hexane. In most instances, this will not significantly affect interpretation and IL classification. However, it will prevent the criminalist from detecting early-eluting compounds such as some light oxygenates. More interestingly, one does not have to wait for the solvent to elute; rather, the instrument parameters may be set to turn the detector off for the much shorter period of time when the solvent is actually eluting. In such instances, it is possible to detect data before the elution of the solvent and detect some light compounds.

In any case, it is necessary for the laboratory to establish what compounds will not be detected in a routine analysis and to acknowledge the scope and limitations of the analysis in the written procedures. Alternatively, if the laboratory utilizes a technique that does not involve the use of a solvent, such as Tenax, which uses thermal desorption (see Subsection 11.5.4), then it would be possible to collect data from the very beginning of the chromatogram. Additionally, it is possible to keep the MS acquiring at all time, with the direct result of having a dominating solvent peak at the beginning of the chromatogram, and the risk of reducing the lifetime of the detector. Modern instruments are particulary suitable to this last possibility. Finally the option of using a heavier solvent, eluting at a later time, to desorb the adsorbent also is discussed in Subsection 11.5.2. Most of the data in this text is presented with a range starting at C_6.

Although chemical composition is a significant factor in the end use of a petroleum product, boiling point range is of equal importance. For example, distillates are marketed for use in both cigarette lighter fluids and diesel fuels; however, it would be difficult to flint-light a cigarette lighter with the higher boiling diesel fuel and it would be quite inefficient to put cigarette lighter fluid in a diesel engine. Thus, the boiling range of an IL can provide important information as to its intended use.

As a consequence, one of the most important steps in data interpretation is the determination of the boiling point range. This typically is accomplished by comparing the unknown chromatogram to that of a reference chromatogram such as the one shown in Figure 9-1. Figure 9-2 shows examples of this type of determination with three chromatograms for which the boiling point range is C_6-C_8, C_8-C_{12}, and C_8-C_{17}, respectively.

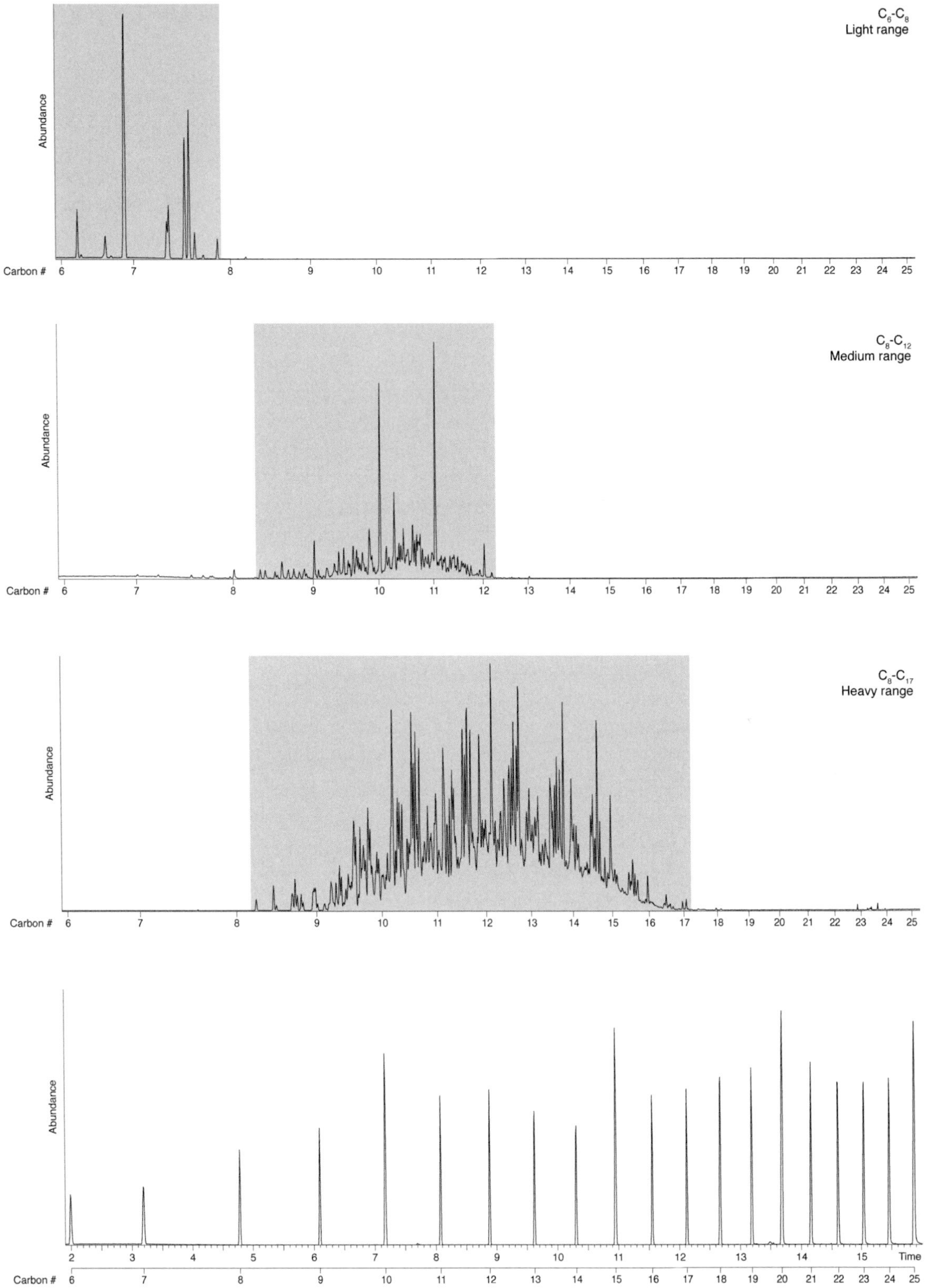

FIGURE 9-2 *Examples of the different boiling point ranges found in ignitable liquids. The bulk of the liquid determines its corresponding carbon number range as indicated by the grey areas. Note that the top liquid may contain compounds well below C$_6$ (usually down to C$_4$), however these are not observable using the given chromatographic conditions. This is a limitation that must be clearly understood.*

Light range IL elute primarily prior to C_9 (n-nonane). Medium range products elute between C_8 and C_{13} and generally encompass a range of less than five normal alkanes. Heavy products either elute from C_8 to C_{20} and above while encompassing a range of five or more normal alkanes or they elute entirely above C_{13}. There is an obvious overlap between medium and heavy products; the distinction is made in the breadth of the boiling point range for a given product. In general, medium range products are significantly tighter whereas heavy products encompass a much broader boiling point range as illustrated in Figure 9-2.

Most products can readily be placed into one of these three ranges, but there are some that do not fit neatly into a single category. ASTM addresses this by recommending the use of descriptive hybrid ranges such as "light-medium" and "medium-heavy" [1]. Petroleum-based products occur throughout the various ranges, nonpetroleum-based ignitable liquids are limited primarily to light- and medium-range products.

9.4 PETROLEUM-BASED IGNITABLE LIQUIDS

9.4.1 Basis for Interpretation

Petroleum-based products are the most commonly available IL and thus the most commonly used liquid accelerants. Among them, gasoline is by far the most common liquid used as accelerant in the United States and probably around the world. Heating and diesel fuels are somewhat less common but still are produced in abundance. All other petroleum products are the result of refining operations responding to market demands. The various fractions are marketed for a wide variety of uses and commonly are found in garages, work sheds, and homes throughout the world. Their presence in a fire investigation as an incidental ignitable liquid or a true accelerant is not uncommon.

With petroleum-based products, the only compounds of interest to the fire debris analyst are:

- All saturated aliphatics (normal-alkanes, isoalkanes, and cycloalkanes)
- The aromatics, namely simple (mononuclear) aromatics, polynuclear aromatics, and indanes, which boil in the range of C_4 to approximately C_{20}.

By evaluating the presence, relative abundance, distribution, and boiling point range of these chemical classes, petroleum products can readily be classified into their appropriate ASTM classes.

Table 9-3 describes the hydrocarbon compound classes common to each of the petroleum-based ASTM classes (except for others-miscellaneous) [7]. Because the ASTM classes are based upon refinery process—designed to remove or transform crude oil components—one can easily deduct from the

		ASTM classes and their chemical composition. It is important to note that the presence of some compounds is dependent on the boiling point range into which the liquid is sub-classified		
Table 9-3				

Class	Alkanes	Cycloalkanes	Aromatics (includes indanes)	Polynuclear aromatics
Gasoline	Present, less abundant than aromatics*	Present, less abundant than aromatics	Abundant	Present
Petroleum distillates	Abundant, Gaussian distribution	Present, less abundant than alkanes	Present, less abundant than alkanes (Absent in dearomatized distillates)	Present (depending on boiling point range), less abundant than alkanes (Absent in dearomatized distillates)
Isoparaffinic products	Branched alkanes abundant, n-alkanes absent or strongly diminished	Absent	Absent	Absent
Naphthenic paraffinic products	Branched alkanes abundant, n-alkanes absent or strongly diminished	Abundant	Absent	Absent
Aromatic products	Absent	Absent	Abundant	Abundant (depending on the boiling point range)
Normal-alkanes products	Abundant	Absent	Absent	Absent
Oxygenated solvents	Composition may vary, presence of oxygenated organic compounds			

*It should be noted that not all gasolines exhibit an aromatic content more abundant than the aliphatic content. While the majority of them do so, it has been observed for many years in Canada that a good number of premium gasolines are constituted of more than 60% of aliphatics (up to 85%) [14]. In such instances, the chromatograms look quite differently than the regular chromatogram shown in the ASTM standards.

types of compounds present which refinery processes were likely involved in the production (see Chapter 7). Additionally, as the name of each class is based on the composition of the liquids, one can quickly have an understanding of what should or should not be present in the resulting GC-MS data for a given class of IL.

Because petroleum products are first separated by fractional distillation, they generally consist of numerous compounds, many of which are not unique to petroleum-based liquids and many of which are found as interfering products (mostly due to pyrolysis) in fire debris substrates. Thus, the presence of any specific chemical is not really significant, whereas the combined presence of various chemicals in the right proportion becomes characteristic of an IL. The greater the boiling point, the more compounds exist, thus usually resulting in unresolved chromatograms. Although mass spectral characteristics of the different chemical classes can provide valuable interpretive information as to the type of compounds present, the identification of specific compounds may be limited due to the similarity of some hydrocarbon mass spectra (particularly isomers) and the inability to completely resolve the various components in the data. In general, absolute identification of compounds is rarely necessary.

Pattern recognition is used to evaluate the significance of the presence of the different compounds in a chromatogram. For example, whereas n-undecane (C_{11}) may be a significant compound in a petroleum distillate, the presence of n-undecane in itself does not mean that a petroleum distillate is present. Rather the presence of n-undecane in relation to other compounds common to petroleum distillates in a specific configuration is essential to data interpretation and IL identification. Figure 9-3 shows that it is the relative abundance of n-undecane, the presence of other compounds found in petroleum distillates, and the overall pattern of data that allows for the identification of this product as a medium petroleum distillate

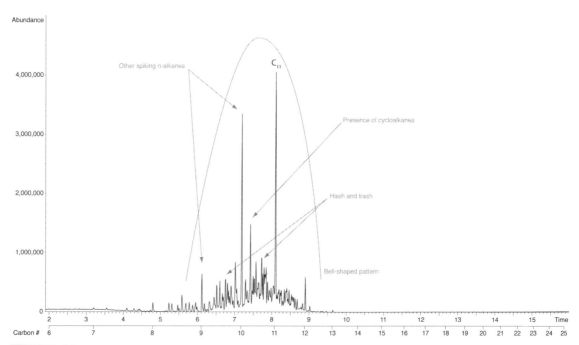

FIGURE 9-3 *The presence of undecane alone is not representative of an ignitable liquid. The presence of C_{11} in combination with a bell-shaped pattern, other spiking n-alkanes ranging from C_9 to C_{12}, as well as cycloalkanes and the typical hash and trash between the n-alkanes, is characteristic of a medium petroleum distillate (MPD).*

(MPD). Thus, data interpretation by pattern recognition is the identification of diagnostic chromatographic patterns.

Pattern recognition is used for the identification of most petroleum products. Single- or few-component IL, including n-alkane products, which contain too few peaks to establish a unique pattern for identification, have different data interpretation requirements. These will be addressed in detail in their respective sections.

9.4.2 Diagnostic Patterns

Gas chromatography provides the mechanisms for separating the various components of petroleum-based ignitable liquids; mass spectrometry allows for a filtering mechanism to develop specific patterns (mass chromatograms abbreviated MC) based upon chemical composition resulting in more diagnostic data. The choice of the most pertinent ions to be used in order to produce mass chromatograms has been the subject of several publications [9–12]. For each class of compounds, specific ions are thus used (see Table 8-6 for a list of these ions for each class).

In Figures 9-4a and 9-4b, the total ion chromatogram (TIC) for a diesel fuel is filtered to extract ions common to specific chemical classes. These extracted ion profiles or chromatograms provide some distinctive information and allow for the visualization of important, but less abundant, compounds; in the example of diesel fuel, simple aromatics, polynuclear aromatics, and indanes that are not distinguishable in the TIC.

Comparing Chromatograms

One can wonder what the best technique is to compare chromatograms. One of the simplest and most efficient manners is to use a light box and place the reference chromatogram in front of it, with the sample chromatogram atop it. Once the retention time and abundance zero are perfectly superimposed, by simply shifting the sample chromatogram left or right (just a couple of millimeters) or back and forth, it is possible to quickly observe the differences and similarities between the two patterns. The technique requires a little bit of training, but is very successful. The eye then scans the complete chromatogram peak after peak or region after region. The sample chromatogram can then be marked with a pen or pencil to emphasize differences and similarities.

For purposes of convenience and to start training this skill, some chromatograms are available for download on the publisher's web site (see note at the beginning of the book). One can print them on transparencies and use them to compare patterns with the chromatograms presented throughout this book. Although transparencies are not necessary when using a light box, these are more convenient to use when a light box is not available (which is probably the case when reading this book).

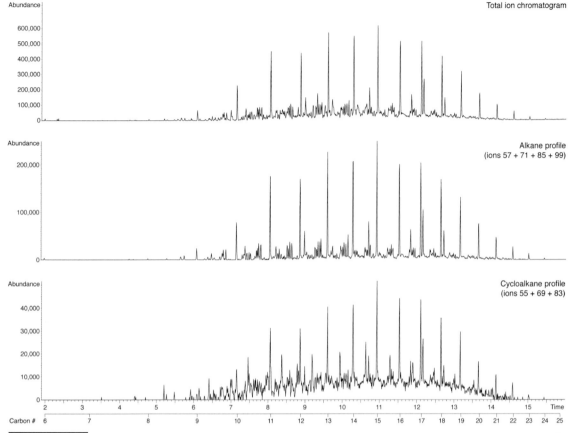

FIGURE 9-4a *TIC of diesel fuel (top), followed by EIPs of alkanes and cycloalkanes. This figure is available for download on the publisher's web site (see note at beginning of book).*

Figure 9-4 represents the sum of ions indicative of the various chemical classes to provide a proportionate representation of the ion abundance across the boiling point range. Single ion chromatograms can also be extracted to provide emphasis on certain diagnostic regions. Figures 9-5a and 9-5b

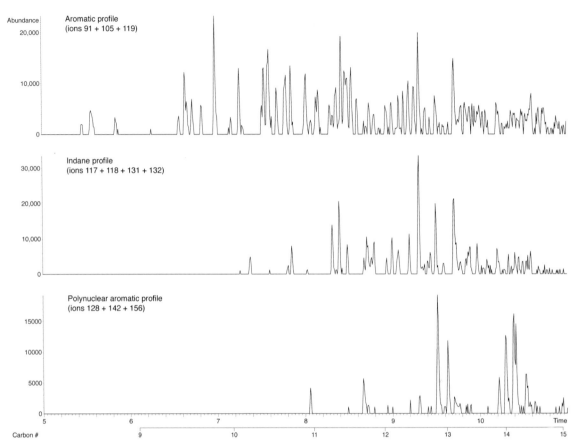

FIGURE 9-4b *Diesel fuel EIPs of aromatics, indanes, and polynuclear aromatics. EIPs allow for a visualization of important, but less abundant, classes of compounds present in an ignitable liquid and not readily observable in the TIC. This figure is available for download on the publisher's web site (see note at beginning of book).*

display the same data in (single) extracted ion chromatogram (EIC) format. The use of summed versus single ion mass chromatograms is largely due to personal preference, however there are specific advantages and drawbacks to each (see the following text box).

Summed v. Single Ion Mass Chromatograms

Although personal preference plays a major role in the choice whether summed ion chromatograms or single ion chromatograms are used, there are serious advantages and disadvantages to each [13]. In the summed version, where two or more ions are used to produce the desired mass chromatogram (MC), a better signal ensues (compare the alkane profile in Figures 9-4a and 9-5a. This usually produces an MC with peaks better distinguished from the background. It works well with the alkane and aromatic series. It also allows for a reduction of the number of MC generated and thus, fewer chromatograms to examine. It also provides a pattern that is more representative of the ratios exhibited in the TIC pattern.

Single ion chromatograms allow for a better distinction between some classes. For example, when separating ions 55 and 83, it is possible to distinguish between pyrolysis products (ion 55 is very prominent in alkenes) and cycloalkanes (ion 83 is more prominent in cycloalkanes than any other alkanes and alkenes). Although there are two MC to look at, each provides specific sepa-

rated information that is not available when looked at jointly on one chromatogram. Similarly, when separating ions 105 and 119, 117 and 131, as well as 142 and 156, whereas the signal for each species is not cumulated, it is possible to observe a pattern evolving in a diagonal from the top-left to the bottom-right with diagnostic patterns for each ion (as shown in Figure 9-5b from about 6.5 to 11.5 min). Additionally, ions such as 142 and 156—typically in much lower abundance than ion 128, with which it often is summed—can be clearly seen in each single ion chromatograms whereas they may be completely lost in the baseline on the summed ion chromatogram, particularly with gasoline summed ion chromatograms (see later). Single ion chromatograms bring some advantages, however they definitely require a global thinking capacity from the user.

To simplify the reading of the text and for the purpose of clarity, the term extracted ion chromatogram (EIC) will be used to mention a single ion mass chromatogram and the term extracted ion profile (EIP) will be used to refer to a summed ion mass chromatogram.

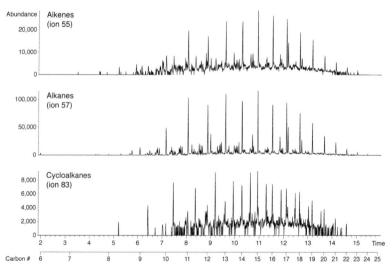

FIGURE 9-5a *EICs of diesel fuel shown in Figure 9-4. When using single ions rather than summed ions, it is possible in this case to separate ion 55 from 83 and obtained different information. In this case, the cycloalkanes are much more obvious in the 83 window when compared to Figure 9-4a.*

Data interpretation should always start at the most general level and then be worked down to the most specific level. The least specific level is based upon the recognition of peaks or groups of peaks in specific boiling point ranges (often this is an early indicator of petroleum v. nonpetroleum products). Any time that a peak grouping encompasses a distinct boiling point (n-alkane) range, it is a good indication that a petroleum-based product may be present. Next, the TIC is evaluated to formally

Specific Nomenclature of Alkylbenzenes and Substituted Naphthalenes

Like the n-alkane series, a shorthand for describing the simple and polynuclear aromatic compounds uses the "C_x-alkyl" prefix in which X is used to describe the number of alkyl radical carbons attached to the benzene ring or naphthalene ring. Thus, the term C_2-alkylbenzenes designates compounds to which two carbon atoms are attached to the benzene ring, such as with ethylbenzene, m-xylene,

p-xylene, and o-xylene. The term C_2-naphthalenes encompasses compounds such as dimethylnaphthalenes and ethylnaphthalenes. Similarly, C_1- and C_2-indanes are also used throughout this text. This nomenclature is well accepted in fire debris analysis and is used throughout the book.

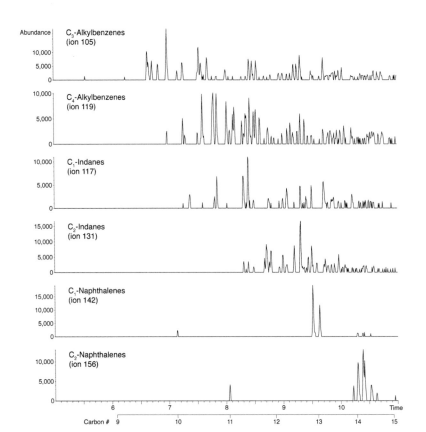

FIGURE 9-5b

In these EICs, peaks of interest can be followed in a diagonal from top left to bottom right. This figure is available for download on the publisher's web site (see note at beginning of book).

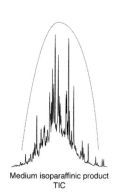
Medium isoparaffinic product
TIC

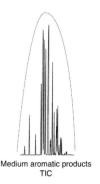
Medium aromatic products
TIC

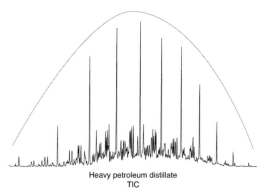
Heavy petroleum distillate
TIC

FIGURE 9-6 *The bell-shaped pattern often is encountered with petroleum products. This is due to the Gaussian distribution of the boiling points of the different components that comprise the mixture, which is a consequence of the fractionation distillation process used in the refining.*

establish the boiling point range and to note any diagnostic patterns associated with different IL class. Then, mass chromatograms are created for each class of compounds and carefully observed for diagnostic patterns. Finally, library searches of pertinent peaks are performed among the different mass chromatograms in order to tentatively identify them and confirm their nature.

The most common diagnostic peak groupings and descriptors used in IL identification are provided in the following paragraphs. Included for each is a rather staid technical description of the pattern and its relative elution location as well as some ordinary descriptive colloquialisms that have evolved in the community and are now common vernacular for data interpretation. These specific patterns provide the basis of the data interpretation rules used to distinguish each IL class.

A/ Spiking n-Alkanes

Perhaps the most easily recognizable pattern is that of the Gaussian distribution (bell-shaped curve) of spiking normal alkanes associated with petroleum distillates as shown in Figure 9-6. This distribution occurs throughout the ignitable liquid boiling point ranges, although it is less distinctive in light products. A similar pattern is observed with the cycloalkanes, when using the MC with the single ion 83 as shown in Figure 9-7.

B/ The Three Musketeers

This grouping of C_2-alkylbenzenes is an important diagnostic grouping for petroleum products for which the aromatics have not been removed. It may be absent if the product underwent significant weathering. It is seen as three peaks, representing four compounds, two of which coelute. This is where the reference to the three musketeers come from: though only three of them are

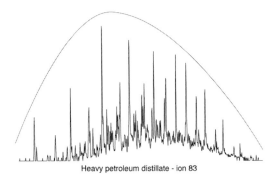

FIGURE 9-7
The bell-shaped pattern is also clearly distinguishable with cycloalkanes by extracting ion 83.

Heavy petroleum distillate - ion 83

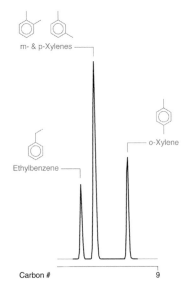

m- & p-Xylenes

Ethylbenzene

o-Xylene

Carbon #   9

FIGURE 9-8
The three musketeers (in bold), a specific pattern constituted of aromatic compounds eluting between C_8 and C_9.

visible, a fourth one is present as in the famous story where D'Artagnan joined Athos, Porthos, and Aramis in their fight. Figure 9-8 shows this group of peaks, where ethylbenzene elutes first, followed by *m*- and *p*-xylenes (coeluting) and, finally, *o*-xylene. The three musketeers elute between C_8 and C_9.

C/ The Castle Group

This grouping of C_3-alkylbenzenes is a very important diagnostic grouping for petroleum products for which the aromatics have not been removed. Eluting between C_9 and C_{10}, as shown in Figure 9-9, the castle group is very evident on the TICs of gasoline and aromatic solvents. This grouping starts with n-propylbenzene followed by 3-ethyltoluene partially coeluting with 4-ethyltoluene, followed by 1,3,5-trimethylbenzene and 2-ethyltoluene. It is referred to as the castle group for its similar profile to the castle found at Disney World (Orlando, Florida, USA). Older nomenclature also refers to this group of peaks as the pseudocumenes. Extraction of the specific aromatic ions results in visualization of this grouping in traditional petroleum distillates as well.

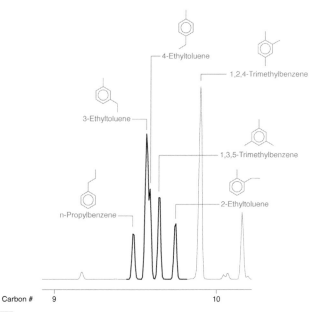

FIGURE 9-9 *The castle group (in bold), a specific pattern composed of aromatic compounds eluting between C_9 and C_{10}. Although 1,2,4-trimethylbenzene is not part of the group per se, it is always present at the immediate right vicinity of the castle group.*

D/ The Gang of Four

The gang of four refers to a distinctive double doublet of C_4-alkylbenzenes as shown in Figure 9-10. This group of peaks elutes in the C_{10} to C_{11} range. It is composed of C_4-alkylbenzenes, which have not been clearly identified due to the fact that there are a great number of isomers. The range shown in Figure 9-10 includes all C_4-alkylbenzenes. At the end of that range, there are two very important components, which are 1,2,4,5-tetramethylbenzene and 1,2,3,5-tetramethylbenzene. Like the castle group, it is a key diagnostic feature of gasoline and can typically be visualized on the TIC of both gasoline and aromatic solvents in the appropriate boiling range. Ion extraction allows for visualization in traditional petroleum distillates as well. With other chromatographic systems, the gang of four may not present any coelution.

E/ The Twin Towers

This grouping consists of 2-methylnaphthalene and 1-methylnaphthalene, which elute around C_{13}. If a petroleum product contains aromatic compounds (i.e., gasoline, aromatic solvents, traditional petroleum distillates) and the chromatographic data includes the C_{11} to C_{12} range, this peak grouping must be present. Visualization on the TIC is dependent on their relative concentration; however, this pair can be readily seen using extracted ion techniques as shown in Figure 9-11. Some gasolines may contain extremely low amounts of methylnaphthalenes.

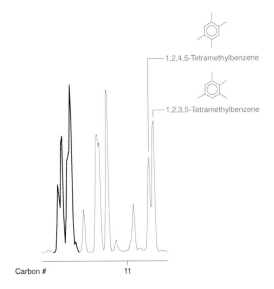

Carbon #   11

FIGURE 9-10

The gang of four (in bold), a specific pattern constituted of C_4-alkylbenzenes eluting between C_{10} and C_{11}. Also, note the presence of two important compounds at the end of the C_4-alkylbenzene range: 1,2,4,5- and 1,2,3,5-tetramethylbenzene.

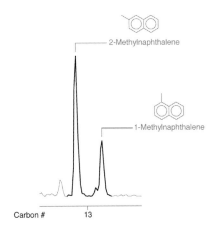

Carbon #   13

FIGURE 9-11   *The twin towers (in bold), a specific pattern constituted of C_1-naphthalenes eluting around C_{13}. This pattern gets its name in reference to the twin towers in New York City as one was a bit shorter than the other one. Note that in ignitable liquids, 2-methylnaphthalene is almost always more abundant than 1-methylnaphthalene.*

F/ The Five Fingers

This grouping of dimethyl- and ethyl-naphthalenes is located around C_{14}. Although it actually is composed of more than five peaks—some are coeluting—the grouping appears like the tip of five fingers sticking out of the baseline. Due to the great number of isomers, besides a couple of peaks, the exact isomers constituting the pattern have not been clearly identified. An example is shown in Figure 9-12. This grouping is specific of petroleum products containing aromatics in the heavy range.

FIGURE 9-12

The five fingers, a specific pattern constituted of C_2-naphthalenes eluting around C_{14}.

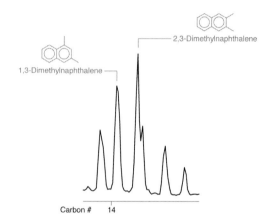

1,3-Dimethylnaphthalene

2,3-Dimethylnaphthalene

Carbon #   14

G/ Pristane and Phytane

Pristane (2,6,10,14-tetramethylpentadecane, $C_{19}H_{40}$) is a C_{19} isoalkane with a boiling point near that of n-heptadecane ($C_{17}H_{36}$). Phytane (2,6,10,14-tetramethylhexadecane, $C_{20}H_{42}$) is a C_{20} isoalkane with a boiling point near that of n-octadecane ($C_{18}H_{38}$). Both occur naturally in crude oil—they are biomarkers—and are considered essential in classifying and identifying petroleum distillates. They are chromatographically displayed as doublets (heptadecane-pristane and octadecane-phytane) with the n-alkane being much more abundant as shown in Figure 9-13. In some rare instances, the

FIGURE 9-13

The two doubles (in bold) C_{17}-pristane and C_{18}-phytane are a specific pattern of petroleum distillates within that boiling range.

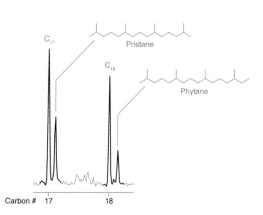

C_{17}

Pristane

C_{18}

Phytane

Carbon #   17   18

relative abundance may be reversed with the pristane and phytane being more abundant.

H/ Hash and Trash

This is a messy pattern that, as its name implies, includes numerous peaks with a notably unresolved baseline. An example is shown in Figure 9-14. Typically limited to medium and heavy range naphthenic paraffinic products and distillates, the envelope consists of the abundant (and thus unresolved) isomers of the various isoalkanes (mixed among the cycloalkanes) found in these products.

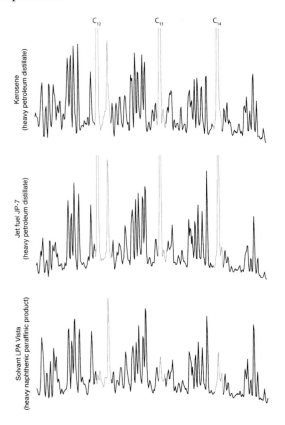

FIGURE 9-14

Typical hash and trash (in bold) found in between alkanes in petroleum distillates in the medium and heavy ranges. Because naphthenic paraffinic products are basically petroleum distillates without this n-alkane content, everything else is almost identical. As a result, one can observe the blatant resemblance in the hash and trash between the two upper chromatograms and the bottom one.

I/Aromatic Petroleum Profile

Although not nearly as abundant in crude oil as the alkanes, aromatic compounds provide for the most easily recognizable diagnostic patterns used in data interpretation of petroleum-based liquids. This is due, in part, to the fact that the aromatic pattern is so similar to the TIC of gasoline. Although the three musketeers, the castle group, the gang of four, the twin towers, and the five fingers described earlier are key features, the aromatic pattern in its totality constitutes an important diagnostic feature.[3] If a petroleum product containing aromatic compounds encompasses the range of C_8 to C_{15}, it must include all the aromatic compounds shown in Figures 9-15 and 9-16 in their relative ratios. The relative abundance coupled with boiling

[3]While the aromatic patterns presented here are common to most gasolines, they may not be exactly the same for all gasolines. One must keep in mind that there are some gasolines that present a dominant aliphatic pattern, thus possibly skewing the resulting aromatic pattern [14].

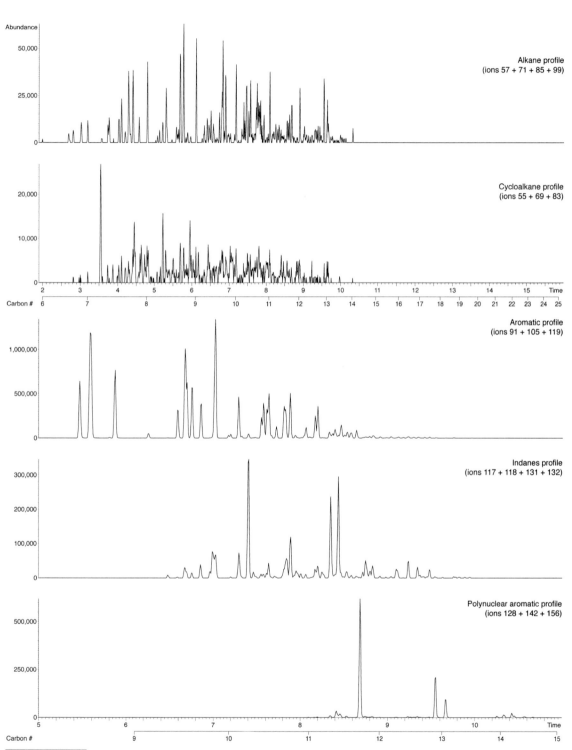

FIGURE 9-15 EIPs of a 75% weathered gasoline, showing the different specific aliphatic and aromatic patterns and their overall relationships. This figure is available for download on the publisher's web site (see note at beginning of book).

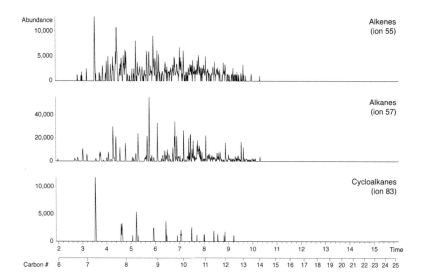

FIGURE 9-16a

EICs of a 75% weathered gasoline, showing the different specific aliphatic patterns and their overall relationships. This figure is available for download on the publisher's web site (see note at beginning of book).

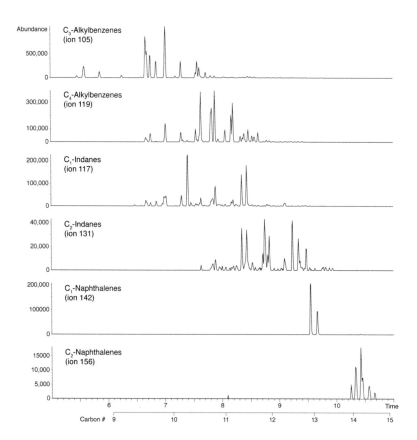

FIGURE 9-16b

EICs of a 75% weathered gasoline, showing the different specific aromatic patterns and their overall relationships. This figure is available for download on the publisher's web site (see note at beginning of book).

range of the various aromatic groups can provide important information as to the IL class. Figure 9-17 details the key aromatic compound grouping encompassing the entire IL range. Note that if one class of aromatic compounds exists in a given boiling range (i.e., simple aromatics) all other (indanes, polynuclear aromatics) eluting in that range must also be present.

Recapitulation of the major aromatic patterns found in crude oil ranging from C_7 to C_{15}. Adapted from "Aromatic compounds in petroleum products," copyright Pinellas County Forensic Laboratory, Florida, USA. Used with permission.

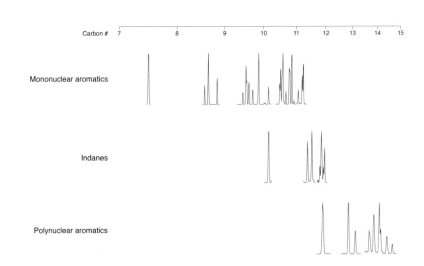

9.4.3 Weathering/Evaporation

Ignitable liquid residues often exhibit a slightly different pattern than that of the raw liquid. Because petroleum-based ignitable liquids consist of compounds encompassing a range of boiling points, they to not evaporate uniformly. The lower boiling compounds logically evaporate at a faster rate than higher boiling compounds. This nonuniform evaporation process, often called weathering, results in the skewing of the chromatogram toward the higher boiling compounds. In Figure 9-18, the same gasoline is reduced by a percentage of the initial volume. As the lighter compounds evaporate away, the right side of the pattern becomes more pronounced. Figure 9-19 shows the same principle with a heavy petroleum distillate (diesel fuel in this particular example).

For some IL classes, notably distillates, this reduction does not typically effect data interpretation; for other classes, however, the difference between fresh and highly reduced liquids is significant. Fire debris analysts should maintain both fresh and reduced exemplars of each ignitable liquid class in each boiling range.

A Word on Weathering

When referring to weathering, fire debris analysts use a system of percentage, which is indicative of the portion removed (evaporated) from the original mixture. As a consequence, a 25% weathered gasoline means that out of 100 ml, 25 ml were evaporated and 75 ml remained. A 90% weathered diesel fuel means that out of 100 ml, 90 ml were evaporated, leaving only 10 ml. When mentioning a liquid that has not been weathered, the term neat liquid is used throughout this text.

One must also understand that while the main pattern of an ignitable liquid is skewed by weathering, most specific patterns seen under Subsection 9.4.2 remains relatively intact. This is due to the fact that these patterns span over a very short time range, and thus all the components constituting them evaporate at a very similar rate. This is the reason why diagnostic patterns include narrow specific patterns rather than wide overall patterns.

9.4.4 Petroleum Product Purity

Petroleum products are refined to meet the specifications of the customer. Manufacture of the final product includes only the amount of cleanup or purification required to meet those specifications. For example, in Table 9-3, when describing the chemical composition of an isoparaffinic product as having no aromatic compounds, the reality is that the aromatic compounds have been removed for the most part; however complete removal may not be required and is definitely not cost effective. Therefore, aromatics may be present at very low levels. In describing the absence of any particular class of compounds, the term "absence" is loosely defined and residual levels (in comparison to a similar range distillate) may be present, but considered negligible.

9.4.5 Interpretation Scheme

Data interpretation, and the resultant IL classification, is a systematic process. All the information presented so far in this chapter provides for the basis of that scheme. The following questions describe the mental process used to evaluate the resultant GC or GC-MS data.

Does the GC pattern on the TIC contain groupings of closely adjacent peaks?
Groupings of peaks in a distinctive n-alkane range are indicative of a possible petroleum product as opposed to a nonpetroleum-based product. Single, few, or extremely well-resolved mixtures of peaks are more indicative of a nonpetroleum product.

What is the boiling range of the pattern?
The boiling range provides important information for determining which diagnostic peak patterns should be evaluated. For example, light petroleum products (LPD) do not contain polynuclear aromatics (PNA) as those elute

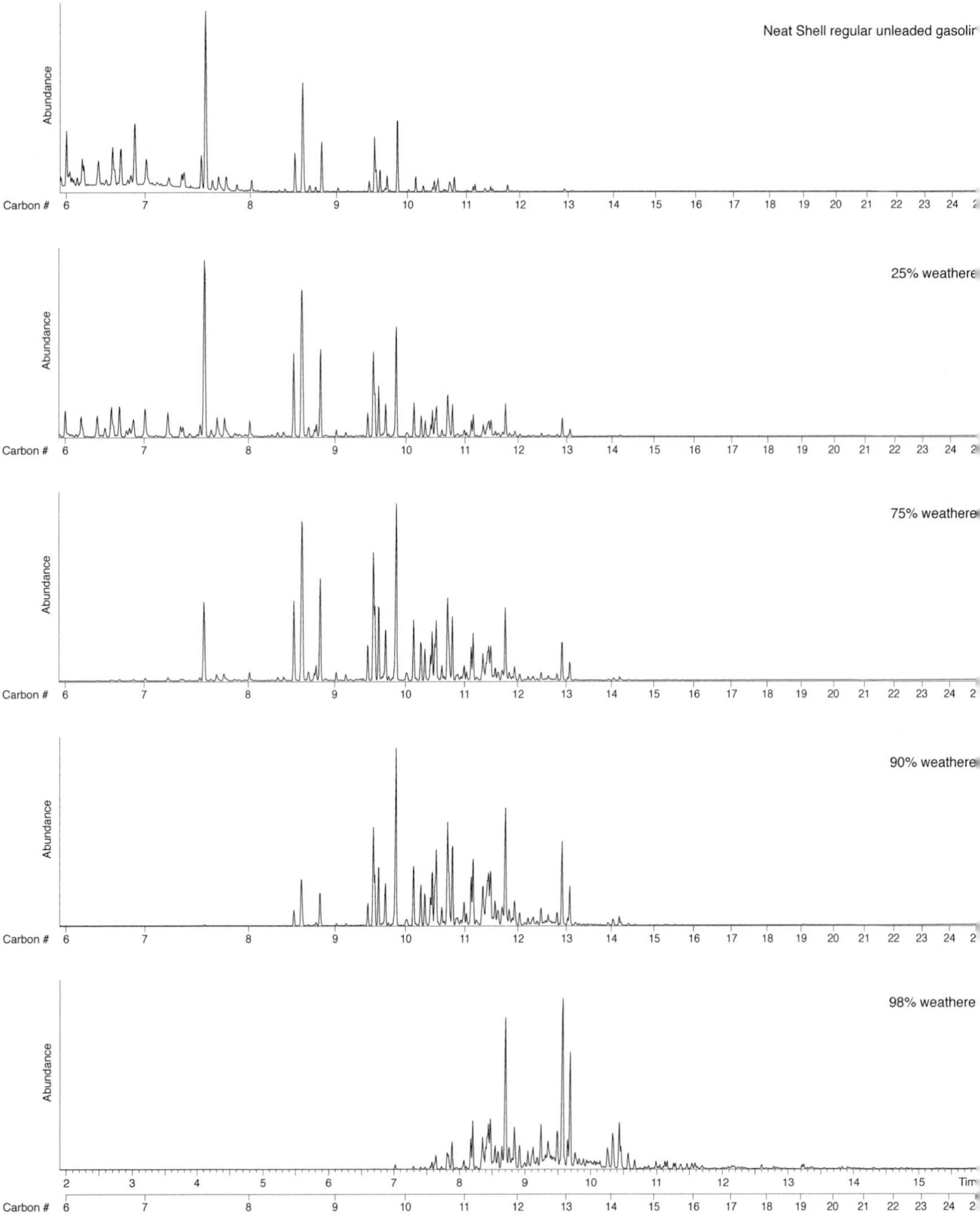

FIGURE 9-18 *Example of the nonuniform evaporation of the components of gasoline. Fresh gasoline (top chromatogram) exhibits a pattern mostly located on the left (light and low boiling point compounds). As the weathering increases, the pattern moves to the right (heavier compounds, higher boiling points), as the relative concentration of light compounds diminishes in the mixture.*

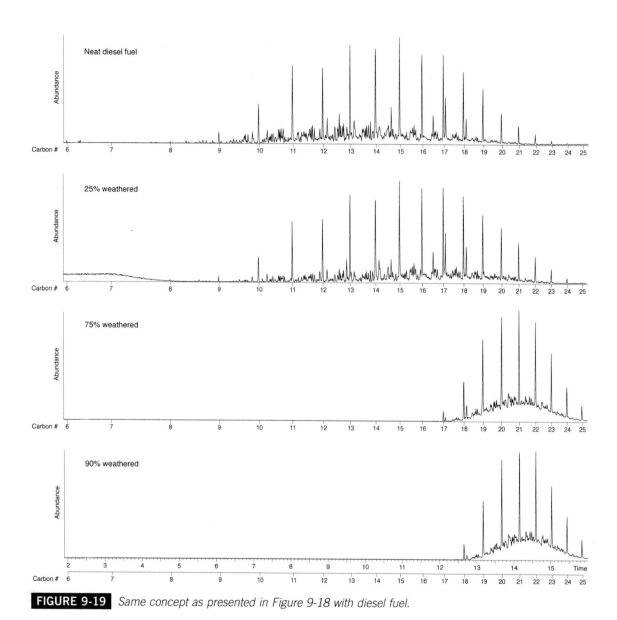

FIGURE 9-19 *Same concept as presented in Figure 9-18 with diesel fuel.*

in the range starting at C_{12}, whereas light products elute in the range of C_4 to C_9. The castle group and gang of four elute in the medium range, thus the presence or absence of those diagnostic groups in a mid-range product would be very significant.

Which mass chromatograms have peaks and which ones do not?
The single most distinctive feature of the petroleum class is the types of chemical compounds present. For example, the absence of aromatic compounds automatically excludes gasoline, traditional petroleum distillates,

and aromatic products. Conversely, the absence of aliphatic compound would exclude isoparaffinic products, naphthenic paraffinic products normal-alkane products, and petroleum distillates.

What is the relative abundance of the various ion classes?
By using mass chromatography, the criminalist may evaluate the relative abundance of aliphatic and aromatic compounds and determine their relative ratios. The relative abundance of aromatics to aliphatic compounds ca be used to determine IL class and can help in determining the presence product mixtures.

What diagnostic peak patterns are evident on the TIC and the mas chromatograms?
The diagnostic peak patterns described in Subsection 9.4.2 are extremel helpful in identification and classification.

What other IL class specific diagnostic features are present?
There are diagnostic features related to each IL class that must be consid ered; they will be presented in the following sections.

9.5 GASOLINE

Gasoline is a blended product manufactured to meet the needs of the auto motive industry while adhering to the requirements of government environ mental regulations. Gasoline is most often predominantely comprised aromatic compounds in the range of C_4 to C_{12} (see Figure 9-20a). Exception may be encountered, such as with some premium gasolines in Canada [14 All gasolines contain alkanes; however, the alkanes are normally not abur dant in fresh gasoline and the resultant mass chromatograms are much les abundant than that of their aromatic counterpart. Aliphatic compounds gasoline vary by lot, location, and manufacturing process. In addition, it more diagnostic in presence or absence rather than in specific pea patterns.

The total ion chromatogram of fresh gasoline is rich in lower boilir aromatic compounds (C_1-, C_2-, and C_3-alkylbenzenes) as shown in Figu 9-20a. The three musketeers and the castle group are easily identified both the TIC and the aromatic EIC. The C_4-alkylbenzenes are present an the gang of four easily recognized. Polynuclear aromatics are present in mo gasolines, however the visualization of 2- and 1-methylnapthalene in fres gasoline is variable due to final concentrations. The extracted ion profil in Figure 9-20b allow for a better observation of the different classes. Indar and methyl indanes are present.

As gasoline evaporates, the lower boiling and more abundant aromat compounds are disproportionately lost. The chromatographic pattern shif to higher boiling compounds (see Figure 9-21). In the C_9 to C_{12} range, the alkanes (notably normal and isoalkanes) are better represented (see EIP in Figure 9-15 and compare the aliphatic:aromatic ratio with Figure 9-20b). The aromatics are still abundant and the C_4-alkylbenzenes (including the gang of four) are still key diagnostic features. The C_3-alkybenzenes are still present in most gasoline exemplars up to 95% evaporated, however the C_2-alkylbenzenes disappear quite rapidly. The PNAs become predominant and the twin towers (methylnaphthalenes) and five fingers (dimethyl- and ethyl-naphthalenes) groups are more easily seen.

The aromatic profile is the most important and most readily diagnostic, however, aliphatic compounds also must normally be present in order to identify gasoline. A lack of aliphatic compounds would indicate an aromatic solvent rather than gasoline. However, in general, aromatic solvents are represented by a much narrower cut (extending on one or two carbon numbers) than the wide range exhibited by gasoline (see Section 9.10 for chromatograms of aromatic solvents). There is a wide variation in aliphatic peak patterns in gasoline as demonstrated with the example in Figures 9-22a and 9-22b.

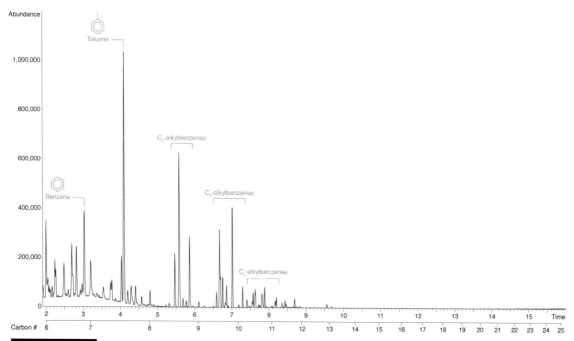

FIGURE 9-20a *TIC of a neat gasoline (unweathered). Gasoline is mostly constituted of aromatics, as seen by the patterns, however there exists some exceptions as discussed earlier.*

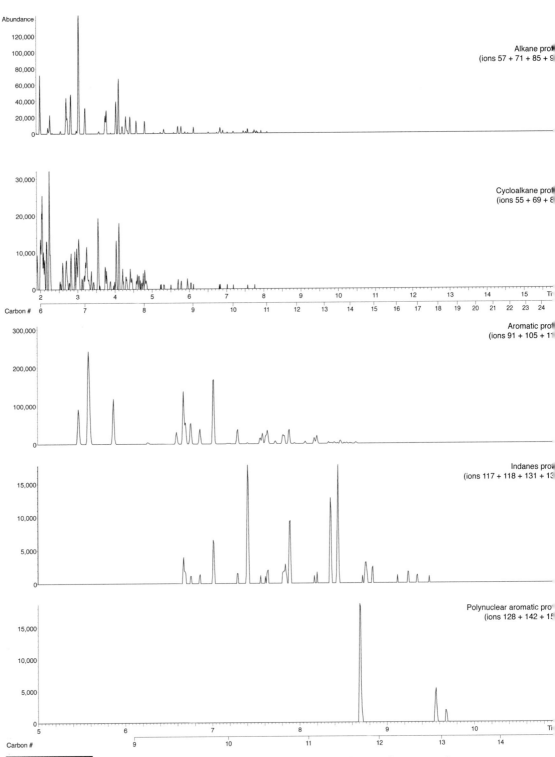

FIGURE 9-20b *EIPs of a neat gasoline, which show the different classes of compounds.*

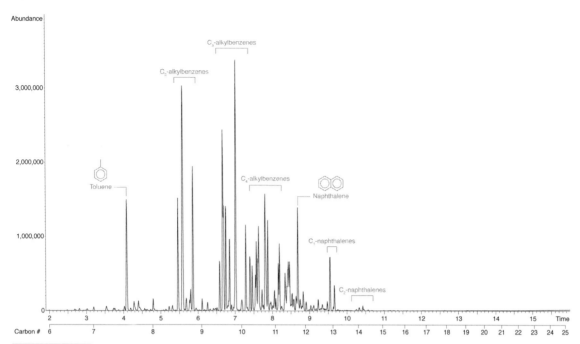

FIGURE 9-21 *TIC of a 75% gasoline. The pattern moves to the right and the naphthalenes are now visible in the TIC.*

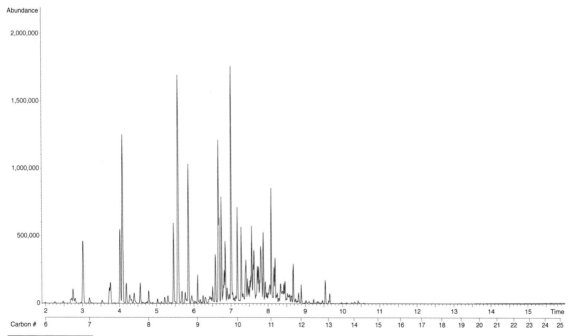

FIGURE 9-22a *TIC of a gasoline with a high proportion of aliphatic compounds. Although the aromatic pattern is still dominant, it is possible to distinguish additional spiking n-alkanes when compared to Figure 9-20a.*

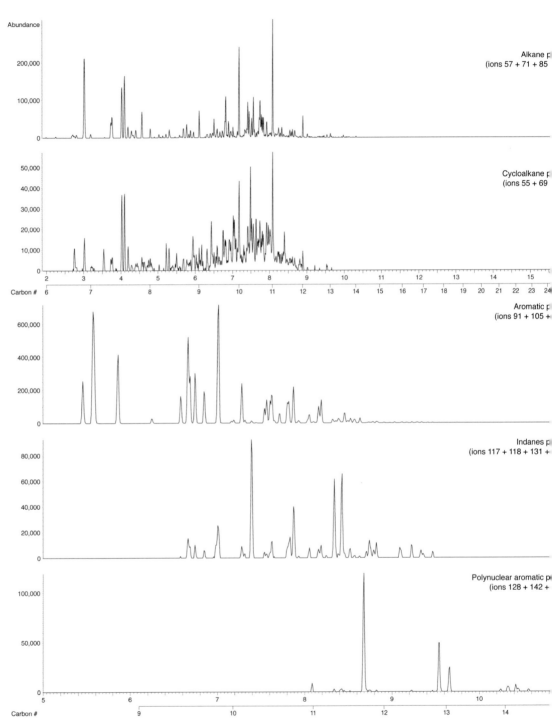

FIGURE 9-22b *EIPs show the high presence of n-alkanes. Compare the aliphatic content to the one show* *Figure 9-20b.*

A Gaussian distribution of spiking n-alkanes with interspersed isoalkanes is not uncommon. An initial evaluation of such data might lead to the erroneous conclusion that a product is a mixture of gasoline and a petroleum distillate; however, remembering that gasoline is a refined distillate, such a composition should not be unexpected. The ratio of the relative abundance of aromatics to aliphatics is very important. Unfortunately, due to the inherent variety in crude oils, refinery processes, product mixing, and extracted ion analysis procedures there is no exact ratio that can be used to differentiate gasoline from a distillate or a mixture of the two. Forensic scientists should analyze a vast array of gasoline exemplars using the same chromatographic parameters and data analysis techniques (extracted ions) to determine normal distribution ranges of aromatic to aliphatic abundance ratios.

9.6 PETROLEUM DISTILLATES

Petroleum distillates are the least processed of the various petroleum products. Of all the petroleum-based IL classes, traditional petroleum distillates best represent the content of raw crude in a given boiling point range. Thus, all classes of compounds (aliphatic and aromatic) should be present in the resultant data. In the latest ASTM standard E 1618, the two classes of "traditional" petroleum distillates and dearomatized distillates were combined to form a single petroleum distillate class [1]. As the name implies, the only difference between a "traditional" distillate and a dearomatized distillate is the aromatic content. Dearomatized distillates have a distinctive lack of aromatic compounds, and that distinction can typically be readily made with neat ignitable liquids [5]. However, in ignitable liquid residues extracted from debris, often the distinction cannot be made, thus the merging of the classes [4, 6].

Traditional petroleum distillates have the characteristic Gaussian distribution of spiking normal alkanes interspersed with less abundant isoalkanes, cylcoalkanes, and aromatic compounds. Figure 9-23 shows the three boiling point ranges of petroleum distillates.

The TIC of a heavy petroleum distillate (HPD), in this case diesel fuel, was shown in Figure 9-4. Its associated EIPs and EICs were shown in Figures 9-4 and 9-5. The cycloalkanes are less abundant than the normal alkanes but are present nonetheless, also in a normal distribution pattern. The presence of the diagnostic doublets of n-heptadecane/pristane and n-octadecane/phytane is clearly evident. Note the bell-shaped curve and predominant alkane pattern in both the TIC and MC. The normal distribution is readily evident in medium and heavy distillates (see Figures 9-24a and 9-24b for the example of an MPD). But, because there are fewer compounds due to the limited number of isoalkanes and cycloalkanes in light petroleum distillates (LPD), the n-alkane pattern is more subtle. Isoalkane and cycloalkane

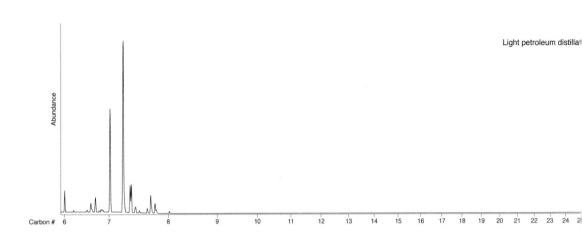

Light petroleum distilla

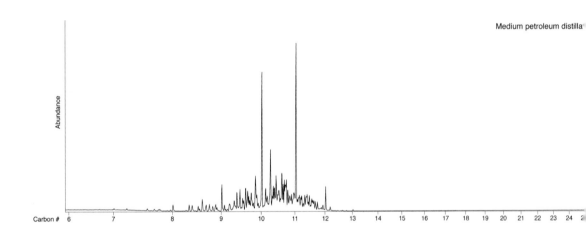

Medium petroleum distilla

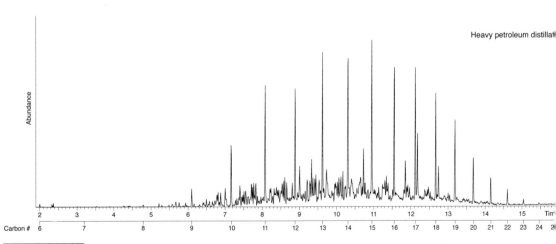

Heavy petroleum distilla

FIGURE 9-23 The three boiling point ranges of petroleum distillates. Note that as the boiling point range increases, so does the spreading of the peaks.

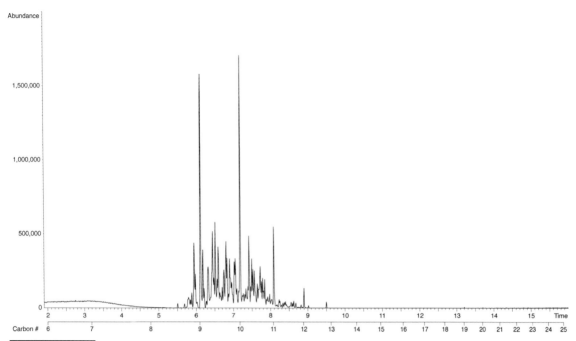

TIC of a medium petroleum distillate.

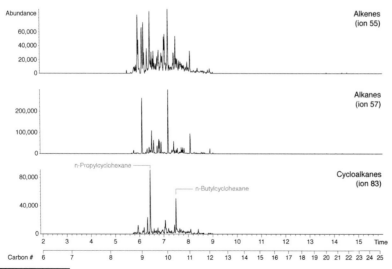

EICs of the MPD shown in Figure 9-24a.

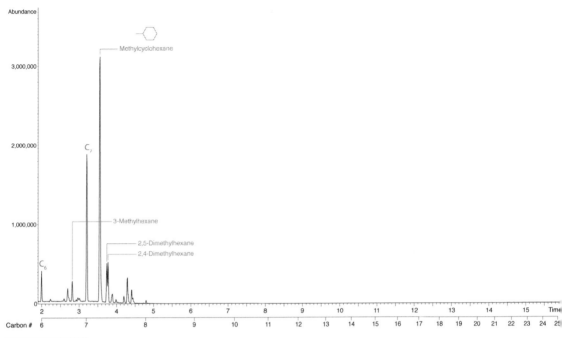

FIGURE 9-25 *TIC of a light petroleum distillate (LPD).*

peaks are more abundant in LPD than their heavier counterparts as shown in Figure 9-25. The most abundant n-alkane in an LPD is typically n-hexane or n-heptane. Chromatograms that start at hexane do not allow for complete visualization of the pattern. This does not preclude identification or classification, but the difference must be understood and acknowledged when interpreting data. An LPD may exhibit the right half of a bell-shaped curve only.

The aromatic profile of an MPD or HPD clearly resembles that of gasoline, again because this is the aromatic content of crude oil in this boiling range (see Figures 9-4 and 9-5). In fact, one of the notable features of the aromatic compounds is the boiling point range, which will necessarily vary based upon the boiling range of the distillate. Naphthalene and C_1 naphthalenes are present in distillates that encompass the C_{10} to C_{12} range. The five fingers group of the C_2-naphthalenes is found in broad range HPD like diesel fuel.

Dearomatized distillates are similar except that they lack any significant amount of aromatic compounds as shown in Figure 9-26. Thus the simple aromatic, indane, and polynuclear aromatic patterns are notably absent or minimally present.

In LPD, aromatics are usually absent or represented by benzene or toluene. This is due to the boiling point range, which does not encompass any aromatics besides benzene or toluene.

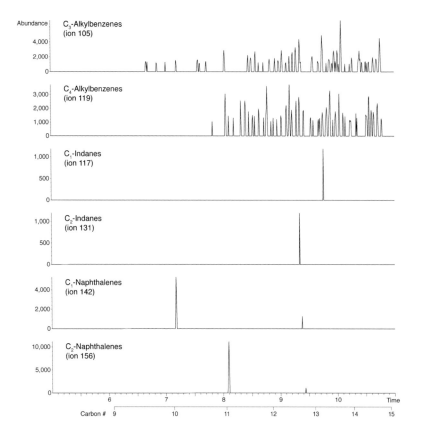

FIGURE 9-26

*EICs from a
dearomatized HPD.
Note that ions
corresponding to the
mononuclear
aromatics, indanes,
and naphthalenes are
no inexistent.*

9.7 ISOPARAFFINIC PRODUCTS

As the name implies, isoparaffinic products (also referred to as isopars
from the name of a brand of isoparaffinic solvents marketed by Exxon
Mobil) are comprised solely of isoalkanes. The petroleum industry takes
specific steps to separate the isoalkanes from the distillate fraction. The
number of isoalkane peaks is related directly to the boiling point range as
the number of alkane isomers obviously increases with the number of
carbons in the molecules (see Table 3-4). Light isoparaffinic products have
fairly clean total ion chromatograms (see Figure 9-27). Medium products
have more peaks, however, they may still display baseline resolution. Heavy
isoparaffinic products result in unresolved peaks with fairly indistinctive
TIC.

The most diagnostic feature of isoparaffinic products is found in the
comparison of the TIC, alkane, and cylcoalkane EIC as seen in Figure 9-28.
These three chromatograms are virtually indistinguishable from each other

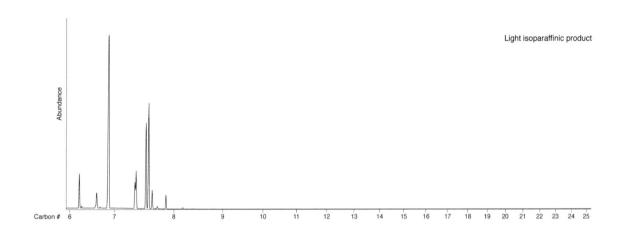

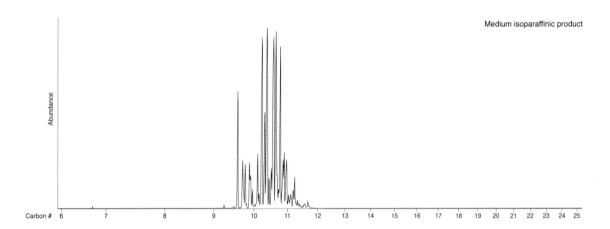

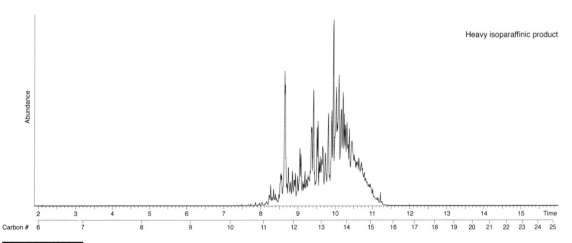

FIGURE 9-27 *The three boiling point ranges of isoparaffinic products. Note that as the boiling point range increases, so does the spreading of the peaks.*

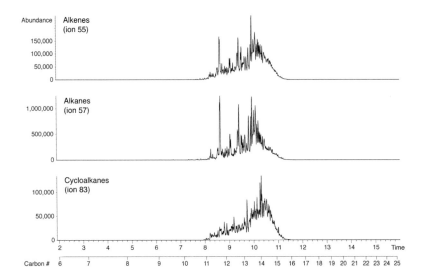

FIGURE 9-28

EICs for a heavy isoparaffinic product. Compare to the bottom TIC of Figure 9-27. Note how there is extremely little difference between the three EICs and particularly the total absence of spiking cycloalkanes in the 83 window.

in terms of pattern and range. The only notable difference is in relative abundance.

This may seem incongruous, as isoparaffinic products do not contain cycloalkanes, however it is logical when considering the mass spectrum of an isoalkane. Although the alkane-indicative ions 57, 71, and 85 are abundant, the fragmentation of alkanes also includes ions 55, 69, and 83 in proportionate ratio to the alkane-indicative ions. Thus, the peaks present in the cycloalkane EIC are similar to the ones in the alkane profile. This is usually typical of isoparaffinic products.

A mass spectral library search of the associated peaks results in a variety of substituted alkanes. Actual identification of each peak is neither practical nor possible, however the loose class identification is an important clue as to the molecular structure of the compounds present.

9.8 NAPHTHENIC PARAFFINIC PRODUCTS

Naphthenic paraffinic products are composed primarily of isoalkanes (isoparaffins) and cycloalkanes (naphthenes). One must envision a petroleum distillate from which the n-alkanes and aromatic fractions have been removed during the refining process. Actually, the n-alkanes are more commonly reduced but often not completely removed, as it is not uncommon to find low abundance of n-alkanes in naphthenic paraffinic products.

The TIC associated with naphthenic paraffinic products can be mentally visualized by taking a dearomatized distillate and chopping off the spiking n-alkanes as shown in Figure 9-29. The resultant chromatogram is an

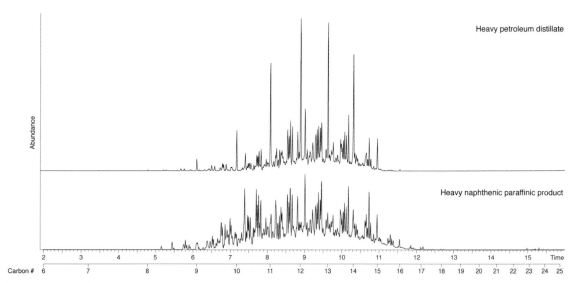

Abundance

Heavy petroleum distillate

Heavy naphthenic paraffinic product

| Time | 2 | 3 | 4 | 5 | 6 | 7 | 8 | 9 | 10 | 11 | 12 | 13 | 14 | 15 |

Carbon # 6   7   8   9   10   11   12   13   14   15   16   17   18   19   20   21   22   23   24   25

FIGURE 9-29 *The difference between a petroleum distillate and a naphthenic paraffinic product consists of the removal of the aromatic content and the n-alkanes. This is well illustrated when looking at the hash and trash of an HPD and a heavy naphthenic paraffinic product.*

unresolved envelope of the numerous isomers of isoalkanes and cycloalkanes in the given boiling point range.

Figure 9-30 shows the three boiling point range of naphthenic paraffinic products. The extracted ion chromatograms are notable in the absence of aromatic compounds (including indanes and naphthalenes). The alkane EIC resembles that of a related isoparaffinic product with distinctive isomer groupings. The resultant alkene profile is very complex and notably unresolved. However, note that the pattern of the cycloalkane EIC is different to that of the alkane EIC. In the naphthenic paraffinic product, one can clearly see the spiking cycloalkanes. This is shown in Figures 9-31a and 9-31b.

A library search of peaks found in a naphthenic paraffinic product will result in numerous substituted alkanes and cycloalkanes. The similarity between the mass spectral data for cylcoalkanes and alkenes may also result in matches to alkene compounds; however, there are no alkenes in petroleum-based ignitable liquids.

9.9 NORMAL-ALKANE PRODUCTS

Normal-alkane products (also referred to as norpars from the name of a brand of normal-alkane solvents marketed by Exxon Mobil) result in the simplest of chromatographic data of all petroleum products. N-alkanes are ultra-pure petroleum products that generally consist of three to five n-alkanes either in series or where every other one is missing (see Figure 9-32). Pattern

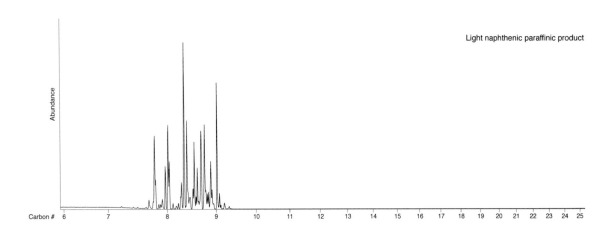

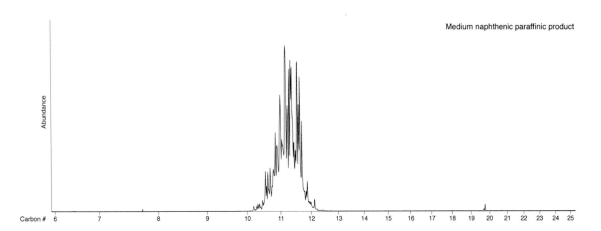

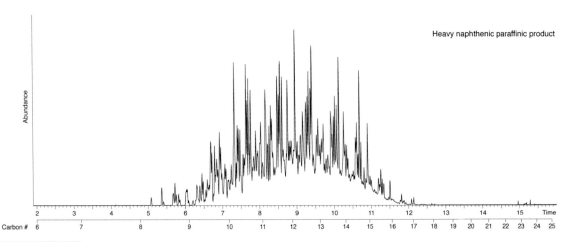

FIGURE 9-30 *The three boiling point ranges of naphthenic paraffinic products. Note that as the boiling point range increases, so does the spreading of the peaks.*

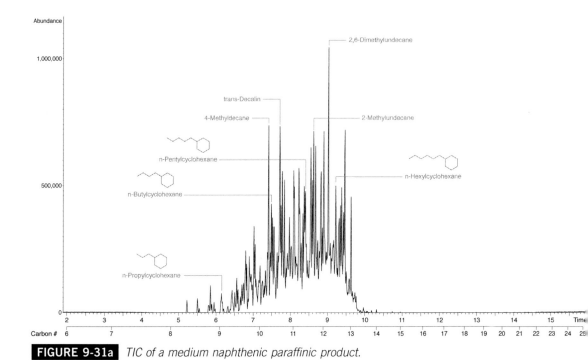

FIGURE 9-31a   *TIC of a medium naphthenic paraffinic product.*

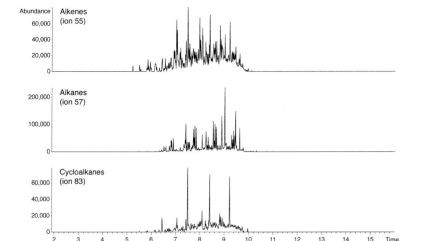

FIGURE 9-31b   *EICs of the medium naphthenic paraffinic product. When compared to Figure 9-28, the difference is quite obvious. The spiking cycloalkanes are clearly visible in the 83 window.*

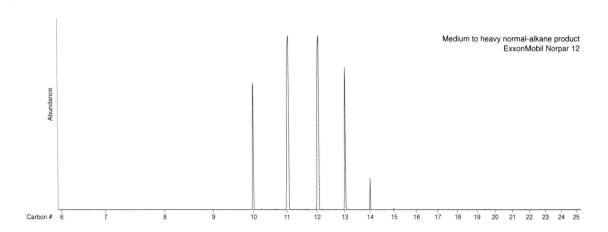

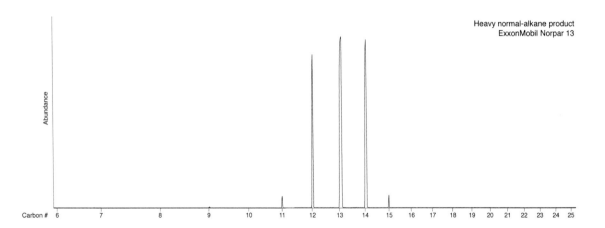

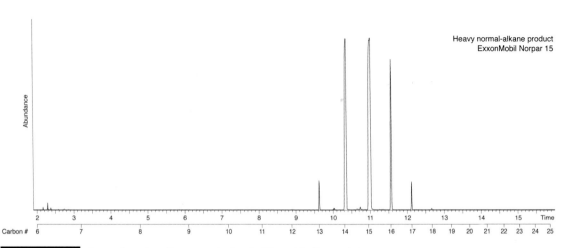

FIGURE 9-32 *Examples of n-alkane products of different boiling point ranges.*

When extracting ions 55, 57, and 83 from a n-alkane product, three identical (abundances aside) EICs are obtained.

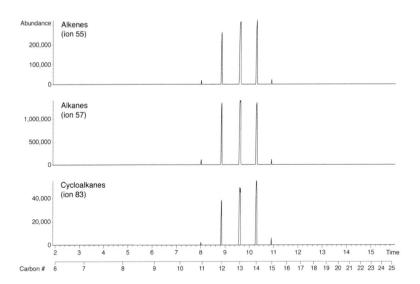

recognition techniques are not reliable for identification of products with so few components, so identification of n-alkane products is necessarily based upon GC retention time and mass spectral identification. That said, the extracted ion chromatograms indicative of alkanes and cycloalkanes are identical in pattern and are identical to that of the TIC as shown in Figure 9-33.

9.10 AROMATIC PRODUCTS

Aromatic products are manufactured through the isolation of the aromatic fraction of crude oil. Unlike the other hydrocarbon classes, the chromatographic data of aromatics is very different from one boiling point range to another. Figure 9-34 shows three examples of aromatic products of three different boiling point ranges.

Usually, aromatic solvents consist of narrow fractions—such as isolated C_8 to C_9 or C_{10} to C_{12}—as shown in the two top chromatograms in Figure 9-34. However, some solvents may exhibit a larger fraction such as the one shown in Figure 9-35. In these cases, this very closely mimics gasoline.

The alkane and cycloalkane EICs of aromatic solvents are notably lacking in data. The abundance of simple aromatics, indanes, and polynuclear aromatics is solely a function of the boiling point range of the aromatic solvent. In general, TICs include distinct boiling point range with fairly well-resolved peaks.

A light aromatic solvent could be comprised of only toluene or include the C_2-alkylbenzenes. Medium products may include the C_2-, C_3-, and/or

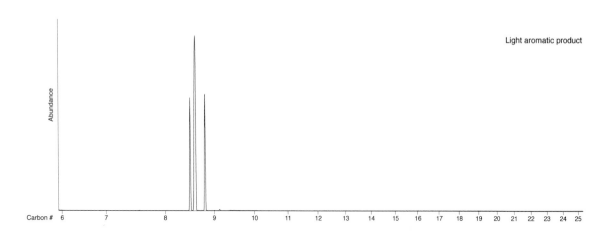

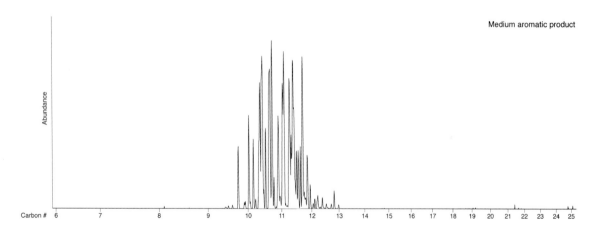

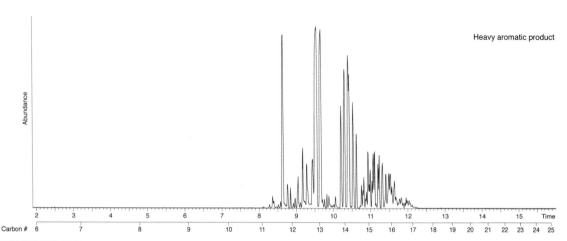

FIGURE 9-34 *The three boiling point ranges of aromatic products. Note that as the boiling point range increases, so does the spreading of the peaks.*

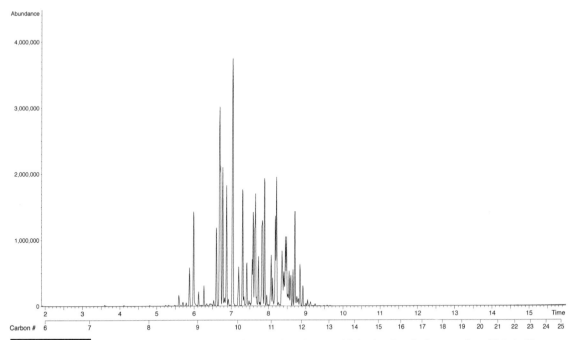

FIGURE 9-35 *Example of a large fraction of aromatic solvent, which closely mimics gasoline. This is Kleen Strip driveway cleaner. The mononuclear aromatic, indane, and naphthalene EIPs or EICs of this solvent matche perfectly those of a weathered gasoline.*

C_4-alkylbenzene groups (including the three musketeers, the castle group, and the gang of four) and the C_1- and C_2-indanes. Heavy aromatic solvents are abundant in polynuclear aromatics. Up to C_{11}, the TIC and mononuclear aromatic EIP are virtually indistinguishable. Above C_{11}, the TIC pattern resembles more closely that of the polynuclear aromatic EIP.

The presence of significant alkanes in either the peak pattern or the mass spectral library search would indicate the presence of gasoline rather than an aromatic solvent. Also, in general gasoline extends over a wide boiling point range (from about C_4 to C_{12}) whereas an aromatic solvent would have a much narrower range.

9.11 NONPETROLEUM-BASED IGNITABLE LIQUIDS

9.11.1 Preamble

Unfortunately, there are no simple rules or pattern recognition techniques that can be associated with the nonpetroleum-based ignitable liquids. Recognition and identification is based primarily on the mass spectrum of key chromatographic peaks and comparison to known reference liquids. The two most common types of nonpetroleum-based ignitable liquids are oxygenated solvents and terpene-based products.

9.11.2 Oxygenated Solvents

Oxygenated solvents are ignitable liquids containing significant oxygenated compounds. Examples of oxygenated solvents include low boiling alcohols (methanol, ethanol, and isopropanol) and ketones (acetone, methyl ethyl ketone). Some examples are shown in Figure 9-36. Due to their high volatility, detection may not be possible under the chromatographic conditions used to separate and identify petroleum-based ignitable liquids. Alternative GC methods must be available to detect compounds that elute before hexane such as program 2 shown in Table 8-4 (see the box "Detecting Light Products" in Section 9.3).

Like n-alkanes, oxygenated solvents typically are comprised of too few compounds to allow for any kind of pattern recognition. GC retention time coupled with mass spectral identification is the accepted method of identification and classification of oxygenated solvents.

It should be noted that oxygenated compounds are often blended with petroleum distillates. Lacquer thinner and many cleaning products use such combinations (see Figures 9-37a and 9-37b). Such mixtures are still classified in ASTM E 1618-06 as oxygenated solvents [1]. In such instances a combination of retention time/mass spectral identification and pattern recognition techniques may be employed.

9.11.3 Terpenes

Turpentine is an ignitable liquid extracted from soft woods that is still commonly used in some parts of the world. D-limonene is a terpene extracted from citrus that is used in hundreds of ignitable and nonignitable products. Figure 9-38 shows an example of a turpentine product. Due to the inherent variety in products, identification is limited to mass spectral identification. However, as will be discussed in Chapter 12, identification of terpenes as an ignitable liquid can be difficult due to the naturally occurring terpenes found in wood building products.

9.12 IGNITABLE LIQUID IDENTIFICATION SCHEME

The identification and classification of ignitable liquids in their raw state is a systematic process. A thorough understanding of the characteristics of crude oil and petroleum refining allows the forensic scientist to easily predict and classify products using total ion and mass chromatograms. The evaluation of the presence or absence of specific peak groupings among different chemical classes and boiling point ranges through GC-MS data provides the basis of classification and identification of most common ignitable liquids. The flow chart in Figure 9-39 provides an overview of the decision-making process associated with petroleum-based ignitable liquid identification. It is clear that

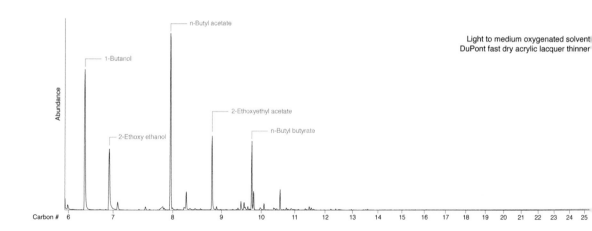

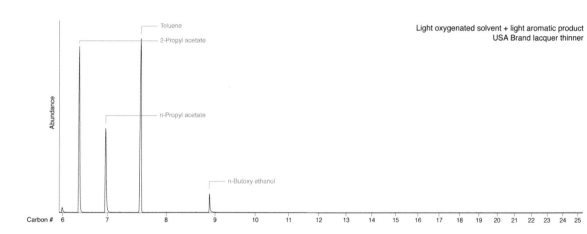

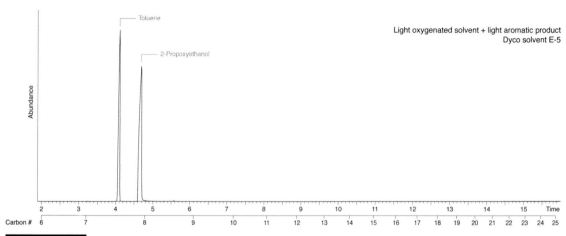

FIGURE 9-36 *Examples of oxygenated solvents.*

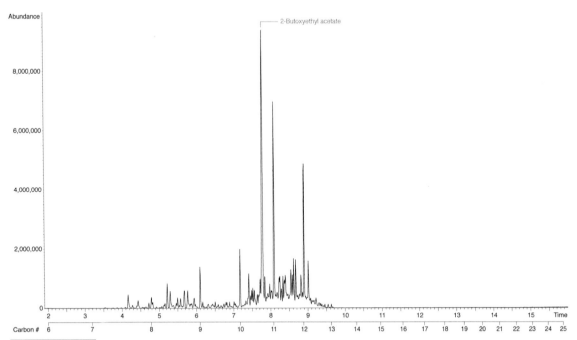

FIGURE 9-37a *TIC of a mixture of a medium petroleum distillate with an oxygenated compound.*

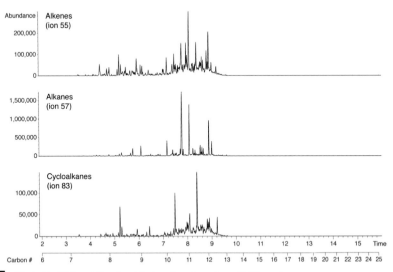

FIGURE 9-37b *Aliphatic EICs of the liquid showing the clear MPD pattern.*

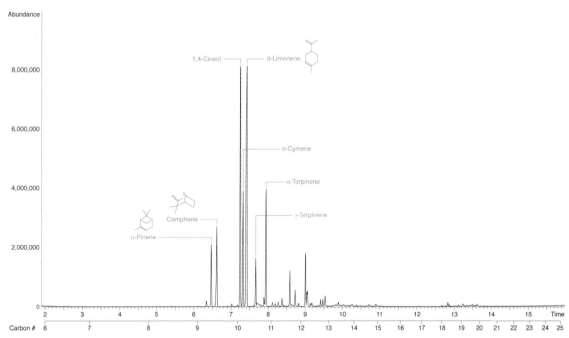

FIGURE 9-38 *Total ion chromatogram of a turpentine product. This pattern does not correspond to any pattern exhibited by petroleum-based liquids.*

the mere presence of the compounds described in the flowchart is not a sufficient criteria to determine the presence of an ignitable liquid: These compounds must exhibit patterns similar or identical to patterns exhibited by comparison (reference) liquids analyzed on the same chromatographic system. Although this process appears quite simple, the presence of interfering products makes it much more complex as we will see in Chapter 12.

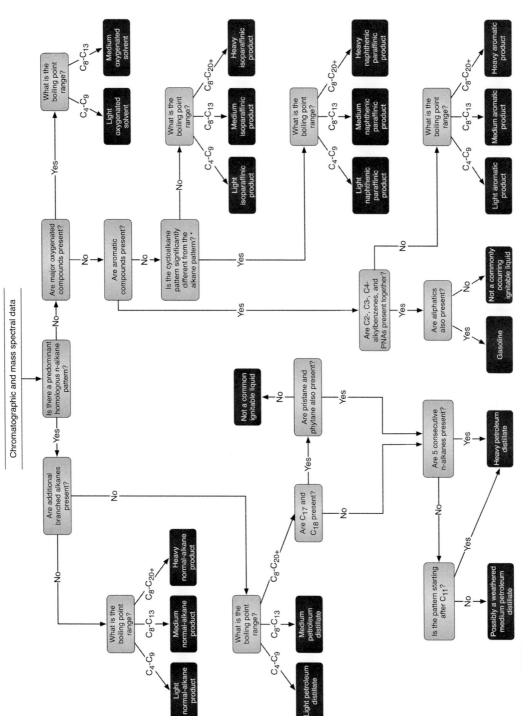

FIGURE 9-39 *Petroleum-based ignitable liquid classification flowchart. Every question related to the presence of specific compounds implies that these compounds must be present in the proper pattern (as compared to a pattern of these compounds from a reference liquid analyzed on the same system).* *Another formulation for this question would be: "Are cycloalkanes distinctively present in the EIPs or EICs?"*

The Ignitable Liquids Reference Collection

One of the permanent projects of SWGFEX is the development and maintenance of the Ignitable Liquids Reference Collection (ILRC). The ILRC is a collection of ignitable liquids that have been analyzed by GC-MS and classified following ASTM E 1618. The collection currently has over 400 formulations, and is continually increasing. General information and chromatographic data for each liquid is available free of charge on the Internet at http://ilrc.ucf.edu. The web site includes a very convenient interface where one can search for an ignitable liquid based on different criteria, as shown in Figure 9-40.

Each liquid is identified by brand name, unique serial number, hydrocarbon range, predominant ion profile, and major peaks present in the chromatogram. For each liquid, an individual file contains an illustration of the chromatogram with identification of the major peaks, the data set available in Agilent ChemStation or Microsoft Excel format, and the MSDS (see Figure 9-41).

Additionally, it is possible to order a sample of the liquid at a reasonable cost so that it can be run on the laboratory's own instrument. The ILRC is a fantastic tool that is very convenient to use and that can quickly help a fire debris analyst find the right comparison liquid.

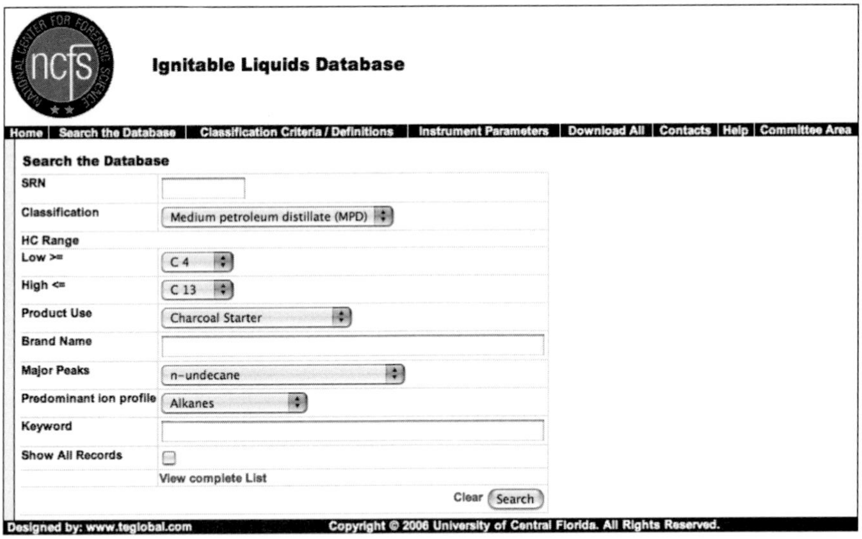

FIGURE 9-40

Search interface of the Ignitable Liquids Reference Collection. Available from http://ilrc.ucf. edu.

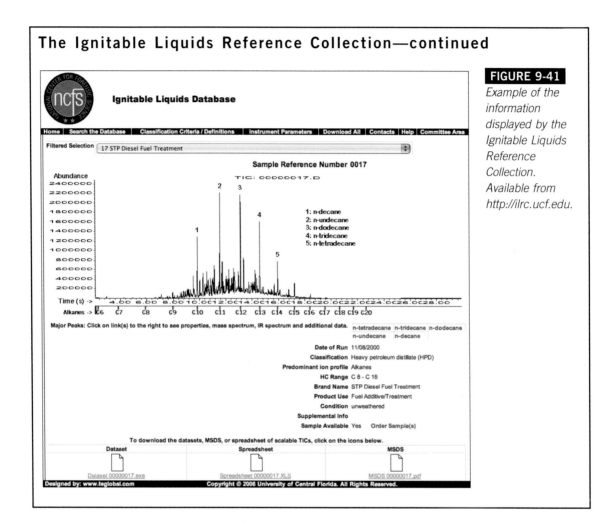

The Ignitable Liquids Reference Collection—continued

Example of the information displayed by the Ignitable Liquids Reference Collection. Available from http://ilrc.ucf.edu.

9.13 COMPARISON OF IGNITABLE LIQUIDS

Contribution from P. Mark L. Sandercock, Royal Canadian Mounted Police

9.13.1 History of Forensic Comparisons of Ignitable Liquids

There has been a long-standing interest in forensic science to compare two or more samples of neat ignitable liquid to determine if they originated from the same source. For example, linking an IL recovered from a container at a fire scene to the contents of a jerry can seized from a suspect's vehicle or residence would provide strong evidence that the suspect was the one who placed the IL at the fire scene. One of the earliest known references to the forensic comparison of petroleum products was published as a technical note in 1953 [15]. This short article described the use of a paper chromatography method to compare four samples of fuel oil. Following on this work, another scientist used a similar paper chromatography method to compare five gasoline samples [16]. For its time, the method worked well, requiring only one to two drops of each gasoline sample diluted in ether, with the separated petroleum fractions observed directly on the paper under ultraviolet light. Twenty years later, in the mid-1970s, forensic laboratories began to use gas chromatography to compare ignitable liquids. The first published example in the literature is the work of Cain who used capillary gas chromatography to compare samples of home heating kerosene for suspected adulteration [17].

Gasoline is probably the most common liquid used by an arsonist to accelerate a fire [18, 19]. Furthermore, another scientist reported that for fire debris cases that tested positive for gasoline, 20% also had a liquid sample available for comparison [20]. For this reason, much attention has been given to the comparison of samples of neat gasoline. In the 1980s, when leaded gasoline was a common automotive fuel, significant differences in lead content between samples of leaded gasoline could be used not only to identify a particular brand of gasoline but also to directly compare two samples [21–23]. However, Hennig observed that compounds eluting in the upper boiling range of the gas chromatograms also showed a significant variation between samples of gasoline [24]. Because leaded gasoline was phased out in many countries during the 1980s and 1990s, new "fingerprinting" techniques were developed to compare gasoline samples based on chromatography [20, 23, 25] and three-dimensional fluorescence spectroscopy, and were reported in the literature [26, 27]. However, these methods were not widely adopted because the visual comparison between different peaks or peak ratios in sample chromatograms described by Hirz [23] and Mann [20, 25] had an element of subjectivity, and fluorescence spectroscopy equipment is not commonly available in forensic science laboratories.

Comparing Samples of Gasoline v. Brand Identification

Forensic scientists often are asked why they do not simply identify the brand of gasoline (e.g., Exxon versus Shell) and use this as a point of comparison. The reason is that in the gasoline retail market a single refinery will have a "sharing agreement" with the other refining companies to supply fuel to service stations other than their own brand. This is done because it is not economic to refine gasoline at one refinery and ship it across a country, or into a neighboring country, when a competitor has a refinery closer by. In those places where there is more than one refinery in the area the relationship between refinery and independent service stations (nonbranded retailer) is even more complicated because the retailer may enter into a short-term contract to purchase fuel from one refinery, and then enter into a new contract with the other refinery that will cause the composition of the fuel to suddenly change as the switch from one refinery to another occurs.

In some parts of the world fuel additives (i.e., detergents, lubricity agents, and dyes) are required by legislation and so analysis for these additives may be one way of identifying a brand. Fuel additives are proprietary and are present in very low concentrations, making analysis for them difficult. Furthermore, fuel additives do not usually change much over time and so analysis for a fuel additive may assist in determining the brand of the fuel, but is unlikely to help differentiate two fuels from the same brand that were purchased at two different retailers (i.e., the comparison would not be very specific). Fuel additives add to the cost of the fuel and so, when not required by legislation, certain additives may be omitted from the fuel altogether.

9.13.2 Application of Chemometrics to the Comparison of Ignitable Liquids

One way of objectively comparing analytical results is to perform a statistical analysis on the dataset. Multivariate analysis, or the statistical analysis of complex chemical datasets such as gas chromatography results, is called chemometrics. One chemometric method, called principal component analysis (PCA), can be used to find which parts of the dataset contain the greatest variation (i.e., information), thus allowing a complex dataset to be mathematically reduced into a simpler dataset. Chemometric methods can be used to compare, or classify, ignitable liquids. For example, Ichikawa and coworkers [28] used chemometric methods to differentiate between samples of premium and regular unleaded gasoline.

In a forensic context, the discrimination of gasoline using chemometric methods was first explored in 1981 by Bertsch et al. [29]. This work subsequently was followed by the extensive research of Mayfield and Henley [30], and later Lavine et al. [31–34], for the classification of jet fuels where it was demonstrated that chemometric methods often could be used to distinguish between fuels within the same class. Potter [35] applied a chemometric technique to discriminate between a small number of gasoline samples, and Tan and coworkers [36] showed that chemometric methods could be used to discriminate between ignitable liquids based on their class. In addition to using chemometrics, Andrews and Lieberman [37] applied artificial neural networks to fluorescence spectra to discriminate petroleum products by class.

9.13.3 Recent Comparisons of Ignitable Liquids

Interest in discriminating between samples of liquid gasoline, as well as other ignitable liquids, has experienced a recent resurgence. Some researchers have employed methods that are not commonly available in most forensic laboratories. For example, analysis of a small set of samples showed that high resolution mass spectrometry could be used to discriminate between and within classes of ignitable liquids [38], whereas gas chromatography isotope ration mass spectrometry (GC-IRMS) has been used to detect small differences in carbon isotope ratios between different samples of unevaporated and evaporated gasoline [39].

Forensic science laboratories around the world typically use GC–MS for fire debris analysis and so this is the instrument of choice for the forensic comparison of ignitable liquids. Following on the work by Mann [20, 25], gasoline samples ranging from unevaporated to 50% evaporated were differentiated by comparing the ratios of sequential peaks obtained from GC–MS analysis [40]. This work was later expanded to include a study of 16 gasoline samples (50% evaporated), extracted from fire debris using headspace analysis, which showed that all samples could be distinguished from each other based on the relative ratios of selected compounds [41]. The discrimination of unevaporated gasoline samples by applying PCA to the C_0- to C_2- naphthalene profiles obtained from GC–MS analysis was reported [42]. This initial work was expanded and the method used to successfully discriminate gasoline samples that were up to 90% evaporated [43, 44]. In another study, multiple regression coefficients were calculated for different samples of unevaporated and evaporated gasoline to determine, first, if the sample was gasoline and, second, to discriminate between samples of gasoline [45]. Covariance mapping, a way to display in a two-dimensional matrix the degree to which two random variables vary together (covariance), was applied to GC–MS data to compare samples of neat ignitable liquids [46]. Covariance mapping also was used to discriminate a set of 10 unevaporated gasoline samples; however, the effects of evaporation on the mapping technique were not addressed in the article [47].

The profiling of petroleum products in order to identify a spill source has received a lot of attention in the environmental forensic literature [48] and the concept described, eventually, may find application in the field of forensic fire investigation as well. For example, some helpful concepts have been described in a four-part series on the effects of refining on finished petroleum products [49–52]. Two studies used pattern recognition analysis to fingerprint spills of heavier fuels such as jet fuel [53, 54]. This research was followed up by a study that used SPME and pattern recognition techniques to classify jet fuels by type [55]. Two-dimensional GC has been used in conjunction with PCA to classify samples of jet fuel [56]. A differential mobility spectrometer (DMS) with a photoionization source interfaced to a gas chromatograph was used to classify samples of diesel fuel and jet fuel [57]. Principal component analysis was applied to GC–MS data in order to distinguish between samples of evaporated kerosene and diesel fuel [58]. N-alkane information was collected from GC-MS data and used to differentiate samples of kerosene from diesel fuel [59]. The use of GC data to distinguish between different sources of medium to heavy ignitable liquids found in environmental spills has been reported [60]. Mass spectra of unfragmented compounds from oil and other petroleum products, obtained from a liquid chromatograph–mass spectrometer (LC–MS), were used to chemically fingerprint different samples [61].

Biomarkers, compounds attributed to the biological formation of petroleum, have been used to characterize heavier ignitable liquids and oils. The methods described in the literature may have application in the characterization and comparison of heavier ignitable liquids that have been solvent-extracted from fire debris. A review of biomarkers, including the use of sesquiterpanes and diamondoids to characterize oils and other petroleum products, has been published [62]. Ratios of compounds from the alkylbenzene, alkylphenanthrene, and sesquiterpane classes were identified by PCA and used to differentiate samples of diesel fuel [63]. Bicyclic sesquiterpanes were used to fingerprint diesel fuels and jet fuels and, in that case, identify the source of a spill [64, 65]. The analysis for diamondoids in gasoline, and their potential use for discriminating samples, has been discussed [66].

The comparison of ignitable liquids is not trivial and, though this area has been explored extensively through research, no single method has been shown to be the best approach in all situations. Perhaps further work with GC-IRMS, in combination with the methods described earlier, will eventually allow neat liquids and fire debris extracts to be reproducibly compared more simply and with greater accuracy. Or perhaps the advent of an altogether new technique will allow any ignitable liquid to be compared to another with relative ease.

REFERENCES

1. ASTM International (2006) *ASTM E 1618-06 Standard test method for ignitable liquid residues in extracts from fire debris samples by gas chromatography-mass spectrometry*, Annual Book of ASTM Standards 14.02, West Conshohocken, PA.
2. ASTM International (2006) *ASTM E 1387-01 Standard test method for ignitable liquid residues in extracts from fire debris samples by gas chromatography*, Annual Book of ASTM Standards 14.02, West Conshohocken, PA.
3. ASTM International (2002) *ASTM E 1618-01 Standard test method for ignitable liquid residues in extracts from fire debris samples by gas chromatography-mass spectrometry*, Annual Book of ASTM Standards 14.02, West Conshohocken, PA.
4. Fire Laboratory Standards and Protocols Committee (2004) *Letter to John J. Lentini, Chair of ASTM Committee E30*, Scientific Working Group for Fire and Explosives.
5. Dolan JA and Stauffer E (2004) Aromatic content in medium range distillate products—Part I: An examination of various liquids, *Journal of Forensic Sciences*, **49**(5), pp 992–1004.
6. Dolan JA and Stauffer E (2004) The effects of adsorption-based extraction methods on the recovery of aliphatic and aromatic compounds in medium petroleum distillates, *56th Annual Meeting of the American Academy of Forensic Sciences*, Dallas, TX.
7. Stauffer E and Lentini JJ (2003) ASTM standards for fire debris analysis: A review, *Forensic Science International*, **132**(1), pp 63–7.
8. Speight JG (1999) *The chemistry and technology of petroleum*, 3rd edition, Marcel Dekker, New York, NY.
9. Kelly R and Martz R (1984) Accelerant identification in fire debris by gas chromatography/mass spectrometry techniques, *Journal of Forensic Sciences*, **29**(3), pp 714–22.
10. Keto RO (1995) GC/MS data interpretation for petroleum distillate identification in contaminated arson debris, *Journal of Forensic Sciences*, **40**(3), pp 412–23.
11. Keto RO and Wineman PL (1991) Detection of petroleum-based accelerants in fire debris by target compound gas chromatography/mass spectrometry, *Analytical Chemistry*, **63**(18), pp 1964–71.
12. Smith MR (1982) Arson analysis by mass chromatography, *Analytical Chemistry*, **54**(13), pp 1399A–409A.

13. Gilbert MW (1998) The use of individual extracted ion profiles versus summed extracted ion profiles in fire debris analysis, *Journal of Forensic Sciences*, **43**(4), pp 871–6.

14. Sandercock PML (2007) *Personal communication to Eric Stauffer*, August 2 2007.

15. Herd M (1953) A paper strip method of examining fuel oil suspected of being identical, *The Analyst*, **78**, pp 383–4.

16. Coldwell BB (1957) The examination of exhibits in suspected arson cases, *Royal Canadian Mounted Police Quarterly*, **23**(2), pp 103–13.

17. Cain PM (1975) Comparison of kerosenes using capillary column gas liquid chromatography, *Journal of the Forensic Science Society*, **15**(4), pp 301–8.

18. Sutherland DA (1999) Fire debris analysis statistics and the use of the latest analytical tools, *Canadian Society for Forensic Science Journal*, pp 11–13.

19. Jackowski JP (1996) The incidence of ignitable liquid residues in fire debris as determined by a sensitive and comprehensive analytical scheme, *Journal of Forensic Sciences*, **42**(5), pp 828–32.

20. Mann DC (1987) Comparison of automotive gasolines using capillary gas chromatography II: Limitations of automotive gasoline comparisons in case work, *Journal of Forensic Sciences*, **32**(3), pp 616–28.

21. Frank HA (1980) Lead alkyl components as discriminating factors in the comparison of gasolines, *Journal of the Forensic Science Society*, **20**, pp 285–92.

22. Chan L (1981) The determination of tetraalkyl lead compounds in petrol using combined gas chromatography atomic absorption spectrometry, *Forensic Science International*, **18**, pp 57–62.

23. Hirz R (1989) Gasoline brand identification and individualization of gasoline lots, *Journal of the Forensic Science Society*, **29**(2), pp 91–101.

24. Hennig HJ (1982) Möglichkeiten der Differenzierung von Mineralölen, Gasölen und Vergaserkraftstoffen mit Hilfe der Gas Chromatographie, *Archiv für Kriminologie*, **170**, pp 12–20.

25. Mann DC (1987) Comparison of automotive gasolines using capillary gas chromatography I: Comparison methodology, *Journal of Forensic Sciences*, **32**(3), pp 606–15.

26. Alexander J et al. (1987) Fluorescence of petroleum products II. Three-dimensional fluorescence plots of gasolines, *Journal of Forensic Sciences*, **32**(1), pp 72–86.

27. Sheff LM and Siegel JA (1994) Fluorescence of petroleum products V. Three-dimensional fluorescence spectroscopy and capillary gas chromatography of neat and evaporated gasoline samples, *Journal of Forensic Sciences*, **39**(5), pp 1201–14.

28. Ichikawa M et al. (1993) Mass spectrometric analysis for distinction between regular and premium motor gasolines, *Analytical Sciences*, **9**, pp 261–6.

29. Bertsch W, Mayfield H, and Thomason MM (1981) Application of pattern recognition to high resolution GC and GC/MS. Part I. Basic studies, *Proceedings of the International Symposium on Capillary Chromatography*, pp 313–34.

30. Mayfield HT and Henley MV (1991) Classification of jet fuels using high resolution gas chromatography and pattern recognition, *ASTM Special Technical Publications*, **1102**, pp 578–97.

31. Lavine BK, Stine A, and Mayfield HT (1993) Gas chromatography-pattern recognition techniques in pollution monitoring, *Analytica Chimica Acta*, **277**, pp 357–67.

32. Lavine BK et al. (1995) Source identification of underground fuel spills by pattern recognition analysis of high-speed gas chromatograms, *Analytical Chemistry*, **67**, pp 3846–52.

33. Lavine BK et al. (1998) Fuel spill identification by gas chromatography genetic algorithms/pattern recognition techniques, *Analytical Letters*, **31**(15), pp 2805–22.
34. Lavine BK et al. (2000) Source identification of underground fuel spills by solid-phase microextraction/high-resolution gas chromatographic/generic algorithms, *Analytical Chemistry*, **72**, pp 423–31.
35. Potter TL (1990) *Fingerprinting petroleum products: Unleaded gasoline*. In: *Petroleum contaminated soils*, editor Kostecki PT, Lewis Publishers, Chelsea, MI.
36. Tan, B, Hardy JK, and Snavely RE (2000) Accelerant classification by gas chromatography/mass spectrometry and multivariate pattern recognition, *Analytica Chimica Acta*, **422**(1), pp 37–46.
37. Andrews JM and Lieberman SH (1994) Neural network approach to qualitative identification of fuels and oils from laser induced fluorescence spectra, *Analytica Chimica Acta*, **285**, pp 237–46.
38. Rodgers RP et al. (2001) Compositional analysis for identification of arson accelerants by electron ionization Fourier transform ion cyclotron resonance high-resolution mass spectrometry, *Journal of Forensic Sciences*, **46**(2), pp 268–79.
39. Smallwood BJ, Philip RP, and Allen JD (2002) Stable carbon isotopic composition of gasolines determined by isotope ratio monitoring gas chromatography mass spectrometry, *Organic Geochemistry*, **33**(2), pp 149–59.
40. Dolan JA and Ritacco CJ (2002) Gasoline comparisons by gas chromatography-mass spectrometry utilizing an automated approach to data analysis, *54th Annual Meeting of the American Academy of Forensic Sciences*, Atlanta, GA.
41. Barnes AT et al. (2004) Comparison of gasolines using gas chromatography-mass spectrometry and target ion response, *Journal of Forensic Sciences*, **49**(5), pp 1018–23.
42. Sandercock PML and Du Pasquier E (2003) Chemical fingerprinting of unevaporated automotive gasoline samples, *Forensic Science International*, **134**(1), pp 1–10.
43. Sandercock PML and Du Pasquier E (2004) Chemical fingerprinting of gasoline: 2. Comparison of unevaporated and evaporated automotive gasoline samples, *Forensic Science International*, **140**(1), pp 43–59.
44. Sandercock PML and Du Pasquier E (2004) Chemical fingerprinting of gasoline: 3. Comparison of unevaporated automotive gasoline samples from Australia and New Zealand, *Forensic Science International*, **140**(1), pp 71–7.
45. Hida M et al. (2006) Discrimination of heat degradation gasoline using different calculation method of regression analysis, *Bunseki Kagaku*, **55**(11), pp 869–874.
46. Sigman ME and Williams MR (2006) Covariance mapping in the analysis of ignitable liquids by gas chromatography/mass spectrometry, *Analytical Chemistry*, **78**(5), pp 1713–18.
47. Sigman ME, Williams MR, and Ivy RG (2007) Individualization of gasoline samples by covariance mapping and gas chromatography/mass spectrometry, *Analytical Chemistry*, **79**(9), pp 3462–8.
48. Stout SA et al. (2002) *Chemical fingerprinting of hydrocarbons*. In: *Introduction to environmental forensics*, editors Murphy BL and Morrison RD, Elsevier Academic Press, London, United Kingdom.
49. Uhler AD et al. (2001) The influences of refining on petroleum fingerprinting. Part 1. The refining process, *Contaminated Soil Sediment and Water*, October issue.
50. Stout SA et al. (2001) The influences of refining on petroleum fingerprinting. Part 2. Gasoline blending practices, *Contaminated Soil Sediment and Water*, December issue.

51. Stout SA et al. (2002) The influences of refining on petroleum fingerprinting Part 3. Distillate fuel production practices, *Contaminated Soil Sediment and Water*, January–February issue.

52. Uhler AD et al. (2002) The influences of refining on petroleum fingerprinting Part 4. Residual fuels, *Contaminated Soil Sediment and Water*, April issue.

53. Lavine BK et al. (2001) Generic algorithm for fuel spill identification, *Analytic Chimica Acta*, **437**(2), pp 233–46.

54. Lavine BK et al. (2001) Authentication of fuel spill standards using gas chromatography/pattern recognition techniques, *Analytical Letters*, **34**(2 pp 281–93.

55. Lavine BK et al. (2001) Fuel spill identification using solid-phase extraction an solid-phase microextraction. 1. Aviation turbine fuels, *Journal of Chromato graphic Science*, **39**, pp 501–7.

56. Johnson KJ and Synovec RE (2002) Pattern recognition of jet fuels: Compre hensive GC × GC with ANOVA-based feature selection and principal compo nent analysis, *Chemometrics and Intelligent Laboratory Systems*, **60**(1–2), p 225–37.

57. Rearden P et al. (2007) Fuzzy rule-building expert system classification of fue using solid-phase microextraction two-way gas chromatography differentia mobility spectrometric data, *Analytical Chemistry*, **79**(4), pp 1485–91.

58. Borusiewicz R, Zadora G, and Zieba-Palus J (2004) Application of head-spac analysis with passive adsorption for forensic purpose in the automated therma desorption-gas chromatography-mass spectrometry system, *Chromatographia* **60**, pp S133–42.

59. Zadora G, Borusiewicz R, and Zieba-Palus J (2005) Differentiation betwee weathered kerosene and diesel fuel using automatic thermal desorption-GC-M analysis and the likelihood ratio approach, *Journal of Separation Science* **28**(13), pp 1467–75.

60. Uhler AD et al. (2005) Identification and differentiation of light-and middle distillate petroleum for NRDA using chemical forensics, *Proceedings of th International Oil Spill Conference*, pp 3580–91.

61. Zahlsen EK and Eide I (2006) Standardizing the novel method fo chemical fingerprinting of oil and petroleum products based on positive elec trospray mass spectrometry and chemometrics, *Energy Fuels*, **20**(1 pp 265–70.

62. Wang Z, Stout SA, and Fingas M (2006) Forensic fingerprinting of biomarker for oil spill characterization and source identification, *Environmental Forensics* **7**(2), pp 105–46.

63. Gaines RB et al. (2006) Chemometric determination of target compounds use to fingerprint unweathered diesel fuels, *Environmental Forensics*, **7**(1), p 77–87.

64. Wang Z et al. (2005) Characterization, weathering, and application of sesquiter panes to source identification of spilled lighter petroleum products, *Environ mental Science and Technology*, **39**(22), pp 8700–7.

65. Stout SA, Uhler AD, and McCarthy KJ (2005) Middle distillate fuel fingerprint ing using drimane-based bicyclic sesquiterpanes, *Environmental Forensics*, **6**(3 pp 241–51.

66. Stout SA, Healey EM, and Douglas GS (2004) Diamondoid hydrocarbons-Appl cation in the chemical fingerprinting of gas condensate and gasoline, *Soil an Sediment Contamination*, **13**(2), pp 191–2.

CHAPTER 10

Preliminary Examination of Evidence

"Can't you smell that smell"

Lyrics of the song "That Smell", Lynyrd Skynyrd (1987)

10.1 INTRODUCTION

When tasked with examining evidence from a fire scene, the forensic scientist must address the specific requests of the investigator submitting the evidence; however, he or she must also ensure that critical information contained within the submitted evidence is exploited and not forever lost. Therefore, the criminalist must approach each case and each item of evidence with the attitude that it may contain more forensic traces than the ones sought by the investigator. As such, there may be more to learn about the fire from the evidence than the mere presence of ignitable liquid residues (ILR). Properly trained fire debris analysts should have an overall foundation in general criminalistics in addition to their in-depth knowledge of ILR analysis. This chapter addresses some of the issues relating to the documentation of evidence and other forensic examinations that may be performed on fire debris samples.

10.2 DOCUMENTATION

Every item of evidence collected from a fire scene and submitted to a forensic laboratory for examination has the potential to be presented in a court of law, in either criminal or civil procedures, or possibly both. Because of this, it is imperative that the forensic scientist sufficiently documents all aspects of his or her examination, from the receipt of the evidence to its final disposition, including all steps in between. There are numerous guidelines for what is considered necessary documentation [1, 2]. The Fire Laboratory Standards and Protocols Committee of TWGFEX has identified the following items as part of the critical documentation that must be established with all evidence submitted [3]:

- A unique identifier assigned to each case or record
- Submission documents
- Identifying information of the submitting parties
- A description of the items submitted
- A record of the chain of custody

Besides these documents, it is also necessary to have adequate notes regarding initial observations and examinations performed on the evidence and sometimes photographs. Additional documentation to support analytical findings and to comply with a laboratory's internal and/or accreditation requirements is also necessary, however the focus of this section is on the preliminary examination of evidence; therefore documentation requirements for those purposes will not be discussed.[1]

An example of a transmittal sheet used to submit fire debris samples to Pinellas County Forensic Laboratory (Florida, USA) is shown in Figure 10-1. A similar transmittal sheet used to submit fire debris samples to a private laboratory is shown in Figure 10-2. These sheets are filled by the submitting party and attached to the evidence sent to the laboratory.

When evidence is initially received into a forensic laboratory, whether directly by the criminalist or through the support staff, the information regarding when it was received, how it was received—by a commercial carrier or directly from an individual—and the condition in which it was received must be clearly documented. If an item of evidence is received via a commercial carrier, the tracking number should be recorded, and if the evidence was received from an individual, then his or her signature, title, and affiliation (agency or company) must be recorded. The condition of the exterior package should indicate if it is appropriately sealed or if there is any damage to it. In most laboratories, this type of documentation is guided by policies and is done as part of standard operating procedures.

---

[1] For note-taking and documentation requirements, a good reference is the ASCLD/LAB (American Society of Crime Laboratory Directors/Laboratory Accreditation Board) manual, which lists its requirements for laboratories accredited under their program [4]. Some introductory forensic science textbooks also provide a good overview [5].

Pinellas County Forensic Laboratory

10900 Ulmerton Road • Largo Florida • 33778

(727) 582-6810 • Fax (727) 582-6822

REQUEST FOR LABORATORY ANALYSIS   Page_____ of_____
PLEASE PRINT

☐ CONTROLLED SUBSTANCES   ☐ FIRE DEBRIS   ☐ OTHER_____

Offense/Incident number_____

Address (if applicable)_____

Subject(s):

Last	First	Race	Sex	DOB	Juvenile	In Custody
_____	_____	____	____	_____	☐	☐
_____	_____	____	____	_____	☐	☐
_____	_____	____	____	_____	☐	☐
_____	_____	____	____	_____	☐	☐

ITEM NO.	QUANTITY	SHORT DESCRIPTION OF ITEMS	SUSPECTED MATERIAL	SPECIAL INSTRUCTIONS

The evidence in this case is part of an official investigation; it has not, nor will it be, submitted to any other laboratory.

Case Officer/Agent (print):_____Date collected:_____
_____

Agency:_____Division:_____Phone number:_____
_____

****

FOR LABORATORY USE ONLY   LABORATORY NUMBER:

Date:_____Received by:_____From:_____# of Containers_____
Date:_____Received by:_____From:_____# of Containers_____
Date:_____Received by:_____From:_____# of Containers_____
Date:_____Received by:_____From:_____# of Containers_____

Request for Analysis Form
1105F-1.revB
Effective: 11-11-02

FIGURE 10-1 *Example of an evidence transmittal sheet used to submit fire debris samples to a crime laboratory in the United States. (Illustration courtesy of Reta Newman, Pinellas County Forensic Laboratory, Largo, Florida, USA.)*

**FORENSIC
AND
SCIENTIFIC
TESTING, INC.**

3069 Amwiler Road, Suite 9, Atlanta, GA 30360 (770) 449-4199
(800) 225-1302

EVIDENCE TRANSMITTAL LETTER

Original report &
Invoice to: _____   Copy of Report To: _____
_____

Phone: (___) _____   Phone: (___) _____

*Insured: _____   Investigation #: _____
*Policy #: _____   Date of Fire: _____
*Claim #: _____   Date Evidence Taken: _____

List of Specimens: Location Taken From:
1.) _____
2.) _____
3.) _____
4.) _____
5.) _____
6.) _____
7.) _____
8.) _____

Examination Requested:

Condition of Scene:
(weathered, altered,
undisturbed, etc.)

Evidence Taken From: _____ To: _____

Evidence Taken From: _____ To: _____

Evidence Taken From: _____ To: _____

Evidence Taken From: _____ To: _____

*Required with third-party billing

FIGURE 10-2 *Example of an evidence transmittal sheet used to submit fire debris samples to a private laboratory. (Illustration courtesy of Doug Byron, Forensic & Scientific Testing, Lawrenceville, Georgia, USA.)*

An inventory of the content of the evidence and its condition should be conducted as soon as it is practically feasible after the initial opening of the exterior package. The initial inventory is often conducted by the criminalist who will perform the subsequent examination. Its aim is to ensure that the items submitted to the laboratory correlate to those listed on the submission paperwork. Any significant discrepancy should be contemporaneously documented and resolved (via the submitter's notification) prior to completion of the analysis [3]. The integrity of the evidence container must be carefully examined and if its condition is not optimal, it must be documented in the laboratory notes. Containers for evidence submitted for ILR analysis should be airtight and not present any damage that may compromise their effectiveness or their ability to prevent the loss or contamination of evidence (see examples in Chapter 6). Often, tamper-evident seals are used on each individual item of evidence; the condition of these seals must be noted and documented as a part of the preliminary examination of evidence. Once the inventory has been conducted and documented and any discrepancies resolved, the fire debris analyst may move on to the initial observation of the evidence.

10.3 INITIAL OBSERVATION

When fire debris samples are submitted with the primary examination request being that of ILR analysis, it is generally not advisable to conduct a thorough physical examination of the evidence prior to its extraction. This is because ignitable liquids, particularly when present in low quantities, can be irrecoverably lost to the environment if the airtight packaging remains open for an extended period of time or if the debris is removed from the packaging for detailed observation and documentation. This does not mean that the evidence should not be examined prior to extraction; it most certainly must. This preliminary examination of the evidence serves four main functions:

I. To confirm that the content of the container is what it is purported to be. By making a quick examination of the evidence, the analyst often can determine if an item was mislabeled or mixed up. Again, any significant discrepancies must be addressed immediately.

II. To ensure that there are no additional layers of packaging that could prevent a headspace-based extraction technique from accessing the sample's headspace. Although it does not happen too often, there are cases in which an investigator places evidence into a plastic bag or other container and then places the entire package into a can or other additional layers of packaging.[2] This is more likely to occur when the material being submitted is a suspected flammable or combustible liquid. Liquids are often double-packaged: first in a glass vial or jar, then into another package to protect the glass and to contain the liquid if the glass container were to break. During this preliminary examination, the criminalist can remove extraneous layers of packaging prior to beginning the extraction process.

III. To ensure a safe extraction procedure. Most of the commonly used extraction techniques require heating the sample, which is in a closed system. If a sample contains a substantial quantity of one of the lighter ignitable liquids, heating it, especially in a closed system, could be dangerous, possibly resulting in a small-scale boiling liquid expanding vapor explosion (BLEVE). In less severe cases, an overpressure could occur, causing the friction lid from a metal can to be propelled from the container, creating both a safety hazard and a potential for contamination and loss. Similarly, clothing with pockets may contain materials that are dangerous when heated.

IV. To select the most appropriate analytical scheme. First, evidence submitted for ILR analysis may be amenable to other examinations, such as DNA, fingerprint, trace evidence, and chemical analysis for hypergolic mixtures or explosive residues. Second, the knowledge gained from a preliminary examination of the evidence may affect the selection of the extraction technique or its conditions. A sample with an alcohol-like odor may benefit from an initial extraction technique that is solventless such as SPME or simple headspace. A sample with noticeable petroleum-like odor may require the parameters used in an adsorption-based extraction to be less robust than those used for samples in which there is no initial indication of an ignitable liquid. A nonporous item of evidence bearing a visible stain may be most efficiently extracted with a small amount of solvent.

---

[2] A true story occurred once with a fire debris analyst who thought that ILR contained in the sample could be lost in a split second when the can was opened. Hence, he thought it was crucial to place the activated charcoal strip (see Chapter 11) inside the container extremely rapidly. He performed so with 18 one-quart cans that were brought to the laboratory by an investigator. He just slightly opened the lid of each can and quickly placed the activated charcoal strip, closing the lid immediately after. He performed in the same manner to remove the activated charcoal strips, thinking in terms of preserving the sample. After performing all the analyses and getting 18 negatives results, without even a peak on any of the chromatograms, a report was written declaring all 18 samples negative for the presence of ILR. A private laboratory was retained to perform a reanalysis of the samples. Upon receiving the evidence and proper preliminary examination, it was observed that each one-quart can contained another one-pint can into which the debris was placed! As such, it was necessary to pull out the one-pint cans and place activated charcoal strips in each one of them in order to perform a proper extraction of the debris. As a result, more than two-thirds of the samples were positive for gasoline.

The permutations are endless; therefore it is important to have a thorough understanding of the strengths and weaknesses of each extraction technique discussed in Chapter 11, and to have at least some knowledge about the sample to be extracted.

In any case, it is crucial to remember that this preliminary examination must be thorough enough to fulfill these four goals while being cursory enough not to compromise the ILR possibly present on the debris.

Organoleptic Examination

Preliminary examinations in fire debris analysis historically have included an organoleptic examination, commonly referred to as a "nasal appraisal" or "smelling the evidence." This step often could provide information regarding the types and/or relative amounts of ILR present or, more simply, regarding a strong smell of plastic decomposition. This information could be very valuable to fire debris analysts as they decide on the best method to extract the evidence. Recognition of a known odor could even provide a clue as to what an appropriate standard might be to include on an autosampler run.

However, the intentional inhalation of a myriad chemicals emanating from fire debris is not really healthy. Chemists routinely are exposed to a variety of chemicals with various health risks associated with them and are trained to use engineering controls to minimize exposure. In this regard, one commonsense engineering control that can be applied is to avoid intentionally inhaling vapors from evidence. In addition to ILR, there is likely a multitude of other carcinogens and unhealthy chemicals that were produced by the heat of the fire by either incomplete combustion or pyrolysis. For these reasons, one cannot recommend conducting organoleptic examination as a routine preliminary step. In any case, the staff must abide by the laboratory policies regarding occupational safety. However, one can also not ignore the forensic intelligence gained from such an examination.

10.4 OTHER FORENSIC EXAMINATIONS

10.4.1 Preamble

There are many other items of forensic interest that may be present in fire debris. The goal of this section is to review, nonexhaustively, the different traces and physical evidence that the fire debris analyst must be aware of and should take into consideration prior to performing ILR analysis. If the forensic scientist is not sure whether the debris harbors potential evidence, other than ILR, he or she should not hesitate to ask the assistance of more experienced colleagues. It is always good practice to confer with specialists in each domain before making any decisions that could be detrimental to another type of evidence. To maximize the evidentiary value of the submitted items, a team approach is desirable. The expertise of a team of specialists, each of whom has an overall understanding of all the applicable forensic disciplines and a detailed understanding of his or her field of specialty will result in minimal destruction of the evidence, and in the maximum amount of intelligence being gained.

Depending upon a sample's suitability for other forensic examinations, the criminalist may need to alter the order in which examinations are conducted in order to best preserve the various types of evidence. Many of the extraction techniques used for the recovery of ILR require moderate heating— in the range of 50° to 80°C—which in itself is not expected to damage other types of evidence (exception possibly made of DNA). The use of other extraction techniques however, such as the solvent wash technique, would almost certainly result in the loss of many other types of evidence.

Additionally, it is important that the forensic scientist have some knowledge of the circumstances surrounding the fire and that he or she discusses the possible examinations with the submitting party, who needs to authorize them. The reason is that the pertinence of these examinations must be determined. For example, if the individual suspected of starting the fire has legitimate access to the site where the fire occurred, then finding his or her DNA or fingerprints there would not demonstrate anything in relation to the fire. However, if these fingerprints or this DNA profile were found on a container for a Molotov cocktail, their significance in relation to the crime is much more pertinent.

10.4.2 Latent Fingerprints

The request to examine evidence for the presence of latent fingerprints is one of the most frequent ones received by a forensic laboratory. When an arsonist obtains and carries fire-setting materials to a scene, such as a delay device, a gasoline can, or a Molotov cocktail, it is possible that fingerprints are deposited on the item. Indeed, these prints may have survived the conditions (fire, extinguishing activities, etc.) experienced by the item. This is the reason why it may be pertinent to examine such items for fingerprints.

Fire does have a deleterious effect on the fragile fingerprints left behind, and the chances for their survival decrease as the intensity of the fire increases. As such, fingerprints are not frequently found on fire debris. In addition to the damaging effect of heat and fire suppression efforts, fingerprints can also be damaged by vapors. This is of concern when both fingerprint examination and ILR analysis are requested. Particularly in cases in which there is a high concentration of ILR remaining, the chances for recovering latent fingerprints of sufficient quality to be of value for identification are rather poor.

Although an item typically described as "fire debris" (see Figure 10-3), containing only remnants of burned, calcined, unidentified debris and powder residues will not contain any fingerprints, there are many other samples submitted as fire debris that may present surfaces susceptible of bearing fingerprints. Such objects may include bottles from Molotov cocktail, containers found at the fire scene, components of incendiary devices such as batteries, or a suicide note. Also, in many instances, a fingerprint may be completely hidden, covered with soot. As a consequence, if an object exhibits surfaces onto which fingerprints could be present and their detection would be of any significance, the analyst must be very careful and consider their potential probative value even in cases in which a fingerprint examination

FIGURE 10-3

The typical content of what is often described as "fire debris"—a mixture of unidentified debris, mostly burned or charred, from which other types of evidence such as fingerprints can never be retrieved.

was not specifically requested. As such, the forensic scientist should handle these objects as little as possible and make sure that he or she does not wipe out these delicate fingerprints from the surfaces.

There has been very little literature vis-à-vis the development of fingerprints on objects that have been exposed to fire. Research conducted by the US Bureau of Alcohol, Tobacco, Firearms and Explosives (ATF) Forensic Science Laboratory and Fire Research Laboratory demonstrated that fingerprints placed on Molotov cocktails, which were then ignited, will survive when properly preserved and promptly examined [6]. Some authors have demonstrated that when fingerprints are covered with soot, it is possible to rinse the surface with water with or without the use of an ultrasonic bath [7, 8]. Other solvents, such as toluene, also have been tested, with limited success [7]. Regular fingerprint enhancement or development techniques vary in effectiveness depending upon the types of surface onto which the prints are present [9]. Research demonstrated that fingerprints have a relatively good chance of surviving a fire if not directly exposed to the flames [10]. The same research also successfully enhanced some fingerprints that were directly exposed to the flames. More recently, a paper published by Stow and McGurry demonstrated that a few of the usual fingerprint enhancement techniques still work on fingerprints exposed to fire [11].

In general, fingerprint examiners classify surfaces as porous, semiporous, nonporous, or adhesives. Among all the different fingerprint enhancement techniques, some of them use solvents such as methanol, ethanol, acetic acid, pentane, petroleum ether, or other proprietary solvents such as HFE7100 or HFC4310. Thus, it would not be very pertinent to perform fire debris analysis after the fingerprint examiner worked on the item with such a solvent. Nevertheless, if solvent extraction was to be used, it has a good chance to wash out the deposit constituting the fingerprint, thus destroying these precious traces. Passive headspace concentration extraction should not interfere with the fingerprint enhancement.

Alternatively, items of evidence may be split so that portions of the evidence that are more likely to have retained latent prints, such as materials with smooth, nonporous surfaces, can be allowed to air dry or be placed in nonairtight packaging to be tested for latent prints. Other types of materials, such as debris, liquids, and textured materials can remain in airtight packaging until they can be tested for ILR.

In cases in which it is deemed appropriate to analyze an item of evidence for both ignitable liquids and latent prints, it is important to process the items with minimal delay. Extended periods of time exposed to ignitable liquid vapors may destroy latent prints. In all instances, the fire debris analyst should meet and discuss with the fingerprint expert and work out the proper sequence of events, keeping in mind that passive headspace concentration extraction does not interfere with subsequent fingerprint enhancement techniques.

10.4.3 Trace Evidence or Microtraces

Microtraces, also referred to as trace evidence, constitute a very broad category of forensic evidence that includes fibers, hairs, paint, glass, soil, and any other types of microscopic items. When in the presence of a sample that might contain such evidence, it is better for the fire debris analyst to directly convene with the trace evidence analyst, as the recognition of such a broad spectrum of evidence often requires the expertise of a specialist. As with latent fingerprints, the recovery of trace evidence is not easy when a fire has caused significant damage. However, it is important to keep in mind that even after being subjected to fire, some of these microtraces are still valuable for future comparison with material found on a suspect, for example. Trace evidence, as with other types of evidence, are also prone to contamination. As such, if trace evidence examinations are to be conducted, it is important that their potential be recognized early on, so that appropriate measures to ensure the integrity of the potential trace evidence can be put into place.

In most instances, the examinations performed on this type of physical evidence are not influenced by passive headspace concentration extraction. However, solvent extraction might dissolve paint particles or (maybe to a lesser extent) fibers, particularly if a solvent such as dichloromethane is used. Other microtraces may also get damaged with the use of a solvent. In such instances, it is crucial to convene first with the specialist, conduct an appropriate preliminary examination, and possibly separate this kind of evidence from the debris.

There is more trace evidence present in fire debris than one might think of. For example, the wick from a Molotov cocktail may provide useful information, especially if it originated from an unusual type of fabric or from an item of clothing. An unusual fabric could provide intelligence regarding its intended use, eventually leading to a potential source. Clothing could potentially bear DNA (see next subsection) or if the wick is only a portion of a piece of clothing perhaps it could be compared with or physically matched to evidence recovered from a suspect source.

10.4.4 Body Fluids

DNA, like fingerprints, can provide a strong associative link between an item of evidence and an individual. In some samples, body fluids or even skin cells containing DNA may be present. They could become very pertinent to the outcome of the investigation. Exploitation of DNA evidence often starts with a detection and identification of the stains, however, trace levels of DNA, also referred to as contact DNA will not appear as stain. This is then followed by an extraction of biological materials, and finally their analysis. The detection of body fluids usually is performed first by a naked eye observation of the item for obvious stains or discoloration. Then, an alternate light source in the UV range or other selected wavelengths is used. This is followed by a chemical detection of the different body fluids, which consists of applying different chemical reagents on the items and observing either a change of coloration or a chemiluminescence. Once stains have been located, the forensic scientist typically swabs the surface with a small piece of humidified cotton or cuts a piece of the item, which will then be used for confirmatory testing and the subsequent DNA analysis.

The three great enemies of DNA are heat, light, and humidity [12]. All three of these elements are present in a fire. However, even under such conditions, DNA samples have survived fires. Sweet and Sweet report a case in which DNA was extracted from teeth of the incinerated remains of a homicide victim [13]. It also has been shown that even after a fire, blood can be detected using luminol [14]. If the fire is not too intense on the stains, the blood still reacts to the luminol. The same authors noticed that soot and bloodstains looked very alike after a fire and could be confused. They recommended the use of an [14]: "alternate light source (ALS) at 415 nm in conjunction with a Tiffen Orange 21 filter and 580 nm in conjunction with a Tiffen 1 (25) Red filter [. . .]."

When preserving fire debris in airtight containers as recommended for fire debris analysis, the humidity factor may accelerate the degradation of DNA. When heating the sample at 80°C overnight for a passive headspace concentration extraction, DNA will be further degraded. If enough material was present in the sample prior to the manipulation by the fire debris analyst, the DNA extraction and analysis will not necessarily be jeopardized. But it is usually not possible to estimate the amount of nondegraded DNA by just looking at the sample. Therefore, when body fluids may be present in the debris, it is recommended to first observe it with the naked eye under natural and selective light prior to the extraction of ILR. One exception would be if the debris contains highly volatile compounds for which exposure to the air could destroy the ILR content. Fortunately, this kind of situation is not often encountered. And if the ILR are extremely volatile, the extraction can always be carried out at room temperature, thus avoiding the need for heating. The criminalist performing the observation of the item for body fluid stains should do it in the shortest amount of time possible. A good practice would consist of freezing the sample prior to its manipulation, which would decrease the loss of volatile compounds during its examination by lowering the vapor pressure of the liquids. Then, if stains are located, the swabbing or cutting is performed prior to ILR extraction. However, the chemical detection of body fluids on the debris itself is not recommended prior to ILR extraction.

Continuing advances in the science of DNA analysis have resulted in techniques that are extremely sensitive. Consequently, if a DNA analysis is to be conducted on evidence collected from a fire scene, all aspects of its handling and collection should be done with this in mind in order to avoid contamination. Incendiary devices or delay mechanisms are often suitable for DNA analysis, and may provide a useful link between a device used to set the fire and the individual who committed the crime. A properly trained criminalist should be aware of the potential sources of probative DNA from evidence associated with a fire. In any case, when dealing with samples susceptible to containing DNA evidence, the fire debris analyst should contact the appropriate specialist and discuss the situation to prioritize the evidence examination. In the meantime, the debris should be frozen to slow down, if not prevent, the degradation of the potential DNA.

10.4.5 Impression Evidence

Impression evidence is a category of traces that includes toolmarks, shoeprints, and tire tracks. Such traces can be found on some objects. One may think of incendiary device components that would have pliers indentations, wire that would have been cut and carry impression evidence from the pair of lineman's pliers, or the shoeprint on a piece of broken glass. When the fire debris analyst is confronted with such evidence, particular care should be taken in the handling of the items. These impressions can be very fragile and will be destroyed by repeated contact with other items when placed in the same container and moved around. These impressions, whenever possible, should be isolated and prevented from contacting any other surfaces or objects.

A typical sequence of examination of such evidence starts with photographing the impression with rulers. Close-up photographs are taken to ensure that all potential individual characteristics are properly documented. Measurements then are taken from the impressions. If the impression is three-dimensional, a casting of it is made using either dental paste or, with larger surfaces such as tire tracks, plaster of Paris. If the impression is not three-dimensional, such as with a shoeprint on glass, a transfer onto a gelatin sheet usually is performed. A sample of the material onto which the evidence is located is also collected, particularly with three-dimensional impressions. This will allow for a comparison with material possibly found on the object and the demonstration of a cross-transfer between the object and the surface, following the Locard's principle of exchange.

When these impressions are located on metals or materials that will not distort under a slight heat increase, passive headspace concentration extraction can be performed without interfering with their subsequent examination. However, if such impressions are present on material that will easily distort (temporarily or permanently) under slight heat, such as some plastics, then the fire debris analyst should consult with the proper specialist and discuss the sequence of examinations to be conducted. Since the debris already experienced fire conditions, it is likely already distorted, so the heat of the extraction procedure will not worsen its condition any further. Also, when the impression is located on some metallic surface, it is important from a toolmarks perspective that the surface not rust. This is typically not compatible with the packaging used for the fire debris (sealed container): If humidity is present, rust develops. This situation must be addressed very rapidly with the firearms and toolmarks examiner. It would be a shame to lose toolmarks evidence because the fire debris sat on the shelf for two weeks prior to its preliminary examination.

10.4.6 Documents

Among the debris submitted to the laboratory, it is possible occasionally to find papers partially burned or almost completely charred. Paper ignites at approximately 230°C (450°F), and when in the form of loose sheets, it burns very rapidly and produces black ashes. If the paper is in the form of stacked sheets, such as in a phone book, it is almost impossible to burn the sheets to completion, as it is difficult for the fire to penetrate due to a lack of oxygen. In any instance, documents can prove to be extremely important in a fire investigation. It is possible that the debris contains a note explaining the planning of the burning of the house, some unpaid invoices or bank statements establishing the motive of the fraud, a suicide note left by a victim, or simply the label of a container of paint thinner that was used to set the house on fire.

When dealing with documents, the fire debris analyst needs to be extremely gentle. If the document is not burned, there is little risk that it will break when manipulated; however, if the document is partially burned or charred (ashes), it will break into small pieces as soon as it is improperly manipulated. It is best for the fire debris analyst to immediately consult with the document examiner as to the best course of action. The questioned document examiner has the experience in handling documents and his or her needs have to be discussed and planned with the needs of the fire debris analyst [15].

Questioned document examiners use many different techniques to examine documents, which depend on the examination requested. However, in almost all instances, they will need to work with the original document. Photographs, and particularly close-up shots, are taken of the handwriting or signature. Often, the photographs themselves are not sufficient, as the examiner must look at the lines and curves on the paper itself in a three-dimensional fashion in order to determine the degree of pressure applied. Also, when working with counterfeit or forged documents, the examiner observes the documents under different lights (ranging from UV to IR) and filters, at different magnifications. Also, when performing ink analysis, besides nondestructive techniques such as spectrophotometry, the forensic scientist usually extracts the ink to analyze it by TLC [16]. One particular aspect of document examination is the observation of indented writings, which is usually carried out with an electrostatic detection apparatus (ESDA). In a notebook, indented writings can be found several pages down from the page onto which the text was originally written. This could be particularly useful when a blank notebook is found at a fire scene, which may have been used to write the fire-setting plan on the original top sheet. Thus, it is extremely important to preserve the document as much as possible for future examination. In no instance should the fire debris analyst perform a solvent extraction on a document without first consulting with the questioned document examiner. Again, passive headspace concentration extraction, and in general all headspace techniques, are the least invasive techniques, and should not create any further damage to the document.

10.4.7 Incendiary Residues and Device Components

Although they are used in relatively few arson fires, the presence of incendiary device components or chemical residues can provide a wealth of information. It is important to realize that the residues resulting from most hypergolic mixtures will not be recovered by the extraction methods typically used for the recovery of ignitable liquids. Whereas the extraction methods discussed in Chapter 11 are optimized for the collection of common liquid accelerants (typically nonpolar, volatile ignitable liquids), the nature of chemical incendiary residues precludes their extraction by such techniques. If a heat-producing chemical reaction was used to start the fire, a detectable residue will most likely be left; however, the criminalist needs to be aware of this potential evidence in order to properly test for it. A preliminary visual examination of the collected evidence may provide an indication; however, it is best if this type of reaction is recognized *in situ* by the fire investigator. Fortunately, it is unlikely that the common means of extracting fire debris for ILR would result in the loss or destruction of chemical incendiary residues.

Hypergolic Mixtures

When two substances ignite spontaneously (without any external heat source) upon their mixing, they form what is called a hypergolic mixture. Combustion occurs as a result of a highly exothermic reaction with a low energy of activation. One well-known application of this type of mixture is rocket propellants, in which hydrazine N_2H_4, monomethylhydrazine NH_2NHCH_3 (MMH), or unsymmetrical dimethylhydrazine $(CH_3)_2NNH_2$ (UDMH) reacts upon contact with dinitrogen tetroxide N_2O_4 as shown in the reaction:

$$(CH_3H)_2NNH_2 \text{ (1)} + 2N_2O_4 \text{ (g)} \rightarrow 2CO_2 \text{ (g)} + 3N_2 \text{ (g)} + 4H_2O \text{ (g)}$$

Because they can ignite easily upon contact, hypergolic mixtures are ideal as rocket fuels. Less commonly known however, are less lofty applications. There are several combinations of readily available materials that have been used as hypergolic mixtures for criminal purposes.

Mixing brake fluids or an antifreeze (both glycol-based products) with calcium hypochlorite $Ca(ClO)_2$—often referred to as "chlorine" for pools or HTH—will react spontaneously and quite violently. The time delay between the two materials coming in contact with one another, the onset of flames, and the rate of reaction can vary significantly, and depends primarily upon ambient temperature and the amount of surface area in contact. Another hypergolic reaction that has seen illicit use is that of sugar, chlorate, and sulfuric acid, usually in the presence of an ignitable liquid; when properly configured, these simple ingredients can result in self-igniting incendiary devices. Hypergolic mixtures have been presented in several underground publications. Although not commonly seen, they can be effective fire starters, and will generally leave a visible residue that can be tested at the forensic laboratory.

When devices are used in setting an incendiary fire, they may serve several purposes. They could be used to falsely indicate an accidental cause, to provide a delay, or for concealment. Tampering with a toaster or bypassing the thermal cut-off (TCO) on a coffee pot placed near ordinary combustibles may initially appear as a fire of accidental origin, although a detailed examination of the device could show otherwise. This type of device usually is submitted to electrical engineers for examination, rather than a traditional forensic laboratory. Devices that may be used to provide a delay can be as simple as a cigarette in a matchbook or a candle surrounded by paper towels, or something much more complex. When materials such as these are used to set a fire, fingerprints, DNA, or other evidence may be recovered; however the investigator must rely upon to recognize the remains of a device, which may be badly damaged. More complicated devices involving timers or other mechanical or electrical components may offer additional leads. These materials may be examined for manufacturer's information, which may provide potential retail sources. Even simple device components, such as containers for ignitable liquids or bags used to conceal evidence, may provide valuable intelligence. The criminalist needs to conduct at least a brief examination of the evidence prior to conducting any other examinations. This helps to ensure that steps will be taken to avoid the loss or damage of other types of evidence that could be exploited from the submitted items.

10.5 DETAILED OBSERVATIONS

Great emphasis was placed on the necessity of an initial cursory examination of the evidence prior to beginning any analytical procedure. Often however, this initial examination is not sufficient to provide the level of detail required for proper data interpretation. As discussed in Chapter 12, the material (substrate) being analyzed will likely contribute to the resulting chromatogram. Knowledge of what the sample described as "debris" actually is provides critical information to the fire debris analyst as he or she begins the complex process of data interpretation. Prior to the extraction of residues, it was not possible to make detailed observations of the evidence without risking the loss of ignitable liquids. Once the extraction has been performed however, the residues of interest have been collected and preserved in the form of an extract, allowing for a more thorough visual inspection.

A detailed visual examination of evidence following extraction may provide important clues as to the relevance of chemical compounds found in the instrumental data. For example, the presence of a polyethylene plastic could be responsible for a homologous series of normal alkanes [17]. Softwoods such as pine will contribute terpenes to an extract—often providing a pattern indistinguishable from the natural product turpentine. Although it is not unusual to be able to easily observe some of these materials in the initial brief examination of the evidence, there are many instances in which a crucial material is not readily observed. Similarly, there are numerous materials that have been shown to contain common ignitable liquids such as adhesives used in many flooring materials [18]; the presence of this type of material within a container of debris will come into play when advising the investigator of the potential sources of the ILR identified in that sample. Figure 10-4 shows the importance of knowing the nature of the materials constituting the debris.

FIGURE 10-4a

The content of the can was spread over a white paper and observed. Particular metallic pieces were pulled aside (on the left).

These pieces revealed to be ferrules for paint brushes.

In this case, a medium petroleum distillate (MPD) was identified in the sample described as "fire debris" by the submitting agency. A thorough examination of the debris showed that there were metal bands present in the debris: the type used as a ferrule to hold the bristles of a paintbrush together and to attach them to the handle of the paintbrush. Because many paints and paint thinners contain MPDs, the presence of these materials that had been hidden in the debris was extremely important. This allowed the criminalist to offer an opinion as to the relevance of the detected MPD and to a possible source. A general knowledge of the types of interferences commonly encountered in fire debris analysis can be practically applied only when used in conjunction with specific knowledge of the particular evidence, which can be acquired only through a detailed visual examination of the debris.

Detailed observations of the evidence submitted can sometimes provide other valuable information as well. In cases in which a device was used as a means to initiate a fire, or in which containers used to transport a liquid accelerant to a scene were left behind, there may be opportunities to determine the source of those materials. This type of information may be as banal as recovering a label's fragments in order to determine the type of bottle used in a Molotov cocktail. Figure 10-5 shows an example of a case in which the remnants of a metal can was present in a debris sample. It was important for the investigator to identify this can, however it was free of any labels. A thorough examination of the debris after ILR analysis revealed pieces of labels that were partially charred and hardly readable. By simply laying out the label extremely carefully on a light table, it was possible to obtain sufficient information to identify the source of the metal can.

Other information, such as mold markings, lot numbers, bottling facility, or date-shift codes may provide sufficient information so as to narrow

FIGURE 10-5 *A/ Overall view of the label. B/ Detailed view of the manufacturer's information that is hardly readable due to the damage of the label. C/ Detailed view of the same area as in B, on the light table. More information is gained. D/ Detailed view of the description of the can on the light table.*

down where a particular device component was manufactured or marketed. This type of data can provide an investigative lead with information regarding where the items were sold at the retail level. Investigators may then seek more intelligence from potential retail outlets through interviews or sales records. This information is most helpful for items that are not mass-produced or that bear date-shift codes, which can aid in narrowing the retail outlet. This information can also be used for comparison purposes, with materials recovered from a suspect. An incident involving the use of a Molotov cocktail made with a Mountain Dew bottle, wicks from a kerosene-type heater, and chunks of candle wax resulted in the recovery of the nearly intact device, and the quick identification of a suspect. A search of the suspect's home resulted in the seizure of Mountain Dew bottles from the same lot, a package of wicks, and the same types of candles. Although this type of evidence is not conclusive by itself, other materials recovered during the

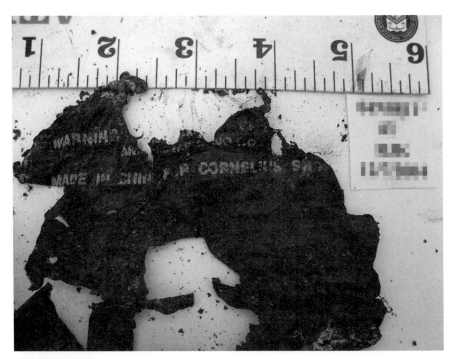

FIGURE 10-6 *Remnants of black plastic recovered from the scene of a fire set by a serial arsonist. Examination of the plastic indicated that it belongs to a thin plastic bag, most likely used to conceal the container of ignitable liquid. Discernible printing on the remains of the bag provided intelligence regarding which area stores used this type of bag, thus providing an investigative lead. (Photograph courtesy of Raymond Kuk, Bureau of Alcohol, Tobacco, Firearms and Explosives, Ammendale, Maryland, USA.)*

search warrant along with additional intelligence that had been gathered throughout the investigation provided additional circumstantial evidence.

In a series of fires that had been set in numerous residences in a major metropolitan area in the United States, the arsonist used plastic bags to conceal plastic jugs of gasoline. In these cases, examination of the bags and jugs provided several important leads. Primarily, the similarity of the construction of the devices, along with the times and locations of the fires, was sufficient to show a link among numerous fire scenes. More importantly though, intelligence obtained from the fire-setting materials provided crucial evidence to the investigation. Information discerned from the surviving remnants of the plastic bags had printing on them that provided potential sources for the bags (see Figure 10-6). In addition, the jugs used to transport the gasoline were examined and mold markings were recovered (see Figure 10-7).

Research into the mold markings provided additional information regarding the mold number, the manufacturing machine, and the manufacturing company. With this information investigators were able to determine that the plastic jugs originally contained a specific brand of fruit juice drink.

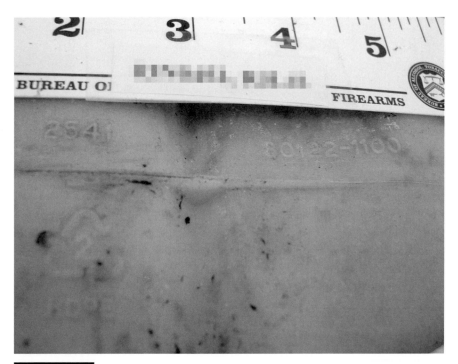

FIGURE 10-7 *The bottom of a jug recovered from the scene of a fire set by a serial arsonist. Container bottoms are generally well protected from the fire, and often survive almost completely intact. Mold markings on this container provided information about its original contents. When label fragments were recovered from a separate fire incident an additional link between the fire scenes was established, and the retail outlet at which the product was sold was identified. (Photograph courtesy of Raymond Kuk, Bureau of Alcohol, Tobacco, Firearms and Explosives, Ammendale, Maryland, USA.)*

Later in the investigation, partial labels from the plastic jugs were recovered. From markings on the labels, the original contents of the jug and the retail store chain could be identified. The investigators used this information to determine where the device components were likely purchased, resulting in surveillance of the stores frequented by the arsonist. Had the criminalist not conducted a thorough examination of the evidence, much of this information would have been lost.

A preliminary examination of evidence prior to its extraction is vital to ensure that the maximum evidentiary potential can be gained from the submitted evidence. It will guarantee that steps are taken to minimize the potential for loss of other types of valuable evidence, and will assist the forensic scientist in developing an appropriate analytical scheme for the recovery and identification of ignitable liquids. In addition, a more thorough examination following the extraction of ignitable liquids is often warranted, in order to provide additional information.

REFERENCES

1. ASTM International (2006) ASTM E 1459-92 *(reapproved 2005) Standard guide for physical evidence labeling and related documentation*, Annual Book of ASTM Standards 14.02, West Conshohocken, PA.
2. ASCLD/LAB (2005) *Accreditation manual*, American Society of Crime Laboratory Directors/Laboratory Accreditation Board, Garner, NC.
3. Fire Laboratory Standards and Protocols Committee (2003) *Quality assurance guide for the forensic analysis of ignitable liquids*, Technical and Scientific Working Group for Fire and Explosives.
4. ASCLD/LAB (2005) *Legacy accreditation manual*, American Society of Crime Laboratory Directors/Laboratory Accreditation Board, Garner, NC.
5. Saferstein R (2004) *Criminalistics: An introduction to forensic science*, 8th edition, Prentice Hall, Upper Saddle River, NJ.
6. Brun-Conti L (2007) Chemical enhancement techniques of bloodstain patterns after fire exposure, *personal communication to Julia A. Dolan*, Ammendale, MD.
7. Shelef R et al. (1996) Development of latent fingerprints from incendiary bottles, *Journal of Forensic Identification*, **46**(5), pp 556–69.
8. Spawn MA (1994) Effects of fire in fingerprint evidence, *Fingerprint Whorld*, **20**(76), pp 45–6.
9. Champod C, Lennard C, Margot P, and Stoilovic M (2004) *Fingerprints and other ridge skin impressions*, CRC Press, Boca Raton, FL.
10. Deans J and Nic Daéid N (2005) The potential for recovery of fingerprints from fire scenes, *17th Meeting of the International Association of Forensic Sciences*, Hong Kong, China.
11. Stow KM and McGurry J (2006) The recovery of finger marks from soot-covered glass fire debris, *Science & Justice*, **46**(1), pp 3–14.
12. Coquoz R (2003) *Preuve par l'ADN: la génétique au service de la justice*, Collection sciences forensiques, Presses polytechniques et universitaires romandes, Lausanne, Switzerland.
13. Sweet DJ and Sweet CHW (1995) DNA analysis of dental pulp to link incinerated remains of homicide victim to crime scene, *Journal of Forensic Sciences*, **40**(2), pp 310–14.
14. Clark BS and Graham GD (2001) Bloodstain pattern analysis after a fire: Effect of heat and flame on reconstruction and interpretation, *53rd Annual meeting of the American Academy of Forensic Sciences Annual Meeting*, Seattle, WA.
15. Ellen D (2006) *Scientific examination of documents: Methods and techniques*, 3rd edition, Taylor & Francis, Boca Raton, FL.
16. Brunelle RL (2000) *Ink analysis*. In: *Encyclopedia of forensic sciences*, editors Siegel JA, Saukko PJ, and Knupfer GC, Academic Press, London, United Kingdom, pp 591–7.
17. Stauffer E (2003) Basic concept of pyrolysis for fire debris analysts, *Science & Justice*, **43**(1), pp 29–40.
18. Lentini JJ, Dolan JA, and Cherry C (2000) The petroleum-laced background, *Journal of Forensic Sciences*, **45**(5), pp 968–89.

CHAPTER 11

Extraction of Ignitable Liquid Residues from Fire Debris

"It is a bad plan that admits of no modification."

Publilius Syrus (~100 BC)

11.1 INTRODUCTION

Ignitable liquid residues (ILR) must be in a suitable form to be analyzed by gas chromatography as described in Chapter 8. Unless a pure liquid is brought to the laboratory, ILR must first be isolated from the debris into a gaseous or liquid phase. This is achieved though the extraction process. This step, the most labor-intensive in the examination of fire debris samples, is carried out by the criminalist right after the preliminary examination of the sample.

There are several different techniques used to perform the extraction. They can be classified in four main categories (see Figure 11-1):

- Distillation
- Solvent extraction
- Headspace
- Adsorption

Each technique presents its own advantages and disadvantages. In general, only one extraction technique is performed for each sample. However, in some instances, it is possible to perform two or more. For example, simple headspace extraction, because of its nondestructiveness and simplicity, is often used as a screening technique prior to performing passive or dynamic headspace concentration extraction or solvent extraction. Some techniques are destructive and cannot be followed by any other extraction or even forensic examination. This is why the decision of which extraction technique to use for a particular sample must be made wisely.

FIGURE 11-1

The different extraction techniques used to isolate ignitable liquid residues from fire debris samples.

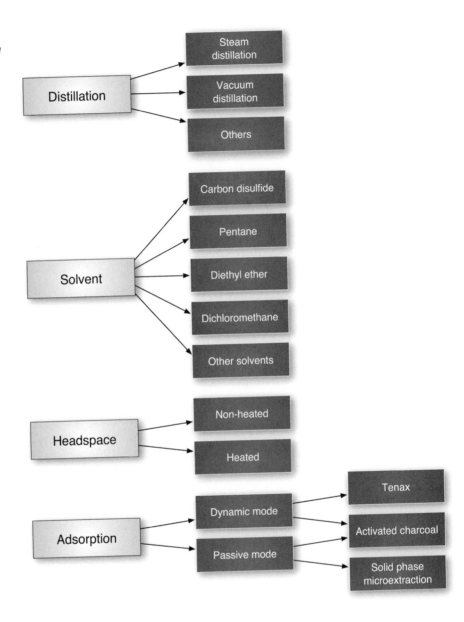

It is important to understand that some extraction techniques presented hereafter have been completely abandoned due to their obsolescence. Distillation techniques are no longer found in any modern forensic laboratories. As a matter of fact, adsorption techniques, and more particularly passive headspace extraction, represent the most commonly used techniques for extracting ILR from fire debris samples. In many instances, depending on the particulars of a sample, solvent extraction is also used. Nevertheless, it is imperative that the fire debris analyst be aware of the different techniques, regardless of their obsoletism, as part of each one's general knowledge of the field.

Each technique is described in detail in the following sections. The final section of this chapter, which starts with a comparison of the different techniques available, presents a short guide on how to choose the proper technique for a given sample.

11.2 DISTILLATION TECHNIQUES

11.2.1 Principle

Distillation was among the first extraction techniques applied to the analysis of fire debris [1]. Distillation is a physical separation based on the vaporization of the different components of the mixture to be separated. Typically, a mixture is heated, vapors are produced, separated, and then condensed back into a liquid. As a result, each component can be separately recuperated in different fractions. Distillation has already been described in Chapter 7, as it is used in the refinery industry to produce petroleum distillates from crude oil. Distillation, in its most rudimentary form, has been used for a few thousand years in the concentration of alcoholic beverages.

Figure 11-2 shows the simplest distillation laboratory set-up. The mixture to be separated is placed in a flask to which a heat source is applied. As the

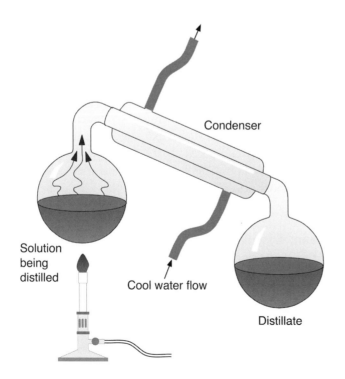

Solution
being
distilled

Cool water flow

Condenser

Distillate

FIGURE 11-2

Illustration of a regular distillation set-up. The solution to be distilled (left) is heated and its vapors go into the condenser, which is cooled by water. Vapors condense and fall into the receiving flask, thus constituting the distillate.

liquid heats, vapors are produced and rise to the distilling head, where a thermometer is often placed to monitor the temperature. As the vapors accumulate at the head, a portion of them enters the condenser, a device that is cooled (typically with cold water) and provokes their condensation. By force of gravity, the liquid then drips down to the receiving flask, which collects the distillate.

Distillation does not allow for a complete extraction of all components from a given mixture. As the total amount of a given component is distributed between its liquid and vapor phases, complete extraction is theoretically and practically impossible. Depending on the circumstances, it is possible to reach an almost complete extraction, although total purification can never be reached. However, this is not an issue in fire debris analysis as it is not a quantitative analysis, but a qualitative one.

Because most fire debris samples are solid in nature, simple distillation as shown in Figure 11-2 is neither suitable nor efficient. Additionally, the nature of the components to be isolated from the debris makes the typical temperatures used in regular distillation quite ferocious, leading to the decomposition of the substrate and any ignitable liquid residues. Thus, other types of distillation have been used successfully in fire debris analysis, such as steam distillation and vacuum distillation. They are described in the following subsections.

Today, distillation techniques are for most part obsolete. Although distillation is the only technique that can isolate a pure liquid from a sample, it is rarely, if ever, performed in modern crime laboratories. The authors do not recommend the use of steam distillation or any other distillation techniques. The only situation in which a criminalist would perform a distillation technique is if the presence of an ignitable liquid can be clearly smelled and if a pure liquid extract is desired. As a matter of fact, the obtaining of a pure liquid is the only argument in favor of the use of distillation in modern days; it brings forth quite an impressive effect to show to the jury during trial a vial with the pure liquid extracted from the sample. However, this advantage is minor compared to the fact that distillation techniques lack sensitivity and are completely destructive to the sample. In any case, these techniques must never be used with samples exhibiting low concentrations of ILR.

11.2.2 Steam Distillation

Steam distillation is a special type of distillation for which the mixture to be distilled is first placed in water, the carrier liquid. The main advantage of steam distillation is that it allows for any VOC, most of which with a boiling point above that of water, to be vaporized at a lower temperature. This is due to the fact that when two immiscible liquids are present in a mixture under constant agitation, the total vapor pressure of the mixture is equal to the sum of each liquid's vapor pressure. Thus, the distillation process is performed at a relatively low temperature (below 100°C), which prevents the decomposition of some organic compounds and the substrate by pyrolysis and allows, to some extent, for the recovery of heavy compounds such as the ones found in heavy petroleum distillates. ASTM has a standard devoted to steam distillation: ASTM standard E 1385-00 [2]. At the time of this writing, the ASTM forensic science committee E30 has decided not to vote on the renewal of this standard, which is doomed to expire anytime soon.

Vapor Pressures and Boiling Points in a Mixture of Immiscible Liquids

When two immiscible liquids are present in a mixture, the total vapor pressure of the mixture is equal to the sum of each liquid's vapor pressure, independently of their concentration, as long as there is enough of each liquid so they can both reach equilibrium. The condition to reach this state is that the mixture must be in constant agitation. If the mixture is let to rest, both liquids will form layers and the vapor pressure of the mixture will equal the vapor pressure of the liquid forming the top layer. The bottom layer will not have any vapor pressure as it is in contact with the top layer, thus preventing any evaporation. Therefore, it is necessary for both liquids to be in constant agitation to let the phenomenon of added vapor pressures to take place.

Consequently, when two immiscible liquids are in a mixture, their boiling point can be greatly decreased. For example, the boiling point (vapor pressure of 101,325 Pa at standard pressure) of water is 100°C, and the boiling point of m-xylene is 138.7°C [3]. When these two immiscible liquids are present in a mixture, their vapor pressures add up to make the total vapor pressure of the mixture. The boiling point of the mixture is still at 101,325 Pa since it is operating at standard pressure, however the temperature required to reach the boiling point is now below 100°C. As a matter of fact, at 93°C the vapor pressures of water and m-xylene are 78,494 Pa and 24,431 Pa, respectively [3, 4]. This adds up to a total vapor pressure of 102,925 Pa, sufficient for the solution to boil. This is the principle on which steam distillation operates.

Figure 11-3 is a schematic representation of the set-up used to carry out steam distillation of fire debris samples. The flask containing the debris sample mixed with water is heated until the mixture boils. Steam and vapors of ILR rise up and eventually reach the condenser. At this point, vapors condense into a liquid phase, which drips down into the receiving tube. Distillates accumulate in the tube and the liquid eventually reaches the return tube, which acts as a reflux system.

Because all VOCs of interest are immiscible in—but less dense than—water, they form a separate layer above it. As the first distillates drip in the receiving tube, a portion of both layers is diverted to the reflux tube and eventually falls back in the sample. Once enough water is present at the

Set-up used to carry out steam distillation of fire debris samples. The vapors escape the liquid and travel to the condenser where they condense and, by force of gravity, the distillate falls down to the receiving flask. The system is tweaked in a fashion that water vapors do not have time to condense and thus, escape in the air. A reflux system is in place to recycle water that would have been collected in the distillate.

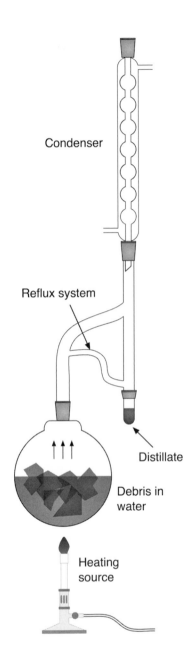

Condenser

Reflux system

Distillate

Debris in water

Heating source

bottom of the receiving tube, the separate layer of VOCs is exclusively present in the receiving tube as shown in Figure 11-4. Once the distillation process completed, it is easy to flush the water layer out and recuperate the layer formed by the VOCs.

It is important to add enough water in the flask to ensure that no further burning of the sample occurs, but not too much either so the distillation

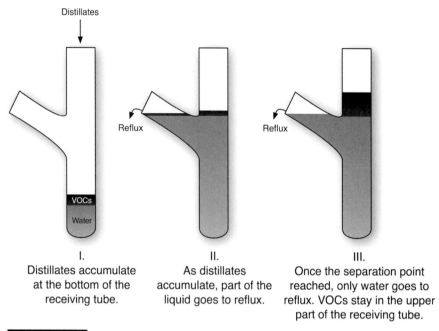

I.
Distillates accumulate
at the bottom of the
receiving tube.

II.
As distillates
accumulate, part of the
liquid goes to reflux.

III.
Once the separation point
reached, only water goes to
reflux. VOCs stay in the upper
part of the receiving tube.

FIGURE 11-4 *Principle of the accumulation of distillates in the receiving tube.*

can be carried out in an efficient manner. A good rule of thumb is to add water to cover approximately half the height of the sample. Once started, the temperature of the distillation should be carefully monitored and the rate of distillation should not be too rapid. The distillation process can take as little as half an hour to as long as a few hours. On average, a distillation takes approximately one hour. The rule of thumb is that if no separate layer is observed in the receiving tube after one hour, the distillation is probably not very successful. If that is the case, it is advised to rinse the trap (receiving tube) with a solvent and analyze the solvent extract [2]. This might save the distillation, but it surely compromises the advantage of isolating a pure liquid.

11.2.3 Vacuum Distillation

Vacuum distillation, also known as reduced-pressure distillation, is a regular distillation technique without the addition of a carrier liquid. By lowering the pressure inside the distillation chamber, the boiling points of the liquids present in the mixture are highly reduced (see Chapter 4). Thus, it is possible to evaporate components at a much lower temperature than the one required at standard pressure. This suppresses the need to heat the sample at very high temperature to isolate the compounds of interest, even heavy petroleum distillates.

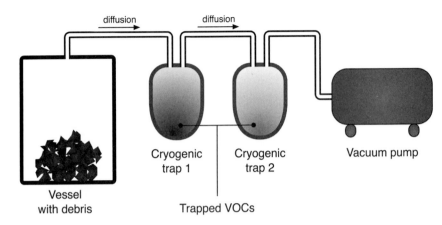

diffusion   diffusion

Cryogenic trap 1   Cryogenic trap 2   Vacuum pump

Vessel with debris   Trapped VOCs

FIGURE 11-5 *Set-up used to carry out vacuum distillation of fire debris samples.*

Vacuum distillation was used since at least the 1940s by Dr. Hnizda [5]. Farrell also described it in 1947 [6]. The main reasons it was developed was to permit large debris to be placed in the distilling vessel (which was not possible with steam distillation because of the flask's shape) and to prevent the destructiveness of regular steam distillation.

Figure 11-5 is a schematic representation of the set-up used to carry out a vacuum distillation of fire debris samples. The sample is placed in a solid vessel connected to the vacuum tubing. The vacuum tubing is then connected to a first cryogenic trap, to a second cryogenic trap, and finally to the vacuum pump. Cryogenic traps are cooled using saline ice, dry ice, or even liquid nitrogen. The vessel does not need to be heated, however if a more rapid distillation or the distillation of heavier compounds is desired, it is possible to heat the vessel. In such instances, the use of infrared lamps has been recommended. Hrynchuk et al. presented a technique in which the vessel was placed inside an oven, which in turn was heated to 100° to 200°C [7].

Once the extraction started, the vacuum pump creates a reduced pressure in the vessel containing the fire debris, resulting in an evaporation of most VOCs present in the sample. The vapors then diffuse throughout the system and a portion of them eventually reaches the first trap, where they condense. A second trap is also placed in line with the vacuum tubing to catch any vapors that would not have condensed in the first one. A third trap can be used if necessary. One of the problems that may arise during the distillation process is the accumulation of water in the traps, which might clog them and compromise the vacuum. After a certain time, components (in liquid or even solid state) start to accumulate in the traps. The vacuum pump is stopped and the distillates can be recuperated from the traps (after reaching room temperature again) either as pure liquid or by rinsing with a solvent.

This technique is a very particular application of distillation that somehow resembles a dynamic headspace extraction concentration (described in Subsection 11.5.3). However, there are two main elements that radically differentiate the two techniques:

I. Even though it operates under reduced pressure, there is no draft of atmosphere in vacuum distillation contrary to dynamic headspace where a draft is created to force the headspace through a tube. In this aspect, vacuum distillation relies solely on the diffusion of molecules throughout the apparatus' volume, as the air throughout the system is quasi still.

II. Vacuum distillation does not use any adsorbent to trap VOCs; it relies solely on their condensation in locations where the temperature has been lowered.

11.2.4 Other Distillations

Other types of distillations using a mixture of ethanol and water or pure ethylene glycol in lieu of pure water were first described in the literature by Macoun in 1952 and Brackett in 1955, respectively [8, 9]. In order to benefit from the maximum of the added vapor pressure phenomenon, the carrier liquid must be completely immiscible in the liquid to be extracted and must boil at the highest practicable temperature. Thus, ethylene glycol appears to be a logical choice at first; it is insoluble in most hydrocarbons and its boiling point (196.9°C) is much higher than the one of water [3].

A/ Ethylene Glycol

Brackett recommends the use of water as the carrier liquid if low boiling point compounds are suspected and ethylene glycol with high boiling point compounds [9]. He demonstrated that the rate and efficiency of recovery of ignitable liquids such as kerosene and diesel fuel are highly increased with ethylene glycol when compared to water. For example, he was able to recover 98% of a given amount of kerosene in 30 minutes with ethylene glycol, whereas it took 270 minutes to recover only 89% with water [9]. Woycheshin and DeHaan compared all four distillation techniques (water, ethylene glycol, ethanol:water, and vacuum) and determined that ethylene glycol offered the best recovery efficiency, however they also demonstrated that it had the worst contamination issues and that the clean-up process was more difficult than with regular steam distillation [10].

B/ Ethanol: Water Mixture

Macoun describes the distillation using the ethanol:water mixture as giving more satisfactory results than regular steam distillation [8]. This is not the opinion of Woycheshin and DeHaan, who demonstrated that the ethanol:water distillation yielded the worst recovery of ILR [10]. Macoun's description of the ethanol:water distillation also involves quite complicated and time-consuming operations to be performed on the sample prior to distillation and on the distillates after the distillation, before being able to recuperate the hydrocarbon layer [8].

11.2.5 Contamination

As with any other extraction techniques, it is crucial to ensure that no contamination is present in the system and the carrier liquid(s) used throughout the distillation process. The apparatus must be very thoroughly cleaned prior to its use. ASTM standard E 1385 recommends cleaning the apparatus using a strong detergent in hot water, followed by an acetone rinse, and a final rinse with hot water [2]. Vacuum distillation apparatus can be cleaned in the same fashion. Finally, when using a carrier liquid such as water, ethanol, or ethylene glycol, this liquid must be first tested to ensure its purity. It is recommended that the liquid is evaporated before testing it to estimate its contamination potential in the worst-case scenario. Subsection 11.3.4 addresses this issue.

11.2.6 Advantages and Drawbacks

The main advantage of all distillation techniques is the obtaining of a neat liquid from the fire debris sample. Unfortunately, this is the only real advantage to using such techniques.

One of the main disadvantages of distillation with a carrier liquid lies in its destructiveness. By placing the sample in water and boiling it for approximately one hour, it is completely altered and no other subsequent examinations can be conducted. Other major disadvantages include the potential for contamination when exposing the sample to a carrier liquid and the lack of convenience when placing the sample in the flask; in most instances, it is necessary to break the sample in smaller parts, which adds up to the destructiveness of the operation.

The use of vacuum distillation remediates the destructiveness of the process because there is no carrier liquid involved and the distillation vessel is much bigger, allowing for larger debris to be placed in it.

Distillation techniques are also very labor-intensive and require a significant amount of time to carry out. They all necessitate constant monitoring and adjustment, otherwise the process can quickly become compromised

This is particularly true for vacuum distillation, which is also highly subject to the loss of the most volatile components. Nevertheless, cleaning-up procedures must be carried out in a very tedious fashion and can be quite time-consuming.

Finally, while there are important variations in the efficiency of the extraction depending on the distillation technique and the nature of the ignitable liquid residues, the general recovery efficiency is quite poor when compared to the other extraction techniques described in the following subsections.

11.3 SOLVENT EXTRACTION TECHNIQUES

11.3.1 Principle

Solvent extraction is a simple method that consists of extracting the debris with solvent in the hope that any ILR present in the debris will flush out in the solvent. It has been in used in fire debris analysis from very early on. Today, solvent extraction is still widely used in crime laboratories and the ASTM standard E 1386 is devoted to it [11].

A solvent is defined as a [12]: "substance that dissolves other material(s) to form solution." When a sample is placed in a solvent, a distribution of the analytes of interest (ignitable liquid residues) occurs between the substrate onto which they are adsorbed and the solvent where they are in solution. This distribution occurs based on the partition or distribution coefficient, which is mostly dependent on the substrate, the solvent, and the nature of the analytes. The criminalist typically does not decide which debris is collected at the fire scene and forwarded to the laboratory, so the substrate is a parameter that cannot be chosen but only taken into account. The nature of the ILR usually remains unknown prior to the analysis, and whereas most ILR are petroleum-based compounds, there is always a small fraction of debris received at the laboratory that contain alcohols or other oxygenated compounds. Thus, it is not a parameter that can be chosen. As a consequence, the forensic scientist is left with the choice of the solvent to use. An appropriate solvent should exhibit the following characteristics:

- Low boiling point
- No chemical interference (dissolution, etc.) with the substrate and the ILR
- Not a potential ignitable liquid used by an arsonist
- Great capability in extracting ILR
- Low tendency to extract interfering products present in the substrate
- No interference with subsequent analysis
- Free of contamination
- Safe and easy to handle
- Inexpensive

More About Solvents

A solvent is a liquid that dissolves a solid, a liquid, or a gas. The resulting mixture is called a solution. When dealing with a solution, the solvent is the component present at the greatest amount. The other components of the mixture are called solutes. The most common solvent is water.

Solvents usually are characterized based on their polarity, solubility, boiling point, melting point, density, and chemical interaction. When dealing with solvents, it is typical to classify them as polar or nonpolar and aqueous or nonaqueous. Solvents also often are referred to as organic when the solvent is composed of an organic molecule. Nevertheless, it is important to remember that many organic solvents are actually soluble in water. In general, polar solvents are miscible in water and nonpolar solvents are not.

Unfortunately, the perfect solvent that would fulfill all these characteristics does not exist. It is important to use a solvent with high extraction efficiency, as this determines the sensitivity of the technique. In fire debris analysis, it is common to consider nonpolar liquids as solvents. The reason lies in the fact that most ILR are nonpolar in nature, or of very limited polarity. Therefore, nonpolar solvents offer the greatest partition coefficient, meaning that the distribution of ILR between the solvent and the substrate is to the advantage of the solvent. The only exception to this rule is the situation in which a more polar ignitable liquid is present in the sample such as ethanol or acetone. In such instance, it is wise to choose a solvent with a higher polarity. This is one of the reasons why it is essential for the criminalist to have knowledge of the circumstances around the collection of the fire debris samples and to be made aware of any possible suspicion regarding the use of an ignitable liquid. Also, the preliminary examination of the debris may bring some clues as to the type of ignitable liquid present and should be integrated in the decision-making process.

Consequently, polarity is an important, if not the most important, characteristic in the choice of the proper solvent to isolate ILR from fire debris samples. Polarity is defined as [12]: "the ability to form two opposite centers in the molecule." In other terms, polarity is used to describe a solvent's dissolving power. Molecules that present a certain symmetry, such as n-alkanes or simple aromatics (benzene, toluene) have almost no dipole moment, and therefore are considered nonpolar or weakly polar. The rule of "like dissolves like" applies here, too. A nonpolar solvent preferentially attracts a nonpolar solute compared to a polar solute.

One of the most convenient manners of classifying solvents based on their polarity is the use of Snyder's polarity indices, p' [13]. Table 11-1 shows some solvents along with their polarity index, boiling point, and solubility in water.

Table 11-1	Some solvents and their characteristics. The solvents in grey are recommended for solvent extraction of fire debris samples. Other solvents are presented for informational purpose only. polarity indices are from [13]. Boiling points have been obtained from [3] and have been rounded up to the next digit. Solubility in water is expressed in %/mass and is measured at 25°C [3]

Solvent	Formula	Polarity Index p'	Boiling Point [°C]	Solubility in water [%]
n-Pentane	C_5H_{12}	0.0	36	0.0041
n-Hexane	C_6H_{14}	0.0	69	0.0011
Cyclohexane	C_6H_{12}	0.0	81	0.0058
Carbon disulfide	CS_2	1.0	46	0.210
Carbon tetrachloride	CCl_4	1.7	77	0.065
Toluene	C_7H_8	2.3	111	0.0531
Diethyl ether	$C_2H_5OC_2H_5$	2.9	35	6.04
Benzene	C_6H_6	3.0	80	0.178
Methylene chloride	CH_2Cl_2	3.4	40	1.73
Acetone	CH_3COCH_3	5.1	56	100
Ethanol	C_2H_5OH	5.2	78	100
Methanol	CH_3OH	6.6	65	100
Water	H_2O	9.0	100	—

Snyder's Polarity Index

The Snyder's polarity index (p') is a measure of the ability of the solvent to interact with various polar test solutes. Snyder actually classified solvents based on their ability to act as proton acceptor, proton donor, and dipole-dipole. In order to estimate their ability for each of these phenomena, he used the solutes ethanol (proton donor), dioxane (proton acceptor), and nitromethane (strong dipole), respectively. Proton acceptor solvents interact strongly with ethanol, proton donor solvents with dioxane, and solvents with strong dipole with nitromethane. He used the solubility measurements (adjusted with the partition coefficient) for a given solvent with each of the three reference solutes and obtained the polarity indices. Finally, he used hexane as a baseline (p' = 0).

11.3.2 Choice of the Solvent

In practice, several different solvents may be used to carry out a solvent extraction of fire debris. The goal is to use a relatively nonpolar solvent (except when in presence of alcohols and other oxygenated compounds for which some polarity is desired) that does not dissolve the substrate and that evaporates very easily. Of course, it helps if the solvent is safe to handle and inexpensive to purchase. The most commonly used solvents are n-pentane

(C_5H_{12}), n-hexane (C_6H_{14}), and carbon disulfide (CS_2). The authors recommend the use of one of these three solvents. Carbon disulfide is a quite efficient solvent, however it is not only very toxic but it also exhibits a very low autoignition temperature $(100°C)$, thus making it dangerous even around boiling water. Pentane and hexane still present some dangers, but are quite safer to handle than carbon disulfide.

When dealing with a sample suspected of containing light oxygenated compounds, it is not recommended to perform a solvent extraction. However, if the sample contains a heavier oxygenated compound, methanol (CH_3OH) or diethyl ether $(C_2H_5OC_2H_5)$ are solvents of choice. However, due to its low polarity methanol is not as efficient if hydrocarbon compounds are present in the debris. If oxygenated compounds are suspected of being present along with hydrocarbons, diethyl ether offers a better compromise. However, coelution issues may arise during the analysis. Finally, if the sample is suspected to contain glycols, it is recommended to use water and, after concentration of the water, to perform a liquid-liquid extraction with diethyl ether.

Other solvents are used or have been used depending on the circumstances. Carbon tetrachloride (CCl_4) has been used extensively in the past, however it is highly poisonous by inhalation, ingestion, or even skin adsorption, which resulted in the fact that it is no longer used in crime laboratories. Diethyl ether is also used on a more sporadic basis. It is convenient as it exhibits a low boiling point, however it is very flammable and slightly polar, thus less efficient on alkanes and other nonpolar molecules. Also, it is slightly soluble in water, which might be inconvenient with wet samples. Acetone (CH_3COCH_3) also has been used, however its polarity is much higher. Additionally, acetone might possibly be a solvent used by an arsonist, thus its use should be avoided. It is also not recommended to use methylene chloride (CH_2Cl_2) as it has the tendency to dissolve many plastics and to extract significant interfering products. ASTM standard practice E 1386 recommends the use of [11] "a suitable solvent, such as carbon disulfide, pentane, petroleum ether, or diethyl ether."

11.3.3 Application

The application of solvent extraction to fire debris samples is a procedure that is achieved in three steps: extraction, filtration, and concentration.

A/ Extraction

First, one must decide if the whole debris will be extracted, or just a portion of it. ASTM standard E 1386 specifies [14]: "If possible, select a representative portion of the sample to extract." However, most samples are not homogeneous and it is nearly impossible to select a representative sample. As such, the criminalist must choose between the whole sample, at which point the problem of the representative sample no longer applies, or a portion of it, at which point something may be missed in the analysis.

Then, a given amount of solvent is introduced in the selected debris and the mixture is agitated for a given time. It is important to choose the amount of solvent wisely. There should be enough solvent to cover a major portion of the debris and to extract sufficient ILR. Conversely, the more solvent used, the more concentration will be necessary and the more light compounds may be lost. If the criminalist wants to extract as much ILR from the sample as possible, it is better to proceed to two consecutive solvent extractions with two small amounts of solvent rather than one extraction using a large one. In general, the solvent does not need to be in contact with the debris for more than a few minutes.

When dealing with nonporous surfaces such as the surface exhibited by a metal plate or the inside of a broken glass bottle from a Molotov cocktail, it is possible to proceed to the rinsing of the surface without soaking the whole item in the solvent. For this purpose, the surface is placed over a beaker and a pipette is used to spray the solvent over the surface until it drips back in the beaker. This process should be repeated about a dozen times at the minimum. The analyst must be careful that the solvent does not evaporate prematurely.

When soaking the debris in the solvent, it is possible to squeeze and release, like in a sponging action, the debris in the solvent several times. This is particularly adapted to cloth materials. A clean rod or beaker can be used to that effect. When removing the solvent from the debris, it is recommended to squeeze the solvent out of the debris as much as possible.

B/ Filtration

Once the solvent is removed from the debris, when necessary, it is filtered as it may contain many impurities detrimental to the subsequent analysis (see Figure 11-6). It is important to remove fine particles as much as possible and as early as possible in order to prevent them from being injected in the GC with the extract at the time of the analysis.

A simple paper filter offers a relatively good manner of filtrating the solvent. When using a paper filter, it is imperative to ensure that the filter itself does not contain any hydrocarbons or other organic compounds that might be extracted by the solvent, subsequently contaminating the extract (see later). Whatman paper filters have always been, in the experience of the authors, very efficient without bringing any contamination. In some instances, too many particles are present in the extract and may clog the filter, leading to a very long and tedious filtration process. When confronted with this scenario, it is also possible to centrifuge the extract and then filtrate the solvent without including the heavy debris.

FIGURE 11-6 *Particles can be present in the solvent both floating and sunken. It is crucial to remove them prior to GC-MS analysis.*

If centrifugation is not feasible because the extract is too large, it is also possible to let the extract rest for several minutes or hours until the sediments settle at the bottom. At that point, the solvent can be decanted very carefully so as not to disturb the particles at the bottom. If such a practice is chosen, it is crucial to keep the extract container closed to prevent the early evaporation of the solvent and any light solute. Alternatively, it is also possible to pass the solvent through a filter, thus separating it from the sediments.

C/ Concentration

Once the extract is free of any undesirable particles, it must be concentrated (if necessary). The concentration of the extract consists of the evaporation of the solvent, with as little as possible evaporation of the ILR it potentially contains. There are several manners to conduct this evaporation. Heating the sample is the fastest one, but it is not recommended. As a matter of fact, the faster the evaporation, the more likely compounds of interest will

Purified N$_2$

Pasteur pipette

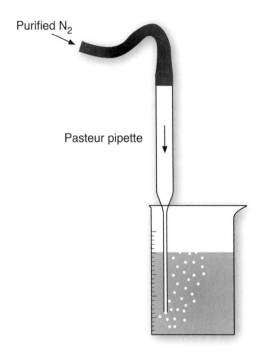

FIGURE 11-7
To concentrate the solvent after filtration, it is possible to subject the solution to a bubble bath of pure nitrogen. This is achieved easily with a Pasteur pipette as shown here. It may be pertinent to place a charcoal trap between the nitrogen tank and the Pasteur pipette if one is not fully sure of the purity of the nitrogen.

evaporate too, particularly light ones. The goal is to perform the evaporation as gently as possible. One simple solution is to leave the extract container under the hood and regularly monitor the progress of the concentration. Another solution consists of running a bubbling gas through the extract (see Figure 11-7). Any inert gas or, more simply, air, is useful to achieve this purpose. However, the criminalist must ensure that the gas is completely free of any contamination. This might require the use of analytical grade gases and filters. The flow rate of the gas must be kept at a minimum: just enough to create bubbles throughout the solvent, but not to create a significant disturbance of the solvent and oversplashing.

The concentration of the extract should reduce the solvent's volume down to 1 to 2 ml. It is important to remember that the sensitivity of the technique is dependent on the final concentration of the extract. However, concentrating the extract from 2 to 1 ml only doubles (without taking into account losses) the concentration of the solutes in the solvent, whereas concentrating from 200 to 2 ml increases their concentration by 100-fold. Thus, the last leg of the concentration process (less than two ml) is not very important compared to the preceding ones. Furthermore, as the solvent quantity diminishes, more analytes evaporate too, particularly light ones. Thus, it is not worth forcing the evaporation to concentrate as much as possible. Anything below 2 ml is fine.

The criminalist should also keep in mind that in some instances it is possible that more than 2 ml of ILR were actually present in the sample and are thus recuperated. In this case, trying to evaporate the extract below that volume would just eliminate more ILR rather than solvent, as the latter had already completely evaporated. This is one of the reasons why it is essential to monitor the evaporation process and pay attention to the color of the extract and its viscosity. If the analyst observes that the color and/or viscosity of the extract is radically changing during the evaporation process and is completely outside the norm of the blank, the evaporation should be stopped and the GC analysis should be carried out at this stage. If no satisfactory results are obtained, it is always possible to continue the concentration. However, the opposite is not possible.

11.3.4 Contamination

The issue of potential contamination of the solvent is very important and must be addressed prior to the extraction of the sample. Solvents used in this process must be of analytical grade and must be verified through the analysis of a blank. Unfortunately, it is not enough to simply inject a blank solvent in the GC and check the baseline for interfering analytes.

As a matter of fact, the blank must undergo the same process as the solvent that will be used in the extraction of the debris. More particularly, the blank must undergo the greatest possible concentration phase that the solvent may undergo. Thus, prior to using a solvent for the extraction, it is important to concentrate a given amount of solvent, after passing it through the filter, so the filter can also be checked at the same time. In any instances, the type of filter used to filtrate solutions must be checked. ASTM standard E 1386 recommends to [11]: "check solvent purity by evaporating to at least twice the extent used in the analysis. . . ." As a general practice, it is very common to use 200 to 500 ml of solvent to extract debris and to concentrate the solution down to 1 to 2 ml. Thus, the authors recommend concentrating the solvent at a ratio of 1,000 to 1 to check for impurities. This does not need to be carried out with each new bottle of solvent; the quality checks performed by reliable chemical companies are pretty thorough. However, this procedure must be carried out every time a new type or brand of solvent is used. It is also recommended that a contemporaneous blank be prepared along with the sample extract to ensure the quality of all materials used in the extraction process.

Additionally, if a gas is used to evaporate the extract, it must also be checked for impurities. This is performed through the production of a blank solvent that undergoes the same evaporation through bubbling than a regular sample. The analyst should perform the contamination check of all three sources (solvent, filter, and gas) at once in order to save time. However, if contaminations are detected in the blank, then it might be necessary to perform these steps separately to identify the source of the contamination and remediate to the problem.

11.3.5 Advantages and Drawbacks

Solvent extraction is a relatively fast and easy technique that requires a slightly more labor-intensive handling of the sample than with simple headspace or passive headspace concentration, but that is more convenient than other extraction techniques. This technique presents a few advantages that render it very useful in some instances:

- It allows for the extraction of compounds from substrates exhibiting strong competitive adsorption and that tend to retain much ILR when subjected to headspace or adsorption techniques.
- It produces an extract not skewed by differences in vapor pressure between the different components (light v. heavy).
- It allows for a much better extraction of heavy components such as the ones present in diesel fuel and other heavy petroleum distillates.

Without entering in one of these three categories, solvent extraction can also be used on very small and clean samples. If a nonporous surface must be checked for ILR, solvent extraction is also the technique of choice as described earlier.

By opposition, solvent extraction presents several serious drawbacks that must be taken into consideration:

- It is destructive. A solvent—sometimes a potential ignitable liquid used by an arsonist—is added to the sample, which could lead to contamination and the failure to identify an ILR.
- Depending on the solvent used, it may create by-products by reacting with the substrate. This is one of the reasons why the use of dichloromethane should be avoided.
- There is a great risk that the low boiling point components of an ILR may be lost during the concentration of the extract. Though this technique provides a great recovery of high boiling point components, it may result in very poor recovery of low boiling point components.
- The efficiency of the procedure, in terms of proportion of ILR recovered, is under controversy. Some literature describes it as a very sensitive method, capable of recovering quantities less than one microliter. In contrast, some literature shows poor sensitivity.

11.4 HEADSPACE TECHNIQUE

11.4.1 Principle

Extracting ignitable liquid residues using a headspace technique is the simplest, fastest, and most convenient manner of doing so. As its name implies, a headspace extraction deals with the components contained in the headspace above the sample rather than the components directly adsorbed onto the substrate. In this regard, the technique relies on the vapor pressure properties of the different components. As seen in Chapter 4, every molecule has a vapor pressure; that is, a certain amount of the liquid molecules vaporizing into the atmosphere above the liquid until equilibrium is reached. As a result, when placing some debris in a closed container, a portion of each ILR component goes into the atmosphere (headspace) until a certain concentration, dependent on the vapor pressure, is reached.

The principle behind headspace extraction is the isolation of this headspace—somehow representative of the ILR present in the sample—rather than the isolation of the components directly adsorbed onto the sample. Because the components in the headspace are not present in the same relative proportions than the ones adsorbed onto the substrate, the analytical results may be significantly skewed, compared to what the ILR content really is, which may lead to an erroneous interpretation of the results. So, the headspace of a sample does not typically depict exactly what is in the sample. As a matter of fact, light components are overrepresented in the headspace compared to the adsorbed ones whereas heavy components are underrepresented. This principle was shown in Figure 4-19: whereas decane is in much higher proportion in the liquid phase (2.33 times more decane than benzene), because its vapor pressure is much lower (as an example its boiling point is 174°C versus 80°C for benzene), it is underrepresented in the headspace. As a result, in that example, benzene is 33.4 times more abundant in the headspace than decane. Thus, one must be very careful when extracting samples with simple headspace and should integrate these parameters in the interpretation of the results. The temperature at which the container is heated during the extraction greatly influences the proportion of the different components in the headspace.

Headspace has been successfully used for more than 30 years in fire debris analysis. Ettling and Adams were the first ones to apply this technique to the extraction of debris [15]. It requires very little apparatus: a syringe and possibly a heating mantel or oven. As it is completely nondestructive and very rapidly carried out, it often is used as a screening tool for a preliminary analysis of the debris, thus allowing the criminalist to choose the most suitable technique and the appropriate parameters. ASTM standard E 1388 is devoted to the headspace extraction of fire debris samples [14].

11.4.2 Application

The simple headspace extraction consists of using a syringe to withdraw a small volume of a fire debris container's headspace and directly injecting that volume into a gas chromatograph. The extraction procedure is performed in three steps: heating, withdrawal, and injection.

A/ Heating

The extraction by simple headspace is highly dependent on the temperature of the sample as it directly relies on the vapor pressure of the components inside the container. Thus, it is important to heat the sample in order to increase the concentration of the analytes of interest in the headspace. In order to do so, the container can be placed in an oven or in a heating mantle. The container should never be heated above 100°C as water vaporizes, which may create some problems. Ideal temperatures are in the range of 60 to 90°C. Once the sample is placed in the oven or in the mantle, it is important to let it equilibrate for a certain time, as the temperature does not increase rapidly inside the sample. Finally, the syringe should also be heated at the same temperature, so the volatiles do not condens in the syringe body when the headspace is drawn. However, some practitioners do not recommend heating the plunger, as the small Teflon head might get damaged. Naturally, it is possible to perform the simple headspace analysis at room temperature, however the resulting chromatograms will be significantly skewed (see Section 11.6).

Prior to heating, care will be taken to prepare a hole in the container for the insertion of the syringe during step B. Unless using bags—for which the syringe can perform the puncture directly—syringes are not designed to puncture metal lids. Thus, a hole is predrilled or punched with a screwdriver or other pointed objects and plugged with a septum or a piece of tape.

B/ Withdrawal

Once the sample has reached the right temperature, it is time to proceed to the withdrawal of the headspace (see Figure 11-8). Attention will be place on the necessity to use a syringe designed to handle gases as opposed to liquids. Typically, the 10-µl syringe used to inject liquid samples in the GC is not airtight (see Figure 11-9). The syringe is placed inside the container by puncturing the septum or the piece of tape. At this point, the entire volume of the syringe is pulled in and out three to four times, then the proper volume is withdrawn.

It is important not to extract too much volume. When estimating the volume that must be withdrawn, one must take into account the volume of the liner in the injector port of the GC (see Chapter 8). It is not a good practice to inject a volume greater than the liner's capacity because it might result in overpressure in the injector and subsequently poor chromatography. Generally, a volume between 0.5 and 1 ml is sufficient.

C/ Injection

Once the proper volume is drawn into the syringe, this one is extremely rapidly extracted from the container and placed inside the injection port of the GC. It is important to proceed to this step as quickly as possible. The analytes inside the syringe eventually escape if the transfer is not rapid enough. The transfer from the container to the injector should not take more than a couple of seconds. For this reason, it is necessary to proceed to step B with the container next to the GC.

FIGURE 11-8

Principle of simple headspace extraction. The debris is heated and the headspace is withdrawn with an airtight syringe.

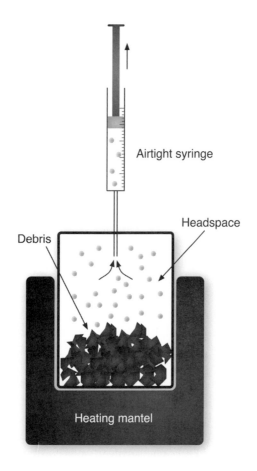

FIGURE 11-9 *With simple headspace, it is necessary to use an airtight syringe. The top syringe is not airtight, it is a 10-µl syringe used to inject liquids into the GC. The bottom one is a 5-ml airtight syringe as distinguished by its Teflon piston head.*

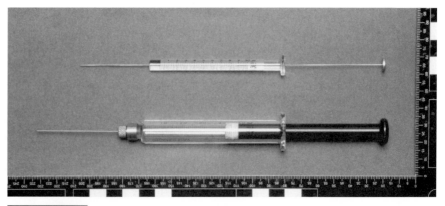

11.4.3 Contamination

The problem of contamination with a simple headspace extraction is extremely limited. It is crucial to ensure that the syringe is not contaminated, but the risk is very limited as it is used to withdraw only vapors and not liquids. By heating the syringe in the oven with the sample, any remnants of vapors would be driven off. A blank sample should be injected prior to any casework sample. For that purpose, the syringe is simply utilized to draw a certain volume of lab air and to inject it in the GC.

As the simple headspace extraction uses the original container, the criminalist does not have to worry about the cleaning of new beakers or other containers. The only tool that must be contamination-free is the object used to punch a hole in the can's lid or the glass canning jar's lid. Finally, if a septum or tape is used to clog the hole, it is important to check for their possible contribution to the chromatogram. This is readily achieved by withdrawing a headspace sample from a blank container that underwent the same preparatory process as the evidence container.

11.4.4 Advantages and Drawbacks

One of the main advantages behind the use of simple headspace lies in its nondestructive nature. This technique does not modify the sample in any fashion and subsequent extractions or other forensic examinations can be performed on the sample afterward. It is also a rapid method that requires little laboratory work. For these two reasons, simple headspace extraction is still often used in some crime laboratories as a screening technique. This technique is also excellent for low boiling compounds such as light oxygenated products or light petroleum distillate. The fact that it is a solvent-free technique makes it extremely suitable for such ILR.

The two main drawbacks with the simple headspace extraction are its poor recovery of heavy compounds and its overall low sensitivity. Skewing of the chromatograms can be quite significant when dealing with heavy compounds and this technique is not suitable to identify such ILR. In addition, the sensitivity of the technique is quite low, usually samples containing less than 10µl of ignitable liquid (in laboratory experiments) do not produce positive results. The reason lies in the fact that there is no concentration of the extract: Only a fraction of the headspace is analyzed.

11.5 ADSORPTION TECHNIQUES

11.5.1 Principle

The principle behind the extraction of ILR from fire debris by adsorption lies in the concentration of vapors on a material having good affinity for the analytes of interest. This material is called adsorbent. Adsorption techniques are actually particular headspace techniques for which the ILR present in the headspace get trapped, and therefore, concentrated, onto the adsorbent.

There are two main modes used in the application of adsorption techniques: passive and dynamic. For each of these two modes, several variations have been developed for the analysis of fire debris samples as shown in Figure 11-10.

In passive mode, the adsorbent is placed in the headspace and subjected to the diffusion of the vapors within the headspace. Thus, the proportion of compounds adsorbed on the adsorbent increases until equilibrium between the adsorbent, the headspace, and the sample's substrate is reached.

In dynamic mode, the headspace above the sample constantly is drawn through the adsorbent. In this fashion, the equilibrium state is never reached. ILR adsorbed on the substrates evaporate in the headspace, which is pumped or pushed out, thus diminishing their concentration. In turn, more molecules adsorbed on the substrate evaporate to compensate for the diminishing concentration in the headspace. After a given time, a quasi-

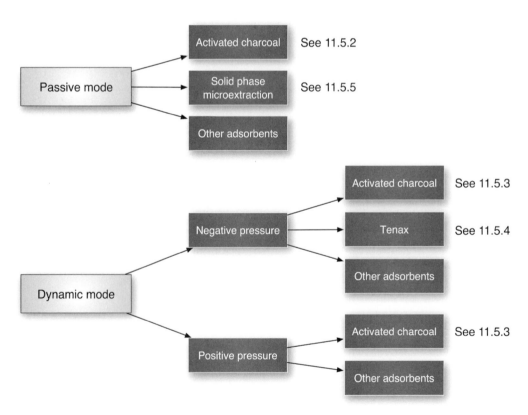

FIGURE 11-10 *The different adsorption techniques used in fire debris analysis.*

Table 11-2	*The different parameters common to all adsorption techniques*		
Adsorbent	**Adsorption**	**Sample**	**Desorption**
Type	Temperature	Competitive adsorption	Type
Number of sites	Time	Amount of ILR	
	Headspace volume	Presence of water	

complete extraction of the ILR adsorbed on the substrate is achieved. Dynamic headspace techniques, although requiring a much more complex apparatus and being quite labor-intensive, offer the best sensitivity of all extraction techniques. Conversely, they are known as destructive techniques as they typically lead to a complete removal of any ILR present in the sample.

There are several parameters influencing the recovery of ILR through adsorption that are common to all variations of the technique. These are relative to the type of adsorbent, the adsorption process, the sample, and the desorption process. Table 11-2 shows these parameters and the following paragraphs describe each of them. It is important to understand that other parameters specific to each type of variation exist. They will be addressed in their respective paragraphs.

A/ Adsorbent Type

The type of adsorbent is probably the most important parameter. It is crucial to use an adsorbent having a great affinity for the types of components found in ignitable liquids, which are mostly nonpolar, as seen in Chapter 7. The most commonly used adsorbent is activated charcoal. In the particular application of (negative pressure) dynamic headspace, Tenax is the adsorbent of choice. In the past, other adsorbents also have been tried in fire debris analysis, however none equaled the affinity exhibited by activated charcoal for ILR. More recently, with the advances in solid phase micro extraction (SPME), other types of adsorbents are used; however, this remains a marginal encounter in fire debris analysis. Each adsorbent type is discussed in their respective subsections.

B/ Number of Adsorption Sites

Because the goal of the adsorption extraction is to collect as many analytes as possible, it is critical that the greatest number of adsorption sites be available. The more adsorption sites, the more analytes are collected on the adsorbent. The number of adsorption sites can be optimized through the manufacturing of adsorption media and the amount used. This is addressed for each adsorbent type in the following subsections.

C/ Extraction Temperature

The temperature of the extraction has a direct influence on the amount of analytes recovered in the adsorbent. The reason lies in the fact that the concentration of the analytes in the headspace increases with the temperature. This concept was introduced in Chapter 4: As the temperature increases, so does the vapor pressure of each compound. Thus, the extraction is more efficient at higher temperatures. Conversely, the higher the temperature, the more undesirable analytes (interfering products) are released from the substrate. Thus, there is a range of temperatures within which the most efficient extraction is carried out. This temperature range is not as dependent on the type of adsorbent used than on the nature of ILR and substrates to be extracted.

D/ Extraction Time

As seen in Chapter 4, the phenomenon of vapor pressure results in constant molecular activity. Once equilibrium is reached, the rate of evaporation of molecules from the substrate (or liquid) to the headspace is equal to the rate of condensation or adsorption of molecules from the headspace to the substrate (or liquid). The same phenomenon occurs with the adsorbent placed inside the headspace to collect ILR. The only difference is that the adsorption media has a greater affinity for these molecules than the sample's substrate. Thus, it is important to leave the adsorbent inside the headspace long enough for equilibrium to be reached. Other phenomena such as displacement and overload also occur and must be taken into consideration. They are discussed for each technique in the following subsections.

E/ Headspace Volume

Although the exact headspace volume is far from critical, it is important to have a minimum amount of headspace. If no volume is available, the transfer of ILR from the substrate to the adsorption medium is severely hampered.

F/ Competitive Adsorption

Competitive adsorption from the substrate is a very important phenomenon that may greatly influence the recovery of ILR. Most substrates are burned and therefore, contain many active adsorption sites retaining potential analytes. Once an adsorption medium is inserted in the headspace and the extraction process started, analytes go from the substrate to the headspace and from the headspace to the adsorption medium. These transfers are all controlled by equilibrium between the different phases. Obviously, the competitive adsorption depends exclusively on the substrate, mostly its composition and its degree of burn. This parameter is completely uncontrolled by the criminalist. However, through the use of an internal standard, the criminalist can estimate the influence of this phenomenon and ultimately have recourse to other extraction techniques, such as solvent extraction, in order to recover ILR.

G/ Amount of ILR

The amount of ILR present in the substrate also influences the outcome of the extraction, mostly through the phenomena of displacement and overload of the adsorption medium [16]. This usually results in some skewing of the chromatogram toward one of the ends, the light or the heavy one, depending on other parameters (as discussed later).

H/ Presence of Water

If a small amount of humidity is present in the sample, and more particularly in the headspace, it should not influence too greatly the capacity of the adsorption medium to fulfill its purpose. However, if an important level of humidity is present, it may influence the efficiency of the extraction by decreasing the amount of analytes of interest adsorbed onto the medium. Nevertheless, this greatly depends on the type of adsorption medium. For example, charcoal is very slightly influenced because of its strong affinity for nonpolar compounds.

I/ Desorption Type

Two desorption techniques are available: thermal and solvent. Thermal desorption is ideal in the sense that it is a solvent-free technique. This greatly simplifies the chromatogram and allows the criminalist to scan for all types of liquids. When using thermal desorption, the only important parameter to consider is the temperature at which the desorption is carried out. Conversely, thermal desorption is not very efficient with some adsorbing media, more particularly activated charcoal.

Solvent desorption is very efficient and allows for the obtaining of a liquid extract that can be archived. It presents the disadvantage of masking some analytes in the chromatogram due to the presence of a solvent peak. However, it is very efficient in the desorption of activated charcoal. On the contrary, some adsorbing media, such as Tenax, cannot be solvent desorbed.

11.5.2 Passive Headspace Concentration Extraction with Activated Charcoal

A/ Principle

In passive headspace concentration extraction with activated charcoal (PHSC), a small piece of activated charcoal is placed inside the headspace of the sample for a certain period of time and at a certain temperature (see Figure 11-11). It is then removed from the container and desorbed using a solvent. Finally, a portion of the solvent is injected in the GC for analysis.

Principle of passive headspace concentration extraction. Activated charcoal is exposed to the headspace of a sample inside a container, which is placed inside an oven.

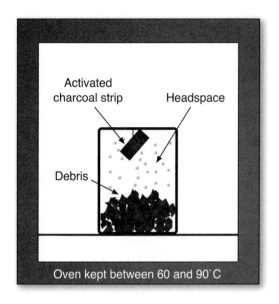

B/ Adsorbent

Activated charcoal can be purchased from many different retailers, however Albrayco Technologies (Cromwell, Connecticut, USA) developed a very convenient activated charcoal strip (ACS) used by most crime laboratories around the globe. This item is much more convenient to use than powdery charcoal. Different charcoal adsorbents are shown in Figure 11-12.

Activated Charcoal Strip and DFLEX Device

The activated charcoal strip (ACS) is composed of a homogeneous mixture of activated charcoal and Teflon embedding. This results in the binding of the charcoal together in a convenient strip of approximately 8 × 20 mm and about 1 mm thick. The strip is manufactured and distributed by Albrayco Technologies, a company located in Cromwell, Connecticut (USA). Strips are sold in bulk packs of 150 units all together or separated in sheets of six. Another device, called the Diffuse Flammable Liquid Extraction (DFLEX), also is manufactured by Albrayco, and consists of an ACS placed inside a metal frame between two permeable Teflon sheets.[1] Each DFLEX comes in separate packaging with a unique serial number.

---

[1] At the time of this writing, DFLEX devices are no longer sold. It appears that the metal used for the device's jacket was purchased through a bulk order Kodak made for their film processing. Because Kodak no longer purchases this "clean" metal, Albrayco is not able to get a supply of clean metal for their jackets. This does not affect the manufacturing of the activated charcoal strips that Albrayco continues to make and sell.

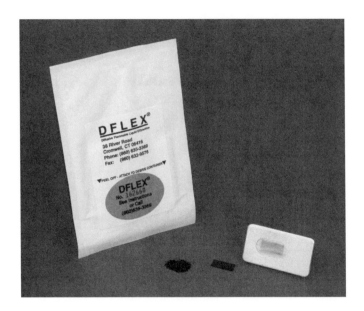

FIGURE 11-12
Different activated charcoal media. The DFLEX device (far right) comes in a sealed package (far left) and contains an activated charcoal strip like the one shown in the middle. The activated charcoal strip measures approximately 8 × 20 mm. Loose granular activated charcoal is shown on the left of the strip.

Prior to the availability of ACS and DFLEX devices, criminalists would use granular activated charcoal placed inside the headspace of the container using different means, mostly improvised ones [17]. For example, Dietz presented a system used to hang activated charcoal inside a can using tea bags as shown in Figure 2-10 [18]. Depending on the source of activated charcoal, contamination issues could arise [19]. With the venue and the convenience of ACS and DFLEX devices, the use of granular activated charcoal became obsolete and is no longer recommended.

C/ Application

The adsorbent is placed in the headspace, as high as possible in the container. There are several manners that can be used to place the adsorbent in the container. The simplest one for metal cans and glass canning jars consists of pinching the ACS onto a paper clip or a safety pin, which is then held on the inner part of the lid by a rare earth magnet placed on the outer part of the lid. A portion of the paper clip or safety pin can be bent at 90° for a better contact. Figure 11-13 shows another example in which the safety pin is held by a string. With plastic bags, it is possible to simply pin the strip on top of the debris with a small straight pin or to hang the strip on a metal wire frame. In any case, it is important to make sure that all material used to hang the pin is free of any contamination.

The sample is then placed in an oven for a certain period of time. The temperature and duration of the extraction are two parameters that may vary depending on the sample. If a sample strongly smells of gasoline, for example, it is possible to carry out the extraction for a short period of time

Illustration of one technique used to hold an ACS into a metal can or a glass canning jar: the strip can be hung with a safety pin or a paper clip and using unwaxed dental floss or cotton string. The string is then just pinched between the lid and the container.

(3–4 hours) and even at room temperature. Newman et al. presented the optimum values to be used with activated charcoal strips in function of time, temperature, strip size, and sample concentration [20]. This article is a reference in the field and should be thoroughly read. In summary, for regular samples the extraction should be carried out for 12 to 16 hours between 60 and 90°C [20]. In any case, it is quite important not to exceed 18 to 24 hours and to stay below 100°C.

ASTM standard E 1412, dealing with PHSC, recommends that the minimum size of ACS be $100\,mm^2$ [21]. A whole ACS is approximately $140\,mm^2$. In practice, it is possible to use a half or a third of a strip, however it is important not to use any smaller size. It is also possible to use a whole strip and then use only half for the desorption step (see Paragraph E/Extracts Archiving).

Figure 11-14 shows different chromatograms of the same SAM[2] obtained under different conditions. This illustrates well the concept of time and temperature dependence of passive headspace concentration.

D/ Desorption

Different solvents are available to desorb ACS. ASTM standard E 1412 confines the user to choose between carbon disulfide, n-pentane, and diethyl ether [21]. However, many recent researchers have explored the possibility of using other solvents and even binary mixtures of solvents [22–27]. The common point between all these studies is that carbon disulfide (CS_2) is

---

[2] SAM stands for "standard accelerant mixture," a name used in the fire debris community for many years to refer to a mixture of ignitable liquids used as a standard to test extraction techniques and GC-MS parameters. The original SAM is composed of gasoline (50% evaporated), kerosene, and diesel fuel in a $1:1:1$ ratio. Some users prefer to make a SAM with gasoline (50% evaporated) and diesel fuel only, still in a $1:1$ ratio. A SAM often is used as a quality control to verify that the GC-MS is working properly.

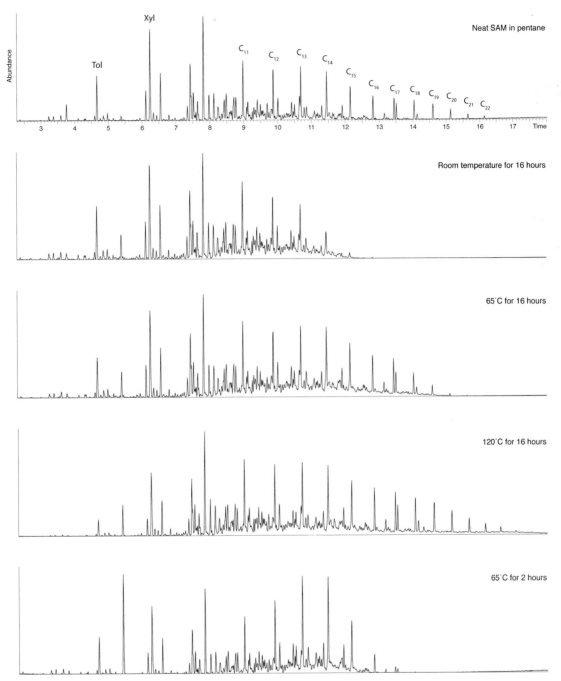

FIGURE 11-14 *Illustration of the effect of the variation of temperature and time with passive headspace concentration extraction on activated charcoal strip. From top to bottom: Neat SAM standard in pentane, extraction on ACS at room temperature for 16 hours, at 65°C for 16 hours, at 120°C for 16 hours, and at 65°C for 2 hours. Note how the pattern moves to the right as the temperature increases. One must take into account these effects when interpreting the chromatograms. These chromatograms were obtained with a different configuration than the one presented in Figure 9-1. Tol = toluene, Xyl = m,p-xylenes.*

definitely the most efficient and most commonly used solvent. To date, no other solvent has been found to have the same efficiency in desorbing activated charcoal strips.

Desorption Capacity: Solubility and Adsorptivity

It is important to understand that the desorption of a compound (the adsorbate) from an adsorbent is a matter of equilibrium, which is governed by two mechanisms: the solubility and the adsorptivity.

The solubility of a compound in the solvent is a crucial parameter as it represents the affinity exhibited by the solvent for the adsorbate. The more the adsorbate is soluble in the solvent, the more likely it is to move from the adsorbent to the solvent.

The adsorptivity is the affinity of the solvent for the adsorbent. This represents the capacity of a solvent to displace an adsorbate from the adsorbent by taking its place. The more adsorptivity is exhibited by the solvent for the adsorbent, the more likely it will displace adsorbed compounds to take their place. It is also said that the solvent wets the strip when it displaces adsorbates to take their place.

The great efficiency of carbon disulfide does not lie as much in the fact that ILR are very soluble in it, but rather in its high adsorptivity for activated charcoal.

Birrer carried out an extensive study comparing dichloromethane (DCM) to carbon disulfide [25, 26]. He concluded that DCM is better in desorbing alcohols and ketones, however it is slightly less efficient in desorbing alkylbenzenes and much less efficient in desorbing alkanes. Additionally, he observed that DCM failed to properly desorb naphthalenes and substituted naphthalenes. Figures 11-15a and 11-15b are brief summaries of the results obtained by Birrer in his study [25].

Hicks et al. also compared the efficiency of dichloromethane to carbon disulfide and concluded that although CS_2 is a more efficient desorbing solvent, dichloromethane [23] "provides a safer alternative without significantly compromising results."

Massey et al. presented a study in which they compared several solvents: carbon disulfide, dichloromethane, diethyl ether, pentane, hexane, a 1:1 mixture of isopropanol and carbon disulfide, and a 1:1 mixture of isopropanol and dichloromethane [22, 28]. Their results are summarized in Table 11-3. Again, it is possible to see that carbon disulfide leads the group, except for alcohols as noted before. Additionally, the authors note that DCM is the solvent that offers the most consistency across the different categories of chemical compounds [22].

More recently, Egli studied some other solvents and the possibility of using binary mixtures of solvents [27]. She determined that cyclohexane, heptane, ethyl acetate, and acetonitrile were clearly less efficient than carbon disulfide. She also showed that diethylamine was better than carbon disulfide for light compounds, however its efficiency seriously decreases with

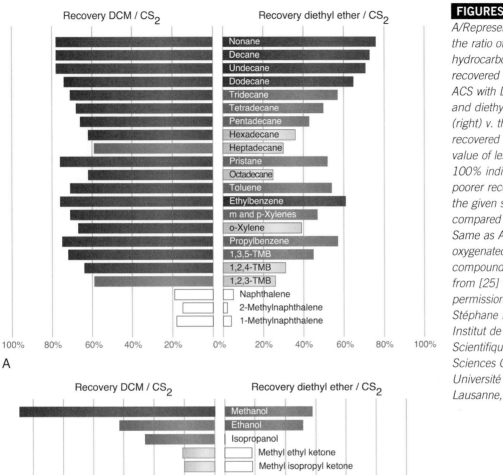

FIGURES 11-15

A/Representation of the ratio of hydrocarbons recovered from an ACS with DCM (left) and diethyl ether (right) v. the ones recovered with CS$_2$. A value of less than 100% indicates a poorer recovery with the given solvent compared to CS$_2$. B/ Same as A/ for oxygenated compounds. Adapted from [25] with permission of Stéphane Birrer, Institut de Police Scientifique, École des Sciences Criminelles, Université de Lausanne, Switzerland.

Table 11-3	Results obtained by massey et al. [22] showing the ranking of desorption solvents for ACS by decreasing order of efficiency		
Rank	**Gasoline**	**Diesel fuel**	**Alcohols**
1	Carbon disulfide	Carbon disulfide	Diethyl ether
2	Isopropanol/carbon disulfide	Hexane	Isopropanol/dichloromethane
3	Isopropanol/dichloromethane	Isopropanol/dichloromethane	Isopropanol/carbon disulfide
4	Dichloromethane	Dichloromethane	Dichloromethane
5	Diethyl ether	Pentane	Pentane
6	Pentane	Isopropanol/carbon disulfide	Hexane
7	Hexane	Diethyl ether	Carbon disulfide

Table 11-4	The aliphatic:aromatic ratios obtained with the desorption of ACS using different solvents [24]. Ratios have been normalized to CS_2.	
Solvents	Volume 200 µl	Volume 1000 µl
Carbon disulfide	1:1	1:1
Pentane	2.4:1	1.7:1
Diethyl ether	2.2:1	1.5:1
Freon	4:1	4:1

alkanes from C_{14}. She also tested the 1:1 binary mixtures dichlorome-thane-pentane, dichloromethane-heptane, diethylamine-pentane, and diethylamine-heptane. She found that dichloromethane-pentane was offer-ing desorption capacity similar to that of carbon disulfide and therefore would make a suitable substitute [27]. Additionally, under her chromato-graphic conditions, this mixture would generate only one peak.

Dolan and Newman presented a very interesting study in which they evalu-ated the difference in the aliphatic:aromatic ratios (from the recovered extracts) for several solvents [24]. Table 11-4 presents these aliphatic:aromatic ratios, which were normalized to the recovery made with carbon disulfide.

More importantly, the authors also studied the efficiency of the binary solution carbon disulfide-pentane to extract a SAM using different relative amounts of each solvent [24]. The goal in mind was to determine what would be the minimal relative amount of carbon disulfide in the binary mixture to reach the same desorbing efficiency as with 100% carbon disulfide. They demonstrated that this absolute amount would depend on the volume of solvent used and the size of the strip. The more solvent was used, the smaller the proportion of carbon disulfide is needed for a given strip. Similarly, the larger the ACS, the greater the proportion of carbon disulfide is needed for a given volume. Thus, they concluded that in order to obtain an efficient desorption, a minimum amount of carbon disulfide was needed to wet the strip [24]. This demonstrates well the high adsorptivity of carbon disulfide, resulting in its high capacity to displace adsorbate from the adsorbent.

Table 11-5 summarizes some of the most common solvents used to desorb ACS along with some properties.

It is recommended to use between 600 and 1,000 µl of solvent per com-plete ACS. Using less solvent may result in a less than efficient extraction. The desorption process is not instantaneous. Research has shown that full equilibrium between the ILR adsorbed on the charcoal and the ILR in the solvent phase is reached after about 20 minutes [25]. However, as soon as the solvent is placed in the vial, most ILRs are transferred into the solvent, so there is no real need to wait that long. A small hand agitation of the vial is

Table 11-5 *The most common solvents used to desorb ACS in fire debris analysis and their characteristics*

Name	Extraction remarks	Health concerns and other hazards	Odor threshold [ppm]	Boiling point [°C]	Density [g/cm³]	Approximate price [USD/l]	NFPA hazard identification system
Carbon disulfide	Best solvent overall. Quite poor desorption of alcohols and other oxygenated compounds.	It affects the central nervous system and the normal functions of the brain, liver, and heart. Human body can absorb CS_2 through breathing and skin. Long-term exposures to small amounts (5 to 10ppm) can lead to neurological behavior troubles. Fertility can also be seriously affected; exposure to CS_2 during pregnancy may lead to birth defects. Autoignition temperature is 90°C.	<0.1	46	1.26	60	Health 3, Flammability 4, Reactivity 0
Pentane	Not a very good desorbing solvent in general. Better with alkanes and alcohols than aromatics.	Exposure can cause headache, dizziness, and passing out. It may affect the nervous system, causing numbness and weaknesses.	400	36.1	0.626	40	Health 1, Flammability 4, Reactivity 0
Hexane	A quite good desorbing solvent with alkanes and heavy compounds. Not good with aromatics or alcohols.	Repeated skin contact can cause irritation. Exposure can cause lightheadedness, giddiness, headaches, and nausea. High or repeated exposure can damage fertility and nervous system. Human body can absorb hexane through breathing and skin.	65–248	69	0.655	60	Health 1, Flammability 3, Reactivity 0

Table 11-5 *The most common solvents used to desorb ACS in fire debris analysis and their characteristics continued*

Name	Extraction remarks	Health concerns and other hazards	Odor threshold [ppm]	Boiling point [°C]	Density [g/cm^3]	Approximate price [USD/l]	NFPA hazard identification system
Diethyl ether	Not a very good desorbing solvent in general. Good with alcohols and oxygenated compounds. Quite poor with alkanes and heavy compounds, slightly better with aromatics.	Breathing diethyl ether can irritate nose and throat, can cause drowsiness, dizziness, vomiting, and irregular breathing. High exposure may affect the kidneys.	<1	34.6	0.713	60	3 / 0 / 0
Dichloromethane	Usually considered second to best desorbing solvent, except for naphthalenes, where is desorbing capacity is quite poor.	It should be handled as a carcinogen. Breathing dichloromethane may irritate the nose, throat, and lungs causing coughing, wheezing, and/or shortness of breathing. It may damage the liver and affect the kidneys and brain. Human body can absorb dichloromethane through breathing and skin.	200–300	40	1.325	35	2 / 1 / 0
Tetrachloroethylene	This solvent should be used to desorb ACS only when checking for light compounds.	It should be handled as a carcinogen. Exposure can irritate mouth, throat, eyes, and nose. It may also damage the liver and kidneys and affect the nervous system. High exposure may damage fertility and cause pulmonary edema. Human body can absorb tetrachloroethylene through breathing and skin.	47	121.1	1.622	60	3 / 0 / 0

recommended to guarantee the homogeneity, however there is no need for the use of a vortex. If desired, the solvent may be extracted from the vial with the strip and placed into another vial, such as one with a micro insert. Also, some practitioners place a drop of deionized water on top of the CS_2 extract to prevent evaporation. This does not influence the analysis, except if oxygenated compounds are present in the extract, in which case they could be extracted from the CS_2 into the water phase, thus diminishing if not suppressing their presence in the CS_2. When the strip is left in the vial for the injection process (autosampler), it is good practice to ensure that the strip does not get in the way of the syringe, to the risk of clogging it. In such instance, it is usually possible to get the strip to "stick" to the inside wall of the vial in a vertical position. This may require a little bit of training to get the right "hand shake."

When checking for alcohols or other light compounds, it is possible to desorb the strip with a heavier solvent, such as tetrachloroethylene (PCE)[3]. In such instance, the GC-MS program must be adapted to reflect the new solvent peak that will elute after a few minutes. Figure 11-16 shows an example of such a chromatogram.

Alternatively, it is possible to desorb ACS via a thermal desorption process. This system has been the subject of studies at the School of Criminal Sciences of the University of Lausanne [29, 30]. Even though thermal desorption using the ATD400 (Automatic Thermal Desorber) is normally carried out with Tenax, it is pertinent here to compare the efficiency of the thermal and solvent desorptions with activated charcoal strips. Studies have shown that for an identical amount of ignitable liquid adsorbed on an ACS, solvent desorption with CS_2 would extract between 13 and 65 times more products with gasoline and between 100 and 690 times more products with diesel fuel when compared with thermal desorption [30]. However, only a very small quantity of extract in the solvent actually is injected and analyzed by the gas chromatograph. As a matter of fact, if 500 µl of solvent are used to extract an ACS and 1 µl is injected in the GC with a split ratio of 20:1, then only 1/10,000 of the extract is analyzed. With the ATD400, the amount analyzed can be reduced to 1/20 or even more. As a result, a thermally-desorbed ACS containing the same amount of ignitable liquid will produce a final chromatogram about 6 to 28 times more abundant with gasoline and up to 4 times more abundant with diesel fuel when compared to solvent desorption [30]. It is important to note that in general, thermal desorption is not as efficient as solvent desorption with heavy compounds.

Even though thermal desorption is much less efficient than solvent desorption, when considering the final outcome, it appears much more

---

[3] Because TCE is the accepted abbreviation for trichloroethylene, it cannot be used for tetrachloroethylene. The abbreviation PCE comes from perchloroethylene, a synonym used to designate tetrachloroethylene.

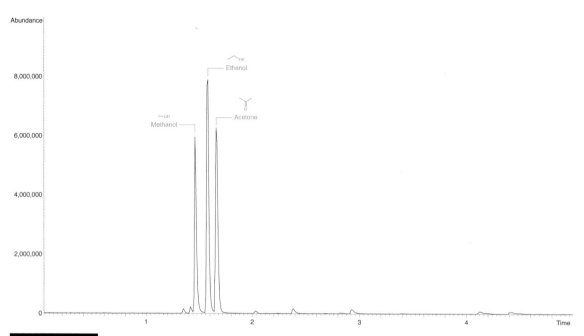

FIGURE 11-16 *Example of a chromatogram obtained with an extract from an ACS desorbed with tetrachloroethylene (PCE). In this case, the mass spectrometer is turned on at 0 min until about 5 minutes, where it is turned off to allow for the solvent to elute. This allows for the detection of very early eluting peaks such as methanol, ethanol, and acetone, three of the most often encountered oxygenated compounds used as accelerants. It is possible to use the same program temperature than the one for regular ILR, and only modify the acquisition timing of the MS. In this case, the temperature program has been changed and does not reflect the one used in Figure 9-1.*

advantageous. This is not to mention the numerous advantages of thermal desorption over solvent desorption (no solvent peak, less laboratory operation, less risk of contamination). Therefore, thermal desorption of activated charcoal strips is an excellent alternative to solvent desorption. The only drawback in this technique is the lack of possibility of archiving samples for future cross-examination. However, studies have shown that the poor thermal desorption efficiency of ACS results in the possible repetition (two- or three-fold) of the desorption of a strip, thus leading one to believe that after only one desorption, the ACS can still constitute an active archive of the extraction.

E/ Extracts Archiving

One of the advantages of using PHSC is the possibility of archiving an extract. It is strongly suggested to take this opportunity. There are several manners through which an extract can be archived:

I. One full strip is used for the extraction. Prior to desorption, it is cut in two halves; one for analysis and one for archiving.

II. Two full strips are used for the extraction. Only one is desorbed and analyzed; the other is archived.

III. One full (or portion of a) strip is used for the extraction. It is then desorbed and a small portion of the extract (left in the same vial as the strip) is analyzed. The lid of the vial then is replaced and the strip with the extract is archived. Alternatively, it is possible to let the solvent evaporate through the hole created by the syringe on the septum of the lid and to preserve the strip "dry." This involves the risk of losing light compounds during the evaporation process.

SWGFEX produced a very informative document regarding the archiving of extracts in fire debris analysis [31].

11.5.3 Dynamic Headspace Concentration Extraction with Activated Charcoal

A/ Principle

In dynamic headspace concentration extraction with activated charcoal (DHSC) the adsorbent is placed in a tube through which the headspace of the sample is drawn. Figure 11-17 illustrates this concept well.

The debris usually is heated and the above headspace is drawn through the tube containing the activated charcoal. After a given time, the process is stopped and the charcoal is recuperated from the tube and desorbed. Although it may be thermally desorbed, this operation is usually carried out with a solvent as for passive headspace concentration, a portion of which is injected in the GC for analysis.

This method is extremely sensitive as it removes the compounds present in the headspace. This provokes an imbalance in the equilibrium between the liquid and the vapor phases of the compounds. Nature reacts by further vaporizing the compounds, in order to reach equilibrium with the vapor pressure. As the headspace sweeping to the adsorbent trap is continuous, the ILR adsorbed on the substrate are slowly transferred to the adsorbent. If the process is carried out for a sufficient time, quasi-total extraction of the ILR is achieved.

B/ Application

Activated charcoal exhibits a high adsorbing capacity and adsorbs a wide range of compounds, thus making it an ideal medium for this application. Additionally, it has a reasonable cost. It is possible to buy activated charcoal and prepare the tubes oneself. Alternatively, it is possible to buy charcoal tubes already prepared. They are usually glass tubes of which both ends must be broken off (such as with medical glass bulbs) prior to use. The tube can then be completely broken down and the charcoal recuperated. Supelco (St. Louis, Missouri, USA) manufactures several of such tubes, called ORBO, at a relatively reasonable cost. A sketch of such a tube is shown in Figure 11-18.

◀FIGURE 11-17

Principle of dynamic headspace concentration extraction.

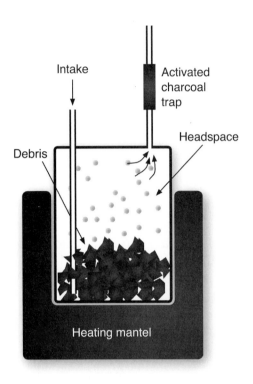

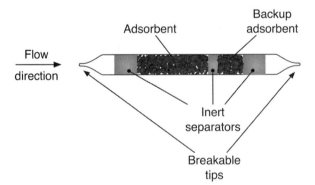

FIGURE 11-18 *Illustration of a commercial activated charcoal tube used for dynamic headspace concentration extraction. The main adsorbent package is used to collect ILR. The backup adsorbent package is used to detect sample breakthrough (see explanation later in the text). Prior to the use of the tube, the two ends are broken off and the tube is placed in line with the headspace flow from the container.*

Preparing Charcoal Tubes

Preparing charcoal tubes is relatively straightforward and may result in cost saving. The process requires clean tubes (preferentially glass ones such as Pasteur pipette cut at the neck), activated charcoal (usually around 20 to 40 mesh), and material to act as plugs or separators (usually glass wool). If necessary, the tube is thoroughly cleaned to ensure that no contamination is present. One of the separators is placed in the tube with a pair of tweezers. Its role is to retain the charcoal inside the tube while allowing the vapors to go through. Thus, it must be tight enough not to loosen during the analysis, but be porous enough to allow a relatively easy draft. Glass wool often is used for this operation, but other materials such as a metal mesh are also adapted. It is crucial to ensure that the material used as plugging material is free of any con-tamination and does not interfere with the adsorption of ILR by the charcoal. Then, a predetermined amount of charcoal is placed in the tube, usually between 200 and 500 mg. The second separator is placed on the other end of the tube to retain the charcoal and the tube is ready. It is important to pack the charcoal quite tightly in the tube and not to leave it loose between the separators. In the latter situation, vapors might go through the tube without contacting the charcoal, and thus, without being adsorbed. If the charcoal is tightly packed, then the vapors will have an optimal contact with it. Also, when one suspects that the sample may have a lot of water, it is possible to place Na_2SO_4 on top of the second separator; this will catch the water that condenses near the top of the tube and prevent it from running back down over the charcoal [32].

In regards to the drawing of the headspace through the charcoal tube, two modes are usually distinguished:

- Positive pressure: In this configuration, a positive pressure by means of compressed gas is applied at the inlet of the container, thus pushing the vapors toward the outlet, that is, the tube with the adsorbent (see Figure 11-19a).
- Negative pressure: In this configuration, a vacuum pump is placed behind the tube with the adsorbent, thus pulling the vapors through the inlet, the headspace, and finally the outlet, that is, the tube with the adsorbent (see Figure 11-19b).

For both applications, and particularly for the negative pressure one, a solid container is required.[4] Thus, this technique must not be applied

---

[4] It should be noted that it is also possible to apply a variation of the positive pressure technique using a charcoal tube in the same manner as described under Subsection 11.5.4 with Tenax [32]. For example, a plastic bag with debris can be heated in an oven after placing two strips of tape in a cross shape somewhere on the surface of the bag. The bag is then pulled out of the oven and a hole is punctured with a needle connected to a charcoal tube (a homemade all-in-one device with a Pasteur pipette works great). By pressing the tube firmly against the layer of warm tape, it is possible to achieve an air tight seal and then, by pressing on the bag, the entire headspace can be pulled out through the charcoal tube.

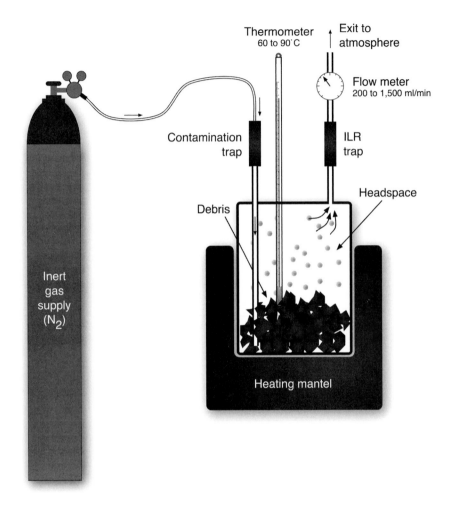

FIGURE 11-19a

Illustration of positive pressure dynamic headspace concentration extraction.

directly to non-rigid containers such as bags. The difference between the two modes in terms of efficiency is negligible. The choice of the pressure mode is dependent on the materials available at the laboratory and the personal preference of the criminalist. Each has its advantages and drawbacks.

In positive pressure, one must have a tank of an inert pressurized gas, preferably nitrogen. This tank is connected to a valve, which is connected to the inlet of the container. The tank must be able to deliver about 40 psi and the gas must be cleaned of any possible contamination, even at low trace level. It is possible to use an activated charcoal trap right before the container's inlet to catch any possible remnants of contamination. The inlet should be located at the bottom of the container whenever possible, so as to sweep through the debris. The charcoal tube is placed at the outlet of the

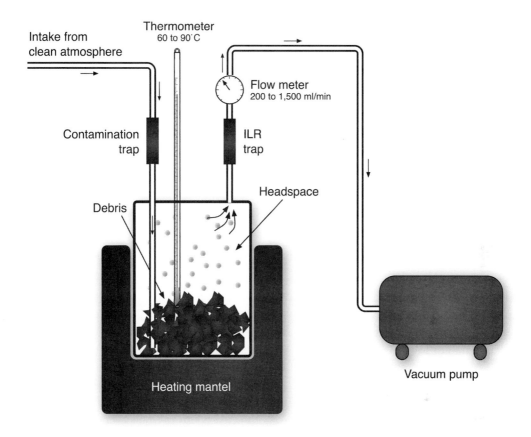

Intake from
clean atmosphere

Thermometer
60 to 90°C

Flow meter
200 to 1,500 ml/min

Contamination
trap

ILR
trap

Headspace

Debris

Heating mantel

Vacuum pump

FIGURE 11-19b *Illustration of negative pressure dynamic headspace concentration extraction.*

container, located at the top of it. All the tubing used in the experiment should be free of any contamination and thoroughly cleaned when necessary. A flow meter is placed after the charcoal tube to control the flow rate, which should be set between 200 and 1,500 ml/min. The sample is then heated. As for PHSC, the sample should not be heated too high as it favors the vaporization of interfering products. A temperature between 60 and 90°C is recommended. A thermometer should be placed inside the container in order to monitor the inside temperature, which may be significantly different than the one exhibited by the heating apparatus. The extraction is carried out for approximately one hour. The parameters—time, temperature, and flow rate—should be the subject of an internal evaluation at the laboratory to determine the optimum values. It is important to keep in mind that these values vary not only from laboratory to laboratory, but also with the sample and the amount of ignitable liquid. Using the same type of containers every time helps reduce the differences between each extraction. Additionally, it is imperative to remember that the flow rate and the extraction time are two dependent parameters. For a slow flow rate, extraction time may be increased and vice versa.

Breakthrough

One of the caveats in dynamic headspace concentration extraction that must be addressed is breakthrough. Breakthrough is due to either the loss of compounds previously adsorbed on the adsorbent because of their premature desorption or the nonadsorption of compounds on the adsorbent. This may be due to several reasons, including a flow rate too high, resulting in an insufficient "residence" time of the compounds in the adsorbent tube to get in contact with the adsorbent, a saturation of the adsorbent not allowing further compounds to get adsorbed, or a dilution of the adsorbed species because of a long-lasting draft through the tube. Prevention of breakthrough is crucial as it leads to the direct loss of ILR and, given the destructive nature of DHSC, once lost, they cannot be recuperated. Breakthrough is prevented through the use of a sufficient amount of charcoal, a moderate flow rate, and an extraction not left running for a long period of time. The crime laboratory desiring to introduce DHSC as a technique for the extraction of ILR should carry out internal studies of breakthrough. This is achieved by placing a second charcoal tube behind the first one and determining the level of ILR found in it based on the different parameters.

In negative pressure, one must have a vacuum pump capable of pulling between 200 and 1,500 ml/min through the system. An activated charcoal trap is placed at the inlet of the container to filter any possible contamination coming from the ambient atmosphere in the laboratory. It is recommended to carry out this operation under a clean hood. This activated charcoal trap should be replaced often to guarantee its efficiency in catching possible contamination. This is a crucial issue that cannot be neglected! The ILR adsorbent is placed at the outlet of the container, followed by the flow meter, and the vacuum pump. The operation is then carried out in the same manner as for the positive pressure mode.

C/ Desorption

Desorption of the charcoal is carried out in the same manner as for passive headspace. The only difference lies in the fact that loose activated charcoal may render the solvent turbid as small particles may float around. In such instances, it is essential to centrifuge the solvent with the charcoal to make sure that no loose particles, as small as they can be, may be injected in the GC, which may seriously and permanently affect the quality of the chromatography. It is also possible to remove the solvent from the charcoal and keep the vial with the solvent only.

D/ Sample Archiving

Because this technique is destructive, it is important to take every possible step to archive a portion of the sample or extract. When using solvent desorption, it is easy to save the remainder of the solvent, after injection of the microliter or so in the GC, and archiving it. The lid of the vial must be replaced and the vial should be kept under refrigeration. Alternatively, it is also possible to split the adsorbent and desorb only half of it. The other portion also should be kept in a sealed vial under refrigeration. Nevertheless, it is also possible to let the solvent evaporate and keep the ILR adsorbed on the ACS. Sandercock published a study demonstrating the proper long-term preservation of ignitable liquids on charcoal at room temperature [33]. He states [33]:

> For the samples of gasoline and diesel fuel deposited on charcoal in this study, no significant change was observed in the chromatograms of the eluted samples over a four year period. No loss of sample from the charcoal, or contamination of the sample by the laboratory atmosphere was observed. Loss of the more volatile compounds in a mixture, (i.e. the "light ends" of a fresh gasoline) may be expected when the sample is initially deposited onto the charcoal and the solvent allowed to evaporate.

Otherwise, it is possible to save a portion of the sample prior to extraction. This depends on the characteristics of the sample, the circumstances of the case, and the appreciation of the criminalist. It is important to remember that if a portion of the sample is archived prior to the analysis, given the fact that a sample is never perfectly homogeneous, the results of the analysis might not be fully representative of the whole sample and ILR may be missed. With thermal desorption, the most appropriate archiving would be to split the adsorbent prior to the analysis.

11.5.4 Dynamic Headspace Concentration Extraction with Tenax

A/ Principle

The principle of dynamic headspace concentration extraction with Tenax is extremely similar to the one with charcoal described in the previous subsection. However, the difference lies in the amount of headspace that is pulled from the sample. Typically, with Tenax, the amount of headspace drawn is about 30 to 60 ml. Thus, there is no constant sweeping of the headspace, rendering this technique much less "dynamic" than the one previously described. Figure 11-20 illustrates the principle of this technique. The sample is heated, a small amount of headspace is drawn through the tube with the adsorbent. The adsorbent is then thermally desorbed and the ILR are analyzed with the GC.

Principle of dynamic headspace concentration extraction with Tenax. The sample is heated and a small volume of headspace is withdrawn with an airtight syringe onto which the adsorbent cartridge has been placed.

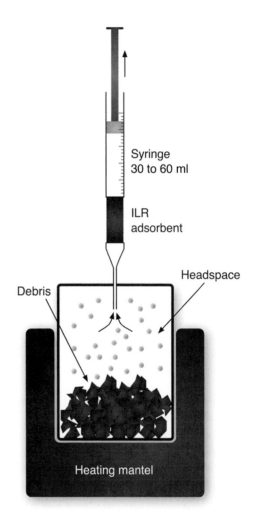

One of the greatest advantages of this technique is the fact that it does not necessitate the use of a solvent, thus the resulting chromatogram does not present any hidden zones. Additionally, as seen in Subsection 11.5.2, thermal desorption leads to a better final sensitivity than solvent desorption.

B/ Adsorbent

Tenax is a white porous polymeric resin based on 2,6-diphenyl-*p*-phenylene oxide (see Figure 11-21) [34]. It is a trademark owned by Buchem BV in the Netherlands [34]. It is a particularly useful adsorbent as it resists high temperature (350° to 400°C), rendering it ideal for thermal desorption—it

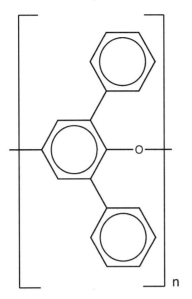

FIGURE 11-21
Chemical structure of Tenax (2,6-diphenyl-p-phenylene oxide).

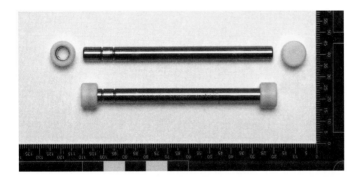

FIGURE 11-22
Tenax tubes provided by Perkin-Elmer for their automatic thermal desorber. The tube's plugs are removed when performing the dynamic headspace extraction.

adsorbs a wide variety of polar and nonpolar compounds, and it has a high adsorbing capacity. Today, it is commonly referred to as Tenax TA, in comparison to Tenax GR, which is mixed with 30% graphite. Tenax is widely found on the market.

C/ Application

The sample is heated to the desired temperature (not to exceed 100°C) and left a few minutes to ensure that the equilibrium is reached between the liquid and vapor phases. Then, a hole is punched through the container with a syringe equipped with a Tenax tube (see Figure 11-22). Approximately 30 ml are drawn from the container very slowly.

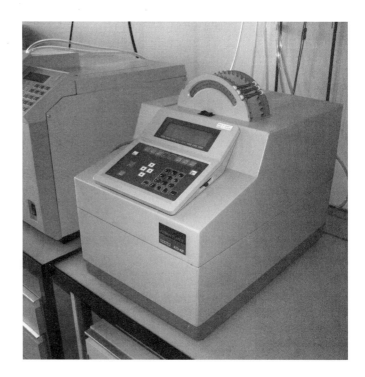

FIGURE 11-23

Photograph of a Perkin-Elmer ATD 400. The Tenax tubes are loaded on the rotary autosampler at the top of the apparatus. The ATD is connected through an insulated line to the adjacent GC. Photograph courtesy of École des Sciences Criminelles, Université de Lausanne, Switzerland.

D/ Desorption

Tenax must be thermally desorbed as it does not resist solvents very well and is completely soluble in carbon disulfide. In order to carry out this operation, a specific apparatus called a thermal desorber (TD) is used. PerkinElmer proposes a line of TDs, called TurboMatrix, with different capabilities [35]. Some are automatic thermal desorbers (ATD) as they include an autosampler capable of holding usually 50 samples. Figure 11-23 shows an older model of TD, the ATD400 (PerkinElmer, Connecticut, USA). This particular model comprises an autosampler with a capacity of 50 tubes.

Figure 11-24 is a diagram summarizing the functioning principle of the ATD400. The tube is brought by the autosampler in the heating chamber, where it is heated to a temperature between 50 and 350°C for a given time. A flow of gas (helium) carries the analytes from the tube to a much smaller trap, also composed of Tenax, where the temperature is anywhere between −100 and 30°C. For the fire debris application, a temperature of −30°C is sufficient. At this stage, it is possible to use an inlet split, which would reduce the amount of analytes transferred to the trap. After desorption of the tube, the trap is desorbed. The trap is very rapidly heated to a temperature between 200 and 400°C and after a very short equilibration time— desorption of the analytes is almost instantaneous—vapors are transferred into the injection port of the GC with the carrier gas flow. At this stage, an

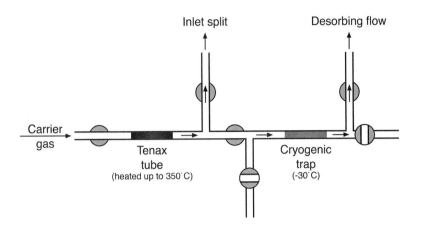

FIGURE 11-24a

First step in the automatic thermal desorption of Tenax tubes: The tube is heated and the carrier gas flow takes the analytes from the tube to a cryogenic trap.

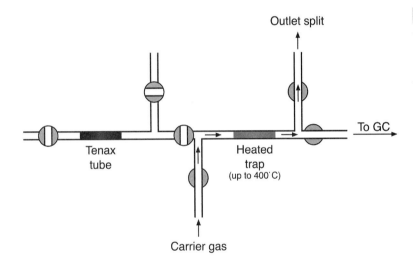

FIGURE 11-24b

Second step: The cryogenic trap is heated very rapidly and the analytes are desorbed into the GC column.

outlet split may be used to reduce the total amount of analytes injected in the GC.

Limited breakthrough data for Tenax and carbon black (activated charcoal) are shown in Tables 11-6 and 11-7 [36, 37]. These breakthrough data are quite important for two main reasons. First, they allow the user to better estimate the parameters used for DHSC as seen in the previous subsection. Second, they allow for a much better understanding of the conditions necessary for the thermal desorption of Tenax, or activated charcoal for that matter. In the adsorption part of DHSC, breakthrough is not desired and the parameters should be tweaked in order to prevent it. Conversely, in the thermal desorption part of DHSC, complete breakthrough is the goal, and thus the parameters should be adjusted to maximize the number of analytes desorbed. The data shown in Tables 11-6 and 11-7 can be compared to provide a better idea of the difference in breakthrough between Tenax and

Table 11-6	Breakthrough data for Tenax TA. The values represent the volume (in liters) per gram of adsorbent necessary to elute the respective organic compound. The higher the volume, the more difficult the compound is to elute. Conversely, the lower the volume, the easier the compound elutes. When in an adsorption phase (when collecting ilr from a debris onto the adsorbent), one wants to be in the part of the table with very high volumes (left part of the table). When in a desorption phase (when desorbing the adsorbent into the gc-ms), one wants to be in the part of the table with very low volumes (right part of the table) [36]

Temperature [°C]	0	20	40	100	200	300
Methane	0.015	0.006	0.003	—	—	—
n-Pentane	25.1	5.00	1.10	0.036	0.001	—
n-Hexane	199	31.6	5.30	0.106	0.002	—
n-Octane	6,300	590	90.0	0.790	0.004	—
n-Decane	50,000	3,900	500	3.55	0.012	—
n-Dodecane	900,000	50,000	5,000	15.0	0.030	—
n-Tetradecane	5,000,000	300,000	25,000	56.2	0.081	0.001
n-Eicosane	150,000,000	6,600,000	420,000	700	0.700	0.007
Methanol	1.30	0.362	0.140	0.0011	—	—
Ethanol	7.90	1.80	0.481	0.021	0.001	—
1-Butanol	400	56.0	11.0	0.194	0.003	—
Benzene	410	70.0	18.0	0.268	0.004	—
Ethylbenzene	12,500	1,400	200	2.00	0.011	—
n-Butylbenzene	250,000	18,000	2,000	11.0	0.030	0.001
Naphthalene	1,500,000	100,000	9,500	40.0	0.038	0.002

activated charcoal. In general, one can quickly appreciate the significant influence of the temperature to the breakthrough data. Also, one can observe the differences in values between Tenax and charcoal and realize that charcoal does not thermally desorb as well as Tenax. Typical conditions for the desorption of a Tenax tube with an ATD400 are shown in Table 11-8 [30].

E/ Sample Archiving

Dynamic headspace concentration extraction with Tenax does not permit for any extract archiving. The thermal desorption does not result in any sample left over. However, this is not necessarily an issue since the technique itself is not considered as destructive. The reason lies in the fact that the volume of headspace drawn from the sample is very small.

It is also not recommended to proceed to the splitting of the sample prior to extraction, as for DHSC with activated charcoal. The technique being

Table 11-7	Breakthrough data for Carbotrap. Same remarks than the ones made for table 11-6. It is interesting to compare the values found in this table with the ones displayed in table 11-6. These values are for a carbon-based adsorbent and may exhibit differences with other carbon adsorbents such as the one constituting the activated charcoal strips [37]					
Temperature [°C]	0	20	40	100	200	300
Methane	0.015	0.009	0.005	—	—	—
n-Pentane	13.0	5.89	2.5	0.22	0.009	—
n-Hexane	200	79.9	30.0	2	0.03	0.003
n-Octane	22,000	7,500	2,500	110	0.6	0.02
n-Decane	3,000,000	1,000,000	330,000	13,000	40.0	0.19
n-Dodecane	23,000,000	8,000,000	3,000,000	110,000	600	3
Methanol	0.600	0.250	0.110	0.010	0.001	—
Ethanol	1.20	0.550	0.250	0.025	0.002	—
1-Butanol	80.0	30.0	11.0	0.675	0.014	0.002

nondestructive, the risk taken by splitting the sample in terms of missing a possible ILR is not worth it.

11.5.5 Passive Headspace Concentration Extraction with Solid Phase Micro-extraction

A/ Principle
Sold phase micro-extraction (SPME) is based on the same principle as PHSC with activated charcoal, except for the nature of the adsorbent and the desorption process. SPME is a sample preparation technique invented in 1989 by Dr. Pawliszyn and his research team of the University of Waterloo (Ontario, Canada). SPME is patented to Dr. Pawliszyn and is licensed exclusively to Supelco [38]. This technique consists of an adsorbent coated on a fiber exposed to the headspace of the sample to be extracted. In this regard, it is identical to the activated charcoal version. The difference lies in the size (much smaller) and type of adsorbent (several types are available). Additionally, the greatest and only advantage of SPME compared to its activated charcoal counterpart is its desorption: it is carried out thermally, directly in the injection port of the GC, thus guaranteeing a maximum sensitivity. Also, SPME is a very quick and easy technique to perform.

Figure 11-25 shows the application of SPME in fire debris analysis. First, the sample is heated. Then, the SPME fiber is exposed to the headspace of the sample for a given period of time, usually in the range of 5 to 10 minutes.

Table 11-8	Typical parameters used to configure an ATD 400 to desorb Tenax tubes for ILR analysis [30]
Parameter	**Value**
Tube conditioning	
Temperature	300°C
Time	10 min
Desorption 1 (Tenax tube)	
Desorption temperature	230°C
Desorption time	10 min
Desorption flow	80 ml/min
Inlet split	No
Trap temperature	−30°C
Desorption 2 (inner trap)	
Desorption temperature	300°C
Rate	40°C/s
Desorption time	1 min
Desorption flow	80 ml/min
Outlet split	40 ml/min
Final split	20:1
Injection	
Valve temperature	225°C
Transfer line temperature	225°C
Carrier gas	Helium

Finally, the SPME fiber is inserted in the GC for desorption and analysis of the ILR.

SPME was first applied to forensic sciences with the analysis of amphetamines in urine samples and methadone and its metabolites in hair. One of the first applications of SPME to fire debris analysis was demonstrated by Steffen and Pawliszyn in 1996 [39]. ASTM developed a standard, E 2154, devoted to SPME [40]. It is important to note at this stage that SPME is not a stand-alone extraction technique for fire debris analysis, as stated under point 4.5 of the ASTM standard [40]: "This practice is intended for use in conjunction with other extraction techniques described in Practices E 1385, E 1386, E 1388, E 1412, and E 1413." To this date, the use of SPME for fire debris analysis in crime laboratories around the world is extremely

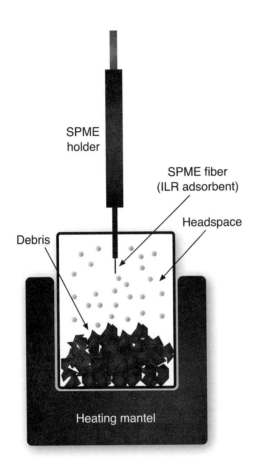

FIGURE 11-25

Principle of solid phase micro-extraction (SPME). The SPME fiber is part of the holder. The fiber is exposed to the headspace of the sample as for passive headspace concentration extraction with activated charcoal.

marginal. As a matter of fact, the only worthy use of SPME would be as a screening technique or when carrying out analysis directly at the scene of the fire. However, simple headspace does a much simpler job for the first reason, and the second reason is extremely rarely, if ever, encountered.

B/ Adsorbent

Figure 11-26 shows a schematic of SPME fiber and its holder [41]. A SPME device is composed of the holder onto which the fiber assembly is located. The fiber is protected inside the needle and is exposed only when needed.

The holder has two positions: In the resting position, the fiber is retracted inside the needle and thus, protected. The needle is used to pierce through the different septa (for the adsorption and the desorption processes). Once the needle is in the proper medium, the fiber is exposed.

There are several coating options available for SPME fibers characterized by the type of adsorbent and its size. To this date, Supelco commercializes

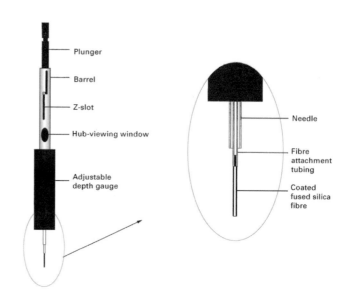

FIGURE 11-26

Schematic of a SPME
holder and its fiber.
(Source: Pawliszyn J
(2000) Extraction:
Solid-Phase
Microextraction. In:
Encyclopedia of
separation science,
editors Wilson I, Poole
C, and Cooke M,
Academic Press, San
Diego, CA, USA
Reproduced with the
permission of Elsevier
Academic Press,
Burlington, MA, USA)

fibers made of polydimethylsiloxane (PDMS), polyacrylate (PA), a combination of PDMS and divinylbenzene (DVB), a combination of PDMS and carboxen, and a combination of carboxen and DVB. The thickness of the different phases ranges from 7 to 100 μm.

Ren and Bertsch presented a very interesting study on the efficiency of the different SPME fibers [42]. They found that a 100-μm PDMS fiber was ideal for compounds ranging from C_{10} to C_{25} and that an 85-μm PA fiber combined with a 75-μm carboxen/PDMS would perform well with compounds from C_1 to C_{10} [42]. For polar compounds, a PA or carboxen/DVB phase would be most adapted. In general, a thick coat is desirable for very volatile molecules and a thin coat is preferred for large, less volatile, molecules. Nevertheless, the thicker the coat, the longer the extraction.

One issue that must be taken into account with SPME is the fact that the number of adsorption sites in a SPME fiber is very limited compared to ACS. Thus, the phenomenon of displacement may quickly arise, leading to some significant skewing in the chromatogram. Additionally, depending on the type of fibers, some compounds may be preferentially adsorbed. For the PDMS fiber, it has been observed that alkanes are more likely to be adsorbed than aromatics, thus leading to a skewing of the chromatogram of some ILR such as the ones from diesel fuel or gasoline [43].

C/ Application

The sample is heated to a given temperature (not to exceed 100°C). The fiber is then inserted in the container and exposed for a given time, usually ranging from 5 to 15 minutes. The fiber is retracted in the needle and the needle is withdrawn from the container. The needle is then inserted in the injection port of the GC and the fiber is exposed for a couple of minutes.

One caveat of using SPME is that the inlet of the injection port may need to be changed to one with a larger hole to fit the wide holder's needle. Additionally, the liner used must also be straight and free of glass wool, or other material usually present in it to retain particles from entering the column. If the liner is not adapted to the SPME technique and the SPME holder, it is likely that the fiber will break when attempting to desorb it. This results in annoying artifacts leading to poor chromatography. The inlet must then be taken apart and cleaned.

Research has shown that the SPME fiber did not adsorb molecules in any significant quantities above C_{15} when an extraction temperature of 40°C is used and above pristane at 80°C [43]. This is a serious issue that may lead to the misidentification of a heavy petroleum distillate.

D/ Contamination

Contamination may become an important issue with the use of SPME as the adsorbent (fiber) is reused. A thorough cleaning of the fiber is necessary between each injection. Additionally, a blank of the fiber after its cleaning must be performed to ensure that it is contamination-free. The fiber typically is cleaned by leaving it in the injection port of the GC or in another injection port of the GC heated to at least 270°C. Higher temperatures may result in the deterioration of the fiber. It is recommended to leave the fiber for 10 to 30 minutes under these conditions. Then, a blank is run. Research has shown that the 100-μm PDMS fiber exhibits significant memory effect. A cleaning of the fiber at 270°C for 63 minutes was not enough to fully desorb the fiber after being exposed to 10 and 100 μl, respectively, of SAM [43].

A fiber is reusable, approximately 100 times according to the manufacturer. Practice has shown differently and a fiber is usually good for approximately 20 to 50 uses. Although the adsorbing capacity of the fiber is typically not influenced for the first 50 to 80 uses, the fiber has the tendency to break away from its support, rendering the fiber assembly obsolete.

Prior to its first use, it is necessary to condition the fiber at a given temperature and for a given time, following the manufacturer's recommendations.

E/ Sample Archiving

It is not possible to preserve any portion of the extract when using SPME. However, SPME is not considered a destructive technique, and thus the archiving of the extract is not necessary. Some of the remarks formulated in the corresponding paragraph in the subsection dealing with Tenax are applicable.

11.6 CHOOSING THE RIGHT TECHNIQUE

11.6.1 Comparison

Table 11-9 summarizes the different techniques presented in this chapter, along with some of their characteristics.

Modern techniques are quite sensitive as most of them detect very small amounts of ILR, down to the 0.1 µl range. Simple headspace is the least sensitive of the most commonly used techniques. This is the reason why it is almost exclusively used as a screening technique.

As seen in Table 11-9, the most labor-intensive techniques are distillation techniques and dynamic headspace with activated charcoal. This is due to the complex laboratory equipment required for these techniques and the permanent surveillance of the operation. The least labor-intensive are simple headspace, dynamic headspace with Tenax (if equipped with an autosampler), and passive headspace with activated charcoal.

Contamination issues are quite moderate with most techniques. With good laboratory practice, they can be eliminated safely. A means to monitor contamination should be incorporated into the quality control procedures for each extraction technique.

| Table 11-9 | The different extraction technique for fire debris analysis. Obsolete techniques have been grayed out. Values given in the table are approximate in nature |

Technique	Sensitivity[1] [µl]	Labor time [h]	Total time [h]	Labor intensity[2]	Contamination issue	Destructive technique?	Archive	Cost[3]	ASTM
Steam distillation	100–500	2.5	2.5	+++	Moderate	Yes	Yes	$$	E 1385
Ethylene glycol distillation	–	2.5	2.5	+++	Moderate	Yes	Yes	$$	–
Ethanol:water distillation	–	2.5	2.5	+++	Moderate	Yes	Yes	$$	–
Solvent extraction	1–10	0.5	1–2	++	Moderate	Yes	Yes	$$$	E 1386
Headspace	10	<0.25	1	–	Little to none	No	No	$	E 1388
Passive headspace with charcoal	0.1	<0.25	12–16	+	Little to none	No	Yes	$$	E 1412
Dynamic headspace with charcoal	0.1	1	2	+++	Moderate	Yes	Yes	$$	E 1413
Dynamic headspace with Tenax	0.1	<0.25	1	–	Little to none	Yes/no	No	$$	–
SPME	<0.1	1	1.5	++	Moderate	No	No	$$$	E 2154

[1] Sensitivity may depend on the nature of the sample, the size of the container, the amount of ILR, and the parameters of the extraction.
[2] +++ very intense, ++ intense, + relatively easy, – very simple.
[3] $$$ most expensive, $$ moderately expensive, $ very inexpensive.

The most important point to remember when choosing an extraction technique is its influence on the resulting chromatogram. None of the extraction technique provides a perfect picture of what the liquid is. There will always be some sort of skewing, as minimal as it can be in some instances, between the chromatogram of the neat liquid and the chromatogram obtained through the extraction process.

Figure 11-27 presents different chromatograms of SAM obtained with a neat injection of the mixture, by simple headspace, passive headspace concentration on activated charcoal, and solvent extraction. It is possible to appreciate the sometimes-significant influence of the extraction technique.

The SAM spans from about C_7 to C_{23} and the chromatogram of the neat liquid is the most representative one that can be obtained. Simple headspace carried out at 80°C suffers from the fact that heavy species are underrepresented in the headspace. As a result, the chromatogram abruptly stops around C_{16}. One critical consequence to this extraction technique is that the criminalist cannot fully appreciate the presence of an HPD, as the two couples C_{17}-pristane and C_{18}-phytane are absent. PHSC usually provides a chromatogram with the pattern most resembling compared to the neat liquid. The ratios between the aromatics from gasoline and the aliphatics from kerosene and diesel fuel are quite well respected. The chromatogram also stops earlier than the neat one (around C_{21} instead of C_{23}), which is due to the fact that the extraction is carried out at 80°C. By increasing this temperature, the heavy end may be slightly better represented. However, it is not necessarily pertinent to check for compounds above C_{22}. Also, increasing the temperature may skew the overall ratios of the chromatogram between the early-eluting and late-eluting compounds. The last chromatogram represents a solvent extraction. Because solvent extraction necessitates the concentration of the extract—in this case, it has been concentrated from 50 ml to 0.5 ml, a 100-fold concentration—the light end of the chromatogram often is diminished, if not lost. As a consequence, the chromatogram does not start before C_{10} and most of the light aromatics—the C_2- and C_3-alkylbenzenes—are lost. If one does not pay particular attention to the castle group, the presence of gasoline will be missed in this chromatogram as the overall pattern resembles the one of an HPD alone. Conversely, the heavy end is quite comprehensively extracted and the chromatogram extends to the same limit as the neat liquid. Finally, a peak (in this case, heptane, a contaminant of the solvent pentane used to perform the extraction) is also present and may interfere with the identification.

Figure 11-28 is similar to Figure 11-27, however the amount of SAM extracted has been decreased from 20 μl to 3 μl. One can readily appreciate the differences in the patterns observed with some chromatograms. With simple headspace, for which 3 μl is already below the usual limit of detection, the alkane patterns is quite different that the one shown with 20 μl. Solvent extraction completely missed the presence of any ignitable

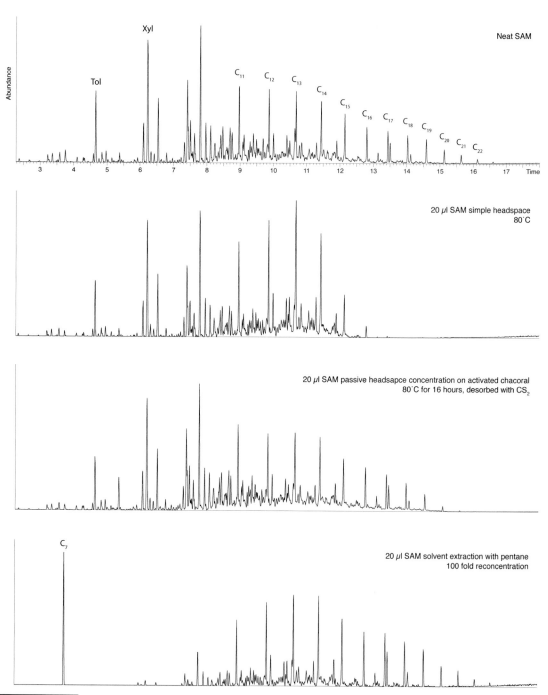

FIGURE 11-27 *Top: Chromatogram of SAM injected as a neat liquid. Second: Chromatogram of 20μl SAM by simple headspace. Third: Chromatogram of 20μl SAM by PHSC. Bottom: Chromatogram of 20μl SAM by solvent extraction. These chromatograms were obtained with a different configuration than the one presented in Figure 9-1. Tol = toluene, Xyl = m,p-xylenes.*

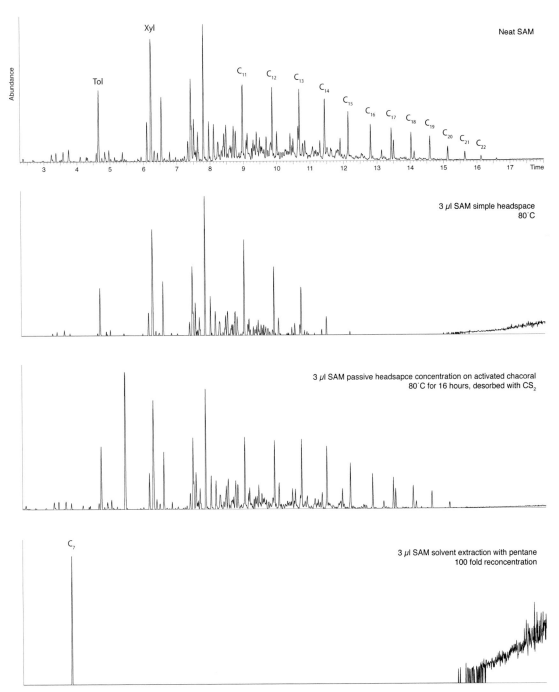

FIGURE 11-28 *Same as Figure 11-27, but the extracts were obtained with 3μl of SAM instead of 20μl.*

liquid. To the contrary, the pattern shown by PHSC is relatively stable and closely resembles the one of the neat liquid and the one obtained with 20 μl. This shows again the great consistency of PHSC and its preferred use.

11.6.2 Making the Choice

The application of extraction techniques does not represent a very difficult laboratory task. The choice of the right technique may be more problematic and if not taken wisely, may not lead to the most optimal extraction technique.

As many laboratories perform fire debris analysis as part of their routine work, they use the same, standardized, technique on every sample. However, in some instances, it is necessary to adapt the extraction techniques, or its parameters, to a given sample. In this case, it is important to fully understand the advantages and drawbacks of each technique, and the influence of the most important parameters to the results obtained.

Simple headspace and SPME should be used only as screening techniques. They provide results that must be confirmed by other techniques. Depending on what is obtained with simple headspace and SPME, the most appropriate technique can be more wisely chosen and its parameters may be adapted. For example, if the screening technique reveals the possible presence of an HPD, the extraction temperature of the regular PHSC may be increased from 60 to 90°C. To the contrary, if a very light compound is suspected, the temperature of extraction may be kept around 60 to 70°C. If a light oxygenate is thought to be present, part of an activated charcoal strip can be eluted with a heavier solvent and the light compounds can be detected.

For most regular samples (more than 95% of them), passive headspace concentration or dynamic headspace concentration with activated charcoal or Tenax are the most valuable techniques.

Solvent extraction must be avoided if the sample cannot be destroyed or if it is suspected to contain light ILR such as alcohols. Solvent extraction is best adapted to heavy ILR on small and relatively clean samples. For example, a small piece of cloth is perfectly adapted to solvent extraction. The rinsing of a nonporous surface would also make a good candidate for solvent extraction. This technique may also be used if adsorption techniques failed. Often results have been obtained with solvent, when none were obtained with adsorption techniques.

When the presence of an IL or ILR is more than obvious during the preliminary examination, the extraction time may be diminished. Because displacement phenomenon takes place with PHSC and the heavy presence of organic compounds, by extracting for a shorter period (such as 4 hours instead of 12), this displacement phenomenon can be minimized. This emphasizes the necessity to perform a preliminary examination of the sample.

There is not one perfect solution to every problem, but by understanding the ins and outs of each technique and the effects of each parameter, the criminalist can wisely chose the right technique for each sample.

REFERENCES

1. Reiss R-A (1911) *Manuel de police scientifique (technique)—I Vols et homicides*, Librairie Payot & Cie, Lausanne, Switzerland.
2. American Society for Testing and Materials (2001) *ASTM E 1385-00 Standard practice for separation and concentration of ignitable liquid residues from fire debris samples by steam distillation*, Annual Book of ASTM Standards 14.02, West Conshohocken, PA.
3. Lide DR (2004) *Handbook of chemistry and physics*, 84th edition, CRC Press, Boca Raton, FL.
4. Ohe S (2003) *Vapor pressure calculation program*, available from http://www.s-ohe.com, last access performed on March 20, 2006.
5. Bennett GD (1958) The arson investigator and technical aids, *Journal of Criminal Law, Criminology and Police Science*, **49**, pp 172–7.
6. Farrell LG (1947) Reduced pressure distillation apparatus in police science, *Journal of Criminal Law and Criminology*, **38**(4), p 438.
7. Hrynchuk R, Cameron R, and Rodgers PG (1977) Vacuum distillation for the recovery of fire accelerants from charred debris, *Canadian Society of Forensic Science Journal*, **10**(2), pp 41–50.
8. Macoun JM (1952) The detection and determination of small amounts of inflammable hydrocarbons in combustible materials, *The Analyst*, **77**, p 381.
9. Brackett JW (1955) Separation of flammable material of petroleum origin from evidence submitted in cases involving fires and suspected arson, *Journal of Criminal Law, Criminology and Police Science*, **46**(4), pp 554–61.
10. Woycheshin S and DeHaan JD (1978) An evaluation of some arson distillation techniques, *Arson Analysis Newsletter*, **2**, pp 1–16.
11. ASTM International (2006) *ASTM E 1386-00 Standard practice for separation and concentration of ignitable liquid residues from fire debris by solvent extraction*, Annual Book of ASTM Standards 14.02, West Conshohocken, PA.
12. Wypych G (2001) *Production methods, properties, and main applications*. In: *Handbook of solvents*, editor Wypych G, ChemTec Publishing, Toronto, Canada.
13. Snyder LR (1974) Classification of the solvent properties of common liquids, *Journal of Chromatography*, **92**(2), pp 223–30.
14. ASTM International (2006) *ASTM E 1388-00 Standard practice for sampling of headspace vapors from fire debris samples*, Annual Book of ASTM Standards 14.02, West Conshohocken, PA.
15. Ettling BV and Adams MF (1968) The study of accelerant residues in fire remains, *Journal of Forensic Sciences*, **13**(1), pp 76–89.
16. Dolan J and Stauffer E (2004) The effects of adsorption-based extraction methods on the recovery of aliphatic and aromatic compounds in medium petroleum distillates, *56th Annual Meeting of the American Academy of Forensic Sciences*, Dallas, TX.
17. Juhala JA (1982) A method for adsorption of flammable vapors by direct insertion of activated charcoal into the debris samples, *Arson Analysis Newsletter*, **6**(2), pp 32–6.
18. Dietz WR (1991) Improved charcoal packaging for accelerant recovery by passive diffusion, *Journal of Forensic Sciences*, **36**(1), pp 111–21.

19. Henderson R (1986) Impurities in activated charcoal, *Arson Analysis Newsletter*, **9**(1), pp 13–19.

20. Tindall Newman R, Dietz WR, and Lothridge K (1996) The use of activated charcoal strips for fire debris extractions by passive diffusion. Part 1: The effects of time, temperature, strip size, and sample concentration, *Journal of Forensic Sciences*, **41**(3), pp 361–70.

21. ASTM International (2006) *ASTM E 1412-00 Standard practice for separation of ignitable liquid residues from fire debris samples by passive headspace concentration with activated charcoal*, Annual Book of ASTM Standards 14.02, West Conshohocken, PA.

22. Massey D, Du Pasquier E, and Lennard C (2002) Substitution of carbon disulfide for desorption of flammable liquid residues from DFLEX™, *16th Meeting of the International Association of Forensic Sciences*, Montpellier, France.

23. Hicks GD, Pontbriand AR, and Adams JM (2003) Carbon disulfide versus dichloromethane for use of desorbing ignitable liquid residues from activated charcoal strips, *55th Annual Meeting of the American Academy of Forensic Sciences*, Chicago, IL.

24. Dolan JA and Newman RR (2001) Solvent options for the desorption of activated charcoal in fire debris analysis, *55th Annual Meeting of the American Academy of Forensic Sciences*, Seattle, WA.

25. Birrer S (2000) *Recherche d'un solvant capable de remplacer le CS2 dans la phase de désorption des membranes DFLEX® utilisées dans la recherche d'accélérants de combustion*, séminaire de 4ème année, Institut de police scientifique et de criminologie, University of Lausanne, Lausanne, Switzerland.

26. Birrer S, Delémont O, Lacarrière JF, and Deharo D (2000) Search for a substitute to carbon disulfide for the desorption of accelerant vapours concentrated on activated charcoal membranes composing the DFLEX® devices, *2nd European Academy of Forensic Science Meeting*, Cracow, Poland.

27. Egli N (2001) *Recherche d'un mélange de solvants capable de remplacer le CS2 dans la phase de désorption des membranes DFLEX® utilisées dans la recherche de substances accélératrices de combustion*, séminaire de 4ème année, Institut de police scientifique et de criminologie, University of Lausanne, Lausanne, Switzerland.

28. Massey D, Du Pasquier E, and Lennard C (2002) Solvent desorption of charcoal strips (DFLEX®) in the analysis of fire debris samples: Replacement of carbon disulfide, *Canadian Society for Forensic Science Journal*, **35**(4), pp 195–207.

29. Pepler R (2000) *Analyse de résidus d'incendie en criminalistique: comparaison des méthodes d'extraction*, Master's thesis, Institut de police scientifique et de criminologie, University of Lausanne, Lausanne, Switzerland.

30. Bapst S (2002) *Opportunité de l'emploi de système d'extraction thermique ATD400 pour la désorption de membranes de charbon actif par rapport à la méthode chimique (CS2)*, séminaire de 4ème année, Institut de police scientifique et de criminologie, University of Lausanne, Lausanne, Switzerland.

31. Laboratory Fire Education and Training Committee (2002) *Standard practice for preservation of ignitable liquid residues in extracts from fire debris samples and questioned liquid samples submitted for ignitable liquid analysis*, Technical and Scientific Working Group for Fire and Explosives.

32. Sandercock PML (2007) *Personal communication to Eric Stauffer*, August 8, 2007.

33. Sandercock PML (1997) Retention of gasoline and diesel fuel samples on charcoal: Evaluation of long term preservation of petroleum residues, *Canadian Society for Forensic Science Journal*, **30**(4), pp 219–24.

34. Buchem BV (2000) Tenax®, available from http://www.buchem.com, last access performed on September 4, 2006.

35. PerkinElmer (2005) *TurboMatrix thermal desorbers for GC*, PerkinElmer Life and Analytical Sciences, Shelton, CT.

36. Scientific Instrument Services (2005) *Tenax TA breakthrough volume data*, available from http://www.sisweb.com/index/referenc/tenaxta.htm, last access performed on April 18, 2007.

37. Scientific Instrument Services (2005) *Carbotrap breakthrough volume data*, available from http://www.sisweb.com/index/referenc/carbotrp.htm, last access performed on April 18, 2007.

38. Pawliszyn JB (1997) *Method and device for solid phase microextraction and desorption*, United States Patent 5,691,206, November 25, 1997.

39. Steffen A and Pawliszyn J (1996) Determination of liquid accelerants in arson suspected fire debris using headspace solid-phase microextraction, *Analytical Communications*, **33**(4), pp 129–31.

40. ASTM International (2006) *ASTM E 2154-01 Standard practice for separation and concentration of ignitable liquid residues from fire debris samples by passive headspace concentration with solid phase microextraction (SPME)*, Annual Book of ASTM Standards 14.02, West Conshohocken, PA.

41. Pawliszyn J (2000) *Solid-phase microextraction. In: Encyclopedia of separation science*, editors Wilson I, Poole C, and Cooke M, Academic Press, San Diego, CA, pp 1416–24.

42. Ren Q and Bertsch W (1999) A comprehensive sample preparation scheme for accelerants in suspect arson cases, *Journal of Forensic Sciences*, **44**(3), pp 504–15.

43. Schelling C (2001) *Evaluation des performances et de la facilité d'utilisation de la SPME comme méthode d'extraction pour l'analyse de liquids inflammables dans des échantillons solides*, séminaire de 4ème année, Institut de police scientifique et de criminologie, University of Lausanne, Lausanne, Switzerland.

CHAPTER 12

Interpretation of Ignitable Liquid Residues Extracted from Fire Debris

"Fighting fire with fire only gets you ashes!"
Abigail "Dear Abby" van Buren, American advice columnist (1918–)

12.1 INTRODUCTION

12.1.1 Principle

When ignitable liquids are analyzed in their pure form, the interpretation of the resulting chromatograms is relatively straightforward. The different categories into which ignitable liquids can be classified have been presented in detail in Chapters 7 and 9. The methodology of interpretation of neat liquids has also been presented in Chapter 9 and a flowchart leading to this clear-cut classification was proposed in Figure 9-39. So far, fire debris analysis does not seem to be a very complex science; however, this is about to change. As a matter of fact, criminalists infrequently analyze neat liquids: Most analyses are carried out on fire debris samples collected from fire scenes. These samples are made of substrates that, in modern days, very often include synthetic polymers. Upon burning, these polymers can produce organic molecules that are either identical to the ones found in ignitable liquids or, at the very least, coextracted with ignitable liquid residues (ILR), thus making their identification more difficult. In addition, the presence of incidental liquids (ignitable liquids that have a legitimate presence in the debris and that are not accelerants used by a possible arsonist) is encountered more often today than a few decades ago. These incidental liquids significantly complicate the interpretation of the results, particularly as modern extraction and analytical techniques are much more sensitive than past ones. Thus, the presence of trace amounts of an incidental liquid that would not even have been detected 20 years ago is largely detected today because of the highly improved detection limit.

All these elements complicate the interpretation of chromatograms obtained from fire debris samples, and the criminalist must be very careful when carrying out this operation. This chapter first introduces how fire debris samples are created, which greatly helps in understanding what they contain in terms of volatile organic compounds (VOCs). Then, the most common materials found among substrates are presented, followed by the introduction to the concept of interfering products. Finally, a primer on how to interpret chromatograms from fire debris will be presented, along with some case examples. It is important to understand that this chapter constitutes a basic interpretation course rather than an advanced one. The reader should pursue his or her training with literature readings and practical examinations of debris.

12.1.2 Creation of the Debris

In order to understand how fire debris samples can contain organic compounds hindering the identification of ILR, it is necessary to study their life, from their birth to the moment when they are analyzed. Figure 12-1 should help with this endeavor.

A/ Raw Material

First, all substrates come from raw materials, which could be as diverse as wood, crude oil, or mineral stones. It is important to realize that although back at the beginning of the century, most household items were manufactured from wood or inert material, today, most of these items find their origin in crude oil, which is the raw material used in modern plastics—the same crude oil as the one used to produce petroleum products such as gasoline or diesel fuel. Already at this stage, one can quickly make the connection between petroleum-based ignitable liquid and products hindering the identification of ILR and that are found in substrates. Nevertheless, raw material can contain many VOCs, even if it is not made from crude oil. For example, some soft wood contains a lot of terpenes, compounds constituting thinners such as turpentine [1].

B/ Manufacture

The raw material must be transformed into the desired object, which could be absolutely anything ranging from simple plywood, to synthetic floor tiles, to foam for couches and other furniture, to plastic containers, to nylon fibers for a carpet. The manufacture of each object obviously cannot be described in this book, however it is important for the fire debris analyst to invest personal time understanding how some objects are manufactured. For example, it is crucial to know that most outsoles are actually

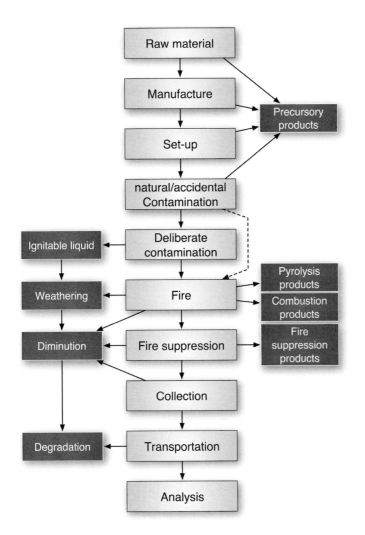

FIGURE 12-1
The different steps (in the middle) to which the fire debris sample is subjected from its creation to its analysis, along with the influences (on the left) to the potential ignitable liquid present in the debris and the different interfering products created (on the right).

glued on the upper part of the shoe. This glue contains many VOCs such as benzene or toluene. Similarly, the printing industry uses solvent during newspaper ink application. This solvent, usually a heavy petroleum distillate such as kerosene, is still present in newspapers long after they have been printed. Another example would concern the presence of normal-alkane and isoparaffinic products in vinyl flooring [2]. These are used as plasticizers, along with some oxygenated compounds, during the manufacture of the flooring, thus their presence is entirely due to the manufacturing process.

Gathering Information on Objects Manufacturing

It is strongly advised that the fire debris analyst gather more information regarding how objects are manufactured, particularly with the most commonly submitted samples. These include carpet, wood, baseboards, newspapers, shoes, clothing, and such. Some books, such as *How things are made: From automobiles to zippers*, may bring some answers or contain links to other more informative sources [3]. There are also web sites that can provide pertinent information. Such an example is "How everyday things are made," available at http:// manufacturing.stanford.edu. However, the information is limited and must always be independently checked as Internet resources are rarely peer-reviewed. The more recent show produced by The Science Channel called "How it's made" is also a great source of information. It is available for free viewing at http://science.discovery. com. The fire debris analyst should also not hesitate to contact manufacturing plants and eventually organize and participate in factory visits. The most pertinent information is gathered from these types of events.

C/ Set-up

Whereas an object such as a toaster is sold as a plug-and-play apparatus (no additional operation is required before its use), there are many building materials that must be set up in their final configuration before they can be used as a part of the household. For example, vinyl flooring, parquet flooring, wooden deck, and carpet must all undergo a specific process to be set up in their intended environment. Vinyl flooring and carpet often are glued to the floor. That glue contains a solvent, usually a medium petroleum distillate. Wooden decks are treated for waterproofing, a treatment that often contains a medium petroleum distillate as a solvent [4].

Again, the fire debris analyst should gather intelligence regarding how things are built and set up in their final configuration. This information is extremely helpful in determining what products can be present in the sample based on the substrate. One good source of such information is found in the classes often offered by home improvement stores. These courses teach how to build or repair a house, and thus, good building practice information is available through this channel.

D/ Natural/Accidental Contamination

Once an object has been set up and is in use, it is subject to all sorts of contamination, both natural and accidental. These contaminations can be known or unknown to the user. For example, when spraying insecticides in an apartment, the insecticide's vehicle is usually a solvent such as a naphthenic paraffinic or aromatic product. This IL will deposit on the surfaces that were sprayed and may persist for a certain time. The substrate is thus contaminated. Another example of contamination has been studied by Cavanagh et al. [5]: Four percent of car mats placed in vehicles became contaminated with gasoline. This contamination is due to the fact that people may carry small amounts of gasoline on their shoe sole mainly by filling up their gas tanks at the gas station—gasoline that will eventually deposit on the car mats upon contact with the shoe sole. It is for this category of interfering products that a comparison sample is most valuable. The proper comparison sample should have been subjected to the same random life than the questioned sample, to the exception of the deliberate contamination (pouring of the accelerant). Thus, natural/accidental contaminations, which cannot be predicted or identified from the nature of the sample itself, can be determined from the analysis of the comparison sample.

E/ Deliberate Contamination

The deliberate contamination of a substrate is defined as the pouring of an ignitable liquid as an accelerant by the arsonist. The result of this event—the presence of ignitable liquid on the substrate—is what must be identified by the fire debris analyst when examining the sample. As shown in Figure 12-1, this step has been placed aside to emphasize the fact that it may not have occurred. Obviously, if all samples submitted to the crime laboratory were known to have been doused with an ignitable liquid, there would be little need for an analysis. But in reality, a crime laboratory receives a good proportion of samples that do not contain any ILR, which are thus identified as negative samples.

F/ Fire

The fire brings significant influences to the VOC content of a substrate. The fire has effect on the ignitable liquid as well as on the substrate. It consumes the ignitable liquid, weathers it, and diminishes its presence. But it also pyrolyzes the substrate and combusts it. All these actions greatly increase the presence of products hindering the identification of any possible ILR.

G/ Fire Suppression

Fire suppression efforts, though a necessary operation, can also contribute to the modification of the products ultimately found in the substrate and to the diminution of the presence of ILR in the substrate. This will all depend on the procedures used by the fire department during the intervention. The use of powder or foam as extinguishing agents produces different effects than simple water. Nevertheless, a water-soluble ignitable liquid will have a much greater tendency to be washed out by extinguishing water than a water-insoluble ignitable liquid. More detailed information will be covered in Subsection 12.3.6.

H/ Collection

Modern collection techniques as seen in Chapter 6 should not bring any further contamination of the debris sample. When hand tools are properly decontaminated and no power tools using an internal-combustion engine are used, the possibility of extra contamination is quasi-nonexistent. However, improper or incomplete collection of fire debris samples can seriously contribute to a diminution of the ignitable liquid present in the sample. This is the reason why it is crucial to perform a very well-though selection of the samples to be collected.

Also, the use of an inappropriate container may seriously contribute to a diminution of the ILR present in the sample. In this particular instance, cross-contamination between debris packed in the same box can also occur (see example in Figure 6-11). This situation can easily be avoided by using proper containers for fire debris evidence.

I/ Transportation

The transportation of the debris itself, as long as the container is appropriate and sealed, should not bring any further contamination. However, if the sample is composed of soil, biodegradation of ILR can occur. This could greatly hamper their proper identification. Thus, the transportation must always be brief and properly controlled. Of course, if soil is known to be present in the debris, the sample must be cooled during transportation to prevent any possible degradation.

J/ Analysis

The difficulty of the analysis is to observe what is inside the sample. Unfortunately, it is not possible to obtain a picture identical to what is inside the sample. There are different effects created by the different extraction techniques, as presented in Chapter 11. Fortunately, these effects are quite well known and can readily be integrated in the interpretation of the results, as long as the fire debris analyst keeps them in his or her mind.

12.2 MATERIALS CONSTITUTING SUBSTRATES

12.2.1 Overview

It would be hopeless to try to make a comprehensive survey of all materials used in all substrates. However, it can be interesting for the fire debris analyst to have a relatively good idea of the composition of most common substrates. Figure 12-2 shows the distribution of the types of different substrates submitted to a laboratory [6].

As one can readily notice, carpet and flooring materials, in general, constitute the majority of the samples. This is very logical as ignitable liquids are most often poured on the floor; all other objects are in relatively small proportion compared to flooring materials. As explained in Chapter 6, it is better to collect porous material: Because the ignitable liquid can soak into the material, there are better chances that residues will survive, compared to a nonporous material into which the liquid cannot penetrate. As such, carpet is often the sample of choice, particularly in US homes, where carpet is very common and where construction is mostly made of wood. In some other countries, concrete is used more often to build floors and carpet may

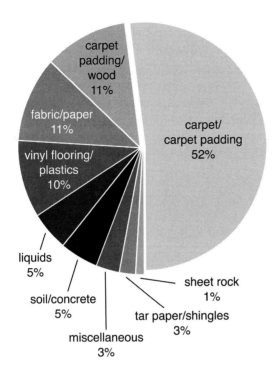

FIGURE 12-2
Distribution of the types of different substrates submitted as fire debris samples to a crime laboratory. Source: [6].

not be as common. As a result, floor tiles or wooden parquet are present. When concrete floors are encountered, it is possible to collect chunks of concrete. Although it may require a little bit of work to obtain the sample, the reward is definitely worth it as concrete is one of the best substrates for ILR, since it is porous and exhibits almost no interfering products.

12.2.2 Description of Some Materials

Substrates of the same type can be composed of different materials. This is well illustrated with carpets, as the fibers can be nylon, polypropylene, polyester, or other polymers. Thus, it is not possible to state with certainty that a given material is made of a given polymer—this would make the task way too simple. However, it is possible to provide a list of the most common polymers used with some materials.[1] This is done as a reference for the reader, who must remain aware that this information is neither comprehensive nor exclusive.

A/ Carpets and Rugs

Carpets usually are made of a main fiber type (monofiber carpet) or a set of different fiber types (multifiber) that constitute the upper part of the

---

[1] This list was compiled in 2001 by carrying out a survey of the different substrates sold in major home improvement retailers in Miami, Florida, USA [7].

Table 12-1a	Different compositions of monofiber carpets and rugs	
Monofiber carpets	**Monofiber rugs**
Polypropylene	Wool
Polyester	Nylon
Polyolefin	Polyolefin
Nylon	Polypropylene
	Modified acrylic (modacrylic)
	Acrylic
	Cotton
	Natural hemp
	Jute
	Sisal
	Seagrass

Table 12-1b	Different compositions of multifiber carpets and rugs			
Multifiber carpets	**Proportion**	**Multifiber rugs**	**Proportion**
Polyolefin-nylon	54%–46% to 92%–8%	Wool-polyolefin	60%–40%
Nylon-PET	92%–8%	Wool-polypropylene	40%–60%
Polypropylene-nylon	81%–19% to 96%–4%	Wool-nylon	n/a

substrate. These fibers are glued on a backing, which is made of a different material, most commonly polybutadiene. A second backing may also be present. As such, a carpet usually contains at least two different polymers in addition to glue. A rug is normally not glued, however it can also be mono- or multifiber and it has a backing. Table 12-1 shows some of the most common polymers found in carpets and rugs [7]. Also, a floor protector—a piece of transparent polymer placed atop a carpet or rug to protect it without hiding it, such as in a place where a chair is located—often is found in modern households and offices. This floor protector is almost exclusively made of polyvinyl chloride (PVC).

B/ Flooring

Synthetic flooring usually is made of PVC or linoleum. Some synthetic flooring materials are also made of polyurethane, but this is not very widespread. Wood flooring can be solid wood or engineered wood (made of several layers of different woods). Commonly encountered woods are red oak, white oak, ash, maple, birch, walnut, cherry, mahogany, Douglas fir, white pine, and yellow pine wood. Sometimes, a layer atop the wood, called covering, may be present. This layer is made of wax or polyurethane.

Vinyl v. Linoleum

Very often people use the two terms vinyl and linoleum (floorings) interchangeably, however these terms do not have the same meaning. Vinyl flooring, sometimes called vinyl composite tile (VCT), commonly refers to a synthetic plastic made of polyvinyl chloride (PVC). Linoleum refers to a material made of a preparation of linseed oil and wood flour or cork dust. This preparation is solidified (due to the polymerization of linseed oil) on a canvas or burlap backing, making a very strong material. Both vinyl and linoleum are used to make flooring sur-

faces, however one must be careful not to confuse the two terms as they present significant differences in their chemistry, and thus in the types of VOCs they may produce.

A quick trick to differentiate vinyl flooring from linoleum is that the latter usually exhibits a uniform coloring through its thickness, while the former usually has a top layer of a given color/pattern and the rest is of different color/pattern. Also, linoleum has the canvas or burlap backing, which is absent on the vinyl flooring.

C/ Wall Coverings

Wall coverings can consist of many different materials. A common wall covering is wallpaper, which is usually made of either paper (cellulosic material) or PVC. Modern wallpapers are almost all made of PVC, or at least, the underlying layer is made of PVC and then other material may be placed on top of it. This material could be paper, wall fabrics, grass cloth, cotton, or silk.

Walls can also be covered with paint, which could be composed of many different polymers. However, paint on walls is usually not an issue in fire debris analysis, due to its relatively thin layer and the fact that it burns away quite rapidly.

Finally, walls can also be covered with curtains or other fabrics. Curtains usually are characterized by a panel (a curtain that just hangs straight down) or a scarf (an ornamental piece of material draped across the rod), and a liner (the fabric on the window side of the curtain). In a monofiber version, the panel, scarf, or liner is usually either polyethylene or cotton [7]. Table 12-2 shows different typical multifiber compositions of curtains [7].

D/ Furniture

Items of furniture can include many different polymers. Furniture upholstery usually is made of nylon, polyester, cotton, or wool. Synthetic foam found in couches and other furniture usually is made of polyurethane or polystyrene. Other plastic parts found in furniture include polyethylene, polypropylene, and polyethylene terephthalate (PET). Wood, which is a cellulosic natural polymer, is also often encountered.

Table 12-2	*Typical compositions of multifiber curtains*		
Multifiber panels and scarfs	**Proportion**	**Multifiber liners**	**Proportion**
Rayon-polyethylene	41%–59% to 75%–25%	Rayon-polethylene	20%–80%
Rayon-acetate	72%–28%	Rayon-acetate	72%–28% to 77%–23%
Rayon-acrylic	80%–20%	Rayon-flax-acetate	56%–8%–36%
Rayon-acrylic-cotton-polyethylene	n/a	Rayon-flax-cotton	62%–10%–28%
Polyethylene-acrylic	77%–23%	Cotton-polyethylene	29%–71% to 47%–53%
Polyethylene-acrylic-polyolefin	50%–41%–9%		
Polyethylene-cotton	21%–79% to 50%–50%		
Polyethylene-metallic fibers	88%–12%		

E/ Other Items

Other items found in a typical household are made of many different materials, and more particularly polymeric material. Polyethylene and polypropylene often are used to make plastic sheeting and enclosures. Plastic cutlery are made of polystyrene for example, as are most appliance housings, and as is a CD case (the CD itself is made of polycarbonate). Synthetic sponges are made of polyurethane with the (usually green) scratching part made of nylon. Polymethylmethacrylate constitutes the shatterproof windows, also called Plexiglas, often encountered in locations with hurricane activity.

Learning More about Polymers

These are just a few examples of the great variety of components found in the different items of a house. The fire debris analyst cannot know all the items and their respective compositions. Thus, it is important to rely on good information resources when the nature of a material must be determined. One such source is "The macrogalleria: A cyberwonderland of polymer fun," developed by the University of Southern Mississippi under the direction of Professor Lon J. Mathias and available at http://pslc.ws/macrog. This web site contains a plethora of information regarding polymers. It is not possible to emphasize enough how this Internet resource is useful to the criminalist to learn about polymers and substrate composition as well as to identify the composition of a given substrate for a specific case. Other resources should be consulted on a regular basis. Also, the fire debris analyst is strongly advised to read composition labels of diverse objects he or she may encounter in every day life. Only by having this sleuthing attitude can one greatly improve his or her knowledge of the substrates found in fire debris samples.

12.2.3 Description Based on Polymers

There are numerous polymers that are commercially available and commonly found in household items. Table 12-3 is a list of some of these most often encountered polymers. Figure 12-3 shows their chemical structures.

Table 12-3	*Most commonly encountered polymers in a household with some of their applications*		
Polymer	**Abbreviation**	**Type**	**Example of use**
Polyethylene	PE	Thermoplastic	Plastic bags, boxes (Rubbermaid), toys, gas tanks, enclosures, bottles, hoses, wiring insulation
Polypropylene	PP	Thermoplastic	Food packaging, textiles, ropes, enclosures, automotive parts, banknotes, outdoor carpets
Polystyrene	PS	Thermoplastic	Appliance housings, disposable cutleries, all kinds of plastic parts used with appliances, molded automotive parts, styrofoam, CD cases, toys
Polyvinyl chloride	PVC	Thermoplastic	Vinyl siding, magnetic cards, piping, conduit, vinyl flooring, shower curtain, rain gear
Polyvinylidene chloride (Saran)	PVDC	Thermoplastic	Food transparent sheets, plastic films, doll hair, shoe insoles, cleaning cloths, tape
Polyvinylidene fluoride	PVDF	Thermoplastic	Paints, electrical wire insulator (particularly the ones getting hot), special coatings, combined with PMMA to make specially resistant containers
Polytetrafluoroethylene (Teflon)	PTFE	Thermoplastic	Nonstick surfaces (cookware), bearings, insulator, treatment for carpets and fabrics
Polymethylacrylate	PMA	Thermoplastic	Used to absorb water in pads, diapers
Polymethylmethacrylate (Plexiglas)	PMMA	Thermoplastic	Synthetic glass, exterior automotive lenses, helmet visors
Nylon (polyamide)	—	Thermoplastic	Fibers, clothing, fabrics, parachutes, ropes, strings
Polyacrylonitrile	PAN	Thermoplastic	Fibers, textiles, outdoor fabrics, precursor for carbon fibers
Poly(styrene-butadiene-styrene)	SBS	Thermoplastic	Shoe soles, tire treads
Acrylonitrile butadiene styrene	ABS	Thermoplastic	Automotive body parts, piping, toys (Lego bricks), enclosures
Poly(styrene-*co*-acrylonitrile)	SAN	Thermoplastic	Plastic with similar applications to PS
Polyethylene terephthalate	PET	Thermoplastic	Drinking bottle, food containers, plastic jars, fibers for clothing or fabrics
Polybutylene terephthalate	PBT	Thermoplastic	Insulation material, solvent resistant material
Polycarbonate	PC	Thermoplastic	Lenses, safety glasses, CDs, DVDs, bottles, headlamp lenses, appliance/computer enclosures, protective films
Polybutadiene	PBD	Elastomer	Tires, hoses, car parts
Polyisobutylene	PIB	Elastomer	Inner tire chamber, airtight material
Polyisoprene	PIP	Elastomer	Rubber, tires, gloves, condom, rubber bands
Polychloroprene (Neoprene)	PC	Elastomer	Wet suits, laptop sleeves, electrical insulation, adhesives

Table 12-3 continued			*Most commonly encountered polymers in a household with some of their applications*		
Polymer	**Abbreviation**	**Type**	**Example of use**
Polyvinyl acetate	PVAc	Elastomer	Adhesive, wood (white) glue, one constituent of latex paint
Polyvinyl alcohol	PVA	Elastomer	Adhesive, combined with PET to make bottles for carbonated drinks (PVA acts as a carbon dioxide barrier), slime, water-soluble films
Polyurethane	PU	Elastomer	Fibers, foam, condoms, carpet parts, hard plastic parts, fabrics (Spandex), paints, upholstery padding, synthetic sponge

12.3 CONCEPT OF INTERFERING PRODUCTS

12.3.1 Definition and Origin

The beginning of the chapter introduced the fact that substrates from fire debris samples contain VOCs that, through their contribution to the chromatogram, may hinder the identification of an ILR. It is time to see with greater details what these products are and what origins they have. Even though one can never predict exactly what contribution the substrate provides to the chromatogram, it is still possible to have an idea of what should be in the sample and the reasons why it is there. This greatly helps the fire debris analyst to interpret chromatograms: Because he or she can better understand which compound comes from what substrates and how they relate to each other, making it easier to better identify what belongs to a possible ignitable liquid and what does not.

In fire debris analysis, interfering products are defined as the set of products (or components) found in a sample and that interfere with the proper identification of ignitable liquid residues [7]. The sources of interfering products are multiple and can be classified in four main categories:

- Precursory products
- Pyrolysis products
- Combustion products
- Fire suppression products

The origin of these products was roughly presented in Figure 12-1. Figure 12-4 shows the more detailed process undergone by the substrate, which explains the presence of all these products. Each category of products is discussed in Subsections 12.3.3 to 12.3.6. It is truly important for the fire debris analyst to fully comprehend these concepts.

12.3.2 Training

This chapter offers an introduction to the concept of interfering products. It provides the reader with the basic principles and some examples, however it

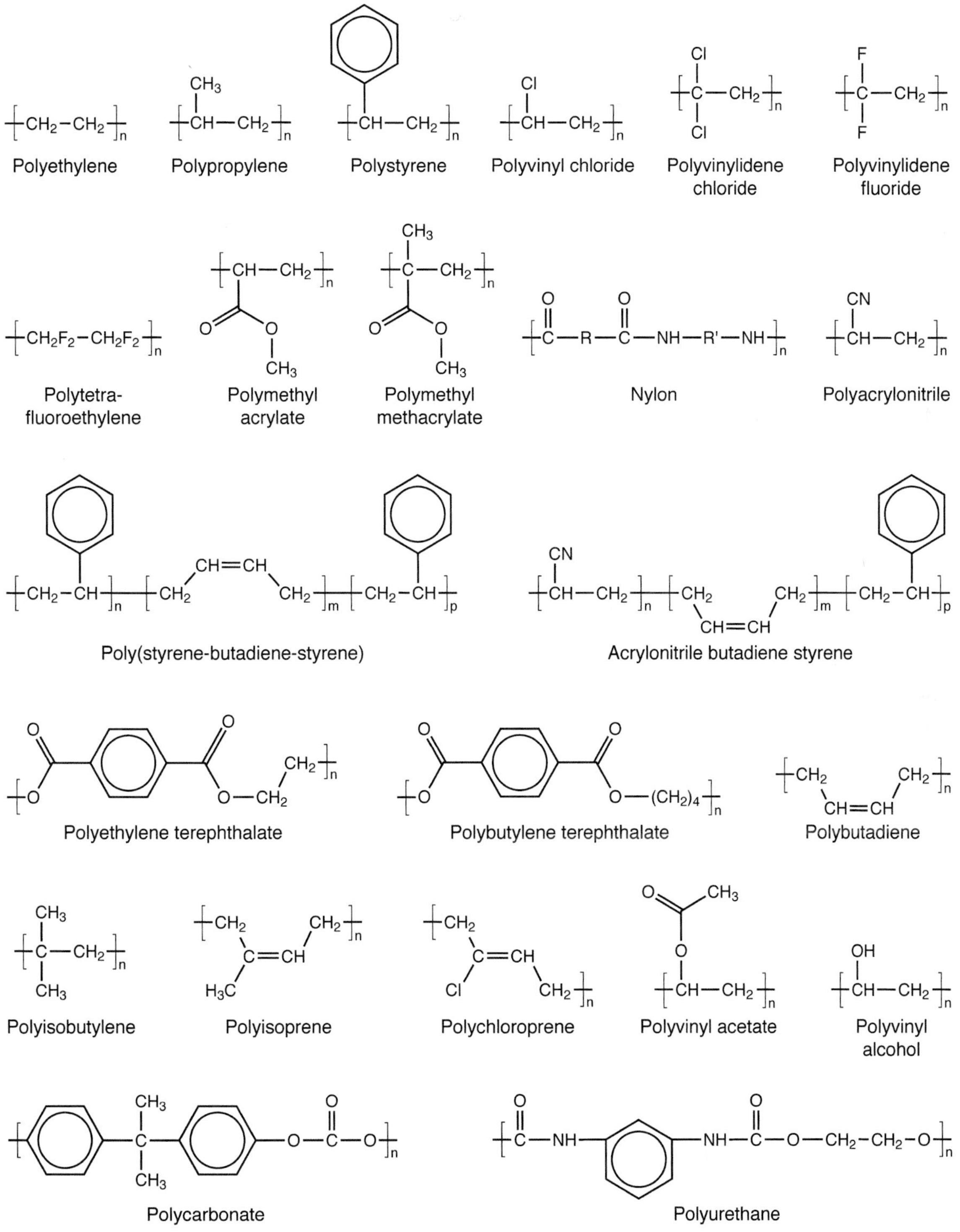

FIGURE 12-3 Chemical structures of the polymers presented in Table 12-3.

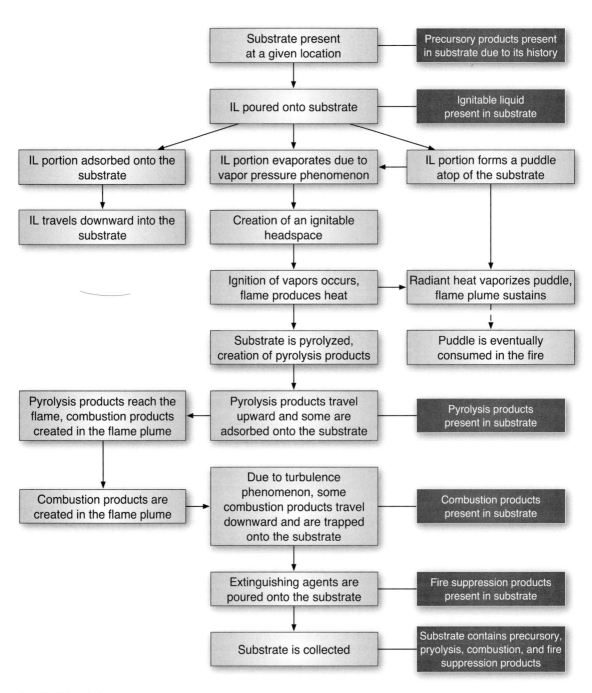

FIGURE 12-4 *Origin of the different categories of interfering products through the steps undergone by the substrate.*

is not a comprehensive resource of all interfering products found in fire debris samples. Such a directory is not even thinkable in terms of comprehensiveness. The only true manner by which a fire debris analyst can train his or her skills in understanding interfering products and improving his or her interpretation of ILR chromatograms is to thoroughly practice this science. It is not possible to emphasize enough how important it is for the criminalist to analyze self-made fire debris samples by obtaining different substrates from different sources, burning them, and looking at the resulting chromatograms (see Figure 12-5). This is the only true manner of obtaining valid and meaningful experience. Substrates should be obtained from all kinds of sources, mostly retail stores. When doing so, keep in mind that there is no control on natural or accidental contamination, which could be problematic. However, by performing repeated analyses on many different substrates, one can better comprehend the usual baseline observed for each type of substrates.

It is also interesting to analyze substrates in both their burned and unburned states. This allows for a differentiation between precursory products and pyrolysis/combustion products. When receiving a comparison sample in a case, the criminalist can very well first analyze the sample unburned and then proceed to its burning and its subsequent analysis.

Burning Samples

Whenever required, a sample should be burned in order to generate pyrolysis and combustion products, so they can be analyzed and their contribution in terms of interfering products evaluated. The simplest manner of burning a sample is to place it in a one-quart or one-gallon can and use a propane torch to ignite it as shown in Figure 12-5.

Some samples will readily ignite and flaming fire will sustain. Others will be difficult to ignite and some will not exactly sustain flaming fires, such as PVC. If that is the case, the propane torch should be constantly applied to the sample to provide sufficient flame to scorch it. Otherwise, the sample can be removed from the can and held with tongs. In this case, more air is provided to the sample, which allows it to burn better.

The sample should be burned between one- to two-thirds of its size. It useless to completely carbonize the sample: one would be left with carbon and some other elements and all organic molecules would be consumed. The ideal is to ignite the sample, let it burn (if possible) until about two-thirds of its size is scorched and extinguish it.

The extinguishment is very important, and there are two manners of conducting it. One method is to place the lid back on top of the can, which starves the fire due to a lack of oxygen and eventually extinguishes it. This technique leads to a great amount of pyrolysis products, as the sample remains hot for a long period of time, and smoldering fire may sustain for a while. During that time, pyrolysis of the sample may continue, thus loading the substrate with pyrolysis products. Practical experiments have shown that a sample extinguished by starvation of oxygen produces up to 10 times the amount of VOCs compared to a sample extinguished with water [7]. This is ideal if the criminalist wants a lot of pyrolysis products, however it may generate even more than what is found in a real fire scenario. The other technique consists of spraying some water on the sample. This should be carried out with a spray bottle and no more than 10 to 20 ml of water should be squirted on the flames. Excessive water may hamper the extraction of the sample. The lid can then be placed immediately on the can, or the sample can be left airing for a while. This may contribute to a certain loss of pyrolysis and combustion products. In any case, the sample should be left to rest for a couple of hours prior to its extraction.

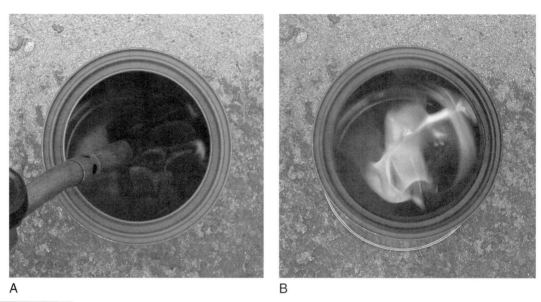

A   B

FIGURE 12-5   *Creation of burned comparison samples. A/ The sample is first ignited with the propane torch until the flame sustains. B/ Fire is sustained until about two-thirds of the sample is burned. (For a full color version of this figure, please see the insert.)*

12.3.3 Precursory Products

Precursory products represent a broad category encompassing numerous sources of products. Figure 12-1 presented the different steps undergone by a substrate and identified the sources of precursory products as originating from raw material, manufacturing process, set-up, and natural/accidental contamination. It is clear that one will never be able to determine all precursory products present in a sample by simple knowledge of its identity. Although some manufacturing processes are constant and involve the use of known products, contaminations can arise from anywhere at anytime and can neither be predicted nor all known. However, by understanding which products arise from the manufacturing process, for example, the interpretation of a chromatogram is rendered much easier as one is not surprised as to the presence of a specific compound or set of compounds in a given sample. Table 12-4 shows some substrates commonly encountered in fire debris samples and precursory products that may be associated with them [7–10]. The fire debris analyst should create a library of chromatograms of precursory products of most common substrates.

Table 12-4	*Typical precursory products (from manufacturing process) found in different substrates [7–10]*
Substrate	**Precursory products**
Adhesives	Aromatics, petroleum distillates, isoparaffinic products
Carbonless forms	Medium normal alkane products
Clothing	Toluene, heavy petroleum distillate, series of aldehydes
Magazines	Heavy petroleum distillate, light aromatics
Newspapers	Heavy petroleum distillate
Plastic bags	Heavy normal alkane products, isoparaffinic products, heavy petroleum distillate
Ropes	Heavy petroleum distillate
Shoes	Toluene, heavy petroleum distillate, glycols
Shop rags	Heavy petroleum distillate
Vinyl flooring	Normal-alkane products, medium isoparaffinic products
Wood (some)	Terpenes (miscellaneous category)

Distillation Products

It is important to understand that most precursory products are distillation products in the sense that they distill out of the debris either as a result of the fire, after the fire, or after the collection from the scene. Typical natural distillation products are terpenes from softwoods. As a matter of fact, distillation is used in the industry to extract these compounds from the raw wood. Distillation products also include the very particular category of products originating from the putrefaction of organic matter such as a body at a fire scene. These may include aldehydes, ketones, alcohols, and even dimethylsulfides.

12.3.4 Pyrolysis Products

The phenomenon of pyrolysis is definitely one of the most important contributors in terms of interfering products. The contribution from pyrolysis products is inevitable in a substrate that has been burned and that is constituted of polymers, natural or man-made. As seen in Section 4.4, there are three main routes through which pyrolysis of polymers occurs. Among them, the two most important ones—random scission and side-group scission—are enormous contributors of interfering products with some given polymers. The fire debris analyst must be well aware of this contribution as pyrolysis products consist largely of molecules identical to the ones found in petroleum products. Fortunately, the diagnostic patterns presented in Chapter 9 are quite specific to petroleum products. Pyrolysis may reproduce a pattern somehow resembling one particular diagnostic pattern, but they have not yet produced a combination of these diagnostic patterns. Thus, pyrolysis products will normally not create a chromatographic pattern that may be confused with an ignitable liquid. However, they will add compounds to a chromatogram, which may mask an ignitable liquid, or distort the diagnostic patterns normally observed.

Figure 12-6 is the total ion chromatogram of pyrolysis products from polyethylene (PE). Polyethylene mostly decomposes by random scission and as a result, as shown in Figure 4-7, a series of alkane-alkene-alkadiene is created. This can be readily seen in Figure 12-6a with the repeating groups of alkadiene-alkene-alkane constituting the main pattern of the chromatogram. The aliphatic extracted ion chromatograms shown in Figure 12-6b renders this picture even clearer.

Note how peak occurrence in the chromatogram in Figure 12-6a spans from beginning to end. This is typical of pyrolysis products, as opposed to most IL, which span over a short range (except for heavy petroleum distillates, which exhibit patterns that have a wider range). Also, note how the pattern repeats itself (even though each group is slightly different and gets more unresolved as time increases), with a constant interval of one methylene group.[2] This is a second indicator of pyrolysis products, as repeating patterns are typically not common with petroleum-based IL. Also, note the similarity of the pattern between the 55 and 83 windows in Figure 12-6b. This is due to a complete absence of cycloalkanes. In this instance, the 83 ions mimic the 55 ions because they are produced by the same molecules. Finally, the difference between the 55 and 57 patterns is due to the saturation of the aliphatic compounds: In the 57 pattern, n-alkanes are predominant, with n-alkenes shown as small peaks, and in the 55 pattern, n-alkenes and n-alkadienes are predominant, leaving relatively short n-alkane peaks.

Figure 12-7a shows the TIC of polypropylene (PP) pyrolysis products. Clearly, the repeating pattern is not as obvious as with polyethylene, but when the peaks are identified (or at least their classes), it is possible to

---

[2] If a pure chain of polyethylene would be pyrolyzed, only n-alkanes, n-alkenes, and n-alkadienes would be produced. However, because there are some cross-linkings between the macromolecular chains of polyethylene, there are some branched alkanes, alkenes, and alkadienes that are produced. This is the reason why this chromatogram does not exhibit a perfect triplet of peaks, but rather small groups of several peaks, mostly dominated by n-alkanes, n-alkenes, and n-alkadienes. A polyethylene with a low amount of cross-linking is called a high density polyethylene (HDPE), and one with a high amount of cross-linking is called a low density polyethylene (LDPE). The higher the polyethylene density, the more closely a triplet pattern will be produced. Also, one can appreciate how the base of each group becomes more and more unresolved as time increases. This is due to the fact that as the molecule contains more atoms, more isomers are possible and thus, present. Thus, the presence of this increasing number of isomers results in the less resolved cluster of peaks.

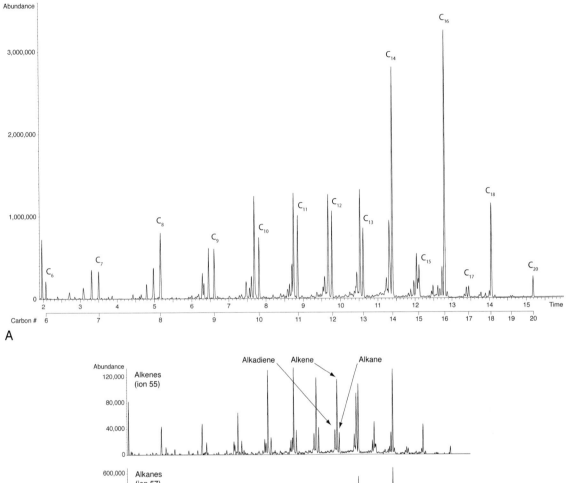

A

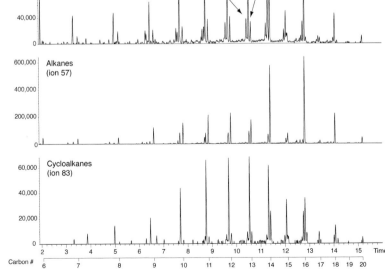

B

FIGURE 12-6 (a) TIC of polyethylene pyrolysis products. This chromatogram was obtained with a different configuration than the one presented in Figure 9-1. (b) EICs for ions 55, 57, and 83 of polyethylene pyrolysis products.

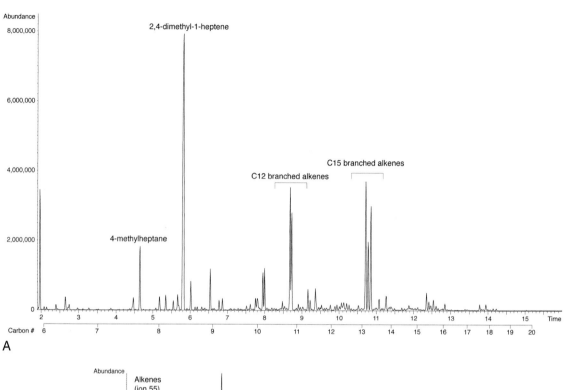

A

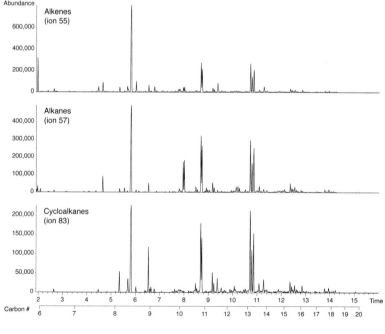

B

FIGURE 12-7 *(a) TIC of polypropylene pyrolysis products. This chromatogram was obtained with a different configuration than the one presented in Figure 9-1. (b) EICs for ions 55, 57, and 83 of polypropylene pyrolysis products.*

realize that the different groups differ by three carbons. When the difference between each group is constant, it is a relatively clear indicator of pyrolysis products, and the difference (of three carbons in this case) usually corresponds to the loss or gain of a monomer. Polypropylene monomer is constituted of three carbon atoms, corresponding perfectly to the pattern shown in this chromatogram. Figure 12-7b shows the extracted ion chromatograms, which again exhibit very close resemblance to one another.

Figure 12-8 shows the TIC of polystyrene (PS) pyrolysis products. Because PS decomposes by both monomer reversion (as shown in Figure 4-9) and side-group scission, it creates a chromatogram composed of styrene as the main peak, followed by many different aromatics. Polyvinyl chloride (PVC) is a polymer that decomposes mainly by side-group scission and thus, would produce many aromatic compounds [11]. Again, although many aromatic compounds that are present in gasoline, aromatic products, and some petroleum distillates are present in PS pyrolysis products, the diagnostic patterns for IL are not present.

Pyrolysis products can seriously complicate the chromatogram, however they are not known to create diagnostic patterns that are typical of IL. However, they will significantly modify them, when both pyrolysis products and IL are present.

Predicting Pyrolysis Products

It is not possible to predict exactly which pyrolysis products will be present in a sample; however, it is possible to proceed to an estimate of these products. In order to do that, one must know the polymer constituting the debris. If the substrate consists of several polymers, the process may quickly become complicated. Then, it is necessary to carefully study the structure of the polymer and identify the different bonds constituting it. By knowing their bond dissociation energy (D), as presented in Table 3-2, it is possible to identify the pathway(s) used by the polymer when undergoing pyrolysis: The weakest bonds usually are broken first. In this fashion, it is possible to estimate what types of compounds are released by the polymer when undergoing pyrolysis. This does not bring the answer regarding all the interfering products present in the sample, but it may explain part of them, which is pertinent information for the interpretation of the results.

12.3.5 Combustion Products

Combustion products differ from pyrolysis products by the fact that they result from an oxidation process, which is not the case for pyrolysis products. Practically, because most pyrolysis occur in an environment in which oxygen is present, some oxidation of the released products will occur, thus creating combustion products. No studies have been published yet in forensic sciences to study the difference between pyrolysis and combustion products. This is likely due to the fact that it is not practically feasible to separate combustion and pyrolysis products. One must remember that combustion

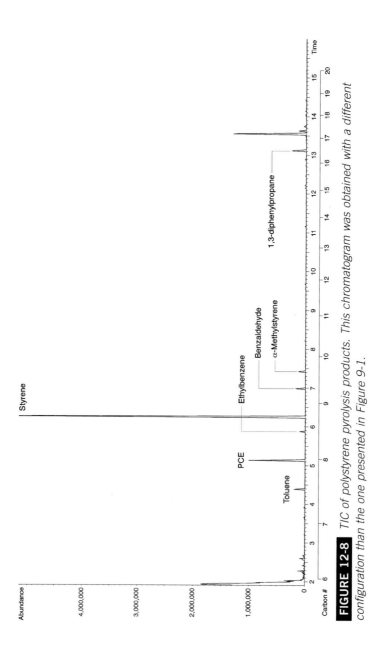

FIGURE 12-8 TIC of polystyrene pyrolysis products. This chromatogram was obtained with a different configuration than the one presented in Figure 9-1.

is a very complex process, which generates many different ions and thus, molecules. As a result, many different products can be released by combustion. The two most important ones, in the burning of an organic substance, are water (H_2O) and carbon dioxide (CO_2). However, these products do not usually interfere with the identification of ILR. Products that are heavier in nature (constituted of more atoms) can become problematic in ILR analysis. Examples of combustion products are benzaldehyde and acetophenone.

Table 12-5 shows the 25 most commonly encountered combustion and pyrolysis products determined based on the analysis of approximately 100 samples of burned substrates [7].

Although the meaning of this table is questionable, one can quickly see that many aromatic products, major components of several types of IL, are among this list. As such, the criminalist must keep this in mind and always look at the big picture when interpreting chromatograms and avoiding the tunnel effect of getting focused on too few components to make a call.

Interfering Products Released by the Burning of Human Fat

DeHaan et al. published a very important and interesting study on the interfering products released by the pyrolysis and combustion of human fat [12]. They demonstrated that human fat, as well as animal fat and tissue, would release many VOCs, including a series of n-aldehydes, n-alkenes, and n-alkanes. The chromatographic pattern would resemble the one from polyethylene pyrolysis products, but with a strong presence of n-aldehydes, ranging from approximately C_6 to C_{13}. This creates a repeating pattern of groups of a few peaks.

These n-aldehydes also are encountered often in samples containing clothing such as T-shirts or pants that have been worn. They may come from sebaceous secretions contained in clothing and, if present without the n-alkenes and n-alkanes, they appear as a series of spiking peaks. Because n-aldehydes have almost the same re-tention times as n-alkanes on a nonpolar chromatographic column such as a DB-1 or DB-5, this pattern first appears as an n-alkane pattern. This is the reason why it is crucial for the criminalist to identify some of these peaks through a mass spectral library search. Also, if one looks closely at aldehyde peaks, it is possible to notice that they exhibit a slight tailing compared to an n-alkane peak.

There is additional literature that could be useful to the fire debris analyst regarding the compounds released upon putrefaction of organic matter. For example, Kamiya and Ose published a study on the odorous compounds produced by the putrefaction of food and Wilkins published an article reporting the VOCs released by various household waste [13, 14]. Important information may be obtained through these different sources.

12.3.6 Fire Suppression Products

During fire suppression activities, the fire department can use several different strategies to combat the blaze. The most common one is to douse the fire with water, however in many instances, additives can be used with water, to create foam for example. Table 12-6 shows the four main fire extinguishing agents [15, 16].

Table 12-5	The 25 most commonly encountered pyrolysis and combustion products encountered in the analysis of approximately 100 burned samples of different substrates commonly encountered in household [7]	
Compound	**Occurrence in [%]**
Toluene	97.1
Styrene	82.4
Naphthalene	73.5
Benzaldehyde	64.7
Ethylbenzene	64.7
Indene	55.9
Phenylethyne	55.9
m,p-Xylenes	35.3
1-Methylnaphthalene	29.4
2-Methylnaphthalene	29.4
Acetophenone	26.5
Furaldehyde	26.5
5-Methyl-2-furancarboxaldehyde	26.5
Tetradecane	26.5
α-Methylstyrene	23.5
2-Ethyl-1-hexanol	23.5
Biphenyl	23.5
Tridecane	23.5
C_{12} branched alkanes	20.6
Dodecane	20.6
Pentadecane	20.6
Undecane	20.6
C_{15} branched alkenes	17.6
o-Xylene	17.6
2,3-Dihydro-1,1,3-trimethyl-3-phenyl-1H-indene	14.7

Agent	Description
Table 12-6	*The four main fire suppression agents and their descriptions*
Water	Most commonly used agent. Acts by cooling down the substrate (due to its high heat capacity) and reducing oxygen concentration (dilution of oxygen by production of tremendous amounts of vapors: 1 liter of water creates 1,700 liters of vapor).
Foam (wet chemicals)	Two types of foam: chemical foam (obsolete) and mechanical foam. Different kinds of mechanical foams (AFFF, FFFP, etc.). All kinds of foam act by isolating the fuel from the oxidizing agent and some foams also act by cooling down the substrate.
Powder (dry chemicals)	Different kinds of dry chemicals, such as graphite or salt powder. Most of the dry chemicals act by inhibiting the chain reaction whereas some also act by cooling effect or by isolation of the fuel.
Gas	Halons (for halogen hydrocarbons) can be used only in special locations due to their serious effect on the ozone layer; they act by inhibition of the chain of reaction. Halons are now prohibited in many jurisdictions. CO_2 (carbon dioxide) is more widespread and acts by reduction of the oxygen concentration and by cooling effect.

Because there are many different brands of foams and powders, a comprehensive survey of their composition cannot be provided here. As illustrative examples, Tables 12-7 and 12-8 show the composition of two major foams and two major powders manufactured by Amerex [17].

Fire extinguishing agents can have two effects on the analysis of ILR: diminishing the amount of ILR recovered (see Subsection 12.4.3 for more details) and contributing to the presence of interfering products. Although the presence of these agents can add peaks to a chromatogram, the number of components is limited and they do not bring any possibility of false positive for ignitable liquids. Different studies exist in this regard. Coulson et al. published a paper for which they studied the Phos-Check WD 881 foam used by the New Zealand Fire Service [18]. That foam contains mostly d-limonene, 1-dodecanol, 2-methyl-2,4-pentanediol, and 1-tetradecanol. They concluded that the use of the foam had no significant interference on subsequent fire debris analysis [18]. McGee and Lang published research regarding the effect of a miscelle encapsulator fire suppression agent, known as F-500 and used in Ontario, Canada [19]. They found that the product would exhibit n-octanol, 2-ethylhexanoic acid, dodecane, and n-decanol in the chromatogram. However, in samples from a real house fire,

Table 12-7	*Typical composition of fire-fighting foams [17]*
Aqueous Film-Forming Foam 3% (AFFF)	
Water	78–81%
Diethylene glycol butyl ether	9.5–10.5%
Urea	3–7%
Triethanolamine	0.1–1%
Methyl-1H-benzotriazole	<1%
Miscellaneous (alkyl sulfate salts, amphoteric fluoro alkylamide, perfluoroalkyl sulfonate salts)	
Film-Forming Fluoroprotein (FFFP)	
Water	>53%
Hydrolyzed protein	<30%
Hexylene glycol	<10%
Miscellaneous (preservative, fluorosurfactants, surface active agents)	

Table 12-8	*Typical composition of fire-fighting powders [17]*
ABC powder	
Monoammonium phosphate and ammonium sulfate	95%
Mica	<3%
Attaclay	<3%
Silicone oil	1%
Calcium carbonate	<1%
Silica (precipitated)	<1%
Yellow pigment	<1%
Regular powder	
Sodium bicarbonate	>93%
Hydrated alumina silicate	<3%
Attaclay	<5%
Silicone oil	<1%

none of these compounds were detected. They concluded that the presence of this miscelle encapsulator did not preclude the detection or identification of common ignitable liquids [19]. A recent study also demonstrated that foam did not interfere with the ignitable liquid recovery and analysis [20].

On an interesting note, although the powder obtained by the manufacturer and analyzed in a study by the author (ES) did not contribute to the chromatogram at all, the same powder from a supplier exhibited the presence of alkanes and branched alkanes [21]. It was determined that the stock of powder from which fire extinguishers were refilled was stored in a shed containing a diesel generator as well as diesel fuel. The powder absorbed the fuel's vapors, which were then released as interfering products during analysis. This example demonstrates one more time that there is no black-or-white knowledge about the composition of substrates and the influence they can have on the fire debris sample.

Another influence that may be created by fire department suppression efforts is the contamination of the scene through the use of internal combustion engines. One phenomenon, which created some polemic in recent years, is the use of positive-pressure ventilation (PPV) at fire scenes. These large fans are used to push the smoke in a given direction, usually through the bottom part of a building toward the back or the top of the building. This helps the fire department to keep a clear view of the inside of the building as they penetrate it, and it is also an integral part of the fire fighting strategy. Lang and Dixon demonstrated that the use of a gasoline-powered PPV resulted in the identification of low levels of gasoline in 3 out of 39 fabric samples placed inside a house in no predictable pattern with respect to time of exposure, location, or substrate type (wet or dry) [22]. They also stressed the fact that the use of a PPV fan at a fire scene must be documented and that the conditions set in the experiment involved a regular use of the fan; if a spill occurs during refueling operation and gas is pushed through the venting action, more important contamination may occur [23]. If other tools using an internal combustion engine are utilized at the scene, such as a chainsaw or a generator, they may also contaminate a specific location. In such instances, it is crucial to document the use of such apparatuses, so that the investigator can know about it when collecting samples and forward this information to the crime laboratory along with the samples.

Finally, contamination of the substrates at a fire scene may also occur through the walking action of the intervening people. However, this is a very rare and unlikely possibility. A recent study demonstrated that even when walking through major quantities of spilled gasoline and then onto the fire scene, no contamination of the scene substrates occurred [24]. As a result, this type of contamination is not likely to be encountered by the fire debris analyst.

12.4 OTHER INFLUENCES ON ILR

12.4.1 Definition

Although the different interfering products have been presented, there are other phenomena that contribute to the modification of the original ignitable liquid that was poured on the substrate. These phenomena can have significant effects on the components constituting the IL. As a result, without even considering the contribution from interfering products, the chromatographic pattern obtained from the ILR extract can be significantly skewed compared to the genuine chromatographic pattern, obtained through the analysis of the neat liquid.

Consequently, the fire debris analyst must be aware of the phenomena leading to a modification of the ILR. These have been classified as weathering, diminution, and degradation. Fortunately, one can understand these phenomena fairly well, and thus estimate their influence on the ILR in a manner relatively accurate. Their effect is not as detrimental as some other unpredictable occurrences significantly contributing to the presence of VOCs in a sample. Hence, the fire debris analyst can relatively easily include weathering, diminution, and maybe to a lesser extent, degradation, in the interpretation of the chromatographic pattern to determine which genuine ignitable liquid is at the origin of the ILR present in the sample.

12.4.2 Weathering

Weathering is a term commonly used in the fire debris analysis community to describe the evaporation effects an ignitable liquid is subjected to. The reason why this term is used in lieu of evaporation is because the causes of weathering are multiple. One can imagine a beaker with some liquid in it just being evaporated under a hood. In practice, the liquid is poured on a substrate and subjected to major environmental stresses: heat, light exposure, and change of headspace due to turbulence. Weathering also is influenced by the substrate onto which the liquid has been poured.

Weathering was presented earlier in Subsection 9.4.3, and its effects on gasoline and a heavy petroleum distillate was shown in Figures 9-18 and 9-19. The reader must make sure he or she understands that phenomenon and its resulting influence well. Because an ignitable liquid is usually composed of tens or even hundreds of different components with different evaporation rates, a skewing of the composition of the liquid takes place with time. The more volatile a compound, the faster the rate at which it evaporates. Thus, weathering typically results in a shift of the chromatographic pattern toward the heavy end (high boiling point components); this is very well illustrated in Figures 9-18 and 9-19.

It is important to understand that a light IL will sustain more weathering damage than a heavy IL, as the components of the latter are not as influenced by regular weathering conditions because of their high boiling points. The overall pattern exhibited by an IL with a very narrow boiling point range does not dramatically change, if it even changes at all, until the product has completely disappeared. The reason lies in the fact that the boiling points of the different liquids' components are sufficiently close to each other so that the difference in their evaporation rate is negligible. This is the reason why the diagnostic patterns presented in Chapter 9 are relatively constant for different ignitable liquids and, more importantly, different stages of weathering of a given ignitable liquid. So, if intrapattern comparison is valuable, it is clear that interpattern comparison may not work as significant changes may occur between two patterns, due to their differences in boiling point range.

The fire debris analyst is advised to weather some liquids such as gasoline, kerosene, diesel fuel, and some medium-range liquids to study the change in chromatographic patterns. One must always keep in mind that ILR extracted from fire debris will rarely exhibit a chromatographic pattern identical to the neat liquid: most often they correspond to a 50% or 75% weathered liquid (less with heavier liquids). Thus, in order to use comparison material that can be fully exploited, it is necessary to create a small library with weathered liquids.

How to Weather a Liquid

The weathering conditions encountered at a fire scene cannot be exactly reproduced at the laboratory, but it is still worth it to weather some reference liquids under laboratory conditions so that they can be analyzed and their chromatographic patterns studied. To weather a liquid, it is simply placed in a beaker and left under the hood, under moderate to heavy ventilation. A magnetic stirrer may be added to keep the liquid uniform. It is important to make sure that the beaker or recipient's walls are not too tall: If that is the case, the headspace will remain mostly steady in the recipient and the evaporation will be very slow. If the walls are short enough, vapors can escape by falling away from the headspace, thus decreasing their concentration in the headspace above the liquid, thus engendering further evaporation of the liquid.

It is important to note that it is possible to weather a liquid by volume or by weight. In fire debris analysis, most people weather a liquid by volume, meaning that a 50% weathered ignitable liquid has a final volume half its original one.

When evaporating liquids such as gasoline, the first half of the volume usually quickly disappears. However, as the liquid weathers, the evaporation rate is slowed down, because the remaining components have a higher boiling point. As such, creating 90+% weathered liquid may take several hours. To accelerate this process, it is possible to moderately heat the recipient by placing it on a hot plate.

12.4.3 Diminution

Diminution of the ILR content of a sample differs from weathering in the sense that it is simply defined by a loss uniform throughout the different compounds of the liquid. This could be the result of fire suppression activities or bad collection/packaging practices. Diminution and weathering are usually phenomena that will occur simultaneously. Although it is semantically correct to define both terms separately, in practice they often will be confused as they can rarely be fully separated.

Water suppression activities can have an important effect on the diminution of ILR. Fire fighters most often use water to extinguish a fire and will thoroughly douse the fire scene until all flaming and smoldering fires disappear. This is done in order to prevent any sort of rekindling that would occur after the fire department leaves the scene, which could have disastrous consequences. As a result, a washing out effect occurs on ILR still present in substrates at the scene. Fortunately, most IL are petroleum-based and these are not water miscible. As a result, the washing out effect is quite limited with petroleum-based liquids and they will likely resist the fire suppression activities unless a particular effort is made to wash out a given surface for a very long period of time. To the contrary, if the IL used as an accelerant is an oxygenated product, it will likely be water miscible and may be very quickly washed out by the extinguishing water. This is definitely a circumstance to take into account when interpreting chromatograms and providing an answer to the fire investigator. Solvent-rinsing phenomena do not act on the different components of an IL in the same manner as evaporation does: It involves other molecular forces, which are not based on the vapor pressure of the components. Thus, patterns exhibited by the weathering of a liquid will likely not be the same as the ones produced through a diminution phenomenon.

The diminution of the amount of ILR recovered can be significant if the conditions necessary to that phenomenon are present. For example, foam is designed to form a film above the substrate to prevent the evaporation of ignitable liquid, thus cutting out fuel supply. If the film is still present in the debris (if the debris is sufficiently wet), studies have shown that this phenomenon takes place. As a result, some components of gasoline are retained by the foam and their recovery, compared to a sample subjected only to water or powder, can be diminished by up to 80% [21].

Finally, collection and packaging of fire debris samples is a very delicate task that must be carried out with the most diligence. As discussed in Chapter 6, if a sample is not collected at the exact proper location, the sample may completely lack the presence of ILR. Similarly, if the container into which the debris is placed is not appropriate, serious diminution of the sample may arise. This is the reason why it is absolutely necessary for the criminalist to ensure that the investigator uses appropriate containers and, if otherwise, to remediate to this problem with proper explanation and preventive techniques.

12.4.4 Degradation

Some soils contain proteobacteria that can degrade petroleum-based ignitable liquids through the metabolization of some of their components. Mainly, there are two types of bacteria fulfilling this function [25]:

- *Pseudomonas fluorescens biovar III:* They degrade only aliphatic compounds.
- *Pseudomonas putida:* They degrade only aromatic components. This bacterium actually is used to remedy soils contaminated by aromatic compounds such as naphthalene. It is also used to degrade polystyrene during its recycling process.

Fortunately, not all soils contain these bacteria and thus, petroleum-based IL will not be degraded by all types of soils. However, for soils containing these bacteria, significant risk of degradation exists. Besides, the relative presence of both bacteria and other parameters also influencing the degradation process, such as the availability of mineral nutrients, the availability of oxygen, and temperature, are not constant from one soil to another [26]. Garden soils usually exhibit a significant bacterial activity. As a result, even though it is possible to affirm that *Pseudomonas*-rich soils will degrade petroleum-based IL, it is not possible to predict with accuracy how and how fast this degradation will occur. Some literature has shown that degradation may be significant, as fast as a couple of days [27]. It is also important to note that some fire extinguishing agents may contain bacteria that will also contribute to the degradation of hydrocarbons as reported by Byron [28].

The different components of an ignitable liquid do not degrade in a uniform manner either. As a consequence, patterns that have been described as characteristics of petroleum-based IL (as seen in Chapter 9) may be significantly skewed by the microbial activity and no longer identifiable. For example, Figure 12-9 shows the TIC of a gasoline after 0, 7, and 14 days of exposure in a soil. One can quickly appreciate the disappearance of the three musketeers, and the distortion of the castle group (particularly between 7 and 14 days). Toluene is also strongly diminished. If one looks only at the castle group at 14 days, the identification of gasoline would be missed as it no longer resembles the original pattern.

Even though exact degradation cannot be predicted, there are general rules that are followed: Normal alkanes and mono-substituted aromatics are degraded before (or at least at a faster rate than) substituted alkanes and polysubstituted aromatics [26]. This is visible in Figure 12-9, in which the heavier aromatic (C_4-alkylbenzenes and higher) patterns are relatively constant throughout the three chromatograms. Figure 12-10 shows another example with diesel fuel at 0, 7, and 14 days of exposure in a soil. It is

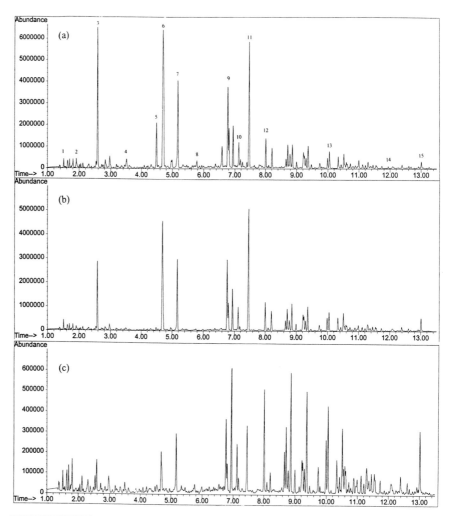

FIGURE 12-9 *Gas chromatograms of Petro-Canada regular grade gasoline after (a) 0 days, (b) 7 days in field soil, (c) 14 days in field soil. Peak identification as follows: (1) benzene, (2) n-heptane, (3) toluene, (4) n-octane, (5) ethylbenzene, (6) para + meta-xylenes, (7) ortho-xylene, (8) n-nonane, (9) meta-ethyltoluene, (10) ortho-ethyltoluene, (11) 1,2,4-trimethylbenzene, (12) n-decane, (13) n-undecane, (14) n-dodecane, (15) 2-methylnaphthalene [internal standard].* Source: Chalmers D, Yan X, Cassista A, Hrynchuk R, and Sandercock PML (2001) Degradation of gasoline, barbecue starter fluid, and diesel fuel by microbial action in soil, Canadian Society of Forensic Science Journal, **34**(2), pp 49–62. *Reprinted with kind permission of the authors.*

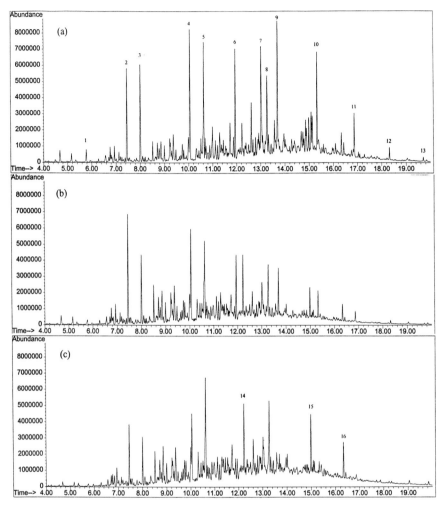

FIGURE 12-10 *Gas chromatograms of Imperial Oil Ltd. P-30 grade diesel fuel (HPD) after (a) 0 days, (b) 7 days in field soil, (c) 14 days in field soil. Peak identification as follows: (1) n-nonane, (2) 1,2,4-trimethylbenzene, (3) n-decane, (4) n-undecane, (5) 1,2,4,5-tetramethylbenzene, (6) n-dodecane, (7) 2-methylnaphthalene [internal standard], (8) substituted-alkane, (9) n-tridecane, (10) n-tetradecane, (11) n-pentadecane, (12) n-hexadecane, (13) n-heptadecane, (14) 2,6-dimethylundecane, (15) 2,6,10-trimethyldodecane, (16) 2,6,10,11-tetramethylhexadecane.* Source: *Chalmers D, Yan X, Cassista A, Hrynchuk R, and Sandercock PML (2001) Degradation of gasoline, barbecue starter fluid, and diesel fuel by microbial action in soil,* Canadian Society of Forensic Science Journal, ***34****(2), pp 49–62. Reprinted with kind permission of the authors.*

possible to see the almost total disappearance of the alkanes, whereas more substituted aliphatics are very little influenced. Again, the bottom chromatogram is no longer representative of what usually is known as a heavy petroleum distillate.

Besides this general rule, it is not possible to predict with greater accuracy the metabolization of the organic compounds present in the debris. In this regard, when receiving soils as a substrate to analyze, the fire debris analyst should always request a comparison sample. This comparison soil can be used by spiking the suspected IL, or a set of different IL, onto it and to see how it degrades after different time ranges of pertinence to the case in question. This is the only true manner in which the microbial degradation can be evaluated.

The criminalist must be well aware of the phenomenon of microbial degradation of petroleum-based IL found in soil samples. This is one reason why the preliminary examination of the fire debris samples must be performed as soon as possible, so that steps preventing this degradation can be taken. In order to do so, the sample should be frozen to at least −5°C [27]. Adding bactericide could be another option, however it may not be as convenient [25]. The fire debris analyst should also take preventive steps with the fire investigators by informing them about this microbial degradation. This is particularly true in locations where the soil is known to be rich in those bacteria. In this case, the investigators should not lose any time bringing the samples to the laboratory and the sample should be refrigerated as much as possible until the time of analysis. In any case, the fire debris analyst must pay particular attention when dealing with a sample containing soil and not call it negative simply because the typical patterns such as the castle group are not perfectly matching a reference IL. The distortion of the patterns should be taken into account as accurately as possible.

12.5 INTERPRETATION KEY

12.5.1 Systematic Approach

The goal of the interpretation is to determine if an ignitable liquid is present in the sample. When dealing with ILR extracts, the chromatogram is constituted of the components from the ILR as well as from the interfering products. The key element is to be able to distinguish the ILR among the comprehensive chromatographic data. Chapter 9 presented the diagnostics patterns used to identify the presence of ILR. The methodology remains identical, however one must now understand that some of these patterns may be modified because of the interfering products and the influences modifying the ILR and thus, these patterns may not exactly match the reference liquid anymore. Consequently, one must sort through the patterns and determine if sufficient similitude are present with the reference liquid, making abstraction of differences that are due to the contribution of the substrate and to modification of an original IL.

The interpretation of a chromatogram should be performed using the following steps:

A. Identify the sample and its substrate.
B. Estimate the typical contribution from that substrate.
C. Determine to which influences the substrate was subjected.
D. Estimate the effect of these influences.
E. Study the TIC from start to end, including peak identification.
F. Study the MC in the regions of interest, including peak identification.

A/ Identify the Sample and its Substrate

The identification of the substrate, if it is possible, is a crucial step. As seen in Sections 12.2 and 12.3, different substrates contribute differently to the interfering products. Even though it is not possible to fully predict the contribution of a given substrate, it is possible to give a rough estimate, sufficient to help in the interpretation of the chromatographic data. This means that the preliminary examination of the debris must be properly carried out.

B/ Estimate the Typical Contribution from that Substrate

One's knowledge and experience is most important here. Based on the substrate, one must attempt to estimate what pyrolysis/combustion products may be generated and what precursory products may be present. A literature research may also prove itself useful when it comes to determine the type of pyrolysis and combustion products released by a given substrate. For example, Blomqvist et al. studied the products released by burning TV sets and other household items [29, 30].

Although it is not possible to determine out of the blue which contamination the item was subjected to, one should include the circumstances surrounding the sample to identify a possible specific contamination. Examples of such contamination would be if the carpet sample comes from a garage mat (possible presence of gasoline or diesel fuel to verify with the investigator regarding the exact use of the garage) or if the sample is a baseboard recently lacquer-treated (possible presence of terpenes or petroleum distillate), or if the sample was wood from a kitchen under-sink cabinet, which contained many cleaning products (possible presence of d-limonene, alcohols, ketones). These are just a few examples to mention, but the list is endless.

C/ Determine to which Influences the Substrate was Subjected

Is the substrate soil? If that is the case, it may be subjected to biodegradation. If the substrate was not collected until four weeks after the fire and the scene was left in the open air in a very warm place such as southern Florida in the summer, then it may be extremely weathered. If the sample is a piece of floor tile that was thoroughly rinsed by the fire department, it may be a victim of diminution. By integrating the exact circumstances around the case, one can properly address all the influences to which the sample was subjected.

D/ Estimate the Effect of these Influences

Biodegradation will selectively consume n-alkanes and simple aromatics before attacking branched alkanes and polysubstituted aromatic compounds. Depending on the IL, the effect can change the chromatographic pattern quite a bit. Weathering will move the chromatogram to the heavy end, thus significantly changing the original pattern of the liquid. Again, it is only by knowing the exact circumstances around the creation of the substrate and its collection that one can attempt to estimate the effect of the different phenomena to which it was subjected.

E/ Study the TIC from Start to End, Including Peak Identification

First, one must look at the TIC from start to end. Remembering that ignitable liquids usually consist of a clean-cut pattern, a chromatogram with peaks spreading throughout the whole width or with groups of peaks here and there, is usually more indicative of a negative sample. When an ignitable liquid is present, a nice clear-cut pattern usually is seen. One must keep that in mind when scrutinizing the TIC. If the ILR present in the sample is in a relatively decent proportion—meaning that it clearly overcomes the background of the sample—the identification is relatively easy and follows the methodology presented in the chapter because the diagnostic patterns will still be easily recognizable. To the contrary, if the ILR present in the sample is at the same level as the background, or even worse, completely lost in the background, this is where the interpretation becomes extremely difficult.

When a cluster of groups appears to be repeating within the chromatogram at given intervals, for which the separation is consistent with the addition of a functional group, there is great chance that these groups are the result of pyrolysis. The diagnostic patterns for petroleum-based ignitable liquids, as described in Chapter 9, do not repeat; they are all quite different from each other. To the contrary, the pattern produced by pyrolysis, mostly through random-scission, consists of clusters of components that are separated by a functional group as perfectly illustrated with polypropylene. Thus, a repeating pattern is usually a good indicator that it is due to pyrolysis.

Then, one must determine if there are distinct contributions to the chromatogram; for example, whether there is a nice group of peaks at the beginning of the chromatogram and a nice group of peaks at the end, with absolutely nothing in-between. This is a suspicion that it may be two different IL, because one ignitable liquid usually consists of compounds within a given boiling range rather than two distinct boiling ranges and because pyrolysis products usually span over a wide area of the chromatogram. Thus, it is important to determine which cluster of peaks may come from one source and which may come from another source. After some training and experience, one can relatively easily see which patterns are independent and which are not.

Finally, one must tentatively identify the main peaks on the TIC by selecting them and running their mass spectra through a library. The important point is to have a good idea of what the major peaks are. Having the knowledge of what interfering products may be present in the sample, one can determine if the major peaks are consistent with the sample or not. If these peaks are all unsaturated compounds or many of them do not produce a very clear match in the MS library, it is likely that they are not the contribution of an IL.

F/ Study the MC in the Regions of Interest, Including Peak Identification

Once one has a good feeling for the TIC, and has identified which patterns are of interest, it is important to look for the diagnostic patterns presented in Chapter 9. For that reason, one must extract ions using mass chromatograms (extracted ion chromatograms or profiles) to observe these patterns. This is an extremely important part of the interpretation. The patterns are then compared to the patterns exhibited by different reference IL, keeping in mind that modification of the patterns exhibited by the sample may have occurred due to the presence of interfering products and influences. Also, when looking at EICs or EIPs, one should identify the peaks that were not clearly visible in the TIC, by running the mass spectrum through the library.

12.5.2 Case Examples
A/ Case Example 1

Figure 12-11a is a chromatogram obtained from a sample with charred wood and unidentified debris (extraction by passive headspace concentration on activated charcoal).

One can see several isolated peaks spread from 4 to 15 minutes and a continuous pattern ranging from about 6 to 10 minutes. A quick mass spectral identification of some of the major peaks revealed the identities shown in the figure. The signal produced by the chromatogram is quite low, as witnessed by the high internal standard peak. Many of the peaks are unidentified by the mass spectrometer, usually a good indication (at least in this case, where little coelution exists) that they do not originate from an ignitable liquid. Among the different peaks, it is possible, however, to

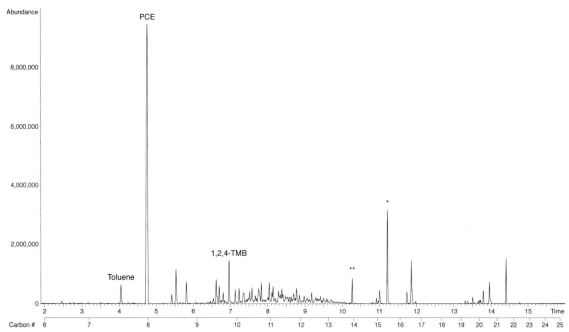

FIGURE 12-11a *Case example 1 TIC (charred wood and unidentified debris). Extraction by ACS 18h @ 60°C, desorption 200 ml CS₂.*

* [1R-(1α,3α,4β)]-4-ethenyl-α,α,4-trimethyl-3-(1-methylethenyl)-cyclohexanemethanol

** 1-ethenyl-1-methyl-2,4-bis[1-methylethenyl]-cyclohexane

recognize some diagnostic patterns such as the three musketeers and the castle group. The presence of these groups is a good indication of the presence of gasoline or an aromatic product. At this stage, it is necessary to extract ions, first aromatic ones, and second, aliphatic ones as shown in Figures 12-11b and 12-11c.

In the aromatic profile, one can clearly identify the castle group. The other profiles, such as with the C₄-alkylbenzenes and the indanes, are also a perfect match to a gasoline reference standard. The ratio of 2- to 1-methylnaphthalenes is not proper, but may very well be due to the low abundance of these compounds and/or to the presence of interfering products. Finally, no C₂-naphthalenes are present, likely due to the very low abundance.

Figure 12-11c shows the presence of n-alkanes and cycloalkanes between 6 and 10 minutes. If one compares the abundance of the aliphatics to the abundance of the aromatic profile, one can see that the aromatic compounds are in a much higher proportion, as witnessed by the TIC.

Therefore, the presence of the proper aromatic diagnostic peaks, the wide range of the patterns (not limited to just one group), and the presence of some n-alkanes and cycloalkanes are all consistent with gasoline. The presence of gasoline is identified in this sample. The sporadic peaks after 10 minutes are merely interfering products.

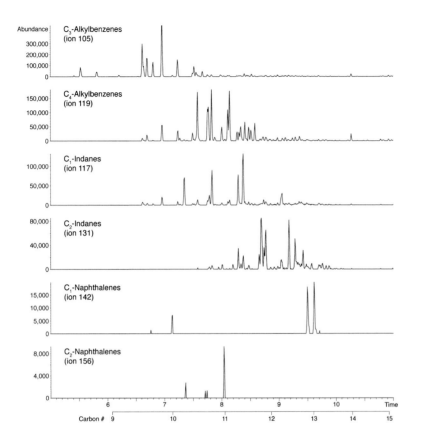

FIGURE 12-11b
Case example 1 aromatic EICs.

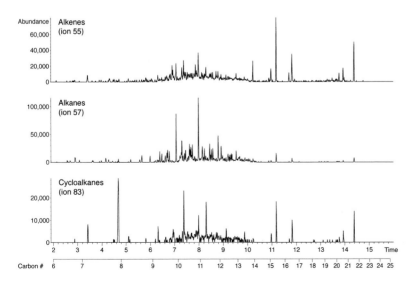

FIGURE 12-11c
Case example 1 aliphatic EICs.

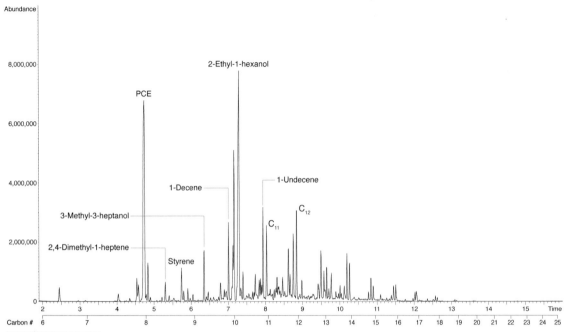

FIGURE 12-12a *Case example 2 TIC (melted plastic and burned cardboard). Extraction by ACS 18 h @ 60°C, desorption 200 ml CS$_2$.*

B/ Case Example 2

Figure 12-12a is a TIC from a sample with melted plastic and burned cardboard. Plastic could be anything from polyethylene to polystyrene, however one usually knows that plastic will produce many interfering products, either by random scission or by side-group scission. Peaks are present from about 4 to 13 minutes and one can appreciate the presence of a repeating pattern that is going decrescendo from about 8 minutes to 14 minutes. This type of repetition is usually a good indicator of pyrolysis products, possibly polyethylene, due to the short interval (one methylene group) between each group of peaks. The main peak is 2-ethyl-1-hexanol, a very common interfering product. Many alkenes are also present as identified in the figure. No clear diagnostic patterns can be recognized from the TIC. The next step consists in looking at the extracted ion chromatograms.

Figure 12-12b is the EIC for aromatic compounds. As one can observe, though many of the compounds typically present in a petroleum product are present, no diagnostic patterns whatsoever can be observed. Figure 12-12c shows some interesting patterns. One can clearly see the repeating compounds that appear to be groups of three or more peaks. Each group consists of an n-alkane preceded by an n-alkene and an alkadiene. Other branched unsaturated aliphatic compounds are present in these groups, too. However, there is no hash and trash corresponding to the pattern seen in

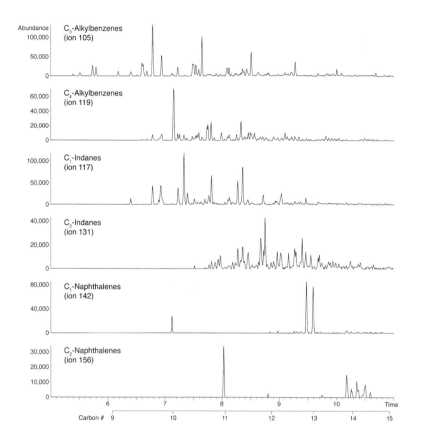

FIGURE 12-12b

Case example 2 aromatic EICs.

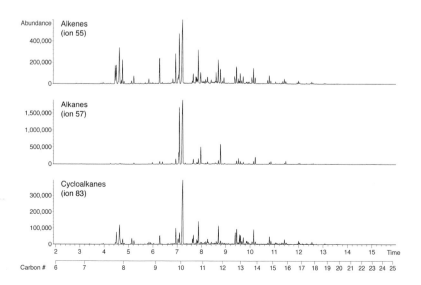

FIGURE 12-12c

Case example 2 aliphatic EICs.

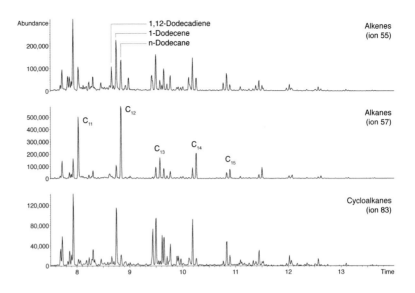

FIGURE 12-12d

More detailed view of Figure 12-12c.

petroleum distillates and there are no cycloalkanes present. Figure 12-12d shows a more detailed view of this repetition of groups of peaks from 7.5 to 14 minutes. When the patterns between the 57 and 83 match that well, it means that no cycloalkanes are present. Furthermore, one can also see the intensity of the peaks in the 55 profile compared to the 57 one. They are in the same range and the unsaturated peaks are much stronger in the 55 profile than the 57 profile. This pattern is typical of pyrolysis products from polyethylene. This sample is negative for ILR.

C/ Case Example 3

Figure 12-13a shows the TIC from a sample of charred wood. The nature of the wood was not identified in this case, however one can expect terpenes and some oxygenated products such as furans. The chromatogram contains relatively few peaks, some of which are identified in the figure. The quasi-totality of these peaks are terpenes, typical natural components of wood. Although the extracted ion chromatograms of this chromatogram did not bring any pertinent information, they are shown in Figures 12-13b and 12-13c so that one can clearly appreciate the complete lack of diagnostic patterns. Figure 12-13a is a typical chromatogram obtained from wood. It is reported as a negative sample, unless one can demonstrate without a doubt that the type of wood present in the sample does not naturally contain terpenes. Even in this instance, one must remember that there are many wood lacquers that contain terpenes and can be applied to the wood, independently of the pouring of an accelerant. The reporting of terpenes in wood should be done with a specific disclaimer.

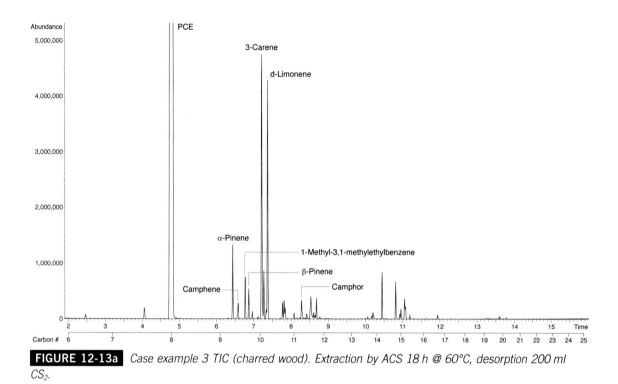

FIGURE 12-13a *Case example 3 TIC (charred wood). Extraction by ACS 18 h @ 60°C, desorption 200 ml CS$_2$.*

D/ Case Example 4

Figure 12-14a is a TIC obtained from a sample of burned vinyl flooring with some foam pad and carpet. From an interfering product perspective, one may expect some chlorinated compounds and some aromatic ones, because the vinyl flooring, made of PVC, will break down by side-group scission. Also, plasticizers used in vinyl flooring may be isoparaffinic products or n-alkane products.

The chromatogram consists of very few peaks spread in a well-defined pattern. Often, when such a nicely well-defined pattern is present, it is very likely that it comes from an ignitable liquid, rather than from interfering products. One may even be able to recognize the castle group between six and seven minutes. The group of three little peaks between 9.5 and 10 minutes consists of unsaturated branched alkenes and is a common interfering product pattern. The aromatic profile shown in Figure 12-14b removes any doubt regarding the castle group pattern. No interesting patterns were developed from the aliphatic extracted ion chromatogram. Fortunately, a comparison sample was brought in by the investigator. The TIC is shown in Figure 12-14c and one can readily see that the narrow pattern observed in the first sample is not there. As a result, a medium aromatic product is identified in the sample.

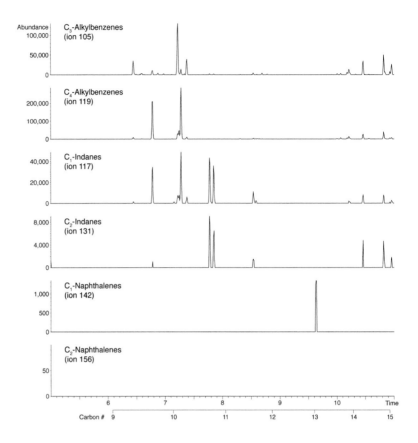

FIGURE 12-13b

Case example 3 aromatic EICs.

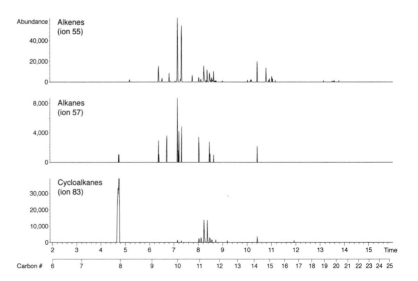

FIGURE 12-13c

Case example 3 aliphatic EICs.

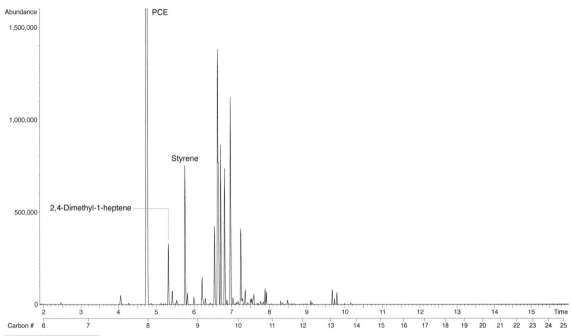

FIGURE 12-14a *Case example 4 TIC (burned vinyl flooring with foam pad and carpet). Extraction by ACS 18 h @ 60°C, desorption 200 ml CS$_2$.*

E/ Case Example 5

Figure 12-15a is the total ion chromatogram of a bulk fibrous material submitted as a fire debris to the laboratory. One can observe the presence of a first pattern, of an approximate Gaussian shape distribution, between five and nine minutes, followed by a series of different peaks until about 13 minutes. The dominant n-alkanes identified in the figure may suggest the presence of a petroleum distillate. The three peaks between 9.5 and 10 minutes are common interfering products as shown in the previous example. The aromatic EIC did not bring any pertinent information, because there are almost no compounds appearing in it. However, the aliphatic EIC, shown in Figure 12-15b clearly shows the n-alkane pattern as well as the presence of cycloalkanes between the n-alkanes. In addition, the sharp cut and the Gaussian distribution as well as the hash and trash matching the one from reference standard allow to conclude that a medium petroleum distillate is present in the sample. The absence of aromatic compounds is not alarming, as this product is of dearomatized type, but still classified as an MPD. All other peaks are simply interfering products contributed by the substrate.

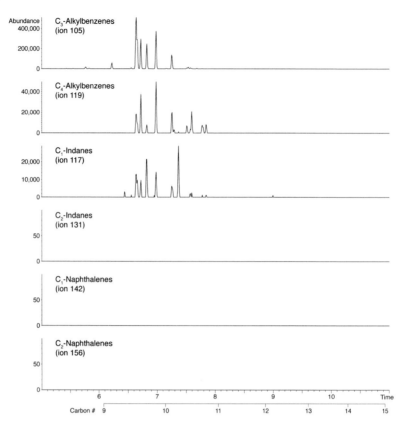

FIGURE 12-14b

Case example 4 aromatic EICs.

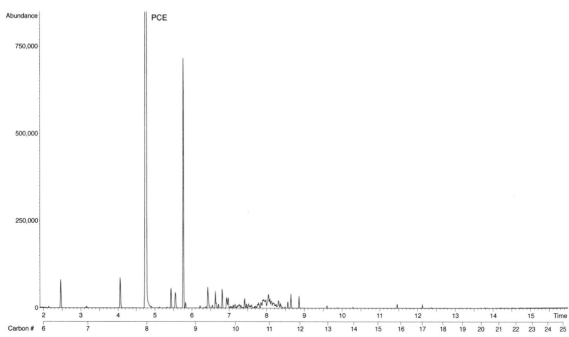

FIGURE 12-14c *Case example 4 comparison sample TIC.*

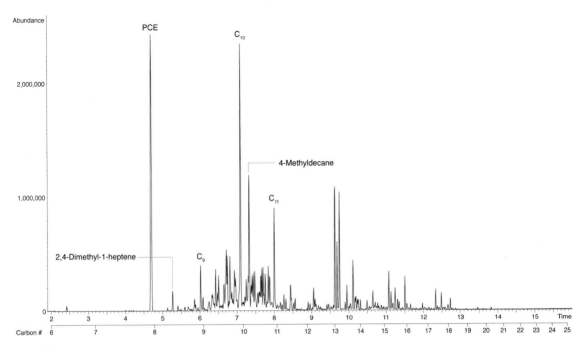

FIGURE 12-15a *Case example 5 TIC (bulk fibrous material). Extraction by ACS 18 h @ 60°C, desorption 200 ml CS₂.*

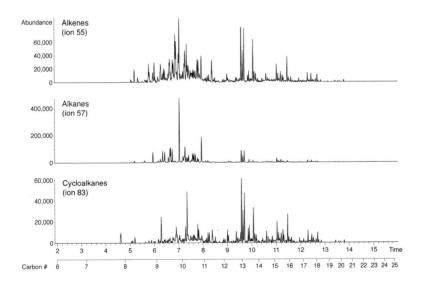

FIGURE 12-15b

Case example 5 aliphatic EICs.

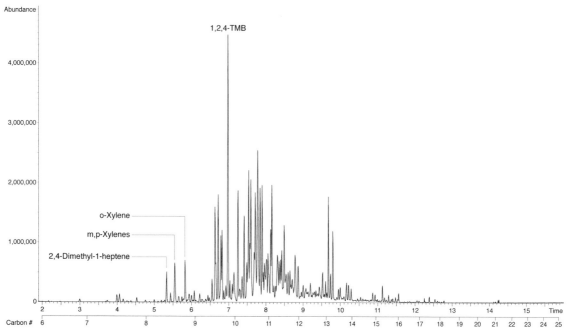

FIGURE 12-16a *Case example 6 TIC (soil, stone, and unidentified debris). Extraction by ACS 18 h @ 60°C, desorption 200 ml CS₂.*

F/ Case Example 6

Figure 12-16a is the TIC from a sample of soil, stone, and unidentified charred debris. The pattern is quite spread out from about 5 minutes to 13 minutes. The tallest peak is 1,2,4-trimethylbenzene, one of the components from gasoline. Other smaller peaks have been identified on the chromatogram, however no obvious pattern can be distinguished.

The aromatic EIC gives a much different, clearer picture of the content of the debris as shown in Figure 12-16b. Many of the aromatic diagnostic patterns are present in their proper shape and proportion. The aliphatic EIC does not provide such a nice pattern (see Figure 12-16c). Some aliphatic compounds are present in the range of six to nine minutes, range corresponding to the aromatic pattern, however no clear n-alkanes or cycloalkanes are present. They are actually lost in the background of interfering products released by the substrate. This sample contains gasoline, as identified by the aromatic pattern. Note that the sample is already heavily weathered.

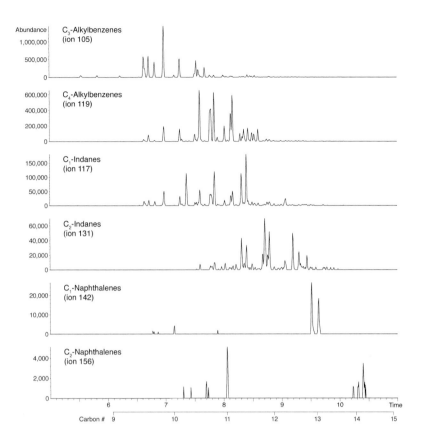

FIGURE 12-16b
*Case example 6
aromatic EICs.*

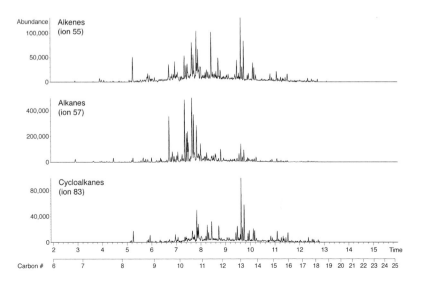

FIGURE 12-16c
*Case example 6
aliphatic EICs.*

G/ Case Example 7

Figure 12-17a is burned paper. One can readily see that there seems to be at least two different, independent contributions to this sample. There is a big hump between 6.5 and 9 minutes and a nicely Gaussian-shaped pattern of spiking n-alkanes between 9.5 and 14 minutes. However, there also seems to be a few other diagnostic patterns, such as the three musketeers and the castle group. The aromatic and aliphatic EIC provide a better picture of these different patterns as shown in Figures 12-17b and 12-17c.

The aromatic profile shows clearly a match between all the patterns and the gasoline reference sample (Figure 9-16b). The aliphatic profile shows the nice spiking n-alkane patterns, however no cycloalkanes seem to be present. This is likely due to the very low concentration in this sample. However, the hash and trash is present and matches well the petroleum distillate standard, not to mention that pristane and phytane are also present. The hump between seven and nine minutes is due to interfering products and often is found in samples. This sample contains a mixture of a heavy petroleum distillate and gasoline.

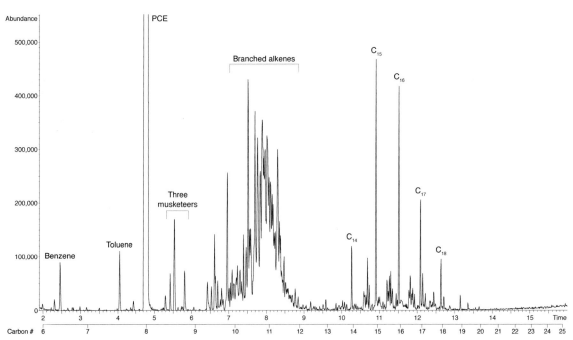

FIGURE 12-17a *Case example 7 TIC (burned paper). Extraction by ACS 18 h @ 60°C, desorption 200 ml CS₂.*

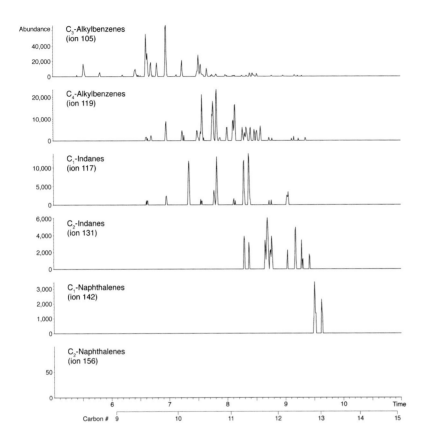

FIGURE 12-17b

Case example 7 aromatic EICs.

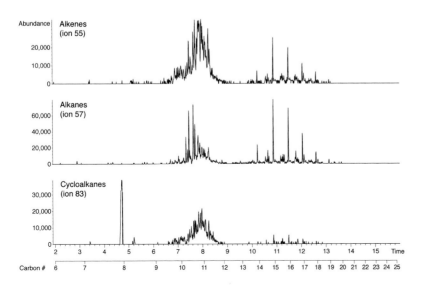

FIGURE 12-17c

Case example 7 aliphatic EICs.

REFERENCES

1. Trimpe MA (1991) Turpentine in arson analysis, *Journal of Forensic Sciences*, **36**(4), pp 1059–73.
2. Wells SB (2005) The identification of isopar H in vinyl flooring, *Journal of Forensic Sciences*, **50**(4), pp 865–72.
3. Rose S and Schlager N (1995) *How things are made: From automobiles to zippers*, Black Dog & Leventhal Publishers, New York, NY.
4. Hetzel SS and Moss RD (2005) How long after waterproofing a deck can you still isolate an ignitable liquid?, *Journal of Forensic Sciences*, **50**(2), pp 369–76.
5. Cavanagh K, Du Pasquier E, and Lennard C (2002) Background interference from car carpets—The evidential value of petrol residues in cases of suspected vehicle arson, *Forensic Science International*, **125**, pp 22–36.
6. Bertsch W and Zhang Q-W (1990) Sample preparation for the chemical analysis of debris in suspect arson cases, *Analytica Chimica Acta*, **236**, pp 183–95.
7. Stauffer E (2001) Identification and characterization of interfering products in fire debris analysis, *Master's thesis*, International Forensic Research Institute, Florida International University, Miami, FL.
8. Higgins M (1987) Turpentine, accelerant or natural ???, *Fire and Arson Investigator*, **38**(2), p 10.
9. Chanson B et al. (2000) Turpentine identification in fire debris analysis, *2nd European Academy of Forensic Science Meeting*, Cracow, Poland.
10. Lentini JJ, Dolan JA, and Cherry C (2000) The petroleum-laced background, *Journal of Forensic Sciences*, **45**(5), pp 968–89.
11. Stauffer E (2003) Basic concept of pyrolysis for fire debris analysts, *Science & Justice*, **43**(1), pp 29–40.
12. DeHaan JD, Brien DJ, and Large R (2004) Volatile organic compounds from the combustion of human and animal tissue, *Science & Justice*, **44**(4), pp 223–36.
13. Kamiya A and Ose Y (1984) Study of odorous compounds produced by putrefaction of foods. V. Fatty acids, sulphur compounds and amines, *Journal of Chromatography*, **292**, pp 383–91.
14. Wilkins K (1997) Gaseous organic emissions from various types of household waste, *Annales of Agricultural and Environmental Medicine*, **4**, pp 87–9.
15. Eishold E and Meyer J (1990) *Les moyens d'extinction*, première édition, Edition Simowa, Pfäffikon, Switzerland.
16. Haessler WM (1974) *The extinguishment of fire*, National Fire Protection Association, Quincy, MA.
17. Amerex (1998) Format material safety data sheets for Amerex products.
18. Coulson S, Morgan-Smith R, and Noble D (2000) The effect of compressed air foam on the detection of hydrocarbon fuels in fire debris samples, *Science & Justice*, **40**(4), pp 257–60.
19. McGee E and Lang TL (2002) A study of the effects of a miscelle encapsulator fire suppression agent on dynamic headspace analysis of fire debris samples, *Journal of Forensic Sciences*, **47**(2), pp 267–74.
20. Geraci B, Shaw W, and Hine G (2007) The suppression of fires using compressed air foam: Does it affect your origin and cause determination?, *Fire & Arson Investigator*, **57**(4), pp 22–5.
21. Stauffer E and Almiral J (2001) Chemistry of fire extinguishing agents and their interference in fire debris analysis, *53rd Annual Meeting of the American Academy of Forensic Sciences*, Seattle, WA.
22. Lang T and Dixon BM (2000) The possible contamination of fire scenes by the use of positive pressure ventilation fans, *Canadian Society of Forensic Sciences Journal*, **33**(2), pp 55–60.

23. Koussiafes MP (2002) Evaluation of fire scene contamination by using positive-pressure ventilation fans, *Forensic Science Communications*, **4**(4).
24. Armstrong AT et al. (2004) The evaluation of the extent of transporting or "tracking" an identifiable ignitable liquid (gasoline) throughout fire scenes during the investigative process, *Journal of Forensic Sciences*, **49**(4), pp 741–8.
25. Kirkbride KP et al. (1992) Microbial degradation of petroleum hydrocarbons: Implications for arson residue analysis, *Journal of Forensic Sciences*, **37**(6), pp 1585–99.
26. Chalmers D et al. (2001) Degradation of gasoline, barbecue starter fluid, and diesel fuel by microbial action in soil, *Canadian Society of Forensic Science Journal*, **34**(2), pp 49–62.
27. Mann DC and Gresham WR (1990) Microbial degradation of gasoline in soil, *Journal of Forensic Sciences*, **35**(4), pp 913–23.
28. Byron DE (2002) The effects of surfactants and microbes on the identification of ignitable liquids in fire debris analysis, *Fire and Arson Investigator*, **53**(1), p 50.
29. Blomqvist P, Rosell L, and Simonson M (2004) Emissions from fires part I: Fire retarded and non-fire retarded TV-sets, *Fire Technology*, **40**(1), pp 39–58.
30. Blomqvist P, Rosell L, and Simonson M (2004) Emissions from fires part II: Simulated room fires, *Fire Technology*, **40**(1), pp 59–73.

CHAPTER 13

Other Techniques of Analysis and the Future of Fire Debris Analysis

"It is not the strongest of the species that survives, nor the most intelligent, but the one most responsive to change."

Charles Darwin, British naturalist (1809–1882)

13.1 INTRODUCTION

Throughout the years, many different techniques have been applied to the analysis of fire debris samples for ignitable liquid residues as shown in Figure 13-1. Some of these techniques were successful and are now widely accepted in the forensic community. Some did not pass the adequate validation procedure and are not suitable for the analysis of ILR and, thus, should not be used. Other techniques have been shown to provide different information with regard to the analysis of ILR and can be valuable for some specific, nonroutine aspects. Finally, one is still under development and might represent the future of fire debris analysis. As previously seen, gas chromatography (GC) and gas chromatography–mass spectrometry (GC–MS) are the only two analytical techniques presently developed and validated for the analysis of ILR. This chapter catalogs all analytical techniques, besides GC–FID and GC–MS, which either have been developed for the analysis of fire debris analysis, or are under development. Other techniques may have been applied to the analysis of ignitable liquids, such as GCxMS [1], however no direct fire debris analysis applications were published.

Even though many of these techniques are inadequate to routine ILR analysis, it is important for the fire debris analyst to be aware of them for the following reasons:

- If the forensic scientist is asked to use an unusual technique rather than a validated one, he or she will be able to argue this request by quickly justifying the reasons why it should not be used.

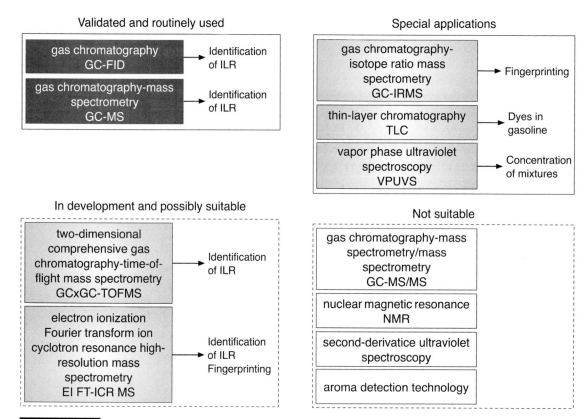

FIGURE 13-1 *Analytical techniques reported in the literature with fire debris analysis applications.*

- Some of these techniques are still under development. They may become the future techniques that will replace presently used techniques. Therefore, as part of continuing education and awareness of the development of science in the field, the analyst should be aware of them.
- During testimony, when asked why a particular technique was used, the criminalist must be able to justify it and explain the advantage of that technique compared to other possible, but not necessarily more suitable, techniques. Indeed, when asked why another technique was not used, rather than having never heard of that technique, the scientist can quickly reply and justify the nonuse of such a technique.
- If, during a case review, the criminalist realizes that the opposing expert is using one of these inappropriate techniques, he or she will be able to quickly pinpoint the weaknesses and limitations of the examination and its subsequent results.

- If the technique is not suitable, it is necessary for the researcher to be aware of the research and literature demonstrating so in order to avoid conducting the same experiments when they already have been done.

13.2 COMPREHENSIVE TWO-DIMENSIONAL GAS CHROMATOGRAPHY–MASS SPECTROMETRY (GCxGC–MS)

13.2.1 Principle

A/ Development

Multidimensional comprehensive chromatography is one of the most recent advances in chromatography even though its first application was performed in the mid 1940s with paper chromatography [2]. It consists of submitting a sample to two chromatographic processes that are coupled together, one after the other each of which providing a separation based on different properties, such as boiling point and polarity. It is a new way to obtain better separation of complex mixtures, which were not always resolved when using only one chromatographic separation.

Unlike in drug or explosives analysis, the chromatographic patterns obtained in fire debris analysis typically will contain several hundred peaks. As seen in previous chapters, in many chromatograms, coelution of peaks occurs and the pattern recognition process is severely complicated. The application of comprehensive two-dimensional gas chromatography (GCxGC) to fire debris analysis could lead to a significant improvement of the identification of ILR [3].

The principle behind GCxGC is simple and is well illustrated with thin-layer chromatography (TLC). Figure 13-2a shows a TLC plate onto which a mixture of analytes has been placed at the bottom left corner. The plate

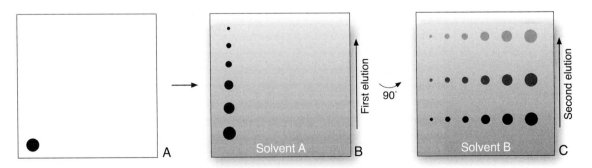

FIGURE 13-2 *Illustration of the principle of comprehensive two-dimensional chromatography using thin-layer chromatography. A/ The plate is eluted with solvent A. B/ Separation of the compounds after elution with solvent A. The compounds are separated based on their shape. C/ After the plate is rotated 90°, it is eluted again with solvent B. The compounds are now separated based on their color.*

is then eluted with solvent A. This solvent separates the compounds according to their size, the larger compounds traveling more slowly than the smaller ones. The result is illustrated in Figure 13-2b, where the compounds are separated into six groups of different sizes. This separation worked well, but there may be more than one compound in each group. Hence, the plate is dried, rotated 90°, and is now eluted with solvent B, which, in this example, separates the compounds according to their color rather than shape or size. The result is illustrated in Figure 13-2c, where the second dimension of separation allowed for the distinction of three classes of color: black, dark grey, and light grey.

This is the principle of two-dimensional chromatography. The term "comprehensive" indicates that all the components of the original mixture undergo both separations [4]. If only one group of compounds is selected to undergo the second separation, the chromatography would be called conventional rather than comprehensive. Conventional two-dimensional chromatography (also called heart-cut chromatography) was used long before its comprehensive counterpart; it is easier to select a cut from the first separation to undergo a second separation, rather than for the whole mixture to go through both separation processes.

B/ Two-Dimensional Gas Chromatography

GCxGC was developed in the early 1990s by Professor John B. Phillips and his student Zaiyou Liu [2, 5, 6]. It consists of two GC columns, which are coupled together via an interface. These two columns are either placed in the same oven or they may be in two different ovens in order to control the temperature of each column independently. The sample is injected through the first column and it eventually reaches the interface where it is transferred to the second column. At the end of the second column, a detector reacts to the presence of analytes and the data is recorded through a computer system, which builds the two-dimensional chromatogram.

GCxGC is truly a hyphenated technique in the sense that the entire sample passing through the first column also passes through the second column, as shown in Figure 13-3.

Therefore, the secondary column has to perform the separation and analysis fast enough to generate at least one complete chromatogram during

FIGURE 13-3

Schematic representation of a GCxGC–MS system.

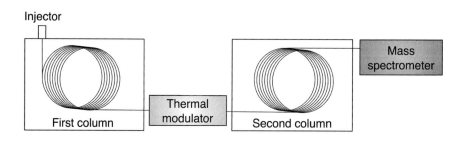

FIGURE 13-4

Modern thermal modulators are very small and can easily fit inside the oven of the gas chromatography. This modulator is produced by Leco Corporation (St. Joseph, MI, USA) under a license, which belongs to Zoex Corporation (Houston, TX, USA). Photograph courtesy of Professor Glenn Frysinger, US Coast Guard Academy, New London, Connecticut, USA.

the time required for a peak to elute from the first column. This is necessary in order to avoid overlapping and to permit possible reconstruction of the two-dimensional chromatogram. Thus, controlling the injection in the secondary column is the most important part of the process. It is carried out by the thermal modulator, which constitutes the interface between the primary and secondary columns. Different systems have been developed and used throughout the years [6–10]. The most recent and efficient system consists of a series of cold and hot jets [11, 12]. This thermal modulator is very compact and can be placed inside the oven of the GC, allowing for a relatively short connection between the two GC columns when placed in the same oven (see Figure 13-4). The operating principle of the thermal modulator is shown in Figure 13-5.

The portion of column running through the modulator, and therefore connecting the primary and secondary column, has no stationary phase. The thermal modulator works in cycles of a few seconds. The start of the cycle is shown in Figure 13-5a. Both tubes provide cold jets and the analytes reaching the thermal modulator condens on the blank column at the first jet. The tube on the left then blows a hot jet as shown in Figure 13-5b, which vaporizes the analytes, allowing them to travel inside the modulator to the second jet. The jet then becomes cold again (Figure 13-5c), thus preventing new analytes from entering. At this stage, a

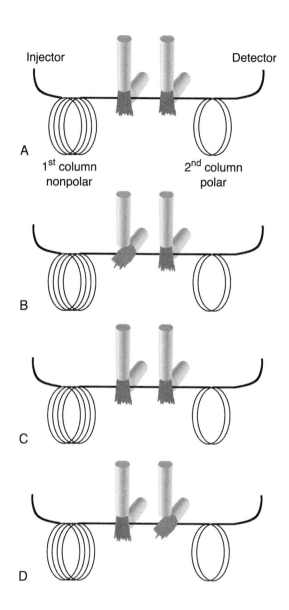

Illustration of the functioning principle of the thermal modulator. A/ Beginning of cycle: both jets blow cold air, analytes concentrate right before the thermal modulator. B/ The left tube blows hot air and the analytes are mobile again. They move into a tight fraction, located between the two jets. C/ The first jet is switched to cold again, thus stopping the entry of analytes in-between the jets. D/ The right tube blows hot air and the analytes are injected as a narrow plug in the second column. Diagrams courtesy of Professor Glenn Frysinger, US Coast Guard Academy, New London, Connecticut, USA. (For a full color version of this figure, please see the insert.)

tight fraction of analytes is trapped at the second jet. This tube starts to blow a hot jet (Figure 13-5d), thus injecting the narrow plug of analytes into the second column. Both jets return to cold and the cycle is repeated. The thermal modulator changes the temperature of the transfer line from about −120°C to about 140°C in a tenth of a second in both directions [13].

The separation processes occurring in the columns have to offer different interactions of the compounds with the stationary phase in order to be truly two-dimensional. For example, the columns are considered independent when the first one separates the compounds according to their boiling points and the second one based on their polarity. The second column is shorter and has a thinner stationary phase than the first one, so the elution is much faster. Examples of typical parameters used with a GCxGC–MS for fire debris analysis are shown in Table 13-1.

Table 13-1	*Some typical parameters used for a GCxGC-MS system to perform fire debris analysis.* Data courtesy of Professor Glenn Frysinger, US Coast Guard Academy, New London, Connecticut, USA

GC	Parameter
Instrument	Agilent 6890
Gas	Hydrogen
Flow rate	0.6 ml/min constant
First column	
Type	Polydimethylsiloxane (phase 007-1, quadrex)
Length	5 m
Internal diameter (ID)	0.1 mm
Film thickness	3.5 µm
Initial temperature	30°C for 4 min
Ramp and final temperature	3°C/min to 200°C
Modulator column	
Type	Blank column
Length	1 m
Internal diameter (ID)	0.1 mm
Second column	
Type	50% silphenylene polydimethylsiloxane
Length	1.5 m
Internal diameter (ID)	0.1 mm
Film thickness	0.1 µm
Initial temperature	35°C for 4 min
Ramp and final temperature	3°C/min to 205°C
Mass spectrometer	
Type	TOF
Brand	Leco Pegasus

Because the second chromatographic separation is carried out in only a few seconds, it is necessary to use a detector rapid enough to obtain adequate resolution even in such a short time span. When using the types of mass spectrometers that are commonly used in fire debris analysis, the scan rate ranges between 2 and 5 Hz. This means that the number of scans on the whole second dimension could be as small as 5 or 10. Unfortunately, this is not sufficient to provide a good resolution. Therefore, detectors with a higher scan rate are necessary. A typically recommended scan rate is at least 50 Hz [14]. When using an FID, a model acquiring at 200 Hz provides adequate resolution. If an MS is considered, it is necessary to use a time-of-flight mass spectrometer (TOFMS) as other types of MS cannot provide the minimum frequency of 50 Hz. In a TOFMS the analytes enter the chamber where they are ionized as in other mass spectrometers. Once ionized, they are accelerated through the ion accelerator toward the detector. The push pulse plate controls this acceleration. Thus, ions are not accelerated on a constant basis, but by cyclic pulses. As each ion receives the same amount of force, its speed will vary depending on its mass. Thus, the heavier ions come out of the ion accelerator at a lower speed than the lighter ions. Ions will reach the detector at different times (of flight) depending on their masses. The detector records the intensity of the ions reaching it versus time. The time factor is then converted into a mass. This technique allows for several hundreds of full scans per second.

The data output of a GCxGC analysis and the data treatment necessary to generate the two-dimensional chromatogram are shown in Figure 13-6 [15]. The two-dimensional chromatogram has the retention time of the primary column on the x-axis and the retention time of the secondary column on the y-axis. The abundance of the peaks usually is expressed using a range of colors or shades of a color. Each colored plot on the chromatogram represents one compound.

When using GCxGC–MS, the chromatogram also has extra information that is not displayed: the mass spectral information. Because most compounds are resolved, each peak yields a mass spectrum that is generally not contaminated with coeluting compounds. Thus, the mass spectrum allows for a much better discrimination between isomers and makes the identification of the compound more straightforward.

13.2.2 Application

The application of GCxGC to the analysis of fire debris was first performed by Phillips, Tang, and Cerven in 1996 [16]. Unfortunately, further development of this application did not follow until the early 2000s, when Professor Frysinger and Professor Gaines from the US Coast Guard Academy gained interest in its fire debris analysis application and received a grant from the National Institute of Justice (USA) to validate this technique. The increase in specificity is the obvious advantage to the fire debris application. One of the reasons lies in the fact that the problem of coelution is significantly reduced.

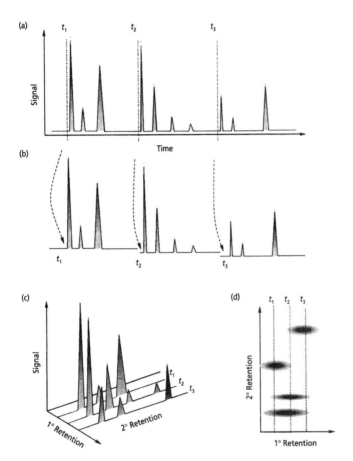

FIGURE 13-6 *Data output of a GCxGC and data treatment necessary to reach it. (a) The raw linear chromatographic signal with t_1, t_2, and t_3 denoting when injections onto the second dimension occurred. (b) The individual slices of the raw data that represent each individual second-dimension chromatogram. (c) The 3-D space into which the computer software places the individual slices of chromatographic data. (d) The final contour plot of the data viewed top-down. Peak heights or intensities are replaced by color.* Source: Harynuk J, Gorecki T, and Campbell C (2002) On the interpretation of GC x GC data, LCGC North America, 20 (9), pp 876–892, Figure 4. Reprinted with permission from the authors.

Figure 13-7 shows a chromatogram of a standard test mix for which all the peaks have been identified.

The first separation, on the x-axis, is based upon boiling point and resembles the separation obtained on a regular one-dimensional system with a nonpolar column. The second separation, visible on the y-axis, is based on polarity. It is possible to distinguish three groups of analytes on the y-axis. The nonpolar compounds, such as the n-alkanes, elute first, followed

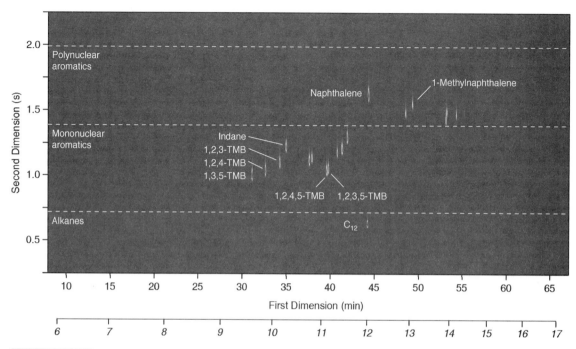

FIGURE 13-7 *GCxGC chromatogram of an ASTM standard test mix. Data courtesy of Professor Glenn Frysinger, US Coast Guard Academy, New London, Connecticut, USA. (For a full color version of this figure, please see the insert.)*

by the aromatics and substituted aromatics. Finally, on the top part of the chromatogram, it is possible to see the polynuclear aromatics. This use of a second dimension leads to a significant improvement in the separation of the analytes in the chromatogram. This has critical potential in fire debris analysis. Figure 13-8 shows a chromatogram of 75% weathered gasoline. Again, it is possible to distinguish the three groups of compounds as previously described. At the bottom are the most popular compounds, including all the aliphatics, ranging from the lighter compounds on the left to the heavier ones on the right. The aromatics, which are located just above the aliphatics, exhibit greater intensity, as expected. Finally, the top portion of the chromatogram represents the polynuclear aromatics and most polar compounds. They are located on the right part of the chromatogram because they are heavier. The patterns characteristic of gasoline as seen in Chapter 9 are readily recognizable. The arrows are pointing at the different groups; arrow A shows the three musketeers, arrow B shows the castle group, arrow C shows the gang of four, and arrow D shows the twin towers. Figure 13-9 shows a detailed view of some of the characteristic patterns of aromatic compounds found in this gasoline sample, along with the equivalent one-dimensional chromatogram.

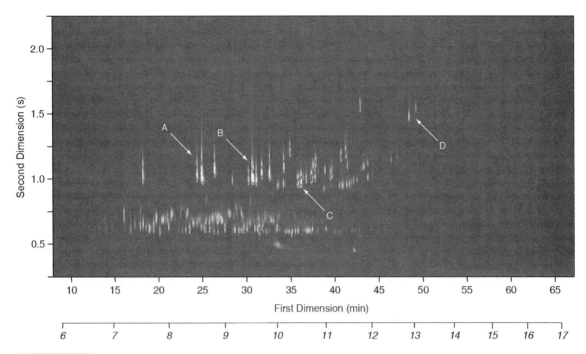

FIGURE 13-8 *GCxGC chromatogram of a 75% weathered gasoline. Data courtesy of Professor Glenn Frysinger, US Coast Guard Academy, New London, Connecticut, USA. (For a full color version of this figure, please see the insert.)*

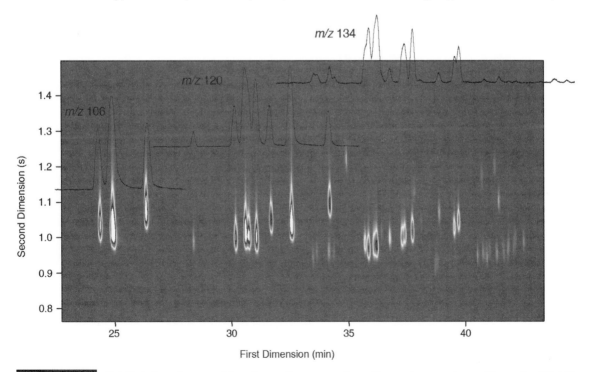

FIGURE 13-9 *Detailed view of some of the diagnostic groups of gasoline and comparison with regular GC–MS data. Data courtesy of Professor Glenn Frysinger, US Coast Guard Academy, New London, Connecticut, USA. (For a full color version of this figure, please see the insert.)*

The one-dimensional patterns usually observed in mass chromatogram are matched to the new patterns observed. With the mass spectral information available in Figure 13-9, all the components in the range of C_2 to C_4 alkylbenzenes, many of which coelute on a regular gas chromatographic system, can now be identified.

Figure 13-10 shows a chromatogram of diesel fuel. Immediately, it is possible to observe the prominent presence of aliphatic compounds. The lower line is much more dense than in the gasoline chromatogram. The n-alkanes are distinguished as some the most intense peaks. They are separated according to their boiling points on the horizontal axis. The cycloalkanes are slightly higher on the y-axis than the alkanes. The pattern exhibited by the aromatics is also recognizable and corresponds to the portion of the patterns previously described for the gasoline sample although, as expected, the aromatics are less abundant in the diesel fuel pattern. Figure 13-11 shows a chromatogram of medium naphthenic paraffinic product. The pattern shown by the naphthenic paraffinic product is interesting. The cycloalkanes are distinguished from the isoalkanes by their position on the y-axis. The overall pattern is very narrow and the aromatic pattern is noticeably absent, which is expected.

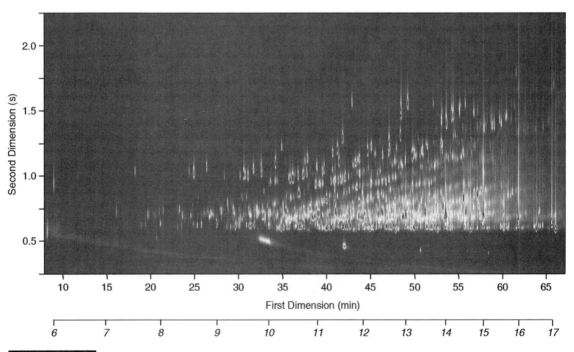

FIGURE 13-10 *Chromatogram of diesel fuel. Data courtesy of Professor Glenn Frysinger, US Coast Guard Academy, New London, Connecticut, USA. (For a full color version of this figure, please see the insert.)*

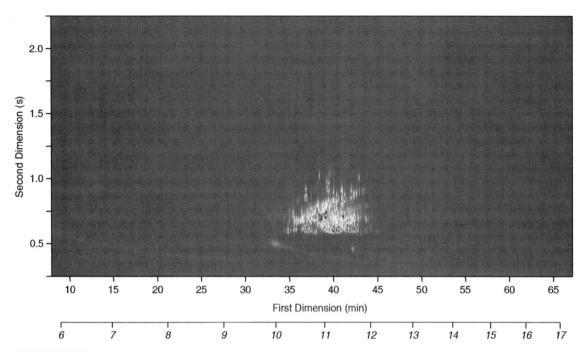

FIGURE 13-11 *Chromatogram of a medium naphthenic-paraffinic product. Data courtesy of Professor Glenn Frysinger, US Coast Guard Academy, New London, Connecticut, USA. (For a full color version of this figure, please see the insert.)*

13.2.3 Advantages and Drawbacks

A/ Peak Capacity

The peak capacity offered by GCxGC is approximately 30,000 peaks, which is several times that offered by traditional GC, which usually exhibits a few hundred [8]. A gasoline sample showing approximately 700 analytes on a GC–MS system will show about 1,250 analytes on a GCxGC–TOFMS system [17].

B/ Discrimination Based on Two Independent Properties

Because there are two different columns, discrimination based upon two different properties (for example, volatility and polarity) is provided by the instrument. This is not the case for GC–MS, which separates based only on one property (usually boiling point in fire debris analysis). This allows for a neat organization of the chromatogram into groups of compounds with similar chemical properties.

C/ Two-Dimensional Chromatograms

The chromatogram resulting from the GCxGC provides a much more complete and a clearer picture of the composition of a mixture of compounds.

It has been stated by some that the interpretation of GCxGC chromatogram is difficult, even to the trained eye, and that it "would be incomprehensible to judge and jury alike" [18]. The same authors criticize the poor gain in resolution exhibited by the second separation [18]. Even though comparing GCxGC chromatograms requires a new learning, it is far from being more difficult than with regular chromatograms. In addition, as seen in the previous figures, the separation presented by the second chromatographic process is not only exceptional, but allows the analyst to resolve almost all previously coeluted peaks. The data generated by a GCxGC–TOFMS system is surely more complicated to handle than the regular GC–MS data, but far from being more difficult to interpret or to understand. The software managing this data is still under development and is improving on a continual basis; it is far more powerful than any software developed for GC–MS systems. It would require an entire book to present the power of the possibilities of data analysis that can be performed with the software. GCxGC is recent and the industry needs to find a standard manner of handling and presenting the data before its full power can be revealed [15]. One thing is certain: The power of the data generated by a GC–MS system is only the tip of the iceberg compared to the power of the data generated by a GCxGC–TOFMS system.

Another claim has been made in very recent literature that it takes as much as 110 to 130 minutes to run a sample with GCxGC [19]. Originally, GCxGC was used to analyze complex mixtures of petroleum distillates such as crude oil, which needed extended run time (up to several hours) in order to obtain full resolution of all peaks. Validation studies of GCxGC–TOFMS for ILR analysis run samples in 40 to 50 minutes, which is slightly longer than a typical corresponding GC–MS run, but that is far from the beliefs of some researchers.

D/ Instrumentation Cost

As previously stated, it is necessary to use a time-of-flight mass spectrometer in order to generate a fast spectrum scan. Also, a thermal modulator and special software are needed to run the instrument. This brings an extra cost when compared to regular GC–MS. A benchtop GC–MS can be purchased for less than USD 50,000, but the cost of a GCxGC–TOFMS can easily reach USD 150,000 or more. This is definitely the greatest limitation in the use of such a system. But as time passes and technology advances, it is expected that the cost will decrease as it did for the GC–MS.

E/ Validation Studies

GCxGC is reliably used in different fields of chemical analysis. Unfortunately, the validation of this technique for fire debris analysis is being conducted by only one laboratory at this time: the US Coast Guard Academy [3, 13, 20]. Once this validation is completed, the technique will have to undergo additional studies in other laboratories prior to becoming accepted by the scientific community. Furthermore, a standard procedure should be developed prior to becoming accepted by crime laboratories around the world.

F/ Compatibility

Data compatibility is a serious problem because very few people are currently using this technique. Data cannot be shared between a laboratory using GC–MS and one using GCxGC–MS. Thus, a transition period will be necessary in order to build libraries or a system for data exchange and peer-review processes to take place.

13.2.4 Final Comments

GCxGC–TOFMS offers an extremely promising future in the field of fire debris analysis. It permits better separation, and, therefore, better specificity of the analysis of ILR. Validation studies are currently in progress, and once they are completed and the cost of benchtop time-of-flight mass spectrometers and comprehensive two-dimensional chromatographic systems decreases, it is likely that more people will use this kind of instrument. This will be the change of technique that will lead to a significant improvement of the analysis of fire debris samples in the future.

13.3 GAS CHROMATOGRAPHY–MASS SPECTROMETRY/ MASS SPECTROMETRY (GC–MS/MS)

13.3.1 Principle

Tandem mass spectrometry (MS/MS) underwent great development during the 1980s. Analysis of explosives, drugs, and toxics were among the first forensic applications of MS/MS and appeared shortly thereafter [21]. Since the late 1990s, a few researchers sought to develop gas chromatography–mass spectrometry/mass spectrometry (GC–MS/MS) for fire debris analysis [18, 19, 22, 23]. Unfortunately, it does not seem that GC–MS/MS offers any practical advantage for the analysis of fire debris. Efforts to publish an ASTM standard on GC–MS/MS have been met with serious opposition from the forensic community, and proposals have been rejected for the past few years. The reason behind the community's rejection of the application of this technique to ILR analysis lies in the fact that not only does it bring no improvement, it also presents some disadvantages, such as a decrease in specificity. There are very few laboratories using GC–MS/MS for routine ILR analysis. Although the use of this technique is not recommended, it is important that the fire debris analyst be aware of it, its principles, its use, and more particularly its lack of suitability for ILR analysis.

MS/MS originally defined a technique that combined two mass spectrometers in tandem [21]. The first mass spectrometer separates the analytes based on their m/z ratio. One ion (commonly referred to as the parent ion) is focused in the collision chamber, located between the first and the second mass spectrometer, where it undergoes further fragmentations into daughter ions. The daughter ions then are analyzed by the second mass spectrometer, which returns a mass spectrum solely based on the parent ion. This has the great advantage of filtering unwanted ions and obtaining a much cleaner mass spectrum. Although the principle just described is a general one, it is then possible to use the two mass spectrometers to favor a parent ion or a daughter ion, depending on the application. As mass spectrometer technology advanced, the ion trap was invented as described in Chapter 8. The ion trap is not physically constituted of two mass spectrometers, but because of its capacity to trap or isolate a specific ion, it is widely used as an MS/MS. The ion trap is actually the instrument used within all publications pertaining to the analysis of ILR by GC–MS/MS.

13.3.2 Applications

The first referenced use of an ion trap detector for the analysis of ILR was published in 1992, however it was not used in an MS/MS mode [24]. MS/MS was first applied to the analysis of fire debris in the late 1990s [22, 25]. Two different approaches to the use of MS/MS have been described in the literature. The first one consists of the optimization of the "parameters and conditions of target compounds in order to obtain maximum sensitivity and specificity for ignitable liquids" [18]. The other one consists of the optimization of the parameters to improve the selectivity, not of target compounds, but rather of classes of compounds. This allows the forensic scientist to use pattern recognition of profiles of classes of compounds [18].

The only differences between the analysis by GC–MS and GC–MS/MS reside in the detector. An ion trap is a much more complicated detector to program than a quadrupole detector, particularly when the ion trap is used in MS/MS mode. There are several parameters, which greatly influence the analytical outcome. The user first has to choose which mode of MS/MS will be used. As stated previously, depending on the approaches, the parameters will then significantly differ. In the target compounds analysis mode described earlier, it is necessary to specify parameters for each compound [26, 27]. In such an application, the user does not obtain a total ion chromatogram as with GC–MS, but obtains a target compound chromatogram that contains only ions from its preselected target ion list.

13.3.3 Advantages and Drawbacks

The primary advantage of this technique is an increase in sensitivity; however, this is not necessarily an advantage to the application of fire debris. Improving the sensitivity of a technique usually results in a decrease of its specificity, which is illustrated by the example of GC–MS/MS. Because

GC–MS/MS seriously reduces the specificity of the analysis of fire debris samples, its significance is also reduced. Here are the three main reasons that explain this reduction in specificity.

A/ Characteristic Patterns

As explained in Chapter 12, interfering products can be classified into two main categories—those that are identical molecules to the ones found in ignitable liquids and those that are different. Because most interfering products are identical molecules to those found in ignitable liquids (such as toluene, xylenes, and methylnaphthalenes), enhancing the sensitivity of their detection is not pertinent. The key in the interpretation of the results is to identify patterns of these molecules that are characteristic to the presence of ignitable liquid residues. This is usually achieved with extracted ion profiles or chromatograms, as demonstrated in Chapters 9 and 12. When the amount of ILR present in the debris is of lower concentration than the interfering products, these patterns are masked and the ratios are skewed, thus preventing a positive identification of ignitable liquids. The sensitivity of GC–MS is already very low and the limitation of the detection of ignitable liquid does not reside in the instrumentation, but in the presence of interfering products. Thus, there is absolutely no need to use a technique that can detect lower amounts of these analytes when the minimum detected is obscured by the presence of interfering products.

B/ No Detection of New Patterns or Molecules

If scientists want to evolve the interpretation of fire debris analysis to the next step, there is a need to find either analytes that are solely specific to ignitable liquids and not to interfering products, or to find other sets of characteristics (such as patterns) that are solely specific to ignitable liquids and that are not disturbed by the presence of interfering products. This was the original intention of the basis of the application of target compound chromatography to fire debris analysis presented by Wineman and Keto [28]. In order to use this approach, it is necessary to analyze and look at the whole content of ignitable liquids and fire debris. Techniques such as GCxGC–MS could perform such research. These goals are not likely to be achieved using GC–MS/MS because the analyst specifies which ion, and thus which molecule, is detected. Thus, even if there were minute amounts of a molecule specific to a type of ignitable liquid, without knowing its presence at first, it would not be detected by GC–MS/MS because the analyst would be oblivious to its presence.

C/ Too Little is a Dangerous World

The use of GC–MS allows the scientist to detect minute amounts of ILR among fire debris samples. Combined with the proper extraction technique, analysts can detect $1/10\,\mu l$ or less of gasoline among debris having a volume of a bout one gallon. At that point, the lower limits of significance already have been reached. Detecting too little is not a good thing, because its significance is greatly diminished. GC–MS/MS allows the user to detect even lower amounts of analytes, which is not only useless, but also dangerous and potentially misleading. The significance of detecting such low amounts is not understood.

13.3.4 Summary

The use of GC–MS/MS is not recommended in fire debris analysis. As demonstrated, GC–MS/MS not only brings no further improvements when compared to GC–MS, but it also brings the interpretation of the results to a doubtful level, which the field of forensic sciences cannot afford.

13.4 GAS CHROMATOGRAPHY–ISOTOPE RATIO MASS SPECTROMETRY (GC–IRMS)

13.4.1 Principle

Isotope ratio monitoring (IRM) is a relatively novel technique. It has been used since the early 1990s to identify common sources of hydrocarbons in the geochemical industry [29, 30]. It led to the development of the identification of common origin of pharmaceutical drugs [29]. Smallwood et al. were able to differentiate gasolines from different areas of the United States using gas chromatography–isotope ratio mass spectrometry (GC–IRMS) [30]. In addition, they showed that some evaporation and water washing of the samples did not influence the outcome of the isotope ratio analysis. Philp et al. used the isotope ratio of carbon and hydrogen to investigate the origins (also known as fingerprinting or tracing) of oil spills [31]. They found that technique very useful and complementary to GC or GC–MS. More recently, Benson et al. published a comprehensive review of the application of IRMS in forensic sciences [32].

Since the beginning of the new century, developments have been undertaken toward the application of this technique to identify a common source of ignitable liquids. Jasper et al. reported that preliminary research has proven the technique promising, however more research is needed to validate it and obtain general acceptance in the forensic community [33–35]. It is very important here to emphasize that this technique is not being developed to replace GC–MS in the identification of the presence of ignitable liquid residues in fire debris samples. It is being developed in order to analyze two ignitable liquids (or residues) and to determine whether they have a common origin or not. This is a tool that would help the investigator when, for example, gasoline from a container found in a suspect's car needs to be compared with gasoline found at the scene of an arson and the question of a possible common source must be answered. As presented in

Chapter 9, several authors have tackled this problem using GC or GC–MS and various data analysis procedures [36–42].

The principle behind the theory that GC–IRMS can help to identify the common origin of petroleum products is based on the fact that the different geological sources of hydrocarbons present different isotope ratios. By using the ratio of ^{12}C to ^{13}C, it is possible to obtain 67 discrete ratios in the range of naturally-varying carbon material [35]. The theory also stipulates that the ratio displayed by one compound of a hydrocarbon mixture is independent of the ratio exhibited by all other compounds. Thus, if each compound can display one of 67 ratios, then, by analyzing only seven molecules, the possibilities of different ratios is already in the trillions. The discrimination power of the isotope ratios of several components of a mixture is very close to one.

13.4.2 Application

The sample is prepared as for regular GC or GC–MS analysis. The gas chromatographic separation conducted with this analytical technique is the same as described earlier in Chapter 8. The difference lies in the detection, after the chromatographic separation, as shown in Figure 13-12.

A GC–IRMS is composed of four main elements: the gas chromatograph, the high-temperature furnace, the water trap, and the isotope ratio mass spectrometer. Once the column exits the gas chromatograph, instead of going into the mass spectrometer as with regular GC–MS, it enters the high-temperature furnace where oxygen is made available. The organic material is burned at about 900°C, which produces CO_2 and H_2O as major combustion products. At the exit of the furnace, the mobile phase continues into a water trap, where the water is removed. Finally, the resulting gases are brought into the isotope ratio mass spectrometer, where the amounts of $^{12}CO_2$ and $^{13}CO_2$ are analyzed.

The results are reported as the difference from the international standard ratio of ^{13}C to ^{12}C in part-per-thousand using the following equation:

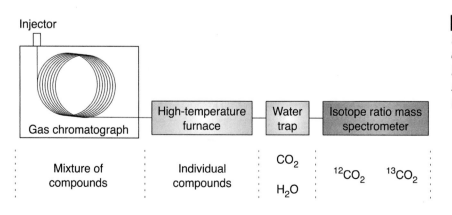

Injector

Gas chromatograph

High-temperature furnace

Water trap

Isotope ratio mass spectrometer

Mixture of compounds

Individual compounds

CO_2

H_2O

$^{12}CO_2$ $^{13}CO_2$

FIGURE 13-12

Principle of gas chromatography–isotope ratio mass spectrometry (GC–IRMS).

$$\delta^{13}C = \frac{R_{sample}}{R_{standard}-1} \cdot 1000$$

where R_{sample} is the $^{13}C/^{12}C$ ratio of the given compound in a sample and $R_{standard}$ is defined as 1.108%.

13.4.3 Advantages and Drawbacks

GC–IRMS definitely appears to be an interesting tool that can be used to link the origins of petroleum products. It might bring the long-awaited answer to the problem of linking ignitable liquids that cannot always be performed with GC–FID or GC–MS for different reasons. Before it can be used on a routine basis, it will need to be completely validated for this particular purpose. This validation procedure should include experiments evaluating the variation of ratios, if any, due to the weathering of ignitable liquids, extraction procedures, and the contribution of interfering products. There will need to be a lot of data analysis to set the thresholds under which two samples can be considered to be from a common origin. There is still a lot of work ahead before a procedure for the interpretation of the results can be laid out.

In addition to the validation of the technique itself, it is necessary to consider the significance of the demonstration of the common origin, as discussed in Chapter 9. Having the techniques and instrumentation to evaluate the ^{13}C to ^{12}C ratio is one thing, but determining its significance with regard to a potential common origin is another.

The instrumentation also has a serious disadvantage that needs to be considered. The gas chromatographic part is identical to its GC–MS counterpart, but everything else is different. The need for a special furnace with a water trap and other connections to a particular mass spectrometer capable of analyzing ratios of ^{12}C to ^{13}C costs about USD 150,000 to 200,000. Given that this technique does not allow the fire debris analyst to conduct regular ILR analysis, but only to compare two liquids or ILR for a common origin, this cost is prohibitive. Again, with technological advances, it is very possible that much less expensive instruments may be available in the near future. In addition, with the other potential forensic applications, such as drug or explosives profiling, it also is possible that this technique may be justified in a crime laboratory, shared between different sections.

13.5 ELECTRON IONIZATION FOURIER TRANSFORM ION CYCLOTRON RESONANCE (EI FT–ICR)

13.5.1 Principle

Rodgers et al. reported the application of electron ionization Fourier transform ion cyclotron resonance (EI FT–ICR) high-resolution mass spectrometry to the analysis of ignitable liquids [43]. EI FT–ICR was developed from the ion cyclotron method for mass determination. This began in the 1940s with the discovery of the Fourier transform technique and continued with the development of soft ionization sources in the early 1990s [44]. The EI FT–ICR MS is a very complex mass spectrometry technique that requires highly sophisticated instrumentation. The mass spectrometer consists of three main parts: the sample source, the ion transfer region, and the analyzer. EI FT–ICR MS offers a very high resolution of masses. A conventional benchtop mass spectrometer offers resolutions of approximately one m/z, whereas this type of mass spectrometry offers resolution down to 1/1000 m/z. This, in turn, allows for the differentiation of molecules with the same elemental composition (and thus with the same nominal mass) but that differ in their total exact masses. Because of the extreme high resolution, a chromatographic separation is not needed for this technique.

13.5.2 Application
The extract is injected through the inlet of the instrument and is brought to the sample source, which ionizes the analytes electronically. They are then brought to the analyzer (ion trap) where the analysis takes place. The overall time of an analysis is less than 10 minutes. The design of the inlet system allows for the hydrocarbons to be analyzed with a minimum of fragmentation, since the goal is to keep as many molecular ion peaks as possible.

The experiments conducted by Rodgers et al. were performed on neat ignitable liquids as well as extracts from fire debris. The extraction procedure performed by the authors consists of a Soxhlet-type extraction in chloroform [43]. The extract was then distilled and evaporated to dryness.

13.5.3 Advantages and Drawbacks
Outside the scope of the research, this technique has not been applied to practical casework for the analysis of fire debris samples. It is not yet a validated technique. The results shown in the literature are interesting and definitely deserve some attention. Being able to differentiate molecules of the same nominal elemental composition but of different configurations is a powerful asset. However, it is not certain that it has a direct application in the field of fire debris analysis. The reasons for this uncertainty were explained in Chapter 12 within the concept of interfering products. If most of the interfering products and, more particularly, pyrolysis products are identical molecules to those constituting ignitable liquids, this technique will not reveal the origin of the molecule itself. Coupling gas chromatography with this analytical technique has been done

in the past, but it will not necessarily add more information in this particular application [45]. Using the EI FT–ICR MS in lieu of a regular MS does not offer an advantage because such a high-resolution MS in fire debris analysis is not necessary.

Nevertheless, this technique allows the researcher to identify about every molecule present in an ignitable liquid. It could become a fantastic tool to discover new molecules or patterns of molecules that are characteristic of the different ignitable liquids. If such research was undertaken and this technique was proven capable of achieving this, it might find a better application in fire debris analysis, at least in the research and development phases. Nevertheless, this technique might be considered in fingerprinting ignitable liquids (determination of common source) as described with GC–IRMS. With such a high resolution, it might be possible to profile origins of ignitable liquids.

Unfortunately, there are other issues that need to be resolved before being able to consider this technique for practical evaluation. For example, the extraction technique previously described (Soxhlet extraction) is not suitable with most of the fire debris samples, notwithstanding the enormous risk of losing the volatile during the drying process. The requirement of injecting the sample without solvent will be difficult to respect. Most modern extraction techniques require the use of a solvent at some point. It would be difficult to use such a technique with real-case fire debris. If no other extraction technique is suitable for the analysis by EI FT–ICR, it is clear that this technique cannot be considered for routine application. The researchers of this technique seem to have a very good grasp of these practical issues because they are working on the compatibility of the activated charcoal strip with their inlet system [43, 46].

Finally, the cost of the instrument and its operation are obviously the main drawbacks that will probably never be overcome. The instrument itself costs several million USD and requires several technicians to operate. Furthermore, it takes a great volume of space and a tremendous amount of maintenance. This cost prohibits its consideration for any crime laboratory.

At this time, it is inconceivable to use such an instrument in routine fire debris analysis. If further developments allow for the determination of molecules or patterns of molecules specific to ignitable liquids, for a better integration with extraction technique, and for a reduction of the cost and operability of such an instrument, it might be possible for this technique to come into fruition in the field of fire debris analysis.

Very recently, the analysis of ILR by proton transfer reaction time-of-flight mass spectrometry (PTR–MS) was developed [47]. While this technique presents differences, it also has the advantages of requiring a less complex instrumentation and allows for direct headspace sampling. Its development should be closely monitored.

13.6 VAPOR PHASE ULTRAVIOLET SPECTROSCOPY

13.6.1 Principle

McCurdy et al. reported the use of vapor phase ultraviolet spectroscopy (VPUVS) for the analysis of ignitable liquid residues from fire debris samples [48]. They base their observations on the absorption maxima of different aromatic components present in some ignitable liquids. They used it as a complementary technique to GC and GC–MS in order to determine the presence of gasoline in a mixture with diesel fuel and to estimate the ratio m-xylene/p-xylene in another mixture.

Ultraviolet spectroscopy is another analytical technique commonly used in analytical chemistry. This method of absorption spectroscopy is based on the fact that when a radiation passes through a substance, the latter may absorb a portion of the radiation. This absorption of different levels of energy (wavelengths) of the radiation is dependent on the different electronic energy levels exhibited by the molecules present in the substance [49]. Transition from the ground state to excited states is shown in Figure 13-13. Different molecules exhibit different energy transitions depending on their chromophores.[1] When the electrons return to their ground states, they usually emit light. If the effect is immediate, it is called fluorescence; if it is delayed, it is called phosphorescence.

Unfortunately, alkanes do not absorb UV in the range detected by the instrument. UV spectroscopy is useful to characterize other organic compounds such as aromatics, alkenes, alcohols, and carbonyls. Another advantage of UV spectroscopy, and absorption spectroscopy in general, is the fact

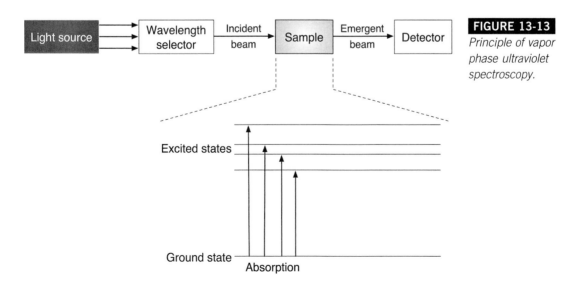

FIGURE 13-13
Principle of vapor phase ultraviolet spectroscopy.

---

[1] A chromophore is a group of atoms that absorbs light at certain wavelengths.

that it is possible to quantify the presence of a component in a solution, based upon the principle of the Beer-Lambert law [49]:

$$A = \log \frac{I_0}{I} = \varepsilon \cdot c \cdot l$$

where A = Absorbance, I_0 = intensity of incident light, I = intensity of emergent light, ε = molar absorptivity, c = molar concentration of solute, and l = length of sample cell.

Thus, by knowing the intensity of the incident and emergent lights as well as the cell length and the molar absorptivity, it is possible to determine the concentration of the solute. However, this task becomes nearly impossible in the presence of a complex mixture.

UV spectroscopy is performed with the help of a spectrophotometer [50]. Modern instruments are usually double-beam spectrophotometers. The deuterium lamp provides wavelengths as short as about 190 nm to about 800 nm (which is visible spectroscopy). Typically, UV spectroscopy is performed in the range of 200 to 400 nm. The light is split and converged toward the sample cell and a reference cell (which constitutes the baseline). The portion of the light exiting the sample (or the reference) is then directed toward the photomultiplier where intensities are detected and recorded versus their frequency. When the cell used in the instrument contains a vapor, the technique is called vapor phase ultraviolet spectroscopy (VPUVS).

13.6.2 Application
McCurdy et al. either analyzed the headspace of the sample by direct sampling with the quartz cell or by dynamic headspace concentration on charcoal followed by desorption with hexane [48]. The hexane extract was then placed in the quartz cell and allowed to evaporate. The result of the analysis is a UV spectrum with the wavelength plotted on the abscissa (x-axis) and the absorbance on the ordinate (y-axis), as shown in Figure 13-14.

13.6.3 Advantages and Drawbacks
The use of VPUVS appears attractive from economical time consumption standpoints. The analytical time is very short (less then a minute) and the preparation can be very simple. Also, the instrument is not very costly and does not require a great amount of maintenance. Unfortunately, the limitations of VPUVS are very quickly reached.

UV spectroscopy is a great tool for characterizing some organic compounds from simple mixtures and for quantifying them when circumstances permit. This technique is not suitable for analyzing complex mixtures, which constitute most of the samples in fire debris analysis. Also, McCurdy et al. recognized that the technique cannot analyze alkanes or polyaromatic

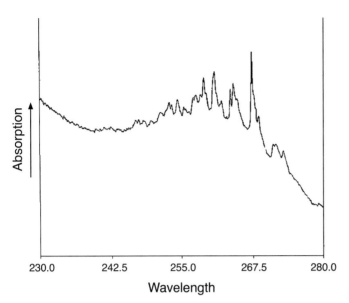

FIGURE 13-14 *Example of a UV spectrum of 75% weathered Amoco regular unleaded gasoline obtained by VPUVS. Source: McCurdy RJ, Atwell T, and Cole MD (2001) The use of vapour phase ultra-violet spectroscopy for the analysis of arson accelerants in fire scene debris, Forensic Science International, 123(2–3), pp 191–201, Figure 13. Reprinted with permission of Elsevier.*

hydrocarbons, thus it cannot be used to detect the whole array of ignitable liquids [48]. Although it is possible to characterize the presence of benzene, toluene, and xylenes with little difficulty, there are only rare instances when this distinction is necessary and pertinent. As seen in Chapters 4 and 12, these compounds are major pyrolysis products and are expected to be present in a great majority of samples that have not been exposed to an ignitable liquid [51]. Therefore, the demonstration of their presence is rarely useful per se. Finally, this technique does not separate the different components present in an ignitable liquid or fire debris samples. Although it is possible to interpret the data with a binary liquid (two component), it becomes impossible when several tens or hundreds of components are present. There-fore, its application to fire debris analysis is extremely limited and is not suitable for the routine analysis of ILR.

When used complementarily with GC–MS, it might offer information in extremely rare and particular situations. McCurdy et al. were able to demonstrate the presence of gasoline within a mixture with diesel fuel using VPUVS [48]. Also, they were able to quantify the ratios of *m*-xylene/*p*-xylene using the same technique when it was not possible using the GC–MS due to coelution of the two peaks. These two cases demonstrate the rare applica-tions of VPUVS in fire debris analysis.

13.7 SECOND DERIVATIVE ULTRAVIOLET SPECTROMETRY

Second derivative ultraviolet spectrometry is the application of a particular mathematical operation to the data obtained from an ultraviolet spectrophotometer. It produces cleaner spectrum and, more importantly, it increases the "fingerprint" of a compound. There have been some sporadic forensic applications, such as in drug analysis [52]. Meal applied second derivative ultraviolet spectrometry to the analysis of ignitable liquid residues [53]. The author demonstrated that among the 150 ignitable liquids analyzed, none presented the same spectra. She also stated that the weathering of the liquids did not influence the original spectrum and that interfering products from substrates did not influence the spectrum to any significant extent. The author presents some spectra and some data, however, she did not identify the criterion necessary to recognize and identify different classes of liquids. Further research would be required in order to attempt to validate this analytical tool. Today, this technique is not valid to perform fire debris analysis and probably never will be.

Important work was also carried out in the 1980s and 1990s with the three-dimensional fluorescence spectroscopy of petroleum products [54–56]. The work primarily focused on the comparison of neat liquids, but it would be possible to imagine extending these concepts to the identification of ILR; however the presence of interfering products may prevent a positive outcome.

13.8 THIN-LAYER CHROMATOGRAPHY (TLC)

13.8.1 Principle

Thin-layer chromatography has been applied to the analysis of fire debris samples with two different purposes: as a cleanup procedure and as a means of identifying dyes in gasoline. This chapter does not review the fundamental principles of thin-layer chromatography. The reader should obtain this information from other texts if needed [57, 58].

13.8.2 Cleanup Procedure

Prior to the arrival of mass spectrometry, criminalists tried to clean ignitable liquid extracts, usually obtained by steam distillation, mainly from alkenes and oxygenates because these products originated mostly from matrices. An acid stripping procedure was used to that effect, which was once an ASTM standard [59, 60]. Aldridge presented a procedure by which the extract is cleaned up using TLC [61]. He used silica-gel plates with a mixture of hexane:benzene (95:5) to elute the analytes. Once the elution ended, he used UV light and Marquis reagent to visualize the compounds on the plate. He explained that the color given by the Marquis test was consistent with the different classes of compounds from the gasoline. Finally, he scraped the plate to recuperate the analytes and dissolved them in a solvent suitable for gas chromatographic analysis.

It is clear that this technique was pertinent and useful at that time. Today, with the venue of the GC–MS and the improvement of the technology, this cleanup procedure is obsolete.

13.8.3 Analysis of Gasoline Dyes

One of the first scientists to use TLC to analyze gasoline dyes was Hausser in Germany [62]. The idea was to discriminate between gasoline brands. In the mid 1970s, the same method was applied successfully in the United States [62]. It was possible to differentiate gasoline brands based on the analysis of the dyes. However, this technique presents important limitations because the dye content would vary over time for a given gasoline brand. The procedure consists of extracting the dyes from the gasoline by passing the gasoline through a column of alumina, which is then rinsed with petroleum ether. The alumina is dried and the dyes are recuperated with acetone. The dyes are then placed on a TLC plate (silicagel) and eluted with benzene, carbon tetrachloride, or a mixture of benzene: carbon tetrachloride (1:1) [63]. Once the plate is eluted, the components are detected under visible and UV lights. This method is relatively insensitive, and requires on the order of 10 ml of sample. Long proposed the use of several different solvent systems for the elution of the plate [64]. He also claimed that it is possible to identify brands and batches of gasoline using this technique.

Although the problem of gasoline branding using dyes is equivalent to any other "fingerprinting" technique for the reasons explained in Chapter 9, Moss et al. used this technique to determine the presence of gasoline from wood samples [63]. They warned that the presence of such dyes in a sample is not enough to determine that gasoline is present, but it supports chromatographic data showing gasoline or helps in cases where the chromatographic pattern is masked by interfering products. They also warned the user not to use diethyl ether to extract the ILR from the debris because it would rinse the dyes off the alumina. They recommended the use of hexane, which allows for both the identification of the dyes by TLC and the identification of the volatile organic compounds portion of the extract by GC.

13.9 AROMA DETECTION TECHNOLOGY

13.9.1 Principle

Barshick studied the possibility of using aroma detection technology to identify ignitable liquid and ignitable liquid residues from fire debris samples [65].

She analyzed different classes of neat ignitable liquids (gasoline, kerosene, diesel fuel, mineral spirit, and lacquer thinner) as well as some residues extracted from fire debris. She concluded that the detection of ignitable liquids from fire debris was feasible; however, more work was needed in order to understand the influence of different parameters. Since then, no research has been published dealing with this particular topic.

The vapors to be analyzed enter the instrument and pass through an array of aroma detectors. Aroma detectors are organic polymer sensors that respond to different volatile compounds. Each sensor consists of a certain organic polymer to which a particular functional group has been added. Each sensor provides a response based on variations in the spatial arrangement of the atoms within a molecule, its ionicity, as well as its hydrophilic and hydrophobic properties. These variations cause changes in the electrical resistance at the surface of the polymer, which is recorded. Barshick used an AromScanner (AromaScan Inc, Hollis, NH, USA, now Osmetech Inc, Rowell, GA, USA) [65]. The sensor number is plotted on the x-axis and the intensity of the response is plotted on the y-axis. Barshick used a neural network software to interpret and differentiate the samples [65].

13.9.2 Advantages and Drawbacks

The time required for the analysis is usually less than five minutes and the instrumentation costs less than USD 10,000. This makes this analytical technique very attractive. The sample preparation is either nonexistent or requires the possible headspace concentration on an adsorbent.

Unfortunately, this technique lacks serious research for this application and, more importantly, for its validation. It is not certain that validation will ever be possible. Barshick's research lacks the analysis of a "blank" fire debris sample. Also, because this technique is used to analyze mostly classes of compounds, similar to infrared spectrometry, it does not appear to be suitable for fire debris analysis because different compounds of the same class characterize different ignitable liquids. As a result, the data presented by Barshick show very little difference between gasoline and kerosene or kerosene and diesel fuel [65]. Therefore, this technique should not be used for fire debris analysis until further research demonstrates its suitability, which is unlikely.

13.10 NUCLEAR MAGNETIC RESONANCE

13.10.1 Principle

Bryce et al. studied the possibility of using nuclear magnetic resonance (NMR) in order to identify ILR from fire debris samples [66]. They used proton-NMR to analyze different gasolines and a few other ignitable liquids in neat solutions as well as in solution with different solvents. They also recovered some liquids from burned wood using steam distillation. They concluded that NMR can be an effective tool that complements existing methods of analysis. No other publication addressing the use of NMR for ILR analysis has appeared in the forensic community since Bryce et al.'s article in 1981.

Certain atom nuclei spin around an imaginary axis. Because the nucleus carries an electrical charge, its spinning creates a magnetic moment; the energy level is dependent on the atom and its configuration within a molecule. If this atom is placed in a magnetic field, it will absorb energy levels corresponding to the magnetic field created by the spin. The absorption of the different energy levels is characteristic of one particular atom in a particular configuration. Thus, a spectrum over a range of frequencies (or representative values of frequency) versus the absorption can be obtained and used to identify the configuration of atoms within a molecule.

The analysis of a sample by NMR is relatively straightforward with regard to sample preparation. The sample can be analyzed either in a pure form or diluted in a solvent. In general, NMR requires a much greater quantity of sample than GC or GC–MS. Sample chambers need to contain about 0.1 ml or more of solution or neat liquid. When in solution, the analytes of interest need to be present at a certain percentage (v/v).

13.10.2 Advantages and Drawbacks

NMR is not a technique of choice for the analysis of fire debris. It does not allow for the observation of the pertinent characteristics necessary to identify ignitable liquids from fire debris samples. NMR does not include a separation technique, nor is it preceded by a separation technique. Thus, potentially hundreds of components are analyzed simultaneously. This does not provide the means necessary to differentiate which signals come from which components. NMR requires a much greater amount of sample than GC or GC–MS. This sample also has to be either in a pure form or in solution in a particular solvent. In addition, NMR is a very high-cost instrument, rarely found in crime laboratories. Bryce et al. also did not define or demonstrate the criteria that would be used in the identification of ILR from NMR spectra [66]. NMR should not be used in the analysis of fire debris unless further research demonstrates otherwise, which is very unlikely.

NMR can be used for other applications in the petroleum industry, such as the determination of the amount of hydrocarbon types in gasoline, because this does not require a specific identification of each hydrocarbon but, rather, an identification of the amount of one type of hydrocarbon, such as aromatic or olefinic [67].

REFERENCES

1. Wang FC-Y, Qian K, and Green LA (2005) GCxMS of diesel: A two-dimensional separation approach, *Analytical Chemistry*, **77**(9), pp 2777–85.
2. Bertsch W (1999) Two-Dimensional gas chromatography. Concepts, instrumentation, and applications—Part 1: Fundamentals, conventional two-dimensional gas chromatography, selected applications, *Journal of High Resolution Chromatography*, **22**(12), pp 647–65.
3. Frysinger GS and Gaines RB (2002) Forensic analysis of ignitable liquids in fire debris by comprehensive two-dimensional gas chromatography, *Journal of Forensic Sciences*, **47**(3), pp 471–82.
4. Cortes JH (1989) *Multidimensional chromatography*, Marcel Dekker, New York, NY.
5. Bertsch W (2000) Two-dimensional gas chromatography. Concepts, instrumentation, and applications—Part 2: Comprehensive two-dimensional gas chromatography, *Journal of High Resolution Chromatography*, **23**(3), pp 167–81.
6. Liu Z and Phillips JB (1991) Comprehensive two-dimensional gas chromatography using an on-column thermal modulator interface, *Journal of Chromatographic Science*, **29**, pp 227–31.
7. Zoex Corporation (year unknown) GC x GC: *A new frontier in separation science*, Zoex Corporation, Lincoln, NE.
8. Venkatramani CJ and Phillips JB (1993) Comprehensive two-dimensional gas chromatography applied to the analysis of complex mixtures, *Proceedings of the 15ᵗʰ International Symposium on Capillary Chromatography*, pp 885–91.
9. Phillips JB and Xu J (1995) Comprehensive multi-dimensional gas chromatography, *Journal of Chromatography A*, **703**, pp 327–34.
10. Phillips JB et al. (1999) A robust thermal modulator for comprehensive two-dimensional gas chromatography, *Journal of High Resolution Chromatography*, **22**(1), pp 3–10.
11. Ong RC and Marriott PJ (2002) A review of basic concepts in comprehensive two-dimensional gas chromatography, *Journal of Chromatographic Science*, **40**(5), pp 276–91.
12. Gaines RB and Frysinger GS (2004) Temperature requirements for thermal modulation in comprehensive two-dimensional gas chromatography, *Journal of Separation Science*, **27**(5–6), pp 380–8.
13. Frysinger GS and Gaines RB (2001) *Methods for improved detection of accelerants in fire debris*, US Coast Guard Academy, New London, CT.
14. Gorecki T, Harynuk J, and Panic O (2004) The evolution of comprehensive two-dimensional gas chromatography (GC x GC), *Journal of Separation Science*, **27**(5–6), pp 359–79.
15. Harynuk J, Gorecki T, and Campbell C (2002) On the interpretation of GC x GC data, *LCGC North America*, **20**(9), pp 876–92.
16. Phillips JB, Tang Y, and Cerven JF (1996) Prospective new method for fire debris analysis using comprehensive two-dimensional gas chromatography, *Pittsburgh Conference*, Chicago, IL.
17. Leco Corporation (2004) Leco Pegasus® 4D GCxGC–TOFMS, Leco Corporation, St. Joseph, MI.
18. Sutherland D et al. (2004) *Identification of ignitable liquid residues in fire debris by GC/MS/MS*. In: *Advances in forensic applications of mass spectrometry*, editor Yinon J, CRC Press, Boca Raton, FL, pp 181–230.
19. Almiral JR and Perr J (2004) *Chapter 8: New developments and quality assurance in fire debris analysis*. In: *Analysis and interpretation of fire scene evidence*, editors Almiral JR and Furton KG, CRC Press, Boca Raton, FL.

20. Frysinger GS and Gaines RB (2004) Comprehensive two-dimensional gas chromatography for analysis of ignitable liquids, *4th Annual TWGFEX Symposium on Fire and Explosion Debris Analysis and Scene Investigation*, Orlando, FL.
21. Yinon J (1991) *MS/MS techniques in forensic science.* In: *Forensic science progress 5*, editors Maehly A and Williams RL, Berlin, Germany, pp 1–29.
22. Sutherland DA (1997) The analysis of fire debris samples by GC/MS/MS, *Canadian Society for Forensic Science Journal*, **30**(4), pp 185–9.
23. Sutherland DA and Penderell KC (2000) GC/MS/MS an important development in fire debris analysis, *Fire and Arson Investigator*, October issue, pp 21–6.
24. Vella AJ (1992) Arson investigation using the ion trap detector, *Journal of the Forensic Science Society*, **32**(2), pp 131–42.
25. Sutherland D and Byers K (1998) Vehicle test burns, *Fire and Arson Investigator*, **48**(3), pp 23–5.
26. Plasencia MD et al. (2000) Improved sensitivity and selectivity for the detection and identification of ignitable liquid residues from fire debris by ion trap mass spectrometry I, *52nd Annual Meeting of the American Academy of Forensic Sciences*, Reno, NV.
27. Armstrong AT et al. (2000) Improved sensitivity and selectivity for the detection and identification of ignitable liquid residues from fire debris by ion trap mass spectrometry II, *52nd Annual Meeting of the American Academy of Forensic Sciences*, Reno, NV.
28. Wineman PL and Keto RO (1994) Target-compound method for the analysis of accelerant residues in fire debris, *Analytica Chimica Acta*, **288**(1–2), pp 97–110.
29. Jasper JP (1999) The increasing use of stable isotopes in the pharmaceutical industry, *Pharmaceutical Technology*, **23**(10), pp 106–14.
30. Smallwood BJ, Philip RP, and Allen JD (2002) Stable carbon isotopic composition of gasolines determined by isotope ratio monitoring gas chromatography mass spectrometry, *Organic Geochemistry*, **33**(2), pp 149–59.
31. Philp RP, Allen J, and Kuder T (2002) The use of the isotopic composition of individual compounds for correlating spilled oils and refined products in the environment with suspected sources, *Environmental Forensics*, **3**(3–4), pp 341–8.
32. Benson S et al. (2006) Forensic applications of isotope ratio mass spectrometry—A review, *Forensic Science International*, **157**(1), pp 1–22.
33. Jasper JP et al. (2002) Putting the arsonist at the scene: "DNA" for the fire investigator?, *Fire and Arson Investigator*, **52**(2), pp 30–4.
34. Jasper JP et al. (2003) An initial report of the arson stable isotope analysis project, *55th Annual Meeting of the American Academy of Forensic Sciences*, Chicago, IL.
35. Jasper JP, Edwards JS, and Ford LC (2001) A novel method for arson accelerant analysis: Gas chromatography/isotope ratio mass spectrometry, *Arson Stable Isotope Analysis*, Niantic, CT.
36. Mann DC (1987) Comparison of automotive gasolines using capillary gas chromatography I: Comparison methodology, *Journal of Forensic Sciences*, **32**(3), pp 606–15.
37. Mann DC (1987) Comparison of automotive gasolines using capillary gas chromatography II: Limitations of automotive gasoline comparisons in casework, *Journal of Forensic Sciences*, **32**(3), pp 616–28.
38. Barnes AT et al. (2004) Comparison of gasolines using gas chromatography-mass spectrometry and target ion response, *Journal of Forensic Sciences*, **49**(5), pp 1018–23.

39. Doble P et al. (2003) Classification of premium and regular gasoline by gas chromatography/mass spectrometry, principal component analysis and artificial neural networks, *Forensic Science International*, **132**(1), pp 26–39.
40. Sandercock PML and Du Pasquier E (2003) Chemical fingerprinting of unevaporated automotive gasoline samples, *Forensic Science International*, **134**(1), pp 1–10.
41. Sandercock PML and Du Pasquier E (2004) Chemical fingerprinting of gasoline: 2. Comparison of unevaporated and evaporated automotive gasoline samples, *Forensic Science International*, **140**(1), pp 43–59.
42. Sandercock PML and Du Pasquier E (2004) Chemical fingerprinting of gasoline: 3. Comparison of unevaporated automotive gasoline samples from Australia and New Zealand, *Forensic Science International*, **140**(1), pp 71–7.
43. Rodgers RP et al. (2001) Compositional analysis for identification of arson accelerants by electron ionization Fourier transform ion cyclotron resonance high-resolution mass spectrometry, *Journal of Forensic Sciences*, **46**(2), pp 268–79.
44. Beu SC et al. (1993) Improved Fourier-transform ion-cyclotron-resonance mass spectrometry of large biomolecules, *Journal of the American Society for Mass Spectrometry*, **4**(2), pp 190–2.
45. Larsen BS, Wronka J, and Ridge DP (1986) An ion cyclotron resonance spectrometer as a gas chromatographic detector. The effect of continuous trapping on performance, *International Journal of Mass Spectrometry and Ion Processes*, **72**(1–2), pp 73–84.
46. Rodgers RP et al. (2002) Forensic analysis of petroleum products by FT-ICR mass spectrometry, *54th Annual Meeting of the American Academy of Forensic Sciences*, Atlanta, GA.
47. Whyte C et al. (2007) Fast fingerprinting of arson accelerants by proton transfer reaction time-of-flight mass spectrometry, *International Journal of Mass Spectrometry*, **263**(2–3).
48. McCurdy RJ, Atwell T, and Cole MD (2001) The use of vapour phase ultraviolet spectroscopy for the analysis of arson accelerants in fire scene debris, *Forensic Science International*, **123**(2–3), pp 191–201.
49. Pavia DL, Lampman GM, and Kriz GS (1996) *Introduction to spectroscopy*, 2nd edition, Saunders Golden Sunburst Series, Orlando, FL.
50. Skoog DA and Leary JJ (1992) Principles of instrumental analysis, 4th edition, Saunders College Publishing, Fort Worth, TX.
51. Stauffer E (2001) Identification and characterization of interfering products in fire debris analysis, *Master's thesis*, International Forensic Research Institute, Florida International University, Miami, FL.
52. Lawrence AH and McNeil JD (1982) Identification of amphetamine and related illicit drugs by second derivative ultraviolet spectrometry, *Analytical Chemistry*, **54**(13), pp 2385–7.
53. Meal L (1986) Arson analysis by second derivative ultraviolet spectrometry, *Analytical Chemistry*, **58**(4), pp 834–6.
54. Alexander J et al. (1987) Fluorescence of petroleum products II. Three-dimensional fluorescence plots of gasolines, *Journal of Forensic Sciences*, **32**(1), pp 72–86.
55. Siegel JA and Cheng N-Z (1989) Fluorescence of petroleum products IV. Three-dimensional fluorescence plots and capillary gas chromatography of midrange petroleum products, *Journal of Forensic Sciences*, **34**(5).
56. Sheff LM and Siegel JA (1994) Fluorescence of petroleum products V. Three-dimensional fluorescence spectroscopy and capillary gas chromatography of neat and evaporated gasoline samples, *Journal of Forensic Sciences*, **39**(5), pp 1201–14.

57. Poole CF, Cooke M, and Wilson ID (2000) *Encyclopedia of separation science*, volume 2, Academic Press, London, United Kingdom.

58. Sherma J and Fried B (2003) *Handbook of thin-layer chromatography*, 3rd edition, revised and expanded, Marcel Dekker, New York, NY.

59. American Society for Testing and Materials (1995) *ASTM E 1389–95 Standard practice for cleanup of fire debris sample extracts by acid stripping*, Annual Book of ASTM Standards 14.02, West Conshohocken, PA.

60. Juhala JA (1979) Determination of fire debris vapors using an acid stripping procedure with subsequent gas chromatographic and gas chromatography/mass spectrometry analysis, *Arson Analysis Newsletter*, **3**(4), pp 1–19.

61. Aldridge T (1981) A thin layer chromatography clean-up for arson distillates, *Arson Analysis Newsletter*, **5**(3), pp 39–42.

62. Pearce WE (1976) Study of gasoline dyes, *Arson Analysis Newsletter*, **1**(3), pp 1–2.

63. Moss RD, Guinther CA, and Thaman RN (1982) The analysis of gasoline dye in fire debris samples by thin layer chromatography, *Arson Analysis Newsletter*, **6**(1), pp 1–14.

64. Long CW (1978) Lab excercise No. 9: Identification of dyes in gasoline, *Arson Analysis Newsletter*, **2**(3), pp 2–4.

65. Barshick S-A (1998) Analysis of accelerants and fire debris using aroma detection technology, *Journal of Forensic Sciences*, **43**(2), pp 284–93.

66. Bryce KL, Stone IC, and Daugherty KE (1981) Analysis of fire debris by nuclear magnetic resonance spectroscopy, *Journal of Forensic Sciences*, **26**(4), pp 678–85.

67. Myers ME, Stollsteimer J, and Wims AM (1975) Determination of hydrocarbon-type distribution and hydrogen/carbon ratio of gasolines by nuclear magnetic resonance spectrometry, *Analytical Chemistry*, **47**(12), pp 2010–15.

CHAPTER 14

Other Possible Examinations Conducted on Fire Debris

"For instance, it would not do much good to try and show arson by producing, shall we say, some rags soaked in linseed oil when it could be proven that the type of business where the fire occurred called for the use of such oil-soaked rags."

Glenn D. Bennett, Commanding Officer of the Arson Squad, Detroit, Michigan, USA (1954)

14.1 INTRODUCTION

Fire debris samples are collected mainly to perform ignitable liquid residues (ILR) analysis. However, in some instances—for example if an investigator suspects that the fire was caused by the spontaneous ignition of some oil—different examinations are requested, such as the analysis of vegetable (and animal) oil residues. In other instances, neither the investigator nor the criminalist is initially aware that there is other pertinent physical evidence present in the sample. Therefore, it is extremely important for the fire debris analyst (1) to be aware that such evidence can be present in the fire debris sample, (2) to be able to recognize it, and (3) to be able to properly examine it or preserve and forward it to the appropriate specialist (as seen in Chapter 10). This chapter deals with some nonroutine examinations that either are requested or are pertinent for some fire debris samples, depending on the circumstances of the case.

Unfortunately, examinations performed on an item of evidence in order to observe one particular characteristic may not be compatible with the examinations performed to observe another one. In such instances, the different specialists should meet together with the investigators and determine the most appropriate sequence of examinations to be performed on the particular item. This determination needs to be based upon:

- the pertinence and significance of the characteristics sought,
- the examination(s) required to observe these characteristics, and
- the compatibility of these examinations.

It is extremely important to weigh each of these elements before making the final call regarding the sequence of examination. Sacrificing one type of evidence in order to preserve another sometimes may be necessary, but it is not a decision that should be made lightly. Once evidence is lost or damaged, it may never be recovered.

This chapter introduces the reader to the examination of vegetable (and animal) oil residues, automotive fluids, flare residues, and homemade chemical bombs. A section dedicated to flash point determination is provided at the end. The reader is referred back to Chapter 10 for information on the examination of other types of forensic evidence.

14.2 VEGETABLE OIL RESIDUES (VOR)[1]

14.2.1 Introduction

Fires caused by the spontaneous ignition of vegetable or animal oils[2] are documented facts [3, 4]. In these instances, where fire investigators suspect that a fire was caused by the spontaneous heating and ignition of vegetable oils, the laboratory can offer some help with the chemical analysis of debris [5]. The fire debris analyst typically handles this kind of examination, although the procedures for extracting and identifying VOR differ significantly from the standard ILR procedures that have been discussed in previous chapters.

Vegetable oils are among the substances that can undergo spontaneous ignition under the right set of circumstances [8]. These substances are widely available in today's market, in such things as food supplies, paint hardeners, and other chemical products.

The analysis of vegetable oil residues (VOR) can be an important step in the investigation of a fire suspected of having been caused by the spontaneous ignition of vegetable oils [1, 2]. When such samples arrive at the laboratory, the fire debris analyst must be aware of the different analyses, how to perform them, and how to interpret the results. The goal of this section is to present, briefly but with sufficient details, basic theory about vegetable oils and the analysis of their residues, how to interpret the results, and the limitations of the analysis.

---

[1] This chapter is only a brief introduction to the analysis of vegetable and animal oil residues from fire debris samples. A comprehensive review of the topic has been published in two articles in Journal of Forensic Sciences and the reader is strongly encouraged to refer to these in order to complete his or her knowledge of the topic [1, 2].

[2] For simplicity, the term "vegetable oil" will be used instead of "vegetable and animal oil"; however, it encompasses both oil sources.

Thermal Runaway and Spontaneous Ignition

In order for the phenomenon of spontaneous ignition to occur, the sequence of events shown in Figure 14-1 needs to take place [6, 7].

This situation illustrates a system that produces heat spontaneously. The heat is dissipated to some extent in its surrounding environment. If the rate at which the heat is produced is greater than the rate at which it dissipates, then the temperature of the system rises. As the tempera-ture of the system rises, the rate of the exothermic reaction that produces the heat increases and the heat generation rate increases. By contrast, the change in heat dissipation rate is negligible. Thus, thermal runaway occurs: the higher the temperature, the faster the production of heat, and so on. At some point, the autoignition temperature of the material is reached and, under the proper conditions, ignition occurs.

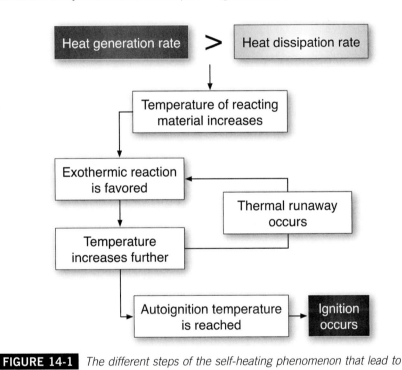

FIGURE 14-1 *The different steps of the self-heating phenomenon that lead to spontaneous ignition.*

14.2.2 Vegetable Oil Composition
A/ Lipids
Vegetable oils are composed mainly of lipids, which are defined as [9]: "naturally occurring organic molecules that dissolve in non-polar organic solvents when a sample of plant or animal tissue is crushed or ground." Lipids are mostly triglycerides (or triacylglycerides, abbreviated TAG), which are glycerol esters of fatty acids [10]. Figure 14-2 shows the chemical struc-ture of a triglyceride.

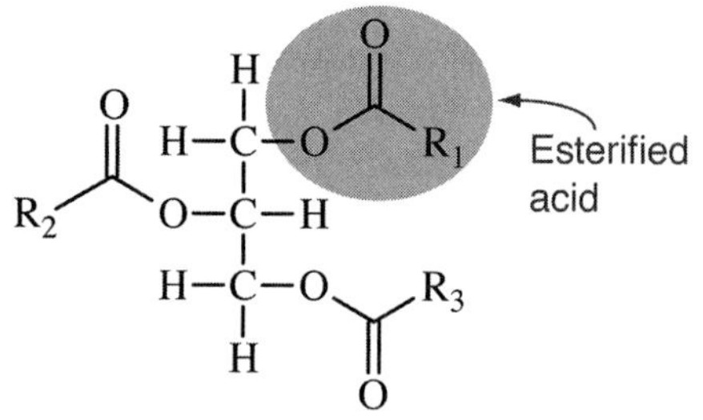

FIGURE 14-2

FIGURE 14-2

Chemical structure of a triglyceride or triacylglyceride (TAG).

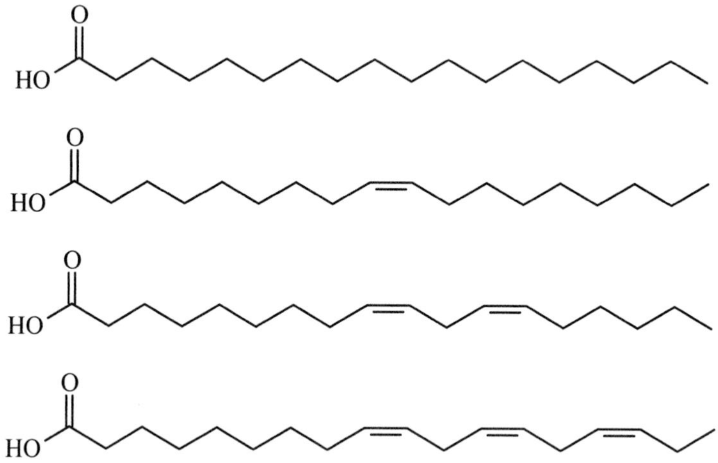

FIGURE 14-3

Different degrees of saturation of fatty acids: saturated fatty acid–stearic acid (top), unsaturated fatty acid–oleic acid (second from top), polyunsaturated fatty acid–linoleic acid (second from bottom), and linolenic acid (bottom).

B/ Fatty Acids

Each of the three positions (one per carbon) on the glycerol structure can carry one fatty acid (FA). Fatty acids are organic aliphatic acids in the form R-COOH occurring naturally in fats and oils [11]. Fatty acids found in TAG commonly range from octanoic acid (C_8) to tetracosanoic acid (C_{24}) in three different types:

- *Saturated fatty acids*: All the bonds in the carbon chain are single bonds.
- *Unsaturated fatty acids*: One or more double bond is present in the carbon chain.
- *Polyunsaturated fatty acids (PUFAs)*: Two or more double bonds are present in the carbon chain.

Figure 14-3 shows examples of the different types of fatty acids. Stearic acid is located at the top. It is a saturated fatty acid with no double bond. Just below is oleic acid with one double bond, making this acid unsaturated.

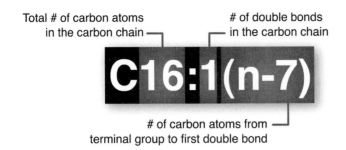

FIGURE 14-4

Fatty acid nomenclature system.

Linoleic and linolenic acids are the third and fourth acids from the top and are both polyunsaturated fatty acids (PUFAs) as they contain two or more double bonds. These four fatty acids represent the most important compounds in terms of VOR analysis.

The names of fatty acids can very quickly become complicated and hard to remember, because of the great number of them. Hence, a system has been developed with respect to the nomenclature of fatty acids [12]. This system is illustrated in Figure 14-4.

The nomenclature consists of using a "C" followed by the total number of carbon atoms in the carbon chain, including the one from the carboxylic group. The total number of double bonds is placed after the colon and is followed by the position of the first double bond from the terminal group. The double bonds are separated by one carbon atom, although there are a few exceptions. Thus, from the formula shown in Figure 14-4, it is possible to retrieve the exact structure of most fatty acids. Figure 14-5 shows the example of three different structures of fatty acids with their respective names based on the rules just explained. Although much of the chemical literature uses the designations just described, the common names are still primarily used in industry.

Table 14-1 shows a list of different fatty acids with their IUPAC name, common name, chemical composition, and molecular weight [1].

14.2.3 Propensity Toward Self-Heating and Spontaneous Ignition

The reason that vegetable oils are subject to self-heating and to possible spontaneous ignition lies in their PUFA content. The exothermic reaction at the origin of the self-heating phenomenon is an autooxidation, which is favored as the number of double bonds increases [13]. The rate of the reaction is highly increased by the number of double bonds. As a result, linoleic acid (C18:2) autooxidizes much faster than oleic acid (C18:1) [14–16]. Also, the presence of a conjugated system of double bonds, such as in eleostearic acid (C18:3), renders the autooxidation process extremely rapid. Thus, the autooxidation of a vegetable oil, and therefore its propensity

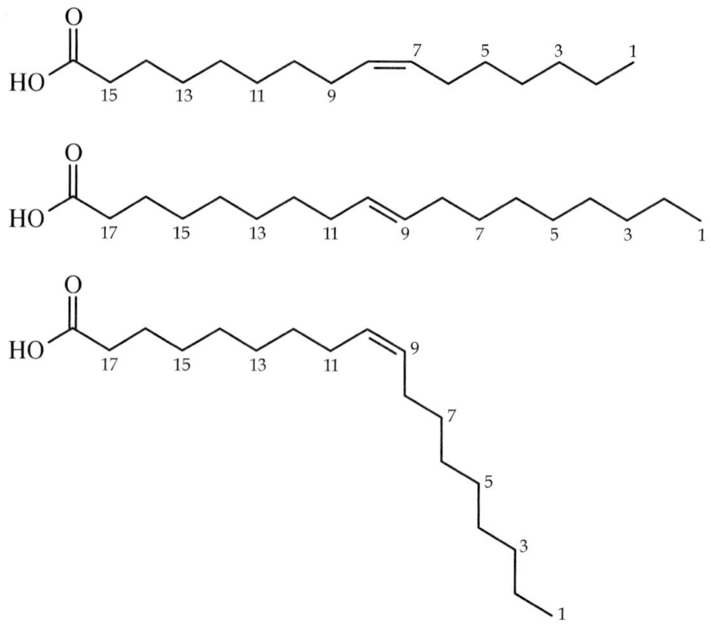

FIGURE 14-5

Examples of three fatty acid structures. Top: C16:1(n-7) cis *configuration. Middle: C18:1(n-9)* trans *configuration. Bottom: C18:1(n-9)* cis *configuration. The* cis *configuration should be drawn as in the bottom example (with the angle). However, to save space, the* cis *configuration usually is drawn flat as shown in the top example.*

toward spontaneous heating, is directly correlated to its fatty acid content, and more particularly to its PUFA content. This is why some vegetable oils exhibit little tendency to self-heat, such as mustard and peanut oils, whereas some exhibit a very high propensity to self-heat, such as linseed and tung oils. Table 14-2 presents some vegetable and animal oils with their respective tendencies toward self-heating [17–19]. Table 14-3 shows their composition [17, 20]. This also explains why petroleum-based products are not susceptible to spontaneous heating.

14.2.4 Forensic Approach

When a fire investigator suspects the presence of vegetable oils as the cause of a fire, the forensic scientist can assist in the investigation. The questions requiring answers pertain to (1) whether there were any vegetable oils present in the debris, (2) whether those vegetable oils were prone to spontaneous ignition, and (3) whether those vegetable oils underwent spontaneous ignition. Figure 14-6 summarizes these questions with the proper forensic approach to answer them.

The detection of fatty acids in nature and in proportions similar those found in known vegetable oil reference materials is sufficient to confirm the presence of a vegetable oil. The determination of the type and amount of

Table 14-1	List of Fatty acids and some of their characteristics [1]			
Designation	**IUPAC name**	**Common name**	**Formula**	**MW [amu]**
C8:0	Octanoic	Caprylic	$C_7H_{15}COOH$	144
C10:0	Decanoic	Capric	$C_9H_{19}COOH$	172
C12:0	Dodecanoic	Lauric	$C_{11}H_{23}COOH$	200
C14:0	Tetradecanoic	Myristic	$C_{13}H_{27}COOH$	228
C16:0	Hexadecanoic	Palmitic	$C_{15}H_{31}COOH$	256
C16:1(n-7)	*cis*-9-Hexadecenoic	Palmitoleic	$C_{15}H_{29}COOH$	254
C18:0	Octadecanoic	Stearic	$C_{17}H_{35}COOH$	284
C18:1(n-7)	*cis*-11-Octadecenoic	*cis*-Vaccenic	$C_{17}H_{33}COOH$	282
C18:1(n-9)	*cis*-9-Octadecenoic	Oleic	$C_{17}H_{33}COOH$	282
C18:1(n-12)	*cis*-6-Octadecenoic	Petroselinic	$C_{17}H_{33}COOH$	282
C18:2(n-6)	9,12-Octadecadienoic	Linoleic	$C_{17}H_{31}COOH$	280
C18:3(n-3)	9,12,15-Octadecatrienoic	α-Linolenic	$C_{17}H_{29}COOH$	278
C18:3(n-6)	6,9,12-Octadecatrienoic	γ-Linolenic	$C_{17}H_{29}COOH$	278
C20:0	Eicosanoic	Arachidic	$C_{19}H_{39}COOH$	312
C20:4(n-6)	5,8,11,14-Eicosatetraeinoic	Arachidonic	$C_{19}H_{31}COOH$	304
C20:5(n-3)	5,8,11,14,17-Eicosapentaeinoic	EPA	$C_{19}H_{29}COOH$	302
C22:0	Docosanoic	Behenic	$C_{21}H_{43}COOH$	340
C22:1(n-9)	*cis*-13-Docosenoic	Erucic	$C_{21}H_{41}COOH$	338
C22:6(n-3)	4,7,10,13,16,19-Docosahexaenoic	DHA	$C_{21}H_{31}COOH$	308

the fatty acids present provides an estimate of the propensity toward spontaneous ignition. However, this estimate must be made with great caution because there are two phenomena that are not taken into account in this analysis:

- Antioxidants, which slow down the autooxidation process, or driers, which increase the rate of the autooxidation process, often are added to oils. This information, unfortunately, is not available when analyzing the fatty acid content of an oil.
- Degradation of the components of an oil is not uniform, thus skewing the fatty acid ratios from what they were in the original oil. As a result, an oil with a great amount of C18:3 and less C18:0 can have this proportion reversed after undergoing self-heating, thus misleading the criminalist on its original self-heating propensity.

Table 14-2	Different vegetable (and animal) oils and their respective tendencies toward self-heating [17–19]	
Material	**Tendency**	**Origin**
Coconut oil	Very slight	Produced from Cocus nucifera (coconut palm), mainly from Indonesia and the Philippines
Corn oil	Moderate	Corn
Cottonseed oil	Moderate	Seeds of cotton
Fish oil	High	Lipid extracted from the body, muscle, liver, or other organ of fish
Linseed oil	High	Crushed flax seeds
Olive oil	Moderate to low	Olive
Palm oil	Low	Flesh of the fruit of the palm tree
Peanut oil	Low	Peanut
Perilla oil	Moderate to high	Perilla is a traditional crop of Asian countries
Rapeseed oil	Moderate	Crushed rapeseed
Soybean oil	Moderate	Soybean
Tung oil	High	Obtained from the nut of the tung tree

FIGURE 14-6

Questions to be answered and the forensic approach in vegetable oil residues analysis.

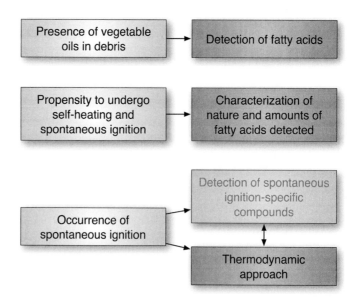

Table 14-3 Some vegetable (and animal) oils and their compositions [17, 20]

Vegetable Oil	C12:0 [%]	C14:0 [%]	C14:1 [%]	C16:0 [%]	C16:1 [%]	C18:0 [%]	C18:1 [%]	C18:2 [%]	C18:3 [%]	C20:0 [%]	C20:1 [%]	C22:0 [%]	C22:1 [%]
Coconut Oil	47	19		9		3	6	2					
Corn oil				11		2	27	59	1				
Cottonseed oil		<1		22	<1	3	19	54	1				
Linseed oil				5		4	22	14	50	<1			
Olive oil				11		2	73	8	<1		<1		
Palm oil		1		44		5	40	10					
Peanut oil	<1	<1		13		2	48	29		1	1	3	<1
Perilla oil				4		4	20	10	60				
Rapeseed oil		<1		3		1	33	15	6		1	<1	<1
Soybean oil				11		4	24	54	7				
Tung oil							4	9	82				

The determination of whether or not a vegetable oil underwent spontaneous ignition cannot be made solely by chemical analysis at this time—this is the reason why it is shaded in Figure 14-6. The mere presence of a vegetable oil susceptible to spontaneously ignite is not a sufficient condition to establish that the phenomenon of spontaneous ignition occurred. This is similar to finding ignitable liquids at a fire scene: it does not mean they were used as accelerants. There are other conditions that must be fulfilled in order to obtain spontaneous ignition, such as proper amounts of oil and substrates, size, shape, and nature of fuel package and its surroundings, as well as initial temperature [21, 22]. A thermodynamic approach is necessary to resolve this problem [23]. However, some recent research provided preliminary results with regard to the possibility of producing compounds or patterns of compounds that are specific to the phenomenon of spontaneous ignition [24]. If such research is further developed and validated in the future, it might be possible that fire debris analysis will focus on the detection of these compounds, which would be indicative of the occurrence of the phenomenon.

14.2.5 Analytical Scheme

There are many different types of analyses that can be performed on vegetable oil and their residues for different purposes [11, 25, 26]. However, when examining fire debris samples for the presence of VOR, the sequence presented in Figure 14-7 should be followed.

A/ Extraction-Isolation

If the liquid to be tested is in a pure form, this step does not apply. Otherwise, the debris needs to be extracted in order to isolate any possible TAGs or free fatty acids[3] (FFAs). In a case where stains can be distinguished on the debris, it may be desirable to extract only a small part of the debris.

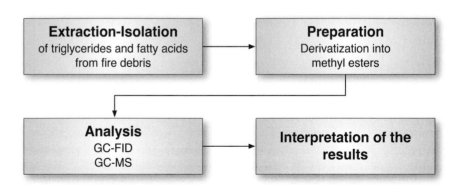

FIGURE 14-7

Analytical sequence used for the analysis of vegetable oil residues (VOR).

---

[3]When fatty acids are present without being part of a triglyceride, they are called free fatty acids.

Although it is much more convenient to work with small samples and it allows for the preservation of the bulk of the sample, only extracting a small portion increases the risk of missing something and of having to repeat the extraction.

Because of the nonvolatility of the components of interest, the only effective extraction technique is solvent extraction. Use of a nonpolar solvent, such as pentane, hexane, heptane, cyclohexane, ethyl ether, or diethyl ether, is best [2, 27–29]. The sample should be extracted for a couple of minutes under agitation and then removed. The solvent can be reconcentrated by gentle heating, although it is best not to heat the extract whenever possible.

B/ Preparation

Because TAGs and FFAs are not readily amenable to gas chromatographic analysis, the extract cannot be analyzed in its present form; thus, it needs to be derivatized. The purpose of the derivatization is three-fold:

I. It lowers the boiling point of the components.
II. It decreases their reactivity.
III. It allows for a separation of the fatty acids from the TAG, which makes the analysis and the interpretation of the results much easier.

The derivatization process removes the acids from the TAG and transforms them into fatty acid methyl esters (FAMEs), as illustrated in Figure 14-8. Other esters can be produced, however they do not present much interest in this particular application [30]. There are many different derivatization techniques available in the literature [1]. Two of the most suitable for VOR analysis are presented in Table 14-4. Table 14-5 shows the characteristics for the methyl esters corresponding to the acids shown in Table 14-1 [2].

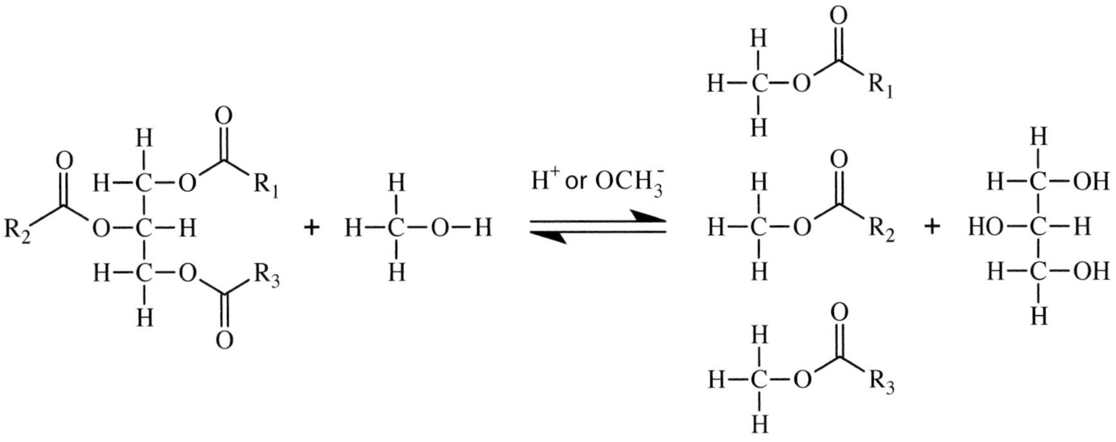

FIGURE 14-8 Principle of derivatization of triacylglycerides into fatty acid methyl esters (FAMEs).

Table 14-4	Recommended derivatization techniques for fatty acid methyl esters

KOH in methanol [31, 32]

- Mix 100 mg extract in solvent with 2 ml of a 2M solution of KOH in methanol

- Shake (vortex)

- Centrifuge for 1 minute

- Remove the upper layer (organic)

Triborofluoride in methanol [32–34]

- Mix 100 mg extract in solvent with 2 ml of a solution 10% BF_3 in methanol

- Heat at 60°C for 5 to 10 minutes

- Cool and add 1 ml H_2O and 1 ml hexane

- Shake (vortex)

- Centrifuge for 1 minute

- Remove the upper layer (organic) and dry it on anhydrous Na_2SO_4

C/ Analysis

Either GC or GC-MS is used to conduct the analysis. If the GC is equipped with a nonpolar column, such as a DB-1 or DB-5, it is possible to conduct the analysis by adapting the temperature program although conditions are not optimized. In this case, however, it is necessary to use a mass spectrometer for the detection because, otherwise, many peaks remain unresolved by the chromatographic system and will require the additional structural information provided by the mass spectrometer in order to be identified. If the GC is equipped with a column specially designed for the analysis of FAMEs, such as a diethylene-glycol phase (DB-Wax or HP-Wax) or a Supelco SP2380 (poly[90% biscyanopropyl/10%cyanopropylphenyl siloxane]), then an FID is sufficient as a detector because all the peaks are fully resolved. Table 14-6 shows the parameters used in a GC-MS equipped with a DB-5 type column.

Figure 14-9 shows the chromatogram of peanut oil, which typically exhibits a relatively low tendency to spontaneously ignite. It is possible to distinguish the main peak at C18:1, followed by C16:0, C18:2, and C18:0. C18:3 is completely absent. An eyeball estimate determines that the proportion of C18:1 is around 50% and the proportion of C18:2 around 20%.

Figure 14-10 shows the chromatogram of Canola[4] oil, which has a moderate tendency to self-heat. Again, the most abundant peak is C18:1, but it

---

[4] Canola oil is a trademark to designate rapeseed oil with a low eruric acid contant. It is also called LEAR for low eruric acid rapeseed. The term Canola comes from the contraction of the terms Canada oil low acid.

Table 14-5	List of fatty acid methyl esters and some of their characteristics [2]		
FA Designation	**FAME Name**	**Formula**	**MW [amu]**
C8:0	Methyl octanoate	$C_7H_{15}COOCH_3$	158
C10:0	Methyl decanoate	$C_9H_{19}COOCH_3$	186
C12:0	Methyl dodecanoate	$C_{11}H_{23}COOCH_3$	214
C14:0	Methyl tetradecanoate	$C_{13}H_{27}COOCH_3$	242
C16:0	Methyl hexadecanoate	$C_{15}H_{31}COOCH_3$	270
C16:1 (n-7)	Methyl hexadecenoate	$C_{15}H_{29}COOCH_3$	268
C18:0	Methyl octadecanoate	$C_{17}H_{35}COOCH_3$	298
C18:1 (n-7)	Methyl octadecenoate	$C_{17}H_{33}COOCH_3$	296
C18:1 (n-9)	Methyl octadecenoate	$C_{17}H_{33}COOCH_3$	296
C18:1 (n-12)	Methyl octadecenaote	$C_{17}H_{33}COOCH_3$	296
C18:2 (n-6)	Methyl octadecadienoate	$C_{17}H_{31}COOCH_3$	294
C18:3 (n-3)	Methyl octadecatrienoate	$C_{17}H_{29}COOCH_3$	292
C18:3 (n-6)	Methyl octadecatrienoate	$C_{17}H_{29}COOCH_3$	292
C20:0	Methyl eicosanoate	$C_{19}H_{39}COOCH_3$	326
C20:4 (n-6)	Methyl eicostetraenoate	$C_{19}H_{31}COOCH_3$	318
C20:5 (n-3)	Methyl eicosapentaenoate	$C_{19}H_{29}COOCH_3$	316
C22:0	Methyl docosanoate	$C_{21}H_{43}COOCH_3$	344
C22:1 (n-9)	Methyl docosenoate	$C_{21}H_{41}COOCH_3$	342
C22:6 (n-3)	Methyl docosahexaenoate	$C_{21}H_{31}COOCH_3$	332

is coeluting with C18:3 (on its left). A C18:1 isomer is also present on the right of the most abundant C18:1 peak. C18:2 is also present. The estimation of the proportion of the different fatty acids is difficult, but C18:1 is present at about 50%, C18:3 at about 15%, C18:2 at about 20%.

Figure 14-11 shows the chromatogram of a linseed oil with a high tendency to self-heat. The chromatogram shows C18:3 as the most abundant peak with about 50% of the total abundance. C18:3 coelutes with C18:2. C16:0 and C18:0 are also present at low levels.

One way of distinguishing between C18:1, C18:2, and C18:3 is to extract the molecular ions using the values shown in Table 14-5. This has been done for the chromatograms of Canola and linseed oils as shown in Figures 14-12 and 14-13.

One can readily appreciate the efficacy of this technique, as it allows one to easily identify which peak comes from which fatty acid.

Table 14-6	Analytical parameters used with a GC-MS system to carry out FAMEs analysis. Parameters courtesy of Doug Byron, Forensic & Scientific Testing, Lawrenceville, Georgia, USA	
Column	Type	Hewlett-Packard HP-5 (5% diphenyl methyl siloxane)
	Dimensions	30 m × 0.25 mm × 1.00 µm
Mobile phase	Carrier gas	Helium
	Flow rate	1 ml/min (manually setup at 170°C)
Injection	Type	Liquid/Autosampler
		Split 20 : 1
	Volume injected	1 µl
Temperatures	Injector	250°C
	Column	220°C for 5 min
		0.5°C/min to 225°C for 0 min
		5°C/min to 275°C for 5 min
		Total run 30 min
	Transfer line	280°C
	Quadrupole	150°C
	Source	230°C
Mass spectrometer	Scanning range	33–400 amu
	Threshold	500
	Solvent delay	2.50 min
	Sampling #	2

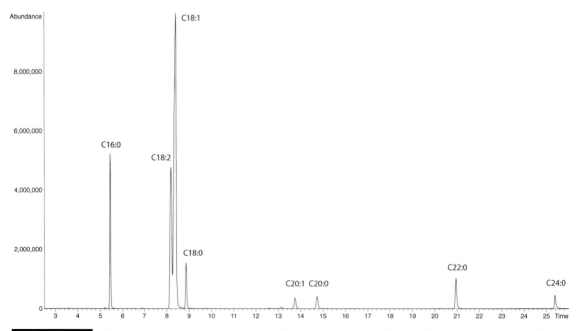

FIGURE 14-9   Total ion chromatogram of peanut oil (range from 2.5 to 26 min). Data courtesy of Doug Byron, Forensic & Scientific Testing, Lawrenceville, Georgia, USA.

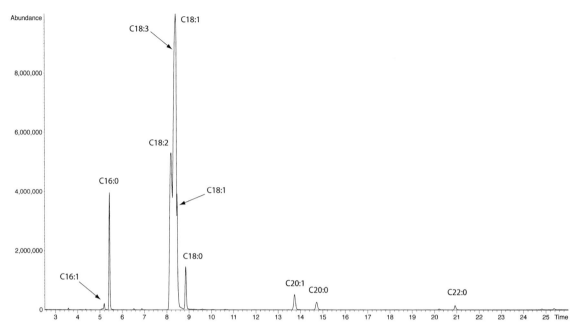

FIGURE 14-10 *Total ion chromatogram of Canola oil (range from 2.5 to 26 min). Data courtesy of Doug Byron, Forensic & Scientific Testing, Lawrenceville, Georgia, USA.*

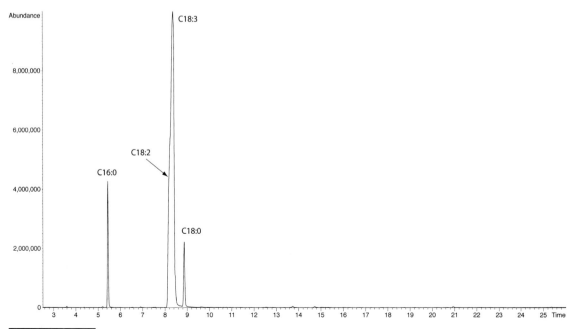

FIGURE 14-11 *Total ion chromatogram of linseed oil (range from 2.5 to 26 min). Data courtesy of Doug Byron, Forensic & Scientific Testing, Lawrenceville, Georgia, USA.*

FIGURE 14-12

Extracted ion chromatogram of Canola oil (range from 7 to 10min). Data courtesy of Doug Byron, Forensic & Scientific Testing, Lawrenceville, Georgia, USA.

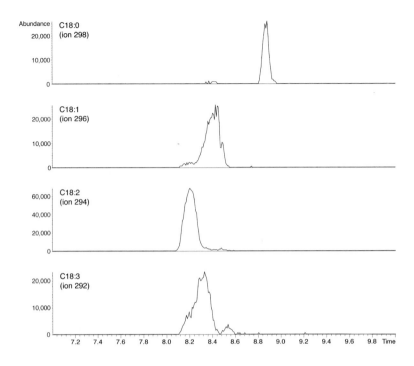

FIGURE 14-13

Extracted ion chromatogram of linseed oil (range from 7 to 10min). Data courtesy of Doug Byron, Forensic & Scientific Testing, Lawrenceville, Georgia, USA.

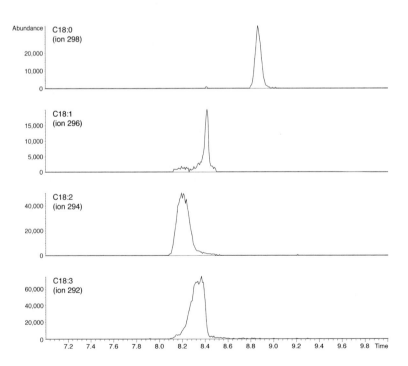

D/ Interpretation of the Results

The most difficult and least developed portion of the analysis of VOR is the interpretation of the results. A DB-1 or DB-5 type column does not allow the user to quantify the relative amounts of fatty acids with any precision. Hence, it is necessary to eyeball the amounts, which is sufficient in most instances. Fortunately, the determination of the exact quantity of fatty acids is not pertinent, because each category of oil presents variations in their oil composition. When a column designed to separate fatty acid methyl esters is used, it is possible to integrate the chromatogram and proceed to a much more accurate quantification of the relative amounts of fatty acids. However, in the present state of the art, this exact quantification is not necessary. After getting an estimate of the relative proportions of saturated, unsaturated, and polyunsaturated fatty acids, and more particularly C18:0, C18:1, C18:2, and C18:3, the user can report a possible propensity to undergo spontaneous ignition based on comparisons with the compositions of known reference samples. The best technique is to compare these estimate proportions to tables of compositions of oils, such as the one shown in Table 14-3. It is possible to find complete tables of compositions of vegetable and animal oils throughout the literature [20].

It is important to understand that there are significant limitations to the conclusions that can be drawn from such an analysis. The nature and amounts of fatty acids recovered and analyzed depends on many parameters in addition to the nature of their parent oils. These parameters include the substrate on which they were found, the extraction procedure, and more importantly, the thermal degradation that they encountered. Nonetheless, the thermal degradation of the components of a vegetable oil will not be consistent throughout. As demonstrated by research, PUFAs degrade faster than mono unsaturated fatty acids and saturated fatty acids, particularly if the oil underwent spontaneous ignition [13, 35, 36]. Thus, a linseed oil that originally contained a major amount of C18:3 might be recovered with its VOR showing only a small amount of C18:3 and a major amount of C18:1. In such instances, the analyst will not be able to observe the presence of linseed oil, but instead will think that it might be an olive oil with a low propensity toward spontaneous ignition: A wrong conclusion. Another major limitation concerns the possible presence of natural and/or artificial antioxidants and driers in the original oil, which significantly affects the kinetics of the autooxidation process, and, thus, its ability to self-heat. As such, even though a certain configuration of fatty acids may be present, the oil's original propensity toward self-heating may be significantly hampered by the presence of antioxidants. Unfortunately, with the present technique, it is not possible to determine the presence of these components from the VOR. As such, one cannot get a complete picture of what the original oil was.

Table 14-7	Guidelines for reporting the results of VOR analysis	
Observations	**Conclusion**	**Disclaimer**
No fatty acid detected	No vegetable (or animal) oil was detected in the sample.	This result does not imply that no such substance was present prior to the fire.
Fatty acid detected, but no PUFAs present	Vegetable (or animal) oil with very slight to low tendency toward spontaneous ignition was detected.	This result does not eliminate the possibility that a substance with a higher tendency toward self-heating was present prior to the fire.
Fatty acids detected, but low amount of PUFAs present (less then 30% C18:2 and less than 10% C18:3)	Vegetable (or animal) oil with moderate tendency toward spontaneous ignition was detected.	This result does not eliminate the possibility that a substance with a higher tendency toward self-heating was present prior to the fire.
Fatty acids detected, large amount of PUFAs detected	Vegetable (or animal) oil with high tendency toward spontaneous ignition was detected.	This result does not necessarily imply that spontaneous ignition occurred.

For these reasons, the criminalist must be very careful when reporting conclusions regarding VOR analysis. Table 14-7 gives some guidance in this regard.

It is important to note that this table is only a guide and is not a clear-cut reference. It also may be a good idea to add a brief explanation stating that the analytical scheme does not test for the presence of antioxidants or driers and that these can significantly decrease or increase the reported self-heating propensity of the oil. While waiting for new research to provide better interpretation guidelines for this type of analysis, the forensic scientist should render his or her conclusions conservatively and with caution and awareness.

14.3 VEHICLE FLUIDS

14.3.1 Introduction

On occasion, the failure of an automotive component involves a fluid, because many systems are fluid-based in vehicles. In such instances, the question of the nature of the fluid involved arises. It might be suspected that the wrong liquid was used, or that the liquid contained contaminants, which caused the failure [37, 38]. In other instances, a liquid suspected to be related to the automotive industry needs to be evaluated and identified [39]. Moreover, when a fire occurs in a garage, it is not uncommon for the fire investigator to sample different fluids found at the scene and forward them to the laboratory for analysis.

In all these situations, the samples usually are forwarded to the fire debris analyst. Because most fluids found in a vehicle are petroleum-based, the fire debris analyst is probably the most qualified person in the lab to identify these liquids. In spite of this, he or she cannot rely on any literature references regarding the characterization of vehicle fluids and often does not know how to interpret the results of such analyses. Hence, it is important to know the different fluids found in a vehicle, their function and composition, how to analyze them, and the criteria used for their identification. This is presented in this section.

14.3.2 The Different Vehicle Fluids

It is obvious that the number and nature of the fluids found in a vehicle will vary depending on the type of vehicle. But, for most part, the basic functions covered by fluids are common to all vehicles. Most of the liquids described next contain additives used to prevent decomposition, improve performance, and decrease wear and tear on the systems into which they operate. These additives are present in a small proportion within the liquids and, although they are the topic of detailed analyses for different purposes, they are of no interest to the fire debris analyst in order to identify the liquid [40]. Therefore, the presence of these additives will not be discussed in this section and only the bulk composition of the liquids is presented.

A/ Engine Oil

The engine oil is used to lubricate the components of the engine. It is found in the engine, where it circulates in a closed system. In some vehicles, the engine oil is routed away from the engine through rubber lines to a cooling radiator, providing an extra cooling system dedicated to the engine oil. Most vehicles contain between 2 and 8 liters of engine oil. Trucks and heavy equipment can contain up to a few dozen liters.

As shown in Figure 14-14, engine oil is usually a clear-brown to dark-brown liquid. It is a petroleum distillate composed of aliphatic compounds ranging from approximately C_{20} to C_{40}.

B/ Automatic Transmission Fluid

Automatic transmission fluid is used to provide propulsion in the propeller and to lubricate the transmission. Vehicles equipped with a manual (stick shift) transmission do not have any automatic transmission fluid. Automatic transmission fluid is found in the transmission case, but usually is routed away from it through a combination of hard steel lines and flexible rubber lines to a separate circuit of the cooling radiator (or sometimes a separate radiator). This controls the temperature of the transmission fluid.

As shown in Figure 14-14, automatic transmission fluids are all red. They may exhibit different shades of red, but the authors have never encountered such a fluid that is not red. Literature states that automatic

General view of the aspect of the different automotive fluids. (For a full color version of this figure, please see the insert.)

Engine oil

Automatic transmission fluid

Power steering fluid
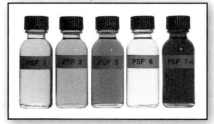

Brake fluid
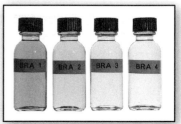

Coolant

Washer fluid

transmission fluids are dyed red so, in case of leakage, it can be differentiated from engine oil [41]. They are petroleum distillates composed of aliphatic compounds ranging from approximately C_{15} to C_{30}.

C/ Power Steering Fluid

Power steering fluid is used to provide hydraulic power to the assisted steering box. Only vehicles with steering assistance will have power steering fluid. Nowadays, almost all vehicles are equipped with assisted steering, but low-cost vehicles and old vehicles from the 1970s or earlier might not have any. It is usually contained in a closed circuit between the steering pump and the steering box. It is not routed outside for cooling purposes.

Power steering fluid is a petroleum distillate composed of aliphatic compounds ranging from approximately C_{15} to C_{30}. Note that some automatic transmission fluids are used interchangeably with power steering fluid. These fluids, such as the Type F Automatic Transmission Fluid, are of red color [42, 43]. As shown in Figure 14-14, there is a wide variety of different colors for power steering fluid. They range from completely transparent to dark red, through shades of yellow and brown.

D/ Brake Fluid

Brake fluid is used to provide hydraulic power in the assisted brake system. It is found in about every vehicle on the road today. It is a closed circuit, but this circuit is not confined to one particular area of the vehicle. It runs from the reservoir to the master cylinder to each brake cylinder at the wheels of the vehicle. It is routed through hard and flexible steel lines.

As shown in Figure 14-14, brake fluids are available in different colors, ranging from transparent to a medium shade of brown. DOT3 and DOT4 brake fluids are very similar and differ only in their boiling point (DOT4 has a higher boiling point than DOT3). Brake fluids are almost all composed of glycols. The only exception to this rule is the brake fluid DOT 5, which is composed of silicone-based chemicals (polydimethylsiloxane). This fluid is designed for racing cars and is not compatible with the other (regular) DOT3 and DOT4 brake fluid systems. Brake fluid does not contain any petroleum distillates. Additionally, a new brake fluid, DOT5.1, was created, which is not silicone-based, but contains glycols like those in DOT3 and DOT4. DOT5.1 is a higher quality of DOT4 brake fluid, thus presenting a higher boiling point. Table 14-8 shows the minimum specifications for dry and wet boiling points[5] of brake fluids [44]. Brake fluids may be important from a forensic standpoint as it is one component of some common improvised hypergolic mixtures.

Table 14-8	Minimum specifications for dry and wet boiling points of brake fluids	
Norm	**Dry boiling point [°C]**	**Wet boiling point [°C]**
DOT3	205	140
DOT4	230	155
DOT5	260	180
DOT5.1	260	180

E/ Gear Lubricants

Gear lubricants are used to provide lubrication in gearboxes and transfer cases. By leaving a thin fluid film between metal parts, metal-to-metal

---

[5] Brake fluid boiling points are evaluated in a dry condition (when the brake fluid does not contain any humidity) as well as in a wet condition (when it contains a small amount of water, usually 3.7%).

contact is avoided, thus preventing excessive wear and tear. Not all vehicles use gear lubricant in their gearboxes. Gearboxes that operate under light load use either engine oil or automatic transmission fluid.

Gear lubricants are found in different shades of brown to dark-brown, similar to the ones shown in Figure 14-14 for engine oils. They are petroleum distillates composed of aliphatic compounds of a heavier range than engine oil. These are very thick fluids.

F/ Fuels

Fuels, when combined with air and the proper ignition source, are used to provide chemical energy to the engine. All vehicles have some sort of fuel, primarily gasoline or diesel fuel. Some vehicles also are equipped with vegetable oil methyl ester derivates- (biodiesel), alcohol-, natural gas-, or liquid petroleum gas-based engines. More vehicles also use electrically powered engines. Because all the fuels pertinent to the fire debris analyst already have been described in previous chapters, they will not be covered here.

G/ Hydraulic Fluid

Some of the fluids previously described can be considered hydraulic fluids. However, the term hydraulic fluids often is used in the heavy equipment or trucking industry. It refers to a fluid used in a hydraulic system, such as the one found in an excavator to lift its bucket or in a tractor to provide propulsion.

Most hydraulic fluids are some shade of brown. They are mostly petroleum distillates composed of aliphatic compounds ranging anywhere from C_{20} to C_{50}. There are also synthetic hydraulic fluids that are composed of aliphatic compounds, polyethers, organic esters, phosphate esters, silicones, or fluoroethers.

H/ Coolant

Coolant is used to fill the engine's cooling system, to act as a heat exchange fluid, to lower the freezing point of water, and to increase the boiling point of water. It is confined to the cooling circuit, which runs through rubber hoses from the radiator to the engine. It is not present in air-cooled engines.

As shown in Figure 14-14, coolant can have many different colors. Usually it is green, but it is also found in yellow and red or orange tints. It is sold as a concentrated solution of glycols in water and needs to be diluted with water prior to use. Ethylene glycol has a sweet taste, but is poisonous and it should never be ingested. Propylene glycol is seeing increased use, due to the fact that it is nontoxic.

I/ Washer Fluid

Washer fluid is used to wash the windshield. It is the only liquid found in a vehicle that is designed to be expelled from the vehicle to the outside environment in a liquid form. It is found in the windshield washer reservoir and usually passes through the pump and then to the windshield through small hoses.

As shown in Figure 14-14, washer fluid is found in many different colors such as pink, blue, yellow, and orange. Some shades are almost transparent. It is composed mainly of water with additives, such as alcohols, glycols, and detergents. It is sold either as a ready-to-use solution, or as a concentrated solution that is diluted with water prior to use.

14.3.3 Analytical Scheme

Because most of these fluids are petroleum products and differ from each other primarily in the range of their cut, the most suitable instrument for a detailed chemical analysis is the gas chromatograph or the gas chromatograph–mass spectrometer. Figure 14-15 describes a useful analytical scheme for these types of fluids. The first two steps, color examination and miscibility testing, bring extra information that will help not only in the choice of the parameters for the GC or GC-MS analysis, but also in the final interpretation of the results.

A/ Color Examination

It is important to look at the color of the liquid. For example, power steering fluid and automatic transmission fluid are of indistinguishable chemical composition. However, automatic transmission fluid is always red, which is not the case for power steering fluid. Thus, observation of the color might offer another piece of information in the analytical scheme.

As seen previously in Figure 14-14, colors exhibited by the different vehicle fluids vary. This is true for new unused liquids. When the liquid is used for even a short amount of time in a vehicle, its color darkens relatively

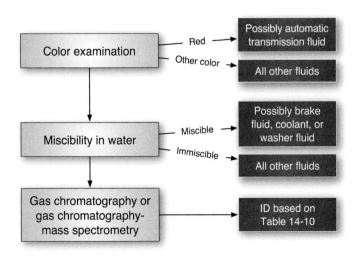

FIGURE 14-15

Analytical scheme for vehicle fluids.

General view of the aspect of some used vehicle fluids. Note how they are all darkened. When held close to the light, it is still possible to discern the red tint of most automatic transmission fluids. (For a full color version of this figure, please see the insert.)

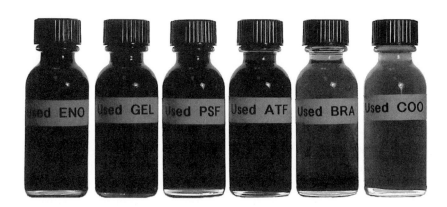

quickly and, with the exception of washer fluid, coolant, and fuel, will come out of the vehicle much darker or even black. This is particularly true with diesel engine oil due to the enormous amount of soot present in it. Figure 14-16 presents some of these liquids in a used state.

When observing the color of a dark or black liquid, it is important to place a sample of the liquid in a relatively narrow vessel and to hold it in front of a powerful lamp in order to try to determine the color or shade of the liquid. Hence, a black automatic transmission fluid will reveal its red tint, which would help in its identification.

B/ Miscibility Testing

If there is enough liquid, a quick miscibility test in water can be performed. It is fast and might provide some information regarding the nature of the liquid. Table 14-9 summarizes the different liquids with their miscibility in water and density.

Table 14-9	*Density and water miscibility of vehicle fluids*	
Fluid	**Miscibility in water**	**Density [g/ml]**
Engine oil	No	<1
Automatic transmission fluid	No	<1
Power steering fluid	No	<1
Brake fluid	Yes	~ or >1
Gear lubricants	No	<1
Hydraulic fluid	No	<1
Coolant	Yes	~1
Washer fluid	Yes	~1

Among the automotive fluids, only brake fluid, coolant, and washer fluids are miscible in water. Also, all other fluids are less dense than water and will therefore form a layer on top of the water.

C/ Gas Chromatography–Mass Spectrometry

A solution of the liquid should be prepared in a suitable solvent, such as carbon disulfide, diethyl ether, or dichloromethane. Depending on the results obtained in the previous examination, the concentration of the solution can be adapted. If the liquid is suspected to be brake fluid or coolant—liquids containing very few components—a one-percent solution is a good starting point. If the liquid is suspected to be engine oil, automatic transmission fluid, power steering fluid, or hydraulic fluid—liquids containing numerous components—a higher concentration might be required, up to a few percent. For liquids suspected to be washer fluid, the solution should be prepared in a heavier solvent such as tetrachloroethylene (PCE), so it elutes later and does not interfere with the very light components, or the liquid may be injected directly into the instrument via wet needle.

The column used on the GC–MS can be the same as that used for ignitable liquids, however, a different temperature program should be used when dealing with heavy samples, such as automatic transmission fluid, power steering fluid, or engine oil. This program should have a higher end temperature, up to 300°C or more, and should stay at that temperature for a much longer period of time (at least 15 minutes). This will allow for heavy components to elute from the column. It is not recommended to analyze very heavy components, such as some hydraulic fluids and gear lubricants using these parameters. For such components, a special high temperature column should be used [45]. Fortunately, these are not submitted very often to the laboratory.

Figure 14-17 presents the TIC of an engine oil. It is possible to observe a quasi-Gaussian distribution pattern starting around C_{20} and ending after C_{40}. The chromatogram does not present any predominant pattern of n-alkanes or other components. It is big mass of continuous peaks.

Figure 14-18 shows the TIC of an automatic transmission fluid. Although a Gaussian distribution pattern is also present, this pattern differs tremendously from the engine oil pattern. First, the range is from C_{15} to about C_{28}. Second, it is possible to distinguish the presence of a dominant n-alkane pattern ranging from about C_{15} to C_{20}. Finally, pristane and phytane are also present. If extracted ions are used, it is possible to see the pattern of cyclo-alkanes ranging from undecylcyclohexane to tetradecylcyclohexane. This is shown in Figure 14-19. It should be noted however that the chemical composition of these fluids can vary greatly. Specifications for engine oils are generally performance-based, meaning that various blends can be used in order to achieve the desired properties. In addition, composition can be

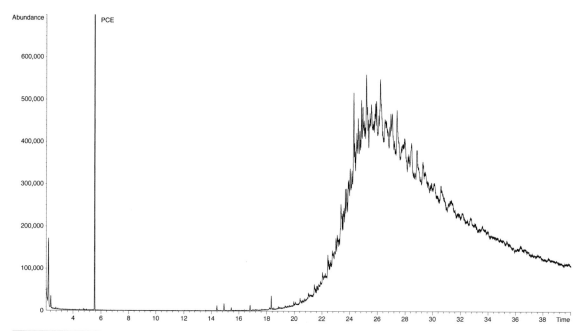

FIGURE 14-17 *Chromatogram of an engine oil. PCE = internal standard.*

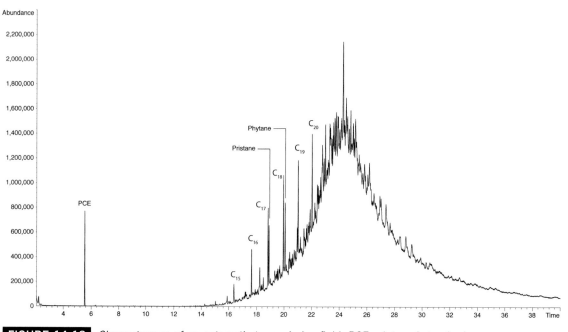

FIGURE 14-18 *Chromatogram of an automatic transmission fluid. PCE = internal standard.*

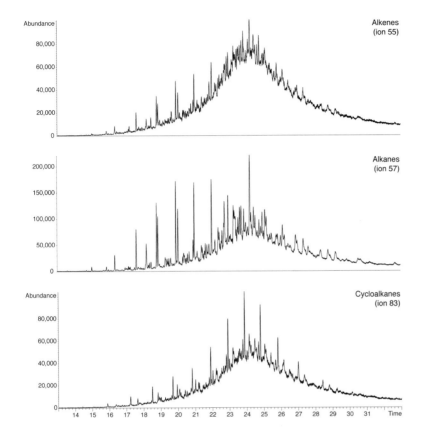

FIGURE 14-19

Extracted ions 55, 57, and 83 for the chromatogram of automatic transmission fluid presented in Figure 14-18. Note the spiking cycloalkanes in the 83 profile between the n-alkanes.

greatly affected by the source of the crude oil. A paraffinic crude oil will result in an oil with a stronger n-alkane component.

Figure 14-20 is the TIC of a power-steering fluid. In this case, this pattern slightly differs from the automatic transmission fluid shown in Figure 14-18 because the presence of n-alkanes is not as dominant. Not all automatic transmission fluids look exactly like Figure 14-18, and not all power steering fluids look exactly like Figure 14-20. Automatic transmission fluids and power steering fluids are usually in the same range in terms of carbon numbers, although some power steering fluids, such as the one shown in Figure 14-20, exhibit a higher range, close to that of engine oil. Some other power steering fluids have shown dominant pristane and phytane peaks, an odd and rare occurrence. In general, automatic transmission fluids and power steering fluids are not distinguishable by GC–MS because they are from the same approximate cut and composition.

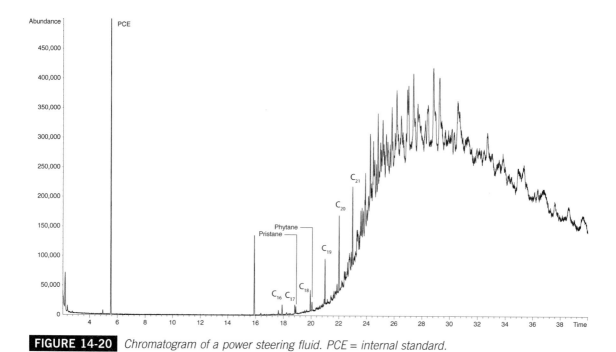

FIGURE 14-20 *Chromatogram of a power steering fluid. PCE = internal standard.*

Figure 14-21 presents the TIC of a DOT 3+4 brake fluid. All brake fluids, except for DOT 5, are composed of a mixture of different glycols. They usually have a range of five to nine different glycols. The pattern is, therefore, very clear and distinct. The peaks are identified on the chromatogram and are all glycols.

Figure 14-22 shows the TIC of a coolant. Coolants are also composed of glycols, mostly ethylene glycol. They usually have a very simple chromatogram of one to two peaks. They are easily distinguished from brake fluid by its fewer components and their lighter nature. There has been an increase in the number of propylene glycol-based coolants, as it is considerably less toxic than ethylene glycol.

Washer fluids are composed of, besides water, methanol or ethanol. Some washer fluids have been encountered that contain ethylene glycol.

14.3.4 Identification Criteria

Table 14-10 summarizes the criteria used to identify vehicle fluids. These criteria are not exclusive and variations in the compositions of the different vehicle fluids may very well occur. It is important to consider Table 14-10 as a general guideline that fits most fluids encountered.

It is also important to remember that it is possible to have a mixture of more than one fluid. It also has been shown that, although brake fluid is

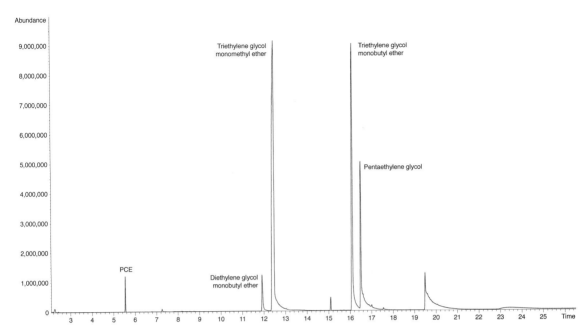

FIGURE 14-21 *Chromatogram of a DOT 3+4 brake fluid. Note the tailing due to the presence of oxygenated functional groups on a nonpolar phase chromatographic column. PCE = internal standard.*

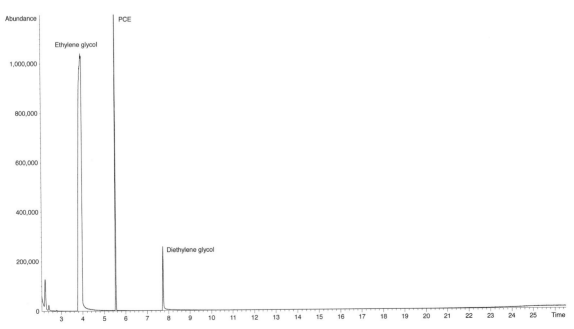

FIGURE 14-22 *Chromatogram of a coolant. PCE = internal standard.*

Table 14-10	Identification criteria for the different vehicle fluids	
Fluid	**Criteria**
Engine oil	Aliphatic compounds ranging from approximately C_{20} to C_{40} without any particular class of compounds dominating the chromatogram
Automatic transmission fluid	Aliphatic compounds ranging from approximately C_{15} to C_{30} with possible predominance of n-alkanes, pristane, phytane, and cycloalkanes
Power steering fluid	Aliphatic compounds ranging from approximately C_{15} to C_{30} with possible predominance of n-alkanes, pristane, phytane, and cycloalkanes
Brake fluid	Glycols, usually between 5 and 10
Coolant	Glycols, usually 1 to 2, confined to ethylene glycol, diethylene glycol, propylene glycol, or dipropylene glycol
Washer fluid	Methanol, ethanol, or less often, ethylene glycol

not miscible with power steering or automatic transmission fluid, a small amount can get dissolved in such fluid and appear in the chromatogram [38].

14.4 FLARE (FUSEE) RESIDUES

14.4.1 Description

Road flares, also called highway flares or railway fusees, were invented at the beginning of the nineteenth century and were designed originally as signals for the railroad industry. They were developed over the years and they are now frequently used on the roads to warn drivers of accidents and road hazards, and as pyrotechnic devices. They are readily available on the market in the United States, and are very accessible. In 1984, there were five manufacturers of road flares in the United States [46].

Road flares consist of a tube, usually made of cardboard, sealed at one end and with a match head on the other one, as illustrated in Figure 14-23. The seal might be made of a wooden plug, waxed paper plug, or gunwad plug. The match head normally is protected with a cap. The cap typically bears the scratching surface on its outer part. When struck with a scratched surface, the match head ignites readily and acts as a primer to ignite the contents of the tube. The flare also has a system to hold it straight up or with a certain inclination. This system could be a metal nail coming out of the bottom plug, two wire legs, a metal stand, or even a cardboard stand. Different types of flares are shown in Figure 14-24. Figure 14-25 shows the typical procedure used to ignite a flare.

Flares are commonly 12 inches long or more. They are characterized by the color of the flame (mostly red) and by the duration of the flame (from

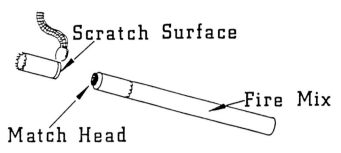

FIGURE 14-23 *Schematic of a typical road flare.* Source: *Dean WL (1984) Examination of fire debris for flare (fusee) residues by energy dispersive x-ray spectrometry*, Arson Analysis Newsletter, **8(2)**, pp 23–46. Reprinted with permission from SEA Limited, Columbus, Ohio, USA.

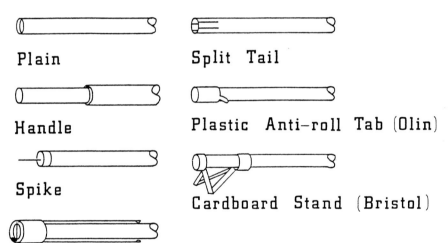

FIGURE 14-24

Different road flares available on the market. Source: *Dean WL (1984) Examination of fire debris for flare (fusee) residues by energy dispersive x-ray spectrometry*, Arson Analysis Newsletter, **8(2)**, pp 23–46. Reprinted with permission from SEA Limited, Columbus, Ohio, USA.

5 to 30 minutes or more). While road flares usually are designed to produce a red flame, other colors, such as yellow or green, are also available.

Arsonists also use road flares to ignite fires [47]. Their primary use is to delay ignition of nearby combustibles, thus allowing for the arsonist to establish an alibi. Flares have been reported to burn at extremely high temperatures, up to 1,450°C (2,650°F) [48]. They are a good, steady source of ignition because they are pyrotechnic devices that contain both the combustible and the oxidant. Also, the flame duration designated by the manufacturer for each flare is fairly reliable. Flare residues might be encountered at a fire scene. There have been very few publications dealing with the recovery of flare residues from fire scene and their subsequent analyses. Dean pre-

FIGURE 14-25

Typical procedure used to ignite a flare. Source: *Dean WL (1984) Examination of fire debris for flare (fusee) residues by energy dispersive x-ray spectrometry,* Arson Analysis Newsletter, *8(2), pp 23–46. Reprinted with permission from SEA Limited, Columbus, Ohio, USA.*

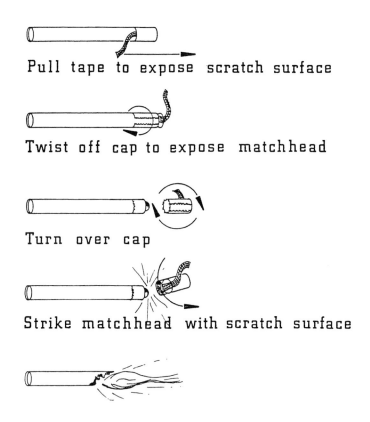

Pull tape to expose scratch surface

Twist off cap to expose matchhead

Turn over cap

Strike matchhead with scratch surface

sented the most comprehensive study on the characterization of flare residues by energy dispersive x-ray spectrometry [46].

14.4.2 Examination of Road Flare Residues

Flare residues are fundamentally different than ignitable liquid residues. They are solid and inorganic. Because they are ashes of a flare, they can be characterized by their elemental composition. The different parts of a flare, as shown in Figure 14-23, are constituted of different chemicals. The mixture contained in the tube contains combustibles and oxidizers in order to sustain the combustion. Metals are present, too, in order to produce the color of the flame. Strontium is used for red flames; barium for green; copper for blue; sodium for yellow; and magnesium for white ones [49]. Table 14-11 shows the range of compositions reported by Dean in his study [46].

In addition to these components, several other chemicals can be found, such as starch, stearic acid, antimony, sawdust, and wax. Even though some recipes had called for the powder mix to be wet with kerosene prior to sealing the tube, this does not seem to be done any longer [50]. The match head may also contain some strontium nitrate, potassium perchlorate, potassium chlorate, and barium chlorate. The scratching surface usually is composed

Table 14-11	Composition of different road flares		
Constituent	Range of concentration in mixture [%]		
	Red flares	Yellow flares	Green flares
Strontium nitrate	59–76	28–63	—
Potassium perchlorate	0–10	6–11	10
Potassium chlorate	0–12	—	—
Potassium nitrate	0–15	—	—
Sulfur	6–19	9–10	10
Barium nitrate	—	0–44	70
Sodium oxalate	—	0–13	—

of red phosphorous mixed with a material with good friction properties, such as glass, quartz, sand, or emery.

It is not easy to recognize the presence of a burned flare among fire debris. They have been reported to leave "creamy white residue that looked like stale cake frosting and had a consistency similar to plaster of Paris (but heavier)" [48]. Sometimes, it is possible to distinguish the general shape and to see a contrast with the rest of the debris. However, this is in a situation where the debris has not been moved around and did not sustain any overhaul. If the debris is moved around, the pattern left by flare residues might be lost.

As the flare burns, the pyrotechnic reaction projects small particles over a reasonably large area compared to the flare itself. Therefore, it is possible to retrieve metal residues from the flare, even several inches away from the flare. Also, the flare burns with the production of white spherical particles.

There are elements other than the chemical composition that must be sought when the presence of a flare is suspected. The cap may be disposed of remotely from the flare itself, or may be found near the flare. It is the primary role of the fire investigator to look for the cap at the scene. Also, it is important for the fire debris analyst to make sure to sift through the debris and look for the possible presence of a cap in the sample. The wad or seal is also an element that can survive a fire. The wooden plug, the metal nail, wire legs, or base can also be in the debris. It is important to keep these elements in mind when examining the debris. Additionally, these elements can all help in the identification of the flare brand. Also, upon inspection of the fire debris, the criminalist should observe the sample and determine if there are any suspicious particles. If so, an elemental analysis of these particles can reveal the presence of metals typical of flare residues. The use of a scanning-electron microscope coupled with an energy dispersive x-ray analyzer (SEM-EDX) provides a very good means of analyzing these particles. Even when flare residues are mixed with debris, the presence of strontium is quickly established with the SEM-EDX. Dean demonstrated that strontium was found in significant quantity in most flare residues, except for those of green flares [46].

14.4.3 Summary

If flare residues are suspected to be present, it is important to examine the debris in search of burned and unburned flare components:

- White spherical particles and slurry masses
- End cap (commonly plastic)
- Seal (wood, paper, wax, metal)
- Stand (wire legs, nail)

Retrieval of the different parts of a flare could possibly lead to the identification of the flare brand. If flare residues are suspected, it is important to perform an elemental analysis of these particles. The presence of strontium is a possible indication of the presence of flare residues. The combined presence of strontium, barium, chlorine, potassium, and sulfur is a very strong indication.

14.5 HOMEMADE CHEMICAL BOMBS (HCBS)

14.5.1 Principle

Homemade chemical bombs (HCBs), also called bottle or acid/caustic bombs, have been used in terrorist activities [51]. They do not commonly lead to a fire, but may generate a great deal of destruction and injuries [52]. There are several different variations of HCBs, however they all mostly produce an increase in pressure inside a closed container. As the pressure increases, the vessel eventually reaches its breaking point and a mechanical explosion ensues. The pressure increase is created by the evolution of a gas due to a chemical reaction. Acid bombs are composed of an acid and a metal, which react together. Caustic bombs are composed of a base and a metal, which react together. The reaction is always exothermic and evolves hydrogen. Following are three examples of chemical equations showing acid-metal reactions as well as base-metal reaction with their enthalpies:

$$Mg + 2HCl \rightarrow MgCl_2 + H_2 \qquad -465\,kJ/mol$$
$$2Al + 6HCl \rightarrow 2AlCl_3 + 3H_2 \qquad -405\,kJ/mol$$
$$2Al + 2NaOH + 6H_2O \rightarrow 2NaAl(OH)_4 + 3H_2$$

The heat released by such reactions is important. The release of hydrogen creates a volume of gas that, when expanded by the generated heat, leads to the overpressurization of the container and its explosion. Of course, hydrogen is also a flammable gas, which may be ignited and may create a flame front.

Most often, an acid bomb is composed of hydrochloric acid (HCl) and aluminum (Al). These two chemicals react very well together and are, in many countries, readily available on the shelf of any common store. Muriatic acid (concentrated [31.5%] hydrochloric acid) can be purchased from any home improvement store in the United States. A regular recipe for an acid bomb consists of using a plastic milk jug (or any soft drink bottle) half full with muriatic acid. Aluminum foil is thrown in the container, which is closed and thrown far away as fast as possible. The time required for these bombs to explode can vary greatly, and is mostly dependent upon the surface area of the reactants. There also have been reports of more complex acid bombs that include a timer used to place the metal in contact with the acid at a given time.

McDonald and Shaw described a new trend of bottle bombs involving pool and spa chlorinated or brominated chemicals, toilet tank sanitizers, or other products designed to slowly release chlorine and/or bromine when placed in contact with water [53]. Figure 14-26 shows some of these products.

The components found in these products usually are composed of cyanuric acid derivatives (trichloroisocyanurate acid, dichloroisocyanurate acid) or hydanthoin derivatives. They revealed that, when combined with solvents other than the water they are designed for, such as alcohols, ammonia, and hydrogen peroxide, there is a very violent release of gas [53]. Figure 14-27 shows the result of the explosion of an HCB made with trichloroisocyanuric acid mixed with isopropyl alcohol in a bottle. The gases released are chlorine or bromine in most instances.

Another variant of the bottle bomb consists of placing dry ice in a plastic bottle [54]. As the dry ice warms up, it sublimates into carbon dioxide gas

FIGURE 14-26a

Typical household products used in the manufacturing of HCBs. Hydrogen peroxide, ammonia, and alcohol products. (For a full color version of this figure, please see the insert.)

FIGURE 14-26b

Toilet bowl cleaner containing chlorinated and brominated hydanthoins. (For a full color version of this figure, please see the insert.)

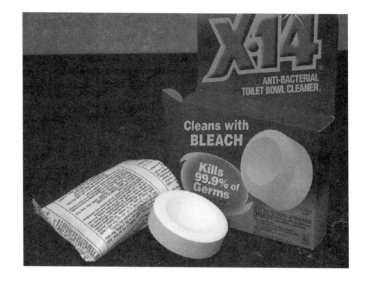

FIGURE 14-26c

Swimming pool products containing di or trichloroisocyanuric acids. Photographs courtesy of Kristin McDonald, Criminalist III, Chemistry Unit, New York City Police Department Crime Laboratory, Jamaica, New York, USA. (For a full color version of this figure, please see the insert.)

and increases the pressure inside the bottle. Eventually, the bottle explodes under the pressure, which might create a significant mechanical explosion.

14.5.2 Laboratory Examinations

The analysis of debris to determine if an acid bomb was used is fairly common due to juvenile activities. Thus, when such a request arrives, it is important that the fire debris analyst be aware of what an HCB is and how to perform the examination to determine its presence among the debris. It is important to remember that, in most instances, the debris forwarded is not the usual burned fire debris seen for ILR analysis. A typical item of evi-

FIGURE 14-27a
The result of an explosion of a mixture of trichloroisocyanuric acid and isopropyl alcohol in a laboratory hood. (For a full color version of this figure, please see the insert.)

FIGURE 14-27b *View of the plastic bottle after explosion. Note the presence of unreacted material at the bottom of the bottle. Photographs courtesy of Kristin McDonald, Criminalist III, Chemistry Unit, New York City Police Department Crime Laboratory, Jamaica, New York, USA. (For a full color version of this figure, please see the insert.)*

dence consists of a burst plastic bottle with residues, possibly liquid residues, in and around it. Figure 14-28 is an example of a plastic bottle that was used as a chemical bomb. Figure 14-29 shows the remaining particles still present inside the bottles. It should be noted that this type of evidence should not be packaged directly into metal cans, but rather into plastic containers.

Depending on the exact type of HCB used, different analyses can be performed. For an acid bomb, the analytical steps are pretty simple. The goal is to detect the presence of residual aluminum (or other metals, such as magnesium) and hydrochloric acid. The following procedure is used at the Miami-Dade Crime Laboratory Bureau (Miami, Florida, USA)[6]:

[6] The authors would like to thank Colleen Carbine, Criminalist I, Miami-Dade Police Department Crime Laboratory Bureau, Miami, Florida, USA for sharing this information.

An example of two bottles that were taped together and used as chemical bomb. Photograph courtesy of Kristin McDonald, Criminalist III, Chemistry Unit, New York City Police Department Crime Laboratory, Jamaica, New York, USA. (For a full color version of this figure, please see the insert.)

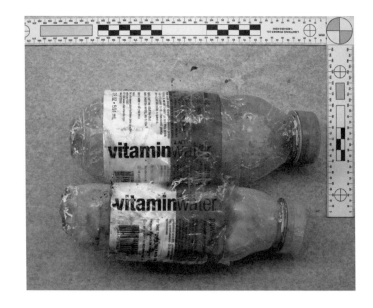

View of the inside of the bottle, where residues are still present and useful for analysis. Photograph courtesy of Kristin McDonald, Criminalist III, Chemistry Unit, New York City Police Department Crime Laboratory, Jamaica, New York, USA. (For a full color version of this figure, please see the insert.)

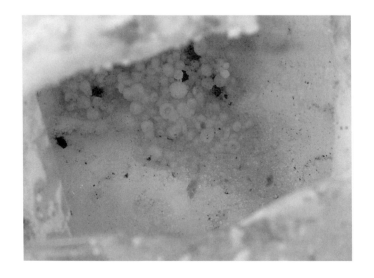

I. Determine the pH if the sample is liquid. The pH should be acidic because, in most instances, all the acid has not reacted.

II. Use the silver nitrate test to test for the presence of chlorine followed by a microcrystalline test.

III. Use a microcrystalline test (with cesium sulphate) to test for the presence of aluminum.

IV. Perform elemental analysis of dried residues by SEM-EDX.

When dealing with the new styles of HCB involving the use of chlorinated and/or brominated compounds, McDonald and Shaw recommend the use of FTIR/ATR in combination with XRD/XRF to identify the residues from such bombs [53].

14.6 FLASH POINT

14.6.1 Introduction

The definition of flash point was presented in Chapter 4. It was also described as an important property of an ignitable liquid because it is the lowest temperature at which a liquid can create a fire hazard when in contact with a proper source of ignition. In many fire investigations, the determination of the flash point of a liquid potentially involved in the fire is an important step. This can be performed on liquids found at the scene in order to evaluate them, or on comparison liquids in order to develop or verify a working hypothesis.

With one exception, all flash point apparatuses works on the same principle. The liquid is placed in a cup, which is heated at a certain rate. A competent source of ignition (typically flame or electrical wire) is brought into the vapor cloud above the liquid at different time intervals. When a flash (brief flame) occurs, it means that the liquid has given off sufficient vapors to be ignited, and, therefore, has reached its flash point.

There are two main classes of techniques used to determine flash points of liquids: closed cup and open cup. The terminology used for these two types of apparatuses is pretty explicit. The open cup apparatus means that the cup is open to the air and the vapors can escape in the surrounding environment, away from the flash point apparatus. The closed cup apparatus implies that the cup into which the liquid is placed is closed until the ignition source is introduced, and, thus, no vapor can escape. Logically, the closed cup apparatus provides lower flash point values than the open cup apparatus. This is because vapors cannot escape; so the lower flammability limit is reached at a lower temperature than if they could escape. For this reason, closed cup apparatuses provide safer values and are usually the preferred method by which flash points are determined. This is why the Occupational Safety and Health Administration (USA) requires that the flash point of flammable and combustible liquids be measured either by a Tag or Pensky-Martens closed cup apparatus [55]. Regardless of which type is used, the test method should be provided along with the measured flash point value.

14.6.2 General Principles

Each technique presents a certain degree of variation, however there are some general principles that are equivalent for all techniques that need to be understood by the criminalist prior to performing flash point testing.

A/ Elements of a Flash Point Tester

Each flash point tester has some common elements. They all have a cup in which the liquid is placed. They also have a heater used to raise the temperature of the cup. A thermometer is present in the liquid to be tested in order to measure its exact temperature at the time of the test. An ignition source, usually a very small flame or an electrical wire that is heated, is present and can be moved into the vapor phase above the liquid at a given time. Finally, closed cup flash point testers have a lid atop the cup where the specimen is located. This lid is movable in order to create an opening for the ignition source to penetrate and enter in contact with the vapor phase.

B/ Ignition Source

As previously stated, each flash point tester has an ignition source, used to ignite the vapor phase above the liquid. Most testers use either a heated electrical wire or a small flame. For those techniques that require the use of a small flame, the size of the flame varies from 2 to 5 mm in diameter depending on the technique, and typically burns butane or propane gas.

C/ Barometric Pressure Correction

Flash point data is always provided for a nominal pressure of 101,325 Pa. Unless the ambient laboratory pressure is also 101,325 Pa, flash points need to be corrected to reflect the difference in barometric pressure. With modern automatic apparatuses, this function is often automatically incorporated. The apparatus has a built-in pressure sensor and a computer performs the calculations. With apparatuses that do not include this function, the flash point value needs to be corrected using the following formula:

$$FP = T + 0.25 \cdot (101,325 - P)$$

where

FP = Corrected flash point for standard pressure in [°C]
T = Measured flash point in [°C]
P = Ambient pressure in [Pa]

D/ Manual, Semi-Automatic, and Automatic Testers

As previously stated, there are automatic, semi-automatic, and manual apparatuses. The degree of automation may vary from one manufacturer to another and from one technique to another. In general, automatic apparatuses perform all the tasks except placing the liquid in the cup. Nevertheless, there are even some manufacturers that produce autosamplers, which provide the user with a carousel carrying a dozen or more samples. The automatic apparatus controls the temperature of the sample, the ignition process, the detection of the flash, and the barometric pressure correction.

A semi-automatic apparatus typically controls the temperature of the specimen, the ignition process, and the barometric pressure correction. By contrast, the flash point detection is left for the user to observe. A manual apparatus is usually very simple and the user has to control and perform all operations.

14.6.3 Precautions

Flash point testing is a measurement that can be taken very accurately and there are several parameters that can influence its outcome. Depending on the technique or on the sample, different precautions need to be taken. However, there are some basic precautions that should be respected in any instance, and a few of them are presented here. It is recommended that the analyst consult and follow all appropriate standards and instructions found in the apparatus' user manual and the appropriate (ASTM) standard method when performing flash point testing.

A/ Loss of Volatiles

The most volatile compounds of a mixture usually have the greatest effect on the value of the flash point. It is important not to lose these volatiles prior to the testing, so the most accurate flash point value can be obtained. The liquid should never be placed in a hot cup, or at a temperature too close to its flash point. This would create a serious risk or premature evaporation of the liquid and a significant increase in its final flash point. Standards recommend placing liquids in a cup at a very low temperature, or at a temperature 15 to 60°C below their expected flash point, depending on the technique used. Depending on which testing needs to be carried out on the liquid, flash point should be performed first, so these volatile components are not lost during other testing.

B/ Repeat Tests on Specimen

The same specimen should never be used twice to perform flash point testing. As the nature of the testing is to heat the sample at or above its flash point, a loss of volatile occurs, thus rendering a second test inaccurate. A fresh specimen must always be used when performing such testing. This may require a significant increase in the amount of sample needed.

C/ Draft-Free Environment

Always perform the test in a draft-free environment. Movement of air around the flash point tester could create undesired motion of the vapor phase and variations in the flash point value. Some apparatuses are designed to protect the cup from small drafts, and some require the use of shields. It is very important to follow the manufacturers' and standards' requirements regarding this.

14.6.4 Pensky-Martens Closed Cup (PMCC)

This test is designed for the analysis of fuel oils, lubricating oils, and other homogeneous liquids, as well as nonhomogeneous materials, such as liquids with solids in suspension and liquids that tend to form a surface film under the test conditions with viscosities above 5.5 cSt at 40°C. This test is dynamic in the sense that the temperature rises at a fast rate and the liquid is constantly stirred, except for the time during which the ignition is applied. Stirring is necessary due to the viscosity of the liquid. The quantity necessary for the test is 75 ml. Some manufacturers have developed special cups that can perform the test with as little as 2 ml; however, these cups are not allowed per the different standard methods. This method allows for the testing of flash point ranging from about 15 to 370°C.

The liquid is placed in the cup and the specimen is brought to a temperature of 15°C or at least 17°C below the temperature of the expected flash point. Heat is then applied in order to raise the temperature of the specimen at a rate of 5 to 6°C per minute. The stirrer revs at 90 to 120 rpm, moving the liquid in a downward motion. The ignition source is then applied at every degree of increase. The stirrer is turned off prior to applying the ignition source and the ignition source is lowered into the vapor phase in 0.5 s and left in the headspace for 1 s. If ignition does not occur, the test is continued. If the flash point is above 110°C, the ignition source is brought into the vapor phase at every two degrees of increase.

There is also an alternate procedure for liquids with solids in suspension or liquids that tend to form a surface film during testing. The procedure is the same, with the exception that the stirrer is set at 250 rpm, and the temperature rises at a slower rate of 1 to 1.5°C per minute. Note that most manufacturers now offer automated or semi-automated Pensky-Martens closed cup testers.

14.6.5 Tag Closed Cup (TCC)

The Tagliabue closed cup test is designed for the analysis of liquids with a viscosity below 5.5 cSt at 40°C or below 9.5 cSt at 25°C, and with a flash point below 93°C. Because of the reduced viscosity, this test does not involve the stirring of the liquid like the Pensky-Martens does. In addition, this test increases the temperature at a much slower rate than the Pensky-Martens. The quantity of liquid required is about 50 ml. Some manufacturers have developed smaller cups that can perform the test with as little as 2 ml, however this option is not allowed per ASTM and IP standards. TCC can measure flash points in the range of 0 to approximately 100°C. Particular circumstances allow the user to go down to −30°C, however the results are not as reliable.

The heat is brought to the cup through an electrically heated water bath, rather than a direct flame or heater as with the Pensky-Martens tester. This allows for a more stable temperature of the specimen in the cup. Indeed, the temperature variation is much slower. The bath is composed of a mixture of water and ethylene glycol at a 1:1 ratio. If the flash point tester is used between 13 and 60°C, the water bath can be only 10% water. The specimen is placed in the cup and the cup is placed in the apparatus. The initial temperature should be 27°C or at least 10°C below the expected flash point. If the flash point is below 60°C, the sample is heated at approximately 1°C per minute. If the flash point is above 60°C, the sample is heated at a rate of approximately 3°C per minute. When the sample is about 5°C below its expected flash point, the ignition source is brought into the vapor phase for every half-degree of increase (or every degree of increase for a flash point above 60°C). The time used to insert the ignition source into the vapor phase and remove it should not exceed one second. The test is pursued until the liquid flashes. Note that most manufacturers now market automatic Tag closed cup testers.

14.6.6 Tag Open Cup (TOC)

The Tag open cup (TOC) method is designed for the analysis of liquids with flash points between −18 and 165°C. It is also designed to measure fire points up to 165°C. Test methods also have been published using TOC to measure flash points of cutback asphalts at temperatures below 93°C. The principle of operation is very similar to the TCC, except that the cup is left open.

14.6.7 Cleveland Open Cup (COC)

This test is designed for the analysis of all viscous liquids and petroleum products (except fuel oils) that have a flash point above 79°C. This test does not involve the stirring of the liquid. The liquid is heated either directly by a burner or by an electrical heater. The quantity needed is about 70 ml.

The specimen is placed in the cup and the cup is placed in the apparatus. Very viscous samples can be heated prior to placement in the cup, however they should never be heated more than 56°C below their flash point. The rate of temperature increase on the sample is fixed at 14 to 17°C per minute until the sample reaches approximately 56°C below its expected flash point. At that moment, the rate is lowered to reach 5 to 6°C per minute for at least the last 28°C below its flash point. Starting 28°C below the flash point, the flame is passed through the vapor phase across the testing cup in a linear fashion. This is repeated for every two degrees of increase. The flame is passed in the opposite direction every other time. The time necessary to pass the flame across the specimen should not exceed one second. This tester also is used to measure the fire point of a substance. In order to achieve this, the test is continued past the flash point until the combustion of the specimen lasts for a minimum of five seconds.

14.6.8 Rapid Equilibrium Small Scale Closed Cup (Setaflash)

This test is designed to determine the flash point of small samples or to determine whether a sample will flash or not at a given temperature and in a very short time. The temperature range over which the apparatus operates is from approximately −30 to 300°C. This method requires a very small sample of a minimum 2 ml or 4 ml if the flash point is above 100°C.

The apparatus is used for two different functions. The first one is called the flash/no flash technique. It consists of setting the apparatus at a given temperature at which the user would like to know whether the specimen ignites or not. Once the apparatus has reached this temperature, the specimen is injected into the cup and the specimen's temperature is equilibrated for two minutes. The lid is open, the flame is placed in the vapor phase, moved out, and the lid is closed. The total time for this operation does not exceed 2.5 seconds. If flash occurred during this operation, then the sample's flash point is below this temperature; otherwise, it is above.

The second use of this apparatus is to determine the exact flash point of a specimen. This practice requires much more than 2 ml of sample because the sample's cup is emptied, cleaned, and refilled with new liquid between each test. This requires about 50 ml of liquid. The sample is placed in the preheated cup as performed earlier for the flash/no flash test. If the flash does not occur, the operation is repeated with a temperature 5°C above the original one. If the flash occurs, the test is repeated with a temperature 5°C below the original one. This operation is repeated until a range of 5°C is determined. Then, the operation is repeated using a 1°C interval. Finally, when a 1°C range is determined, a more accurate flash point can be determined using a 0.5°C variation.

Note that there is no automatic apparatus for this method. Some apparatuses have semi-automatic functions, such as an integrated timer, or a button activating the opening/closure of the lid and motion of the flame.

14.6.9 Continuously Closed Cup (CCC or CCCFP)

The continuously closed cup flash point technique is used to measure the flash point of fuel oils, lubricant oils, solvents, and other liquids. This technique relies on a completely different approach than the ones previously described. It depends on the principle that when a liquid flashes, an instantaneous increase of pressure occurs above the liquid as a result of the combustion. Instead of observing a flame, the apparatus measures that pressure increase, which is deemed to be at least 20,000 Pa. CCC can measure flash point over the range of −25 to 400°C. Flash point values below 10 and above 250°C suffer from poorer precision. This technique has the significant advantage of using an extremely small quantity of sample: One ml is enough to perform the testing. The method employs a stirring magnet, rotating at

250 to 270 rpm inside the cup. The ignition is also different from other flash point testers: This technique uses an electrical arc to induce ignition. Although the mechanism for measuring the flash point is different, extensive validation studies were conducted in order to establish a correlation between this test method and other accepted methods.

The liquid is placed inside the cup, which is positioned inside the apparatus. The cup is then raised to the lid, where it makes a closed, but not sealed, volume of 4 ml. The lid and cup are made of metal with good heat conduction properties. The lid is then heated, which transmits the heat to the cup. The test is usually started at about 15°C below the expected flash point. The temperature is raised at different rates, up to 5.5°C per minute. The arc is applied at intervals of 1°C. In general, the increase of pressure takes place within 100 ms of the arc. When the pressure increase reaches 20,000 Pa or above, the specimen has reached its flash point. After each arc, 1.5 ml of air is injected in the cup. The pressure in the cup remains at ambient pressure, except during injection of the air, and at the flash point. This technique was developed very recently and is very promising for forensic applications because it requires extremely small samples. It is also advantageous because the testing is performed in a couple of minutes. Finally, the system also allows for easy and automatic sample loading.

14.6.10 Other Techniques

There are other techniques available on the market, such as the Pensky-Martens open cup and the Abel closed cup. These techniques are not used very often and, therefore, will not be discussed in this chapter.

14.6.11 Standards Available

Each technique has several standards that have been developed. IP methods are developed by the Energy Institute in United Kingdom and are found in the Standard Methods for Analysis of Petroleum and Related Products, and British Standard 2000 Parts (2005 edition) found at http://www.energyinstpubs.org.uk. ISO methods are developed by the International Organization for Standardization and are found in the International Classification for Standards (ICS), volume 75.080 Petroleum and related technologies – Petroleum products in general, found at http://www.iso.org. ASTM methods are developed by ASTM International and are found in the Annual Book of Standards, volume 05.01 Petroleum Products and Lubricants (I) and volume 06.01 Paint – Tests for Chemical, Physical, and Optical Properties; Appearance, found at http://www.astm.org. EN methods are developed by the European Committee for Standardization (CEN) in the Catalogue of European Standards, volume 75.080 Petroleum products in general, found at http://www.cenorm.be. A listing of some pertinent standards follows.

Pensky-Martens Closed Cup

- ASTM D 93 standard test methods for flash-point by Pensky-Martens closed cup tester
- ISO 2719:2002 determination of flash point—Pensky-Martens closed cup method
- EN 2719:2002 determination of flash point—Pensky-Martens closed cup method

Pensky-Martens Open Cup

- IP 35 determination of open flash and fire point—Pensky Martens method

Tag Closed Cup

- ASTM D 56 standard test method for flash point by Tag closed tester
- IP 304 flash point closed cup equilibrium (obsolete, last printed in 2002)

Tag Open Cup

- ASTM D 1310 standard test method for flash point and fire point of liquids by Tag open-cup apparatus
- ASTM D 3143 standard test method for flash point of cutback asphalt with Tag open-cup apparatus

Cleveland Open Cup

- ASTM D 92 standard test method for flash and fire points by Cleveland open cup (joint with IP 36)
- IP 36 determination of flash and fire points—Cleveland open cup method
- ISO 2592:2000 determination of flash and fire points—Cleveland open cup method
- EN 2592:2001 determination of flash and fire points—Cleveland open cup method

Small Scale Rapid Equilibrium (Setaflash) Closed Cup

- ASTM D 3278 standard test methods for flash point of liquids by small scale closed-cup apparatus
- ASTM D 3828 standard test methods for flash point by small scale closed tester
- IP 523 determination of flash point—rapid equilibrium closed cup method
- IP 524 determination of flash/no flash—rapid equilibrium closed cup method

- ISO 3679:2004 determination of flash point—rapid equilibrium closed cup method
- ISO 3680:2004 determination of flash/no flash—rapid equilibrium closed cup method
- EN 456 determination of flash point—rapid equilibrium method

Continuous Closed Cup

- ASTM D 6450 standard test method for flash point by continuously closed cup (CCCFP) Tester

Abel Closed Cup

- IP 170 determination of flash point—Abel closed cup method
- IP 304 flash point closed cup equilibrium (obsolete, last printed in 2002)
- ISO 13736:1997 determination of flash point—Abel closed cup method
- EN 13736:1997 determination of flash point—Abel closed cup method
- ISO 1516:2002 determination of flash/no flash—closed cup equilibrium method
- ISO 1523:2002 determination of flash point—closed cup equilibrium method

REFERENCES

1. Stauffer E (2005) A review of the analysis of vegetable oil residues from fire debris samples: Spontaneous ignition, vegetable oils, and the forensic approach, *Journal of Forensic Sciences*, **50**(5), pp 1091–100.
2. Stauffer E (2006) A review of the analysis of vegetable oil residues from fire debris samples: Analytical scheme, interpretation of the results, and future needs, *Journal of Forensic Sciences*, **51**(5), pp 1016–32.
3. Vassiliades J (2000) Spontaneous combustion—The invisible danger, *The Journal*, April issue.
4. Dixon B (1992) Spontaneous combustion, *Le Journal de l'Association Canadienne des Enquêteurs Incendie*, March, pp 18–21.
5. Stauffer E (2004) Mastering the analysis of vegetable oil residues, *4th Annual TWGFEX symposium on fire and explosion debris analysis and scene investigation*, Orlando, FL.
6. Ettling BV and Adams MF (1971) Spontaneous combustion of linseed oil in sawdust, *Fire Technology*, **7**(3), pp 225–36.
7. Cunliffe F and Piazza PB (1980) *Criminalistics and scientific investigation*, Prentice-Hall, Englewood Cliffs, NJ.
8. National Fire Protection Association (2004) *NFPA 921 guide for fire and explosion investigations*, Quincy, MA.
9. McMurry J and Fay RC (1998) *Chemistry*, 2nd edition, Prentice Hall, Upper Saddle River, NJ.
10. Christie WW (2001) *Triacylglycerols—Structure, composition and analysis*, available from http://www.lipidlibrary.co.uk, last access performed on April 19, 2005.

11. Gunstone FD and Norris FA (1983) *Lipids in foods chemistry, biochemistry and technology*, Pergamon Press, Headington Hill Hall, Oxford, United Kingdom.
12. Christie WW (2002) *What is a lipid?—Definitions*, available from http://www.lipid.co.uk, last access performed on April 19, 2005.
13. Hess PS and O'Hare GA (1950) Oxidation of linseed oil—Temperature effects, *Industrial and Engineering Chemistry*, **42**(7), pp 1424–31.
14. Litwinienko G, Daniluk A, and Kasprzycka-Guttman T (2000) Study on autoxidation kinetics of fats by differential scanning calorimetry. 1. Saturated C12-C18 fatty acids and their esters, *Industrial & Engineering Chemistry Research*, **39**(1), pp 7–12.
15. Litwinienko G and Kasprzycka-Guttman T (2000) Study on autoxidation kinetics of fats by differential scanning calorimetry. 2. Unsaturated fatty acids and their esters, *Industrial & Engineering Chemistry Research*, **39**(1), pp 13–17.
16. Christie WW (1982) *Lipid analysis*, 2nd edition, Pergamon Press, Headington Hill Hall, Oxford, United Kingdom.
17. Abraham G and Hron RJ (1999) *Oilseeds and vegetable oils*. In: *Wiley Encyclopedia of Food Science and Technology*, editor FJ Francis, John Wiley & Sons, New York, NY, pp 1745–55.
18. Cote AE (2003) *Fire protection handbook*, 19th edition, National Fire Protection Association, Quincy, MA.
19. Gunstone FD and Herslöf BG (2004) *Lipid glossary 2*, The Oily Press, Bridgewater, England.
20. Hilditch TP and Williams PN (1964) *The chemical constitution of natural fats*, 4th edition, Chapman & Hall, London, United Kingdom.
21. Bowen JE (1983) Phenomenon of spontaneous ignition is still misunderstood by some, *Fire and Arson Investigator*, **34**(2), pp 23–4.
22. Fire Findings (1994) Spontaneous combustion not instantaneous, *Fire Findings*, **2**(2), pp 1–3.
23. Küchler B and Martin J-C (2003) Self-heating and spontaneous combustion—A discussion, FEX-FO-07, *3rd European Academy of Forensic Science meeting*, Istanbul, Turkey.
24. Coulombe R and Gélin K (2001) Spontaneous ignition of vegetable oils: Chemical composition, *13th Interpol International Forensic Science Symposium*, Lyon, France.
25. Riva G and Calzoni J (2004) Standardisation of vegetable oils, *International South Europe Symposium—Non-Food Crops: From Agriculture to Industry*, Bologna, Italy.
26. Tyman JHP and Gordon MH (1994) *Developments in the analysis of lipids*, The Royal Society of Chemistry, Cambridge, United Kingdom.
27. Nic Daéid N, Maguire C, and Walker A (2001) An investigation into the causes of laundry fires—Spontaneous combustion of residual fatty acids, *Z. Zagadnien Nauk Sadowych (Problems of Forensic Sciences)*, XLVI, pp 272–7.
28. Coulombe R (2002) Chemical analysis of vegetable oils following spontaneous ignition, *Journal of Forensic Sciences*, **47**(1), pp 195–201.
29. Ehara Y, Sakamoto K, and Marumo Y (2001) A method for forensic identification of vegetable oil stains—Rapid analysis of carboxylic acids with methyl esterification using purge-and-trap gas chromatography/mass spectrometry, *Journal of Forensic Sciences*, **46**(6), pp 1462–9.
30. Christie WW (1995) Are methyl esters of fatty acids the best choice for gas chromatographic analysis?, *Lipid Technology*, **7**, pp 64–6.
31. Christie WW (1990) Preparation of methyl esters—Part 2, *Lipid Technology*, **2**, pp 79–80.

32. American Oil Chemists' Society (1997) *Preparation of methyl esters of fatty acids. Sampling and analysis of commercial fats and oils*, AOCS official method Ce 2–66.

33. Christie WW (1990) Preparation of methyl esters—Part 1, *Lipid Technology*, **2**, pp 48–9.

34. American Society for Testing and Materials (1998) *ASTM D 2800-92 standard test method for preparation of methyl esters from oils for determination of fatty acid composition by gas-liquid chromatography*, Annual Book of ASTM Standards 06.03, West Conshohocken, PA.

35. Keto R (2003) Spontaneous combustion: A laboratory investigation, *30th Meeting of the Mid-Atlantic Association of Forensic Scientists*, Annapolis, MD.

36. Gunstone FD and Hilditch TP (1945) The union of gaseous oxygen with methyl oleate, linoleate, and linolenate, *Journal of the Chemical Society*, **105**, pp 836–41.

37. Lloyd JBF (1982) A note on the detection and determination of mineral oil contamination in brake fluids, *Journal of the Forensic Science Society*, **22**, pp 289–90.

38. Stauffer E and Lentini JJ (2003) Contamination of brake fluid by power steering fluid, *Journal of Forensic Sciences*, **48**(4), pp 798–803.

39. Stauffer E and Lentini JJ (2002) Forensic identification of vehicle fluids, *16th Meeting of the International Association of Forensic Sciences*, Montpellier, France.

40. Evans J and Hunt T (2004) *The oil analysis handbook*, Coxmoor, Oxford, United Kingdom.

41. Crouse WH and Anglin DL (1984) *The auto book*, 3rd edition, McGraw-Hill, New York, NY.

42. Exxon Mobil (2001) *Mobil ATF type F: Ford type automatic transmission fluid*, Exxon Mobil Corporation, Irving, TX.

43. Pennzoil (2001) *Type F automatic transmission fluid*, Pennzoil, Houston, TX.

44. National Highway Traffic Safety Administration (2001) Motor vehicle brake fluids, *Code of Federal Regulations*, Title 49, Volume 5, Chapter V, Part 571, Standard N°116.

45. Lloyd JBF (1982) Capillary column gas chromatography in the examination of high relative molecular mass petroleum products, *Journal of the Forensic Science Society*, **22**, pp 283–7.

46. Dean WL (1984) Examination of fire debris for flare (fusee) residues by energy dispersive X-ray spectrometry, *Arson Analysis Newsletter*, **8**(2), pp 23–46.

47. Fireant Collective (2001) *Setting fires with electrical timers: An Earth Liberation Front guide*.

48. Fire Findings (1995) Fusees get extremely hot, leave telltale signs of their presence, *Fire Findings*, **3**(2), p 5.

49. Akhavan J (1998) *The chemistry of explosives*, The Royal Society of Chemistry, Cambridge, United Kingdom.

50. Davis TL (1943) *The chemistry of powder & explosives*, GSG Associates, San Pedro, CA.

51. Assistant Deputy Chief of Staff for Intelligence—Threats (2005) *A military guide to terrorism in the twenty-first century*, US Army Training and Doctrine Command, Fort Leavenworth, KS.

52. Center for Disease Control (2003) Homemade chemical bomb events and resulting injuries—Selected States, January 1996–March 2003, *Morbidity and Mortality Weekly Report*, **52**(28), pp 662–4.

53. McDonald K and Shaw M (2005) Identification of household chemicals used in small bombs via analysis of residual materials, *55th Annual Meeting of the American Academy of Forensic Sciences*, New Orleans, LA.

54. Division of Fire Safety (2005) *Bottle bombs*, Department of Community Affairs, New Jersey.

55. Occupational Safety and Health Administration (2004) Flammable and combustible liquids, *Code of Federal Regulations*, Title 29, Subchapter B, Part 1910, Subpart 1910.106.

CHAPTER 15

Education, Training, and Certification

"An education isn't how much you have committed to memory, or even how much you know. It's being able to differentiate between what you do know and what you don't."

Anatole France, French author (1844–1924)

15.1 INTRODUCTION

All the technical aspects of fire debris analysis are worthless if not properly applied by competent analysts. Proper application goes well beyond following sets of written instructions. For most crime laboratory applications, although the quality of analytical findings from a given instrument may be defined by stringent procedures, the value of the conclusions drawn from those procedures and results is highly dependent on the knowledge, abilities, and experience of the criminalist who interprets those results.

Most forensic scientists in the United States specialize in specific types of analyses. In some cases the specification is very distinct: seized drug analysis, DNA analysis, fire debris analysis, DUI toxicology, hair and fiber analysis, and so on. In other cases, the occupation is more general (analytical chemistry, biochemistry, trace analysis) in that more than one forensic discipline is included in a given job description. Each specialty appeals to forensic scientists with different personal characteristics, and cross-training in different specialties is not uncommon.

Because of its nature, fire debris analysis requires subjective interpretation of results and thus, it is included often under the job description of the trace analyst. However, since the instrumentation used in fire debris analysis is virtually identical to that used by the drug analyst, it is very common to find fire debris analysts under the general analytical chemistry arm of the laboratory as well. Regardless whether an analyst cross-trains from another discipline or starts his or her forensic career as a fire debris analyst, there are specific personal, educational, and training qualifications that ultimately define the quality of work and the value of the contribution to the laboratory, the investigation, and the science in general.

Various organizations within the forensic science community, both independently and jointly, have worked to define minimum requirements for personnel qualifications in a forensic laboratory. These groups have set down minimum recommended standards for selecting, training, and evaluating forensic scientists. An external, and thus independent and objective, evaluation of a scientist's knowledge, skills, and abilities is becoming an increasingly important tool to the criminal justice community in their quest to find ways to separate facts from junk science and objective forensic scientists from charlatans.

The information presented in this chapter is aimed at different groups of people. For the student, it gives guidance on how to become a successful candidate for a position as a fire debris analyst in a crime laboratory. For laboratory management, it is a resource for evaluating candidates and for developing and maintaining a meaningful training program. For the educator, it is a resource for ensuring that graduates have the industry-recognized basic skills for succeeding in their chosen profession. For the rest of the criminal justice community, it provides resources for evaluating the quality and abilities of potential or purported experts.

15.2 PERSONAL CHARACTERISTICS

The downfall of any well-meaning laboratory, especially a public laboratory, is the perception of "cops in lab coats." Every scientist must be able to separate the science from the situation's emotional state. The analysis of evidence from even the most atrocious crimes must be treated with complete objectivity. So, although somewhat trite, the most important personal attributes of any forensic scientist are objectivity and integrity. A candidate who wishes to become a criminalist simply to help "get the bad guys off the street" should be viewed with extreme caution. Although everyone should take pride in the work they do to help the criminal justice community, all work performed and all conclusions reached by the forensic scientist must be based solely on the objectivity of the science. Forensic scientists are truth-seekers, not case-makers.

Fire debris analysis requires subjective interpretation of the data obtained in the course of analysis. Factors such as substrate use, manufacture, and decomposition properties must be considered in the recognition of any potential ILR. Because every case is unique, a successful analyst must be capable of extrapolating and adapting information from a number of sources when drawing conclusions.

Because fire debris is a general term for a combination of substrates with individual chemical properties, all of which are affected by fire in a number of different ways, the fire debris analyst must be an enthusiastic lifelong learner. Changes in manufacturing of materials, addition of new synthetic materials, advances in petroleum refining and product marketing are constantly occurring. Fire debris analysis goes well beyond gas chromatography and mass spectrometry. As a consequence, fire debris analysts must be both intelligent and inquisitive and, in general, dedicated to continued learning.

Finally, except in rare instances, the forensic scientist must be able to pass a background check. It is important that educators thoroughly counsel students pursuing a forensic science curriculum that the moral standards are necessarily very high. The general rules of "don't lie, steal, cheat, or do drugs" are very apropos. Even problems with creditors can cause an applicant not to pass a background investigation. Integrity is a crucial quality that all forensic scientists must display. A great level of trust is extended to criminalists upon their hiring by a crime laboratory. Therefore, all legitimate laboratory managers are going to do everything in their power to ensure that their applicants are trustworthy before becoming new hires. To reach this purpose, many laboratories incorporate drug testing, extensive background investigations, and—almost exclusively in the United States—polygraph testing. When becoming a forensic scientist, one's ethic must be irreproachable.

15.3 EDUCATION

A number of organizations have defined minimum education requirements for fire debris analysts. The specific requirements for each are provided in Table 15-1.

In general all recognize the importance of a degree in a natural science or forensic sciences with a strong emphasis in analytical chemistry. Traditional chemistry degrees are recognized for their value in providing a very

Table 15-1 *Recommended education standards for fire debris analysts*

Organization	Recommendation
Scientific Working Group for Fire and Explosives (SWGFEX) [1]	Minimum of a Bachelor's degree or equivalent in a natural science, which includes lecture and associated laboratory classes in general, organic, and analytical chemistry.
American Board of Criminalistics (ABC): Fire Debris Management Committee [2]	Minimum of a Bachelor's degree in a natural or applied science, such as biology, chemistry, physics, forensic science, or criminalistics.
American Society of Crime Laboratory Directors/Laboratory Accreditation Board (ASCLD/LAB) [3]	Baccalaureate degree in a natural science, criminalistics, or a closely related field.

well-rounded scientific background, however they lack the job-specific education unique to the criminal justice field. Forensic science or criminalistics degrees generally lack some of the upper level chemistry coursework, however those that require general and organic chemistry as well as analytical/instrumental analysis are appropriate for routine analysis. Note that laboratories looking for skills in method development or research attributes will be drawn more toward the natural science degrees. Most federal and many state and local laboratories require a minimum of 30 hours of traditional chemistry for consideration. For the most part, preference in hiring natural science versus forensic science graduates is highly dependent on the organizational culture of the hiring laboratory.

There are numerous colleges and universities that offer somewhat ambiguous forensic science and criminalistics degrees, making it difficult to distinguish a true forensic science curriculum from a criminal justice program. As a result, there have been instances in which highly qualified analysts with forensic science degrees have been overlooked in favor of natural science graduates. The Technical Working Group on Education and Training in Forensic Science (TWGED) has defined specific core curricula for forensic science degrees in order to separate true forensic science programs from pseudo-forensic science programs that are primarily criminal justice in content [4]. If a significant number of schools adopt these recommendations, it has the potential to make forensic science degrees the more preferred choice for hiring. The TWGED recommendations for forensic science undergraduate degrees as they pertain to the fire debris analyst are provided in Table 15-2 [4].

Bachelor degrees are generally sufficient for the type of work performed, however, because of the increase in popularity of forensic sciences that has developed from widespread (and generally unrealistically glamorous and exciting) works of television and literary fiction, the number of people pursuing a forensic science degree is exceeding the number of position available. Thus, candidates with higher degrees (Masters or PhD level) in chemistry or forensic science have a significant advantage in the present job market.

15.4 TRAINING

15.4.1 Principle

Forensic science training should include a combination of on-the-job training in specific methodologies coupled with in-depth academic training in both theory and practice as it applies to every aspect of a given discipline (see Figure 15-1). Training should never end with just what the criminalist does; it should also include what happens externally that affects what the criminalist observes and the interpretation of the results. SWGFEX has identified a minimum level of training for fire debris analysts in a document

Table 15-2	TWGED sample curriculum for forensic science undergraduate degrees (chemistry/trace evidence/controlled substances) [4]
Category	**Specific Classes**
University general education (36–40 hours)	Courses required by the university constituting general education
Forensic science core (6 hours)	Forensic science survey Forensic professional practice
Forensic science laboratory (9 hours)	Forensic chemistry internship Microscopy Physical methods
Natural sciences core (34–38 hours)	Biology I Calculus General chemistry I and II Organic chemistry I and II Physics I and II Statistics
Specialized core (12 hours)	Inorganic chemistry Instrumental analysis Quantitative analytical chemistry Physical chemistry
Additional courses (19 hours)	Advanced instrumental analysis Drugs Introduction to criminal justice Legal evidence Analytical toxicology Materials science Pharmacology Public speaking

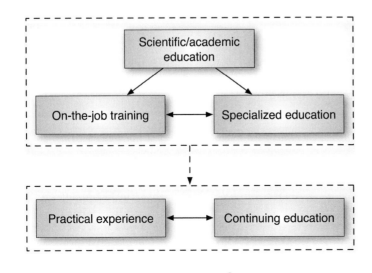

FIGURE 15-1

Typical training scheme for a fire debris analyst.

entitled "Training Guidelines for the Fire Debris Analyst" [5]. The general outline of topics included in this program along with comments regarding each element is provided hereafter. That document includes lists of educational resources and more specific recommendations regarding required depth of knowledge. Note that most of these topics have been addressed in great detail in this book and, where applicable, chapter references have been included.

15.4.2 Basic Topics

A/ Chemistry and Physics of Fire (Chapter 4)

The basis of fire investigation is knowledge of fire: what it is, how it spreads, and what effects it has on materials. Although this is not "working" knowledge that a fire debris analyst will access on a daily basis, it is the most basic foundation of fire and thus must be thoroughly understood in the proper context.

B/ Chemical Composition of Petroleum Products (Chapters 3, 7, and 9)

This heading ideally should be expanded to include all classes of ignitable liquids and common incendiary devices and not just petroleum-derived products. However, the most common analyses performed on fire debris are for the presence of ignitable liquids, which are typically petroleum products, so such an emphasis is warranted. It follows that an in-depth knowledge of the composition of petroleum products (and other ignitable liquids and materials) is a necessity. Basic organic chemistry must also be included so structures and nomenclature as well as physical and chemical properties are understood.

C/ Refinery Processes (Chapter 7)

Continuing in the same vein, the knowledge of how ignitable liquids are produced is equally important to the fire debris analyst. Without this very fundamental knowledge, hydrocarbon combinations produced by substrates can easily be mistaken for those that are found in ignitable liquids. By understanding petroleum refinery processes, the analyst can more easily understand the significance of chromatographic patterns and the likelihood that they were produced by the substrate rather than from a petroleum-derived liquid or vice versa.

D/ Effects of Fire (Chapters 4 and 12)

Understanding impact of fire (heat) on liquids and solids is critical to data interpretation. It is absolutely essential that the forensic scientist understand the concepts and effects of evaporation, heat stress, pyrolysis, and combustion. This is an introductory theme that is further defined in topics dedicated to data interpretation.

E/ Health and Safety Risks: Chemical, Biological, and Physical

Laboratory safety and chemical hygiene are basic training for any laboratory, however there are some additional risks or concerns that should be noted by the fire debris analyst including the production of toxic chemicals as a result of thermal degradation and the use of dangerous extraction solvents. Common laboratory engineering controls are typically sufficient for minimizing risks. Other risks associated with fire scene response should be addressed whenever applicable [6].

F/ Investigative Process: Origin and Cause *(Chapters 1 and 5)*

Although many fire debris analysts do not respond to fire scenes, it is still important that they have a fundamental understanding of how a scene investigation is conducted. The investigation will result in determining what, if any, evidence is submitted to the laboratory for analysis.

G/ Incendiary Devices *(Chapter 14)*

Not all arsonists use ignitable liquids. When ignitable liquids are used, delay devices may also be implemented to facilitate escape or coordinate timing. Recognition of these devices can be crucial to an investigation. The criminalist must be aware of the different types of devices and incendiary chemicals that may be present in laboratory samples so that they can be properly recognized, analyzed, handled, and preserved.

H/ Evidence Collection, Documentation, Packaging, Preservation, and Chain of Custody *(Chapter 6)*

The very fundamental, but essential, aspects of evidence preservation including how it is handled, collected, transported, stored, and maintained must be well understood. Because of the sensitivity of today's analytical techniques and the prevalence of petroleum-based ignitable liquids in the environment, a certain potential for contamination exists if precautions are not addressed. It is not sufficient that precautions are taken; documentation of those precautions is essential to the establishment of the chain of custody and the court admissibility of the evidence. The onus is on the criminalist not only to guarantee the proper handling of evidence, but also to prove to a large extent that those precautions were observed. Training must include both practical and legal aspects and pitfalls of evidence handling.

I/ Other Evidence *(Chapters 10 and 14)*

Although the great majority of examinations associated with fire investigation is that of ignitable liquid detection and classification, as with any crime, other material of evidentiary value may be found and other types of analysis may be beneficial to the investigation. Therefore, the fire debris analyst must have sufficient training in both the recognition of other types of evidence and the understanding as how to best preserve and prioritize these items of evidence.

J/ Recovery and Separation of Ignitable Liquid Residues (Chapter 11)

One of the key activities of the fire debris analyst is the separation and recovery of ILR from debris. Even though every laboratory has procedures as to the process, each sample is different and must be subjectively evaluated to determine the best extraction technique and the optimal parameters in the context of that particular sample. An in-depth knowledge of each technique including theory, advantages, and limitations is absolutely essential. It should be noted that there are a number of techniques that are not routinely used but that are accepted in the field. Even if a given extraction technique is not employed by a laboratory, the analyst should still have extensive knowledge of its process in order to effectively evaluate results from opposing laboratories or forensic scientists.

K/ Theory of Gas Chromatography (Chapter 8)

It is simply not possible to be a good fire debris analyst without a thorough understanding of gas chromatography. This is not only the fundamental, but also the only instrumentation suitable for separating the components of ignitable liquids. The fire debris analyst must have in-depth understanding of the underlying GC theory.

L/ Practical Gas Chromatography (Chapter 8)

Knowing the theory about a complex instrument is good but not sufficient. One must also master the instrumentation hardware and software. This is the goal of the teaching of practical gas chromatography, which includes the operation of the instrument, maintenance, and troubleshooting.

M/ Gas Chromatography–Mass Spectrometry (Chapter 8)

GC–MS is the industry standard for ignitable liquid analysis and classification. A less than complete understanding of the instrumentation and its operation can easily lead to erroneous results and conclusions. Training should focus on both hardware and software, to include operation, maintenance, and troubleshooting, as it applies to fire debris analysis.

N/ Classification, Interpretation, and Identification of Ignitable Liquid Residues (Chapters 9 and 12)

Once the theory of GC is mastered, the practical aspects of applying it to fire debris must be learned and understood. The concept of pattern recognition is not complex, however its application is. A significant proportion of any training program should be dedicated to pattern recognition techniques, as these are the meat of the training. Once the instrument has generated data, properly interpreting those results as to their significance in the context of the investigation is vital. This is where most of the previous subjects are brought together to produce the end results. Ideally, this portion of the curriculum includes numerous examples and scenarios along with an extended list of practical exercises dissecting the effect of each stage of the analysis and how they will affect the final conclusions.

O/ Report Writing *(Chapter 16)*

The old adage of "it's not what you say, it's how you say it" definitely applies to forensic science and is specifically important when the results are more subjective such as in the case of ignitable liquid analyses. The Fire Laboratory Standards and Protocols Committee of SWGFEX is presently working on a standard on report writing, however there is no current published guide for reporting fire debris results, although ASTM standards do address some of the pertinent issues. Hence, there are a multitude of examples of results that appear similar but read very differently. Training should consist of both a laboratory's policy on reporting fire debris results, and on the good and the not-so-good examples still found in the everyday practice. The importance of objective, scientific reporting must be stressed, along with the needs of the investigative community.

P/ Courtroom Testimony and Presentation Techniques

The best of forensic scientists can be discredited by poor testimony. Training should include legal terms, definitions, and case law; the more esoteric aspects of testimony should also be addressed. Public speaking and lawyer's tactics should also be integral parts of the training program. Observations of actual testimony should be employed whenever possible.

Q/ Quality Assurance/Validation and Methodology *(Chapter 16 and 17)*

There is no way to adequately express the importance of quality assurance in a forensic laboratory. Extensive training on how to prevent problems, how to detect them when they do occur, and how to properly address them is very important for the new criminalist as well as for the manager. The results are only as good as the quality that goes into them. Therefore, the concepts of preventive and corrective actions are critical to quality work of unquestionable value. Industry standards for quality assurance including accreditation, standardization, and certification requirements and recommendations should be explored alongside laboratory-specific quality assurance requirements.

15.4.3 Other Recommended Topics

A/ History of Fire Debris Analysis *(Chapter 2)*

Although not essential knowledge to the analyst, knowing how the science evolved is interesting and can offer a lot of insight as to the importance of where the science is presently.

B/ Innovations and the Future of Fire Debris Analysis
(Chapter 13)

As fire debris analysis has a history, it also has a future. Advancements over the last 20 years have completely redefined both analysis and interpretation. The next ten years may be equally as exciting. It is important that criminalists stay current on new techniques and advancements in science so that they will be prepared to properly implement, refine, and improve upon them in the future.

C/ Forensic Science and Fire Investigation Resources

There are a multitude of resources available to the forensic scientist; some of them from very unlikely places. In the course of training, analysts will, by default, come across many of them and find more on their own. Some formalized recognition of those resources by the community can only aid in furthering the education and qualifications of the new fire debris analyst.

15.5 CONTINUING EDUCATION

15.5.1 Principle

It cannot be stressed enough that every forensic laboratory should be a learning organization and that all forensic scientists should be dedicated to lifelong learning. It is absolutely essential that the fire debris analyst stay current in scientific advancements as well as in new interpretations of old information. In general, it is recommended that each forensic scientist receive at least 20 hours of continuing education per year and per discipline. There are numerous ways by which this can be achieved including subscribing to technical journals or attending formal training courses and forensic science organization meetings and symposia.

15.5.2 Scientific Journals

Most laboratories subscribe to a number of forensic journals. It is recommended that the criminalist also stay current with other publications including those related to instrumentation and processes, quality assurance, and petroleum refinery advances. Table 15-3 presents some recommended publications, which often bring pertinent information to the field of fire debris analysis.

15.5.3 Courses and Conferences

Although technical reading is certainly beneficial, it cannot compare to the opportunities for technical advancement provided by formal training opportunities. In the United States, the ATF (in partnership with the National Center for Forensic Science) offers two one-week training classes:

Table 15-3	*Recommended scientific journals for the fire debris analyst*	
Forensic topics	**Chemical/physical topics**	**Fire and arson topics**
Canadian Society of Forensic Science Journal	Analytica Chimica Acta	Combustion and flame
Crime Laboratory Digest	Analytical Chemistry	Combustion science and technology
Environmental Forensics	Chromatographia	Fire and arson investigator
Forensic Science Communications	Journal of Analytical and Applied Pyrolysis	Fire and materials
Forensic Science International	Journal of Chromatographic Science	Fire safety journal
Journal of Forensic Sciences	Journal of Chromatography A	Fire technology
Science & Justice	Journal of High Resolution Chromatography	Fire findings
Z. Zagadnien Nauk Sadowych (Problems of Forensic Sciences)	Polymer degradation and stability	Journal of fire science

Basic Fire Debris Analysis and Advanced Fire Debris Analysis. In parallel, the FBI has a one-week fire debris analysis course. Additionally, many of the national and regional forensic science associations provide specific training in mass spectrometry, gas chromatography, and quality assurance. These training opportunities might not be focused directly on fire debris analysis, nevertheless they are very informative and beneficial to the fire debris analyst.

In addition, professional organization meetings including those of the *International Association of Forensic Sciences*, the *American Academy of Forensic Sciences* (USA), the *Forensic Science Society* (UK), regional forensic science associations, and SWGFEX generally set aside a portion of their annual programs for the presentation of fire debris related research and workshops. Less formalized training can be of significant value as well. There are several Internet-based programs of related topics including petroleum refining, gas chromatography, mass spectrometry, quality assurance, and fire investigation. For example, Agilent Technologies offers free e-Seminars that are of great value [7].

15.6 MEASURE OF COMPETENCE

Once a forensic scientist is fully trained in performing fire debris analysis, laboratories must continually evaluate his/her competence in order to provide their client—the criminal or civil justice community—objective reassurance. This evaluation process can be completely internal or, preferably, it may involve both internal and external reviews of the analyst's knowledge, skills, and abilities.

Internally, most laboratories rely on competency or proficiency testing to evaluate the forensic scientist's performances. The terms competency and proficiency testing often are used interchangeably; however, they have different meanings to different organizations. The SWG and TWG communities have defined competency testing as a method for reviewing individual performance and proficiency testing as a method for evaluating the laboratory system [1, 8]. Some laboratories define competency testing as performance tests conducted at the end of training and prior to assuming casework and proficiency testing as periodic performance tests conducted after an analyst is fully trained and is actively analyzing casework. For the purpose of this text the SWG/TWG definitions will be used.

In a quality laboratory, criminalists should be competency-tested at least once a year in each discipline in which they perform analysis. Ideally, competency and proficiency tests should mimic actual casework as closely as possible. Whenever possible quality assurance samples should be submitted as an actual case, for which the criminalist is unaware that the test is a competency test. Unfortunately, creating "real" fire debris case samples for competency testing is very difficult and thus many laboratories rely solely on testing specific aspects of an actual analysis (i.e., separation or interpretation). Alternatively, reanalysis of casework is also employed to evaluate a fire debris analyst's performance.

Competency/proficiency tests may be created in-house, purchased from a vendor, or developed through interlaboratory cooperation. Accredited laboratories are required to analyze at least one test per year purchased through an approved third-party provider. Forensic scientists in accredited laboratories must be tested at least annually; however, the tests may come from any source, including internal tests.

While successful results generally indicate that both the laboratory and the criminalist are achieving their goals in terms of analysis and quality assurance, unsuccessful results do not necessary indicate incompetence on the part of the forensic scientist. Most competency tests also serve as proficiency tests in that many aspects of the quality system are evaluated in the process. There are situations where a forensic scientist can achieve the wrong result following a laboratory protocol that is actually flawed. As such, he or she is not necessary in error due to his or her own incompetence but rather because of the failure of the system. An example would be a test in which a light petroleum product was applied to fire debris. By laboratory policy, the sample was analyzed by solvent extraction, which resulted in negative results. The criminalist followed policy; however, the limitations of the technique resulted in the false negative results. The error is in the protocol, not the application or interpretation of the results obtained. When a proficiency test is properly applied, information discovered regarding deficiencies in laboratory protocols can be used to improve procedures.

15.7 CERTIFICATION

15.7.1 Principle

The most objective measure of a criminalist's ability and competence comes from a total external review of education, training, knowledge, and competence. This type of external review is available in the form of certification.

It is important to understand the difference between certification and accreditation. Accreditation is the external review and assessment of the quality system of a laboratory. The goal of accreditation is to ensure that a laboratory has an adequate system in place to achieve quality results. Although personnel standards are an important part of accreditation, the focus is on the system as a whole rather than on the individual's abilities and accomplishments. Certification is the external recognition of a person's qualifications and competence.

The certification of fire debris analysts is provided by the American Board of Criminalistics (ABC). It is one of the most recognized and reputable certifying organizations in the US forensic community. Currently, the ABC is the only recognized organization certifying fire debris analysts.

The value of a valid certification to a forensic scientist is significant. In a highly competitive job market, certification provides potential employers with an objective measure of competence. In the court system, where judges and juries can be inundated with technical information beyond their ability to understand, external certification of a criminalist provides them with a resource for separating the knowledgeable from the charlatan. This is especially beneficial to the new forensic scientist who can benefit greatly from citing certification as a part of their qualifications.

15.7.2 ABC Certification Process

The ABC certification process is a three-part continuous assessment of a fire debris analyst's qualifications and competency. Part I is a credentials review to ascertain that the candidate has the minimum educational qualifications, training, and experience for certification. Part II is a practical assessment of knowledge related to forensic sciences in general and fire debris analysis specifically. This is assessed using multiple-choice tests developed and maintained by subject matter experts representing various regional and national forensic science associations. Part III is an ongoing annual review of continuing education and competency testing results.

ABC is currently in a state of change. To date, ABC has divided its certifications into three categories: diplomate, fellow, and technical specialist. In addition, a fourth category is that of affiliate. Although an affiliate is not a certificate holder, the title designates that the individual has successfully completed the requisite examination, and is eligible to become certified once the experience requirements are accomplished. The diplomate certificate required a minimum of a bachelor's degree in a natural science or forensic sciences, two years experience in the field, and the successful completion of the General Knowledge Examination (GKE). Fellow certificates were awarded to those who had achieved diplomate status and successfully had passed a specialty exam in their area of expertise and a practical examination in the form of a proficiency test. Fellows were also required to successfully complete external discipline-specific competency testing each year to maintain their certification. Finally, the technical specialist certificate was awarded to forensic scientists in specific disciplines who took and passed a technical specialist exam in lieu of the GKE and specialty exam. Technical specialist certificates were available only in the disciplines of seized drug analysis and molecular biology.

The face of ABC certification changed in early 2007. In an effort to increase the number of forensic scientists holding certificates in their respective disciplines, ABC moved to a new testing format. Candidates are now required to take a single comprehensive exam that encompasses their area of expertise along with a general knowledge component. Seven new exams were developed including a new Fire Debris Analysis Certification Examination. These exams encompass both the core knowledge, skills, and abilities previously tested by the GKE, as well as specific fire debris analysis related material. Approximately 40% of the 220 exam questions are related to core topics including legal aspects, evidence handling and preservation, and ethics. The remaining 60% are devoted strictly to the theory and application of fire debris analysis.

The distinction between diplomate and fellow in the new system is determined primarily by proficiency testing and participation in active casework. A criminalist who has met the professional and educational requirements, passed the written exam, and successfully participates in annual proficiency testing gains fellow status. Scientists that are not proficiency tested, including administrators who no longer perform casework but maintain all other continuing education requirements, are awarded diplomate certificates. The Technical Specialist certification was removed from the program.

The core knowledge component of the examination is designed to assess the candidate's knowledge in all areas of forensic sciences. The premise for this is that even though much of forensic science is performed by discipline-specific forensic scientists in the United States, knowledge of other types of evidence as well as a general understanding of their collection and analysis is critical to evidence recognition and preservation.

Examples of core and fire debris analysis specific questions are provided in Tables 15-4 and 15-5 [9, 10]. The most current study guides and testing information can be found on the web site of the ABC (http://www.criminalistics.com).

15.7.3 ABC Fire Debris Fellows Distribution

Although there are about 600 ABC certificate holders (with more than a quarter from California), there are only 23 people certified in fire debris analysis [11]. Figure 15-2 shows the distribution of these forensic scientists. Note that 22 of them are in the United States and one is from Switzerland. Fire debris analysts are encouraged to get more involved with the certification process and to take the test.

Table 15-4	Sample test questions for the General Knowledge Examination [9]

1. **In collecting evidence from a gun at a homicide crime scene, one should first:**
   A. photograph the gun.
   B. unload the gun.
   C. dust the gun for fingerprints.
   D. remove a blood stain from the barrel.

2. **The chain of custody is:**
   A. documented proof of the integrity of evidence.
   B. a document presented in lieu of testimony by an expert.
   C. documented proof the evidence was analyzed.
   D. documented proof of where the prisoner is being kept.

3. **An MSDS is:**
   A. a document of chemical safety.
   B. an instrument for chemical analysis.
   C. a technique for testing DNA.
   D. a type of explosive material.

4. **Which one of the following arrangements lists the colors in order of decreasing wavelength?**
   A. Orange, violet, blue, green
   B. Orange, green, blue, violet
   C. Violet, blue, green, orange
   D. Violet, green, blue, orange

5. **Marquis is a reagent used to detect:**
   A. cocaine.
   B. heroin.
   C. marijuana.
   D. PCP.

Table 15-5	Sample test questions for the Fire Debris Analysis Specialty Examination [10]

1. Which class of ignitable liquids is MOST affected by evaporation or burning at the fire scene?
   A. Gasolines
   B. Medium petroleum distillates
   C. Heavy petroleum distillates
   D. Light petroleum distillates

2. Which of the following statements describe capillary columns?
   I.   They were developed by Golay in 1958.
   II. They exhibit lower pressure drop per unit length than packed columns.
   III. They handle very large sample sizes.
   IV. They require instrument modification on units originally equipped for packed columns.

   A. I and II, only
   B. II, III and IV
   C. I, II and IV
   D. II and IV, only

3. Which of the following contribute to the difficulty of individualizing gasolines extracted from fire debris?
   I.   Lack of an n-alkane series.
   II. Refining and marketing practices.
   III. Changes in composition during storage.
   IV. Changes caused by fire exposure.

   A. I and IV, only
   B. III and IV, only
   C. II, III and IV
   D. I, II, III and IV

4. Which of these automotive products can react spontaneously with calcium hypochlorite producing intense flame?
   A. Automatic Transmission Fluid
   B. Motor Oil
   C. Gear Oil
   D. Brake Fluid

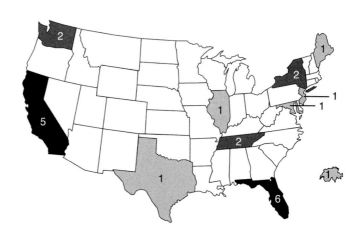

FIGURE 15-2

Distribution of the ABC fire debris certified criminalists. Twenty-two are present in the United States and one in Switzerland.

REFERENCES

1. Fire Laboratory Standards and Protocols Committee (2003) *Quality assurance guide for the forensic analysis of ignitable liquids*, Technical and Scientific Working Group for Fire and Explosives.

2. American Board of Criminalistics (2004) *Eligibility requirements for ABC certification*, Wausau, WI.

3. ASCLD/LAB (2005) *Accreditation manual*, American Society of Crime Laboratory Directors/Laboratory Accreditation Board, Garner, NC.

4. TWGED (2004) *Education and training in forensic science: A guide for forensic science laboratories, educational institutions, and students*, Technical Working Group for Education and Training in Forensic Science, National Institute of Justice, US Department of Justice, Washington, DC.

5. Laboratory Fire Education and Training Committee (2000) *Training guidelines for the fire debris analyst*, Technical and Scientific Working Group for Fire and Explosives.

6. Technical Working Group on Fire/Arson Scene Investigation (2000) *Fire and arson scene evidence: A guide for public safety personnel*, National Institute of Justice, US Department of Justice, Washington, DC.

7. Agilent Technologies (2005) *e-Seminars*, available from http://www.chem.agilent.com/scripts/education.asp, last access performed on February 9, 2006.

8. SWGDRUG (2005) *Part II: Quality assurance*, Scientific Working Group for the Analysis of Seized Drugs.

9. American Board of Criminalistics (1996) *Sample test questions—ABC General Knowledge Examination*, available from http://www.criminalistics.com/cert_diplomate.cfm, last access performed on March 20, 2007.

10. American Board of Criminalistics (1996) *Sample test questions—ABC Fire Debris Examination*, available from http://www.criminalistics.com/cert_fellow_firedebris.cfm, last access performed on March 20, 2007.

11. American Board of Criminalistics (2007) *Membership directory*, available from http://www.criminalistics.com/mem_memdirectory.cfm, last access performed on March 20, 2007.

CHAPTER 16

Standardization

"If you think of standardization as the best that you know today, but which is to be improved tomorrow; you get somewhere."

Henry Ford, American industrialist (1863–1947)

16.1 INTRODUCTION

Three cans of debris from a fatal fire are submitted to a laboratory for analysis to determine if any ignitable liquid residues (ILR) are present. The laboratory performs an analysis, issues a report, and subsequently the fire debris analyst testifies in a high profile murder case. The laboratory report indicates that a heavy petroleum distillate, examples of which include kerosene, some lamp oils, and some charcoals starters, was present in two of the three items.

An opposing expert is employed, who, in turn, refutes the initial findings. His report indicates that no identifiable ignitable liquids are present and that the data obtained by the initial analysis represent condensation of asphalt (shingle) pyrolysis products rather than a petroleum distillate. He, too, provides testimony in the trial.

Which expert's findings will the jury find the most credible? They will (hopefully) base their opinion on the qualifications of the expert and defensibility of the analysis they chose to perform. But, how can lay witnesses assess the qualifications and methodology of scientists and scientific analysis? Is one witness correct because he or she holds a PhD, whereas the other one holds only a Bachelor's degree? Is the expert who used the newest, cutting edge technology more likely to be correct than the expert who used an older technique?

This scenario is not uncommon. Often lay people are required to give credence to expert witnesses based largely on scientific concepts that they do not fully understand. Recognizing this, court systems are constantly looking for authoritative independent measures of competence and scientific validity. Fortunately, in the arena of forensic fire debris analysis, these independent measures are well established in the forms of certification, accreditation, and most importantly, standardization.

Ideally, certification provides for an external mechanism to ensure that practicing forensic scientists possess and maintain sufficient theoretical and practical knowledge to perform quality analysis and reach reasonable conclusions (see Chapter 15). Likewise, accreditation provides an external mechanism to ensure that the management and operational structures of a laboratory are sufficient to produce quality work (see Chapter 17). Finally, and still ideally, standardization provides defined minimum requirements for procedures and applications to ensure quality analytical results. Together these three elements make up the quality triangle used in forensic sciences (see Figure 16-1).

Quality analysis and the development of accurate conclusions depend upon the three distinct factors of management, personnel, and process. Each is interdependent upon the other. Properly trained personnel are required to execute the processes. Well-defined management is needed to obtain personnel, supplies, and equipment to conduct processes. Widely accepted and well-defined methodology generally results in reliable results. External measures and defined criteria for each of these elements—in the form of certification, accreditation, and standardization—are used to elevate the quality of the work performed in a crime laboratory. This is used to provide proof of integrity to the outside world. This is not to say that unaccredited laboratories, uncertified analysts, and the use of nonstandard techniques will result in inaccurate results; however, it is much more difficult to prove reliability without these external measures. Indeed, an accredited laboratory, employing certified forensic scientists using standardized methods, is not a bullet-proof guarantee that the work performed is reliable. Too often, news agencies report malpractice from crime laboratories that have applied the famous

FIGURE 16-1

Representation of the quality triangle.

Certification   Accreditation

Standardization

quality triangle in their practice. In the United States, one may remember the recent case of the three Duke lacrosse players accused of rape for which the director of a private ASCLD/LAB accredited laboratory intentionally decided not to report results favorable to the defense, a serious ethical misdeed [1]. So, even with a fully accredited laboratory, one must rely on the integrity of its workers.

16.2 DEFINITION OF STANDARDIZATION

Standardization is the creation and acceptance of uniform analytical processes and quality testing procedures within an industry. In the forensic science community, standardization is a well-fought battle between those fractions that want to create uniformity and consistency in forensic analyses and those that want to maintain the creativity and individuality that has both helped and hurt forensic sciences. Fortunately, most forensic scientists now understand that those ideals are not mutually exclusive and that forensic sciences can continue to grow and improve in a world of well-defined quality standards.

With too-frequent media coverage of laboratories performing substandard work, along with judicial concerns regarding the accuracy and reliability of competing interpretations of results, the judicial community, and the general public at large, has an almost desperate need to know what is, in essence, "right." Published standards—developed and maintained by experts and practitioners—are essential to the integrity of forensic sciences.

In the United States, the forum into which forensic sciences, as well as most other testing, production, and construction industries have adopted for creating, maintaining, and publishing quality standards is ASTM International. ASTM International is a voluntary consensus standard development organization with over 30,000 members representing thousands of industries [2].

16.3 ASTM TECHNICAL COMMITTEE STRUCTURE

Currently, fire debris analysis is the best represented forensic discipline at ASTM. In the late 1980s, ASTM approached the forensic science community to develop standards for forensic science [3]. A group of fire debris analysts (likely called arson analysts at that time) were sufficiently concerned about the very inconsistent and subjective nature of fire debris analysis in the United States. This group had the initiative to use the ASTM standards development process through the ASTM Committee E30 on Forensic Sciences to develop, publish, and maintain minimum standards for fire debris analysis. The ASTM Committee E30 on Forensic Sciences was originally formed in 1970, currently counts approximately 700 members, and has produced about 50 standards addressing various disciplines of forensic sciences [4].

ASTM membership is voluntary and the use of standards in forensic sciences is also voluntary. There are two levels of membership and three levels of participation in ASTM. The intent of ASTM is to include the input of practitioners, manufacturers, suppliers, testers, and consumers in the standard's development process. Thus, anyone can join and be a member of an ASTM technical committee. ASTM is divided into main technical committees primarily based upon their function. E30 is the main committee for forensic examinations.[1] Each main committee is then divided into sub-committees. Subcommittee membership is granted by application based on the applicant's qualification and interests. Table 16-1 provides a listing of the 10 subcommittees that currently exist under the E30 designation. The responsibility of fire debris standards falls under the immediate duties of the Criminalistics subcommittee designated E30.01.

Subcommittees, in turn, can form task groups to develop or revise new standards. Other professional organizations, including SWGFEX, can work to propose new standards and assist in the revision of existing standards. As an example, the Fire Laboratory Standards and Protocols Committee has

Table 16-1	List of the 10 subcommittees acting under the ASTM E30 Committee on Forensic Sciences
Designation	**Name**
E30.01	Criminalistics
E30.02	Questioned Documents
E30.05	Engineering
E30.11	Interdisciplinary Forensic Science Standards
E30.12	Digital Evidence
E30.90	Executive
E30.91	Long Range Planning
E30.92	Terminology
E30.93	Awards
E30.94	Liaison

[1] Another committee called ASTM Committee E52 on Forensic Psychophysiology also was created in 1998, but even though it includes the term "forensic," it does not deal with issues that are generally accepted as forensic ones, since it deals exclusively with polygraph examination.

suggested the revision of the classification system of ignitable liquids in two ASTM standards and has submitted a new standard for approval.

16.4 ASTM STANDARDS DEVELOPMENT

ASTM standards are consensus-based documents. As such, the membership must come to a consensus agreement as to the scope and content of each standard. Each standard and revision is voted on by all main committee and subcommittee members and all negative ballots must be objectively addressed by the membership.

The standard development process is tedious. First, a member, organization, or task group proposes a new standard to the subcommittee for adoption. The standard must be written following a very strict format [5]. The proposed standard is reviewed and eventually balloted to the subcommittee. Each member of the subcommittee is required to vote. They may vote "affirmative," "affirmative with comment," "negative with comment," or they may simply abstain. All negative votes must be accompanied by an explanation that details the basis of the voter's opposition. All negative ballots are returned to the subcommittee members and must be addressed. The subcommittee will then discuss, debate, and vote on every negative ballot, as to whether the voter's argument is persuasive or not. Persuasive (justified) concerns typically result in substantive changes to the proposed document, which lead to a reballoting of the standard back to the entire subcommittee. This process continues, often over the course of months or years, until a version of the standard is amiable to the subcommittee membership; that is, any remaining negative votes are determined to be nonpersuasive. The standard is then forwarded to the main committee where the entire process is repeated. Once consensus approval is received from the main committee, the document is forwarded to the ASTM staff for editorial review and publication.

All ASTM standards must be reviewed by the membership every five years. At that time the membership can vote for reapproval (as is), revision (changes), or withdrawal based upon the state of the science and industry at that time. Substantial changes can be proposed anytime within that five-year period as well; however, the same process of balloting is utilized. Because every reapproval, revision, or withdrawal must be done with the consensus of both the subcommittee and the main committee, the process can be slow and tedious; however, the end document generally provides for a good representation of the minimum requirements for the production of both quality work and defensible practice.

16.5 TYPES OF STANDARDS

There are six primary types of ASTM standards: classification, guide, practice, specification, terminology standard, and test method. At ASTM, the term "standard" is generic to all these documents [5].

Classifications are, as the name implies, documents providing a systematic means for grouping things with similar characteristics. There are not currently any standalone fire debris classification standards. The ignitable liquid classification described in various chapters of this text is published as a table within two of the test methods rather than as its own standalone document.

Guides are documents providing direction and assistance in decision-making processes without requiring a set course of action. Some test methods are introduced originally as guides to allow users more freedom in using and/or adopting the standard. At this time, there are no published ASTM guides for fire debris analysis, however the two primary test methods E 1387 and E 1618 (see later) were both initially published as guides. They were subsequently converted to test methods in the course of the revision processes.

Practices are documents providing a set of instructions for the application of a specific task that does not generate actual test results by itself. All fire debris extraction standards are standard practices because they provide instructions as to how to extract ignitable liquids from debris, but do not actually result in interpretive data or test results. Specifications are tightly defined requirements for materials or supplies used in various processes. There are not any ASTM specification standards currently published for fire debris analysis. One such example of a specification that may concern fire debris analysts is *ASTM D 260-86 standard specification for boiled linseed oil* [6]. There are many specifications also pertaining to the petroleum industry and the quality of diesel fuels, gasolines, and other ignitable liquids that can be of great use to the fire debris analyst.

Terminology standards are, in essence, glossaries providing a common language and definitions. There is one ASTM terminology standard for forensic sciences developed by the subcommittee E30.92 on terminology. It is *ASTM E 1732-96a(2005) standard terminology relating to forensic science* and it includes various entries related to fire debris analysis [7].

Test methods are standard documents providing a set of instructions for analyses or operations that actually produce results. A test method must produce some type of measure from which a conclusion can be made. In fire debris analysis, there are currently two standard test methods *E 1387-01 standard test method for ignitable liquid residues in extracts from fire debris samples by gas chromatography*, and *E 1618-06 standard test method for ignitable liquid residues in extracts from fire debris samples by gas chromatography-mass spectrometry* [8, 9].

All forensic science standards are published in volume 14.02 of the ASTM Annual Book of Standards. The membership fees include one copy of either an electronic version or a printed version of any of the ASTM Annual Book of Standards. Standards can also be purchased individually through ASTM International's web site. It should be noted that in 2003, all public crime laboratories in the United States received a free copy of volume 14.02, which includes all the standards produced by E30.

The ASTM standards provide an excellent resource for laboratories and criminalists to develop and perform high quality defensible fire debris analysis. However, these standards represent minimum criteria and require that the fire debris analyst have and maintain a comprehensive knowledge of the theory and application of each technique. Most of the practices provide parameter ranges (temperature, volume, etc.) that must be optimized to the specific sample and scenario. An untrained forensic scientist cannot and should not feel that they can simply perform an examination using a standard practice and/or standard method. It is the combination of extensive training, scientifically sound methodology, and effective laboratory management that will ensure quality results.

16.6 STANDARD PRACTICES FOR FIRE DEBRIS ANALYSIS

The ASTM standard practices for fire debris analysis all relate to the separation of ignitable liquids from sample matrices, in order to carry out instrumental analysis. The list of the different ASTM standard practices for fire debris analysis is shown in Table 16-2 [10–16]. The theory and use of these practices was covered in Chapter 11. Table 16-2 represents the state of the ASTM standards as of the writing of this text; however, it should be noted that these standards are under constant review and some revisions should be published in the near future. It is recommended that practitioners monitor ASTM International's web site to see the most current revision at any given time.

Each practice includes general instructions to perform the sample extraction. Methodology ensuring quality results, including the use of blanks (negative controls) to detect contamination and positive controls to ensure efficiency, are detailed within the individual standards. Limitations of each technique, including explanations as to when they are not appropriate for use and what classes of IL may not be effectively recovered are well explained.

Each practice results in the collection of an ignitable liquid residue that is then analyzed utilizing one of the ASTM test methods described in Section 16.7.

16.7 STANDARD TEST METHODS FOR FIRE DEBRIS ANALYSIS

The standard test methods providing instructions as to the analysis, interpretation, and reporting of ignitable liquid extracts from fire debris exist

Table 16-2	List of the ASTM standard practices devoted to fire debris analysis. Note that items in grey are either no longer active or have not yet been accepted

Designation	Title	Original Date	Current Revision (Reapproval)
E 1385	Standard practice for separation and concentration of ignitable liquid residues from fire debris samples by steam distillation	1990	withdrawn
E 1386	Standard practice for separation and concentration of ignitable liquid residues from fire debris samples by solvent extraction	1990	2005
E 1388	Standard practice for sampling of headspace vapors from fire debris samples	1990	2005
E 1389	Standard practice for cleanup of fire debris sample extracts by acid stripping	1990	withdrawn
E 1412	Standard practice for separation of ignitable liquid residues from fire debris samples by passive headspace concentration with activated charcoal	1991	2005
E 1413	Standard practice for separation and concentration of ignitable liquid residues from fire debris samples by dynamic headspace concentration	1991	2005
E 2154	Standard practice for separation and concentration of ignitable liquid residues from fire debris samples by passive headspace concentration with solid phase microextraction (SPME)	2001	2001
TBD	Standard practice for preserving ignitable liquid samples and ignitable liquid residue extracts from fire debris samples	—	under consideration

as complementary documents under the designation E 1387 and E 1618. E 1387 pertains to ignitable liquid analysis by gas chromatography alone; E 1618 is more specific to analysis by gas chromatography–mass spectrometry.

The only significant difference in the documents is in the use of mass spectrometry (see Chapters 8, 9, and 12) in analyzing and interpreting ignitable liquid (IL) data and in the precautionary statements included in E 1387 on the limitations of not using mass spectrometry in IL analysis. It is now generally accepted that gas chromatography–mass spectrometry is the gold standard for fire debris analysis and that gas chromatography alone should be limited to only the most straightforward cases.

Both documents provide instructions for the analytical process including relevant quality control checks in terms of instrument calibration and analysis of controls (text mixtures) necessary to establish that the instruments are working properly. The analysis of a test solution consisting of n-alkanes and aromatic compounds is used to establish detection limits, and to ensure appropriate resolution and reproducibility. With the exception of dilution of neat liquids, sample preparation and handling is referenced to the standard practices described in Table 16-2.

The most important information in E 1387 and E 1618 is the data analysis, ignitable liquid classification scheme, and data interpretation sections. The data analysis section provides instructions to establish appropriate instrumental parameters to obtain meaningful data. This includes directions on the use of alkane ranges, pattern matching, extracted ions (including ion selection), and target compounds.

The ASTM ignitable liquid classification scheme (see Table 9-1) provides a systematic method of classifying IL based upon chemical composition, boiling range and chromatographic characteristics. Originally developed by the then Bureau of Alcohol, Tobacco, and Firearms (ATF)[2] and the then National Bureau of Standards (NBS)[3] in the early 1980s, this scheme has evolved over the course of the years to include the eight IL classes subdivided into three boiling point ranges that are recognized and used today (see Chapter 9) [17].

A section on data interpretation provides instructions on how to interpret chromatographic results in the presence of interfering compounds. In general, the standard requires IL identification based upon pattern recognition by direct comparison with known ignitable liquid reference materials. The significance of extraneous compounds, missing components, and environmental contaminants (petroleum-laced backgrounds) also is addressed.

The report section provides instructions as to what should be incorporated in the text of a report, including recommendations to use terms and examples that are easily understood by the nonscientist (i.e., investigator, prosecutor). It should be noted that the classification scheme was proposed as a cataloging system and a basis for common terminology among fire debris analysts. Although it may be used to report results, it is not a requirement of ASTM to use it as such.

REFERENCES

1. Neff J, Niolet B, and Blythe A (2006) Lab chief: Nifong said don't report all DNA data, *The News & Observer*, available from http://www.newsobserver.com/114/story/522112.html, last access performed on December 16, 2006.
2. ASTM International (2007) *About ASTM International*, available from http://www.astm.org/cgi-bin/SoftCart.exe/ABOUT/aboutASTM.html?L+mystore+iubk5973+1174403583, last access performed on March 20, 2007.
3. Fultz ML and Culver J (1995) Analysis protocols and proficiency testing in fire debris analysis, *International Symposium on the Forensic Aspects of Arson Investigations*, Federal Bureau of Investigations, Fairfax, VA.

[2] Currently the Bureau of Alcohol, Tobacco, Firearms and Explosives.

[3] Currently the National Institute of Standards and Technology (NIST).

4. ASTM International (2007) *Committee E30 on forensic sciences*, available from http://www.astm.org/cgi-bin/SoftCart.exe/COMMIT/COMMITTEE/E30. htm?L+mystore+iubk5973, last access performed on March 20, 2007.

5. ASTM International (2006) *Form and style for ASTM standards*, ASTM International, West Conshohocken, PA.

6. American Society for Testing and Materials (1991) *ASTM D 260-86 Standard specification for boiled linseed oil*, Annual Book of ASTM Standards, West Conshohocken, PA.

7. ASTM International (2006) *ASTM E 1732-96a Standard terminology relating to forensic science*, Annual Book of ASTM Standards 14.02, West Conshohocken, PA.

8. ASTM International (2006) *ASTM E 1618-06 Standard test method for ignitable liquid residues in extracts from fire debris samples by gas chromatography-mass spectrometry*, Annual Book of ASTM Standards 14.02, West Conshohocken, PA.

9. ASTM International (2006) *ASTM E 1387-01 Standard test method for ignitable liquid residues in extracts from fire debris samples by gas chromatography*, Annual Book of ASTM Standards 14.02, West Conshohocken, PA.

10. ASTM International (2006) *ASTM E 2154-01 Standard practice for separation and concentration of ignitable liquid residues from fire debris samples by passive headspace concentration with solid phase microextraction (SPME)*, Annual Book of ASTM Standards 14.02, West Conshohocken, PA.

11. ASTM International (2006) *ASTM E 1413-00 Standard practice for separation and concentration of ignitable liquid residues from fire debris samples by dynamic headspace concentration*, Annual Book of ASTM Standards 14.02, West Conshohocken, PA.

12. ASTM International (2006) *ASTM E 1412-00 Standard practice for separation of ignitable liquid residues from fire debris samples by passive headspace concentration with activated charcoal*, Annual Book of ASTM Standards 14.02, West Conshohocken, PA.

13. American Society for Testing and Materials (1995) *ASTM E 1389-95 Standard practice for cleanup of fire debris sample extracts by acid stripping*, Annual Book of ASTM Standards 14.02, West Conshohocken, PA.

14. ASTM International (2006) *ASTM E 1388-00 Standard practice for sampling of headspace vapors from fire debris samples*, Annual Book of ASTM Standards 14.02, West Conshohocken, PA.

15. ASTM International (2006) *ASTM E 1386-00 Standard practice for separation and concentration of ignitable liquid residues from fire debris by solvent extraction*, Annual Book of ASTM Standards 14.02, West Conshohocken, PA.

16. American Society for Testing and Materials (2001) *ASTM E 1385-00 Standard practice for separation and concentration of ignitable liquid residues from fire debris samples by steam distillation*, Annual Book of ASTM Standards 14.02, West Conshohocken, PA.

17. National Bureau of Standards (1982) AAN Notes, Arson Analysis Newsletter, **6**(3), pp 57–9.

CHAPTER 17

Accreditation

"Quality means doing it right when no one is looking."
Henry Ford, American industrialist (1863–1947)

17.1 INTRODUCTION

Accreditation is a system of formal recognition that an organization (laboratory) has in place to produce quality results by ensuring that the organization (in this case the laboratory) meets predefined quality standards. Accreditation is a process designed to continually challenge and improve laboratory operations through a process of periodic assessments of its quality system as well as appropriate preventative and corrective actions. Accreditation encompasses all aspects of laboratory operations including management, scientific process, personnel, equipment, and physical plant.

In the United States in the early 1980s, a group of proactive laboratory directors took the initiative to formally define minimum quality standards (criteria) for forensic science laboratories knowing that if the forensic community did not take the lead in creating an accreditation process, an outside agency likely would. As a result, one of the first organizations to get involved with forensic laboratory accreditation was the American Society of Crime Laboratory Directors/Laboratory Accreditation Board (ASCLD/LAB). ASCLD/LAB was established in the early 1980s by the American Society of Crime Laboratory Directors (ASCLD) in response to public concerns about inconsistency and inadequacy in forensic laboratories across the United States [1]. ASCLD/LAB now exists as a completely separate entity from ASCLD.

In the United States, accreditation, then and now, is a voluntary process as a whole, although some states (including New York and Texas) have mandated it for all public forensic laboratories. To further encourage accreditation, many federal grant awards are limited to accredited laboratories as is access to some data systems, such as the Combined DNA Index System (CODIS). Today in the United States, there are two basic structures for laboratory accreditation:

- The traditional ASCLD/LAB program, now called ASCLD/LAB Legacy.
- Programs based on the norm ISO/IEC 17025. ASCLD/LAB operates a program based on ISO/IEC 17025 under the auspices of ASCLD/LAB International. Other accrediting organizations, including Forensic Quality Services-International (FQS-I), also offer ISO/IEC 17025 accreditation services [2].

Since 2004, the European Network of Forensic Science Institutes (which encompasses 54 laboratories from 31 countries as shown in Figure 17-1) defines accreditation or "a clear plan to obtain accreditation in the near future" as a requirement for membership [3]. In 2005, the ENFSI issued an even stronger policy stating that [4]: "[. . .] it is the policy of ENFSI that all member laboratories should have achieved or should be taking steps towards EN ISO/IEC 17025 compliant accreditation for their laboratory testing activities." Most countries outside the United States use their own national accreditation body, which is based on ISO 17025. For example, the Royal Canadian Mounted Police (RCMP) uses the Standards Council of Canada (SCC), the Australian Federal Police (AFP) and organizations in New Zealand use the National Association of Testing Authorities (NATA), and the Forensic Science Service (FSS) uses the United Kingdom Accreditation Service/National Accreditation of Measurements and Sampling (UKAS/NAMAS).

FIGURE 17-1

Geographical distribution of the different laboratory members of ENFSI.

As of December 2004, no ENFSI laboratories had been accredited through ASCLD/LAB and none of the 16 laboratories seeking accreditations was planning to do so with ASCLD/LAB [5].

In Europe, 17 laboratories were accredited in 2004 (representing 32.7% of the ENFSI membership) and it is expected that by 2009, 35 laboratories would be accredited (67.3% of ENFSI membership) [6]. The majority of these accredited or seeking-accreditation laboratories use ISO/IEC 17025 standards [6]. It is also estimated that more than 94% of the laboratories either have a quality assurance system in place or are developing one [6].

The key to accreditation is documentation. In order to obtain accreditation, a laboratory must not only do quality work, but must also objectively prove that they do quality work. Quality is defined by accuracy and reproducibility. A well-documented quality system is an essential requirement to ensure reproducible work from case to case, analyst to analyst, and process to process. The goal of the accrediting body is to help an organization raise the level of performance to meet the industry-defined minimal requirements for quality work. Through the evaluation of casework, policies, procedures, proficiency testing, and other quality documents, a laboratory performance is assessed, recommendations for improvement are made, and the quality of forensic science in the laboratory and throughout the community is raised.

17.2 ASCLD/LAB

ASCLD/LAB began as a small organization in the early 1980s. One of the first tasks was to define a set of objective criteria used to evaluate the performance of forensic laboratories in order to ensure their capability to produce reliable and accurate results. As of February 17, 2007, ASCLD/LAB has accredited 330 laboratories as shown in Table 17-1 [7]. It is somewhat

Table 17-1	Distribution of the different laboratories accredited by ASCLD/LAB	
	Number of Accredited Laboratories	
Laboratory type	**ASCLD/LAB Legacy**	**ASCLD/LAB International**
State	174	6
Local	94	6
Federal	12	10
International (non-US)	10	0
Private	14	4
Total	**304**	**26**

ironic to note that none of the non-US laboratories actually have chosen the newer ASCLD/LAB International program. But one must keep in mind that ASCLD/LAB remains an American organization developed for American laboratories and that their international program is still fairly new. It is little known from an international perspective and most countries use their own national accreditation body based on ISO 17025.

ASCLD/LAB is managed by an executive and administrative staff. This staff is overseen by a Board of Directors that is elected by the Delegate Assembly. The voting members of the Delegate Assembly are representatives from each ASCLD/LAB accredited laboratory. All changes to the content and scope of accreditation criteria must be made through the vote of the Delegate Assembly. The interpretation of existing criteria is the responsibility of the Board of Directors. Finally, the day-to-day operations of ASCLD/LAB are managed by the executive staff.

Until 2000, all inspections were conducted exclusively by volunteer inspectors [1]. However, the increase in applications for accreditation and the need to achieve greater consistency among inspections resulted in the addition of paid staff inspectors. Volunteer inspectors are still used for all inspections; however most are now led by staff inspectors who are intimately familiar with the program.

In 2004, ASCLD-LAB created a second mechanism to achieve accreditation based on a compilation of three key documents:

- ISO/EIC 17025 general requirements for the competence of testing and calibration laboratories [8]
- ASCLD/LAB Legacy accreditation manual [9]
- ILAC-G19:2002 guidelines for forensic science laboratories[1] [10]

Eventually, the ASCLD/LAB Legacy program will be completely replaced by the International program. However, for the near future laboratories may seek accreditation and reaccreditation in either program. Under the Legacy program, accreditation is awarded by discipline; fire debris analysis is accredited as part of the "Trace" discipline. In the International program, accreditation is awarded at the subdiscipline level and thus, fire debris analysis is awarded as fire debris analysis.

17.3 ASCLD/LAB LEGACY PROGRAM

Achieving and maintaining ASCLD/LAB Legacy accreditation requires compliance in three areas:

---

[1] ILAC is the International Laboratory Accreditation Cooperation, which is an organization of laboratory and inspection accreditation bodies.

- Meeting the defined criteria for laboratory operation and management
- Maintaining an effective proficiency testing program
- Maintaining an ongoing process of internal assessment and improvement

The culminating event of these actions is an external audit by ASCLD/ LAB inspectors every five years. Accreditation or reaccreditation is awarded only after a laboratory has met the requirements as interpreted by the external auditors and the Board of Directors.

The heart of the ASCLD/LAB Legacy program is the accreditation manual [9]. This document defines the criteria that a laboratory must meet in order to obtain accreditation. Each criterion is rated as essential, important, or desirable. In order to fulfill the requirements for accreditation, the laboratory must meet 100% of the essential criteria, 75% of the important criteria, and 50% of the desirable criteria [9].

The criteria are broken into three distinct chapters of the manual [9]:

- Laboratory management and operations
- Personnel qualifications
- Physical plant

Of the three, laboratory management and operations encompasses the most difficult aspects of the accreditation. This section provides criteria for the highest-level management participation, evidence control, training programs, document management, internal auditing, reagent preparation, equipment maintenance, analytical processes, and case management and reporting.

Personnel qualifications criteria address the requirements for managers, analysts, and technical support staff in terms of formal education, job knowledge, as well as competency and proficiency testing. Job knowledge is assessed primarily based upon an interview and training records; comprehensive assessments of the extent of a given forensic scientist's knowledge are not typically possible. As accreditation is designed to evaluate the laboratory as a whole, individual assessments are limited. Comprehensive measurement of a criminalist's knowledge, skills, and abilities is provided through the process of certification (Chapter 15). Although ASCLD/LAB does not currently require certification of personnel, it can certainly provide objective evidence that the individual meet the criteria for job knowledge. ASCLD/LAB requires annual proficiency testing of the laboratory and competency testing of forensic personnel prior to independently conducting casework. Proficiency testing is a method of evaluating the laboratory system, as well as the competence of each individual, by analyzing simulated casework. At least one proficiency test provided by an approved external supplier is required for every discipline. Additionally, each forensic scientist must be tested annually in each discipline in which they do casework.

The physical plant criteria all relate to the facilities where forensic examinations take place. Most of the criteria in this section are rated important or desirable with the exception of security, which is rated essential. The security criteria are designed to ensure the safety, security, and integrity of the laboratory, evidence, and personnel. Other key physical plant criteria are space, design, and health and safety [9].

In the Legacy manual, criteria are presented as questions. For example, Criteria 1.4.1.3 is an essential criterion asking [9]: "Is evidence stored under proper seal?" Included in the text is the principle behind the criterion, often providing important information as to what documentation or objective evidence is required to meet the criterion. In this instance, the minimum requirements of a proper seal are given in the text. Laboratories are expected to provide, within their quality documents, definitions and procedures for ensuring that they meet prescribed criteria.

It is important to understand that the accrediting bodies, in this instance ASCLD/LAB, do not provide policies or procedures to laboratories. They provide criteria that the laboratory's policies, procedures, and quality documents must include. For example, the Legacy program requires that a laboratory use procedures generally accepted in the field and that the technical procedures are documented [9]. They do not specify what those procedures are or what specific text they must refer to. The burden is on the laboratory, if challenged, to provide proof that the procedures are accepted in the field and are properly documented. Although standardized methods, such as ASTM standards for fire debris analysis (see Chapter 16), can certainly be used to meet these criteria, currently they are not required by ASCLD/LAB.

Often, laboratories will define procedures more stringently than required by ASCLD/LAB criteria. First, ASCLD/LAB will ensure that the laboratory quality documents meet the minimum criteria. Then, they will verify that they meet the requirements of the laboratory's own policies. Often laboratories will meet the definition of the criteria but fail to meet their own policies. Such occurrences result in a negative scoring of those criteria as laboratories are expected to meet both their own minimum standards and the ones defined by the accrediting body.

Laboratory accreditation is defined as an improvement process and not a pass/fail exercise. Most inspections result in findings where a laboratory has room for, or need of, improvement. When an essential criterion results in a "NO" grade, the laboratory must take, and document, appropriate corrective actions to meet the prescribed criterion. Upon completion of those corrective actions, accreditation is granted. External audits are required only every five years, but internal audits based on the ASCLD/LAB criteria are required annually.

Through an on-going process of review, the accreditation requirements have become more refined and more stringent. As a result, forensic sciences, as a whole, have improved to a level where public confidence in accredited laboratories is significantly higher than when the process first began over 25 years ago.

17.4 ISO/IEC 17025

The introduction of a program based on ISO/IEC 17025 brings the forensic science laboratory accreditation to an even higher standard of excellence than compared to the original ASCLD/LAB Legacy Program. ISO/IEC 17025 is the accreditation standard chosen by the majority of the laboratories around the world, except for the United States where less than 10% of the laboratories use it.

The partnership of the International Organization of Standardization (ISO) and the International Electrotechnical Commission (IEC) has resulted in the development of a number of international standards dedicated to various materials and processes. From a forensic laboratory standpoint, the most important ISO/IEC document is the standard *ISO/EIC 17025 General requirements for the competence of testing and calibration laboratories* [8]. This document provides the internationally recognized general requirements for maintaining an effective testing and/or calibration laboratory. As all crime laboratories are testing laboratories (and some are calibration laboratories as well), this document brings forth an internationally recognized process for assessing the competence of forensic laboratories.

ISO/IEC 17025 originally was published as ISO Guide 25. Guide 25 resulted from the efforts of ILAC to establish consistency for laboratory accreditation requirements throughout numerous countries. In 1999, it gained the status of an international accreditation standard under the designation ISO/IEC 17025:1999. The most current version is ISO/IEC 17025:2005, where efforts were made to harmonize the quality system aspects of ISO 9000:2000 registration. In the United States, whereas the ASCLD/LAB Legacy program resulted in monumental improvements to the forensic community, ISO/IEC 17025 brings the accreditation to a new level, which is compatible on an international scale.

Because ISO/IEC 17025 is a general document applicable to any and all testing laboratories, the accrediting body usually issues supplemental requirements to ensure that all key aspects of a forensic laboratory are assessed. In the case of ASCLD/LAB International, the supplemental documents include the elements of the Legacy program that are not directly stated in the 17025 document, as well as significant portions of the ILAC-

G19 document *Guidelines for forensic science laboratories* [10]. The supplemental document is titled "ASCLD/LAB-International Supplemental Requirements for the Accreditation of Forensic Science Testing and Calibration Laboratories" [11]. Other accrediting organizations develop or adopt their own supplemental requirements based on the scope of the laboratory's services and the mission of the accrediting body.

Assessments are based on the ISO/IEC 17025 standard, the supplemental documents issued by the accrediting body, and the laboratory's own quality manual, policies, and procedures. For the most part, the standard places the onus on the laboratory to define how to meet the standard's criteria; however the laboratory must be able to provide objective proof of this compliance. Conversely, assessors, when evaluating the competence of the laboratory, must be able to provide objective proof of nonconformance to any of these documents.

In the ASCLD/LAB International model, all requirements of the standard and supplemental document are assessed for conformity. All nonconformities are further assessed as to their impact on the work product of the laboratory and must be corrected through a documented corrective action process. They are classified in two different levels [11]:

- Level 1 nonconformities have significant impact on some of the quality of the laboratory operation. They must be resolved prior to gaining accreditation or reaccreditation.
- Level 2 nonconformities have minimal impact. They must be corrected prior to the next annual on-site visit.

The main ISO/IEC 17025 document is divided in two main sections: management requirements and technical requirements [8]. As the name implies, the management requirements address the quality management aspects of the laboratory and the technical requirements address the operational/analytical aspects of the laboratory.

Quality management requirements include all aspects of an effective organizational and administrative operation and require that they meet the needs of the client; a well-documented quality system including a quality manual that defines personnel roles, objectives, and related structures; a system of document control that defines all internal and external quality documents including the quality manual, policies and procedures, as well as records; management of supplies and equipment; effective corrective action procedures; and internal and external auditing.

The technical requirements include all technical aspects related to generating quality laboratory results including personnel qualifications, physical plant considerations, test methods, equipment, traceability, sampling, and reporting.

REFERENCES

1. ASCLD/LAB (2007) *History*, available from http://www.ascld-lab.org/dual/aslabdualhistory.html, last access performed on March 20, 2007.
2. Forensic Quality Services (2005) *ISO/IEC 17025 accreditation services*, available from http://www.forquality.org/accreditation.htm, last access performed on March 20, 2007.
3. ENFSI (2004) *Framework for membership*, document BRD-FK-001 issue N˙003, Board, European Network of Forensic Science Institutes.
4. ENFSI (2005) *Policy document on the standards of accreditation*, document QCC-ACR-001 issue N˙003, Standing Committee for Quality and Competence, European Network of Forensic Science Institutes.
5. ENFSI (2005) *Summary report on the accreditation surveys in 2004*, document QCC-ACR-002 issue N˙002, Standing Committee for Quality and Competence, European Network of Forensic Science Institutes.
6. Malkoc E and Neuteboom W (2007) The current status of forensic science laboratory accreditation in Europe, *Forensic Science International*, **167**(2–3), pp 121–6.
7. ASCLD/LAB (2007) *Laboratories accredited by ASCLD/LAB*, available from http://www.ascld-lab.org/legacy/aslablegacylaboratories.html, last access performed on March 20, 2007.
8. ISO (2005) ISO/IEC 17025:2005 *General requirements for the competence of testing and calibration laboratories*, International Organization for Standardization, Geneva, Switzerland.
9. ASCLD/LAB (2005) *Legacy accreditation manual*, American Society of Crime Laboratory Directors/Laboratory Accreditation Board, Garner, NC.
10. ILAC (2002) ILAC-G19:2002 *Guidelines for forensic science laboratories*, International Laboratory Accreditation Cooperation, Rhodes, NSW, Australia.
11. ASCLD/LAB (2004) *ASCLD/LAB-International accreditation program*, American Society of Crime Laboratory Directors/Laboratory Accreditation Board, Garner, NC.

Abbreviations

Note: When an abbreviation is identical for the technique and the related apparatus, only one of the two definitions is provided. For example: GC applies to gas chromatograph and gas chromatography, however only the last one is provided.

°C	Unit degree Celsius or centigrade
°F	Unit degree Fahrenheit
°K	Unit degree Kelvin

A

AAN	Arson Analysis Newsletter (USA)
ABC	American Board of Criminalistics (USA)
ACS	Activated charcoal strip
ADC	Accelerant detection canine
AFFF	Aqueous film-forming foam
AFP	Australian Federal Police (Australia)
AIT	Autoignition temperature
AKI	Anti-knock index
ASCLD	American Society of Crime Laboratory Directors (USA)
ASCLD/LAB	American Society of Crime Laboratory/Directors Laboratory Accreditation Board (USA)
ASTM	American Society for Testing and Materials now ASTM International (USA)
ATD	Automatic Thermal Desorber
ATF	Bureau of Alcohol, Tobacco, Firearms and Explosives (USA)

B

bbl	Unit barrel
BC	Before Christ
BDE	Bond-dissociation energy
BKA	Bundeskriminalamt (Germany)
BLEVE	Boiling liquid expanding vapor explosion
BP	Boiling point

C

CAA	Clean Air Act (USA)
CAAA	Clean Air Act Amendment of 1990 (USA)
CADA	Canine Accelerant Detection Association (USA)
CAS	Chemical Abstracts Service
CCC	see CCCFP
CCCFP	Continuously closed cup
CCD	Charge-coupled device
CD	Compact disc
CE	Capillary electrophoresis
CEN	European Committee for Standardization
CI	Chemical ionization
COC	Cleveland open cup

D

D	Bond-dissociation energy
D-ABC	Diplomate of the American Board of Criminalistics
DC	Direct-current
DCM	Dichloromethane
DFLEX	Diffuse Flammable Liquid Extraction (Albrayco, Cromwell, Connecticut, USA)
DIP	Direct-inlet probe
DHSC	Dynamic headspace concentration extraction
DNA	Deoxyribonucleic acid
DOT	Department of Transportation (USA)
DUI	Driving under the influence
DVB	Divinylbenzene

E

ECD	Electron-capture detector
EI	Electron ionization
EIC	Extracted ion chromatogram
EI FT-ICR	Electron ionization Fourier transform ion cyclotron resonance
EIP	Extracted ion profile
EM	Electron multiplier
EN	Euronorm
ENFSI	European Network of Forensic Science Institutes
EP	End point
ESDA	Electrostatic detection apparatus

ETBE	Ethyl *tert*-butyl ether
eV	Unit electron Volt

F

FA	Fatty acid
F-ABC	Fellow of the American Board of Criminalistics
FAME	Fatty acid methyl ester
FBI	Federal Bureau of Investigation (USA)
FCC	Fluid catalytic cracking
FDA	Fire debris analysis
FFA	Free fatty acid
FFFP	Film-forming fluoroprotein
FID	Flame ionization detector
FPD	Flame photometric detector
FQS-I	Forensic Quality Services-International (USA)
FSS	Forensic Science Service (United Kingdom)
FTIR	Fourier transform infrared spectrometry
FTIR/ATR	Fourier transform infrared spectrometry/attenuated total reflectance

G

g	Unit gram
GC	Gas chromatography
GC-FID	Gas chromatography-flame ionization detection
GCxGC	Comprehensive two-dimensional gas chromatography
GCxGC-MS	Comprehensive two-dimensional gas chromatography-mass spectrometry
GC-MS	Gas chromatography-mass spectrometry
GC-MS/MS	Gas chromatography-mass spectrometry/mass spectrometry
GKE	General Knowledge Examination
GLC	Gas-liquid chromatography
GSC	Gas-solid chromatography

H

H	see HETP
HCB	Homemade chemical bomb
HDPE	High density polyethylene
HETP	Height equivalent to a theoretical plate
HPD	Heavy petroleum distillate

HPLC	High-performance (or high-pressure) liquid chromatography
HRR	Heat release rate

I

IBP	Initial boiling point
ICS	International Classification for Standards
IEC	International Electrotechnical Commission
IL	Ignitable liquid
ILA	Ignitable Liquid Absorbent (Ancarro, Johnston, Iowa, USA)
ILAC	International Laboratory Accreditation Cooperation (based in Australia)
ILR	Ignitable liquid residues
ILRC	Ignitable liquids reference collection (TWGFEX, USA)
IP	Institute of Petroleum
IR	Infrared
IRCGN	Institut de Recherche Criminelle de la Gendarmerie Nationale (France)
IRM	Isotope ratio monitoring
IRMS	Isotope ratio mass spectrometry
ISO	International Organization for Standardization
IUPAC	International Union of Pure and Applied Chemistry

K

Kb	Kauri-butanol value
Kc	Distribution constant in chromatography
kcal	Unit kilocalorie
kg	Unit kilogram
kJ	Unit kiloJoule
kPa	Unit kiloPascal

L

l	Unit liter
L	Column length (in chromatography)
LC	Liquid chromatography
LCD	Liquid crystal display
LDPE	Low density polyethylene
LFL	Lower flammability limit
LKA	Landeskriminalamt (Germany)
LPD	Light petroleum distillate
LSR	Light straight run

M

M	Molar
MC	Mass chromatogram
MEMS	Microelectromechanical systems
MIE	Minimum ignition energy
MIK	Methyl isobutyl ketone
MMH	Monomethylhydrazine
mmHg	Unit millimeter mercury (pressure)
mol	Unit mole
MON	Motor octane number
MPD	Medium petroleum distillate
MS	Mass spectrometer or spectrometry
MSDS	Material safety data sheet
MS/MS	Tandem mass spectrometry
MTBE	Methyl *tert*-butyl ether
MW	Molecular weight
m/z	mass-to-charge ratio

N

N	Number of theoretical plates
NAMAS	National Accreditation of Measurements and Sampling (United Kingdom)
NASA	National Aeronautics and Space Administration (USA)
NATA	National Association of Testing Authorities (Australia)
NBS	National Bureau of Standards, now NIST (USA)
NFPA	National Fire Protection Association (USA)
NIJ	National Institute of Justice
NIST	National Institute of Standards and Technology (USA)
nm	nanometer
NMR	Nuclear magnetic resonance
NPD	Nitrogen-phosphorous detector

O

OSHA	Occupational Safety and Health Administration (USA)
OT	Open-tubular

P

Pa	Pascal
PA	Polyacrylate
PAH	Polycyclic aromatic hydrocarbon(s)

P_AS	Portable Arson Sampler (Tooele, Utah, USA)
PCA	Principal component analysis
PCE	Tetrachloroethylene
PDMS	Polydimethylsiloxane
PE	Polyethylene
pg	Unit picogram
PHSC	Passive headspace concentration extraction
PID	Photoionization detector
PMCC	Pensky-Martens closed cup
PMMA	Polymethyl methacrylate
PNA	Polynuclear aromatic (hydrocarbon)
PON	Pump octane number
PP	Polypropylene
ppm	Part-per-million
PPV	Positive-pressure ventilation
PS	Polystyrene
PTR-MS	Proton transfer reaction time-of-flight mass spectrometry
PUFA	Polyunsaturated fatty acid
PVC	Polyvinyl chloride
Py-GC	Pyrolysis-gas chromatography
PyP	Pyrolysis products

R

RCMP	Royal Canadian Mounted Police (Canada)
RdON	Road octane number
RF	Radio frequency
RFG	Reformulated gasoline
RI	Refractive index
RIC	Reconstructed ion chromatogram
RON	Research octane number
RVP	Reid vapor pressure

S

SAE	Society of Automotive Engineers now SAE International (USA)
SAM	Standard accelerant mixture
SCC	Standards Council of Canada (Canada)
SEM-EDX	Scanning-electron microscope energy x-ray dispersive analyzer
SFC	Supercritical fluid chromatography

SI	Système international (international system of units of measurement)
SIM	Selected ion monitoring
SPME	Solid phase microextraction
STP	Standard temperature and pressure
SWG	Scientific working group
SWGFEX	Scientific Working Group for Fire and Explosives (USA)

T

TAG	Triacylglycerides
TCC	Tag closed cup
	Target compound chromatography
TCD	Thermal conductivity detector
TCE	Trichloroethylene
TCO	Thermal cut-off
TD	Thermal desorber
TEL	Tetraethyl lead
TIC	Total ion chromatogram
TLC	Thin-layer chromatography
TLV	Threshold limit value
TOC	Tag open cup
TOFMS	Time-of-flight mass spectrometry
TWG	Technical working group
TWGED	Technical Working Group on Education and Training in Forensic Science (USA)
TWGFEX	Technical and Scientific Working Group for CCD Fire and Explosives (USA)

U

UDMH	Unsymmetrical dimethylhydrazine
UFL	Upper flammability limit
UK	United Kingdom
UKAS	United Kingdom Accreditation Service (United Kingdom)
UNEP	United Nations Environment Programme
USA	United States of America
USD	United States dollars
UV	Ultraviolet

V

VCT	Vinyl composite tile
VOC	Volatile organic compound(s)

VOR	Vegetable (and animal) oil residues
VP	Vapor pressure
VPUVS	Vapor phase ultraviolet spectroscopy

X

XRD	X-ray diffraction
XRF	X-ray fluorescence

Y

YAG	Yttrium aluminum garnet

Z

Z	Atomic number

Index

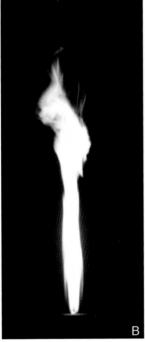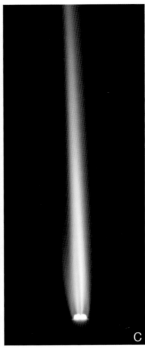

FIGURE 4-4

Example of complete, partial, and incomplete combustion with an acetylene torch where the availability of oxygen is increased from the left to the right. A/ The generation of heavy soot is typical of an incomplete combustion. B/ The bright yellow flame is due to the incandescence of some carbon particles. C/ The blue flame shows a complete combustion, where no particles of carbon are generated.

FIGURE 4-10

Incipient stage of a room fire. (Photograph courtesy of Steven J. Avato, Bureau of Alcohol, Tobacco, Firearms and Explosives, Falls Church, Virginia, USA.)

FIGURE 4-11

Ceiling layer development. (Photograph courtesy of Steven J. Avato, Bureau of Alcohol, Tobacco, Firearms and Explosives, Falls Church, Virginia, USA.)

FIGURE 4-12

Preflashover condition. (Photograph courtesy of Steven J. Avato, Bureau of Alcohol, Tobacco, Firearms and Explosives, Falls Church, Virginia, USA.)

FIGURE 4-13

Flashover. (Photograph courtesy of Steven J. Avato, Bureau of Alcohol, Tobacco, Firearms and Explosives, Falls Church, Virginia, USA.)

FIGURE 4-14 *Full-room involvement. (Photograph courtesy of Steven J. Avato, Bureau of Alcohol, Tobacco, Firearms and Explosives, Falls Church, Virginia, USA.)*

FIGURE 5-1a
These irregularly shaped patterns are the results of particular ventilation conditions. Because of the important crawl space below the flooring, fresh air was brought from the bottom, thus accelerating the burning of holes in the wooden planks.

FIGURE 5-1b
In this case, burning material falling from the ceiling created these irregularly shaped burn patterns.

This room underwent flashover, thus creating these irregularly shaped burn patterns. None of these three burn patterns were the results of the pour of an ignitable liquid.

This irregularly shaped pattern is part of a trailer of ignitable liquid that was poured on the floor of an apartment.

FIGURE 5-2b

The irregularly shaped
patterns present in
this room are actual
pour patterns,
confirmed by
laboratory analyses
positive for gasoline.
Note that the general
shapes very closely
resemble the ones
presented in Figure
5-1.
(Photographs courtesy
of Blair Darst,
Cunningham
Investigative Services,
Grayson, Georgia,
USA.)

FIGURE 5-3

This pool-shaped
pattern is the result of
the pour of an
ignitable liquid. Note
the close resemblance
to Figure 5-1b.

FIGURE 5-4 *This pool-shaped pattern presents spots where the carpet was protected and did not sustain burns. These areas were protected because of the presence of difference objects. If the floor is uneven, a raised area usually burns prior to a lower area, because the liquid accumulates in the latter and protects it from burning. The resulting pattern would be called a doughnut-shaped pattern. (Photograph courtesy of Keith Bell, Holland Investigations, Atlanta, Georgia, USA.)*

FIGURE 5-11 *A fire investigator holding an FID electronic sniffer with a stick probe at a fire scene.*

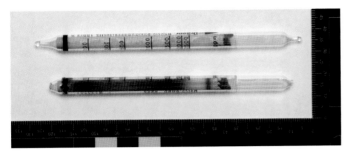

FIGURE 5-13 *Examples of unreacted and reacted Dräger tubes. Note the dark coloration of the reactant inside the bottom tube, indicating the positive reaction. Also, note the scale along the side of the top tube.*

FIGURE 5-20

Example of the use of ILA with 500 μl of diesel fuel. The neat blue delineation indicates the presence of diesel fuel. (Photograph courtesy of François Rey, Institut de Police Scientifique, École des Sciences Criminelles, Université de Lausanne, Switzerland.)

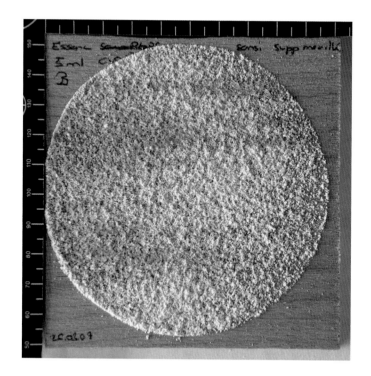

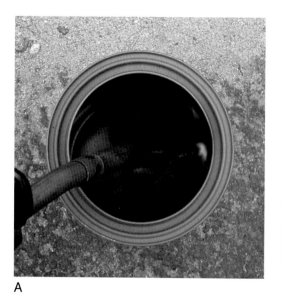

A

B

FIGURE 12-5 *Creation of burned comparison samples. A/ The sample is first ignited with the propane torch until the flame sustains. B/ Fire is sustained until about two-thirds of the sample is burned.*

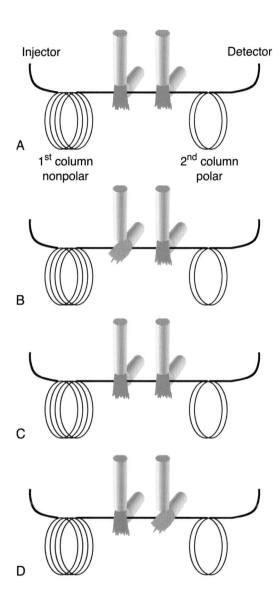

Injector

Detector

A

1st column
nonpolar

2nd column
polar

B

C

D

FIGURE 13-5

Illustration of the functioning principle of the thermal modulator. A/ Beginning of cycle: both jets blow cold air, analytes concentrate right before the thermal modulator. B/ The left tube blows hot air and the analytes are mobile again. They move into a tight fraction, located between the two jets. C/ The first jet is switched to cold again, thus stopping the entry of analytes in-between the jets. D/ The right tube blows hot air and the analytes are injected as a narrow plug in the second column. Diagrams courtesy of Professor Glenn Frysinger, US Coast Guard Academy, New London, Connecticut, USA.

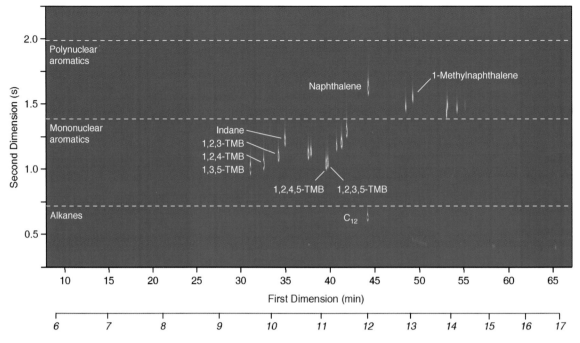

FIGURE 13-7 *GCxGC chromatogram of an ASTM standard test mix. Data courtesy of Professor Glenn Frysinger, US Coast Guard Academy, New London, Connecticut, USA.*

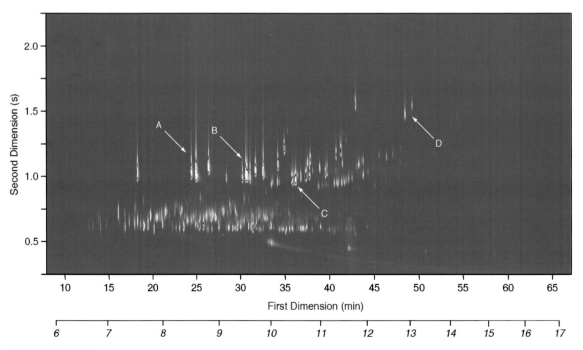

FIGURE 13-8 *GCxGC chromatogram of a 75% weathered gasoline. Data courtesy of Professor Glenn Frysinger, US Coast Guard Academy, New London, Connecticut, USA.*

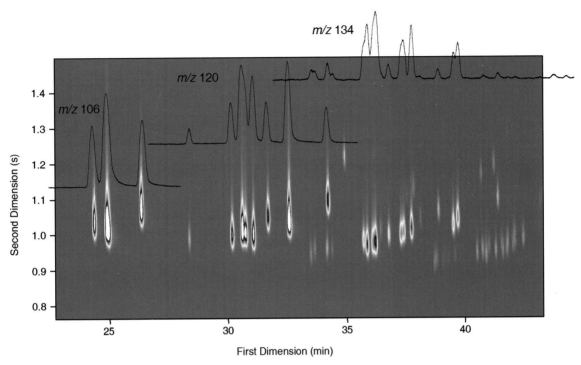

FIGURE 13-9 *Detailed view of some of the diagnostic groups of gasoline and comparison with regular GC–MS data. Data courtesy of Professor Glenn Frysinger, US Coast Guard Academy, New London, Connecticut, USA.*

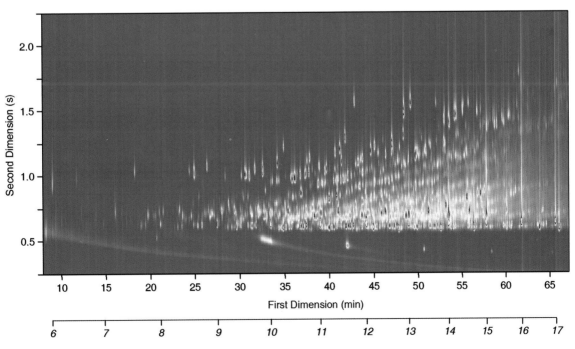

FIGURE 13-10 *Chromatogram of diesel fuel. Data courtesy of Professor Glenn Frysinger, US Coast Guard Academy, New London, Connecticut, USA.*

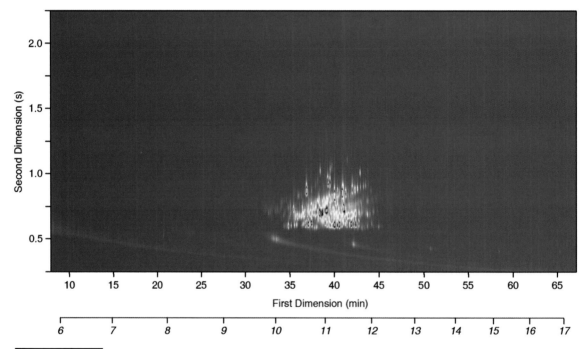

FIGURE 13-11 *Chromatogram of a medium naphthenic-paraffinic product. Data courtesy of Professor Glenn Frysinger, US Coast Guard Academy, New London, Connecticut, USA.*

Engine oil

Automatic
transmission fluid

Power steering fluid

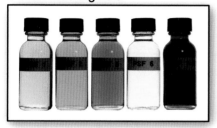

Brake fluid

Coolant

Washer fluid

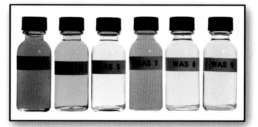

General view of the
aspect of the different
automotive fluids.

General view of the
aspect of some used
vehicle fluids. Note
how they are all
darkened. When held
close to the light, it is
still possible to discern
the red tint of most
automatic transmission
fluids.

FIGURE 14-26a

Typical household products used in the manufacturing of HCBs. A/ Hydrogen peroxide, ammonia, and alcohol products.

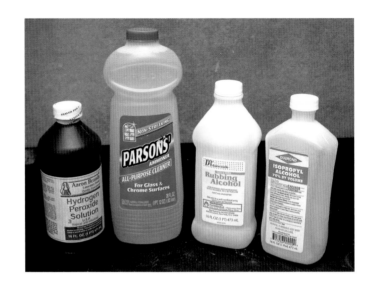

FIGURE 14-26b

Toilet bowl cleaner containing chlorinated and brominated hydanthoins.

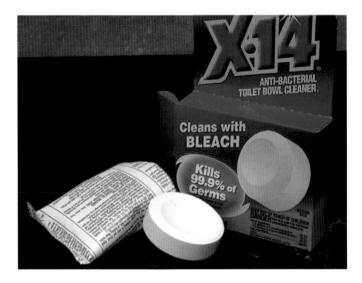

FIGURE 14-27a
The result of an explosion of a mixture of trichloroisocyanuric acid and isopropyl alcohol in a laboratory hood.

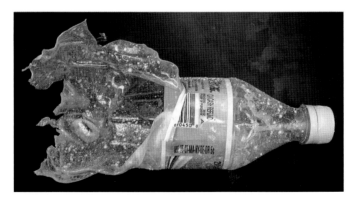

An example of two bottles that were taped together and used as chemical bomb. Photograph courtesy of Kristin McDonald, Criminalist III, Chemistry Unit, New York City Police Department Crime Laboratory, Jamaica, New York, USA.

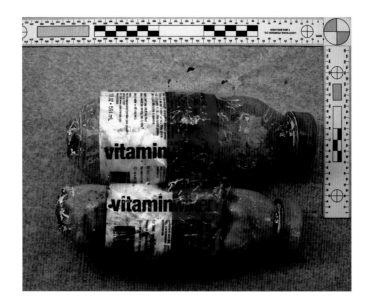

View of the inside of the bottle, where residues are still present and useful for analysis. Photograph courtesy of Kristin McDonald, Criminalist III, Chemistry Unit, New York City Police Department Crime Laboratory, Jamaica, New York, USA.

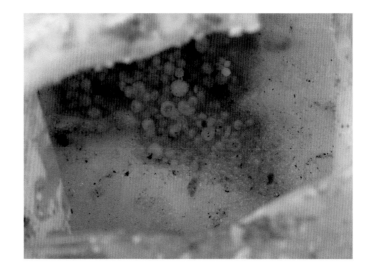